DISCOVER FRANCE

THE GREAT BOOK OF TRAVELS

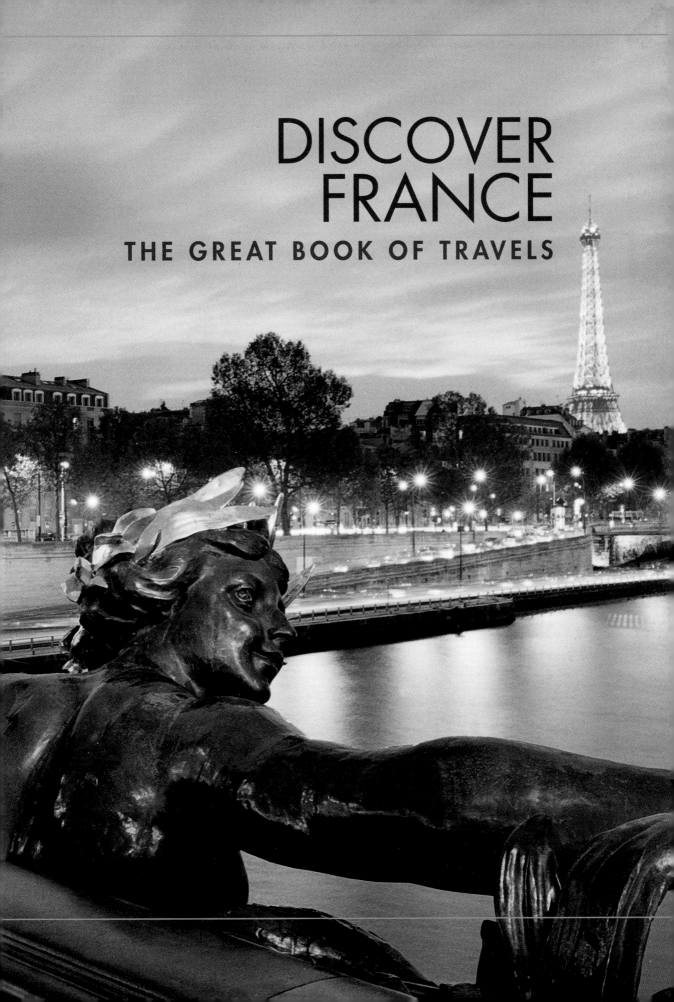

DISCOVER FRANCE

THE GREAT BOOK OF TRAVELS

France is a country with a rich and fascinating past as well as a legendary art of living – its *savoir vivre* – which makes every day of travel in that country a special experience. Its regional diversity is amazing – from Brittany with its Celtic and Gallic culture and the romantic Alsace, via the bustling world city of Paris and the Champagne region with its limestone landscapes, to the many enchanting châteaux of the Loire, as well as Burgundy with its great culinary traditions, right up to the high mountains of the Pyrenees and the Alps, which boast Europe's highest mountain, and onto the fragrant Midi and the spectacular coasts of the Mediterranean and the Atlantic.

"Discover France" presents this mesmerizing European country in all its glorious variety. The first, more extensive section in the book explores the country by following the twelve "most scenic drives" – whether this be along the classic routes, such as the Via Turonensis pilgrim trail, or off the beaten track, such as through the Massif Central. To finish, the book contains detailed descriptions of the 35 historic city centers, monuments and natural landscapes in France that have now been declared UNESCO World Cultural and Natural Heritage Sites.

With informative texts, some 600 color photos, detailed route maps and a 176-page fully indexed France travel atlas, "Discover France" provides an extensive overview of the spellbinding diversity you can expect to find here, encouraging you to set off and explore its attractions yourself.

Twelve routes take you through France's most beautiful natural and most famous cultural landscapes – to the country's most compelling travel destinations, to unique cultural monuments, to pulsating cities and to dreamy villages. The map below shows all the routes at a glance.

A longer introductory text on each chapter provides an initial summary of each respective route, the most popular provinces and regions, as well as their special natural, historic and cultural features. The main text then describes towns and attractions along the route, each one numbered for easy reference. Additional texts in the side panels contain suggested detours and discuss various interesting topics in more detail. Vibrant metropolises such as Paris, Marseille, Strasbourg, Nancy and Toulouse are presented on separate pages with detailed city maps and descriptions. An information box on each route, containing travel

tips and addresses, accommodation options, tourist office websites and addresses and notes for safe driving make it easy to prepare for a trip through this lovely country.

Touring maps at the end of each chapter indicate the main route and all detours, using the numbers used in the text. Icons mark the type and location of specific sights worth visiting, and major places are given extra emphasis with color photographs.

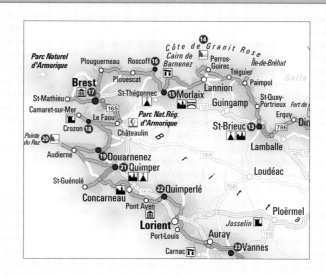

Famous Routes

- 🖼 Rail route
- 🖼 Sea route

Natural landscapes and nature monuments

- 🏔 Mountain landscape
- ◪ Extinct volcano
- 🌋 Active volcano
- ⛰ Rocky landscape
- ⨼ Gorge/canyon
- 🕳 Cave
- ◿ Glacier
- ⬱ Desert landscape
- ◺ River landscape
- 🌊 Water fall/rapids
- ⬱ Lakeland
- ♨ Geyser
- 🌴 Oases
- 🦌 National park (fauna)
- 🌿 National park (flora)
- ⛰ National park (culture)
- ◩ National park (landscape)
- 🅠 Nature park
- 🌐 Biosphere reservation
- ⬱ Coastal landscape
- ⬱ Island
- 🏖 Beach
- 🐠 Underwater reservation
- 🦁 Zoo/safari park

Cultural monuments and cultural events

- ⬚ Pre- and early history
- 🏛 Ancient Middle East
- 🏛 Greek Antiquity
- 🏛 Roman Antiquity
- ♀ Etruscan culture
- ✡ Jewish cultural site
- ☪ Islamic cultural site
- 🕆 Christian cultural site
- ⚱ Phoenician cultural site
- 🏛 Minoan culture
- 🖼 Prehistoric rock images
- 🛡 Vikings
- ▩ Cultural landscape
- 🏰 Castle/fortress/fortifications
- 🏠 Palace/château
- 🏭 Industrial monument
- 🏛 Memorial
- 📡 Space telescope
- 🏙 Historic cityscape
- 🏙 Skyline
- 🎵 Festivals
- 🏛 Museum

- ⬚ Fossil finds
- 🦓 Game reserve
- 🐋 Whale watching
- 🦭 Protected area for sea lions/seals

- ◉ Theater
- 🌐 World exhibition
- ⚬⚬ Olympic city
- 🏛 Monument
- ⬚ Tomb
- ⬚ Market
- 🏛 Caravanserai
- ⊠ Battlefield

- 🚰 Dam
- 🗼 Interesting lighthouse
- 🌉 Exceptional bridge

Major sports and leisure destinations

- 🏁 Racetrack
- 🏟 Arena/stadium
- 🎿 Skiing area
- ⛵ Sailing
- 🤿 Diving
- 🛶 Canoe/rafting
- ♨ Spa/thermal spring
- 🏖 Beach resort
- 🎡 Recreational park
- ♠ Gaming casino
- 🏇 Equestrian sports
- 🎣 Deep-sea fishing
- 🏄 Surfing
- ⚓ Sea port

France's Most Scenic Drives

It would be a shame to stay in just one place when you're in France – instead you should drive along its charming country roads and explore the country. The twelve routes described here range from a tour along the chic and urbane Mediterranean coast to degustation and exploration in the Champagne, from a drive along the storm-battered Atlantic coast to a journey around the wildly romantic island of Corsica, from the Route Napoleon through the French Alps to the Route des Vins around the vineyards of the Alsace.

Across the North of France

You perhaps need to look a little more closely than you would elsewhere but you do then realize that there are indeed a few gems to be discovered in this rather harsh landscape: romantic streams, forests, moors, nature parks, as well as a great deal of culture and history in towns with striking cathedrals and bell towers. The area of France between Lorraine and the Channel coast boasts a wealth of treasures, some of which are UNESCO World Heritage Sites.

Given the diversity of its landscape and its coastline, extending from the Atlantic to the Mediterranean, France is almost a mini-continent in itself. Visitors tend to head to the south of the country, of course, and so the north is somewhat unknown territory at times even to Francophiles. Undeservedly, though, for the landscape in this region has more to offer than most people realize. The north does not reveal its charms to everyone at first glance, however; exploring this part of France needs to be done at leisure.

Lorraine is just one of twenty-six regions in France today but over one thousand years ago, it was a European state in its own right: Lothringen, as Lorraine is known in German, acquired its name in the ninth century from Lothair I following the division of the Frankish

kingdom in 843. The present-day Netherlands, parts of Belgium, Luxembourg and the Rhine provinces all used to belong to Lorraine and the state changed hands several times during the course of its history. In the 18th century Lorraine was in fact even subject to a former Polish king before then becoming entirely French, only to fall into Germans hands on

another two occasions before ultimately forming part of France. Battlefields and war cemeteries are a sad and chilling reminder of the darker days of Franco-German conflict – particularly World War I, the bloodiest battles of which were fought right here.

Traces of this turbulent history are still to be found everywhere, such as in Metz, for in-

stance, the capital of Lorraine. The town has many churches, the origins of which date back to Roman times, while the 19th century left a legacy of Prussian buildings. Of more disparate splendor is the city of Nancy, formerly a royal seat and boasting city squares of consummate artistic perfection that are testimony to the grandeur of the 18th century. Further to the north, near the borders with Luxembourg and Belgium, the route takes you through a romantic landscape: the Ardennes, forested mountain ranges and river valleys. Nature parks line the route before it heads west – to Nord-Pas-de-Calais and the Picardie. Here in the north the proximity to Flanders is obvious: both Lille and Arras boast the Flemish façades usually associated with Belgium. A little farther to the south, in the direction of

Above: An unknown painter belonging to the Flemish School recorded the march of the Brotherhood of Saint Barbara in Dunkerque (Dunkirk) in this painting from 1633. Saint Barbara is one of the Fourteen Holy Helpers and the patron saint of miners. The work is now on display in Dunkerque's Musée des Beaux-Arts.
Left: The Protestant Temple Neuf in Metz was consecrated in 1904 by German Emperor Wilhelm II himself.

Paris, is an architectural gem waiting to be discovered, a true highlight: Amiens Cathedral, a masterpiece of Gothic architecture. This stretch of the route, too, is multifaceted: the cathedrals are as much part of the surroundings as the windmills and the canals of Flanders. Not to be forgotten are the bell towers that are especially numerous and remarkable here in the Nord-Pas-de-Calais.

Water, too, is of course part of this landscape: marsh and moorland areas can be explored in flat boats on canals or rivers, such as the Somme, its estuary a habitat for countless rare birds and as such it is subject to special protection. And then there's the sea that here, too, gives the countryside its very own character. There are of course the industrial plants and large ports as well but you're more likely to come

across steep cliffs along the coast, even proper chalkstone cliffs like those on the other side of the Channel in England, visible from here with the naked eye. Of course there are also fine, sandy beaches and dunes as well as seaside towns whose charm perhaps lies in the very fact that they are not as well known as the famous, chic but often crowded resorts of the Mediterranean.

The gentle hues of this coastline have always been greatly valued by painters. The name given to this stretch of coast by the painter Edouard Lévêque around a century ago has been retained to this day: Côte d'Opale – the Opal Coast.

Left: Art Nouveau windows in the Musée de l'Ecole de Nancy.
Right: The lions of Flanders with the crest above the Old Stock Exchange in Lille.

The Excelsior Brasserie in Nancy boasts exquisite Art Nouveau surroundings.

From Lorraine to the English Channel: our route begins in Lorraine, sweeps to the south via Nancy and Metz, then follows France's northern border before finally crossing Picardie and Nord-Pas-de-Calais. The attractions en route include castles, romantic moorland landscapes and the seaside resorts along the coast.

① Sarreguemines Directly on the border with Germany's Saarland, just a short distance south of Saarbrücken, is Sarreguemines (or Saargemünd in German). This Lorraine town belongs to the Moselle département. Both the French and the German names refer to a river confluence, this being where Saarland's Blies flows into the Saar. International trade played a role early on in the town's history, it being situated on the trade route between Flanders and Italy in the late Middle Ages. Sarreguemines developed an important stoneware industry at the end of the 18th century. The Musée de la Faïence commemorates this prosperous era of ceramic production, and an annual international ceramics contest also ensures that this tradition is maintained. The museum of stoneware technology housed in the historic Mill on the Blies is also worth a visit. The idyllically situated casino on the Saar – which is a cultural center and not a gambling den – is also an interesting sight to seek out, as is the baroque Church of St-Nicolas.

Top: The mighty façade of the Hotel de Ville (city hall) in Nancy dominates the south side of Place Stanislas.

Travel information

Route profile
Length: c. 1,300 km (808 miles), without detours
Time required: 10–14 days
Start: Sarreguemines
End: Dunkerque
Route: Sarreguemines, Epinal, Lunéville, Nancy, Metz, Thionville, Arlon, Bouillon, Monthermé, Charleville-Mézières, Lille, Douai, Arras, Amiens, Abbeville, Boulogne-sur-Mer, Calais, Dunkerque

Safe driving:
The drink driving limit is 0.5 mg per ml. The speed limits are 50 km/h (30 mph) in built-up areas, 90 km/h (55 mph) on open roads, 110 km/h (70 mph) on dual carriageways, 130 km/h (80 mph) on highways (less if raining).

When to go:
During the winter months the weather in northern France can be rather unpleasant; the ideal time for a journey is therefore the time between May to September, when the maximum daily temperatures average 25 °C (77°F). However, this will also be the busiest time of year in the coastal resorts.

Where to stay:
Hotel rooms and gîtes (houses/ villas for rent) can easily be booked over the Internet. While the Maison de la France does not have its own booking service, it does provide useful links in the "Organize your Trip" section of http://us.franceguide.com.

View of the Moselle in Epinal, with the Romanesque Church of St-Maurice in the background.

planned. The Château de Lunéville played an important role in the history of Lorraine as well as in European history on one occasion: the last (Polish) Duke of Lorraine, Stanislaw I Leszczynski, died on the premises in 1766; with his death, the entire Duchy of Lorraine fell to France. The Peace of Lunéville between France and Austria was signed here in 1801, ending the Second Coalition War against Napoleonic France and confirming a series of French territorial claims, including French sovereignty over the occupied territories to the left of the Rhine.

4 St-Nicolas-de-Port The small town of St-Nicolas-de-Port on the outskirts of Nancy is the administrative center for the commune of the same name. The town owes much to Saint Nicolas, including its name: the saint's remains were exhumed in 1087 and shipped to Bari on the Adriatic Coast; it was from there that a crusader brought a finger joint from the popular saint as a reliquary to present day St-Nicolas in 1090. The town soon became an important pilgrimage site and the growing crowds means that ever-larger churches had to be built – culminating in the present basilica built in the 15th and 16th centuries and designed by Simon Noycet. The splendid late-Gothic building is impressive in its dimensions alone: the 28-m-high (92-ft) columns are considered to be the largest in France. The basilica, which has undergone major restoration work following damage incurred during the French Revolution and World War II, still houses the precious reliquary from Saint Nicolas, who was subsequently elevated to patron saint of Lorraine.

5 Nancy See page 18.
From Lorraine's former capital the route goes to Liverdun.

2 Epinal Heading southwest, the journey continues to Epinal on the Moselle River. The castle ruins above the town date back to its founding by the bishops of Metz. Of importance from an art historical perspective is the former abbey Church of St-Maurice, its robust tower being reminiscent of a stronghold. Also worth seeing are the vivid stained-glass windows in the Church of Notre Dame, the rose garden and the art museum. It was for the popular prints by the printing company Pellerin that Epinal became particularly famous in the 19th century, however. The *Images d'Epinal*, narrative image sequences – were printed in large quantities in the late 19th century and are considered to be the forerunners of comics.
The town's location on the Moselle River and on a small canal also contributes to its particular charm. From Epinal it is worth taking a short detour to the Château d'Haroué (see column on the right), before continuing to Lunéville.

3 Lunéville The small duchy enjoyed a considerable boost in the 18th century when Leopold, Duke of Lorraine transferred his residence from occupied Nancy to Lunéville at the start of the century. The comprehensive building works included the construction of a rococo-style castle under the direction of the architect Germain Boffrand. The building with its extensive grounds is considered an 18th-century masterpiece and is sometimes referred to as the "Versailles of Lorraine". It unfortunately suffered extensive damage as a result of a fire in 2003; restoration work is currently being

5 Nancy See page 18.

Detour

Château d'Haroué

Château d'Haroué is situated between Nancy and Epinal, set in the midst of an extensive park. This part of the Lorraine Plateau is known as the Saintois.
Château Haroué was built between 1720 and 1732 by the renowned master builder Germain Boffrand, on the site of two older fortresses. Boffrand integrated some of the surviving sections of the medieval fortresses into the new castle. Artists from Lorraine, including Jean Lamour and Barthélemy Guibal, were largely responsible for the decorative elements; the park was designed by Emilio Terry. It was commissioned by Marc de Beauvau-Craon whose descendants still occupy the castle to this day. At the height of its fame, Haroué repeatedly played host to illustrious personalities such as King Louis XVIII or Grand Duke Leopold of Lorraine, for example.

The aerial view reveals the vast dimensions and layout of Château d'Haroué

The building in its present form, classified as an historic monument in 1983, is still a reminder of this era of courtly life, whereas the older sections remain as testimony to times of war when a castle really did function as a fortification and a refuge.
The enormous extent of the castle belonging to the small village of Haroué is illustrated by a few facts and figures: the complex features 365 windows, 52 chimneys, twelve towers and four bridges. Parts of the interior with the historical decor, furniture and paintings are open for guided public tours.

Nancy is known as the "City of the Golden Gates", and this epithet is best shown to be appropriate in the beautifully worked wrought-iron railings by Jean Lamour on the famous Place Stanislas, which could probably be described as one of the most attractive squares in Europe. On its southern side, the railings with gilded rocaille features in front of the

Amphitrite Fountain form the end of the Park Pépinière. In Greek mythology, Amphitrite is the wife of the sea god Poseidon; the figure that was immortalized here was allegedly based on one of Stanislas Leszczyński lovers. The construction of the entire complex, comprising a central as well as side arches, is reminiscent of Roman triumphal arches.

Nancy

Thanks to its outstanding buildings, the former capital of Lorraine has been able to retain the image of a royal seat to this day. The new town with its planned layout, where the streets intersect at right angles to one another like a grid, extends to the south of the Old Town.

One of Nancy's landmark features are its large city squares dating from the 18th century, their uniform façades making them one of the most important

The Arc Héré triumphal arch at the north end of Place Stanislas

examples of absolutist urban planning; a number of them have therefore been included in the list of UNESCO World Heritage Sites. The loveliest is the Place Stanislas. Its overall enchanting appearance is created to no small extent by the superb decorative wrought iron railings by Jean Lamour.

The Place de la Carrière, formerly a tournament square, is reached via a triumphal arch commemorating Louis XV. To the west are the many Renaissance buildings of the Old Town. The Franciscan monastery with the ducal tombs and the Porte de la Craffe, the last surviving medieval city gate in Nancy, are further sightseeing attractions not to be missed. The new town of Nancy is dominated by its imposing Notre-Dame Cathedral, built in the 18th century.

The city owes a particular cultural treasure to the 19th-century iron industry of Lorraine: iron and glass, which was also produced in Lorraine, were important style elements of the Art Nouveau, a major feature of Nancy.

The St-Etienne Cathedral towers up between the rooftops of Metz.

6 Liverdun To the west of the highway from Nancy to Metz is the small town of Liverdun set on high ground above a bend in the Moselle. It has an attractive, historic Old Town with arcade buildings, particularly around the Place d'Armes. The Church of St-Euchaire from the 12th century is still recognizable as a Cistercian building. The town, once the secondary residence of the bishops of Toul, also has an arched bridge over the Moselle, a railway bridge dating from the year 1855.

7 Pont-à-Mousson The small town of Pont-à-Mousson on the Moselle River owes its name to the fact that there has been a bridge spanning the Moselle here since the ninth century (the present-day bridge is a modern construction, however).
The town itself is even older, the Romans having established a fort on the hill above the Moselle. The former Premonstratensian abbey stands on the banks of the river; it now houses a cultural center.

The streets in the town center are especially attractive, particularly those featuring pergola buildings around the Place Duroc; the most interesting is the building depicting the seven deadly sins (16th century). The small town of Pont-à-Mousson even used to be a university town and it was only at the end of the 18th century that the Jesuit-founded university was closed here and moved to Nancy.

8 Gorze The village of Gorze lies off the road to Metz and belongs to the western part of the Parc Naturel Régional de Lorraine. The Bishop of Metz founded a Benedictine monastery here in the eighth century. This monastery initiated an influential reform movement within the Benedictine order in which 160 monasteries participated in the 11th century; the movement was part of a reorientation of the church in which the influential Cluny monastery in particular played an important role. The early-Gothic

abbey church still survives and boasts a Judgment Day scene above one of the portals.

9 Metz The present-day capital of the Lorraine region, situated at the confluence of the Seille and Moselle Rivers, has always had a key influence on the country's history. The name refers to what was once a Celtic settlement, captured by the Romans in 52 BC. With its strategic location, the town quickly grew to become one of the largest in Gaul – larger than Paris and during the Middle Ages it was at times the second-largest city in the Holy Roman Empire (after Cologne). The free city-state with its countless churches and monasteries was part of the empire, enjoyed brisk trade with Italy and was successful in setting itself apart from the Duchy of Lorraine. The city was conquered by the French in the 16th century; following the Peace of Westphalia in 1648 Metz officially became part of France. Metz fell into German hands again from 1871 to 1918

(as it did from 1940 to 1944 as well), before the city was ultimately returned to France. These changes have left visible traces in the city's architecture: the German and Prussian buildings from 1871 to 1918 are clearly distinguishable among the French buildings.
The monuments from earlier eras are of more importance than the legacies of the late 19th century, however, and these include the St-Etienne Cathedral in particular. Construction of the splendid cathedral – presenting its most attractive side to the beholder standing on the bridge over the Moselle – was begun in 1220 and it was consecrated in 1546. The west façade has undergone numerous design changes, the last being in the neo-Gothic style of the 19th century. The interior dimensions are especially impressive, with extraordinary lengths (123 m/404 ft) and apex heights (42 m/138 ft). The fact that the aisles have been kept relatively low further reinforces this impression of height. Also unusual are the giant windows, designed by prominent artists from different centuries, the oldest dating from the 13th century. The rose window in the west was made by Hermann von Münster in the 14th century, while the 20th century added works by Marc Chagall (the choir ambulatory and the northern transept).
St-Pierre-aux-Nonnains is considered to be the oldest church in France, its oldest components dating from the 4th century. The Church of St-Maximin, first written mention of which was made in around 1000, is worth visiting for the choir windows designed by Jean Cocteau. A secular building

Above: The Gothic Cathedral of St-Etienne in Metz with its fine stained-glass windows.

19

View from the Grund district of the small Alzette River and the fortress-like Old Town of Luxembourg.

Detour

Luxembourg

North of Thionville this detour takes you not only to a very attractive city in its own right but also into the heart of the second smallest country in the European Union: to the Grand Duchy of Luxembourg, the last still sovereign grand duchy in the world. The small nation's landscape does not differ much from that of the countries it borders of course: the north is mostly characterized by the Ardennes highlands, called Osling here, with mountain forests and deep river valleys. The flatter Gutland region in the south is better suited to agriculture, but the land here has to be shared with the few towns and the industrial areas. The landscape knows no borders, however, and so part of it is now protected by a joint German-Luxembourgian nature park. The city of Luxembourg, the capital of Luxembourg, is also situated in the south of the grand duchy.

This small nation, now known particularly for its strong financial sector, was not only a founder member of the European Economic Community (EEC) in 1957, but it was also elected as the seat of important EEC and now EU authorities; Luxembourg is thus also one of the main cities of the European Union.

The Petrus Valley, which separates the upper town from the railway station district, is a scenic feature of the city. The pathways through the pleasant valley are popular with strollers, cyclists, joggers

In addition to the Cathedral of Notre-Dame and the Palais Grand Ducal, Luxembourg's sightseeing attractions include the Luxembourg Fortress as well as the casemates and tunnels hewn out of the rock since the 17th century. Some 16km (10 miles) of these old fortifications are still accessible today. The modern district on the Plâteau du Kirchberg, reached via the impressive Pont Grand Duchesse Charlotte bridge, is home to international finance centers and many EU institutions.

worth seeing is the Porte des Allemands, a double gate in the old ramparts, commemorating the Teutonic Order's one-time presence in the city. Several museums provide insights into the city's history. The French poet Paul Verlaine (1844–1896), the German linguist Leo Weisgerber (1899 to 1985) and the French dramatist Bernard-Marie Koltès (1948–1989), among others, were also born in Metz.

10 Thionville North of Metz is Thionville, center of the French steel industry since the 19th century. "Theodonis villa" dates back to the Carolingian era; the town then belonged to Luxembourg before falling into French hands in the 17th century. Important legacies from the past include a number of palatial buildings around the Cours du Château, the Porte de Clarisses city gate and the Tour aux Puces (the Tower of Fleas), the remains of the Luxembourgian castle complex. The Château de la Grange with its

moats on the outskirts of the town is a popular daytrip destination. A detour to Luxembourg (see column on the left) is also to be recommended.

11 Arlon The route now heads north, parallel to the border with Luxembourg, reaching Arlon shortly after crossing the border into Belgium. The city is situated on a hill close to the source of the Semois River. It can trace its history back to a Roman settlement, making it one of the oldest towns in the country. The hilltop enclosure dating from Roman times is still recognizable in parts; this enclosure also includes the third-century Roman tower (Tour romaine). Excavations have revealed Roman burial sculptures recording everyday scenes from the lives of the Roman inhabitants. These finds are now on display in the Musée Luxembourgeois and are well worth a visit. The remains of Roman baths as well as the Basilique Romaine are further reminders of the city's founders.

12 Ardennes From Arlon the route now heads west through the Ardennes, an expansive, at times heavily wooded, plateau traversed by river valleys. Rocky outcrops define the landscape in some places, while barren moorland is dominant in others. Many beautiful hiking and cycling trails crisscross the region.

Geologically, the Ardennes form part of the Rhenish Massif and are especially characteristic here in south-east Belgium where the foothills extend as far as Luxembourg and France. In the north-east they are bordered by the High Fens. Part of this landscape is protected by a nature park.

13 Bouillon Situated directly on the French border is Bouillon, idyllically located on a bend in the Semois River. Towering above the town on a rocky outcrop is a fortress from the 11th century, said to have been built by Godfrey, Duke of Lower Lorraine. Today the Château Fort attracts a great

The Place Ducale at the heart of Charleville is based on the Place des Vosges in Paris.

Detour

Valenciennes: Musée des Beaux-Arts

Valenciennes today is something of an austere industrial location but it does boast an important artistic legacy, both the painter Jean-Antoine Watteau (1684–1721) and the sculptor Jean-Baptiste Carpeaux (1827–1875) having been born here. Works by the artists can be viewed in

Crucifixion Group by Abraham Janssens van Nuyssen

many visitors as the view from there over the town and the river is truly magnificent. The interior of the fortress is also worth exploring – the dungeon and the torture chamber or the "Godefroy de Bouillon" room where the crusaders are said to have taken their vows in front of the wooden cross. The history of the town and the crusades is detailed in the Musée Ducal.

Not far from Bouillon, located in a large loop in the river, is the Giant's Grave (Tombeau du Géant), it is so called because the wooded area here does indeed resemble the outline of a giant coffin.

⑭ Monthermé This pretty little town – now again part of France – is situated on both sides of the Meuse River. Its historical buildings include the Church of St-Léger, as well as the remains of the Laval Dieu monastery, abolished during the French Revolution. It is mainly the magnificent landscape that draws the visitors, however; rock climbers enjoy testing their skills on the Roche à Sept Heures and on the Rocher des Quatre Fils d'Aymon.

⑮ Charleville-Mézières A short way to the west of Sedan is Charleville-Mézières situated on a bend in the Meuse River. The capital of the Ardennes département first came into being in 1966 with the merger of the previously separate towns of Mézières and Charleville, separated from one another by the river. Mézières was the older of the two towns, an important economic center and even a garrison town as of the 16th century. Charleville was founded in the early 17th century as a ducal seat.

The city's drawing board design is still recognizable in the layout of the streets that intersect at right angles. The most important architectural monument in the Mézières section of the city is the Basilica of Notre-Dame with its Gothic and Renaissance elements. The royal wedding of Charles IX and Elizabeth of Austria was cele-

brated here in 1570. The Place Ducale forms the central point of Charleville, from an urban-planning perspective a highly accomplished city square reminiscent of the Place des Vosges in Paris.

The Charleville section of the city is where the great French poet Arthur Rimbaud (1854–1891) was born and where he spent his childhood. The Musée Rimbaud, housed in a former mill, commemorates the city's famous son, whose work influenced symbolist, surrealist and Dadaist poets decades later.

⑯ Parc Naturel Régional de L'Avesnois The Avesnois regional park – located not far from the border with Belgium – protects a traditional cultural landscape: rivers and lakes, wooded hills, meadows and blossoming hedgerows, with

Top left: A magnificent medieval fortress watches over the little town of Bouillon.
Top: Historic buildings in the Place Ducale in Charleville.

the city's Musée des Beaux-Arts. The museum building with its generous dimensions was built in th early 20th century and underwent extensive renovations in 1995, during which it was also expanded to cover some 4,400 sq m (47,344 sq ft).

On display are outstanding works by the great Flemish masters, including Van Dyck, Bosch, Brueghel and Rubens. The religious art collection in the Rubens Room is especially worth seeing, but other genres – such as landscapes, still life and portraits – are of course also represented. The main attention is naturally focused on the city's two prominent artists, Watteau and Carpeaux, whose work is on display in the sculpture garden.

Lille

Lille, Europe's "Capital of Culture" in 2004, is the French university city with the highest proportion of students among its residents. Lille, its name being derived from an island in the Deûle River ("L'Ile"), was once part of the Spanish Netherlands. Today its one-time affiliation to historic Flanders is still evident.

The Old Stock Exchange was completed in 1653, before Lille became part of France, as an ensemble of several buildings grouped around a courtyard.

The opera and belfry at the Place du Théâtre

The lions of Flanders above the entrances are a visible legacy from the period of its construction. The carefully restored complex with its narrow columns and ornamental pediments is considered by many to be the loveliest building in Lille. The Place du Général de Gaulle, its namesake having come from Lille, also features buildings with attractive façades.

The Fine Art Museum, one of France's most important art museums and thanks to the size of its permanent collection the second-largest after the Louvre, is housed in the Palais des Beaux-Arts. The master fortress builder Vauban began the construction of a magnificent defense complex directly following Lille's capture by King Louis XIV. The remains of the citadel are now part of a popular park.

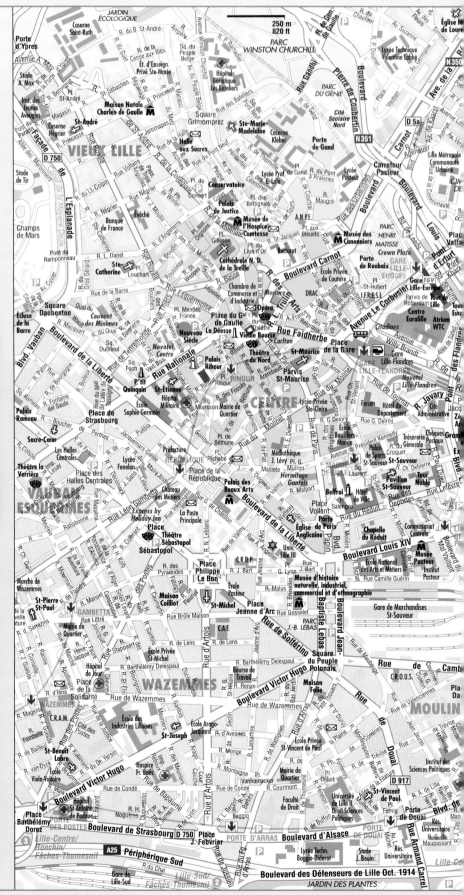

The Place du Général de Gaulle in Lille is dominated by the Old Stock Exchange (La Vieille Bourse), built in the style of the Flemish Renaissance.

tranquil villages in between, some of them still surrounded by protective walls. In the Ecomusée in Fourmies in the south-east of the park, interested visitors find out about the important role played in the Industrial Revolution by what is such an idyllic region today.

⑰ Parc Naturel Régional Scarpe-Escaut The Scarpe-Escaut regional park, named after the region's two most important rivers, extends to the north of Valenciennes, which it is well worth making an excursion to (see page 21). The landscape protected by the park since 1968 was previously a huge area of industrial wasteland for decades. This stretch of land was the heart of a black belt of coalmines, stretching from Bethune across the frontier toward Liège until the 1960s; slag heaps characterized the landscape, both the Scarpe and Escaut Rivers were heavily polluted, and after the Germans felled the last of the forests in World War I, a barren landscape was all that remained. The park therefore also tells the story of a successful renaturation process: woods have been reforested and the wasteland turned into a recreational area with plenty of options for hikers and cyclists, with mountain-bike trails, and swimming and canoeing on the lake. The park's wetlands are now also a sanctuary protecting a great many bird species, including the now rare bluethroat.

Only a few ruins still serve as reminders of the area's early development by monks, including the tower of the abbey of St-Amand and the gatehouse of the abbey of Marchiennes, now housing the park center. The fortified town of Condé to the north testifies to the great wealth and prosperity of the Duc de Croy in the 18th century.

⑱ Lille See page 22.
The route then continues via Lille to Douai.

⑲ Douai South of Lille, in the northern French coalfields, is the town of Douai, rich in tradition. Dating back to a Roman fortress, the town has shared the same fate as many northern French towns, belonging to Flanders, then to Burgundy, next to the Spanish Netherlands and ultimately to France during the course of its turbulent history. Douai was a coal-mining town for a long time but that is now history too, the last of the rich coal mines having finally closed down in 1990.

Today the heart of the town bears no traces of the mining era, retaining instead its 18th-century architecture. The most important monument is typical for the North of France where a great many impressive belfries (bell towers, *beffroy* in French) were built in the Middle Ages, twenty-three of them having been declared UNESCO World Heritage Sites in 2005. These include one of the loveliest bell towers in the region, the belfry of Douai. The tower, 64 m (210 ft) high, dates from the 14th and 15th centuries and stands tall above the roofs of the Old Town, affording an impressive panoramic view. The tower's large chimes sound on the hour and every half hour. Also worth seeing is the Church of St-Pierre and the Musée de la Chartreuse that is part of a Carthusian monastery.

⑳ Lewarde Historic Mining Center/Centre Minier Anyone wanting to know what life was

like as a coal miner and how coal was mined underground ought to pay a visit to the Mining History Center of Lewarde, directly to the south-east of Douai. The Centre Historique Minier de Lewarde is one of the

Top: The courtyard of the Old Stock Exchange in Lille.
Above: The belfry in Douai is one of the loveliest of its kind.

The weeping angel with the symbols of transience was created by Nicolas Blasset in 1628 for Amiens Cathedral.

largest French mining museums; tour guides, usually former coalminers themselves, will take you down the shaft in a small cage and tell you all about coalmining. The mine was operative from 1930 to 1971.

㉑ Arras Further to the southwest, situated in the historical border region between France and the Netherlands, is the town of Arras, dating back to a Celtic settlement. The town's territorial affiliation changed frequently during the course of history until such time as the fortress built by Vauban guaranteed a permanent link with France. Arras once more found itself close to a military front in World War I, suffering severe war damage but being rebuilt again later.

Arras today boasts an attractive historic center with the two large squares, the Grand' Place and the Place des Héros, being especially remarkable, lined as they are with buildings featuring carefully restored façades in the Flemish style of the 17th century. The late-Gothic style Hôtel de Ville is also remarkable; it was rebuilt after sustaining heavy damage in the war. Les Boves, the underground caves running beneath the whole of the town center, are a particular attraction in Arras, this labyrinth of passageways having been in existence since the 10th century. The caves served as a hiding place and shelter in both world wars. The cathedral, an important example of 18th-century church architecture, and the Musée des Beaux-Arts in the abbey church of St-Vaast, are also worth seeing.

Maximilien de Robespierre (1758–1794), one of the most controversial figures of the French Revolution, was born in Arras. In World War II, Antoine de Saint-Exupéry created a literary monument to the town with his novel *Flight to Arras*.

㉒ Amiens From Arras the journey continues initially in what is an almost exactly southerly direction, then heading south-west; the destination is Amiens, capital of the Somme département and of the Picardie region. In Roman times, Samarobriva, situated at a crossing over the Somme River, was one of the most important towns in the region, and apparently Julius Caesar stayed here on occasion. The heavily fortified town fell to the Franks in the fifth century, later to Burgundy and ultimately to France. The city of Amiens owes its worldwide fame to one single building in particular: Amiens Cathedral, a UNESCO World Heritage Site dating from the 13th century. The Gothic church is one of the loveliest and the largest in the whole of France. About 145 m (478 ft) long, the transept 70 m (231 ft) wide, and the central nave with a height of 42.3 m (139 ft), the building has a volume of around 200,000 cu m (7,062,933 cu ft). The use of innovative technology meant that the cathedral was completed in a record time of around 50 years, an extraordinarily short period at that time. It served as a model for many other churches of that period, such as Cologne Cathedral. The ornamentation and decorative sculptures are overwhelming: the main portal alone with its superb Last Judgment scenes features around 3,000 statues; inside, the choir stalls are a masterpiece of woodcarving, boasting no less than about 4,000 figures in around 400 different scenes. The brightness of the cathedral's nave is also astonishing and impressive: in accordance with Gothic ideals, the walled surfaces were greatly reduced in order to allow for large windows.

Amiens has many other attractions on offer in addition to the cathedral. The city tower, or belfry, stands on the Place au Fils, but its great bell was destroyed in World War II. The Musée de Picardie in a 19th-century building displays worthwhile regional art exhibits.

Amiens Cathedral also houses the tombs of countless church dignitaries – seen here that of Canon Adrien de Hénencourt.

Les Hortillonnages provide for a very special experience: this marsh area of 300 ha (741 acres) fed by the Somme and Avre Rivers was converted into a kind of floating market garden which has supplied the city of Amiens with vegetables and flowers since the Middle Ages, although only seven of originally one thousand gardeners still work here today. Taking a flat-bottomed boat along the small waterways affords an unusual way to explore the displays.

Finally, the city of Amiens is also associated with the name of a well-known French writer: Jules Verne (1828–1905), one of the pioneers of science fiction. Although not born in Amiens, he spent much of his life here. The author, who was also a city councillor, lived with his family in the building that now houses the Centre Documentation Jules Verne.

㉓ Grottes de Naours Directly to the north of Amiens the route passes the Caves of

Naours where you can visit a kind of underground town 33 m (108 ft) beneath the surface. For centuries, the caves served as a refuge for the residents of the surrounding area during times of war, and they still did so during World War I. This cosmos beneath the ground comprises no less than 300 caves that can today be explored on a trail of some 2 km (1.2 miles) in length.

㉔ Abbeville Departing Amiens in a north-westerly direction, following the Somme River, you reach Abbeville, the next large town, after about 45 km (28 miles). This was the scene of brisk shipping activity in the Middle Ages as Abbeville was an important port on the English Channel, but over time Somme estuary silted up and so access to the sea eventually disappeared (existing to this day via a small channel only). Following two world wars, there is not much of medieval Abbeville left to see but the

late-Gothic collegiate Church of St-Vulfran is still a reminder of the town's former status.

㉕ Le Crotoy Following the Somme toward the estuary you will reach the small seaside resort of Le Crotoy. It lies on the northern side of a bay in the English Channel and the beach of fine sand therefore has the advantage of facing south. The resort also benefits from its proximity to the nature reserve, the Parc Ornithologique du Marquenterre, which is worth a

detour. A large folk festival at the end of September draws a great many visitors every year, when the flocks of sheep pass through the town while being

**Top left: The city tower with the town hall on the Place des Héros in Arras. Top middle and right: Illuminations recreate the original shades of Amiens Cathedral. Judgment Day scenes and Christ as Bon Dieu adorn its main portal.
Above: A fishing boat on the mud flats off Le Crotoy.**

The dunes on horseback: a beach activity with a difference at Le Touquet-Paris-Plage.

Detour

Parc Naturel Régional des Caps et Marais d'Opale

A nature park is not a national park: it can incorporate entire towns and may even be densely populated – these are precisely the sort of conditions that provide sufficient reason to protect natural landscapes from potentially damaging encroachment and it is also the objective of the regional Caps et Marais d'Opale nature park, the perimeters of which roughly lie within the triangle between Touquet-Paris-Plage, St-Omer and Calais. The park's landscape is very diverse: the coast features river estuaries, dunes as well as steep

Harsh coastal landscapes near Cap Blanc-Nez

chalk cliffs. Inland there are forests – and then there is a unique landscape near Saint-Omer: the moorland and marshes of the Marais. This stretch of land has been cultivated for centuries with narrow canals and water channels ensuring that vegetables could be grown. It is also a refuge for wildlife, from crested grebes and muskrats to tench, roach and pike. Today visitors are able to glide along the network of waterways by boat to explore the nature park.

driven back from their summer grazing on the salt marshes to their winter quarters.

The little town of Le Crotoy boasts an unusually high number of important personalities who have spent time here during the course of its history, including Joan of Arc, the writer Jules Verne, the perfumer Guerlain, and the novelist Colette and the painter Henri de Toulouse-Lautrec.

26 Le Touquet-Paris-Plage Continuing from the Somme estuary along the coast toward the north you soon catch sight of the popular seaside resort of Le Touquet-Paris-Plage, usually referred to just as Le Touquet. The little town on the estuary of the Canche River is focused entirely on tourism: there are hotels and restaurants, a casino and golf courses – and a big white sandy beach.

The resort was only founded in the 19th century, however, and the "Paris by the sea" epithet probably derives from the fact that the relaxed seaside resort

was very popular with Parisians for a long time. It was also a resort for the wealthy British who spent weekends here and built some outstanding villas in the 19th and 20th centuries that are today protected and can be seen on a city trail.

27 Boulogne-sur-Mer Heading north along the Opal Coast takes you to the heart of this charming section of coastline. The first larger town on the Côte d'Opale itself is Boulogne-sur-Mer. The town's strategic location on the Channel coast has been of relevance since Roman times; the Romans began their invasion of Britain from here and it was from this settlement – initially called Gesoriacum and later Bononia – that they maintained their links with Britain. Well over one thousand years later, in 1805, another European emperor came up with a very similar idea: Napoleon considered conquering England from Boulogne-sur-Mer and he amassed his Grande Armée there; a column, the Colonne de

la Grande Armée, commemorates his bold intention.

Today Boulogne-sur-Mer is a vibrant seaside town; the port in the north is considered to be the largest fishing port in France. The beach and port belong to the lower town, the Ville Basse. Here you'll find one of the newer tourist attractions, the excellent Nausicaá aquarium.

The more traditional attractions are to be found in the upper town, the Ville Haute. The Notre-Dame Basilica with its giant dome and Corinthian columns dates from the 19th century. Inside, it is worth seeing the statue of Mary, Notre-Dame de Boulogne, decorated with precious stones. The castle (13th C.) houses the renowned Château-Musée, its reputation extending well beyond the town itself; its remarkable exhibits include a collection of Egyptian and Greek ceramics, for instance. From Boulogne-sur-Mer it is worth making a detour to the Parc Naturel Régional des Caps et Marais d'Opale (see column on the left).

A sailing regatta on wheels on the sandy beach at Le Touquet-Paris-Plage.

28 Cap Gris-Nez The loveliest part of the Opal Coast landscape is reached a little farther to the north, where several headlands jut out into the Channel. The first of these is known as the Cap Gris-Nez, "gris", or grey, because the promontory consists of grey rock. Directly adjacent to the prominent lighthouse are the remains of a German bunkers from World War II, forming part of the Musée du Mur de l'Atlantique. There are also some remains of an English fortress originally built by Henry VIII who wanted to have a base in France. On a clear day you can see England from here.

29 Cap Blanc-Nez A little to the north-east is yet another headland, the impressive Cap Blanc-Nez, where cliffs of marl and white chalk drop steeply down to the sea. Here, too, there are German bunkers as reminders of World War II; they are part of what was known as the Atlantic Wall, with which the occupying Germans had

hoped to protect themselves from a British invasion. It also features an obelisk, erected in memory of the Dover Patrol, the Royal Navy's effort to keep German U-boats out of the Channel during World War I. At a height of more than 130m (427 ft) you have a great view of the sea and the coast from here. Even the famous white cliffs of Dover can easily be seen from here when the weather is fine.

30 Calais Shortly after Cap Blanc-Nez you will catch sight of Calais on the Opal Coast. The name of this town is known around the world yet only comparatively few visitors come here to visit the town. Calais owes it fame to its vast port facilities – it is the second largest passenger port in Europe after Dover. The English Channel is especially narrow here, it is just 34km (21 miles) to Dover, meaning that England is visible in the distance, and so it was only natural that shipping traffic with England

should be concentrated here. This trading importance meant that Calais was in fact subject to English rule for a long time: Edward III of England besieged and captured the fortress of Calais in 1346/47 and developed it into a strategically important English bridgehead on the European continent. Calais has long since been returned to the French, with trade and passenger ferry traffic continuing to dominate the economy. The French entrance to the Channel Tunnel at Coquelles is also located close to the port city. Despite its eventful history, present-day Calais does not boast a great many legacies from the past; the bombing raids by both German and Allied air forces left very little of the historic Old Town still standing. The fortress-like Church of Notre-Dame (from the 13th to 15th centuries) and the city hall, built in the early 20th century in the style of the Flemish Renaissance, are worth seeing. It is also worth visiting the Musée des Beaux-Arts et

de la Dentelle with its unusual combination of exhibits comprising sculptures by Rodin, German and Flemish paintings, works by contemporary artists and also lace *(dentelle)*. Calais' most famous artwork stands in front of the town hall: the world famous sculpture entitled *The Burghers of Calais (Le Monument aux Bourgeois de Calais)* created by Auguste Rodin in 1895. The bronze sculpture (twelve casts of which exist worldwide, by the way) commissioned by the city of Calais alludes to a legend, according to which King Edward III of England, who besieged Calais in 1346/47, is said to have offered to spare the city and to protect it from being plundered in the event of

Top left: The grey cliffs of the Cap Gris-Nez protrude as a headland between Boulogne-sur-Mer and Calais.
Top right: The wonderful play of natural shades and light in the Parc Naturel Régional des Caps et Marais d'Opale.

The Burghers of Calais – the expressive work by the sculptor Auguste Rodin

surrender, if Calais were to deliver six of its most prominent citizens to the English – to face death by hanging. Six citizens did in fact volunteer for this fate – and were then pardoned by the English king. The statue with its very detailed clothing and body language reflects the inner turmoil and fear of the six volunteers and is considered to

be one of the most important and best-known Impressionist sculptures there is.
From Calais it is worth taking a detour to the extraordinarily well-preserved little town of Saint-Omer.

31 Dunkerque North-east of Calais and not that far from the Belgian border is Dunkerque

(English: Dunkirk). The city has its origins as a fishing settlement in the seventh century. Fishing for herring and cod provided an important economic base for a long time. The port's strategic location also ensured that the history of Dunkerque was very eventful of course: over the course of the centuries the city has belonged to Flan-

ders and Burgundy, to the Netherlands and to England, before ultimately falling to France. During World War II, Dunkerque was largely destroyed in what became known as the Battle of Dunkirk – and as Hitler had declared the coastal towns along the Atlantic Wall to be "fortresses" that were not to be surren-

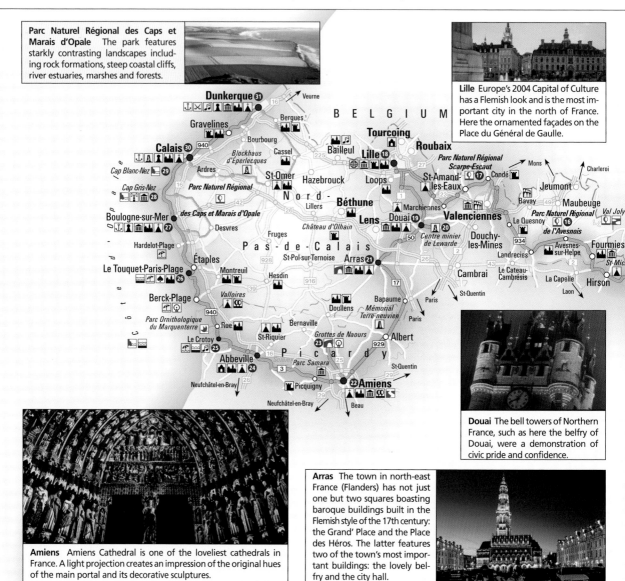

Parc Naturel Régional des Caps et Marais d'Opale The park features starkly contrasting landscapes including rock formations, steep coastal cliffs, river estuaries, marshes and forests.

Lille Europe's 2004 Capital of Culture has a Flemish look and is the most important city in the north of France. Here the ornamented façades on the Place du Général de Gaulle.

Douai The bell towers of Northern France, such as here the belfry of Douai, were a demonstration of civic pride and confidence.

Amiens Amiens Cathedral is one of the loveliest cathedrals in France. A light projection creates an impression of the original hues of the main portal and its decorative sculptures.

Arras The town in north-east France (Flanders) has not just one but two squares boasting baroque buildings built in the Flemish style of the 17th century: the Grand' Place and the Place des Héros. The latter features two of the town's most important buildings: the lovely belfry and the city hall.

Ready to leave for the next catch: fishing trawlers in the port of Dunkerque

dered at any price, the ruined city also had to endure a nine-month siege by Allied troops toward the end of the war.

The search for a cohesive urban development in Dunkerque today is therefore fruitless; the reconstruction work focused on the needs of the port and of industry. The fate of Dunkerque is thus similar to that of Calais: many people journeying to and from England use the ferry connections to Britain, whereas the city itself remains largely ignored and undiscovered.

If you have the time to explore, however, you'll indeed discover a number of fascinating sights: the 15th-century belfry, for instance, or the "Liar's Tower", the Porte de la Marine, a gate forming part of the former town defenses, the town hall from the early 20th century or the Church of St-Eloi from the 16th century (with its neo-Gothic façade). The Musée des Beaux-Arts is certainly worth a visit. The Musée Portuaire, located in a former tobacco warehouse, details the history of the city and the port, and for a closer look you can take a boat tour of the port.

The corsair Jean Bart (1650–1702) was one of the city's most famous residents who rose from simple ship's boy to commander of the French fleet under Louis XIV. He is commemorated by a statue in the city, and a square and a school also bear his name.

Metz The architecture in the capital of Lorraine also serves as a reminder that the city was once subject to German rule. The neo-Romanesque Temple-Neuf, for instance, was consecrated by the German Emperor Wilhelm II in person in 1904.

Nancy The former capital of Lorraine boasts squares of outstanding beauty and design. The Place Stanislas (above) is lined with gilded railings and by the town hall.

Bouillon The Château Fort here on the border with France is the largest and best-preserved medieval fortress in Belgium. The fort provides a splendid view over the town and the bend in the Semois River.

Epinal The little town's very appealing location on the Moselle River is what sets it apart from other sights. The Canal des Vosges links the city with the Saône and Rhône Rivers and it also has a marina.

Route 2

Normandy and Brittany

The territory extending out into the Atlantic and the English Channel in north-western France is not exactly lovely, but the romantic windswept coast and the luscious green interior radiate a sense of magic that captivates even the most unsentimental visitors. Indeed, across the entire region between Le Havre and Nantes, every stone seems to have a story to tell.

Powerful Atlantic surf, jagged rocky bluffs and shimmering white limestone cliffs scattered with long, deserted sandy beaches. On the coastlines of Normandy and Brittany the dynamic forces of nature are unfettered and the aesthetic is that of an ancient world. Augmenting the scene are sleepy fishing villages and vibrant port cities, elegant seaside spas and jolly family resorts.

Thousands of years of human history here have left so much behind that the entire region could be considered an open-air museum. Castles and manors, abbeys and cathedrals, meticulously preserved Old Town centers, half-timbered houses and stone buildings all attest to periods of power and prosperity.

Stout fortifications and sentry towers are reminders of wars and feuds. Normandy was ruled

by the Celts, Romans and Germanic tribes until the fifth century, before the Vikings and Normans claimed the area as theirs. The war between England and France lasted for centuries before the Huguenots devastated the land. But all of this was nothing compared to the German occupation in 1940. Within four years, all of Normandy had become a battlefield until allied troops land-

ed on Calvados and Cotentin beaches on June 6, 1944, generally known as "D-Day". The territory was eventually liberated in September of 1944, but by then many of the cities had been reduced to ash and rubble. Today, Normandy is experiencing what is arguably the most peaceful era in its long history. The roughly 30,000-sq-km (11,580-sq-mi) region is primarily involved in agriculture, and is characterized by pastures with stone walls, fields and apple orchards.

The coastline, which is about 600 km long (373 mi), makes Normandy a popular summer destination in July and August, when (not only) the French come to the lovely resorts and stunning beaches in droves. From there you can make interesting excursions to the famous rock island monastery of Mont Saint-Michel.

Before the Common Era, Brittany was home to a culture that continues to mystify the scientific world: Who were the people of the megalith culture? Were the menhirs, the stone monuments from between 5,000 and 2,000 BC, used as solar or lunar calendars? Were they fertility symbols, cult sites or processional avenues? There are still no clear-cut scientific explanations for any of these puzzling questions.

After 500 BC, the history becomes clearer. For around this time, the Celts came and settled in the area, which they called "Armor" or "Land by the Sea". Although they were evangelized around AD 500, they preserved many of their "pagan" customs and legends, as well as their Breton language. Certain Celtic character traits are also still in evidence: imagination and defiance are

The picturesque fishing port of Saint-Guénolé on the Bigouden peninsula forms the south-western tip of Brittany (left).
The impressive Norman coastline of chalk cliffs, known as falaises, near Étretat north of Le Havre. Worth seeing in the city's environs are in particular the Falaises d'Amont and the Falaises d'Aval (above), which have inspired artists through the ages with their wildly romantic rugged shapes.

particularly prominent, fuelled on by a healthy dose of pride. Brittany, which covers an area of roughly 27,200 sq km (10,499 sq mi), is France's quintessential agricultural regions. But Brittany is also an important fishing center and almost every sea bass ("loup de mer") or monkfish you eat in Europe comes from its waters. It also specializes in early vegetable exports as well as meat and dairy processing. And with its 1,200-km (746 mi) coastline, it ranks second only after the Côte d'Azur among France's tourism regions.

The wind and the stones, the green the meadows and the wild Atlantic ocean spray –

**Left: The La Latte fortress on the Breton Côte d'Armor.
Right: The port city of Saint-Malo on Brittany's north coast was built on a granite island.**

these are the elements that created Brittany reputation. That said, it did not achieve true international fame until the emergence of the comic book stories of Asterix and Obelix. Indeed, they are the best-known Bretons after King Arthur and have delighted readers around the world since the first comic strip by René Goscinny and Albert Uderzo appeared in 1959. The only downside is that their village unfortunately does not exist anywhere Brittany.

Fishing is still one of the main activities in the coastal villages of the Cotentin peninsula.

Detour

Cotentin Peninsula

The Cotentin Peninsula, washed by the sea on three sides, is the most impressively primeval landscape in Normandy. The coastline here is mostly craggy and wild, but there are long, sandy beaches between the jagged rocks. In the south the peninsula protects a vast moorland area from the interior, whereas in the north the landscape is reminiscent of Ireland or southern England, with rolling hills, verdant green meadows and dry-stone walls. The landing of the beaches in Normandy by Allied troops on June 6, 1944, is remembered in many local towns here. At La Madeleine, for instance, a museum commemorates the soldiers who

Fishing boats in the port of Barfleur in the north of the peninsula

landed at Utah Beach. Massive fortifications, which were built by the Germans as part of the Atlantic Wall to protect against a British invasion of the continent, can be seen near Crisbec. A memorial parachutist doll hangs from the church spire of Sainte-Mère-Église, and there is also a war museum.

The most important city in the area, Cherbourg, emerged from World War II virtually unscathed, and the streets and narrow rows of houses still exude the atmosphere of the 18th and 19th centuries. The umbrellas of Cherbourg, the inspiration in 1963 for the title of the award-winning film, *Les parapluies de Cherbourg*, are still produced. Since a merger in 2000, the city is now officially known as Cherbourg-Octeville.

This tour of the Norman-Breton coast takes you first from vibrant city of Paris to the wildly romantic limestone cliffs of Normandy and the beaches where Allied forces landed in 1944. Brittany then offers a unique natural and scenic experience and enchants visitors with the mysteries of prehistoric cultures and myths.

1 Paris See Route 6. Highway A 13 is a good way to get to Normandy from Paris, and leads you along the impressive Seine River valley.

2 Rouen This Norman city is home to one of France's largest seaports, despite its inland location. However, what really fascinates visitors is the historic Old Town.
The ancient alleyways snake between crooked half-timbered houses, churches with extravagant ornamentation, the magnificent Notre-Dame Cathedral and the remains of the massive fortifications.

3 Fécamp This is where the road meets the Côte d'Albâtre, the Alabaster Coast, where the bizarre limestone cliffs drop more than 110 m (361 ft) down to the sea. Fécamp was once famous for two things: its fishing port and its tasty Bénédictine herb cordial. The Sainte-Trinité Church of the Benedictine abbey still stands today.

4 Étretat This village was one of the fishing villages that was considered "picturesque" among a group of artists in the 19th century. It is situated in a bay enclosed on both sides by romantic cliffs. The Notre-Dame

Church dating from the 13th century is astonishingly large for such a small town, and is well worth visiting.

5 Le Havre This city at the mouth of the Seine was occupied by the Germans in World War II and subjected to massive bombing raids by the Allied forces. The town and the port were later rebuilt in concrete to the plans of Auguste Perret. The Pont de Normandie, a cable-staid bridge with the longest span of any bridge in Europe, links Le Havre with Honfleur. The art museum houses a collection of impressionist and cubist works.

6 Honfleur This port city is steeped in tradition and considered the most beautiful city on the Côte Fleurie, the Flower Coast. The architectural gems

Granville has an upper town featuring fortifications and a lower town that sprawls around the port.

Travel information

Route profile
Length: approx. 1,400 km (870 miles)
Time required: 10–14 days
Start: Paris
End: Nantes
Route: Paris, Rouen, Le Havre, Honfleur, Caen, Brest, Quimper, Nantes

When to go:
The ideal time to visit Normandy and Brittany are spring and fall, as the resorts get very busy in midsummer. There is no worry about the heat – the temperatures are on average around 15 °C (59°F) in May, around 18 to 20 °C (64 to 68°F) in June to September, and cool down to 15 °C (59°F) in October.

Information:
Normandy:
www.normandie-tourisme.fr
Brittany:
Tel: (+33) 2 99 36 15 15
www.brittanytourism.com

Ferry connections:
Condor Ferries offers connections from Poole, Weymouth via Jersey and Guernsey to St Malo and Roscoff:
www.condorferries.co.uk
Brittany Ferries travel from Cork, Plymouth, Poole and Portsmouth to Roscoff, Cherbourg, St Malo and Caen:
www.brittany-ferries.co.uk
LD Lines go from Newhaven to Dieppe and Portsmouth to Le Havre:
www.ldlines.co.uk

of the old port, the wharfs lined with narrow row houses, and the steep, hilly Sainte Catherine quarter exude fishing village romanticism and an artistic flair. The small but informative Musée de la Marine is housed in the 14th-century church of St Étienne.

7 Deauville This town is the epitome of sophisticated seaside resorts. In the mid-19th century, the rich and famous came in droves to the expensive luxury hotels, many of which still exist today. The heart of Deauville is the casino, and among the legendary places is the Promenade de Planches, which is constructed of wooden planks.

8 Caen Nearly completely destroyed in World War II, Caen is now a modern city, but its

great historic pride are the two abbeys of Abbaye-des-Dames and Abbaye-aux-Hommes. It is worth making a detour out to the Cotentin Peninsula, on which are located the town of Cherbourg and other villages such as the attractive port of Barfleur. From Coutances at the south-western end of the peninsula, continue southward on the D 971.

9 Granville The "Monaco of the North" is today a mix of medieval city and fishing village. The impressive Old Town is perched high above the center on a cliff. As in Deauville, one of the most famous buildings is the casino, opened in 1910. The fashion designer Christian Dior

Proud citizens' houses from the 17th century line the port of Honfleur (above).

Spectacular rock formations are the hallmarks of the seaside resort of Étretat on the Alabaster Coast. West of the city lies
the breathtaking steep coast of Falaise d'Aval with the Porte d'Aval, a rock arch created by erosion whose shape is reminiscent of an elephant's trunk. In front of this a rock pyramid juts steeply into the sky, known to the coast's inhabitants as

L'Aiguille – the needle. High and low tide have a particularly strong effect on the Alabaster Coast. The rock tunnel linking the Porte d'Aval with the next section of the beach is free-standing at low tide. It is thus a bit of an adventure to get from one part of the beach to another. Artists, including Monet, have always been inspired by the bizarre features of this coast.

The Côte de Granit Rose is at its most beautiful when the sun immerses everything in an orange light as here the lighthouse of Ploumanach. The entire coastal scenery is embued with a fairytale ambience at such times.

Detour

Dinan

Dinan, perched high above the Rance Valley, is one of the most impressive walled cities in Brittany. It is dominated by a mighty fort that contains the residential tower of Duchess Anne and dates back to the 14th century. The wall, which is 3 km long (2 mi), still contains sixteen towers and gates and almost completely encircles the picturesque Old Town. Every other year, Dinan celebrates the Fête des Remparts.

The Old Town quarter itself possesses a lovingly preserved its medieval character, with narrow alleyways, half-timbered houses, patrician houses and attractive churches.

It is clear that the city was prosperous in its day and that the trade in products like fabrics, canvas, wood and grains was lucrative, particularly

View of Dinan with the Gothic bridge across the Rance River.

in the 18th century. The sites that are worth seeing include the St Sauveur Church, which was partially built in the 12th century and has a late-Gothic gable, and the St Malo Church, built in the 15th-century with window panes telling the history of the town.

Also worth a visit is the Franciscan monastery, which today houses a school, but the Gothic cloister can also be viewed. Walkers will find rest and relaxation in the greenery of the English Garden near the Tour Sainte Catherine viewpoint.

spent his childhood in the pinkish house with exotic garden. Today, it is the Dior Museum. Heading toward Avranches on the D 973, which runs right along the coast, you'll enjoy magnificent views of the Bay of Mont Saint-Michel.

10 Mont-Saint-Michel France's most-visited attraction is not a place of peace and tranquility, but it is a place of magic. Its location on a conical mountain in the middle of a bay is simply sensational – the tides render the mountain either as an isolated island in the ocean or as a rock island surrounded by sand. Hermits lived in the first houses of worship in the area until, according to lore, Saint Aubert was charged in the eighth century by Archangel Michael to build a sanctuary on the mountain. Further development on the structure began in the 13th century. The church of Notre-Dame-sous-Terre, the new abbey church, the three-tiered monastery complex, the cloister and the Salle de Chevaliers are the most interesting areas. The D 155 heads out of the Bay of Mont St-Michel toward the Côte d'Emeraude, the Emerald Coast, where some of the most beautiful towns of the Breton north coast can be found.

11 Saint-Malo This medieval city of the corsairs was badly destroyed in World War II but rebuilt after 1945. The Ville Close, the Old Town with its granite houses from the 17th and 18th centuries, as well as the promenade along the ramparts are among the the highlights. The road to Dinard heads over the 750-m-long (0.5 mile) dam-cum-bridge of the tidal power station over the Rance. Its lock is 65 m (213 ft) long.

12 Dinard The second-largest seaside resort in Brittany is a

garden city nestled neatly into a hilly landscape. A walk along the Promenade du Clair de Lune is a must. Dinard was and still is a favorite meeting place for the international jet set.

A detour from here takes you 22 km (14 mi) south to Dinan, a picturesque little town perched high above the Rance River (see left).

If you prefer to forego this detour you can head along the scenic coastal road via Cap Fréhel to the capital of the Côte d'Armor, St-Brieuc, situated some 3 km (2 miles) inland.

13 Saint-Brieuc This city has a nicely preserved Old Town with gorgeous half-timbered houses, including the Hôtel des Ducs de Bretagne. The twin-towered cathedral from the 13th century, which was modified over the 18th and 19th centuries, looks like a fort.

14 Côte de Granit Rose Off the coast from the fishing port of Paimpol is the Ile-de-Bréhat, a birdlife reserve with red gran-

ite rock formations like the rest of the nearby eighty-six islands. It is of course this stone that gave the entire coast the name Côte de Granit Rose. Also worth seeing is the fishing town of Ploumanach just a few miles further north and Plougrescant at the mouth of the Jaudy River north of Tréguier. The chapel in the small seaside resort of Perros-Guirec is also made from red granite.

From Lannion, the road continues along the coast to Finistère, the "end of the earth", and it is here that Brittany shows its most attractive side: the Atlantic crashing along the wild, craggy cliffs and lighthouses standing on wave-battered reefs. The picturesque

Mont Saint-Michel, the monastery on the rocky island (above), is a unique structure in the history of church and fortress architecture. Right: Château de Brest (12th–17th C.) in the port of the city of the same name, is one of France's most important naval bases.

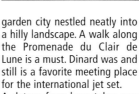

The Benedictine monastery on Mont Saint-Michel is today administrated by the Monastic Fraternities of Jerusalem, an order of nuns and monks founded in 1975, who also conduct the services at the abbey church.

fishing villages feature houses of solid stone and famous walled church courtyards.

⑮ Morlaix This port's Old Town is well worth seeing for its well-preserved medieval houses. The town is dominated by a massive railroad viaduct. If you're interested in the vicarages and calvaires turn onto the N 12 here into the Elorn Valley and head toward Saint-Thégonnec (see p. 40).

⑯ Roscoff There is a regular ferry connection to England and Ireland from this busy spa resort. The town has a number of beautiful old fishermen's houses, and the laboratory for oceanographic and marine biol-ogy research here is renowned around the world.

⑰ Brest This city was transformed into France's largest naval port by Cardinal Richelieu in the mid-17th century. In

Pointe de Saint-Mathieu is a unique complex atop a 30-m-high (98 ft) headland, approximately 20 km (12 mi) west of Brest. The complex includes a 36-m-high (118-ft) lighthouse, a square signal tower, the ruins of a former Benedictine abbey church, Notre-Dame-de-Grâce, whose western façade is from the 12th century (the rest was built between the 13th and 16th cen-

turies), and the village church of Saint-Mathieu. The lighthouse itself was built in 1835, using the stones from the church ruins, and helps sailors navigate along the Côte des Abers in Brittany.. As the waters off the Breton coast are considered among the most dangerous, the lighthouses are not just romantic but have an important function as life savers.

This lonely Breton house high up on top of the Pointe du Raz rock is a home for individualists and romantics.

Detour

The "calvaires" of Brittany

Among Brittany's most famous tourist attractions are the ornate granite calvaires, or calvaries. Some of the most beautiful ones are found in the Elorn Valley between Morlaix and Brest, and three well-signposted routes, the "Circuits des Enclos Paroissiaux", connects the most interesting of them.

Calvaires typically depict the biblical figures of the Passion story grouped around Christ on the cross as well as the apostles and saints. They were primarily created by Breton artists during outbreaks of the plague. All of the calvaires stood in "enclos paroissiaux", or walled churchyards, and the faithful enter through an imposing gate, or "porte triumphale". The church and charnel house or ossuary (ossuaire) were built with the calvaires to create a grandiose church complex. Local communities actually competed

The St.-Thégonnec calvaire, with rich ornamentation

with each other to design the most beautiful vicarages.

One of the most impressive calvaries is the Saint-Thégonnec village calvaire built in 1610. It portrays an enthralling version of the Passion of Jesus Christ and also includes the local saint, Saint Thégonnec, after whom the village is named. According to legend, the saint had his cart drawn by a wolf after his donkey was eaten by a pack of wolves. The pulpit in the church of Saint-Thégonnec is also worth seeing.

World War II it was reduced to rubble. Once rebuilt, it was one of the most modern cities in the country and is once again an important naval base. The Pont de Recouvrance, with pylons 64 m (210 ft) high and a total length of 87 m (285 ft), is the longest drawbridge in Europe. Brest's research center and Océanopolis maritime museum are located at the Moulin Blanc yachting marina.

A short detour west takes you to the Pointe de St-Mathieu, famous for the lighthouse inside an old monastery. From Brest, take the N 165 highway along the Bay of Brest to Le Faou, a town with interesting medieval granite houses made. The D 791 will take you to the Crozon Peninsula with its stunning coastal cliffs.

18 Crozon The main town on the peninsula of the same name is a popular resort. Lovely

beaches are tucked between steep cliffs, and you can take a boat to explore the picturesque coastal grottos. Four headlands extend out into the sea here. On one of them is Camaret-sur-Mer, once France's most important lobster and crayfish port. The Château Vauban, a fort built according to designs by Louis XIV's master military engineer, Vauban is worth seeing. West of Camaret-sur-Mer are the Alignements des Lagatjar, quartzite menhirs arranged in a U-shape in three rows. There are fine views from the peninsula's most beautiful cape, Pointe de Penhir.

19 Douarnenez This city has interesting historic districts and is one of the most important fishing ports in Brittany. The maritime museum displays a collection of boats and all sorts of fascinating information on shipbuilding.

Popular spa resorts in the vicinity invite you to spend a day on the beach.

20 Pointe du Raz This cliff drops 70 m (230 ft) to the sea and is the westernmost point of France. It is also one of the most visited places in Brittany. Countless visitors do the half-hour climb over the rocky ridge to the top every day. And for good reason: the view from the top reveals a primeval landscape of rocks and cliffs amid the surging waves of the Atlantic is spectacular.

Offshore is the tiny island Ile de Sein. It is flat and has hardly any vegetation, but the charming white houses shimmer invitingly across the ocean. Far out at sea, the mighty lighthouse of Phare d'Ar-Men, built on a rock in the sea in 1881, helps ships navigate the dangerous waters from up to 50 km (31 mi) away.

In Quimper, flower-bedecked and richly ornamented timber-frame houses line the Rue Kéréon up to the Saint-Corentin Cathedral.

Carnac

Carnac and the surrounding area are home to the largest megalith field in the world. Roughly 3,000 megaliths, also known as menhirs, are spread over several areas, all

21 Quimper The capital of Finistère is a pretty old town with pedestrian zones, lined with quaint medieval houses and imposing church spires.
It is particularly worth seeing Saint-Correntin Cathedral with its magnificent 15th-century stained-glass windows and twin 76-m-high (249 ft) spires. You can gain a good insight into local Breton history and culture at the Musée Départemental Breton.
Point-l'Abbé, south of Quimper, is a small town whose ornate lacework and embroidery made it famous well beyond the limits of Brittany.
On the way to Quimperlé you will pass Pont Aven, where Paul Gauguin painted and developed the expressionist style of painting together with Emile Bernard between 1886 and 1889. The Musée de Pont-Aven provides an insight into this time. A well signposted foot-

path takes visitors from the banks of the Aven River to the painters' favorite spots. The city has many commercial galleries and attracts artists to this day.

22 Quimperlé This small city has a lower town picturesquely situated on a headland between the Isole and Ellé rivers and boasting some very

charming old houses. The circular Sainte-Croix Church, founded in the 12th century, is also well worth seeing.
The port city of Lorient has no less than five ports, including one of the most important fishing ports in France. In Auray, roughly 18 km (11 mi) before Vannes, you should not miss the detour to the approximately 3,000 prehistoric standing stones of Carnac. From there continue across the peninsula to Quiberon.

23 Vannes The capital of Morbihan is a great destination for all romantics.

Top: view from the 72-m-high (236-ft) steep cliff of the Pointe du Raz in Finistère to its most recognizable landmark, the storm-battered lighthouses. Above left: timber-framed houses in front of Quimper's Saint-Corentin Cathedral.

fenced in to protect them from vandalism. The largest and most beautiful of them are the Alignements de Kerzhero. The stony witnesses of a history date back to the Neolithic period, roughly between 4000 and 2000 BC. There are also prehistoric burial mounds, the most interesting of which is the 12-m-high (39 ft) St Michel tumulus crowned by a chapel. From above, you can get a wonderful view over the landscape of standing stones. If this doesn't satisfy your passion for prehistory, don't worry: you can also visit the dolmens (tomb chambers) in the surrounding area.

An approaching thunderstorm above the isolated Berg en Lan Castle on the Quiberon peninsula.

Detour

Quiberon

Millions of years ago, the stunning Quiberon Peninsula was an island. Now it is connected to the mainland by a narrow isthmus and is home to an upscale holiday paradise with a wide range of resort and water sports on offer. The Côte Sauvage, or wild coast, is a series of craggy rock cliffs that is repeatedly broken up by small, sandy bays. The east coast features wide, sandy beaches that are perfect for relaxing family breaks as well as for those interested in swimming, wind surfing and sailing. Thalasso therapies are also on offer in Quiberon.

Brest France's largest naval port was almost completely destroyed in World War II. Today Brest is one of the country's most modern cities.

Côte de Granit Rose Picturesque pink and reddish rocks characterize the northernmost tip of Brittany. They have been beautifully shaped by the wind and waves.

Cap Frehel On a clear day you can see as far as Saint Malo and the Channel Islands from the reddish cliffs of the cape. You can get the best panorama views of the 70-m-high (230-ft) cliffs while on a boat tour.

Pointe de St.-Mathieu Looks can be deceiving: the lighthouse 20 km (12 miles) west of Brest stands not on top of the old monastery walls (12th–16th centuries), but behind them.

Pointe du Raz France's most westerly point is a 70-m-high (230-ft) rock formation in the Atlantic. The climb up takes about thirty minutes.

Carnac Now a spa resort, this location was even popular in prehistoric times: 3,000 menhirs (from 4000–2000 BC) and other stone monuments attest to human settlements.

The promenade along the port of the small town of Le Croisic on the spit of land west Saint-Nazaire.

And the medieval alleyways, the partially preserved ramparts with its defiant towers and the many charming half-timbered houses attract thousands of visitors every year. Valuable archeological finds from the region are displayed in the Musée d'Archéologie du Morbihan, in the 15th-century Château Gaillard, once the seat of the Breton parliament.

If you do not wish to go directly to Nantes from Vannes on the highway you should take the 30-km-long (19 mi) detour to the coast, for example to the small fishing and pleasure-boat port of the village of Le Croisic, at La Roche-Bernard.

㉔ Nantes The journey ends in Nantes, which vied for centuries with Rennes to be the capital of Brittany. It eventually lost once and for all in the late 19th century.

This city at the mouth of the Loire River was once the most important port city on the Loire, and magnificent build-ings in the Old Town attest to this. The Château des Ducs de Bretagne is an impressive fortress surrounded by a moat.

The grand Cathedral of Saints Peter and Paul, the Art Nouveau city squares as well as the elegant 18th-century arcades in the picturesque Old Town enchant visitors to Nantes.

Limestone coast near Étretat This village and the nearby glorious cliffs ("falaises") was popular with artists like Monet and Courbet in the 19th century.

Deauville This elegant seaside resort was already popular in the mid-1800s. Luxury hotels, the casino and the Promenade des Planches still prosper here today.

Paris The capital of France is also the country's cultural center. If you want to explore the city's numerous museums (Louvre, Musée d'Orsay and others) and enjoy its special ambience, make sure you allow plenty of time.

Dinan A mighty castle towers over Dinan, considered one of the most idyllic towns in Brittany. Miles of walls with sixteen gates surround the Old Town quarter on the left bank of the Rance River.

Saint-Malo The granite houses in the Old Town quarter and the boardwalk on the ramparts are impressive here. The former corsairs' city has been restored to its original state.

Mont Saint-Michel This cone-shaped island mountain with its magical location in a tidal bay, is one of the country's most popular attractions. It was built up in the 8th century, and again from the 13th century onwards. Three million visitors come to the small island every year to visit the Benedictine monastery.

43

The Champagne Region

The most famous sparkling wine in the world comes from Champagne, in north-eastern France. Ancient towns with Gothic churches and medieval alleyways lined with timber-framed buildings are a reminder of the important status once enjoyed by this region. Champagne brings with it the promise of tranquil countryside and lively towns.

Champagne comprises a chalk and limestone plateau landscape forming the east of the Paris Basin. It extends from the upper reaches of the Oise River for around 200 km (124 miles) to the south as far as the Yonne, bordering on the Île de France in the west. Its western section, the dry *Champagne pouilleuse* (poor Champagne), which is also known as the *Champagne crayeuse* (chalky Champagne), is largely comprised of poor soils and water-permeable chalk, for a long time used for extensive agriculture only in the form of sheep pasture and pine plantations. Only since the 19th century has this part of the region seen an increase in agricultural activity based on large leasehold operations. The undulating plains, still used mainly for sheep grazing, enable only meagre agricultural yields, while the deep-

rooted vines on the sunny slopes produce the acidic wine forming the basis of the famous champagne. Directly adjacent to the chalk areas and extending to the east in concentric circles is the *Champagne humide*, or the wet Champagne, made up of sandy and clay soils. With abundant water and forests, it is a livestock breeding area of a great many individual farms. The iron reserves to be found between Champagne and Lorraine saw the establishment of heavy industry there in the 19th century. In the north-east the Champagne landscape is characterized by the Ardennes, an undulating, forested area of hills rising up to 500 m (1,641 ft). The Ardennes are traversed by the Meuse and the Semois.

When Caesar conquered Gaul in 57 BC he made Durocortorum, presentday Reims, the capital of "Campania", as it was the junction of eight roads. Reims remains Champagne's most important city to this day.

In the year 451 the combined Roman, Visigoth, Burgundian and Frankish armies defeated Attila, the king of the Huns, about 20 km (12 miles) north of Troyes. The archbishop of Reims baptized Clovis, the king of the Franks, in 496, as a result of which Reims became France's coronation city. First referred to as a Frankish duchy in the sixth century, Champagne developed into a medieval county in the 10th and 11th centuries, with Troyes as its capital. Champagne was one of the most important fiefdoms in France in the 12th century. It was at this time that the famous Champagne fairs became established in the towns of Troyes, Lagny, Bar-sur-Aube and Provins. The economic prosperity of this period is still reflected in the magnificent buildings today. In 1792 revolutionary troops achieved their first victory over the Prussian and Austrian armies near Valmy. In World War I, on the other hand, the battlefields of the Marne came

In the picturesque town of Troyes the timber-framed buildings (above) in the area surrounding the St-Jean Church make for an atmospheric backdrop. Champagne's gentle, hilly landscape is dominated by vineyards as far as the eye can see. Extensive meadows are a feature of the high plateaus (left).

to symbolize the inhumanity and heavy losses of trench warfare. Champagne's international reputation is based on its luxury sparkling wine, champagne. The world famous wine-growing region extends from Aisne in the north via Épernay as far as the Yonne and is divided into Montagne de Reims, Vallée de la Marne, Côte des Blancs and Côte des Bars. Other gourmet delicacies include Ardennes ham the local cheese varieties, such as the soft Langres and Chaource cheeses.

The area is still only visited by relatively few tourists but has a great deal to offer. In the north the castles and forts testify to its long history as a border region. There are outstanding

Left: The victory monument in Verdun. Right: The reliquary in the Saint Clotilde Basilica in Reims.

art monuments and medieval timber-framed buildings to be admired in Troyes, Reims, Charleville-Mézière, Châlons-en-Champagne and Chaumont.

The landscape guarantees tranquility and diversity: it ranges from the forests of the Ardennes and the Argonne through to the open plains with their cereal fields and gently undulating hills planted with grapevines, then giving way to an area of lakes in the south with leafy oak forests and rivers.

Together with the Cathedral of Notre Dame and the Palace of Tau in Reims, the Abbey of St-Remi has been a UNESCO World Heritage Site since 1991.

The Musée St-Rémi in Reims

The city's other two World Heritage Sites – the Palais du Tau Episcopal palace and the Abbey of St-Remi – tend to be overshadowed, although undeservingly so, by the imposing Reims Cathedral. The Abbey Church of St-Remi, just 1 km (0.6 miles) to the south of the cathedral, is the most magnificent early-Romanesque church in northern France. Built in the 11th century, it houses the tomb of Saint Remigius as well as the Altar of the Three Baptisms from 1610. The

Top: sculptures in the St-Rémi. Abbey Church. Above: The museum in the Palais du Tau recalls the coronations of Reims.

museum in the monastery buildings holds artworks dating from Antiquity through to the Middle Ages, a military history collection as well as ten superb wall tapestries depicting scenes from the legend of Remigius. The Palais du Tau, the Episcopal palace situated directly opposite the cathedral, was built in 1690 based on plans by the Versailles architects de Cotte and Hardouin-Mansart. It houses the cathedral museum with numerous original statues.

With its gently, hilly landscape, Champagne is ideal for leisurely drives to superb Gothic architectural highlights, through the vineyards to the famous champagne cellars or else to Verdun with its poignant memorial to World War I. The many pretty villages along the way are also an open invitation to stop and linger a while.

1 Reims Reims was one of the most prosperous towns in Gaul and over the centuries that followed went on to develop into one of the most important cities in present-day France. Under Carolingian rule, the prestige that the bishops of Reims had acquired through the Christianization of the

Franks earned them the privilege of anointing the new king and Reims was France's coronation city from the 10th century through to 1825. On 17 July 1429 Joan of Arc led Charles VII to be anointed in the cathedral. With its uniformity, its harmonious structure and the wealth of graphic ornamentation, this impressive 13th-century church is considered a masterpiece of the High Gothic period. The cathedral, together with the Episcopal Palace of Tau and the Abbey of St-Remi (see the column on the left), is a UNESCO Cultural World Heritage Site. The twin city of Charleville-Mézières to the north-east of Reims is easily accessible via the N 51 expressway and the A 34 autoroute.

2 Charleville-Mézières The city lies in a picturesque location on the Meuse River close to the Belgian border. The Place Ducale forms the central point of neoclassical Charleville. It was laid out at the beginning of the 17th century based on

Notre-Dame Cathedral in Reims was for centuries the coronation church of French kings. Particularly impressive are the west façade, richly decorated with statues, and the interior (pictures top).

Travel information

Route profile
Length: c. 900 km (560 mi)
Toe required: 1–2 weeks
Start and end: Reims
Route: Reims, Verdun, Chaumont, Bar-sur-Aube, Troyes, Châlons-en-Champagne, Épernay, Reims

Notes:
Gradients of often more than 5 % have to be negotiated.

Driving notes:
A-roads are *autoroutes* (highways, expressways). Important main traffic links are the national routes which carry N-numbers. D-roads are smaller departmental roads. Watch your speeds – there are many fixed radars as well as unmarked, mobile ones.

Weather information:
Météo France,
Tel 08 99 71 02 + No. of the département
www.meteofrance.com

Information:
Champagne region:
Comité départemental du tourisme de la Marne
13 bis, rue Carnot – BP 74
51006 Châlons-en-Champagne
Tel/Fax: 03 26 68 37 52
www.tourisme-en-champagne.com
www.champagne-ardenne-tourism.co.uk
www.reims-tourism.com

Champagne (drink):
www.champagne.fr
Wine tourism: www.champagne-tourisme.com

Reims Cathedral is a high-Gothic masterpiece, rebuilt after 1211 on the remains of an earlier building that had burnt down. It is unusually uniform in style despite the long construction period of around 100 years. The Gothic buttresses literally lead the eye of the beholder toward the heavens. Some of the stained-glass windows are the work of Marc Chagall.

German and French troops fought bitter battles in the forest area of Bois des Caures during the first days of fierce fighting in the trenches around Verdun.

the example of the Place des Vosges in Paris. The medieval city of Mézières lies to the south of Charleville at the narrowest point in the Meuse River's horseshoe bend. Every three years in October the city is the scene of an international puppet festival. The D 764 follows the Meuse River as it meanders here in deep gorges through the rocky Ardennes, for 20 km (12 mi) upstream.

❸ Sedan From 1424 the strategically important location on the edge of the Ardennes, and above the Meuse River, became the site of a fortress that was expanded, in several stages, to become the largest stronghold in Europe. The textile industry that has been of great importance for Sedan since the Middle Ages is commemorated in the Musée des Anciennes Industries located in the royal Le Dijonval factory founded in 1646.

❹ Mouzon The pretty town of Mouzon 18 km (11 miles) south-east of Sedan is reached via Bazeilles, which boasts a superb castle. The impressive Church of Notre Dame was consecrated in 1231 and is a particularly lovely example of early-Gothic architecture. The nearby felt museum (Musée du Feutre) tells you all you ever wanted to know about the manufacture and use of felt.

❺ Forêt d'Argonne The D 964 and the side roads heading south take you to the Argonnes, a range of hills along the border with Lorraine with picturesque valleys and forests. In Varennes-en-Argonne there is a museum detailing the arrest of Louis XVI and Marie Antoinette as they fled in 1791. From there Les Islettes, famous for its faïence and tiles, is reached via Lachalade with its impressive Cistercian abbey.

14 km (8 ½ miles) to the south-east in the elevated Beaulieu-en-Argonne are the ruins of a Benedictine abbey with a giant grape press from the 13th century. Heading east after a short while the D 603 will take you to the small town of Clermont-en-Argonne, worth a visit simply for its 16th-century Saint Didier Church and Saint Anne Chapel. About 14 km (8 ½ mi) to the north, the Butte de Vauquois still bears the scars of the bitter battles from World War I. They are indicative of the next destination along the route, the infamous fortress town of Verdun, scene of such hard-fought battles during World War I. Verdun is reached around 30 km (19 miles) after Clermont on the D 603.

❻ Verdun Verdun is known around the world primarily on account of the tragic events of World War I. In 1916/17 the city's environs were the scene of some of the war's most gruesome battles, costing the lives of almost 800,000 people. Verdun has declared itself a city of peace and forgiveness and attracts large numbers of visitors throughout the year. There are still a great many testimonies to the war to be seen in the city's surroundings (see column on the right) but the city also played an important historical role a long time before World War I. In 843 Charlemagne's empire was divided into three by the Treaty of Verdun: a west, a central and an east Frankish kingdom, the nuclei of the French and German nations. As part of the central kingdom Verdun belonged to the Holy Roman Empire from 925, with the city ultimately falling into French hands in 1648. This was followed by the expansion into a fortified city by Vauban (from 1675). The defenses were reinforced further after 1871 and a double band

The Douaumont Ossuary houses the bones of several hundreds of thousands of casualties. The walls and ceiling bear the countless names of fallen soldiers.

of forts erected around the city. Vauban built the citadel on the site of the Abbey of St-Vanne founded in 952, of which only the Tour de Vanne remains. The diverse facilities ranging from a large-scale bakery to operating theatres and munitions depots were linked by some 7 km (4 miles) of corridors. The magnificent citadel can be viewed from the comfort of a narrow-gauge railway.

Verdun comprises the upper town with the citadel and the Notre-Dame Cathedral, as well as the lower town with its commercial areas. The cathedral's Episcopal palace today houses the Centre Mondial de la Paix. The Douaumont Ossuary, a memorial to the war's countless dead, is situated close to Verdun. You leave Verdun in a southerly direction and follow the Voie Sacrée (Sacred Way) along the D 1916. During World War I this road constituted the city's last link with the hinterland. It was the lifeline across which all supplies were carried and along which the French soldiers were brought to the front.

7 Bar-le-Duc The town marks one end of the Voie Sacrée. The former capital of the Duchy of Bar lies in the midst of the delightful Lorraine landscape. The Place Saint Pierre, surrounded by buildings dating from the 14th to 18th centuries, forms the focal point of the upper town. The new castle, built after 1567, with the Musée Barrois boasting a comprehensive archeological collection as well as works by French and Flemish painters, is reached via the former main street, the Rue des Ducs-de-Bar. From Bar-le-Duc the Route follows the D 635, reaching St-Dizier on the other side of the Pays Barrois plateau.

8 St-Dizier The town is an important traffic junction at which several major roads intersect. It is also the capital of the arrondissement of the same name, counting around 31,000 inhabitants. Situated on the banks of the Marne River, St-Dizier is also close to the largest artificial lake in Europe, the Lac du Der-Chantecoq. It regulates the water level in the Marne, serves as a water reservoir and has developed into a popular recreation site for the region. Following the destruction of the nearby town of Vitry-le-François by the troops of Charles V in 1544, St-Dizier held off their attacks for six months. Legend has it that King Francis I later described the residents of St-Dizier as "braves gars", or valiant chaps, from which the residents' nickname, the "bragards", is derived. You leave St-Dizier via the N 67, following the Marne. The Roman aqueduct near Eurville-Bienville is worth a stop.

9 Joinville With just under 5,000 inhabitants, the fourth largest town in the Haut-Marne département has retained the

Left: Around 800,000 German and French soldiers lost their lives in the trench battles fought near Verdun. The Douaumont Ossuary is the most haunting memorial to this war (left). The Monument du Mort Homme on one of the once embattled hills bears the inscription: "Ils n'ont pas passé" – "They did not pass."

Verdun: Fortresses of World War I

Verdun became one of the main pillars of the French defense during World War I. The front ran directly north of the town between 21 February 1916 and August 1917, attacks being carried out with the utmost ferocity on both sides. Following initial German successes, French resistance increased and gruesome battles were fought in the trenches on both sides covering what was in fact a small area. The battlefields lie to the north of the town on both sides of the Meuse River. You leave Verdun on the D 603 in the direction of Etain, passing the French war cemetery of Faubourg-Pavé first of all. After 6 km (4 miles)

A cannon in Fort Vaux

on the D 112 in the direction of Dieppe-sous-Douaumont you come to the memorial to the builders of the Maginot Line and Fort de Souville. Further east a side road takes you from the D 913 to Fort de Vaux.

After passing the French national cemetery you then reach the monumental Douaumont Ossuary (Ossuaire de Douaumont). It houses the mortal remains of some 130,000 unknown French and German soldiers. The building, with a length of 137m (452 ft) and a tower 46m (151 ft) high, is the most important French monument to World War I. To the north-west of the Ossuaire you'll find yet another memorial, the Fort de Douaumont (1885).

General Charles de Gaulle lived in the Boisserie in Colombey-les-deux-Églises from 1934 to 1970.

Charles de Gaulle

Charles de Gaulle was one of the most important French politicians of the 20th century. He marked the post-war years in France like no other. Following World War I, during which he was wounded several times, de Gaulle participated in the French military mission in Poland during the Polish-Soviet War of 1919/20.

When World War II broke out de Gaulle held the rank of colonel. He disapproved of the policies of Marshall Pétain and appealed to the French people from exile in London via the BBC on 18 June 1940. De Gaulle founded the "Free French" movement in London on 25 June 1940. He entered liberated Paris as head of the provisional French government in 1944 and was celebrated as a liberator.

Charles de Gaulle resigned from the office of president in January 1946 in disapproval of the constitution of the French Fourth Republic. Following the Fourth Republic's failures in French Indochina and in the wake of the Algerian crisis, de Gaulle agreed

to be nominated again as president in 1958. He drew up a new constitution which he intended to be the foundation of the Fifth Republic. De Gaulle won the elections in 1958 and became president shortly thereafter. He then undertook decisive measures to revitalize the country. During his time in government France also became a founding member of the EEC (European Economic Community). Charles de Gaulle died in 1970 and was buried in Colombey-les-Deux-Églises.

tranquil charm of a French provincial town. Legend tells us that Joinville was founded by Jovinus, a Gallo-Roman senator, who is said to have built a fortress here in 354.

The sightseeing attractions include the surviving town's defenses dating from the 16th and 17th centuries, the Church of Notre Dame (12th C.), as well as the Château du Grand Jardin, its Renaissance garden enjoying a reputation that extends well beyond the regional boundaries. Following the Marne in a southerly direction you will reach the city of Chaumont after driving along the N 67 for 50 km (31 miles).

⑩ Chaumont The city lies on a plateau between the Marne and Suize Rivers. The best view of the city and the Marne Valley is to be had from the impres-

sive railway viaduct, some 52 m (171 ft) high and about 654 m (2145 ft) long, built in 1856. Chaumont was the seat of the Counts of Champagne until 1329, with the 11th-century dungeon being the only part of their castle still surviving. With 28,000 inhabitants this otherwise modest and sleepy town is transformed into a hive of activity every year in May, usually around Whitsun, when a 24-hour race demonstrates everything you can do with a bicycle in all its forms. Known as "Les 24 Heures Solex", the race competitors include scooters, bicycles with auxiliary motors, in four different racing categories, from straightforward factory models through to converted racing machines. From Chaumont the D 619 takes you back into the heart of Champagne.

⑪ Colombey-les-Deux-Églises One of the worldwide most famous Frenchmen used to reside in the small village from 1933: Charles de Gaulle (see column on the left). His house, La Boisserie, is open to visitors. On a hilltop in the village a pink granite Cross of Lorraine, 43 m (141 ft) high, commemorates the General and former President of France and stands symbolic for the Free French forces led by him. Continuing in a south-westerly direction through the vineyards of Champagne will bring you to a famous medieval spiritual center, the once powerful Clairvaux Abbey.

⑫ Abbaye de Clairvaux The abbey was founded in 1115 on a remote site in southern Champagne by the 25-year-old Cistercian monk Bernard de

The appealing Côte des Bars landscape is one of the four largest wine-growing regions in Champagne.

Bernard of Clairvaux

Bernard of Clairvaux was born in around 1090 near Dijon. He entered the monastery of Citeaux in 1113 from where he was sent off just two years later to found the monastery of Clairvaux in the west of the Champagne region, becoming the monastery's first abbot. This primary abbey of the Cistercian order instigated a renewal of both monastic community life and also of monastic architecture and the layout of abbeys. At that time the Cistercian order was considered a stricter alternative to the Benedictine order. As a result of these key measures und due to his importance as Doctor of the Church Bernard is venerated by the Cistercians as the order's greatest saint next to the order's three founding fathers.

Depiction of Saint Bernard during the foundation of the Abbey in Clairvaux

Using his diplomatic and oratory skills, Bernard worked on behalf of Pope Eugene III for the successful organization of the Second Crusade (1147–1149). In Speyer, Germany, in 1146, Bernard was successful in persuading the German King Conrad III as well as his adversary Welf VI, a member of the Welf dynasty, to participate in the crusade. Bernard was subjected to criticism following the defeat of the crusaders. At the same time, he enjoyed growing influence under his former student, Pope Eugene III. Bernard died in 1153 at Clairvaux where he was also buried. He was canonized as early as 1174. His remains were transferred to Troyes in 1792.

Fontaine who later became known as Bernard of Clairvaux, one of the most prominent personalities in church history (see column on the right).

The abbey is one of the four primary abbeys of Citeaux – the original monastery from which the Cistercian monks derive their name. Clairvaux was the starting point of an important network with numerous monasteries in France, Belgium, Italy, Spain and Portugal being founded by the abbey in Champagne. The fact that, within a century or so, the abbey stood at the forefront of more than 300 monasteries belonging to the Cistercian reform movement is due largely to Saint Bernard's personal efforts. This leading status resulted in ever-grander buildings being built in several construction periods, concluding

with the Great Cloister in the 18th century. The monks were expelled during the French Revolution and the state purchase of the abbey in 1808 saved the former abbey buildings only for these to be now isolated and converted into the largest prison in France. The church built in around 1140 was demolished in 1819.

The site of the old abbey with its rich history has now distanced itself from the events of its more recent past. The prison still exists, but the prisoners are now kept in modern buildings, while the abbey attempts to play a role reflecting its original spiritual orientation. The monastery buildings have since been opened to visitors.

⓭ **Bar-sur-Seine** The town is characterized by its picturesque timber-framed buildings

dating from the 15th to 17th centuries and is the main center in Champagne's Côte des Bar region. The Church of St-Étienne, combining Flamboyant Gothic, Renaissance and neoclassical style influences, boasts beautiful Troyes windows dating from the 16th century.

You leave Bar-sur-Seine via the D 4, driving through the tranquil beauty of the Champagne landscape. All within close proximity are intensively farmed valleys alternating with expansive meadows on high-lying ground, while the slopes boast one vineyard after the other. It is this mosaic landscape that makes the region so picturesque. Directly on the D 4,

Top: Holy Sepulcher sculptures in the St-Jean-Baptiste Basilica in Chaumont.

Château Bligny lies in the midst of Champagne's gentle, hilly landscape surrounded by vineyards.

halfway to Bar-sur-Aube, is one of the most attractive châteaux in north-eastern France.

⑭ Château de Bligny The château was built in the 18th century by the Marquis de Dampierre who acquired the property in 1733. Bligny is one of the two larger châteaux to be seen in Champagne. Built on a slope, the property overlooks the village and the Landion valley. The Landion River rises directly beneath the cellar of the château. Following the Marquis de Dampierre the château then belonged to the Baron de Cachard at the beginning of the 19th century whose planting of a large vineyard initiated the property's wine-making activities. Château de Bligny has been open to visitors since 1999. The château's wine cellar bears the Route Touristique du Champagne certification. It is worth taking a little time for the ongoing journey via the D 44 and D 4. The gently undulating landscape in which the villages are set is an invitation to linger. "La route,

qui monte et descente, c'est la douce France", according to one saying, meaning "the road that climbs and descends again, that is sweet France".

⑮ Bar-sur-Aube The "other" Bar located on the Aube River was an important fair town in the Middle Ages. The wooden galleries on the west and south sides of the Church of St-Pierre are still recognizable as former market halls today. The main altar in the church originally came from Clairvaux Abbey. The town was the scene of a major battle in 1814 between Napoleon and his opponents, while fierce fighting between German and French troops took place here in 1870. A champagne market is held in the town in the second weekend in September every year. Brienne-le-Château is reached via the D 619 and the D 396.

⑯ Brienne-le-Château One of the biggest attractions in this small town is the Château de Lomenie, built in the 18th century on a hilltop just out-

side the town and visible from afar. It was restored and converted in 1814, and today houses a clinic. For a long time the history of the region was determined by the Counts of Brienne, one of the most prominent aristocratic families in medieval France, producing statesmen, diplomats and crusaders. Brienne-le-Château became known as the place where Napoleon Bonaparte underwent his training having studied at the royal military

academy here for five years (1779–1784). He left the city toward the end of his studies which he then completed at the École Militaire in Paris. On 3 April 1805 – now as Emperor of France – Napoleon visited Brienne-le-Château again en route to Italy and the coronation. Like Alsace, Brienne, too, is renowned for its sauerkraut and the Fête de la Choucroûte en Champagne is celebrated here on the third Sunday each year in September.

Many appealing details are to be discovered among the carefully restored timber-framed buildings in the medieval lanes of Troyes.

⑰ Forêt d'Orient Nature Reserve Brienne-le-Château lies in the midst of an expansive nature park and local recreation area boasting several large lakes. The three largest lakes – the Lac d'Orient, the Lac du Temple and the Lac Amance – are not natural lakes but manmade. On approaching the water you'll become aware of a row of trees, some of which may be almost completely submerged in the water, depending on the seasons. This is due to the fact that the water levels can fluctuate greatly during the course of the year, reaching their maximum in July and their minimum toward the end of October when the trees then stand completely on dry land again. This highlights the importance of the lakes, which serve as a water reservoir and thus also as protection against flooding. All three lakes are linked with one another via canals and thus form a large, single water reservoir. The city of Troyes is reached via the D 619 in a westerly direction.

⑱ Troyes Formerly the main center in Champagne, Troyes lies on the Seine River, the river splitting into several arms here. In 451 the Catalaunian Plains north of the city were the scene of a battle between the Roman legions, together with their allies the Burgundians, the Franks and the Visigoths, and the army of Attila, king of the Huns. In the 10th century the city fell to the Counts of Champagne who built churches and hospitals, as well as founding the trade fair that still takes place today. From the 12th century Troyes was the venue for two of the six fairs for which Champagne was famous and where goods originating from as far as the Netherlands and Italy were traded. In 1284 Champagne came into the possession of the French crown through marriage. The status of the city, subsequently in English hands, fluctuated during the Hundred Year's War (1337–1452) and the increasing shift in trade from land to sea routes. The English were expelled nine years later and Joan of Arc was able to lead the dauphin to his coronation in Reims. The some 15,000 jobs provided today by the knitting industry date back to the manufacturers of caps and socks, the so-called "bonnetiers", first written mention of whom was made in 1505. The textile industry prospered in the 16th and 17th centuries despite the general decline in the town's status. It was an industry largely in the hands of the Huguenots and hence the issuing of the Edict of Nantes in 1685 with the subsequent exodus of Protestant Huguenots was a very serious blow for the textile industry in Troyes.

In addition to its historic and economic importance, Troyes is also a major city of the arts. The ateliers in existence since the 13th century developed their own style during the Renaissance, known as the Troyes School. Its most outstanding representatives were the sculptors Jean Gailde and Jacques Julyot. The city's stained glass attained high prestige between the 14th and 17th centuries, and they adorn the city's churches and many buildings in the region. The historic Old Town of Troyes is vaguely reminiscent of a champagne cork in

Top left: The St-Pierre-et-St-Paul Cathedral in Troyes is one of the most important Gothic churches in the Champagne. Middle left: The magnificent furnishings of Château de Bligny date from the 19th century. Right: The city of Troyes is famous for the large number of its picturesque timber-framed houses, all dating from the Middle Ages.

The Champagne vineyards, here near Champillon close to Épernay, give the landscape an almost Mediterranean charm.

the basilica boasts abundant Flamboyant ornamentation, Flamboyant being the term used to refer to the last late-Gothic style period in both France and England. It is characterized by the overlapping of specific types of tracery producing winding, flame-like and elongated teardrop shapes. The D 3 then continues to Châlons-en-Champagne.

㉓ Châlons-en-Champagne
Elegant town houses as well as lovely timber-framed buildings are what characterize this wine-trading city. It used to be the capital of the Celtic Catalaun and was administered by bishops in the Middle Ages, earning the city its many church buildings such as the St-Étienne Cathedral, the Collegiate Church of Notre-Dame-en-Vaux as well as the Church of St-Jean.
The bishops suppressed the ambitions of its citizens, however, and thus the city's economic development, ensuring that agriculture remained one of the most important economic sectors to this day. The city was called Châlons-sur-Marne up until 1998. The St-Étienne (St Stephen's) Cathedral features stained-glass windows dating from the 12th to the 16th centuries and the cathedral treasure is also on display. The Collegiate Church of Notre-Dame-en-Vaux with its four spires is without doubt one of the loveliest churches in Champagne. The adjacent Musée du Cloître has splendid architectural sculptures and capitals on display. Châlons' magnificent churches remain as testimony to the city's importance as a textile trading place in the 12th and 13th centuries in particular. The market hall dating from the 19th century is well worth visiting from a culinary and an architectural perspective in particular. It is situated to the

its layout – the Episcopal and aristocratic quarters around the cathedral (cité) form the head, and the market and artisan areas (bourg) the plug. Most of the buildings are timber-framed, the loveliest of which are to be seen in the area surrounding the Church of St-Jean. The narrow Ruelle des Chats has an especially picturesque medieval charm. In addition to the magnificent Troyes Cathedral with its five naves and wonderful windows, the Church of St-Urbain in particular is one of the finest examples of Gothic architecture in Champagne. It was built in 1262–1286, on the orders of Pope Urban IV who came from Troyes.

⑲ Longsols The route from Troyes continues on the D 960 in a north-easterly direction via Piney before then reaching the little village of Longsols via the D 126. The Church of St-Julien-et-St-Blaise with its extensive collection of paintings is especially worth visiting in Longsols.

The village on the edge of the Forêt d'Orient National Park is an ideal stop to relax and linger. It is also not far from here to the next destination, the fortress town of Vitry.

⑳ Vitry-le-François Vitry lies on the Marne River at the point where the Canal de la Marne à la Saône, the Canal latéral à la Marne and the Canal de la Marne au Rhin meet. The town owes its name to King Francis I who had it rebuilt in the mid-16th century as a fortress town with a checkerboard layout to the plans of the Italian architect Marini after it had been destroyed by the troops of Charles V. The town was not rebuilt on exactly the same site, however. The previous site (just to the north of the town) is now the site of the village of Vitry-en-Perthois, which was formerly known as Vitry-le-Brûlé. It was rebuilt again following the extensive destruction of World War II in 1940. The impressive Church of Notre

Dame at the Place d'Armes is representative of the French neo-classical style. The village has a number of inviting champagne cellars open to visitors. The N 44 follows the Marne Valley northward, turning right after around 10 km (6 miles) into the valley of the Fion River, a Marne tributary.

㉑ Saint-Armand-sur-Fion
This is a typical Champagne village with timber-framed buildings and still bursting with medieval charm. The picturesque buildings all nestle beneath an elegant, pink-hued Gothic church dating from the 13th century, the foundations of which rest upon the remains of an even older building.

㉒ Notre-Dame-de-l'Épine
The late-Gothic Notre-Dame-de-l'Épine Basilica is a place of pilgrimage is situated about 6 km (4 miles) north-east of Châlons-en-Champagne to Châlons and is visible from a long way off. Built between 1406 and 1527,

Visiting the many rustic wine cellars around Épernay is a real treat for wine connoisseurs as well as for incurable romantics.

south of the town hall and the city museum. The Porte Sainte-Croix to the south of Châlons-en-Champagne was built in around 1770 for the arrival of Marie Antoinette, the future mistress of King Louis XVI.

24 Épernay The town on the Marne River constitutes the second most important center for champagne production after Reims. The chalk subsoil here is traversed by tunnels up to 100 km (62 miles) in length in which 200 million bottles are stored at temperatures of 9 to 12°C (48.2 to 53.6°F). Some of the best-known firms open to visitors in Épernay include Moët & Chandon (founded in 1743), Mercier, Pol Roger and De Castellane. To the east of the town hall is the Avenue de Champagne and it is just that: here you will find one famous champagne house after another, most of them having being built in the 19th century. This is also where you will find the Château Perrier that houses the town museum. The De Castellane wine cellars, easily recognizable by the impressive tower, also include a museum. The major destruction suffered during the course of Épernay's history, however, means that there are now very few historical buildings still in existence. In the village of Hautvillers 6 km (4 miles) to the northwest is the abbey where Dom Pérignon was once cellar master. He lies buried in the local church. The area surrounding Épernay also includes the Château de Condé, one of the most prominent châteaux in the region. This lovely Renaissance château, together with

**Top left: The St-Julien-et-St-Blaise Church is the most famous sight in Longsols.
Right: The Marne meanders past the Champagne vineyards toward Épernay.**

Outstanding wines mature in the chalk cellars of Moët & Chandon in Épernay.

Champagne: The King of Wines

Wine has been produced in Champagne since Gallo-Roman times but it was only toward the end of the 17th century that Dom Pérignon, cellar master at the Abbey of Hautvillers, managed to achieve a natural fermentation that caused the wine to effervesce. Champagne subsequently became the preferred celebratory drink among the European aristocracy. Today production amounts to around 350 million bottles annually, although the Champagne vineyards cover no more than about 30,000 hectares (74,130 acres).

Champagne is produced using a special process. The majority of the basis wines ferment in steel tanks at low temperatures. Following the initial fermentation they are blended with wines of earlier vintages to form a *cuvée*. The champagne is then bottled and mixed with sugar and yeast. A second fermentation takes place in the sealed bottles, a process that usually takes between 15 and 18 months. Noble champagnes can take up to 15 years to mature, however.

The bottles are stored at an angle and shaken regularly, ensuring that the yeast gradually rises to the neck of the bottle. It is removed by freezing the neck of the bottle so that, when the bottle is opened, the frozen deposit shoots out of the bottle. This small loss is offset by adding a solution of sugar and wine, the concentration of which determines the character of the end product, ranging from *brut* (very dry) to *sec* (dry) and *demisec* (semi-sweet) to *doux* (sweet). After being recorked the champagne still needs to be stored for a long period before it goes on sale. Champagne's chalk soils are ideal for the maturation process – the caves known as the *crayères* and which can be visited in Reims und Épernay for instance, extend for some 250 km (155 miles), providing the best conditions for maturation.

The chalky soils around Reims and Épernay, together with the Pinot Noir, Pinot Meunier and Chardonnay grapes, give the sparkling wine its incomparable character. In addition, the climate of the region, the measures taken to reduce the quantity of grapes and the yield restrictions, all contribute to making champagne the king of wines.

Many champagne cellars, like Piper-Heidsieck here, are open to visitors for visits and tastings.

Champagne brands

The largest champagne producers in fact own just some ten percent of the wine-growing area in the Champagne region. They traditionally have to buy in the greater part of their grapes. These come from the more than 14,000 vintners in Champagne, some of whom have less than 1 hectare (2.5 acres) of vineyard at their disposal.

Moët & Chandon has been the brand leader in champagne sales for many years. The most prestigious is the famous

Champagne is still the preferred drink whenever there is something to be celebrated.

Dom Pérignon, commanding at least 100 euros per bottle (for a 2006 vintage, for instance). Moët & Chandon is the brand most frequently sold in the gastronomy sector. Piper-Heidsieck is by far the largest producer among the three renowned Heidsieck champagne labels. The third most famous champagne label – Louise Pommery – is a Cuvée Prestige, named after the wife of Louis-Alexandre Pommery who founded the champagne label in Reims in 1856.

The dark blue Pinot Noir grapes grow best on the sunny slopes of the Montagne de Reims near Verzenay.

between Épernay and Reims. Its landscape with its characteristic elevation constitutes the very first foothills that become the slopes of the Île-de-France. It is characterized by the contrasts between wooded plateaux, the numerous hillside slopes of the renowned Champagne wine-growing area as well as by the at times deep Marne Valley cutting through the landscape. Verzy Forest is a particular attraction for nature lovers. It is the only area in France where the "Fau de Verzy", a dwarf tree belonging to the beech family, is to be found, with some 800 trees growing here. It is from these Faux de Verzy trees that the forest takes its name and this population of rare trees can be viewed on a special nature trail. The tree, also known as twisted or parasol beech, has contorted, stunted, misshapen branches and short, twisted trunks that seldom reach a height of more than 15 m (49 ft). With their drooping branches the crowns of these beeches look like umbrellas or mushrooms. The Montagne de Reims serves also as an important recreation area for the residents of the nearby town and features a well-signposted network of hiking trails.

It is well worth enjoying some rest and recreation in this attractive nature park before returning to the vibrancy of Reims, the start and end point of this route through the Champagne region.

Top links: A windmill stands out on the horizon near Verzenay south of Reims above the vineyards of Pinot Noir grapes that will later be used to make champagne. Above left: The Verzenay wine museum situated next to the lighthouse is the ideal stop for anyone wanting to learn more about champagne production.

its park full of big, old trees, is situated in the little village of Condé-en-Brie. The cobbled courtyard is enclosed on three sides by the residential quarters, offices and the tower. The present-day château is thought to have been built on the foundations of a 12th-century fort. Confiscated by King Louis XIV in 1711, the Château de Condé then became the property of the Marquis de La Faye who

commissioned the French architect Jean-Nicolás Servan, also known as Servandoni, with the rebuilding of the château in the baroque style.

Today the château is in the private possession of the Rochefort family. Today the complex is open for private and groups visits on guided tours. The château with its reconstructed original-style interior has been a protected historical monument

since October 1979. Visitors are able to admire not only the original stone tiles dating from the 16th century, but also the many valuable art treasures including the ballroom decorated in the trompe-l'oeil style and the "salon" designed by Jean-Baptiste Oudry.

㉕ Montagne de Reims Nature Park The Montagne de Reims Nature Park extends

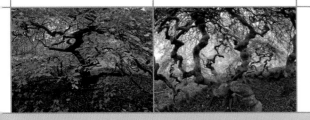

"Fau de Verzy" refers to a special kind of beech tree, a dwarf beech, around 800 of which are to be found in the Montagne de Reims nature park.

Charleville-Mézières The Place Ducale, laid out in the early 1600s and based on the Place de Vosges in Paris, forms the heart of the city of Charleville situated on the Meuse River.

Sedan Near the Belgian border, the town lies in a strategically important position, a fact that has repeatedly earned it a keyrole during times of war, as during the Franco-Prussian War of 1870/71 and World War I. The fortress with its robust ramparts is the most important building.

Reims The city on the Vesle River is a center of champagne production. Reims Cathedral (now a UNESCO World Heritage Site) is a major work of French Gothic architecture and was the coronation church for French kings for centuries.

Épernay Champagne fans in particular enthuse about this town located among rolling hills and on the Marne River – it is the famous champagne cellars that draw them.

Verdun A town whose name has achieved a tragic fame as a result of the battles fought here in World War I costing the lives of countless soldiers on both sides. Battlefields and cemeteries remain as testimonies to the war.

Bar-le-Duc The main town in the Meuse département has an upper and a lower town. The new castle, built in the 16th century by the Dukes of Bar, forms the focal point of the upper town.

Chaumont The Counts of Champagne built a fortress here in the 11th century but only the dungeon still survives today. The most impressive structure in the town is the railway viaduct from 1857, its 50 arches and impressive height of 52m (171 ft) having made it a landmark for the town of Chaumont.

Châlons-en-Champagne The town was called Châlons-sur-Marne up until 1998. It lies close to the Catalaunian Plains where, in 451, King Attila with his army of warlike Huns suffered a devastating defeat. The city's most important architectural legacies date from the 11th and 12th centuries: the Collégiale Notre-Dame-en-Vaux, the St-Étienne Cathedral and a number of churches worth visiting.

Troyes The Celts were the first to establish a settlement on this site and the Romans, too, established themselves here. It was in the late Middle Ages that the city enjoyed great prosperity when it developed into one of the most important trading centers in Champagne. With its cathedral and many attractive historic buildings Troyes has retained its medieval flair.

Through Burgundy

This delightful 1,100-km (690-mi) journey begins in Sens south of Paris and takes you through the wine-growing region of the Côte d'Or, past elegant aristocratic estates and into Dijon, the capital of Burgundy. From there it continues to the caves, Romanesque churches and Charolais beef cattle of southern Burgundy before winding over to Nevers on the Loire and finishing up in Vézelay, one of France's most beautiful villages and a starting point for the Way of St James pilgrimage.

"Bon voyage in France's paradise of churches and vineyards," is how connoisseurs of Burgundy send their friends off into the region between the Saône and Loire rivers. The southernmost of Burgundy's four départements is aptly named Saône-et-Loire, and features all of the vital elements. The water in the lovely rivers and streams feeds the fertile pastures; undulating vineyards and the leafy green forests of the Morvan provide wine and tranquility; and in the 19th century fire in the former iron foundries transformed the small town of Le Creusot into an industrial powerhouse where Eugène and Adolphe Schneider competed with German giants Krupp in Essen. These days the smokestacks are decommissioned, the air is clean and an interesting technology and cultural center provides insights into the area's history.

A land of comfort and ease awaits its guests in Burgundy. Europe has no shortage of regions where the landscapes are varied, and where thousands of years of history have left behind buildings of great beauty along with artistic treasures of the highest order. But there is

more to Burgundy. Even in the high season locals still outnumber tourists. The region's wine is some of the best in Europe and the same applies to Burgundy's cuisine. And because most northern French and Europeans typically head straight for the Mediterranean, they often see nothing more than the autoroutes in Burgundy, despite the region's obvious benefits for people who simply want to enjoy life.

One tip for visitors who may tire of the seemingly endless roads: Burgundy also features numerous waterways and navigable canals – some of them are hundreds of years old – so getting out of your car and onto a houseboat for a few days or a week is a tempting option. And you don't even need a boating license. Depending on the number of locks you probably won't even travel more than

150 km (95 mi) in one relaxing week, and these jaunts add variety to what might be long periods on the highways.

Burgundy's ancient cities survived the two world wars with either none or only very limited damage, and their historic centers have been lovingly preserved despite rapid growth and metropolitan dimensions in all four départements of Burgundy: Auxerre in the Yonne département in the north, Nevers on the Loire in the Nièvre département in the west, Chalons-sur-Saône in the south in the Saône-et-Loire département and Dijon in the Côte d'Or département.

Green forests and pastures, river valleys, vineyards and parks welcome visitors in every corner over Burgundy, however, it is the hills and woodlands of the Morvan that form the verdant core of the region. The

Above: The cloisters of the magnificent Fontenay Abbey, founded in 1118 by Bernard of Clairvaux.
Left: Exquisite church art from the 15th and 16th centuries can be enjoyed in the Cathedral of Saint-Étienne in Sens on the Yonne River. Here we see the three Magi coming to worship the newly born Jesus Christ.

Parc Naturel Régional du Morvan was established in 1971, and with an area of 175,000 ha (432,425 acres) it is one of the largest nature parks in Europe. The lumberjacks and ferrymen of the Morvan have now been relegated to the confines of the museum, but in their stead are hikers, cyclists, equestrians and whitewater rafters who have discovered the area's recreational highlights.

Tours through Burgundy tend to be a series of pleasurable encounters with history, from ancient Celtic tribes via the Middle Ages to modern Europe, and from sumptuous art and religious treasures to the palaces and villas of Burgundy's dukes.

Left: A richly decorated tympanum in the Gothic abbey church of Vézelay.
Right: Remnants of the past in a small Burgundian village.

Particularly beautiful are the plentiful sacred Romanesque and Gothic buildings, found even in the smallest of villages – and all these cultural gems are accompanied by the most exquisite culinary delights and top-quality wines in the local taverns and gourmet oases.

A sculpture in the apse chapel of the Gothic Cathedral of St-Étienne in Sens

During its heyday in the 14th and 15th centuries, Burgundy, today a region in France, was one of the most important independent territories in Europe – a kingdom, a duchy and the Free County of Burgundy. Its rulers invited the best artists from all over the continent here, and their extensive artistic work can still be admired in many places today.

1 Sens It is not far from Paris to the Yonne River, which flows from the Morvan through the historic bishop's see of Sens and ultimately into the Seine. The city is already in Burgundy, but the Yonne divides Sens from its western suburbs.

The main market square is a lively part of the city, as is the north-south transit axis, but visitors soon recognize the stark contrast between commotion and calm when they enter the alleyways of the Old Town around the extraordinary Romanesque-Gothic ensemble of the Cathedral of St-Étienne. Begun in 1140, its massive square towers, the precision tracery on imposing walls and a glorious four-centered arch all add to the charm of this edifice, which is one of the first examples of the French Gothic style. At the time, Sens was the seat of the archbishop while Paris was just a diocese, a fact

reflected in the cathedral and its nearby bishop's palaces. The south tower, which had collapsed centuries before, was only rebuilt in the 1700s, this time in the style of a small Renaissance campanile. Exquisite ivory carvings are displayed in the treasure chamber's (trésor) glass cases. Some came from Asia while others made their way via Italy, for example the cylindrical reliquary whose sides are decorated with figures from biblical stories.

In Sens visitors can stroll between the half-timbered houses in the Old Town lanes, stumble across fairy-tale street names like Lion d'Or (Golden Lion) or Tambour d'Argent (Silver Drum), saunter along the quays of the Yonne or explore the remnants of the city's old ramparts on the Boulevard du Quatorze Juillet. The rampart walls were built of massive natural stone blocks in the fourth century.

Back on the D 606 it is only about 30 km (19 mi) to your next destination on the route.

2 Joigny This city perched on a hillside above the Yonne has a lovely promenade to while

away the time, a charming Old Town with labyrinthine lanes, inviting cafés and shops, well-preserved half-timbered houses and two churches. There is a valuable Madonna in the St-Thibaut Priory and the St-Jean Church holds the grand marble tomb built for a countess of Joigny in the Renaissance. There are virtually no signs of medieval art or architecture here – after a fire in 1530, only ruins of Joigny's Old Town remained, and yet another catastrophe occurred in 1981: on the Cour de Miracles a number of historic buildings collapsed after a gas explosion. It is in that spot that the Jean de Joigny Cultural Center was later established.

Take the D 606 to continue on the route from Joigny to the cathedral city of Auxerre.

3 Auxerre The ensemble that is Auxerre features three imposing hills, each with its own medieval church, overlooking

Travel information

Route profile
Length: c. 1,100 km (685 mi) (without detours)
Time required: approximately four weeks
Start and end: Sens
Route: Sens, Auxerre, Semur-en-Auxois, Saulieu, Dijon, Beaune, Tournus, Mâcon, Nevers, Vézelay

Special considerations:
Be aware that parking spaces are rare in Old Town centers. If possible, park outside the Old Town and walk.

Safe driving:
Headlights are required in rain and snow. The speed limits also drop in rain, from 130 to 110 and from 110 to 100, and from 90 to 80 km/h.

Information:
Comité Régional du Tourisme de Bourgogne:
www.burgundy-tourism.com
21006 Dijon Cédex,
Tel: 03 80 28 02 80

Dijon:
www.visitdijon.com/en
Beaune:
www.beaune-tourism.com
Mâcon:
www.macon-tourism.com/uk/index.php

Houseboats:
Houseboat tours on the Canal du Nivernais start from Auxerre. For information and bookings go to:
www.holidayboat.net
www.europeafloat.com
www.rentaboat.net

Burial scene at the Hôtel-Dieu, the former hospital in Tonnerre

the Yonne and its bridges. All this is enclosed by a pentagon-shaped series of boulevards that were built along the path of the former city walls. Today these roads lead traffic around the historic center.

With its river connections to the Mediterranean, Auxerre boasted a busy port even back in Roman times. The bishop, Germanus of Auxerre, was later canonized but died on a journey in the Italian city of Ravenna. Queen Clotilde had the Abbey of St-Germaine d'Auxerre built over his grave in the sixth century. In the crypt of the former abbey hang reddish and ocher paintings from the ninth century that are among the oldest of their kind in France. They depict the stoning of St Stephen.

The most beautiful of the city's religious edifices is the Gothic St-Étienne d'Auxerre Cathedral. Its façade features detailed stone reliefs which, despite the ravages of time, still climb gloriously up the imposing towers. The crypts are adorned with unusual frescoes that portray a unique version of Jesus Christ on a white horse escorted by the Angels of the Apocalypse.

This religious center is surrounded by worldly gems, with charming antiques shops, lovely half-timbered houses, and a number of museums including a beautiful art museum, a museum of archeology and the Musée Leblanc-Duvernoy where you can see how the affluent citizens of Auxerre once lived,

with tapestries, a number of paintings, valuable furnishings, crystal glasses, ceramics and porcelain on display. Auxerre is also to this day renowned for its gourmet restaurants. One of the premier addresses in all of Burgundy is Barnabet, on the Quai de la Republique. The ground floor houses a brasserie

while the floor above features an excellent restaurant.

After about 35 km (22 mi) on the D 965 you'll reach the town of Tonnerre.

4 Tonnerre Many of the region's, and even some of the country's, most famous stone buildings were constructed using the light-colored materials from the Tonnerre quarries: the Church of Vézelay, the abbeys of Pontigny and Fontenay, and the Panthéon in Paris.

But it is not solely because of its stone that most visitors make their way to Tonnerre. They come to see the famous Hôtel-Dieu (Hospice of God). Originally founded in 1293, this hospice precedes the more famous one of the same name in Beaune by about 150 years. According to the foundation

Top left: Joigny with the towering Church of St-Jean. Above: Auxerre on the Yonne with the Cathedral St-Étienne (foreground) and the Abbey of St-Germain (background). Left: The Old Town of Auxerre with the city gate and the Tour d'Horloge.

The charming town of Semur-en-Auxois is located in the middle of Burgundy on a rocky promontory overlooking the Armançon River valley. Four towers of the former castle and remains of the ramparts still bear witness to the once mighty fortifications. In among the historic houses is the Church of Notre Dame, a Burgundian Gothic masterpiece. After being badly

damaged during the French Revolution, Viollet-le-Duc, a pioneer of heritage site conservation in Europe, began renovations on the church in 1844. Worth seeing in particular are the richly decorated portal of the vestibule featuring a burial scene of Jesus Christ from 1490 and some magnificent late-medieval stained-glass windows.

Rural idyll on the Chablis, the river from which the region gets its name

Detour

Chablis

The name alone makes the hearts of wine enthusiasts and connoisseurs beat faster and they'll enthuse about the region's viticultural delights. On the steep banks of the Serein River and a short way into the hinterland you will discover the Chardonnay vines from which the white Chablis wine is pressed. The grapes are known around the world for their dry, fruity and elegant character. Vintners and dealers differentiate between Petit Chablis, Chablis, Chablis Premier Cru and Chablis Grand Cru and it is well worth taking the trip to Chablis to taste the wines yourself, made from the vines cultivated in more than 4,000 ha (9,884 acres) of vineyards in the municipal area and the Serein Valley.

The Domaine Long-Depaquit Winery holds a special place in the long history of Chablis vintners. When the church was dispossessed of its lands during the French Revolution, the brother of the abbot of Pontigny saw his chance and took it. Simon Depaquit bought the best plots from among the vineyards the monks had cultivated and founded a company that still exists today. The last descendant of the family passed away without children in 1967, but the historic business was taken over by the Bichot family of wine dealers and vintners from Beaune. Tastings are still held in the winery's pavilion.

The wine cellars at the Obédiencerie Monastery

charter, the facility was open to the homeless in need of shelter, the hungry in need of food, and the sick in need of treatment. The 100-m-long (330-ft) hall has a beautiful vaulted ceiling and an impressive gabled roof; it also allowed for large numbers of people to congregate or receive help. A brook flowed in a stone canal down the length of the building and at the altar is a statue of Moses kneeling at the thornbush before Mary. Benefactors and sponsors were given burial plots within the facility in the hope of receiving salvation for their souls.

Tonnerre also has a mysterious spring, the Fosse Dionne, the source and run of which are still concealed within the limestone. For hundreds of years the women of Tonnerre washed their clothes in the well.

5 Tanlay Just a few miles east of Tonnerre a narrow road branches off the main road to the Château de Tanlay. With four impressive corner towers, this enchanting castle stands proudly on an island within a moat, virtually unchanged since it was completed in the mid-1600s. It is not unified in style – when the first owner Coligny d'Adelot, ran out of money for the project in 1550, one hundred years passed before it work continued.

Some remnants of the building's early years remain. At that time the Catholic Church and the Calvinists fought over the future of France. Gaspard de Coligny, the brother of the original owner, was also an admiral in the French army, as well as a leader of the Huguenot League. It is believed that he stopped at Tanlay for secret negotiations, which is why one of the four towers is called the Tour de la Ligue. Coligny perished, however, during the infamous Saint Bartholomew's Day Massacre, in which Catherine de' Medici (widow of Henry II) allegedly ordered all of the key players on the Protestant side of the French Wars of Religion elimi-

nated. One of the eight-sided tower rooms contains a satirical ceiling fresco in which the protagonists of both religions are depicted as Greek deities – naked and with simple-minded expressions, a commentary on the meaningless power struggles among the religions.

The D 905 takes you along the Brenne River through the small town of Montbard to Abbaye de Fontenay.

6 Abbaye de Fontenay This isolated Cistercian monastery building became a UNESCO World Heritage Site in 1981. Unlike Cîteaux, the Abbey of Fontenay no longer houses monks but you can still make out some of the former facilities such as the chapter room, the monk's hall with its small parlor, a hospital ward, a guesthouse and the blacksmith's shop. The simplicity and clarity of Cistercian architecture are well suited to the woodland area, but when you imagine the everyday life of the monks

Clear, strict lines define the Romanesque cloister in the Abbey of Fontenay.

Vercingetorix

Most people know the two Gallic comic strip heroes Asterix and Obelix. Of course they did not really exist, but those interested in history will know of the real Gallic hero, Vercingetorix, who was born in the Auvergne in about 80 BC. At a gathering of Gallic tribal leaders in the Morvan he was able to unite all of the various clans against the Roman forces who were threatening their territory and livelihood. Together they went into battle to fend off the far superior Roman army.

At Gergovia, near the present-day city of Clermont-Ferrand, the Gauls achieved a victory against the Romans thanks to their courage and

Vercingetorix monument

you'll shudder at the degree of deprivation they endured. These pious souls slept with little more than their robes on stone floors barely covered with straw, and the windows were but holes in the wall. The average life expectancy of a monk in those days was 35 years. Your path now leads back toward Montbard and to the next stop a short way farther south.

7 Semur-en-Auxois On the valley floor below Semur-en-Auxois, the small Armançon River flows leisurely past tidy garden terraces and around a steep rock spur. Just east of the city, amidst an undulating pastoral landscape, you can go for a relaxing swim in Lac du Pont and stay in the nearby hotel. This small town more or less in the heart of Burgundy has a pleasant rural ambience. In the center of the Old Town – the *bourg* – cars are banned, and the steep roofs and narrow alleyways are the features that define the townscape around

the main square. The ramparts with the Porte Sauvigny gate and two other imposing portals once provided protection from hostile attack.

The architectural highlight here is the Notre-Dame Collegiate Church, a masterpiece of Burgundian Gothic. Eugène-Emmanuel Viollet-le-Duc (1814–1879) was one of the first European promoters of monument conservation and an enthusiastic fan of the Gothic style that developed in Burgundy. As a result, he dedicated himself to preserving the church which had suffered severe damage during the French Revolution. Naturally, the porch portal with its fine decorative figures is small compared to that of the Cathedral of St-Étienne in the wealthy town of Auxerre, but the masonry skills required to complete them were of a similar caliber.

The Gothic vaulting inside the church along with the colorful capitals, late-medieval glass painting and the sculpture of

the entombment of Christ in a side chapel all required the highest order of craftsmanship. The north portal features a banquet scene relating to the alleged travels of the Apostle Thomas to India. After the resurrection of Christ, he is said to have gone there to establish the first Christian congregations, but he was accused by the Indian King Gondolfus of embezzling the money entrusted to him. Thomas then freely admitted to having handed the money out among the poor. In the scene, a dancer leaning far over backward in front of the

Top left: With its four stout round towers, the beautiful castle chapel and the so-called round hall in which the Huguenots met in 1570 to discuss their fate, Château Tanlay is among the most resplendent Renaissance buildings in France.
Top right: Semur-en-Auxois with the collegiate church of Notre Dame and the imposing round towers of the former citadel

cunning. Not long after that, however, in 52 BC at Alesia (present-day Alise-Sainte-Reine) near Semur-en-Auxois, it came to a decisive battle, which Caesar chronicled in detail in his magnum opus *De bello gallico*. After a relatively short and unsuccessful battle against the Roman invaders, Vercingetorix retreated with the rest of his troops to Alesia. The Romans then laid siege to the town, using every means at their disposal. Following a lengthy period that led to starvation within the settlement and one short final battle, Vercingetorix proceeded alone to the Roman camp to surrender to the future leader of the Roman Empire.

The Gallic leader spent six years in jail in Rome and was ultimately killed when the Romans claimed victory in 46 BC. In 1846, Napoleon III had a monument erected in his honor on the battlefield of Alesia in Alise-Sainte-Reine.

The monastic buildings and the Abbey Church of Fontenay were designed according to the strict rules of the Cistercian Order and its founder Bernard of Clairvaux. All of the structures are plain and unadorned; only the cloister has sculpted capitals. Not even the walls of the triple-nave Notre Dame of Fontenay Basilica are plastered, and the floor consists of tramped-down

earth and mud. The 66-m-long (218-ft) and 17-m-high (56-ft) edifice has no benches to sit on, and the only obvious decoration is a large statue of Mary dating from the 13th century. Other than the Burgundian nobility from the 13th century, who are buried in the chancel, this house of worship is only open to monks.

The ducal palace on the colonnaded Place de la Libération in the center of Dijon

Mustard from Dijon

Dijon has many attractions, but the most famous culinary product from the capital of Burgundy often comes in small round jars: mustard, in all of its unique varieties and flavors. This long tradition is still as successful as ever, despite the fact that the raw materials – mustard plants – have long since been cultivated outside of France; most of the mustard manufacturers in Burgundy import it from Canada these days. (In fact, nearly 90 percent of the world's raw materials for mustard production come from there.)

The art of creating this delicious condiment lies in the varying degrees of spiciness, and hosts who

An inviting mustard store in the heart of Dijon

wish to satisfy the individual tastes of their guests will often set the table with numerous styles. However, there are so many different styles of flavorings that you could never cover the entire spectrum even if you tried. The accents range from garlic and raspberry to Indian chili peppers, which give the already broad variety of Dijon mustards a distinctly exotic tone. Often such flavored mustards are sold in decorative hand-painted china pots

Of course, there is no shortage of specialty shops in Dijon, especially in the Old Town where some of them still feature the traditional wood and glass storefront. The selection and competition among the vendors is particularly feverish in the renovated Les Halles market halls. Below the impressive cast-iron columns and the high roof visitors will invariably discover numerous mustard stalls among the usual cheese, vegetables, meats and other delights.

banquet table looks similar to the type of dancers one might still see in India today.

The D 980 connects Semur with nearby Saulieu.

8 Saulieu Foodies and art lovers alike will enjoy Saulieu, situated on the edge of the Morvan Forest on the central of three north-south routes between Paris and Lyon. Saulieu was originally a postal station, but trade later brought its real wealth. The St-Andoche Basilica recalls Saint Andochius who suffered a martyr's death here in Burgundy. The masterful capital sculptures depicting biblical scenes in the five nave bays (12th century) draw thousands of visitors to St-Andoche every year. For those who love animal sculptures, the Musée François Pompon features works by this native son of Saulieu.

Saulieu also owes some of its fame to Bernard Loiseau's gourmet restaurant Côte d'Or. Sadly, Loiseau took his own life when Michelin revoked his star, but his former employees decided to carry on with his cooking traditions. Small side streets in town lead to the château of Châteauneuf-en-Auxois.

9 Châteauneuf-en-Auxois The astounding number of beautiful and historically significant châteaux in Burgundy is also evident at Châteauneuf-en-Auxois and its surroundings. The castle, whose well-fortified walls and imposing keep were built in the Middle Ages, towers over the neatly manicured village ensemble with charming hotels and restaurants. The museum on the premises possesses a collection of steel engravings depicting Burgundian buildings. In the chapel from 1481 is the elaborate tomb of Philippe Pot surrounded by mourners dressed in black. Pot was an advisor to the Burgun-

dian dukes and the one who commissioned the chapel.

10 Dijon The city of Dijon (see p. 71) is connected to the other rivers of the region by the Canal de Bourgogne. The highways from Germany to Paris and from Belgium to the Mediterranean all cross each other here. In 1851, Dijon also became a train stop on the Paris to Marseille line.

Settled since Gallic times and selected as the location for the

Above: The medieval castle and village of Châteauneuf-en-Auxois. Below: Inside the Fine Arts Museum in Dijon.

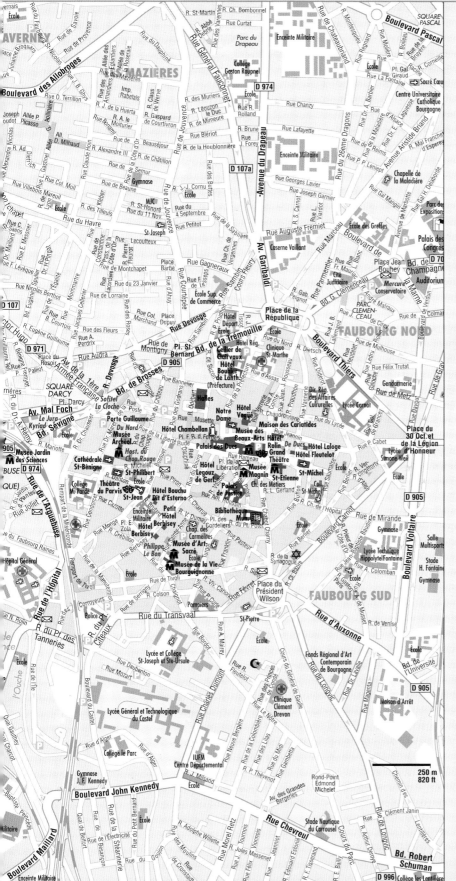

Dijon

The historic capital of Burgundy is located on the western edge of the Saône Plateau. It is an important trading center and famous for its mustard.

Dijon is a metropolis where you can still go for a stroll. Whether you are there to get a closer look at the shops in the Old Town, take in the beautiful wooden-framed storefronts, visit the

Rue Musette and narthex of the Notre-Dame Church

Musée de la Vie Bourguignonne, a history museum utilizing the latest technology, or enjoy a *kir* at one of many charming bars, there is always something down-to-earth to the place.

Kir is a refreshing beverage made from blackcurrant liqueur and white wine that was invented after World War II by Félix Kir, mayor of Dijon. The European perspective of the city can be seen in the Musée Magnin, housed in a 17th-century building with French, Italian and northern European masterpieces dating from the 17th to the 19th centuries.

The architectural magnum opus in Dijon is the Church of Notre Dame (12th C.) with its gorgeous Gothic figures including the Black Virgin (12th C.), one of the oldest wooden sculptures in France. The symbol of the city is the colorful Jacquemart figure that rings the bells every hour. Philipp the Bold (1342–1404) brought the bell ringer back to Dijon from Belgium and installed it here in the year 1383.

The origins of the ducal palace (Palais des Ducs) in Dijon go back to Burgundy's heyday, but there are very few architectural elements left from that time besides the Philippe le Bon tower. Renovations here began in 1681 and were intended to give the governor of the province of Burgundy and the two official tribunals based here a more representative – that is, baroque

– ambience. The greatest architects of the time were involved in the remodel, among them Jules Hardouin-Mansart, the chief court architect of Louis XIV. It was his design that was ultimately chosen for the Place Royal (now Place de Libération) in front of the palace. One of the most splendid baroque halls in the palace is the Salle des États (above).

Interior of the Romanesque-Gothic Church of Notre Dame in Beaune

Castrum Divio by the Romans, Dijon became the capital of the Capetian dukes, a family that produced the French kings until the 19th century and which also spawned the Valois and Bourbon lines. In the late Middle Ages, Burgundy experienced the age of the "grand dukes" until the death of Charles the Bold in 1477. His daughter Maria married German Emperor Maximilian, who ruled thereafter. In 1493, Maximilian had to cede Burgundy to the French crown. These old tales live on in the walls of Dijon, most visibly in the Palais des Ducs et des États de Bourgogne, the ducal residence on the broad Rue de Rameau. The palace complex was given its present look in about 1700 by Jules Hardouin-Mansart, the preferred architect of Louis XIV, but the monumental tombs of the Burgundian dukes are hundreds of years older than the palace itself. They are the works of several artists, among them Dutchman Claus Sluter, who was famous for his "beautiful style" that also possessed very expressive and realistic designs.

A quick jaunt on the D 974 takes you to the most famous vineyards in the world.

⑪ Clos de Vougeot It is no coincidence that the Confrérie des Chevaliers du Tastevin (a brotherhood of wine enthusiasts) established its headquarters in the Clos de Vougeot, a commanding medieval château that looks out over the heart of the Côte de Nuits region south of Dijon. Indeed, it is here that the world-renowned Burgundy wines are produced – a splendid location for specialists to taste and promote the area's most valuable asset. In November connoisseurs dress up in elegant red and gold robes and berets for the Burgundy wine festival "Les Trois Glorieuses". Heading east for a few miles you come to Cîteaux, quickly reached from the vineyard town of Nuits-Saint-Georges or directly from Dijon.

⑫ Cîteaux The original structures in the birthplace of the Cistercian Order (1098) have fallen into disrepair, but it is still worth visiting this unembel-

lished monastery complex. Even nine hundred years later it is an impressive reminder of the beginnings of this early reform movement focused on a simple and industrious life dedicated to respecting Creation. At the abbey store you can sample some of the products the monks grow and harvest on their land. Customers sing the praise of their cheeses and honeys.

⑬ Aloxe-Corton Nearby and just a few miles north of Burgundy's wine capital Beaune, is Aloxe-Corton, a small and very old town that was mentioned during the short reign of the

Roman Emperor Otho (AD 32–60). Charlemagne also got involved with Aloxe-Corton due to the revenues generated by vineyards in the area. The old church in the town was in fact torn down in 1891, but two châteaux can still be visited here. The smaller of the pair, Château de Corton-André, is worth a look for its exterior alone. Only rarely does one see color-fired roof tiles used in such impressively decorative ways as the ones on the steep castle roofs here.

Several miles away is the commercial hub of Burgundy's wine region, Beaune.

Designed in Cîteaux:
the tomb of Burgundian
court official Philippe Pot

Wine from Burgundy

The term Burgundy among red wine enthusiasts typically conjures up the excellent, rich, full-bodied wines of the region, most of which are pressed from the Pinot Noir grape. Exceptions to this are the Bourgogne Passetoutgrains and the Bourgogne Grand Ordinaire, which are made from the Gamay grape. The fact that more focus is placed on quality rather than quantity even applies to the wines that receive no more than the Appéllation Bourgogne Contrôlée, which puts a strict limit on output. To classify the wines of a higher quality, the areas are divided into villages and lots that are dedicated to the better wines. Premier Cru and Grand Cru are the names used to refer to these sought-after areas. Compared to the much larger vineyard estates of the Bordeaux wines, Burgundy's vintners see themselves at a clear disadvantage.

A true century wine!

Their wines are less established and their vines are more vulnerable to pests than those in Bordeaux.

Yet lovers of the best Burgundy wines are ready to spend as much money for exquisite bottles of Musigny or Chambertin as they are for exceptional vintages from Bordeaux.

The term for white whine in Burgundy is Chablis, and in the town of the same name in the Yonne département east of Auxerre, visitors can taste this delightfully dry drop in a number of places. Chablis wines are predominantly pressed from the Chardonnay grape (Aligoté grapes have become very rare). In addition to the Chablis vineyards there are two other areas where white wines are produced: on the Côte de Beaune (mostly with less acidity) and in the Mâconnais in southern Burgundy.

⑭ Beaune Many visitors to Beaune find the city so inviting that they rearrange their schedules to stay longer. However, the Old Town inside the ring of boulevards can get very crowded in the summer.

The first destination for all visitors is the Hôtel-Dieu. The well-proportioned columns creating shady courtyard arcades, decorative gabled roofs and the lavish furnishings in the infirmary and the kitchen have earned the Beaune Hôtel-Dieu its undisputed reputation as the most beautiful Renaissance hospital in Europe. The neat rows of beds may be the work of eager museum employees, with a degree of organization that does not reflect the true reality of a hospital from the early modern age. Still, the exhibition rooms provide plenty of interest.

The foundation was a generous gesture by the social-minded chancellor of Burgundy, Nicolas Rolin, and his wife Guigone. Indeed, the charter remains and the initials N & G will catch your eye often as you make your way around the complex. One room

holds the most valuable object of the house: the sizable *Last Judgment* (c. 1445–50) painted by Rogier van der Weyden.

There is more to see in Beaune than you could manage in two days, however: monasteries, churches, wine cellars and restaurants, the renowned Musée du Vin de Bourgogne and the Musée Marey, dedicated to the inventor of chronophotography, the doctor Étienne-Jules Marey, who in 1882 was able to capture twelve images in one second on a glass plate. The Parc de la Bouzaize, west of the city, features playgrounds and animal enclosures.

Heading south out of Beaune, take the D 974, which branches at Chagny toward the Château de Cormatin. The entrance is on your right after about 60 km (40 mi) down the road.

⑮ Château de Cormatin Several years ago a new owner rescued this lovely Renaissance château advancing decay. It now radiates with its new façade and numerous towers. Most likely built about four hundred years ago by Jacques II

Androuet du Cerceau, the lordly brilliance of this château is clearly visible from the outside, but the splendor continues inside with mostly original furnishings from the 17th century all the way to the Belle Époque of the 19th century. We are assured that lapis lazuli and gold leaf were used on the crown molding for the blue-white-gold beamed ceilings. The list of guests at the château is long and includes dramatist Corneille, writer Lamartine, opera singer Chaliapin and President Gorbachev, for example.

An expansive park with mythological symbols in the style of the Renaissance completes the relaxing visit to the splendid Château de Cormatin.

Heading east, follow the D 14 to your next destination.

Burgundian château grandeur: Château du Clos de Vougeot rising above the vines in the Côte de Nuits (top left), the Château de Cormatin (top right) after its rescue from decay, and the Château de Corton-André with its colorful roof tiles (middle left).

Once a year in July, the courtyard of the Hôtel-Dieu in Beaune springs to life for a few weeks during the Festival International d'Opéra Baroque de Beaune. The music ranges from cheerful to dramatic and fills the open spaces and halls of this former charitable almshouse and hospital, which was founded in the 15th century and treated patients until 1971. One of the most

impressive elements of the inner courtyard is the roof which features glazed tiles in four colors (yellow, red, brown and green) and arranged in diamond shapes. Today the complex serves not only as a sociohistorical monument to early health-care facilities of the highest order but also as a museum and a home for the elderly.

The Benedictine Abbey of Cluny – still an impressive architectural complex, even after the destruction of what was once the largest church in the world

Cluny – past grandeur

All religions have a need to reinvent themselves. Who still knows that the largest Catholic church once stood in Cluny? Yet it was from this non-descript village in the 10th century that the revolutionary Cluniac Reforms were launched. It all started in 910 when the Benedictine Abbey of Cluny was established here, but the morally and politically appealing reforms quickly created the need for larger houses of worship. The cornerstone of the third abbey church was

Inside the steeple of the Abbey Church

laid by Abbot Hugo in 1088, and just fifty years later Pope Innocent III was able to consecrate the massive structure. "Free from all influence from kings, bishops and counts" was the blessing he imparted on the building, but such idealism of faith proved short-lived.

It is, however, worth trying to imagine this impressive five-nave church which once measured 200 m (660 ft) in length. A model at the Musée d'Art et d'Archéologie clearly shows how small even the monumental remnants of the west façade of Cluny III are in comparison to the abbey's former size. The same applies to the Clocher de L'Eau Bénite (the Holy Water Tower) and the 13th-century Gothic front façade. From the parlor in the Tour de Fromages (Tower of Cheese) you can enjoy great views of the abbey grounds and the medieval churches of St-Marcel and Notre Dame. The Maisons Romanes, 12th- and 13th-century homes, are also fairly well preserved.

⑯ Tournus The delightful cities along the Saône south of Beaune follow one another like pearls in a necklace: Chalon-sur-Saône, Tournus and Mâcon. Tournus is the quietest of the three towns, but at least one famous painter comes from here: Jean-Baptiste Greuze (1725–1805), a pioneer of neo-classical painting and a creator of charming and docile genre images of everyday life. He headed off to Paris where he experienced both the French Revolution and Napoleon. In 1868 a monument was dedicated to this son of Tournus, which stands in front of the town hall. Paintings by Greuze can be seen in the Musée Greuze, which also has a department for archeology.

Tournus established itself as a city after becoming a pilgrimage destination famed for the relics of two martyrs who had been buried here prior to the year 1000. In the sixth century an abbey was built to honor the preacher Valerian and in the ninth century monks from Normoutier in western France were given refuge in Tournus after being chased from their monastery by the Normans. Since they carried with them the remains of St Philibert, Charles the Bald, grandson of Charlemagne, saw fit to give them the abbey and town of Tournus. At the end of the 10th century they started building the Abbey of St-Philibert. An unknown master builder created a monumental triple-nave interior infused with Romanesque styles and impressive walled-in columns made of carved natural stone. The church was restored in the 19th and 20th centuries and the famous Georgian goldsmith, Goudji, created goblets for the services and a silver reliquary tabernacle.

The streets and squares of Tournus still reflect an authentic version of the long history this city has enjoyed. The environs also feature beautiful Romanesque churches (Uchizy, Chardonnay, Ozenay) and châteaux (Château d'Ozenay and the ruins of Château Brancion on a rocky promontory). Cuisery, 7 km (4 mi) to the east,

is a town of antiques, antiquarian books and galleries.

The N 6, parallel to the Autoroute du Soleil, for 30 km (19 mi) will take you to Mâcon.

⑰ Mâcon The route continues from one wine town to another, and from the Côte d'Or département to the Saône-et-Loire département: Mâcon faces the Saône River with the lively Quai Jean-Jaurès and the many-arched Pont Saint-Laurent. Along the riverbank are plenty of café and restaurant terraces, and of course buildings with elegant façades. The city is not as rich in unusual architecture and art treasures as Dijon or Beaune, but pedestrian-friendly Mâcon is a relaxing place with many original shops, charming lanes dotted with snack bars, architectural gems like the Maison de Bois, an 18th-century apothecary, and the Musée Lamartine. There is even a trail, the La Route Lamartine, dedicated to this poet from the early French Romantic period that takes you to several châteaux where he spent his time.

The St-Laurent Bridge and the banks of the Saône in Mâcon; in the background the towers of the former Vieux St-Vincent Cathedral

Detour

Parc Naturel Régional du Morvan

"A natural citadel of pink granite, green forest, springs, brooks, fox-gloves and ferns", wrote Hans Roth of the Morvan, a German expatriate to France. French and German nature lovers rave about this green heart of Burgundy, which is large enough to allow the crowds of tourists in summer to enjoy their lakes without disturbing the tranquility of the forest. Smaller cities are dotted in and around this green heart: Saulieu, Château-Chinon and Quarrée-les-Tombes, which gets its name from the mysterious sarcophagi there.

If you're interested in finding out more about the recreational facilities within the Parc Régional du Morvan

The most amazing sight, however, and one with a much longer history, awaits visitors 10 km (6 mi) west of Mâcon: the Rock of Solutré, which rises out of the vineyard landscape like the bow of a giant ship. Archeologists uncovered about 100,000 horse and reindeer skeletons at the foot of this monolith in the 19th century. So what happened here 20,000 years ago? At the Musée Départemental de Préhistoire de Solutré, which leads into the rock formation itself, visitors can see documentation of the theories that try to explain this mysterious discovery.

Follow the N 79 until you reach Cluny from where you take the D 980 (N 80) toward Autun.

⑱ Autun Depending on whether you stop at the former mining and industrial areas around Monceau-les-Mines or

The glorious churches of Burgundy: St-Philibert high above the Saône banks in Tournus (top) as well as St-Lazare in Autun (right).

Le Creusot, it takes two to three hours to get from Mâcon to Autun, a settlement founded under Emperor Augustus and a popular destination for lovers of medieval sculpture. Many of the original images here have been copied millions of times throughout history.

First you see the remains of the city walls, the core of which were built when the town was still called Augustodunum during the early Roman Empire. Saint Symphorian suffered his

martyrdom here under Roman rule, but it is said that the relics of Lazarus were also brought to Autun from Palestine. Regardless, construction on the St-Lazare Cathedral began in the upper town around 1120, and the result was a masterpiece of Burgundian Romanesque architecture. Restoration work on the west portal led to the discovery of a hidden tympanum and the script of the artist stating, "Gislebertus hoc fecit" (Gislebertus created this). It

Top: Château de Bazoches, once owned by master-builder Vauban. Above: Nature in the Morvan

you should head to St-Brisson where there is a 19th-century château on the edge of the village as well as the Maison du Parc with its arboretum, herbularium, fruit orchards, botanical garden and a number of museums (Ecomusée du Morvan, Musée de la Résistance).

The central nave of the
Romanesque-Gothic
St-Cyr-et-Ste-Juliette
Cathedral in Nevers

was an odd find, since only the columns and buttresses illuminated by the clerestory in the nave feature such an abundance of capitals with figures in them. Even more impressive are the sumptuous Romanesque sculptures in the adjacent Musée Rolin. This is also where the unusual, masterfully designed figure of Eve from the north portal is displayed: a sinuous woman crawling through the undergrowth and brush.

The numerous Roman ruins of Augustodunum are also very much worth seeing: the largest ancient theater in Gaul, city gates and the 24-m-high (79-ft) ruins of a temple dedicated to the two-headed god Janus from the first century AD.

From Autun you can take a worthwhile detour into the Parc Naturel Régional du Morvan (see p. 79, right column).

The D 978 takes you west through the Morvan toward the Loire and Nevers.

⑲ Nevers Emerging from the mountains you'll descend to the Loire. Among the towers of the city of Nevers, the St-Cyr-et-Ste-Juliette Cathedral is recognizable. During his military campaigns in Gaul, Caesar made camp once at the confluence of the Loire and the Nièvre. In 52 BC the settlement was burned down by the Aedui, a Gallic people who ruled the region at the time. In the sixth century, the Gallic-Roman city was annexed by the Kingdom of Burgundy and later became an archbishopric. Power in the region shifted frequently among various feudal lords, coming from Flanders, Italy and France, but in 1659 Cardinal Mazarin bought the entire Nevers Duchy for 1.2 million livres. The city of Nevers, the capital of the Nièvre département, has the Gonzaga dynasty of Mantua to thank for the numerous workshops that have made it the hub of French ceramics production.

Allied bombing raids on the German-occupied Nevers during World War II caused widespread destruction. Even the grand cathedral with its elegant stepped towers opposite the Renaissance ducal palace was destroyed. Fortunately, however, the entire structure was rebuilt, including the dramatically high and masterfully designed central nave. Contemporary artists replaced the shattered stained-glass windows. Begun in the Romanesque style, as seen in the two choir terminations and the west apse, Nevers Cathedral was later given Gothic décor, as seen in the east apse. The St-Étienne Church in the north-east of the city, not far from the Porte de Paris (18th C.) is even older (1097).

The memory of Bernadette Soubirous (1844–1879) is also alive and well in Nevers. A young girl from southern France, Bernadette's visions of Mary, and the alleged healing properties of the spring that appeared, transformed Lourdes into a destination for the faithful and the sick. The increasing attention inspired her move from Lourdes to a hospice of the Sisters of Charity in Nevers where a chapel was built after her death. It is still visited by large numbers of pilgrims. Her slight body lies in a glass shrine there with a delicate smile.

Continue on the A 77/N 7 parallel to the Loire, but not following its meanders, until you reach La Charité-sur-Loire.

⑳ La Charité-sur-Loire The cathedral in La Charité-sur-Loire was begun in 1052 and developed over the years into an imposing five-nave colossus called Sainte-Croix-Notre-Dame – a double name that suits both its size and grandeur. One part of the north side aisle served the congregation of Ste-Croix as a parish church. The Grande Cour du Prieuré, the main quadrangle of the priory abbey, is currently being restored but the right side aisle has a beautiful tympanum of the Epiphany. The town's impressive Musée Municipal has some treasures of Art Nouveau artisanry from the likes of Émile Gallé, the Daum brothers and René Lalique.

㉑ Château de Bazoches This fortress-like castle is outside of town and closely connected to the name Sébastian le Prestre Vauban (1633–1707), France's foremost fortress builder. But Vauban did not build this castle on the edge of the Morvan; he was just its first owner, having bought it in 1675. Today it is a museum.

㉒ Vézelay It would be difficult to find a more suitable conclusion to your tour through Burgundy than this charming hillside town. Home to the Basilica of St Mary Magdalene, Vézelay's religious history began with the founding of a Benedictine monastery in

Jesus Christ giving
blessings in the west portal
of the Basilica of St Mary
Magdalene in Vézelay

Le Creusot – crystal and steel

It was a region full of iron and coal, and it was these natural resources that defined life in the area around Le Creusot from the Middle Ages. Two attempts to make the region prosper failed, however. The first was in about 1785, when Queen Marie Antoinette founded a crystal factory here but was unable to get it off the ground due to the French Revolution

**Smelting works in
Le Creusot, 1866**

in 1789. Two British fellows tried later to establish a canon factory, but they too failed.

Today the name of the château, La Verrerie, still recalls the royal crystal facility that once existed here. The Schneiders, a family of industrialists, moved in later and became steel magnates. Now the castle has been transformed into a museum called the Musée de l'Homme et de l'Industrie where visitors can familiarize themselves with the history of the city and the Schneider family. The last Schneider died in 1960 and so the dynasty abandoned the Creusot business; the blast furnaces have now been decommissioned.

The Centre des Techniques focuses on technological history from steam engine railways and nuclear power to the high-speed TGV trains.

For a unique experience there is a small private theater in an unusual location: the Petit Théâtre, established in 1905 in a decommissioned glass furnace in the château's park, shaped like a cone. Among the many small theater rooms, this *théâtre de la poche* (pocket theater) is probably one of the very smallest.

the Cure River valley in the ninth century. Norman attacks inspired the construction of a new building on the hill in 1096. Relics of Mary Magdalene then made the location a holy pilgrimage site.

Despite a disastrous fire and the damaging military consequences of the second crusade – Bernard of Clairvaux mobilized Vézelay in 1146 – the

town's religious and political importance was not impaired in any way. Vézelay's rising star first began to fall in the 13th century, when the "real" relics of Mary Magdalene turned up in Provence.

The period of hibernation lasted until the 19th century. Today a million people visit Vézelay every year to see the stunning architecture and artwork. The

surrounding region is also a popular destination for hikers, cyclists and horseback riders.

Via the bridge of La Charité-sur-Loire, the Via Lemovicensis takes visitors to the former Ste-Croix Monastery (top). The St-Cyr-et-Ste-Juliette Cathedral dominates the riverside panorama in the town of Nevers (above).

The Ste-Madeleine Church in Vézelay owes its rescue to Prosper Mérimée, the author of the novella *Carmen*. He was the supreme protector of historic monuments in France from 1834 until 1860, and in 1840 he drew the attention of the architect and restorer Viollet-le-Duc to the cathedral. By 1861 it had been returned to its former glory.

The Ste-Marie-Madeleine Basilica in Vézelay, a UNESCO World Cultural Heritage Site

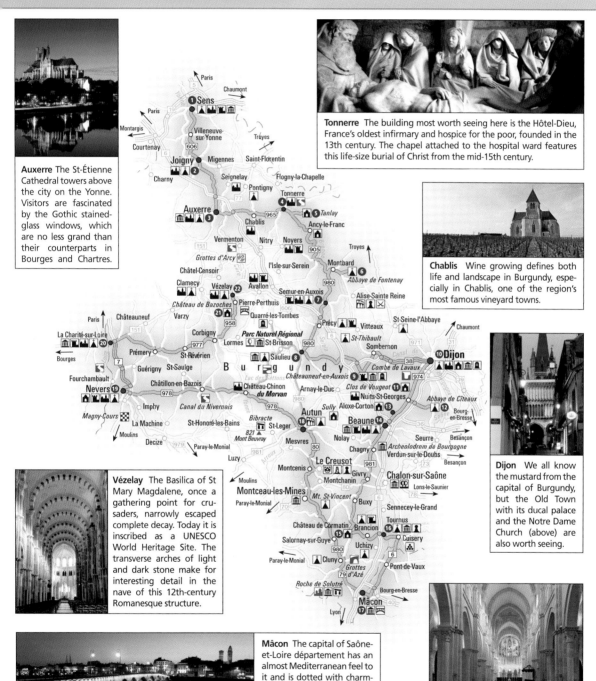

Auxerre The St-Étienne Cathedral towers above the city on the Yonne. Visitors are fascinated by the Gothic stained-glass windows, which are no less grand than their counterparts in Bourges and Chartres.

Tonnerre The building most worth seeing here is the Hôtel-Dieu, France's oldest infirmary and hospice for the poor, founded in the 13th century. The chapel attached to the hospital ward features this life-size burial of Christ from the mid-15th century.

Chablis Wine growing defines both life and landscape in Burgundy, especially in Chablis, one of the region's most famous vineyard towns.

Dijon We all know the mustard from the capital of Burgundy, but the Old Town with its ducal palace and the Notre Dame Church (above) are also worth seeing.

Vézelay The Basilica of St Mary Magdalene, once a gathering point for crusaders, narrowly escaped complete decay. Today it is inscribed as a UNESCO World Heritage Site. The transverse arches of light and dark stone make for interesting detail in the nave of this 12th-century Romanesque structure.

Mâcon The capital of Saône-et-Loire département has an almost Mediterranean feel to it and is dotted with charmingly unique shops. Visitors can enjoy lovely views over the river from the city's cafés and restaurants. Left in the picture is the St Laurent stone bridge from the 14th century.

Beaune This wine-trading town is one of the most beautiful in Burgundy. The Collegiate Church of Notre Dame is its main sight.

Route 5

On the road in Alsace

Picturesque vineyards, gourmet havens like Barr and Riquewihr, monasteries and castles at Haut-Koenigsbourg and Mont Sainte-Odile, venerable cities like Obernai and Colmar, superb views over the Rhine Valley – you can experience all this on your tour of the region which reveals equally strong influences from both German and French cultures.

When people talk of the Alsace, they automatically think of vineyards and romantic towns with half-timbered houses covered in geraniums, of medieval art and fine cuisine, of storks nesting along the Rhine, of Riesling and of sauerkraut. But France's smallest region is more than just what the tourist clichés would have you think. Tucked between the Palatinate in Germany and the Swiss Jura mountains, Alsace stretches from the Rhine to the west across the lowland plains, over the soft rolling foothills and into the higher, almost alpine reaches of the Vosges range. It is a microcosm of Western Europe in the middle of the continent, looking back on a turbulent history, with a strong sense of autonomy, and an impressive density of art monuments and high-ranking museums that are the envy of much larger provinces.

It is true. The first thing a newcomer notices here is the charming landscape: undulating hills with row after row of grapevines; picture-book vineyard towns with historic city walls and gates; labyrinthine ranks of red shingle-roof houses; and church towers visible for miles across the countryside. Massive monastery walls, myth-enshrouded castles or

ancient ruins also overlook many of the region's idyllic villages, but the jewel in Alsace's crown is the imposing crest of the Vosges Mountains, which rise above 1,400 m (4,620 ft) and are a paradise of peace and rejuvenation for hikers as well as winter and water sports enthusiasts.

The region's vibrant outward appearance is a reflection of its turbulent history, which accompanies visitors every step of the way. The relics of its early development under the Romans can be seen in the great museums of Strasbourg and Colmar, and the historic monuments of the Romanesque and Gothic periods are still visible everywhere. Among the five-star religious sights are the cathedrals in Strasbourg and Thann, the Mont St-Odile monastery in the Vosges and Matthias Grünewald's Isenheim Altarpiece at the Musée d'Unterlinden in Colmar. One secular site that is of a similar rank is the Château du Haut-Koenigsbourg, built in around 700 by the Hohenstaufen and later reconstructed under Kaiser Wilhelm II.

The region was part of the Holy Roman Empire throughout the Middle Ages before becoming part of France at the end of the 17th century. In more recent

Above: Riquewihr is surrounded by rolling hillsides and vineyards. This picture-book Alsatian town with its medieval Old Town is a popular stop for visitors on the Alsatian wine route, or Route des Vins.
Left: Impressions of Petite France, the former tanners' quarter in the Alsatian capital Strasbourg.

times it has been used as a sort of territorial punching bag by rival powers in Paris and Berlin. As a result, the region's inhabitants were subject to four official nationality and language reversals between 1870 and 1945. Its location on the border between three countries has however become its boon instead of its bane. A multilingual population, an exciting mélange of culinary, architectural and artisanal traditions, and the creativity and dynamism of the people have all served to bolster the self-confidence of the region. Alsace has produced many a free-spirited thinker, including reformer Martin Bucer, humanist Sebastian Brant and

Left: The castle and church in Eguisheim. Right: Half-timbered houses on the Rue des Écoles bridge in the Petite Venise district of Colmar.

doctor and Nobel Peace Prize winner Albert Schweitzer to the Dadaist Jean Arp and illustrator Tomi Ungerer. An enterprising spirit also thrives here, as can be seen in the commercial and industrial estates that have flourished in the lowlands and around Mulhouse for centuries.

The city of Strasbourg is a fine example of the harmonious fusion of past and future. Its 400,000 inhabitants not only take fastidious care of their picturesque Old Town and the grand cathedral, but they are also the proud guardians of a vibrant cultural environment

and a lively youth scene. The city also plays host to the headquarters of the European Parliament, whose delegates have been meeting and residing in the so-called Boomerang, an elliptical wing of the complex featuring a 60-m (200-ft) tower and built in 1999.

The Virgin Mary with Jesus oversees the main portal of Strasbourg Cathedral with its many sculptures.

Strasbourg Cathedral

This late-Gothic sandstone structure was built between the 12th and 15th centuries and is one of the most important examples of Western architecture anywhere. The highlight of the cathedral is the west façade with its rich relief figures, filigree tracery, the famous rose window and the 142-m-high (469-ft) north tower. The

The cathedral's west façade with its fine rose window

original windows, the early-Gothic Pillar of Angels, the pulpit, the Silbermann organ and the nearly 20-m-tall (66-ft) astronomical clock are also worth a closer look.

The Route des Vins d'Alsace snakes its way for some 170 km (106 miles) along excellent but often very windy roads from Marlenheim west of Strasbourg southward via Obernai and Colmar to Thann. The journey back then traces a wide arch to Sélestat along the Route des Crêtes, climbing over passes often rising to more than 1,200 m (3,937 ft) high.

1 Strasbourg See p. 90. After a stroll through the Alsatian capital, the D1004 first takes you west to Marlenheim and on to a small detour to Saverne. After returning to Marlenheim, follow the signs for the Route des Vins d'Alsace to the south.

Alsace is a little-known paradise for wine connoisseurs, so it is no coincidence that the Alsatian wine route leads right through the middle of the region. Over 5,600 wine-growing families live in the area west of the Strasbourg-Mulhouse axis, which stretches beautifully between the foothills of the Vosges mountain range and the Rhine lowlands.

2 Marlenheim This gem of a small town, whose old customs house is the official starting point for the Route des Vins d'Alsace, provides a wonderful

Top: The Ponts Couverts across two arms of the Ill. In the background are the Petite France quarter and the cathedral.

foreshadowing of the visual and culinary feast that awaits. Leaving behind its charming

half-timbered houses, wine taverns and wine cellars, you are presented with one idyllic vineyard town after another tucked between rolling hills covered in grape vines. Poplar-lined avenues create an almost southern European feel. Marlenheim still has an impressive number of buildings from the

Travel information

Route profile
Length: c. 350 km (without detours)
Time required: at minimum of 4–6 days
Start: Strasbourg
End: Sélestat
Route: Strasbourg, Saverne, Molsheim, Obernai, Barr, Andlau, Kintzheim, Ribeauvillé, Kaysersberg, Colmar, Rouffach, Guebwiller, Thann, Vieil Armand, Col de la Schlucht, Munster, Ste-Marie-aux-Mines, Sélestat

Special notes:
The Alsace boasts many well-marked hiking trails:
www.club-vosgien.com
If you prefer to explore the region by bike or mountain-bike, you'll find Information on: www.tourisme67.com

Information:
Comité Régional du Tourisme d'Alsace
20 A, Rue Berthe Molly
F-68005 Colmar cedex,
Tel: 03 89 24 73 50,
Fax: 03 89 24 73 51,
contact@tourisme-alsace.com
www.tourisme-alsace.com

Office de Tourisme de Strasbourg et sa Région
17 Place de la Cathédral,
BP 70020, 67082 Strasbourg cedex, Tel: 03 88 52 28 28
www.otstrasbourg.fr

For further information try:
www.francethisway.com/ regions/alsace.php
http://de.franceguide.com
http://alsacetourism.com
http://about-france.com/ regions/alsace.htm

Looking down the Rue Mercière you'll see the western elevation of Strasbourg Cathedral with the richly adorned central portal, the rose window and the north tower. The sculptures on the embrasures depict the prophets, while in the tympanum scenes from the life of Christ are represented – the Passion, the Harrowing of Hell, the Resurrection and the Ascension.

Today three museums are based at Strasbourg's Palais Rohan, the former residence of the prince-bishops, not far from the cathedral: the Musée des Arts Décoratifs, boasting one of the most exquisite porcelain collections in France; the Musée des Beaux-Arts, which holds a collection of Gothic paintings up to the 18th century; and the Musée Archéologique. The city

palace, built around a three-part courtyard, is regarded as the most important Baroque structure in Strasbourg. The elevation facing the Ill River features particularly lavish designs. The *Hortus Conclusus* horse sculpture by Mimmo Paladino in the foreground was part of a temporary exhibition and is today on the roof of the Musée d'Art Moderne et Contemporain.

Strasbourg

The Alsatian capital is sometimes referred to as the "carrefour de l'Europe", the crossroads of Europe, not only in geographical terms but also in political and cultural ways.

The city is located at the point where the Ill, the Rhine-Marne Canal and the Rhine-Rhône Canal flow into the Rhine, and it is home to a number of European institutions including the Council of Europe, the European Court of Human Rights and the European Parliament. The former bishop's see also has at least three universities, numerous museums of notable stature, theaters, operas and a large number of gourmet restaurants. The main attraction, however, is the Old Town. Sited between two arms of the Ill, Strasbourg's center has been lovingly preserved despite widespread damage sustained in World War II. Its cozy wine bars, romantic half-timbered houses and the numerous quays provide for a truly unique ambience.

The most significant building in the city is the Cathedral of Our Lady, a particularly splendid late-Gothic creation. To the left of its western portal is the Maison Kammerzell, arguably the most beautiful half-timbered house in the city with exquisitely detailed carvings. But the narrow streets and squares around the cathedral, such as the Rue Mercière, Rue Gutenberg, the Fish Market or the Place Marché-aux-Cochons-de-Lait, are all adorned with charming houses featuring oriels, dormer windows and plentiful woodwork.

South of the church is the Palais Rohan, a baroque archbishop's residence with state rooms and first-class museums including the Museum of Decorative Arts and the Museum of Fine Arts.

The "Petite France" quarter in the western Old Town, the former tanners' district, has many lanes, bridges, jetties and old mills. The European quarter on the north-eastern edge of the city, by contrast, is home to the various futuristic structures of the European Parliament and the Council of Europe.

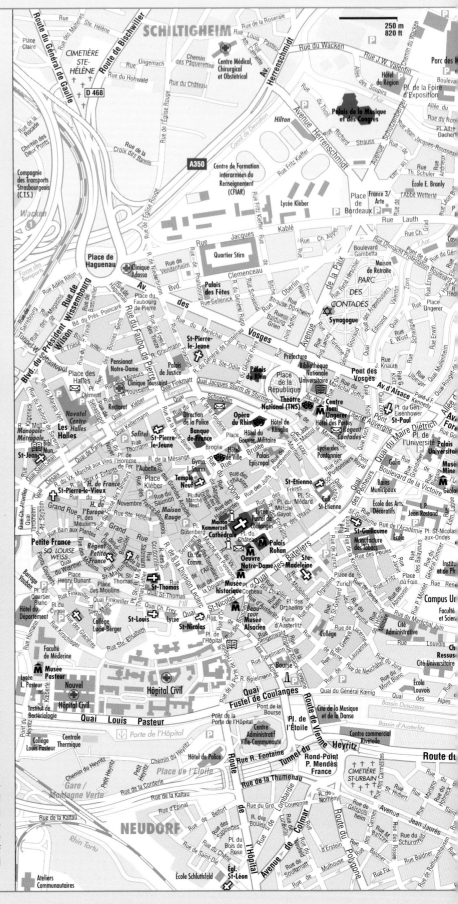

The twin towers of the Church of Saints Peter and Paul and the belfry rise tall above the sea of houses in Obernai.

13th to the 16th centuries while the Château La Petite Sorbonne dates from the 1800s and the 12th-century Sainte-Richarde Church was rebuilt in the 18th century. Only the sculptured south portal remains of the original Romanesque structure.

3 Saverne This industrial and commercial town is often called the Gate to Alsace due to its location on the pass that leads to the highlands of Lorraine. It has a pretty Old Town with half-timbered houses in narrow lanes and a number of stately buildings, dominated by the Château des Rohan. It was built by the Rohan family who in the 18th century provided many Strasbourg bishops; the château in Saverne was their summer palace. The museum beyond the castle's impressive 140-m-long (460-ft) façade of Vosges red sandstone is also worth a visit. Take a stroll in the Grand'Rue and through the pedestrian Old Town, or visit the vast

18th-century rose garden on the other side of the Rhine-Marne Canal. For fine views of the surrounding countryside, take the 5-km (3.5-mi) mountain road to the 800-year-old castle ruins of Haut-Barr.

4 Molsheim Partially surrounded by fortification walls, this historic university town and bishop's see was a center of the Counter-Reformation in the 16th century. Particularly impressive among the numerous old buildings are the Porte des Forgeron gate, the late-Gothic Jesuit church, and "La Metzig", a guild house on the town hall square designed in the style of the Alsatian Renaissance. The municipal museum provides the fans of classic cars with fascinating documentation of the life and works of Ettore Bugatti, who built his legendary automobiles here between 1909 and 1939. Modern Bugattis are today again assembled in Molsheim.

5 Mutzig The main attraction in this famous brewery town is the fortress outside the city. Built in Wilhelminian style in 1893, it is one of the best-preserved specimens of its time. Mutzig's town hall is home to a curiosity as well: a grimacing automaton sticks its tongue out and waggles it ears every thirty minutes, on the hour and at half past.

6 Rosheim The village features a showpiece of Alsatian Romanesque architecture, protected by late-medieval walls and gates: the Church of Saints Peter and Paul from the 12th century. Old fortifications, a number of city gates, and a Romanesque church tower can also be seen in the nearby village of Boersch.

7 Ottrott An exception to the white wine rule in Alsace, Ottrott is a rare source of red wine in the area, the Rouge d'Ottrott, made from Pinot

Noir grapes. It also has an aquarium with exotic fish. Above the town are the ruins of two former castles rising out of the wooded hills, Lutzelbourg and Rathsamhausen.

8 Obernai Allegedly the birthplace of Saint Odile of Alsace, the Old Town of Obernai, with its tangled maze of alleys, half-timbered houses, gables and courtyards is one of the most beautiful around. At its heart is the market square with a Renaissance town hall, the old grain storehouse, the belfry and the Six Bucket Fountain. A stroll along the well-preserved fortification walls takes you all the way around the village.

9 Mont Sainte-Odile It's impossible to miss Mount St Odile towering over the entire area. The monastery complex

Top: The 18th-century Château des Rohan dominates the townscape of Saverne.

The "Wistub zum Pfifferhüs" wine tavern in Ribeauvillé serves delicious specialties from the Alsace.

Wine in Alsace

Wine growing began as far back as the first century when the Romans first introduced the vines to the Gauls of the Vosges region; and today the wines produced in the region are famous around the world. It is in particular the white wines that have captivated wine lovers for centuries, produced from the grapes that flourish on the sun-drenched southern and south-eastern slopes of the Vosges foothills. Vintners here have resisted the use of additives for dozens of generations and they still press some of the most full-bodied dry wines which are highly aromatic and boast a great bouquet. Over an area of 13,000 ha (32,000 acres) between Guebwiller and Marlenheim, some 5,600 vineyards produce more than one million hectoliters (26 million gallons) each year, just over one-third of which is exported. The elegant drop is typically bottled in the slim green "flûtes" and enjoyed in green-stemmed Alsatian glasses.

Varietal wines are the highlights in Alsace, and the main grapes grown here are Muscats, Gewürztraminers (also known as Tokaji d'Alsace), Pinot Gris and the classic Rieslings, all of which carry the designation "Appellation d'Origine Contrôlée" (AOC), the French sign of quality wines from a defined growing area. Characteristic mid-range grape varieties that thrive in the Alsace include the Pinot Noir, Sylvaner and Pinot Blanc. The top wine produced in fifty-one vineyards in forty-seven communes are awarded the coveted "Appellation Grands Crus d'Alsace" status, an indication of the highest quality. The Zwicker or Edelzwicker served in many of the wine taverns is a blend of different grapes.

The sheer variety and superb quality of these exceptional wines alone is a good enough reason to take a trip along the "Route des Vins d'Alsace" and explore the local produce between Marlenheim and Thann. For additional historical and viticultural information you should pay a visit to the wine museum at Burg Kientzheim near Sélestat.

perched on the 760-m (2,500-ft) peak was completed at the end of the 7th century by Sainte Odile, patron saint of Alsace. It is encircled by the more than 10-km-long (6-mi) "Pagan's Wall", up to 3 m (10 ft) high. The region's most important pilgrimage site, it also enjoys spectacular views of the Vosges foothills. Inside there are a number of interesting chapels.

⑩ Barr Time seems to have stood still for centuries in Barr, the wine city par excellence of the Bas-Rhin département. A small gem of a museum here is La Folie Marco, a baroque patrician house that provides insights into how local people lived in the 17th to the 19th centuries.

⑪ Mittelbergheim Originally part of the Abbey of Andlau, romanticism and Renaissance still radiate from buildings such as the old tithe barn. The nearby Zotzenberg region produces superb wines. Mittelbergheim is also one of the "100 most beautiful villages in France".

⑫ Andlau Below the ruins of two castles sits a little wine-growing town with a Romanesque church, the only remains of a once famous abbey. The crypt and portal of the church are particularly noteworthy. After these cultural joys, the road now takes you to the towns of Itterswiller and Blienschwiller, Dambach-la-Ville, Scherwiller, Orschwiller, and Bergheim, wine villages that look as if they were taken straight out of a picture book.

⑬ Kintzheim Exciting experiences await visitors – especially children – in this town. Attractions include the Cigoland stork park, the Montagne des Singes monkey mountain with its free-ranging Barbary monkeys and the Volerie des Aigles at the castle where, weather

permitting, over 80 birds of prey put on impressive shows in the courtyard.

⑭ Haut-Kœnigsbourg Resplendent on a rocky promontory, this imposing castle was owned by the Hohenstaufens in the mid-12th century. Razed during the Thirty Years' War it was rebuilt in around 1900 by Kaiser Wilhelm II as a reminder of the glory of Prussia and the House of Hohenzollern. Today its true-to-original furnishings, the knight's halls and armories give us an idea of everyday life in the late Middle Ages.

⑮ Ribeauvillé This village is overlooked by the ruins of three castles and surrounded by three Grand Crus, particularly high-ranking vineyards. As such, it is one of the wine-growing towns in the region that you really should not miss. Its Old Town is traffic-calmed and boasts many half-timbered houses. Particular highlights include the town hall with its collection of silver, the Butcher's Tower, the Pfifferhüs restaurant and the fascinating and informative viticulture museum.

⑯ Riquewihr This town gladly calls itself the "Pearl of the Wine Route" – and quite rightly too. No other wine-growing village has such an untouched, uniform and expansive 16th-century heart as Riquewihr. The imposing gate towers, long rows of

An idyllic spot in the former free imperial city of Kaysersberg on the Weiss River

Renaissance houses and no fewer than five museums are splendid evidence of centuries of prosperity here. Not even the gauntlet of memorabilia and trinket shops on the Rue de Gaulle or the swarms of tourists traipsing around the town in the high season can spoil its genuine charm.

17 Kientzheim The most impressive sight here is the castle, whose former owner, Lazarus von Schwendi, was the first to introduce the Pinot Gris or Tokaji d'Alsace wines to the area in the 16th century. It is owned now by the Wine Confrèrie of St-Etienne d'Alsace, which documents the tradition and history of Alsatian wine in the Musée du Vignoble et des Vins d'Alsace.

18 Kaysersberg This former free imperial city and birthplace of Nobel Peace Prize winner Albert Schweitzer is rich in history and in architectural monuments. It features all of the characteristics of a romantic Alsatian hamlet. Highlights of any stroll through town include the Holy Cross Church (12th–15th centuries), the Pont fortifié, a fortified bridge over the Weiss River as well as the Musée Schweitzer and the ruins of the Château Impérial.

19 Colmar The capital of the Haut-Rhin département is the culmination of all things beautiful in this region. The Old Town here is traversed by the Lauch River and boasts a new

**Above middle: The picturesque village of Hunawihr at the foot of the Vosges range, between Ribeauvillé and Riquewihr
Left: Perched high above the Zorn River, spread across three hills and linked by gangplanks and stairs, are the ruins of the Château de Haut-Barr, dating from the 12th-century.**

Christmas cheer among the half-timbered houses of "Petite Venise" in Colmar.

postcard-worthy view around nearly every corner: the Collegiate Church of St-Martin, the charming tanners' quarter and the lovely Petite Venise district. Friends of the fine arts find their way quickly to the world-renowned Musée d'Unterlinden. The focal point of its outstanding collection of medieval art is Matthias Grünewald's Isenheim Altarpiece, a unique masterpiece of Western painting that perfectly captures the transition from late-Gothic to Renaissance styles. Martin Schongauer's *Madonna in the Rose Garden* (1473) is the eye-catcher in the nearby Dominican Church.

20 Turckheim Further along the route you will come across one delightful vintners' town after another, Turckheim being one of them, boasting very well-preserved medieval city fortifications and an enclosed historic Old Town. Every night from May until October a singing night watchman here makes his rounds through the charming streets.

21 Eguisheim Below the ruins of three castles and protected by a double city wall, this picturesque town and the birthplace of Pope Leo IX (11th century) is designed in concentric circles around an earlier castle. An ensemble of attractive half-timbered houses abundantly bedecked with flowers invites visitors for a meander through the crooked lanes.

22 Rouffach This historic town features a wealth of houses with gables and bow fronts from past centuries to keep your attention as you wander through the streets.

The Musée d'Unterlinden in Colmar is home to the world-famous Isenheim Altarpiece by Matthias Grünewald.

Turckheim (left) and
Eguisheim: picture-book
Alsatian villages with
geranium-bedecked houses

The Humanist Library in Sélestat holds thousands of volumes from the 16th to the 18th centuries and is one of the most important cultural treasures of Alsace.

The main sights are the grain storehouse from 1544, the Witches' Tower (13th–15th C.), the Renaissance town hall and the impressive but incomplete Church of Notre-Dame, built between the 11th and the 19th centuries and featuring Romanesque and Gothic styles.

㉓ Guebwiller This center of the textile industry possesses a

more urban feel. The late-Romanesque Church of St-Léger and the bulky, neoclassical Church of Notre-Dame deserve mention here, but there is also a fabulous detour to make about 5 km (3.5 mi) west of Guebwiller to a town in the middle of the forest: Murbach. It features the last remnants of a once significant Benedictine abbey including its choir, transept, and two towers of an outstanding Romanesque church.

㉔ Thann The wine route reaches its final destination at the mouth of the narrow Thur Valley. At first it seems industrial and a bit less than inviting, but the surprisingly beautiful Old Town boasts the St-Theobald

Cathedral, the most significant Gothic structure in Alsace after the cathedral in Strasbourg. The 76-m-high (250-ft) filigree tower and the double portal of the west façade with its 500 figures are highlights of the monumental building.

From Cernay, 6 km (4 mi) east of Thann, the Route des Crêtes winds its way along serpentine roads through dense forest up to the crest of the Vosges range. The road, built by the military during World War I, continues for about 100 km (60 miles) and is one of the most spectacular scenic routes in the region.

㉕ Vieil Armand After a few miles, on top of what was once called the Hartmannswiller-kopf, you come to an impressive monument with 30,000 soldier's graves overlooked by a peace sign. It recalls the bloody history of the region. From here, you curve your way into the Vosges Nature Park, a paradise for hikers with treeless hilltops, so-called "ballons", high meadows, moors, passes and lakes.

㉖ Grand Ballon About 20 km (13 mi) after Cernay you reach the highest peak in Alsace at 1,424 m (4,670 ft). Where once the Celtic sun god Belen was worshipped is now a radar and weather station. There are also ski lifts, hotels and restaurants. The panorama from here extends over the High Vosges to the Black Forest, the Jura range and, if the

visibility is particularly good, as far as the Alps.

Green meadows, bare hilltops, ski lifts and (until about May) the odd snowfield line the route now heading north-west via Le Markstein and the Col d'Hahnenbrunnen.

㉗ Col de la Schlucht Once you have reached the pass at 1,159 m (3,825 ft), where the German-French border used to be until 1919 and for centuries an important road has connected the Upper Rhine with Lorraine, it is time to take a break at a Ferme-Auberge (inn) perhaps to sample the locally produced Munster cheese and enjoy a relaxing stroll in the fresh mountain air.

㉘ Munster A nice little detour from here leads on a twisting road to the mountain pass and into the Vallée de Munster. The town of the same name on the Fecht River dates back to a Benedictine monastery founded in the seventh century that was virtually completely destroyed in World War I. Still, it is primarily famous among connoisseurs for the very "fragrant" and flavorful Munster cheese produced on local farms in the region.

Head about 4 km (2.5 mi) east from here to Gunsbach to see the house where the Franco-German theologist, physician and medical missionary Albert Schweitzer spent part of his childhood. There is a small museum in memory of the "doctor from Lambarene" who won the Nobel Peace Prize in 1952. Back on the Route des Crêtes you follow the main ridge over a number of other passes.

㉙ Ste-Marie-aux-Mines The first thing to catch your eye in this old mining town are the Renaissance town houses. On the outskirts of town you can visit two silver mines. Give yourself at least three hours and be sure to bring sturdy shoes and warm clothes.

㉚ Sélestat This town in the valley on the banks of the Ill marks the end of the tour. Due to its industrial and commercial centers, Sélestat is not really the most attractive place at first, but the Old Town still has a few gems worth seeing. In particular, the late-Romanesque Church of St-Foy and the Bibliothèque Humaniste provide evidence of the town's former spiritual importance in the 15th and 16th centuries.

Middle left: The autumn landscape in the Vosges Mountains is particularly vibrant and beautiful at sunrise.

Plumes of mist and the last rays of the sun bathe the ridges of the Vosges and the Grand Ballon in mysterious shades of light.

Haut-Barr The castle here was built in the 12th century atop three separate rocks near Saverne and once held a strategic position between the Zorn Valley and the Alsatian lowlands of the Rhine. The ruins that are preserved today reflect the structure built at the start of the 16th century by Archbishop Manderscheidt.

Strasbourg The watchtowers of the Ponts Couverts (covered bridges) once formed a part of a larger fortification. They connect several branches of the Ill River. The main attraction of the capital of the Alsace, however, is its Cathedral of Our Lady, one of the finest late-Gothic structures.

Obernai One of the most beautiful fountains in Alsace was built here in 1579: the decorative Six Bucket Fountain.

Hunawihr Surrounded by vineyards, Hunawihr is located halfway between Ribeauvillé and Riquewihr, nestling in the foothills of the Vosges Mountains.

Rosheim The Church of Saints Peter and Paul goes back to the 12th century. Its sculpture work is a gem of the Romanesque while its tower dates from the 14th century.

Murbach From Guebwiller it is worth taking a detour to Murbach where the ruins of a once-important Benedictine abbey are tucked away in the forest.

Colmar The Isenheim Altarpiece at the Musée d'Unterlinden is a masterpiece of Western painting by Matthias Grünewald – and a big draw for tourists. The three panels were painted between 1505 and 1516 for the Monastery of St-Anthony about 20 km (13 mi) away in Isenheim.

Map labels:

Sarrebourg, Saverne, Haut-Barr, Marmoutier, Obersteigen, Willgottheim, Marlenheim, Wasselonne, Westhoffen, Ergersheim, Ittenheim, Nideck, Achenheim, Strasbourg, St-Dié-des-Vosges, Mutzig, Molsheim, Entzheim, Rosheim, Illkirch-Graffenstaden, Bœrsch, Ottrott, Obernai, Mont Sainte-Odile, Barr, Andlau, Mittelbergheim, St.Martin, Blienschwiller, Epfig, Dambach-la-ville, St.-Dié-des-Vosges, Lièpvre, Scherwiller, Sélestat, Ste.-Marie-aux-mines, Haut-Kœnigsbourg, Épinal, Thannenkirch, Ribeauville, Kintzheim, Freiburg (D), Fraize, Le Bonhomme, Col du Bonhomme (949), Riquewihr, Bergheim, Hunawihr, Gérardmer, Parc Naturel, Kaysersberg, Kientzheim, Ingersheim, Col de la Schlucht (1139), Turckheim, Gunsbach, Winzenheim, Colmar, Reinkopf 1304, Hohneck 1362, Munster, Eguisheim, Metzeral, Guebersch-wihr, Freiburg (D), Régional des Ballons, Col d' Hahnenbrunnen (1180), Kruth, Murbach, Soultzmatt, Rouffach, Remiremont, le Markstein, Guebwiller, des Vosges, Grand Ballon 1424, Vieil Armand 956, Soultz-Haut-Rhin, Ballon d'Alsace 1250, Willer-sur-Thur, Thann, Cernay, Pulversheim, Freiburg (D), Wittelsheim, Pont-d'Aspach, Mulhouse, Belfort, Basle (CH)

Route 6
Via Turonensis

The Via Turonensis was mainly traveled by pilgrims from the Netherlands and northern France on their way to Santiago de Compostela. Today, there are still pilgrims who follow the Camino de Santiago (St James' Way) and its various "side streets" on foot for religious reasons, but most are simply interested in seeing the wonderful sights along the way.

Four different trails originally led pilgrims through France to the tomb of St James in Santiago de Compostela – the Via Tolosana from Arles through Montpellier and Toulouse to the south-western part of the Pyrenees. The Via Podensis took pilgrims from Le Puy through Conques, Cahors and Moissac to the Franco-Spanish border. The Via Lemovicensis had Vézelay as its starting point and continued through Avallon, Nevers and Limoges. And finally, the fourth route, the Via Turonensis, also known as the "magnum iter Sancti Jacobi" (the Great Route of St James) was named after the city of Tours, though which it passes. The pilgrims started at the tomb of St Dionysius in St-Denis before heading through Paris, down the Rue St-Jacques to the church of the same name, where only the tower still

stands on the right bank of the Seine. The tomb of St Evurtius was the destination in Orléans, while the tomb of St Martin, who was often com-

pared to St James, attracted the pilgrims to Tours. In Poitiers, there were three churches on the itinerary: St-Hilaire, Notre Dame la Grande and Sainte-Radegonde. The head of John the Baptist was the object of worship in St-Jean-d'Angély, and pilgrims would pray at the tomb of St Eutropius in Saintes. Bordeaux was also the custodian of important reliquaries such as the bones of St Severin and the Horn of Roland.

The pilgrims of the Middle Ages would most certainly have been amazed and would have shaken their heads at the buildings that the modern pilgrims along the Via Turonensis today find so fascinating. Whereas the largest and most beautiful buildings in the Middle Ages were erected to honor and praise God, modern man seems mostly obsessed with himself and his comforts.

Pilgrims nowadays are most interested in visiting the many châteaux along the Via Turonensis. Perfect examples of absolutism are just outside Paris in the Île-de-France – the enormous palace complex of Versailles and the château of Rambouillet which, as the summer residence of French presidents, continues to be a center of power. Many other magnificent structures are scattered along the Loire River and its tributaries, the Indre, Cher and Vienne rivers, including the colossal Château de Chambord, a dream in stone realized by Francis I, the Château de Chenonceau, and others like Beauregard, Chaumont, Valençay, Loches, Le Lude and Langeais.

The area around Bordeaux is home to a completely different kind of château. Médoc, Bordeaux and Entre-Deux-Mers are names that make the wine-

Above: With its round towers and its roofscape of countless chimneys and lanterns, Château Chambord, located amid extensive forests, almost looks like a Disney castle.
Left: Situated in front of the Louvre's two wings, the glass pyramid by I M Pei has marked the main entrance to the world-famous museum since 1989.

lover's heart skip a beat. This region is home to many great wines, in particular red wine. The wineries around Bordeaux, most of which look like palaces in the middle of vast vineyards, are referred to as châteaux and include internationally famous names such as Latour, Mouton-Rothschild and Lafitte-Rothschild. Last but not least, today's "pilgrims" are attracted to destinations that are far off the beaten track and would have seemed rather absurd as a destination to the pilgrims of the Middle Ages – namely, those on the Atlantic coast. The sandy beaches and coves of the Arcachon

Basin and the stretches of coast further south on the Bay of Biscay provide wind and waves for windsurfers and surfers. The

elegant life of the 19th century is celebrated in the venerable seaside resort of Biarritz and, from here, it's not much further

to the Aragonian part of the Camino de Santiago, which stretches along the northern coast of Spain.

Left: The Entrance of Joan of Arc into Orléans, painting by Jean Jacques Scherrer. Right: In the Médoc, on the Gironde's left bank, extends one of the best red wine terroirs in the world, and this vineyard.

The Opéra Garnier, one of Paris' two opera houses, was built in an opulent neobaroque style between 1860 and 1875.

St-Denis Basilica

The St-Denis Basilica was built in the 12th century in a northern suburb of Paris on the site of the funeral chapel of the first bishop of Paris, Saint Denis. The martyr was beheaded around AD 250 in Montmartre and allegedly managed to reach this place with his head in his hands.

The monastery that was founded here in the sixth century was transformed into a church in the 12th century following the plans of Abbot Sugers (1081–1151). It is considered one of the founding structures of the Gohic style: ogival arches, rib vaulting, window roses – all the elements that endow Gothic buildings with a lightness and make them strive toward heaven, were used here for a first time. Until Louis XVIII all French rulers were buried here. The magnif-

The St-Denis Basilica was the first important church built in the early Gothic style.

icent tombs give visitors an excellent overview of twelve centuries of French funereal art.

The Via Turonensis follows the classic French route of the St James' pilgrimage trail. Starting in the Île-de-France, you'll head to Orléans on the Loire, continue downstream past some of the most beautiful and famous Loire châteaux and then, from Saumur onward, make your way south into the Gironde to Bordeaux. Prior to arriving in Biarritz, you stop in St-Jean-Pied-de-Port, the final stop for pilgrims before the strenuous crossing the Pyrenees.

❶ St-Denis The actual pilgrim route begins in St-Denis, north of Paris. During the heyday of the Camino de Santiago pilgrimages, this town was located north of the former city limits and was the meeting place for the pilgrims coming from Paris. The French national saint, Saint Denis, is buried in the city's cathedral. The basilica, where almost all of France's kings are entombed, is considered the first masterpiece of Gothic architecture.

❷ Paris See pp. 102–107. South-west of Paris is Versailles. The name of the palace is intrinsically tied to the Sun King, Louis XIV, and is a symbol of the peak of absolutist power attained by the king.

❸ The Palace of Versailles Louis XIII first had a hunting lodge built on the site where this magnificent château now stands. Under Louis XIV, the lodge was gradually expanded to the immense dimensions we know today, followed by some insignificant extensions like the opera, built under Louis XV.

During the reign of the Sun King, Versailles was the place where anyone who wanted to have any sort of influence in the State had to stay. In addition to the opulent reception rooms such as the Hall of Mirrors, the Venus Room, the Hercules Room or the Abundance Salon, there are also the king and queen's lavishly furnished private chambers. The opera, completed in 1770, is a real gem.

Beyond the water features of the Bassin d'Apollon is the vast park with the Grand Trianon, Petit Trianon and Le Hameau. The Grand Trianon was built under the orders of Louis XIV – one wing for himself and the other for his mistress, Madame de Maintenon. The Petit Trianon was built for Louis XV's mistresses. Le Hameau is almost an absurdity – a small village with a farm, dairy, mill and pigeon house, where Marie Antoinette played at being a "farmer", a game that did not win her any fans among supporters of the revolution – she wound up under the guillotine on the Place de la Concorde.

❹ Rambouillet Although the palace is the summer residence

A modern focal point next to the equestrian statue of Napoleon was created by the Louvre's glass pyramid designed by I M Pei.

Detour

Chartres

Chartres Cathedral is impressive even when seen from afar, as it rises like a mirage high above the wide expanse of level cereal fields of the Beauce region. And when regarded close up, it proved to be a miracle of Gothic engineering, most of which was constructed in the second half of the 12th century.

The façade is worth seeing thanks to its rich sculptural ornamentation, especially in the portal area. However, the greatest treasure is inside the cathedral: stained-glass windows of a quantity and beauty as they are unlikely to be found anywhere else. The colorful stained-glass windows represent biblical as well as historical scenes, thus putting into easy-to-understand images information for the faithful who to the most part could neither read nor write. Also of exceptional beauty are the rose windows, which also contain an extensive number of illustrations within their delicately chased tracery. The

The western façade of Chartres Cathedral

southern and the western rose windows depict the Last Judgment, whereas the eastern rose window is dedicated to the Blessed Virgin Mary.

Travel information

Route profile
Length: c. 1,100 km (684 mi)
Time required: 10–14 days
Start: Paris
End: Bayonne
Route: Paris, Versailles, Orléans, Blois, Amboise, Tours, Saumur, Poitiers, Saintes, Cognac, St-Émilion, Bordeaux, St-Jean-Pied-de-Port, Bayonne

Getting around in Paris:
In the capital you are advised to make use of the public transportation network. Information and timetables for métro, buses and trains on: www.parisinfo.com

When to go:
The best seasons for visiting the Île-de-France and the Loire are spring and fall, when the Loire valley is at its most beautiful, bathed in all shades of red. Weather information from: http://france.meteofrance.com (in French).

Information:
• Way of St James: www.chemins-compostelle.com/sommaire.html
• Office du Tourisme et des Congrès de Paris, 25 rue des Pyramides F-75001 Paris www.parisinfo.com
• Office de Tourisme de Chartres Place de la Cathédrale F-28000 Chartres Tel: +33 (0)2 37 18 26 26 www.chartres-tourisme.com
• Office de Tourisme & de Congrès d'Orléans 2 Place de l'Etape F-45056 Orléans cedex 1 Tel: +33 (0)2 38 24 05 05 www.tourisme-orleans.com

of the French president, it can be visited most of the time. The building consists of wings designed in different architectural styles including Gothic, Renaissance and baroque. This palace only became royal property in 1783, when Louis XVI acquired it as a hunting lodge. The park and the adjacent Rambouillet forest are ideal places to take a relaxing stroll. On the way to Orléans to the south of Paris, it's worth making a detour to Chartres, a city that is inextricably associated with its monumental Gothic cathedral, one of the largest in Europe.

⑤ Orléans This city's cathedral, Ste-Croix, is built in Gothic style, though only very small parts of it date back to the Gothic period. The original

Top: The Champs-Elysées are the most magnificent boulevard in Paris, culminating at the Arc de Triomphe.

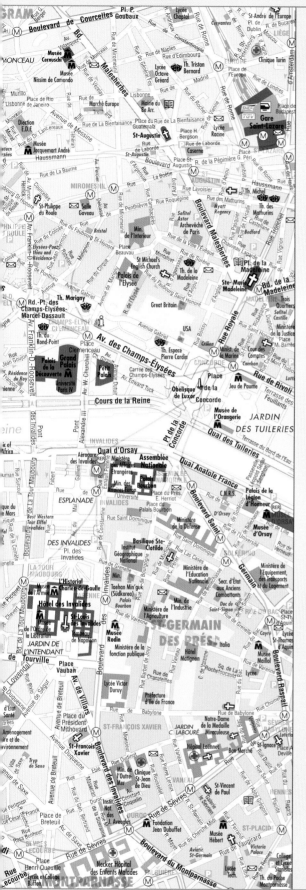

Paris

The French capital is a city of thrilling contrasts – rich in tradition and at the same time avant-garde, enormous in size and yet captivatingly village-like. Paris is also the seat of government and home to several universities, a global center for fashion and art, incredibly multicultural and yet still very much the epitome of all things French.

Throughout its long history, Paris has continually been in a state of expansion. The city always appeared to be bursting at the seams. Today, greater Paris covers an area of about 105 sq km (40 sq miles) and is home to some twelve million people – more than twenty percent of the entire population of France. This city's non-stop growth is not least due to the fact that Paris does not accept any rivals. The nation's capital has always been unchallenged in its political, economic and cultural significance. Worth seeing on the south side of the Seine: the Eiffel Tower, the symbol of Paris built for the World Fair in 1889. The iron construction, towering some 300 m (984 ft) over the city, took engineer Gustave Eiffel just sixteen months to complete. The viewing platform, accessed by elevator, is one of the city's major attractions; the Hôtel des Invalides, a complex crowned by the Dôme des Invalides, built by Louis XIV for the victims of his numerous wars.

Worth seeing on the north side of the Seine: probably the most magnificent boulevard in the world, the Champs-Elysées, with the Arc de Triomphe providing a great view of the streets radiating from its center; the Place de la Concorde, an excellent example of wide boulevards and geometric plazas that gave the French capital its "big city" look during its renovation in the 19th century; the park complex Jardin des Tuileries, which leads up to the Louvre; the Place Vendôme with its upscale shopping; the Palais Garnier, an opulent 19th-century opera house; and the 17th-century Palais Royal.

Worth seeing in the artists' and entertainment district of Montmartre (not shown on the map): the historic Moulin de la Galette with its outdoor garden restaurant; the Sacre Coeur basilica on top of the hill, with fantastic views of the city; the Montmartre cemetery as well as the Père Lachaise Cemetery (east, beyond the map), one of three large cemeteries built around 1800 with the graves of numerous celebrities (Montmartre: Hector Berlioz, Jacques Offenbach, Heinrich Heine; Père Lachaise: Edith Piaf, Oscar Wilde,

The Eiffel Tower, the famous symbol of Paris

Marcel Proust, Sarah Bernhardt). All the cemeteries have detailed maps available at the main entrance.

In the northern suburb of St-Denis (beyond the map): early-Gothic church of St-Denis, the burial place of the French kings, and the Stade de France, a giant new football stadium.

No fewer than nine bridges link Île de la Cité Seine island with the two riverbanks (Rive Droite and Rive Gauche) as well as the nearby Ile St-Louis. The history of settlement in Paris began on the Ile de la Cité – here a view of its eastern tip – in the third century. Notre-Dame Cathedral, however, which together with the square in front of it forms the geographic center of

the capital, was built only much later. The vast Gothic church with its two distinctive double towers was completed in the 14th century. Alongside the cathedral, some other medieval buildings can also be seen on the generally quiet island in the river: the Sainte-Chapelle palace chapel, the Conciergerie and the Palais de la Cité law courts.

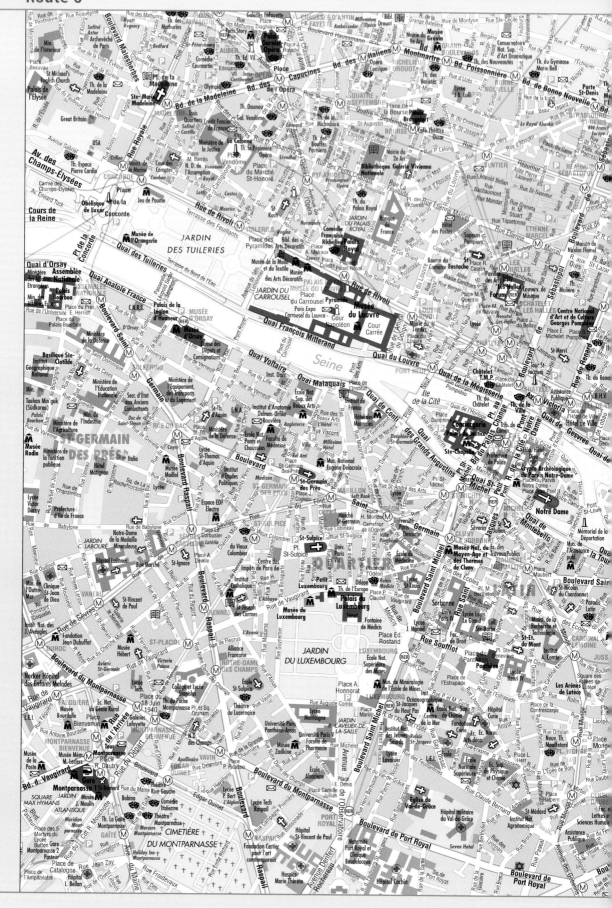

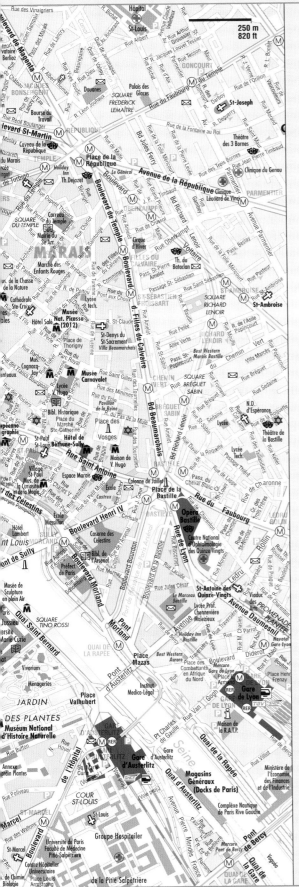

Paris

The historic center of the metropolis on the Seine is relatively easy to navigate, and most of the sights can be reached on foot. However, you should allow yourself copious amounts of time – after all just wandering around the Louvre could keep you busy for days.

During the Middle Ages, when Paris was arguably the most important city in Europe, three factors determined the city's development and status – the church, its royalty and the university, all of which have left their mark on the historic city center. Thus, on the Île de la Cité – the city's oldest core settlement where the Romans, Merovingians and Carolingians based their dominions – stands one of France's most

both 68-m-high (223-ft) towers; the former palace chapel of Ste-Chapelle, a high-Gothic masterpiece; the Conciergerie, part of the medieval royal palace; Pont Neuf (new bridge), one of the most beautiful bridges on the Seine; and the idyllic Île St-Louis, south-east of the Île de la Cité, with its Renaissance buildings. Worth seeing north of the Seine: the Louvre, first a medieval castle, then the royal residence until the

Bronze fountain on the Place de la Concorde

splendid and most powerful cathedrals: Notre Dame. As of 1400, medieval royalty focused their power on the northern banks of the Seine at the Louvre, which was begun in 1200 as part of a first ring of fortifications and developed into a magnificent residence over the centuries. On the other side of the river, in the Latin Quarter, professors and students united to establish the Sorbonne, the famous university, at the end of the 12th century. The Seine riverbank between Pont de Sully and Pont d'Iéna, with its grand buildings, is a UNESCO World Heritage Site. Worth seeing on the Île de la Cité: the early-Gothic Cathédrale Notre Dame (12th/13th centuries), of which you can climb

17th century, then rebuilt and made into one of the largest art museums in the world; the Centre Pompidou, a cultural center with exemplary contemporary architecture; and the Hôtel de Ville, the 19th-century town hall at the Place de Grève.
Worth seeing in the Marais district: the romantic Place des Vosges; the avant-garde Opéra National de Paris; the Gothic church of St-Gervais-et-St-Protais; the Picasso museum; and the Hôtel Carnavalet's museum on the city's history.
Worth seeing south of the Seine: the Latin Quarter, steeped in history; the St-Germain-des-Prés and Montparnasse districts of artists and intellectuals; and the Jardin du Luxembourg park.

The Sun King, Louis XIV, is glorified in the 20 large ceiling paintings of the 73-m-long (240-ft) Hall of Mirrors in the Château of Versailles by the court artist Charles Lebrun. The symmetric mirror surfaces facing the seventeen windows opposite them are assembled from 357 individual mirrors. They virtually "carry" the garden inside the palace. The vast room was used

mainly as a promenading ground as well as for receptions and festivities. It has rather more negative symbolic values concerning the relationship between Germany and France – in 1871 the German Empire was proclaimed from here, and in 1919 Germany had to sign the Peace Treaty here. Both occasions were perceived as humiliation by the one or the other.

Orléans is located at the northernmost point of the Loire bend. It became famous thanks to Jeanne d'Arc, the Virgin of Orléans. Seen here the Pont Georges V and the Sainte-Croix Cathedral.

Jeanne d'Arc (Joan of Arc)

Jeanne d'Arc was born in 1412, the daughter of a rich farmer in Domrémy in the Lorraine region. At the time, France had been heavily involved in the Hundred Years War with England since 1337, and the English had advanced as far as the Loire. At the age of thirteen, Jeanne began hearing voices telling her to join forces with the French heir apparent, Charles VII, and expel the English from France. After she recognized him in Chinon, despite his disguise, people started believing in her divine mission.

The gilded statue of Jeanne d'Arc standing on the Pont Alexandre III in Paris

Jeanne got the support of Charles VII and went with the French army to Orléans, which was besieged by the English; with her help, the city was liberated on 8 May 1429. Jeanne also persuaded Charles VII to take the dangerous road to Reims to be crowned. The ceremony took place in July 1420 in the Reims cathedral.
However, the farmer's daughter from Lorraine, who was now France's heroine, had enemies too. In 1430, the Burgundians, who were allied with England, succeeded in imprisoning Jeanne and handed her over to the English. Jeanne was accused of heresy and witchery. She was condemned and burned at the stake in Rouen on 30 May 1431. Posthumously, her conviction as a witch was overturned in 1456, and in 1920 Jeanne d'Arc was granted sainthood as a martyr.

building, destroyed during the French Wars of Religion, was rebuilt under Henry VI, and the architects of the 18th and 19th centuries continued to use the Gothic style.
The Maison de Jeanne d'Arc was the home of the woman who liberated the city in 1429. The half-timbered house was destroyed in World War II, and rebuilt faithful to the original. Only very few of the beautiful old houses and aristocratic palaces were spared the wartime destructions, among them the Hôtel Toutin, with its stunning Renaissance courtyard. Of course, Orléans wouldn't be complete without a statue of Jeanne d'Arc, erected on the Place du Martroi in 1855.
Before heading on to Blois, it's well worth making a detour to the beautiful moated castle of

Sully-sur-Loire, some 40 km (25 miles) south-east of Orléans.
From Orléans, you have two options for reaching Chambord, which is some way outside of the Loire Valley – either along the right bank of the Loire to Mer and across a bridge there, or along the left bank of the Loire on small country roads.

6 **Chambord** King Francis I had this château built on the site of an older hunting lodge. Lost among the extensive forests, the result was a vast dream castle with an incredible 440 rooms and 70 staircases. The entire complex resembles a castle, featuring corner towers, ramparts and a moat. Leonardo da Vinci was apparently also involved in its construction, designing among other features

the elaborate double-helix staircase whose two spirals are so ingeniously intertwined that the people going up the stairs cannot see the people going down, and vice versa.
Alas, Francis I did not live to see the completion of his château, and work was not continued on the palace until the reign of Louis XIV. Louis XV gave Chambord as a gift to the Elector of Saxony, who had it gloriously renovated. The château fell into temporary neglect after his death.

7 **Blois** In the first half of the 17th century, Blois was the center of political activity in France. The town revolves around its château. Only rarely can the individual building phases be as easily recognized as here. The oldest section of

The Pont Gabriel, a stone bridge across the Loire, is the emblem of Blois together with its château. In the background on the left the towers of the church of St-Nicolas can be seen against the sky.

the château is Louis XII's wing, constructed in red brick with white limestone decorations. The Francis I wing is far more opulent, built in the Renaissance style yet still displaying traces of French Gothic in parts. The king had his heraldic animal, the salamander, displayed in many parts of the château. What really catches your eye is the Renaissance-style staircase tower in the interior courtyard, from where the royal family could attend and watch events.

Noble palaces such as the late-15th-century Hôtel Sardini, the Hôtel d'Alluye (1508) and the Hôtel de Guise in the heart of Blois, testify to the fact that, apart from royalty, numerous other aristocrats also had their residences along the Loire. The St-Louis Cathedral is not Gothic and only dates back to the 17th century, the previous building having been extensively destroyed by a hurricane. An especially lovely half-timbered house, the Maison des Acrobates, is located on the cathedral square. If you are interested in Gothic churches, make sure you pay a visit to the supber 12th-century St-Nicolas. Its interior was inspired by Chartres Cathedral.

8 Cheverny This castle, built between 1620 and 1634, is still owned by the family of the original builder, Henri Hurault, the comte de Cheverny. It is also probably thanks to this fact that the castle still contains a large part of the original, opulent interior décor and furnishings. The ceiling frescoes in the dining hall and bedroom are particularly worth inspecting, as are its collection of furniture, superb tapestries and various objets d'art.

9 Chenonceaux Powerful women played a major role in the history of this romantic pleasure palace. Cathérine Briçonnet supervised its construction in the early 16th century while her husband was in Italy. After Thomas Bohier's death, the building fell into the hands of the king and Henry II gave it as a gift to his mistress, Diane de Poitiers, who had the structure enlarged and continued as a bridge over the River Cher. Following Henry's death, his wife, Catherine de' Medici, claimed the castle for herself, and it is thanks to her idea that the bridge was roofed with a gallery in the Florentine style.

After Catherine de' Medici, Louise de Lorraine, the widow of the assassinated Henry III, proceeded to live a life of mourning in what was actually a bright, cheerful-looking castle. A lively spirit of intellectual pursuits returned in the 18th century with the arrival of the commoner, Louise Dupin, who saved the castle from the destructions of the revolution.

Only very little remains of the original furnishings, but Renaissance pieces have been used to give an impression of what the

Large picture: The Renaissance Château of Chenonceaux is an extravagant bridge structure spanning the small Cher River. The two-tiered gallery was commissioned by Catharine de' Medici to the designs of Philibert Delorme.

The Château of Amboise, towering above the town of the same name on the Loire, was commissioned by Charles VIII in 1490. It was built by Italian master-builders on the foundations of a medieval castle – and rang in the beginnings of the Renaissance in France.

interior might have looked like. Located in the bridge pier is the superb kitchen, where copper pots and pans still hang in an orderly fashion.

⑩ Amboise Perched on a hill sloping steeply into the Loire is France's first major Renaissance château. Although only parts of the construction have been preserved, they are still very impressive in their size and grandeur.
Following an expedition to Italy in 1496, Charles VIII brought back with him Italian artists, craftsmen and works of art to decorate the palace. The interiors of the mighty towers were constructed in such a way that a rider could get to the upper floors on his horse. The Chapelle-St-Hubert is a fine example of Gothic architecture. Not far from the château is the Le Clos-Lucé mansion, where Leonardo da Vinci spent the final years of his life. Francis I had brought the Italian universal genius to come to France, and a small museum displaying models of Leonardo's inventions pays homage to this great Italian artist.
The small town located below the château, a row of houses, and the clock tower all date back to the time of this region's heyday. From Amboise, a minor road leads through the central Loire Valley to Tours.

⑪ Tours This is the town that gave the Via Turonensis its name, and the tomb of St Martin here was an important stop for St James pilgrims. Revolutionaries demolished the old St-Martin Basilica at the end of the 18th century. The new St-Martin Basilica, in neo-Byzantine style, contains the tomb of the saint, consecrated in 1890. It is an example of the monumental church architecture of the time, one that made use of many different styles. The St-Gatien Cathedral is the city's most important historic church. The two-storey cloister provides a great view of the towers' tracery and the finely carved flying buttresses.
In some parts of the Old Town, like the Place Plumereau, you could be forgiven for thinking you were back in the Middle Ages. Charming half-timbered houses with pointed gables and often ornately carved beams are proof of the wealth of the merchants at the time. The historic rooms of the Château Royal (13th century) house a waxworks cabinet.

⑫ Villandry The last of the great castles to be built in the Loire during the Renaissance (1536) fell into ruin in the 19th century and its Renaissance gardens were then transformed into an English-style landscape garden. The Spanish Carvallo family eventually bought it in 1906 and it is thanks to them that the castle has been renovated and the gardens were returned to their original Renaissance style. Visitors of the castle today are mostly those interested in historic landscaping, whether flower or vegetable beds, everything is laid out artistically and trees and hedges are perfectly trimmed into geometric shapes.

⑬ Azay-le-Rideau This château on the Indre, built between 1519 and 1524, captivates visitors with the harmony of its proportions and its romantic location on an island in the river. However, it did not bring its builder, the mayor of Tours, Gilles Berthelot, much luck. Like other French kings, Francis I could not tolerate his subjects openly displaying their wealth. Without further ado, he accused the mayor of infidelity and embezzlement, and seized the castle.

⑭ Ussé The Château d'Ussé was built on the walls of a fortified castle in the second half of the 15th century. With its turrets and crenellations, as well as its location at the edge of the forest, it's easy to see how it was the inspiration for authors of fairy tales. The Gothic chapel houses an important work of art from the Italian Renaissance, a Madonna in terracotta by the Florentine sculptor Luca della Robbia.

⑮ Saumur Horse lovers around the world should be very familiar with the name Saumur. The cavalry school, founded in 1763, is still

The defiant structure of the Château of Saumur, located on a rocky ledge, has succeeded in preserving its original 14th-century appearance with the four towers despite later enlargements of the complex.

in the surrounding area in numerous limestone caves.
From Saumur, the westernmost point of the journey through the Loire valley, the road heads 11 km (7 miles) back toward Fontevraud-l'Abbey.

⑯ Fontevraud-l`Abbaye This abbey was founded in 1101 and continued to exist right until the early 19th century. In the tall, bright church (consecrated in 1119) is the tomb of Eleanor of Aquitaine. Southwest France was "annexed" to England when Eleanor married Henry Plantagenet, the future King Henry II of England. Eleanor's husband as well as their son, Richard the Lionheart, are also buried in Fontevraud. The 16th-century cloister is the largest in all of France. However, the abbey's most original structure is the monastery kitchen, which almost looks like a chapel with six transepts.

⑰ Chinon This fortress-like château situated high above the banks of the River Vienne played a very important role in French history. It was here that Jeanne d'Arc first encountered Charles VII and recognized him despite his costume and the fact that he was hiding in among his courtiers and that she had never seen him before. It is for this reason that the large tower, the Tour de l'Horloge, houses a small museum dedicated to her.
Large parts of the castle, originating from the 10th to 15th centuries, are only ruins now.

France's national riding school. The castle was built in the second half of the 14th century and is located on a hillside above the city. Today, it houses two museums, an art museum and the Musée du Cheval.
In the Old Town, half-timbered houses like the town hall on the Place St-Pierre, which was created in 1508 as a patrician palace, and the numerous 17th-century villas are all worth a look. In the Gothic church of Notre Dame de Nantilly, the side aisle, which Louis XI had built in a Flamboyant style, has a prayer chapel that an inscription identifies as the royal oratorio. On rainy days there are two interesting and unusual museums worth visiting: a mask museum (Saumur is a major center for the production of carnival masks) and a mushroom museum. These precious fungi are grown

Large picture: Chinon, located at the confluence of the rivers Vienne and the Loire, is dominated by a mighty castle dating back to the tenth century. Above left: The Fontevraud Abbey Church stands out thanks to its strictly defined Romanesque shapes.

113

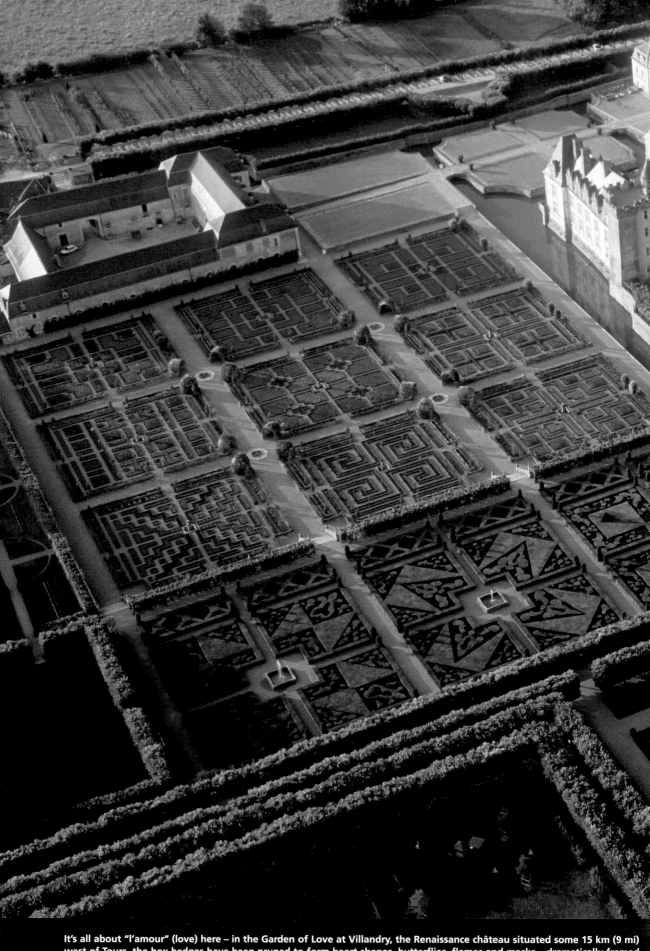

It's all about "l'amour" (love) here – in the Garden of Love at Villandry, the Renaissance château situated some 15 km (9 mi) west of Tours, the box hedges have been pruned to form heart shapes, butterflies, flames and masks – dramatically framed and surrounded by red flowers. In addition, the park also features a water, a music, a vegetable and a herb garden. Even the

vegetables are planted so that their colors make geometric patterns. The plants are fed via a subterranean irrigation system. An aerial view of the complex reveals a highly original masterpiece of horticulture, featuring squares, diamond shapes, labyrinths, crosses and circles like some overdimensioned, symmetrical ornament.

Altar and choir of the Notre-Dame-la-Grande Church in Poitiers, built in the Poitevin Romanesque style.

Romanesque church art in Poitiers and Parthenay-le-Vieux

The Romanesque style of the Poitou region is typified, for the most part, by rich sculptural decorations. The façade of the former collegiate church of Notre Dame la Grande in Poitiers, completed in the mid-12th century, is a particularly good example. Above the three portals, as well as to the left and right of the large second-floor window, is an ornately sculptured series of images depicting themes from the Old and New Testament: Adam and Eve, the prophet Moses, Jeremiah, Josiah and Daniel, the Tree of Jesse, the Annunciation, the birth of Christ, the twelve apostles and, in the gables, Christ in the Mandorla with two angels.

The church of St-Pierre in nearby Parthenay-le-Vieux was built in the late 11th century. The most striking

The west façade of Notre-Dame-la-Grande in Poitiers

part of this building is the eight-cornered transept tower, but the most beautiful features here are also the decorative figures on the façade. Samson's battle with the lion is depicted here, as well as the horseman, which is typical for the Romanesque style in Poitiers. The fairy Melusine, which appears more than thirty times, is an original element.

A highlight of any visit to the castle mountain are the magnificent views from here over the Vienne valley.

⑱ Châtellerault This town, no longer of much significance, was once an important stop for pilgrims on the Camino de Santiago. Pilgrims would enter the town, as did Jeanne d'Arc, through Porte Ste-Cathérine.
The church of St-Jacques, the destination of all pilgrims on the Camino de Santiago, was furnished with an ornate carillon. Some of the town houses, such as the Logis Cognet, still alow you to imagine what life was like in the 15th century.

⑲ Poitiers This historic city, which was an important stop for pilgrims on the Camino de

Santiago, found an important patron in Duke Jean de Berry. Thus it was a center of religious and scientific life into the second half of the 16th century, and its churches still attest to this today.

⑳ Marais Poitevin The marshland located west of Poitiers and stretching all the way to the coast seems to have remained stuck in time. The most important and often the only means of transport in the Venise Verte (Green Venice) is one of the flat-bottomed boats. The Romanesque churches of Parthenay-le-Vieux, some 50 km (31 miles) west of Poitiers, are well worth a visit. The route takes you back to Poitiers before the journey continues on to St-Jean d'Angély.

㉑ St-Jean d'Angély Although it has now paled into insignificance, this town was once an important destination for St James pilgrims as it was here that they had the opportunity to pay their respects to the head of John the Baptist. Only ruins remain of the Gothic church, but a row of beautiful half-timbered houses, the Tour de la Grosse Horloge (clock tower) dating from 1406, a beautiful fountain (1546), and the 17th-century abbey enable modern visitors to take a trip back in time.
It's worth making a detour to the port city of La Rochelle on the Atlantic, and from there an excursion to the Île de Ré.

㉒ Saintes The capital of the Saintonge looks back on a long

A degustation in a cellar in Cognac, the birthplace of the world-famous brandy

Detour

La Rochelle and Ile de Ré

A detour to Île de Ré first takes you to La Rochelle, an important port town since the 11th century and considered one of France's most beautiful cities. In 1628, Cardinal Richelieu besieged the town, which again and again during its history managed to take the wrong side in the political debate of the day – over 23,000 people died during the brutal occupation.

Today, its main attraction is the Atlantic port, where yachts bob up and down in a picture-perfect scene. The city's best-known tourist sites are down by the Old Port – the Tour St-Nicolas and the Tour de la Chaîne. In times of war, an iron chain was stretched between the two towers to

Promenade in the yachting marina of St-Martin

protect the port from enemy ships. The town hall (1595–1606) is built in Renaissance style with a stunning arcaded courtyard.

The Île de Ré – also known as the "White Island" – is connected to the mainland by a 4-km-long (2.5-mile) bridge. Vineyards and salt marshes dominate the scene, with pretty villages of flower-bedecked houses dotted in between. The main town on the island is St-Martin-de-Ré, with a citadel that was constructed in the 17th century by the famous fort builder, Vauban.

St-Clément-des-Baleines near the north-western tip of the island is also interesting – it has two lighthouses worth seeing.

history, traces of which can still be seen today. The Arc de Germanicus, which was originally the gateway to a bridge, dates back to Roman times. When the bridge was demolished, the arc was saved and rebuilt on the right bank. The ruins of the amphitheater, dating back to the 1st century and today overgrown with grass, once seated 20,000 people.

There are also impressive remains from the Middle Ages. The Abbaye aux Dames was founded in 1047, and the Romanesque church was built in the 11th and 12th centuries. The Gothic St-Pierre Cathedral dates from the 13th and 14th centuries and the tower was added in the 17th century. The St James pilgrims prayed in the spacious crypt of the church of St-Eutrope, (late 11th C.), at the tomb of the city's saint. From Saintes you head southeast toward Cognac.

㉓ Cognac This town, on the banks of the Charente, today very much revolves around the drink of the same name, which experts will discern the scent of as they stroll through the town. The Valois Castle, from the 15th and 16th centuries, has a cognac distillery. An exhibition at the town hall allows you to get a better understanding of the history and production of the precious brandy, which takes between five and forty years to mature. Some of the distilleries offer interesting tours of their facilities. You head south-west from here to Pons before continuing on to Libourne.

㉔ Libourne This small town is a typical bastide, a fortified town, built at the time when South-West France was being fought over by England and France (1150–1450). Every bastide town was originally surrounded by a wall, and they all feature a grid-like layout and a large central market square. Libourne was founded in 1270 and was for a long time a very important port on the River Dordogne for shipping wine out of the region. Today, visitors will enjoy taking a stroll around the city's lively Place Abel Surchamp.

Large picture: Two impressive towers, Chaine and St-Nicolas, guard the entrance to the port of La Rochelle, at one point the largest in the country.

Noble wines produced from Merlot and Cabernet franc grapes mature in oak barrels in the cellars of Château Ausone near St-Émilion.

㉕ St-Émilion Soaring out of the sea of vineyards that belong to the St-Émilion appellation, which produce very high-quality wines, is the small town whose beginnings date back to a monastery. The sizeable rock-hewn church here (9th–12th centuries), whose understated facade faces the pretty market place, is a special attraction. The collegiate church was built in the 12th century and its main aisle is Romanesque in style. Don't miss having a look at the very well-preserved cloister.

The donjon, a relic from the royal fort, towers high above St-Émilion where the Jurade wine confrèrie meets to test the new wines. Every year, from the tower platform, the members ceremoniously declare the grape harvest open.

㉖ Bordeaux This venerable city on the Garonne has long been dominated by trade – predominantly the wine trade. An historic event had a profound effect on the city – in 1154, Bordeaux fell under English rule and, thanks to their huge interest in the region's wines, trade boomed. Even when Bordeaux was again part of France, it still maintained a close relationship with the British Isles.

The Place de la Comédie, with the neoclassical columned façade of the Grand Théâtre, is an ideal place to start a stroll through the city. The Esplanade des Quinconces here is considered the largest square in Europe. You shouldn't miss seeing some of the city's churches. The St-André Cathedral was built between the 13th and 15th centuries and fascinates

Right: St-Émilion, with its rock-hewn church dominated by the belltower, is one of the leading wine villages in the Bordeaux region.

The interior of the Église
Monolithe of St-Émilion, a
church hewn from the rock

Bordeaux is a major city in the south-west; since 2007 the Old Town of this historic center of the wine trade has been listed as a UNESCO World Cultural Heritage Site. The city on the Garonne is renowned for its magnificent neoclassical architecture. One of its most attractive squares is the vast Place de la Bourse, which was laid out in the first half of the 18th century, not

far from the river. Much of the square consists of shallow water basins; in a prominent spot stands the Fountain of the Three Graces. At its sides the square is flanked by the impressive former maritime stock exchange and the Hôtel des Douanes – today a toll museum. A short way from here starts the Old Town with its alleyways, shops and restaurants.

The Pont du Pierre spans the Garonne River in Bordeaux. In the background the spire of the St-André Cathedral.

Detour

Château Mouton-Rothschild

Detour

Château Mouton-Rothschild

In France's wine-growing regions, the term "château" does not refer to a palace, but rather a large vineyard. And one of the Bordeaux region's most famous vineyards worldwide among its many châteaux is the Château Mouton-Rothschild in Pauillac on the Gironde. Predominantly Cabernet Sauvignon grapes are grown here to make the top-ranking red wines, on about 80 ha (198 acres) of land. Baron Philippe de Rothschild came up with the idea to make his wine bottles into small works of art. As a result, for over half a century artists have been creating labels for the property's top red wines. The list of contributing artists reads like a *Who's Who* of modern

In the Château's park

art – Jean Cocteau (1947), Georges Braque (1955), Salvador Dalí (1958), Juan Miro (1969), Marc Chagall (1970), Pablo Picasso (1973), Andy Warhol (1975) and Keith Haring (1988). You can admire these works of art, as well as many other exhibits, in the château's wine museum.

visitors with its Porte Royale, a magnificent portal lavishly decorated with sculptures. Next to from the church, there is the Tour Pey-Berland, a free-standing tower. St-Michel was built somewhat later, in the 14th/16th centuries, and is furnished in 17th-century baroque style. Those following in the footsteps of Camino de Santiago pilgrims should pay a visit to St-Seurin. The worship of St-Severin (St-Seurin) was an important part of the route.

Bordeaux has a lot more to offer than just St James relics – the city gates of Porte de Cailhau, Porte d'Aquitaine, Porte de la Monnaie and Porte Dijeaux, for example. The Pont de Pierre (a stone bridge) and the tall, modern bridge, Pont d'Aquitaine, dating from 1967, are also worth a look.

If you are interested in the region's world-famous vineyards you should make the 50-km (31-mile) journey along the Gironde to the grand Château Mouton-Rothschild in Pauillac.

㉗ Les Landes This is the name given to the landscape typical of the area south of Bordeaux – flat, sandy earth with sparse pine forests. The forests were planted by hand and are still used for their lum-ber by-products, predominantly for the extraction of resin.

The region's capital is Mont-de-Marsan, located somewhat off the beaten track in the south-east and counting some interesting Romanesque houses, the 15th-century Lacataye don-jon and several very pretty parks among its attractions.

㉘ Dax This small town on the Adour is one of France's most frequently visited thermal spa resorts. Water at a temperature of 64°C (147°F) bubbles out of the Fontaine de la Néhé.

The 17th-century cathedral here is also worth seeing, but the apostle gate from the earlier Gothic building is more significant in an art-history context. A visit to the Musée Borda in a beautiful city palace and a stroll along the banks of the Adour round off the visit.

If you feel a strong attraction to the seaside, you can drive 40 km (25 miles) from Dax to the southern end of the Côte d'Argent and then continue further on to the Côte des Basques around Biarritz.

On the other hand, if you are more interested in breathing in the mountain air in the Pyrenees, then you should continue south-east along this scenic route to Orthez.

㉙ St-Jean-Pied-de-Port In the Middle Ages, this mountain town was already an important stopover point for pilgrims – and the last one before the strenuous crossing of the Pyrenees over the Roncesvalles Pass and across the Spanish border. "Saint John at the Foot of the Pass" manages to preserve its medieval character even today. The banks of the Nive River are lined with houses dating from the 16th and 17th centuries, and the Gothic church of Notre Dame du Bout du Pont also stands here.

㉚ Bayonne The capital of the Basque country is a densely settled area but it has managed to retain much of its charm in its center with bridges on two rivers, large squares and rows of houses packed closely together around the Gothic cathedral of Ste Marie. Its city festival is famous, held every year on the second week-end in August.

Above: The Old Town of Bordeaux hugs the left bank of the Garonne. The river here flows around a halfmoon-shaped bend, and this is also the reason why Bordeaux is referred to as "Port de la Lune", or Port of the Moon.

Bordeaux boasts not only generous squares but also romantic spots in the Old Town.

Paris France's capital is, and remains, the city of love, zest for life, the arts, haute couture and haute cuisine. Allow plenty of time for a visit – or come again – to explore the Eiffel Tower, Montmartre, the Louvre, the Champs-Elysées and the Arc de Triomphe – and any number of chic cafés.

Orléans This beautiful city on the Loire is the city of Jeanne d'Arc – her statue stands in the Place du Martroi and the place where she lived is now a museum.

Amboise The Château d'Amboise is one of the most important château on the banks of the Loire. Italian artists played a major role in its construction – and it is seen as the cradle of the Renaissance.

Blois The château where Catherine de' Medici spent much of her life and the cathedral are the heart of this Loire town, once a political powerhouse but rather more sedate today.

La Rochelle This old port city is both a fishing town and a busy seaside resort. Arcades and quaint houses characterize the "St-Tropez on the Atlantic".

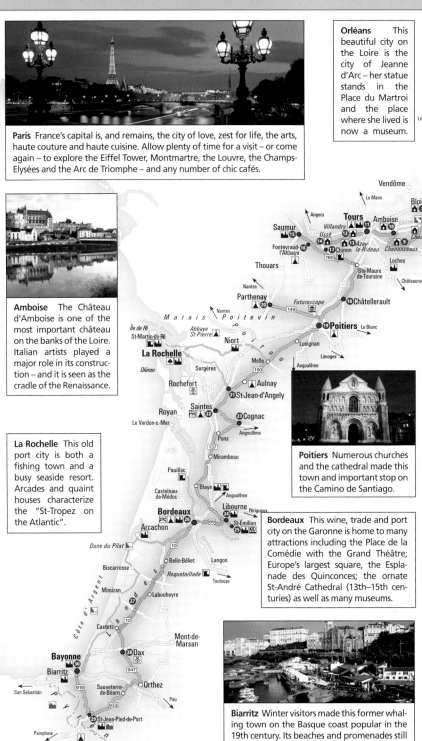

Poitiers Numerous churches and the cathedral made this town and important stop on the Camino de Santiago.

Bordeaux This wine, trade and port city on the Garonne is home to many attractions including the Place de la Comédie with the Grand Théâtre; Europe's largest square, the Esplanade des Quinconces; the ornate St-André Cathedral (13th–15th centuries) as well as many museums.

Château de Chambord With 440 rooms, a wide moat, and scores of towers, chimneys, gables and a wide moat, this dream castle is truly one of a kind. Leonardo da Vinci is aid to have created one of the château's seventy staircases, an intricate double-helix spiral.

Biarritz Winter visitors made this former whaling town on the Basque coast popular in the 19th century. Its beaches and promenades still enjoy huge popularity.

St-Émilion Amid the vineyards stands the fortress complex of t-Émilion, with its famous cathedral and rock-hewn church.

Route 7
Limousin, Dordogne, Périgord

Most people know the cities of Limoges and Toulouse, but what exactly lies in between? It is where you will find a diverse cultural and natural landscape which ranges from the lush Limousin in the north, to the wooded plains of the Périgord around the Dordogne and the limestone plateau of the Quercy, to the broad Garonne Valley in the south-west.

From the old porcelain city of Limoges, the route heads directly up to the high plateaus of the Limousin region – the vast mountain landscape which forms the westernmost ridge of the Massif Central. The peaks easily reach heights of 900 m (2,953 ft), and the climate is fittingly harsh. There is more stony ground and moors than arable land; the few farmhouses are scattered far and wide. A little farther south is the Bas-Limousin, with its much milder climate. Heathlands of birches and pines alternate with grassland, gorse fields, and chestnut groves, before the scenery changes to that of fruit plantations sprawling over sunny, gently rolling hills in the Vallée de la Corrèze. Heading farther south, the Dordogne Valley forms the border between the Limousin and Quercy regions. The landscape

around the tranquil Dordogne was once settled by the Gallic Petrocorii tribe, giving it its present-day name of Périgord. The region presents itself as a harmonious landscape whose

marshlands, as well as numerous grottos and dripstone caves with impressive prehistoric rock paintings, attract visitors seeking peace, tranquility and relaxation.

South of the Dordogne lies the limestone world of plateaus and gorges of the Quercy. This region stretches from the Massif Central to the Aquitaine lowlands, and its main centers are Cahors in Haut-Quercy and Montauban in Bas-Quercy. The entire district is dominated by the *causses*, as the vast limestone plateaus are called here. The high plateaus are crisscrossed by dry valleys, the *combes*, which enable a degree of pasture farming and, in favorable locations, even winegrowing – as in the Cahors AOC region. The showpiece of the Quercy region is the Causse de Gramat, which enchants visitors with unique natural monuments, like the giant Gouffre de Padirac, a vast grotto with an underground lake. The narrow valleys which persistently cut through the tableland are also impressive.

Above: The Dordogne River meanders through wide, fertile valleys. The forests often grow all the way down the slopes right down to the riverbanks. Pictured here is the view from the rocky promontory on which the fortified town of Domme is perched across the wide meanders and loops of the gentle river.
Left: The Abbey of Brantôme, founded by Charlemagne in a picturesque spot directly on the banks of the Dronne River

The journey from Conques is particularly interesting from an architectural and historical perspective. The Abbey of Ste-Foy, built here from the mid-11th-century onward, is considered one of the finest Romanesque churches in all of France, while the Ste-Cécile Cathedral is the best example of the southern French Gothic. Toulouse is one of France's most famous art strongholds, and Montauban's cathedral is a rare neoclassical religious structure.

The return leg north begins in Agen as we leave the Garonne Valley behind us. After crossing the Lot River, the route once again heads into the heart of the Périgord region. The Dordogne Valley re-appears as a veritable treasure chest between Bergerac and Sarlat-la-Canéda, featuring both an enchanting landscape and many historic towns and edifices. We return to Limoges after visiting the prehistoric caves of Lascaux.

Right: The delightful maze of medieval lanes in the fortified town of Cordes-sur-Ciel.
Left: Sunflowers are a cheerful sight in summer, growing in large fields all over the south.

A bronze sculpture of Mary holding the body of Jesus outside the St-Aurélien Chapel in the old butchers' district of Limoges

This route heads through a tranquil region in the heart of France which has lots to offer in the way of landscape, culture, cuisine and wine cellars. Whether it be prehistoric evidence, famous religious buildings or proud fortresses and impressive châteaux, they all attest to the cultural and historic importance of this region.

1 Limoges With its cathedral the capital of the Limousin and the city of porcelain sits in a picturesque spot high above the Vienne River. The oldest part of town is the Cité. The best access provides the Pont St-Étienne, built in 1210 and featuring eight arches. The St-Étienne Cathedral, built between the 13th and the 16th centuries, dominates the town. Particularly attractive is the late-Gothic portal of St John, worked in fine granite and completed in 1530. The massive, 62-m-high (203-ft) bell tower is still Romanesque in its lower part, whereas its upper four stories are Gothic in style. The most beautiful piece inside the cathedral is the rood screen, made from limestone in 1533. It boasts a gallery of suspended keystones.

You can find out about the manufacture of porcelain at the Musée Adrien-Dubouché, which impressively traces the development of all the ceramic, porcelain and glass arts. The Musée municipal de l'Évêché has all manner of interesting information on different types of enamel work.

The route continues along the A 20 autoroute. You'll reach the 73-m-high (240-ft) Mont Gargan peak via the D 15 and the D 12. From here you can enjoy panoramic views extending from the Monédières Massif in the south-east across the hills of the Marche in the north to the mountains of the Limousin in the west. The D 3 now takes you to Uzerche.

2 Uzerche Uzerche "the Virgin" received its epithet because no one had ever managed to take the town located above a bend in the Vézère River.

Accordingly, it boasts a wealth of picturesque city palaces and town houses, many dating

Travel information

Route profile
Length: c. 1,000 km (6214 mi)
Time required: about 2 weeks
Start and end: Limoges
Route: Limoges, Tulle, Rocamadour, Cahors, Figeac, Conques, Rodez, Albi, Cordes (with a detour to Toulouse), Montauban, Moissac, Agen, Domme, Sarlat-la-Canéda, Grotte de Lascaux, Périgueux, Brantôme, Limoges

When to go:
Spring and autumn are the best times to travel. It can get very hot from June to August. The winters, however, are fairly cold in the upper reaches.

Information:
Comité Régional du Tourisme en Limousin

30, cours Gay-Lussac
87003 Limoges, Cédex 1
Tel: 05 55 11 05 90
www.tourismelimousin.com
Comité Départemental du Tourisme de la Dordogne
BP 2063, 24002 Périgueux
Cedex, Tel: 05 53 35 50 24
www.dordogne-perigord-tourisme.fr

Pech Merle: open daily April to November; tickets are best reserved in advance. Information Tel 05 65 31 27 05 and www.pechmerle.com
Lascaux II: closed January, varying opening times rest of year. Information:
Tel: 05 53 51 95 03 and www.lascaux.culture.fr
NB: Bring warm jackets or jumpers for a cave visit, even in midsummer!

Sculptures of the Apostles and the saints in a side chapel of the St-Étienne Cathedral in Limoges

from the Gothic period and featuring proud conical roofs, turrets and portals. The Porte Bécharie of the former city fortifications is preserved, while the Romanesque Church of St-Pierre dates back to the 11th century. Its three-naved crypt is the oldest in the Limousin.
On the D 1120 it is now but a stone's throw to Tulle.

3 Tulle The town extends over several miles along the deeply cut Corrèze valley. It has frequently been heavily fought over since the Hundred Years'

War, most recently on 8 June 1944, when French resistance fighters victoriously entered the town. Only one day later the Germans returned and immediately hanged 99 citizens in public as a "punishment"; a further 101 later died in camps. The Enclos quarter of the town has a medieval feel, with historic houses, narrow lanes and steep flights of steps. You can't miss the 12th-century Notre-Dame Cathedral with its 73-m-high (240-ft) bell tower. Inside, in the left side aisle, it holds a wooden statue dating

from the 16th century of John the Baptist, Tulle's patron saint. The saint's birthday is ceremoniously celebrated each year with a *tour de la lunade* (change of the moon) procession. The most attractive secular building is the 16th-century Maison de Loyac, featuring a richly ornamented façade.
Vie the D 940 you'll reach Bretenoux and the mighty château of Castelnau near the village of Prudhomat.

4 Château de Castelnau-Bretenoux Visible from afar, the castle sits high above the confluence of the Dordogne and Cère rivers. It is defined by its vast belt of protection walls and its proud towers. The building dates back to the 13th century but did not attain its

Top left: St-Étienne Cathedral in Limoges and arched bridge across the Vienne River
Top right: Uzerche panorama above a bend of the Vézère
Left: The Gothic cloister in Tulle's Notre-Dame Cathedral

The white gold of Limousin

Hard porcelain with a high kaolin content and a high firing temperature started to be manufactured in Limoges in 1771, and this was followed by the very successful production of soft porcelain with a lower kaolin content and a lower firing temperature. Soft-paste porcelain was gradually developed to become Limoges' main specialty. Instead of kaolin, it contains a melt (paste) of sand, alum, alkali compounds as well as alkaline earth

A Limoges porcelain plate

compounds. This composition, more akin to glass, is what makes the porcelain slightly translucent, a quality much rated at the time.

127

An underground lake in the bizarre cave world of the Gouffre de Padirac

Old Town idyll in Cahors.
During the Middle Ages, the
city was a major finance
and banking center.

present extent until the Hundred Years' War, when the irregular triangular shape with its three round towers and three concentric rings of ramparts was built. The ensemble was able to accommodate 1,500 men and 100 horses. The wide panoramic views from its historic ramparts are one of the attractions. In 1896 the local opera singer Jean Mouliérat began to restore the château's rooms which today feature beautiful décor, magnificent furnishings and valuable tapestries. The oratory has 15th-century stained-glass windows.

Via well-signposted bendy country lanes you'll return to one of the most amazing show caves in southern France.

5 **Gouffre de Padirac** The karst of the Causse de Gramat conceals, at about 100 m (328 ft) depth, an extensive system of caves, lakes and a river. The corridors that are known today extend over more than 20 km (12.5 mi). Access to this subterranean world is via a 32-m-wide (105-ft) chasm, which opens out to a rubble cone at a depth of 75 m (246 ft). From there you descend another 28 m (92 ft) to the underground river. Open to the public at the bottom of the cave are some 400 m (437 yds) to walk on foot and a further 500 m (547 yds) by boat. Flat-bottom boats take visitors across the crystal-clear water, at a constant temperature of 11°C (51.8°F), into a unique fairytale world. At the end of the boat trip, is the surprising Grande Pendeloque and the Lac de la Pluie (rain lake). This stalactite is part of a 78-m-high (256-ft) sinter formation. The Grand Pilar alone is 40 m (131 ft) tall, while the Salle du Grand Dôme has an overwhelming 91-m-high (299-ft) cupola.

Via the village of Padirac and the D 673 you'll reach a spectacular pilgrimage destination.

6 **Rocamadour** The small town was built in a breathtaking location into the walls of a rock rising some 150 m (492 ft) above the Alzou. It is not known whether Saint Amadour ever really existed, but this has not dented his reputation. Until the Reformation the pilgrimage to the obscure saint was one of the most famous in Christendom. A "Black Madonna" has been here since the 13th century,

venerated today in the Notre-Dame Chapel. The St-Michel Chapel is richly decorated inside and out with frescoes. Those on the exterior walls date from the 12th century, those in the choir from the 13th. To appreciate the extent of the entire complex you'll have to climb the 233 steps of the Via Sancta, not forgetting a visit to the Musée d'Art sacré Francis Poulenc. The treasury holds objects of the pilgrimage treasure.

The D 673 and the D 820 now take you to Cahors, beautifully located in a bend of the Lot.

7 **Cahors** The capital of the Quercy and of the Lot département was in the 13th century one of the largest cities in France, and traders from Lombardy made it the foremost banking center in Europe. This proud past is still evident today when you approach the city via the magnificent seven-arched

Pont Valentré. A grand testimony to medieval fortification, it boasts three towers, each 40 m (131 ft) high and still featuring machicolations. The two outer towers also had lockable gates and portcullises, while the central tower housed the command post. Cahors' St-Étienne Cathedral is one of the most unusual domes churches in the South-West. Its Romanesque nave was enlarged by Gothic chapels in the 13th century, while the façade was not completed until a century later. The 12th-century Romanesque north portal is impressive. In the choir and in the first dome, frescoes from the 14th century are preserved. All around the cathedral there are numerous houses from the Gothic and Renaissance periods for you to discover.

Continue upriver along the Lot and you'll quickly reach the next highlight.

8 **Grotte du Pech-Merle** The dripstone cave is particularly fascinating thanks to its prehistoric wall paintings, dating back to about 20,000 years.

**Left: The buildings in the pilgrimage site Rocamadour look chiseled out of the rock.
Above: The Old Town of Cahors seems to sit on a peninsula in a bend of the Lot**

The Pont Valentré in Cahors, today the city's main landmark – and as such it features on the local Cahors wine bottles and corks –, is an unusual example of a medieval defense structure. On the one hand, it serves as a bridge over the river Lot, but it once also had an unmistakable military purpose. The defense building, erected in the early 14th century, thus features

three 40-m-high (131-ft) towers with machicolations, while the bridge piers have also been reinforced with tapering bastions. The bridge itself was never actually captured. A legend surrounding a pact made with the devil during construction is told by the keystone subsequently placed in the central bridge tower, which depicts the devil trying in vain to rip out the stone.

The chapterhouse of a monastery destroyed by the Protestants became the Chapelle Notre-Dame-de-Pitié in Figeac in 1622.

Several halls follow one another along 1,200 m (1,312 yds) of cave. The Chapelle des Mammouths depicts larger-than-life mammoths, and in one corridor you can see the renowned spotted horses. The Galerie de l'Ours has impressive stalacmite columns, and the Salle de Combel contains the bones of cave bears. At the Musée Amédée-Lemozi you can gain an insight into the pre- and early history of the Quercy.

A few miles farther south, on the left bank of the Lot, you'll enter a medieval world.

9 St-Cirq-Lapopie Castle and village are huddled around an 80-m-high (262-ft) rock above the Lot. The village owes its double name to its patron saint, Saint Cyrus, and to the aristocratic La Popie family,

who ruled here in the Middle Ages. The once mighty fortress was demolished by Henry of Navarre in 1580. The ruins do, however, still afford magnificent views from the highest point of the rock. The vast village church was built as a fortified structure in the 16th century. St-Cirq-Lapopie's narrow lanes are lined with Gothic timber-framed houses. Many now have restaurants, art galleries and souvenir stalls.

The road along the Lot right bank takes you to Cajarc.

10 Cajarc In this small but lively town the former French President, Georges Pompidou, had his second home. The Centre d'Art Contemporain Georges Pompidou, an arts center, was opened here in 1989, making Cajarc one of the foremost re-

gional centers of contemporary art. The writer Françoise Sagan was born in Cajarc.

Continuing along the right bank of the Lot, then taking the D 662, you'll soon reach the next stop on the route, Figeac.

11 Figeac A stroll around this small trading town on the Célé will again take you into a medieval environment. Many of the buildings here date from the 13th to 15th centuries. They all follow the same basic design: the ground floor is broken up by large pointed arches, a gallery runs along the floor above, and the open storage space at the top is covered by a flat roof. The 13th-century Hôtel de la Monnaie is a typical example. Also worth a visit is the Place des Écritures. A giant reproduction of the Rosetta

Stone was set in the floor here. The Stone was found during Napoleon's Egypt campaign in 1799, and with its help Jean-François Champollion, a native son of Figeac, for the first time deciphered Egyptian hieroglyphics. The Musée Champollion is dedicated to his work.

Follow the Lot upstream until the D 901 branches off south; from here it is not far to the next stop on the route.

12 Conques The Abbaye de Ste-Foy stands hidden here in remote woodland above the Dourdou River. In the ninth century, a tiny monastery stood here, while the reliquary of Sainte Foy was kept at another abbey, in Agen. It was then stolen by a monk from the Conques Abbey who thus transformed the place into a desti-

This 15th-century burial scene in the Notre-Dame Cathedral of Rodez was worked in polychrome stone.

nation for pilgrims and a stop on the way to Santiago de Compostela in Spain. The pilgrims brought with them the wealth that made it possible to build this beautiful basilica church between 1050 and 1135. Its central nave soars up 22 m (72 ft) and has three arched floors. The columns count no fewer than 250 richly adorned capitals. The tympanum depicting the Last Judgment is one of the masterpieces of medieval sculpting. The treasury at Conques is also unique; it contains precious items from the ninth to the 16th centuries. The most valuable piece is a gold-plated reliquary of Sainte Foy, studded with rock crystals and gems. The body of the statue dates from the ninth century, the head probably from the fifth century. The reliquary shrine was allegedly donated by Charlemagne.

From Conques continue south on the D 901 which will take you directly to Rodez.

⑬ Rodez The Aveyron flows around the town which clearly demonstrates the medieval separation of worldly and clerical powers. The Place du Bourg is the commercial center, while the Place de la Cité next to the cathedral the spiritual heart. Originally built as a fortified church in the 13th century, the cathedral with its fortress-like west façade clearly dominates the town. Its walls are made from a reddish sandstone which glows in the right light as if illuminated from inside. The 87-m-high (285-ft) tower is adorned with a tip reminiscent of a stone flower bouquet. The Gothic interior is characterized by rows of tall columns. Eye catchers are an excellently worked 16th-century rood screen and an entombment made from polychrome stone. The choir stalls feature rich

Top: The castle ruins, the fortified church and the houses of St-Cirque-Lapopie sit perched on an 80-m-high (-ft) rock above the Lot. Left: Ste-Foy Abbey in Conques, charmingly nestled into green hills

Ste-Cécile Cathedral is the focal point of the Episcopal city of Albi, which became a UNESCO World Cultural Heritage Site in 2010.

The painter of the Moulin Rouge

The late-Impressionist painter Henri de Toulouse-Lautrec was born in Albi on 24 November 1864 as the offspring of one of France's oldest aristocratic families. At the age of 18, he went to Paris to become a qualified painter. The district of Montmartre, with its Place Pigalle, Place Blanche and the Moulin Rouge, quickly became his second home.

As a painter of the Belle Époque, Toulouse-Lautrec created lithographs for posters and illustrations in newspapers and magazines. In 1885, the "Le Mirliton" cabaret theater was opened by Aristide Bruant, and the young painter designed numerous posters for this, bearing the Bruant

Portrait of Miss Dolly from the Star in Le Havre, **1899.**

motif (trademark red scarf). From 1888 onwards, he focused on what was probably his most famous subject: people from circuses, nightclubs and the demimonde. His four-toned *Moulin Rouge – La Goulue* lithograph brought him overnight fame in 1891. He captured the spirit of the times with scenes from Parisian nightlife, and gave poster advertising a crucial boost using color lithography. Three hundred and fifty-one large-size posters have been preserved.

Henri de Toulouse-Lautrec died at his family's Château de Malromé (in the Gironde) on 9 September 1901 at just 36 years of age. He left most of this works to his hometown of Albi, which opened the Musée Toulouse-Lautrec to house these in 1922.

carvings dating from the 15th century and depicting many a strange creature – a winged lion can be seen and also a naughty boy baring his behind.

The N 88 takes you in a south-westerly direction to Albi.

14 Albi The town on the Tarn River is dominated by its Ste-Cécile Cathedral. The Gothic brick building dating from the late 13th century has a mighty 78-m-high (256-ft) fortified tower that looks like a threatening exclamation mark, and in contrast a sumptuously decorated porch made from white limestone. The vast interior is overwhelmed by the rood screen, the largest in France. It was carved from stone by local masters around 1500. The chapter room with its valuable choir stalls feature interesting carvings; it is surrounded by richly adorned stone work. Its outer walls feature painted statues of the prophets and other figures from the Old Testament. The high altar's back wall is adorned with a Last Judgment painted onto stone and dating from the 16th century. The Palais de la Berbie, former see of the archbishop, houses the Musée Toulouse-Lautrec which owns more than 800 works by this native son of the town.

From Albi the D 600 takes you north-east to Cordes.

15 Cordes The fortified little town sits atop a conical hill above the Cérou valley. In its steep lanes you'll spot many a house from the Gothic period. Beautiful examples are the Maison Ségulier with its sculpture-bedecked façade and the Maison du Grand-Veneur.

A worthwhile detour takes you to Toulouse, via the D 922 and

Right: Rood screen and choir of Albi's Ste-Cécile Cathedral are resplendently fashioned in the Gothic Flamboyant style.

One of the most attractive "bastides", the fortified villages in South-West France, is Cordes(-sur-Ciel) in the Cérou River valley.

Bastide towns of the Périgord

Bastides are fortified towns (the Occitan word "bastida" means just that), in the South-West of France, that were built during the 13th century by the English or the French in record time in order to strengthen their positions after the Albigensian Crusade and before the start of the Hundred Years' War.

The feudal lords granted new settlers important privileges. For the price of a parcel of land and the adjoining agricultural fields the settlers received charters containing the right of asylum, inheritance and freedom from military service. A representative of the king was responsible for the collection of taxes, while the town was administered by a council elected by the inhabitants.

Bastide towns: Larressingle (top), Monpazier (above).

All bastides were laid out to the same plan: wherever the terrain allowed, roads and lanes were clustered at right angles around a central market place. It was not unusual for the bastide to be built around an existing structure, often a castle or a fortified church. At the heart of it was always a rectangular square with a market hall, surrounded by arcaded walkways. One particularly attractive example of such a bastide is the Old Town of Domme, once only accessible via the Porte des Tours.

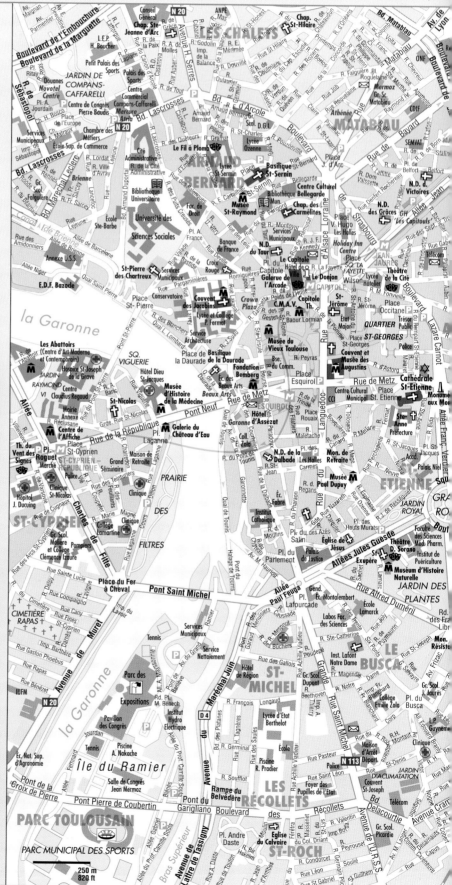

Toulouse

The capital of the Languedoc region was founded by the Romans. It experienced its heyday as a trading city during the Renaissance, as evidenced by the Old Town district around the Hôtel de Ville. This area, as well as the Place St-Georges and the Rue Alsace-Lorraine, always pulsate with life.

Toulouse's greatest attractions, however, are two churches. The 12th-century St-Sernin Basilica, with its 115-m-long (377-ft) nave, is one of Europe's largest Romanesque churches, and has

A beautiful ensemble: the Garonne River, the Pont Neuf and Toulouse

an unusual octagonal bell tower with decorative arcades. Both doorways are Romanesque masterpieces. Behind the chancel is the vast 18th-century tomb of St-Sernin. The holds numerous relics from the 11th and 12th centuries. Meanwhile, the Church of the Jacobins (begun in 1216), which holds the tomb of Thomas Aquinas, is Gothic in style, and impresses visitors with its virtuoso ribbed palm-tree vault.

Toulouse became a Romanesque stronghold in the Middle Ages, because of its location on the Via Tolosana, one of the four pilgrimage routes to Santiago de Compostela. The finest sculptures from this time are housed at the Musée des Augustins, in two cloisters of the former Augustinian monastery.

If you are more interested in technology and engineering make sure you visit the Cité de l'Espace, where you can find out about the conquest of space.

Many lavish palaces were built in Toulouse thanks to its once flourishing trade. In the heart of the Old Town, the giant 18th-century Capitol – named after the Capitouls (mayors) – is home to the town hall and a theater. Inside, the magnificent ceiling paintings in the Salle des Illustres attest to the city's glamorous past.

The masterly worked artistic capitals in the cloister of the St-Pierre Abbey in Moissac

the A 68 (see page 136). From there the A 20 brings you to the town of Montauban.

⑯ Montauban Much more than just the smaller sister of Toulouse, this town was once the capital of the "Protestant Republic" of southern France. Around the Place Nationale stand proud town houses from the 17th century. The Notre-Dame Cathedral, built in 1685 as a counter to Protestantism on the orders of Louis XIV, is a rare example in France of a neoclassical church structure. The 14th-century Pont-Vieux is also worth seeing.

The most important attraction, however, is the Musée Ingres which is housed in the former Papal palace. Dominique Ingres, who was born here, bequeathed his entire estate to Montauban. Along with many paintings it comprises more than 4,000 illustrations which are exhibited on a rotation basis. His most famous painting, *The Vow of Louis XIII*, is displayed in the cathedral.

Via the D 927 you'll quickly get to Moissac.

⑰ Moissac Situated on the north bank of the Tarn amid vineyards, the village is home to the St-Pierre Abbey, one of the oldest in the country. The complex was founded in the seventh century by a Benedictine monk and survived raids by Arabs, Normans and Hungarians. In 1047 it joined the Abbey of Cluny and experienced a heyday thereafter under the Abbot Durand de Bredon. During the 12th century, St-Pierre was the most important monastery in the South-West of France.

Also from this time date the portal of the Abbey Church and its cloister. The south portal, completed in 1115, is one of the earliest works of Romanesque sculpture in the Languedoc region. Its lunette depicts

the Last Judgment with the Enthroned Christ in Majesty above the clouds, holding the Book of Life in his left hand and surrounded by the symbols of the four Evangelists as well as the 24 Elders of the Apocalypse wearing gold crowns, after the Revelation of St John. The central pillar is carved from a single stone and depicts a lion and figures of old men, while the side pillars show St Peter and the Prophet Isaiah. The 11th-century cloister comprises 76 beautifully adorned arcades and features impressively light and elegant columns. The effect is increased thanks to the combination of white, green, pink and gray marble. The capitals are finely sculpted with flowers, wild animals and scenes from the Old and New Testaments.

Moissac has also earned an Appellation d'Origine Contrôlée for its Chasselas grapes.

The D 813 will quickly take you to the next stop, at Agen.

⑱ Agen The capital of the Lot-et-Garonne département is also the center for the cultivation of plums in France, a fruit introduced in the 11th century by Crusaders returning from the Middle East. The monks of the local abbeys first dried the sweet plums and sold them to improve their finances. Today some 40,000 tonnes (44,092 tons) of prunes are produced each year in and around Agen. If you're after more than just plums, visit the small Musée Municipal des Beaux-Arts. Here you'll find works by Goya and Corot as well as the beautiful

Vénus du mas. This Greek marble statue dating from the first century BC was found in a field near Agen in 1876.

⑲ Domme The royal bastide town of Domme was founded in 1281 by Philipp the Bold on a rock 150 m (492 ft) above the Dordogne, in order to gain control over the valley and the advancing English troops. Once heavily fortified, the village was matched to the terrain and built on a trapezoid plan. Preserved today are the ramparts dating from the 13th century and countless houses from the Gothic period. The Porte Delbos and Porte des Tours city gates date from the 13th century, while the Hôtel de Ville was built in the 14th century. Also worth seeing are the ancient

Porte des Tours – the way into the bastide of Domme high above the Dordogne

Armagnac – France's oldest spirit

Armagnac has been distilled from wine in the center of the Gascogne region since time immemorial. A distillery in the Landes département was officially accredited in documents as early as 1461, and is housed in the Musée de l'Armagnac in Condom. Today, Armagnac is subject to strict laws. Only eleven specified varieties of grapes can be cultivated over an area of approximately 15,000 ha (37,065 acres). The name, origin and production process are also legally governed by the Appellation Contrôlée.

The wine can only be pressed without the addition of either sugar or sulphur. Armagnac is only distilled once, after which the brandy is

Armagnac matures in wooden barrels to become one of the finest brandies.

decanted into new barrels made from Gascogne holm oak wood. While cognac is stored in the oldest possible barrels, Armagnac is always left to mature in new barrels, which give it its special bouquet and typical amber color. As with other brandies, Armagnac becomes better – and more expensive – the longer it has matured in the barrels.

market hall with its quaint wooden galleries.

The best views of the Dordogne valley can be enjoyed from the Belvédère de la Barre. A large dripstone cave extends inside the rocks underneath Domme; its 500-m-long (1650-ft) corridors served as a safe haven for the inhabitants during times of war. The entrance to the cave is in the market hall. At the end of a visit, a panoramic lift takes you up the side the rock back to the top, with a view over the Dordogne thrown in.

A short way west of Domme, in a lovely spot on the steep banks of the Dordogne, stands the Château of Castelnaud-la-Chapelle, which has an exhibition of medieval war machines. From Domme the D 46 takes you to Sarlat-la-Canéda.

㉒ Sarlat-la-Canéda Hardly anywhere in France are the Middle Ages, the Renaissance and the 17th century still as omnipresent as in this ancient bishops' see in the Périgord noir. The Rue de la République is surrounded by picturesque old lanes and richly adorned patrician town houses. The focal point of the city is the Place du Peyrou with the former cathedral of St-Sacerdos dating from the 16th and 17th centuries and the historic Episcopal palace with Gothic windows and a gallery in the style of the Italian Renaissance. Along the Rue des Consuls stand the most attractive 16th- and 17th-century town houses where wealthy merchants and clerical dignitaries once lived. Sarlat is also famous for its farmers' market,

which takes place every Saturday on the Place de la Liberté. The D 704 continues directly to Montignac and France's most famous cave.

㉑ Grotte de Lascaux The sheer number and the density of the preserved paintings in the 250-m-long (820-ft) cave have made it the most significant prehistoric site in Europe. Its walls are covered with some 1,500 rock paintings and engravings, which gave it the epithet of the "Sistine Chapel of Prehistory". Painted in around 17,000 BC, the images mostly depict animals. One exception is

Above: A lively scene at the Place de la Liberté in Sarlat-la-Canéda, where the farmers' market takes place each week

The Dordogne river valley is lined with numerous castles and palaces, and a particularly striking example of these can be seen in Castelnaud-la-Chapelle near Domme. The 13th-century castle complex is dominated by the square keep, or donjon, which gave the lords of the castle a good view of the right riverbank. Inside, Castelnaud's château and bailey house a

fascinating and much-visited museum of medieval warfare, displaying weapons and suits of armor, as well as the armorer's workshop. The most spectacular exhibits include the reconstructed *trébuchet*, a giant medieval catapult. The castle itself is a private property, and listed as an historic monument by the Ministry of Culture.

Candelabra and capitals
in the St-Front Cathedral
in Périgueux

Culinary Périgord and Quercy

A nearly indispensable ingredient in the Périgord or Quercy cuisine is the truffle, a black mushroom growing underground that is both extremely rare and expensive. However, it is versatile and refines everything with its unique aroma. Whether *foie gras*, pâtés, poultry, jellified meat terrines, salad or egg dishes – and indeed: *crème brûlée*! – they all achieve perfection with the help of this mushroom. The ultimate in luxury is the *truffe cendrée*, an entire truffle cooked in the chimney.

Another local delicacy is *foie gras*, the liver of forcefed ducks or geese, the pride of the South-West. A *foie entier* or whole liver is just that, 100% liver, *parfait de foie gras* contains 75 %, but *pâté, mousse* or *ga-*

Preparations for the production of *foie gras* (top) and walnut oil (above)

lantine contain only 50%. The third main pillar of cooking in the South-West are the fattened ducks themselves. Their breasts are eaten as *magrets de canard*, their gizzards on salads as *gésiers*. *Confits* are fried duck or goose pieces conserved in their own fat. At one time, they were conserved in stoneware jars, but today confits are available mainly in glass jars or tinned.

the bison attacking a schematic representation of a human being with a bird's head. In order to protect the paintings from damage caused by the perspiration of the visitors the cave was closed to the public in 1963. In 1983 finally, a replica cave named Lascaux II was opened. A faithful copy recreated using the same materials as in the original cave, it grants visitors an impressive experience without damaging the original.

Via the D 67 and the D 6089 you'll quickly reach the next stop, Périgueux, the capital of the Dordogne département.

㉒ Périgueux The town in the gentle valley of the Isle dates back to the Vesunna springs which were venerated by the Celtic Petrocorii tribe. The Ro-

mans developed it as one of the most beautiful cities in the Aquitaine region. Today, the city of Périgueux has two centers, each one marked by a domed church. Above the Cité and the former Roman town towers St-Étienne, while farther east the Byzantine-looking St-Front Cathedral with its domes and turrets dominates the medieval center of town. St-Étienne was the city's first Christian cult site and until 1669 its was also the Episcopal church. Its oldest parts date back to the 11th century and its dome is the largest in the Périgord. St-Front, built in the 12th century, is one of the largest churches in the South-West. Its most beautiful feature is a monumental walnut-wood retable depicting the Ascension

of the Virgin Mary. Grouped around the cathedral is the Old Town where many houses date back to the Gothic and Renaissance periods.

The route next continues on the D 939 to Brantôme.

㉓ Brantôme The historic abbey in the lovely Dronne valley was founded by Charlemagne in 769, although the present abbey buildings all date from the 18th century. It has a particularly remarkable 11th-century *clocher* or bell tower, standing separate from the church on a rock. Its four Romanesque floors are stepped like a pyramid. With its triangular gables and stone pyramid as a crowning finish it is unique within the entire region. The best views of the abbey can be enjoyed from the bridge. Underneath the abbey is an extensive network of caves with exceptionally bizarre dripstone formations. Via the D 78 and the N 21 you get back to Limoges.

Top: The church of St-Front in Périgueux reminds of Sacré-Coeur in Paris – the domes were created by the same architect. Middle: The cave of Lascaux holds some of man's oldest rock paintings.

The Benedictine St-Pierre Abbey on the banks of the Dronne River in Brantôme.

Périgueux St-Front Cathedral (12th C.) is one of the largest in South-West France and with its many turrets and domes it seems vaguely Oriental in appearance.

Domme This royal bastide town is spectacularly perched on a rock above the Dordogne. Large parts of the fortifications – such as the Porte des Tours – are preserved.

Agen Juicy prunes have made Agen famous. One special attraction is the Pont Canal – one Garonne side canal that is taken across the river via a brick-arched bridge.

Moissac This small town on the banks of the Tarn is known for the Romanesque portal of its Abbey Church (early 12th C.) and its exquisite cuisine.

Limoges The world-famous city of enamels and porcelain on the Vienne River is dominated by its monumental cathedral (13th–16th C.). The great Impressionist painter Pierre-Auguste Renoir (1841–1919) is a native son of the city and learned porcelain painting here in its youth.

Rocamadour The medieval village and its seven churches spectacularly clings to a rocky precipice high above the banks of the Lot River. It is a major pilgrimage site.

Cahors The Pont Valentré is a mighty defensive bridge from the 14th century across the Lot River. It is one of the reasons why this city was never taken by its enemies.

Toulouse This congenial industrial and university city on the Garonne is the main center in the South-West alongside Bordeaux. The splendid Pont Neuf featuring seven basket-handle arches is the oldest of all Garonne bridges. Typical of its Old Town are the red brick houses which shimmer pink, red or purple depending on the light.

Albi St-Cécile Cathedral dominates the city on the Tarn that was listed as a World Cultural Heritage Site in 2010 together with the surrounding Episcopal district. Henri de Toulouse-Lautrec was born here, and a museum displays a selection of his works.

Roussillon, the Pyrenees, Aquitaine

This is a route for all those who love the seaside just as much as the mountains.
From the historic province of Roussillon's deep blue Mediterranean coastline it travels
along, and at times over, the peaks of the Pyrenees, ending with the often turbulent
waters of the Atlantic in the Bay of Biscay in the French Basque region.

With the exception of a small detour to Andorra, the route travels solely through France but it explores areas with their own language and culture. The east, on the Mediterranean, is home to the French Catalans who, in some respects, feel themselves to be more closely linked to the people of Spanish Catalonia than their fellow French citizens and who maintain their own traditions and language. It is therefore not unusual in Perpignan, Prades or any of the other towns along the eastern section of the route to see a spontaneous gathering on a square on a warm summer evening with people dancing the sardana hand in hand. The Basque people, who live in the western Pyrenees, have retained their own characteristics and language to an even greater degree. It is not unusual here to see the French town names

on the road signs sprayed over so that drivers are only able to read the Basque equivalents. Unlike in Spain, however, there is no radical separatist movement, such as the ETA, in the French Basque region.

This route affords plenty for nature fans to discover, with the

mountains of the Pyrenees providing a series of sensational displays such as the Cirque de Gavarnie in the Pyrenees National Park. Here you can admire the flora and fauna as well as the magnificent rock faces and numerous waterfalls while hiking or walking.

To the delight of art fans there are also Romanesque masterpieces to be seen, particularly in the Catalan style, in Elne and in Serrabone and St-Bertrand-de-Comminges, for example. The Gothic style is to be found in Bayonne, for instance, yet there are often little-known churches to be seen along the way in small towns, churches with their very own appeal and still testimony to an elementary piety. There is also a series of museums displaying masterpieces from different centuries. An important destination for believers is Lourdes, the small

village that became a pilgrimage site of international status in the 19th century on account of a miraculous healing attributed to the Virgin Mary. Hordes of pilgrims from all over the world flock to Lourdes today, often the sick as well, in the hope of being healed.

Sport fans will find what they are looking for both along the coast and in the mountains. The latter are inviting not only for rock-climbing or hiking, but also for winter sports. A variety of skiing resorts have been developed both in the French Pyrenees and in Andorra. There is plenty of beach action along the Mediterranean in Collioure and the adjacent towns, as well as on the Atlantic side in the elegant seaside resorts of the Belle Époque, such as Biarritz.

Traces of history are to be found in many places along this route. Still standing in

Above: Looking over the Val du Fenouillet and the Corbières Hills it is the 2,784-m-high (9,134-ft) Pic de Canigou (in the background left), the easternmost mountain peak of the Pyrenees, that catches your eye.
Left: From the Pointe St-Martin headland a white lighthouse watches over the elegant seaside resort of Biarritz.

Perpignan is the Palace of the Kings of Majorca, even though it has lost some of valuable furnishings over the course of time. Henry of Navarre who, as King Henry IV, united a country divided by wars of religion, was born in Pau.

A memorial in Gurs commemorates the internment of Jews and political prisoners in a camp there during the German occupation of France in World War II. King Louis XIV spent time in St-Jean-de-Luz on the Atlantic coast while waiting to marry Maria Theresa, the Spanish infanta, a marriage that concluded the Treaty of the Pyrenees and brought peace between Spain and France.

Left: Believers from all over the world come to Lourdes.
Right: The St-Michel-de-Cuxa abbey lies embedded in the mountain landscape.

Whatever other interests visitors to France may have, the country remains first and foremost a nation of culinary delights and superb wines. How about a hearty Basque piperade for instance, a tasty omlet made with tomatoes and bell peppers and some air-dried Bayonne ham, or a spicy salt cod stew? You could wash it all down with a glass of wine from the Mediterranean coast, such as a Corbières. Bon appétit et bon voyage.

The Romanesque capitals
of the singing gallery in
the Church of Notre-Dame
in Serrabone

Detour

Elne and Collioure

Anyone driving from Perpignan to
Collioure along the coast passes
through Elne, a little town of about
6,500 residents that was founded
back in Roman times when it bore
the name Illiberis. Elne was a bishops' see from the sixth century until
1602, and the Ste-Eulalia Cathedral,
built between the 11th and 14th
centuries, a legacy of this era, stands
at the highest point on the hill over
which the Old Town of Elne sprawls.
Of particular interest from an art perspective are the capitals in the cloister with their lovely plant and animal
motifs, as well as Bible scenes.

The little town of Collioure, with its
romantic location on the Côte
Vermeille, also looks back over a
long history. The site was probably
first settled in prehistoric times. The
kings of Majorca built the Château
Royal here in the 13th century, which

The church of Notre-Dame-des-
Anges in the port of Collioure

was then extended into a bastion in
17th century by the master fortress
builder Vauban. The Church of Notre-
Dame-des-Anges, dating from the
17th century, boasts an interesting
feature, its steeple having also served
as a lighthouse in earlier times. There
is no denying the influence of nearby
Spain in the church interior, with the
altars flaunting the opulent style of
the Spanish baroque.

Modern art fans are drawn to the
Hostellerie des Templiers not simply
for the food. Many of the artists that
frequented the establishment – such
as Matisse and Picasso – became
friends with the former owner and
left him a number of their works.

**The autoroute is of course the quickest way to travel
between the Mediterranean coast and the Atlantic coast,
but it would mean missing out on so many gems along the
way! The routes nationales (N roads) and routes départe-
mentales (D roads) take you to numerous attractions, all
of which are worth the extra time spent driving.**

① Perpignan The starting
point for this journey is the
administrative capital of the
Pyrenées-Orientales département, also the center of French
Catalonia. The focal point of
life in the town is the Place de
la Loge, with the late-Gothic
Loge de Mer and the Hôtel de
Ville dating from the 14th century. The town's landmark is Le
Castillet, the only tower from
the city wall still standing. In
the 14th century the kings of
Majorca originally intended
that the Cathedral of St-Jean
Baptiste should be larger and
more magnificent than it in
fact became by the end of their
rule. Directly adjacent to the
cathedral is the town's oldest
church, St-Jean-le-Vieux, built

shortly after the year 1000. The
Palais des Rois de Majorque
was the residence of the kings
of Majorca from the late 13th
century when they spent time
on the mainland; it is situated
on a hill to the south of the Old
Town. Only a few features, such
as the splendid arcades, still
serve as reminders that this
was once the backdrop for a
grand court.

From Perpignan it is worth
making a detour to the towns
of Elne and Collioure (see column on the left).

② Prieuré de Serrabone The
priory is reached via a turnoff
to the left in a southerly direction and continuing on a short
stretch of narrow, very winding

road. The exterior of the solitary priory church from the
14th and 15th centuries seems
very plain. Surprisingly, the interior features a freestanding
singing gallery, its column capitals being among the best that
the Roussillon has on offer in
terms of Romanesque style features. There are animal motifs
as well as angels, the Evangelists or The Lamb of God.

The route continues through
the Têt Valley via Ille-sur-Têt in
the direction of Prades.

③ Prades The town comes
into view after a few miles.
Shortly before the entrance to
the town is the hamlet of Eus
on the top of a high hill. Prades
would certainly still be a sleep-
ing beauty in terms of tourism
if Pablo Casals (1876–1973),
the famous Spanish Catalan
cellist, had not settled here in
1939. It was under the aegis of
Pablo Casals that the Festival
of Prades was founded in 1950

Music is everywhere in Prades, once home to Pablo Casals – even the angels in the church are musicians.

A further performance venue is situated just a few miles south of Prades, the Benedictine St-Michel-de-Cuxa abbey, its bell tower visible from a distance. The abbey had a turbulent past. Monks settled here as early as the 9th century, but the buildings still in existence today were built between the 10th and 12th centuries. The abbey was an important spiritual center during the entire Middle Ages. The St-Michel-de-Cuxa abbey enjoys a superb location with a view of the Pic de Canigou (2,784 m/9,134 ft). In order to reach St-Martin-du-Canigou you need to return to Prades and then continue along the N 116 up until the turnoff for Vernet-les-Bains.

4   St-Martin-du-Canigou
The abbey, accessible by foot only or with a 4x4-vehicle, lies at a height of 1,055 m (3,461 ft) on top of a solitary, isolated rocky peak. Both churches – the

Travel information

Route profile
Length: c. 700 km/435 miles (without detours)
Time required: about 7 days
Start: Perpignan
End: St-Jean-de-Luz
Route: Perpignan, Prades, Font-Romeu, Tarascon-sur-Ariège, Foix, Tarbes, Lourdes, Pau, Bayonne, Biarritz, Cambo-les-Bains, Espelette, Ainhoa, Ascain, St-Jean-de-Luz

Safe driving:
Many of the Pyrenean mountain roads are very narrow and zigzag up and down the mountains. Often you look down at sheer drops, so the route is only recommended for drivers who do not suffer form vertigo. In winter, special winter equipment is required for the mountain roads. All your round you

need to take special care for the countless cyclists who try to conquer the classic passes as their heroes in the Tour de France. Carrying snow chains in the car is obligatory in winter. Information on roads: www.pyrenees-pireneus.com/CIRCULation_routes.htm

When to go:
The route is suitable for any time of year, but spring and autumn are the best seasons, avoiding snow, ice and heat, although the latter is not so oppressive in the mountains.

Further information:
www.sunfrance.com
www.tourisme-midi-pyrenees.com
www.tourisme-hautes-pyrenees.com
www.tourisme-aquitaine.fr

lower church of Notre-Dame-sous-Terre and the upper church of St-Martin – date from the 11th century. The present buildings are all 20th-century reconstructions; most of the monastery was heavily damaged by an earthquake in 1428, falling into ruin thereafter. The cloister with its Romanesque and Gothic capitals, is a particular draw. A steep but short path leads to a viewing platform affording stunning views over the mountains and valleys.
The N 116 now leaves the Massif du Canigou and heads for the mountainous landscape of the Cerdagne. The D 618 soon branches off to the west in the direction of a health and winter sport resort that became

Above left: The Cathedral of St-Jean Baptiste in Perpignan, capital of the Roussillon
Above right: The Orgues d'Ille-sur-Têt rocks; in the background the Massif du Canigou

The Cathedral of Saint Marie in St-Bertrand-de-Comminges features some quite unusual details.

The Solar Furnace at Odeillo

Odeillo, situated in the Eastern Pyrenees close to the winter sport resort of Font-Romeu at an altitude of 1,800 m (5,906 ft), is one of the places in France experiencing the most sunshine: around 3,000 hours a year. The first experiments aimed at utilizing solar energy took place here as early as the 1950s. The "four solaire", the solar furnace, was built here in the 1960s and went into operation in 1970 as the only one of its kind in the world.

The giant parabolic reflector, mounted directly on a 45-m-high (148-ft) office and laboratory building, comprises approximately 9,500 individual

The parabolic reflector of the Odeillo solar furnace

sections, each with a side length of 45 cm (18 inches), thus directing an overall surface area of 2,000 sq m (21,520 sq ft) toward the sun rays. Temperatures of up to 4,000 °C (7,232 °F) are reached at the focal point. The complex, which is jointly operated by the CNRS (Centre national de recherche scientifique) and the University of Perpignan, is used exclusively for research into the use of solar energy and for the testing of materials.

popular in the beginning of the 20th century.

⑤ Font-Romeu The town lies at an altitude of 1,800 m (5,906 ft), while the skiing area with its guaranteed snow extends from 1,700 to 2,500 m (from 5,578 to 8,293 ft). The hermitage of Notre-Dame-de-Font-Romeu with its statue of the Virgin Mary dating from the 12th century is worth a visit. Of considerably more interest, however, is the nearby solar furnace at Odeillo (see column on the left).

From Font-Romeu you take the D 618 initially, and then the N 20 along the main ridge of the Pyrenees as far as the detour to the small Pyrenean Principality of Andorra (see column on p. 149).

⑥ Tarascon-sur-Ariège Following the detour to Andorra you need to go back as far as the turnoff after Font-Romeu and then continue in a northerly direction via the N 20, also signposted as the E 9 here.

The historic Old Town of this small place with its winding alleyways and romantic squares extends along both sides of the Ariège River. Markets that drew visitors from all corners, from the rest of France, from Spain and from Andorra, used to be held beneath the clock tower situated high up on a rocky outcrop from the 19th century until the 1960s.

Today most visitors are drawn to the Parc de l'Art préhistorique to the west of the town with its very graphic presentation of the prehistoric past. Legacies from this era are to be found in 15 caves in close proximity of the town alone. Slide shows, films and presentations provide an introduction to the working techniques used by our Stone Age ancestors.

Following the N 20, just a few miles further to the north, you

will reach the very attractive small town of Foix.

⑦ Foix This little town is worth visiting at the end of July/beginning of August in particular when the medieval festival is staged here against the romantic backdrop of the Old Town. The calendar of attractions includes singing minstrels, knights doing battle and horse riders performing stunts, and there is of course an historic market ensuring that nobody goes hungry. The Old Town of Foix with its timber-framed buildings and the towering fort, built between the 11th and 15th centuries, provides the perfect backdrop for these and many other activities. The main tower houses a museum of local history.

From Foix the route continues along the D 117 as far as St-Girons and from there along the D 618 via the Col de Porte d'Aspet as far as the N 125 to St-Bertrand-de-Comminges.

⑧ St-Bertrand-de-Comminges This town is reached after just a few miles on the N 125. Access is via three medieval gates (Porte l'Hyrisson, Porte Major and Porte Cabirlone), dominated by the Cathedral of Sainte Marie towering up in the upper town. The church is of tremendous significance from an art

Above right: The monastery of St-Martin-du-Canigou in a spectacular location once offered its pious inhabitants the solitude of the mountains. Right: Foix' medieval fort

Pictured here is the high altar with stained-glass windows (left) as well as the mausoleum of Saint Bertrand (far left).

Detour

Andorra

The independent constitutional principality, with an area of 468 sq km (181 sq miles) one of the smallest countries in Europe, has two heads of state: the French president and the Spanish bishop of Urgell. During the rule of the Franco dictatorship it provided refuge to a great many Spanish refugees. When import duties were abolished in the 1950s Andorra developed into a shopping paradise. The majority of Andorra's residents are now employed in retailing and tourism.

Andorra la Vella, the capital of the principality where Catalan is the official language, is divided into a less attractive modern section and the Old Town. The seat of government is

License plate number for Andorra

situated in the latter, in the Casa de la Vall, a building dating from the 16th century. In Santa Coloma, 3 km (1.9 miles) from the center of Andorra la Vella, stands the church of the same name, a Romanesque building, although only some of its murals still survive.

Another remarkable Romanesque church is Sant Miguel d'Engolasters. Andorra's national shrine lies in the principality's main valley, the Valira d'Orient: the Santuari de Meritxell with the patron saint of Andorra, Our Lady of Meritxell. The original statue dating from the 12th century, together with the church, was destroyed by fire on 8 September 1972, Andorra's national day. The new building designed by star architect Ricardo Bofill houses a copy.

Jardin and Musée Massey in Tarbes. The latter houses paintings and archeological collections.

historical perspective even though it has continually been subjected to conversions over the centuries, combining Romanesque, Gothic and Renaissance elements. The cloister with its three galleries, the bell tower and the portal are Romanesque, while the nave with the choir and a number of the capitals are in the Gothic style. The choir stalls with their carvings date from the Renaissance and are worthy of closer attention as the skilled carver did not lack a sense of humor. The organ, too, has an outstanding reputation and concerts are sometimes held here.

The area around the cathedral boasts a whole series of attractive timber-framed buildings, including one particularly outstanding example: the Maison Bridaut from the 15th century. Around 2 km (1.2 miles) outside St-Bertrand-de-Comminges is the Chapel of St-Just (12th century) standing in an open field near Valcabrère, surrounded by tall cypress trees and with an impressive Romanesque portal. The route continues via the N 125 and the D 817 to Tarbes.

❾ Tarbes This small town situated on the banks of the Adour River is a familiar name among horse fans as it is here that the tough tarbais breed of horses is bred. Horse-riding tournaments take place here in summer. The Jardin Massey, a public garden with a great number of plants and trees, the late-Gothic cloister of a former monastery and the Musée Massey, where European paintings and archeological finds from the region are on display, appeal to both nature and art fans alike. The Maison Natale du Maréchal Foch commemorates the life of Marshal Ferdinand Foch (1851–1929), the supreme commander of the Allied forces in World War I, who was born here.

From Tarbes one of the most-visited destinations in France, Lourdes, is just a stone's throw away along the N 21.

❿ Lourdes The famous pilgrimage destination at the foot of the Pyrenees also has plenty on offer for non-pilgrims. The

majority of visitors head for the sacred buildings: the Basilique Supérieure, beneath which is the crypt; Bernadette Soubirous, the girl who had the miraculous visions, was present during its consecration in 1866. The neo-Gothic basilica was unable to accommodate the crowds of pilgrims, and so the neo-Byzantine Basilique de Rosaire was built, but the two churches were still unable to cater for the countless pilgrims. The Basilique St-Pie X was eventually built in 1958 to mark the centenary celebrations; it can hold 20,000 pilgrims. The

The cloister in the Jardin Massey in Tarbes, relocated here from the abbey of St-Sever-de-Rustan

Espace Saint Bernardette is another venue for the faithful. Everything in Lourdes revolves around the miracles attributed to the Virgin Mary; it is the focus of the souvenir shops and film shows about Bernadette. There is a series of museums, including the house where the saint

and Pau are a natural wonder of remarkable dimensions. There are around 20 caves spread over five levels, their stalactites and stalagmites all creating their very own magic. Make sure you bring a warm top, even in summer! A light railway takes visitors through

birthplace of Henry of Navarre who, after he had converted to Catholicism, was crowned as King Henry IV of France. The Old Town is still dominated by the imposing castle building. The oldest sections of the castle date from the 12th century, with the fortifications having

The town's promenade, the Boulevard des Pyrénées, heads eastward from the castle. It runs high above the valley on the edge of the cliff on which the Old Town is situated and affords a wonderful view of the Pyrenees Mountains. The abundant flower beds and palm

was born and the Musée Grevin, a waxworks museum, dedicated to her life.
There are other things to see in Lourdes. The hilltop fort has dominated the town since the 11th century. It has housed the Musée Pyrénéen since the 1920s, an interesting folklore museum covering the culture and traditions of the region. A detour to the Cirque de Gavarnie (see pp. 152/153) is highly recommended.

🔟🔟 **Grottes de Bétharram** The caves located between Lourdes

some of the caves, many of which bear imaginative names, such as The Abbey or The Fairy Castle. A boat trip on the underground lake in one of the caves is also a very special experience.
Back in the daylight, the route follows the D 937/938 to Pau.

🔟🔟 **Pau** The present-day capital of the Pyrénées-Atlantiques département used to be the capital of the province of Béarn at a time when the town was important for the whole of the French kingdom, being the

been built in the 14th century. The elements that are typical of the château today are 16th-century additions built in the Renaissance style. The interior was commissioned by Louis Philippe, the Citizen King, in the mid-1800s, while Napoleon III added a new tower. The tortoise shell, said to have served Henry IV as a cradle, is one of the more bizarre exhibits.
Not far from the castle is the Tour de la Monnaie, originally built as an additional fortress tower and in which coins were minted up until the Revolution.

trees provide for a touch of southern flair and this is a good opportunity to enjoy the lovely fresh air after visiting the rather gloomy castle.
Pau enjoyed a major upsurge in tourism in the 19th century when an English doctor declared it to be one of the few places where those suffering from tuberculosis could recover.

Left: The Basilica of Notre Dame du Rosaire in Lourdes, the destination of millions of pilgrims. Above: Château de Pau with its defiant towers

Cirque de Gavarnie and Grande Cascade

The Cirque de Gavarnie is one of the most frequently visited and most popular tourist destinations in the Pyrenees after Lourdes. You will need to park your car in the small mountain village of Gavarnie, which is situated at an altitude of 1,365 m (4,479 ft), and then proceed either on foot or horseback to the imposing cirque at an altitude of 1,700 m (5,578 ft).

The impressive cirque with a diameter of just over 4 km (2.5 mi) was formed by a glacier. The semi-circular cirque is surrounded by the peaks Grand Astazou (3,071 m/10,076 ft), Marboré (3,248 m/10,657 ft), Pic de la Cascade (3,073 m/10,083 ft) and Taillon (3,114 m/10,217 ft). The different bedding planes are clearly visible in the almost perpendicular rock faces. In a number of places there are waterfalls contributing to the overall spectacle, such as the Grande Cascade, where one of the highest waterfalls in

Above: On the way to the Cirque de Gavarnie. Right: The Grande Cascade waterfall.

Europe plunges down 422 m (1,385 ft). Its hidden location meant that the Cirque de Gavarnie only became a popular travel destination in the 19th century. Prominent writers, too, visited the cirque and reported on their findings. The German writer Kurt Tucholsky (1890–1935), however, found little pleasure in the spectacle as he recorded in his Book on the Pyrenees: "The road ends in Gavarnie, at a bend, and there the pride of the Pyrenees stands in front of its audience. The rock faces stand in a gigantic semi-circle, with a little snow above, and the whole thing is nice to look at. But that is it – and why so much fuss is made about it I do not know". The French writer Victor Hugo (1802–1885), meanwhile, extolled the virtues of the Cirque: "It is both mountain and wall, it is the most enigmatic of constructions by the most enigmatic of all architects, it is nature's colosseum, it is Gavarnie".

This is where you can go for a swim after trying your luck at the roulette table: the Grande Plage in Biarritz with the Casino Municipal.

Consequently, the English in particular came to Pau and settled here, their influence still being visible today in the Park Beaumont and the casino buildings. Typically British sports such as polo or cricket are also played here, which is unusual in France.

The quickest route from Pau to Bayonne is via the D 817 or the A 64 autoroute but the appealing little town of Oloron-Sainte-Marie is well worth the short detour via the N 134 and the D 24.

⑬ Oloron-Sainte-Marie The town was of great importance in the Middle Ages as one of the stops for pilgrims en route to Santiago de Compostela in Spain, situated as it was on the Via Tolosana, one of the French Ways of Saint James. The 12th-century Church of Ste-Croix and parts of the Cathedral of Ste-Marie, particularly the portal with its wealth of sculptures, date from this period. The Cathedral of Ste-Marie was largely destroyed by fire and then rebuilt in the 16th to 18th centuries.

In addition to folklore displays, the Maison de la Patrimoine also documents one of the most disturbing periods of German-French history, namely the Gurs detention camp, in which the French Vichy government detained political prisoners and Jews. Anyone wanting to gain a deeper insight into this topic is able to do so as the route continues toward Bayonne. After about 15 km (9 miles) the D 936 passes the memorial at the site of the former camp. Next to the memorial is also a cemetery for those who died in the "Hell of Gurs". The route then continues along the D 936 to Bayonne.

⑭ Bayonne The capital of the French Basque region lies on the confluence of the Adour and the Nive Rivers. The two rivers divide the city into the Grand Bayonne, Petit Bayonne and St-Esprit districts. The main sightseeing attractions, in particular the Cathedral of Ste-Marie, are situated in Grand Bayonne. Construction of the cathedral was begun in the 13th century and it exhibits strong northern French Gothic influences. The stained-glass Renaissance windows from the 16th century are especially worth seeing. The cloister belonging to the cathedral is reached not via the nave but from the street outside. It is one of the largest in France, its filigree pointed arch a high-Gothic masterpiece, affording wonderful views of the cathedral's two steeples. Also in Grand Bayonne is the Château Vieux, built in the 12th century on the site of a former Roman fort. The interior is not open to the public but it is still worth taking a stroll around the fortifications.

With its lively artist and student population as well as its numerous restaurants, Petit Bayonne is a particular draw for tourists and locals alike in the evening. The famous air-

The bulk of sand that is the Dune du Pilat, the largest shifting dune in Europe, on the Côte d'Argent

dried Bayonne Ham is a taste experience not to be missed. The Musée Basque, one of the largest folklore museums in France, documents its production. There are also informative exhibits relating to agriculture and sheep farming, shipping and fishing, as well as the traditional games and sports, local music and popular dances from the Basque region. The museum also stages temporary exhibitions in the 15th-century Château Neuf, the castle standing in Petit Bayonne.

Almost 10 km (6.2 miles) from the center of Bayonne, and in fact merging with it, is Biarritz.

⑮ Biarritz This seaside resort was a society meeting place during the Belle Époque. In the 1850s, Empress Eugénie declared the town to be her preferred resort, thus attracting other members of high society. Many of the hotels, such as the Hôtel du Palais, still bear the stamp of this era. Two popular sights for leisurely strolls along the coast are the 44-m-high (144-ft) lighthouse (1834) to the north of the town and further south the Rocher de la Vièrge, a cliff with a statue of the Virgin Mary, reached via a jetty. Also situated directly on the water's edge is the Art

Deco building housing the Musée de la Mer. In addition to information about marine life and fishing, the lower floor features an aquarium with living plants and creatures from the Bay of Biscay.

Those with a sweet tooth should not miss the Musée du Chocolat where the information on the growing of cocoa and the making of chocolate is of course followed by the "practical part" with chocolate treats available for tasting.

Opposite the Hôtel du Palais it becomes evident that Biarritz was also home to a colony of Russians during its heyday for here the many towers of the Orthodox St-Alexander Nevsky Church are to be seen.

The direct route from Biarritz to St-Jean-de-Luz follows the coast for around 15 km (9 mi), through built-up areas all the

**Left: The richly sculpted portal of the Cathedral of Ste-Marie in Oloron-Sainte-Marie.
Above: View over the Nive and typical Basque timber-framed buildings in Bayonne. Above left: Biarritz, the Ste-Eugénie Church in the foreground**

Detour

Côte d'Argent

The Côte d'Argent is the section of coast between the Bassin d'Arcachon and Biarritz, where it becomes the Spanish-French Côte Basque. In addition to its excellent bathing facilities, the Côte d'Argent also offers a unique natural environment. The 2.7-km-long (1.7-mile) and 500-m-

The Cap Ferret spit of land and the Bassin d'Arcachon

wide (1650-yd) Dune de Pilat is the highest dune in Europe, fluctuating between 105 and 120 m (345 and 394 ft) in height. The Parc ornithologique du Teich on this stretch of coast is also worth exploring.

Biarritz attracts the attention of visitors with its elegant townscape dating back to the Belle Époque and sandy beaches ideal for walks along the sea. The former fishing village was "discovered" in the mid-19th century by the Countess of Montijo and her daughter Eugénie, whose future husband Napoleon III built her a summer residence here in 1854 – now the Hôtel du

Palais. Biarritz thus became popular with the crowned heads and upper nobility of Europe, developing into one of the most elegant seaside resorts on the Atlantic. The Grande Plage with the Casino Municipal (in the picture on the right) is especially famous; the beach extends as far as Pointe St-Martin with the white lighthouse (in the background).

The coastal landscape near Biarritz possesses its very own bleak charm.

way. There is a short detour, however, through the hinterland of this much-visited stretch of the coast, allowing for interesting insights in the Basque way of life.

⑯ **Basque Villages** A visit to some of the Basque villages makes it clear just how proud the Basque people are of their own culture and individuality. A separatist movement exists in the French Basque region too

but it is not as radical as the Spanish equivalent. The D 932 takes you to Cambo-les-Bains, which is called Kanbo in the Basque language.

Continuing along the D 20 you will reach the first Basque village, namely Espelette, its Basque name being Ezpeleta. This is the heart of the area where the small chili peppers, known in French as "piment d'Espelette", are grown. Once they have been harvested, the

peppers are strung together in long chains and hung on the walls of the houses to dry, the majority of the houses being typical Basque timber-framed buildings. Espelette is also known for the breeding of Pottoks, a Basque pony breed. A small castle with a tower dating from the 11th century now serves as the seat of the local municipal administration.

The route then continues along the D 20 to Ainhoa, considered

to be one of the most attractive villages in France. Ainhoa' main street is lined on both sides with the characteristic Basque timber-framed buildings that, in the past, used to offer refuge for pilgrims journeying along the Way of St James, among others. The Notre-Dame-de-l'Assomption Church, dating from the 13th century, boasts a double gallery, a feature found in many of the Basque churches.

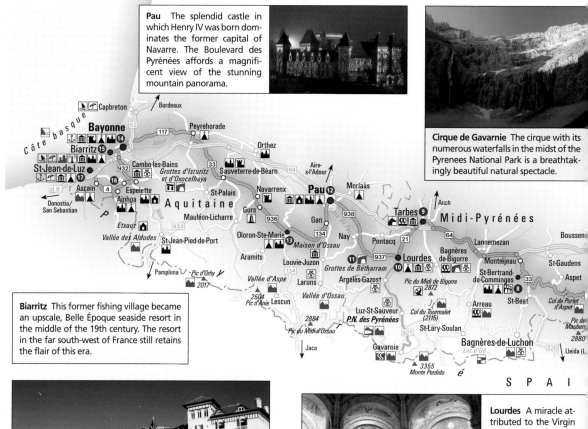

Pau The splendid castle in which Henry IV was born dominates the former capital of Navarre. The Boulevard des Pyrénées affords a magnificent view of the stunning mountain panorama.

Cirque de Gavarnie The cirque with its numerous waterfalls in the midst of the Pyrenees National Park is a breathtakingly beautiful natural spectacle.

Biarritz This former fishing village became an upscale, Belle Époque seaside resort in the middle of the 19th century. The resort in the far south-west of France still retains the flair of this era.

St-Jean-de-Luz It was here, where Spain is very close by, that Louis XIV married the Spanish infanta Maria Theresa in a typical Basque church featuring galleries of several floors.

Lourdes A miracle attributed to the Virgin Mary in 1866 made this little town at the foot of the Pyrenees world famous. It is now visited every year by millions of pilgrims from all over the world seeking relief and healing.

The port of St-Jean-de-Luz
and the Maison de l'Infante
with its towers

The last stop, located on the D 918, before returning to the more urban – and urbane – environs of St-Jean-de-Luz, is Ascain, yet another typically Basque village, bearing the Basque name of Azkaine. As in many of the Basque villages, here, too, the pelota wall forms a focal point of village life. The church with its easily recognizable extensions from the 16th and 17th centuries even boasts a three-floor gallery.

The route now continues to the little town of St-Jean-de-Luz shortly before the Spanish border, and returning to the coast, via the D 918.

⑰ St-Jean-de-Luz The greatest and most significant historical event in this small town, bearing the Basque name of Donibane Lohizune, was the marriage of King Louis XIV and the Spanish infanta Maria Theresa in 1660. The town's most interesting buildings are also closely related to this event. The Maison Louis XIV, an almost fortress-like building with corner turrets, was where the king lived for a month while waiting for his bride. The Spanish infanta and future queen of France lived in the Maison de l'Infante, its painted wooden ceilings only having been uncovered in the 1990s. It also houses a museum documenting the events of 1660.

The royal coupled were married in the St-Jean-Baptiste Church, the construction of which was not yet complete at that time. The richly decorated altar retable is an eye catcher, as are the galleries with their three floors on the side and five floors at the rear.

The historic heart of the town is then the ideal place for a relaxing stroll along the fishing port and the coast with its many bathing opportunities.

...trand-de-Comminges The Cathedral of Ste-... with the adjacent cloister is one of the archi-...al highlights of this tour.

Foix The little town at the confluence of the Ariège and Arget Rivers comes alive with a medieval festival at the beginning of August each year.

Eus One of the loveliest villages in France is located near Prades on a rocky outcrop high above the banks of the Têt. The Pyrenees provide a dramatic backdrop.

Andorra The dwarf state in the heart of the Pyrenees draws visitors with its attractive natural landscape, hiking and skiing opportunities – and duty-free shopping. Several Romanesque churches exist in the area around the capital Andorra la Vella.

Grottes de Bétharram A fascinating wonder world comprising some 20 underground dripstone caves extending over five levels and even featuring an underground lake. A light railway brings visitors to the "abbey" or "fairy castle" rocks formations. It is also possible to take a boat trip on the lake.

Perpignan The capital of French Catalonia boasts a number of important historic buildings, such as the cathedral, the Palais des Rois de Majorque, the Loge de Mer and the Church of St-Jean-le-Vieux.

Route 9

Through the Massif Central

The Massif Central is a sparsely wooded low mountain range just south of central France, near the city of Clermont-Ferrand. Most tourists bypass the extremely isolated region, allowing you to discover the remote landscapes here in peace, and to observe otters by the crystal-clear streams in the valleys and deep gorges.

Coming from the direction of the Bourbonnais, this route through the ruggedly romantic Massif Central has a lot of surprises in store. In this, Europe's largest and oldest volcanic landscape, which borders the Limousin region in the west, the Rhône-Alpes in the east, and Causses, Aubrac and the Cévennes in the south, some of the rivers appear to be completely untouched by mankind. Elemental forces, such as fire, water, rivers and volcanoes, all formed lumps of lava covered in green "velvet", granite massifs folded into sharp jags and deeply cratered volcanoes. Ever since the 1990s and the development of transport routes this region has been attracting an increasing number of visitors. The Massif Central, one of Europe's last intact landscapes, is at its best in early October; ; in winter, some sections

are very difficult to access due to the harsh weather.

The geographic conditions here mean that the natural flora and fauna are still very similar to

those once discovered by the Celtic Arverni tribes, who first made the area accessible by building bridges and paved roads. The region is named af-

ter these old Gauls, who used iron weapons to seize the land from the Ligures in the sixth century BC. Despite suffering a crushing defeat by the Romans in 121 BC, the Arverni were able to retain their independence in the present-day Auvergne. Even today, we can still find traces of their chieftain Vercingetorix, who fiercely resisted the Roman occupiers during the Gallo-Roman era until succumbing to Caesar in the Battle of Alesia in 52 BC, when Gaul became a Roman province.

The Auvergne region was primarily known for cattle breeding and the manufacturing of ceramics. The present-day town of Clermont-Ferrand, the starting point of this route, became the capital. Celtic culture is today still very apparent in the dolmens and menhirs, such as those in St-Nectaire, as well as Celtic customs, conventions

Above: All roads head steeply uphill in the capital of the Haute-Loire département, Le Puy-en-Velay. This town also marks the start of the Via Podiensis pilgrimage route, which takes the faithful on the Way of St James through the Pyrenees to Santiago de Compostela in Spain.
Left: A late-summer evening sunset in the Livradois-Forez Regional Nature Park.

nd religious rites that are still practised today.

he region became part of rance in the sixth century. Mighty counts and the French royal family fought over the Auvergne from the Middle Ages onward until King Louis XIV confirmed his absolutist claim to power in 1665.

While enjoying the thermal pas and the excellent local ood, for instance at Le Mont Dore and Chaudes-Aigues, you may also wish to listen to the many legends and stories that re woven around the castles nd palaces situated along the oute. The Romanesque church

Left: Typical Romanesque ornamentation on a red background in the St-Austremoine Church (12th C.) in Issoire
Right: Yellow daffodils growing in the wild, a pretty sight at the Col de la Croix St-Robert.

buildings, like those in Brioude, attest to the first tourism heyday which occurred from the 10th century onward as a result of religious pilgrimages.

You should also make sure that you regularly leave your car or motorbike behind. Not only is it worth discovering this paradise on foot and enjoying it on

horseback, but exploring the rapids and mysterious gorges by canoe and kayak, for example in Vic-le-Comte, is another pleasure not to be missed.

Orcival attracts visitors with its shingle-roofed houses and its pyramidal Notre-Dame Church. The latter is one of the finest Romanesque buildings in the Auvergne.

"Chabatz d'entrar" is what people say in the Occitan language to welcome visitors to the Massif Central. Apart from its hospitality, the Auvergne region, situated far away from the well-trodden tourist routes, is also worth visiting for its extinct volcanic cones, Romanesque religious buildings, castles and palaces, as well as impressive gorges.

❶ Clermont-Ferrand The twin cities of Clermont and Ferrand can look back on a long history. The Arverni settled here in Celtic times, and the Romans were initially held back by Vercingetorix, whose statue overlooks the hustle and bustle of Place de Jaude. The prospering Roman city of Augustonemetum became the cultural center of the West Frankish Kingdom.

The medieval Old Town is home to the symbol of Clermont, which has borne its name since the eighth century: the Gothic Notre-Dame de l'Assomption Cathedral (start of construction: 1248; completion: 19th century), featuring a Romanesque crypt from the 10th-century. The Romanesque Notre-Dame-du-Port Basilica (12th C.) is typical of the local Auvergnat Romanesque style. It is characterized by the gabled lintel of the doorway in the southern transept. The Auvergnat princes founded another thriving town named Montferrand Castle

(12th C.), which became part of Clermont-Ferrand in 1731. The city experienced a great economic boom in the 19th century as a result of Michelin tire factory based here.

❷ Puy de Dôme Some 30 km (19 miles) west of Clermont-Ferrand you will get to France's youngest volcanic massif, the Monts Dôme, which has been extinct for only 4,000 years in some parts. On the horizon, the Puy de Dôme (1,464 m/4,803 ft), the highest peak in the mountain range, towers over the roofs of Clermont's Old Town, the Ville Noire (black city).

❸ Orcival The tiny town of Orcival is situated just off the road to Bourboule. The unusual location of the Notre-Dame d'Orcival Basilica (12th C.) is linked to a legend according to which the Virgin Mary appeared by a spring in the pilgrimage town. It is said that a statue of Mary found nearby later caused all church walls to

collapse until the basilica was erected at the present site.

This basilica is one of the best examples of Romanesque churches in the Auvergne. Its design is strictly based on the graduated architecture of the so-called Auvergnat pyramid, as can be seen for example in

the pyramidal intermediate level leading to the tower. The eastern wing is home to strikin

Above: The Puy de Dôme slumbers under a green blanket of plants. On the summit you'll find both an observatory and a transmitter site.

Travel information

Route profile
Length: c. 1,000 km (621 mi) (without detours)
Time required: at least two weeks
Start: Clermont-Ferrand
End: Billom
Route: Clermont-Ferrand, Orcival, Puy de Sancy, Bort-les-Orgues, Mauriac, Saint-Flour, Saugues, Le Puy-en-Velay, Château Polignac, Lavaudieu, Brioude, Blesle, Issoire, Billom

Safe driving:
The upper reaches may be covered in snow and ice until late into spring. Some passes are temporarily closed in winter. Public transportation does not offer an alternative to your own car as there are only few connections. You can find up-to-date informa-

tion at www.sncf.com and www.ter-sncf.com.

Weather and climate:
The summers can be very hot in the Massif Central, rain showers are possible at any time. Weather forecasts: http://france.meteofrance.com or Tel 08 99 71 02 XX (XX = number of the département).

Information:
Comité Régional de Développement Touristique d'Auvergne
Parc Technologique
Clermont-Ferrand La Pardieu
7 allée Pierre de Fermat – CS 50502
63178 Aubière Cédex,
Tel: 04 73 29 49 99
www2.auvergne-tourisme.info
www.massif-central.fr
www.clermont-ferrand.fr

The most important church in Clermont-Ferrand is the Notre-Dame de l'Assomption Cathedral, which was built from 1248. It was made from black volcanic rock hailing from the town of Volvic – which is why it is black in appearance and has earned the epithet of *cathédrale noire*. Shown here is one of the portals with a richly ornamented tympanum.

Today the 1,464-m-high (4,803-ft) Puy de Dôme is quite simply the symbol of the Auvergne, but at one time, the highest peak in the Monts Dôme volcanic range was considered a holy mountain. The Gauls and the Romans venerated the god Mercurius Dumias here, and so an impressive monument, a temple of Mercury, was built on the summit in the first century

ac. In more recent times an aerial was added, a prominent landmark. At any time of year the roughly one-hour walk along an historic Roman road from the Col de Ceyssat to the summit of the Puy de Dôme is a great experience. The views extend up to 300 km (186 miles) on a clear day. A short way to the north is the Puy de Côme (bottom left) with its double crater rim

From the Puy de Sancy, the highest peak in the Massif Central at 188 m (617 ft) you can see as far as the French Alps on a clear day.

Into the Chaudefour Valley

It is an amazing experience to hike through the middle of a giant strato-volcano in the Vallée de Chaudefour Nature Reserve, on the north-eastern slope of the Puy de Sancy. The reserve, accessed via a road leading off the D 36 and heading down into the valley between Le Mont-Dore and Besse-et-St-Anastaise, forms a fascinating cirque.

The natural history information center, with its flora and fauna exhibits, is a good starting place for hikes. To ensure the wealth of botanical treasures is preserved, the valley can only be crossed on foot. Picking plants is strictly prohibited.

To compensate, there are plenty of stunning scenes to enjoy: moufflons, various species of reptiles, and a biotope of small moors can all be

Wildflower meadow in the nature reserve

found at altitudes of between 800 and 1,800 m (2,625 and 5,906 ft). The upper regions of the valley are home to rare vegetation and bizarre rock formations, while the lower parts and valley floor are a luminous green. The Puy Ferrand and Puy de la Perdrix peaks, the Cascade de la Biche waterfall and the fairytale rock landscape, comprising the unusual Dent de la Rancune (tooth of resentment) rock stack, the Roche Percée (pierced rock), the Crête de Coq (cock's crest) and the Roc de la Perdrix (partridge rock), are all extremely impressive.

tiered window which create a fascinating play of diffused light inside.

4 Le Mont-Dore At the foot of the Puy de Sancy, coming from the D 996, do as the Gauls and Romans once did and take it easy in the 33 hot springs at the thermal and alpine-air climatic health resort; the springs reach temperatures of 44°C (111°F). Rheumatic, asthmatic and other (bronchial) diseases are soothed by the warm water rich in carbonic acid and silicon, but also by Le Mont-Dore's (the golden mountain) location at an altitude of over 1,000 m (3,281 ft). However, the valley situated between tall rock faces in the upper reaches of the Dordogne also offers attractive sporting facilities for skiing and hiking enthusiasts.

Just 1 km (0.62 miles) south of the Le Mont d'Or, the 30-m-high (98-ft) waterfalls of the Grande Cascade provide a breathtaking backdrop for walkers.

The wooden carriages of the Funiculaire du Capucin, a cable railway dating from 1897 and heritage-listed, takes you from the Office de Tourism to the Salon du Capucin station, perched at a height of 1,286 m (4,219 ft), at the comfortable speed of 1 m (1.6 yds) per second.

From the clearing, it takes roughly an hour to reach the Pic du Capucin summit via well groomed zig-zag trails. The only reason you will be struggling for air will be the breathtaking sight over the Monts-Dore massif.

5 Puy de Sancy The route heads along the D 36 to the highest point of the Massif Central (1,885m/6,185 ft), the Puy de Sancy, offering the most spectacular views of the Auvergne and beyond, into the Monts Dore region, Europe's largest volcanic district, with its many vast plateaus, crater lakes, jagged crests, trough-like valleys and steep rubble slopes.

Extending over an area of 800 sq km (309 sq mi), the Monts Dore are older than the Monts Dôme and were deeply indented by Ice Age glaciers and heavy rainfall after the volcanoes spat out ash, slag and lava at the end of the Tertiary period. The lava of the Puy de Sancy weathered so much that the volcanic vent became the summit. Taking the cable car from the valley station, situated around 4 km (2.5 miles) south of Le Mont-Dore, to just below the summit region, floating over meadows, rock faces and mighty waterfalls, gets you in the mood for the half-hour climb to the top of the volcano.

Alternatively, an approximately three-hour hiking trail over the Puy de Chabane, Puy Redon and the Pas de l'Ane heads along the mountain crest from the Chastreix-Sancy cable car station to the Puy de Sancy, where you will be rewarded with a panoramic view of the

Château de Val – once perched atop a rocky outcrop, now at almost the same level as the Barrage de Bort-les-Orgues dam

high plateaus of the Cézallier in the south and the Monts Dôme in the north.

It is worth making a detour to the Vallée de Chaudefour (see side column on page 166).

6 St-Nectaire Divided into St-Nectaire-Le-Haut and the thermal spa of St-Nectaire-le-Bas, this town is one of the most beautiful in France.

Thanks to its spectacular location, the St-Nectaire Church is among the most impressive Romanesque churches in the Auvergne. It was built on the Mont Cornadore, a conical basalt hill, in the 12th century. Here, too, the tiering of the transept, known as *massif barlong* or the Auvergne-style crossbar, stands out as typical of the Auvergnat Romanesque. It is worth seeing one of the most famous works of Romanesque sculpture, the statue (12th C.) of St Baudine, plated in gilded copper and previously adorned with jewels. The saint is said to have saved the

area from a dragon. Equally interesting is the painted statue of the Basilica of Notre-Dame du Mont Cornadore.

In the valley you'll find the thermal spa, with around forty hot springs and the amazing *fontaine pétrifiante*, a petrifying spring. The mineral water is rich in carbon dioxide, encrusting and ultimately fossilizing plants and animals within six to fourteen months.

At the Maison du St-Nectaire, everything revolves around the famous circular cheese of the same name, which is characterized by its white, yellow or red rind, its nutty taste and its "volcanic temperament".

7 Bort-les-Orgues and Château de Val The château built by Guillot d'Estaing in 1440 glistens like gold in the bluish-black waters of the artificial lake near the climatic spa resort of Bort-les-Orgues in the Dordogne Valley. Six towers with conical roofs and oriels

surround the castle. Upon arrival via the D 922, an iron-clad gate, whose arch is decorated with a bas-relief of the d'Estaing family's coat of arms, leads you into the Château de Val, and you will soon find yourself inside one of the best-preserved castles in the Haute-Auvergne region.

After following the D 922 in a southerly direction for a few miles, you will reach Mauriac.

8 Mauriac The Romanesque Notre-Dame-des-Miracles Church (12th C.) in the so-called "good city of Upper Auvergne" is one of the most famous religious buildings in Haute-Auvergne. The stunningly carved tympanum above the western portal is worth seeing, as is the elaborately decorated polychromatic Romanesque baptismal font made from trachyte.

The St-Pierre monastery situated opposite the church was founded by a princess during Merovingian times, but was

secularized during the French Revolution. It is worth visiting the Romanesque chapterhouse, which dates back to the 11th century and continues to gleam in its old splendor.

Parts of the Gallo-Roman ruins, the foundations of a Romanesque church (9th C.) and the monastery's cloister (14th/15th C.), can also be visited.

9 Château de la Trémolière At the edge of Anglards-de-Salers, accessible via the D 22 from Mauriac, lies the former manor of the Montclar family, containing ten wall tapestries (16th C.) from Aubusson's workshop. Depictions of animals, dragons and unicorns alternate with villages, castles

Top left: Salers cattle graze on the Puy de Sancy.
Top middle: The towers of the Château de la Trémolière are clustered closely together.
Top right: Romanesque interior of the St-Nectaire Church.

An urban gem in the remote Cantal region: the town of Salers with its houses built from dark volcanic rock

Viaduc-du-Garabit

Until 1884, deep gorges made it very difficult for the people around St-Flour to sell the region's predominantly agricultural products and to lead their cattle safely through the difficult terrain to the marketplaces. This need for attentive cowherds or "garde boeufs", colloquially pronounced as "Garabit", eventually prompted a project enabling the foothills of the Massif Central to be crossed: with its apex 122 m (400 ft) above the valley floor, the Viaduc-du-Garabit, a 564-m-long (1,850-ft) single-track railway arch bridge built using some 3,900 tonnes (4,290 tons) of iron, has spanned the Truyère River valley since the end of the 19th century.

For about 25 years, the viaduct, which has become a tourist attraction and the pride of the region's in-

An elastic iron structure with 678,768 rivets: the Viaduc-du-Garabit

habitants, remained the world's tallest bridge. Its height has been visually reduced to 95 m (312 ft) since the construction of the Barrage de Grandval, which as built in 1955 to 1959 to dam the Truyère.

The viaduct's creator, Gustave Eiffel (1832 to 1923), was later nicknamed the "iron magician" for his technically complex and artistic usage of iron as a building material, as in the double-jointed bridge constructed as a steel trussed arch. The fame he achieved with the Garabit Viaduct eventually helped him win the contract to build the Eiffel Tower (1889) that was named after him, for the 1889 World's Fair in Paris.

and towns on the "tapisseries d'Anglards-de-Salers".

⑩ Salers The Place Tyssandier d'Escous is the focal point of this fairytale medieval town built completely from dark lava. The central square in the picturesque town at the western foot of the Massif Central was named after the farmer who created the famous red Salers cattle here by selectively crossbreeding the local cattle in the 19th century. The well-preserved town is one of France's most beautiful villages. It received its present look during its heyday in the Renaissance.

Every year, around 400,000 tourists rouse Salers from the slumber into which it sank when the law court was moved to Aurillac in 1790. Visitors love the stately manors at the Grand' Place (15th–18th C.), the late-Gothic burial site in St-Matthieu (15th–16th C.) and the Maison des Templiers (15th C.), once a hospice for pilgrims on the Way of St James to Santiago de Compostela in Spain.

The latter displays typical Auvergne-style living quarters and cheese-making utensils.

⑪ Puy Mary The steep slopes of what is perhaps the finest of the Auvergne's mountains, the Puy Mary (1,787 m/5,863 ft), are often still covered in snow even in May. It is all the more enjoyable to climb the almost symmetrical "Auvergne-style Pyramid": the view from the top is ample compensation for the effort and considered by many the most spectacular in the Auvergne. Stunning vistas unfold in the mountainous landscape around the Puy Mary, along with the moufflons and chamois on the slopes of the Cantal, the radial, rugged glacial valleys, the steep crests and nearby summits, as well as hundreds of wildflowers, including yellow gentian, which put on a superb display particularly in the spring.

The starting point for the climb is the highest point of the "King of the Auvergne Passes", the Pas de Peyrol (1,588 m/

5,210 ft), which is also the highest pass in the Massif Central. The last 200 m (656 ft) or so to the summit can easily be climbed from the car park in around 45 minutes, including the return trip.

⑫ Allanche/Monts du Cézallier At an altitude of approximately 1,200 m (3,937 ft) between the Cantal Mountains and the Monts Dores, it is rare to come across a fellow human being. Allanche, the center of the Cézallier, is situated along the river of the same name and, with its gray houses and defense walls, looks like the Auvergne of yore.

⑬ St-Flour The basalt-stone town of St-Flour, perched atop a steep basalt plateau above the Ander Valley, is a shopping paradise for regional souvenirs. The hometown of former French president, Georges Pompidou (1911–1974), has a pleasantly medieval feel. The fortified, military-style Gothic Cathedral of St-Pierre was built during the

The starting point for a tour to the Gorges de l'Allier: Villeneuve d'Allier on the river of the same name

Detour

Into the gorges of the Allier

With its waterfalls, rapids and straits, it appears as if the Allier was purpose-made for kayaking and rafting. From Brioude, the upper reaches of the Allier run through the southern Velay. The folding of the Alps resulted in fracture zones, and the river follows these through the Massif Central in a north-south direction. White-water enthusiasts love the Gorges de l'Allier, the gorges of the river's upper reaches. Some of the gorges here are carved several hundred feet deep into the hills.

You can canoe down the calmer waters of the Allier near Pont-du-Château. The sections through the gorges are rated as having degrees

Bridge to St-Ilpize near Villeneuve d'Allier

time of the Hundred Years' War and the English-Gascon brigand gangs (1400–1466). The Porte des Roches city gate, which has been preserved from the city's defense complexes, today still has a portcullis. The Musée de la Haute Auvergne houses hurdy-gurdies and other traditional, regional items and handicrafts, as well as Gallo-Roman findings. The rows of houses in this town nestled between the plateaus of the Margeride and the volcanoes of the Cantal make for a delightful sight.

The technical wonder that is the Viaduc-du-Garabit spans the Truyère Valley not far from St-Flour (see side column on page 168 opposite).

14 Saugues The center of the Margeride region is towered over by the Tour des Anglais (12th–13th C.), a fortified tower which had once been taken over by marauding released mercenaries. The town is yet another of the stops along the Way of St-James pilgrimage

route to Santiago de Compostela. The Bête du Gévaudan is said to have killed and devoured up to 100 women and children in the 18th century. The mystery surrounding the wolf-like beast is today still unsolved and is further intensified at the Musée Fantastique de la Bête du Gévaudan.

15 Monistrol-d'Allier The most important stop for white-water enthusiasts in the Allier Valley (see column on the right) is situated along the D 589. In this remote canyon, a *train touristique* is the only form of company for kayakers. This train follows a track of curving tunnels built into the rock in 1864 to connect the Massif Central's capital with the Provence. Monistrol is also a stop on the pilgrimage route to Santiago de Compostela.

16 Le Puy-en-Velay The capital of the Haute-Loire département, nestled between peaks created out of lava, is home to a variety of bizarre, unusual

and impressive attractions, as well as numerous legends and traditions.

Ever since the 10th century, pilgrims from Germany, France and Switzerland have followed the Via Podiensis from here to St James's tomb in Santiago de Compostela. Perched atop the Aiguilhe (80 m/262 ft), one of the bizarre volcanic outcrops, the Romanesque chapel of St-Michel d'Aighuile (1100) today stands at the same site where a temple of Mercury had been erected during Gallo-Roman times. There are rock plugs dotted around the town, including the basalt columns of Espaly-Saint-Marcel.

Church interiors in Le Puy-en-Velay: a Black Madonna, the replica of an original that allegedly came from the Orient, is housed in the Notre-Dame du Puy cathedral (top left), while the interior of the St-Michel d'Aiguilhe Chapel, perched atop a basalt peak, exudes a Romanesque spirit in its interior (top right).

of difficulty of III and IV, which means that they are only suitable for experienced kayakers, but beginners can enjoy rafting and "hot-dogging" – a ride in a two-seater inflatable canoe accompanied by sports teachers. Canoes and kayaks can be hired at several points along the Allier. And even anglers get lucky in these wild waters.

The D 585 follows the increasingly narrow gorge from Brioude to Langeac, with the steep slopes dropping down as far as 500 m (1,641 ft). Many hiking routes lead to spectacular lookout points over the Velay and Margeride. There is also an Allier Gorges Train which allows you to enjoy the stunning scenery and spectacular views in comfort.

Churches and statues of the Virgin Mary perched spectacularly on top of basalt cones define the townscape of Le Puy-en-Velay. The Romanesque St-Michel d'Aiguilhe Chapel sits on its rock plug as if on a pinpoint, high above the pilgrimage town and dominated only by the Notre Dame de la France Statue on the Rocher de Corneille. In the background is the Notre Dame Cathedral.

Auvergne's largest fresco can be seen in the refectory of the Lavaudieu Benedictine Abbey: Mary is depicted as a queen surrounded by angels and apostles (circa 1220).

The Notre-Dame du Puy Cathedral, a UNESCO World Heritage Site, was built in the 11th and 12th centuries as a pilgrims' stop on the route to Santiago. Thereafter, it was extended to such a degree that it had to be supported with gigantic foundations and pylons to prevent it from falling off Mont Anis. Romanesque architecture and Moorish elements adding an Oriental character, as well as an allegedly curative Druidic "fever stone" and a Black Madonna, are some of the cathedral's unusual and attractive features. The city of Le Puy and the flourishing trade in lace-making sprang up around this focal point of the Marian pilgrimage town. The cathedral's Cloître, a Romanesque cloister, is a stunning work of art with colorful arcades whose capitals display characters from medieval fables.
A 16-m-tall (52-ft) red statue of Mary, which is more striking than it is pretty and which was cast from Crimean War cannons, was set up on the basalt rock known as the Roche Corneille above the city's rooftops in the 19th century. However,

Le Puy-en-Velay became famous for its green Puy lentils, a recognized *appellation* that made it to the gourmet restaurants of large cities around the world and are even made into sweets.

17 **Château Polignac** The view over southern Auvergne from the château's tower is spectacular. Built on the site of a former temple of Apollo, Château Polignac was perched on a basalt plateau around 6 km (4 miles) north-west of Le Puy-en-Velay and virtually impenetrable in the Middle Ages. However, it was left to slowly fall into disrepair by the mighty Polignac family in the 16th century and only ruins of the walls remain today.

18 **Lavaudieu** The picturesque hamlet is home to the ruins of a beautiful 11th-century Benedictine abbey. It is worth taking the time to admire the Romanesque cloister in the St-André Church, which is the only one in the Auvergne to have survived the French Revolution intact and not fallen into disrepair. The twisting, polygonal, smooth, cylindrical columns are very

artistic. The St-André Church, with its octagonal spire, houses Italian-style frescoes. The old stone bridge over the Senouire River is another attraction.
Continue along the N 102 to the town of Brioude.

19 **Brioude** Once known as Benigna Brivas ("the gentle one"), this town situated on a terrace above the River Allier, is today a lively little place in the north-east of the Haute-Loire département and, unlike the rest of the Velay in the Haute-Loire, forms part of the historic Auvergne region. The beheading of a Roman legionnaire around the year 304 during the persecution of the Christians saw the small town, which sprang up around the St-Julian Basilica built upon his tomb, become a stronghold for pilgrimages. Although the basilica, whose construction lasted from the 11th to well into the 13th century, is the largest Romanesque church in the Auvergne region, it differs from comparable buildings in terms of its building material (volcanic tuff) its variety of hues and some specific architectural features,

uncommon to the typical Auvergnat Romanesque. The colorful Allier pebbles used to create the beautiful mosaic flooring also contribute to St-Julian's rich color scheme.

20 **Blesle** One of the "plus beaux villages de France", Blesle is situated at the end of the Gorges de l'Alagnons, near the A 75 highway. All of its historic buildings have been preserved thanks to its isolated location in the gorges. Here, you can stroll down avenues of plane trees and among the half-timbered houses, and visit the Musée de la Coiffe (museum of traditional headdresses), the St-Martin Tower (14th C.), the Notre-Dame de la Chaigne Chapel (17th C.), the Romanesque church of St-Pierre, the Benedictine convent, and the donjon at the castle of the Barons of Mercur (11th C.).

21 **Issoire** The Auvergne's economic and industrial center,

Top: Christ is depicted with the symbols of the four Evangelists on this fresco in the St-Julian Basilica in Brioude.

Bird's eye view of Issoire
with the St-Austremoine
tower (left of center)

Detour

Parc Naturel Livradois-Forez

Between the forests of the Bois Noir in the Monts du Forez and the Velay in the south, over an area of 700 sq km (270 sq mi), extends the Livradois-Forez Nature Park, established in the 1980s. The remote landscape takes its name from the Livradois and Forez mountain ranges, which are separated by the Dore Valley. Some 180 villages in the environs of Thiers, Bas-Livradois, Haut-Livradois, the Monts du Forez and the plains of Ambert form part of this region, steeped in legends. Plants that flourish here include the common butterwort and the sundew, and the hazel grouse and the freshwater pearl mussel are among the animals at home in the park.

The Parc Naturel Livradois-Forez

Guided walks in woods and mountains are organized between May and November. Along the "Route des Métiers" (trail of crafts), century-old regional crafts are demonstrated. Here you can watch basket weavers, wood carvers, charburners, cattle breeders, organic farmers, sculptors and potters at work.

situated in the Allier Valley, is additionally home to an award-winning wine. Aluminum is also produced here, and the aviation industry is an important creator of jobs.

Issoire was almost completely destroyed during the religious wars of the 16th century. Yet a stroll down the narrow, winding lanes of the carefully restored Old Town still transports you back to the Middle Ages.

The Auvergnat Romanesque style of architecture is exemplified by the eastern façade of the St-Austremoine Church (12th C.): the tiered pyramid formed by the crossing tower, chevet, choir ambulatory and radial chapels dominates the townscape.

The center of the Old Town, the Place de la République, is dominated by the Tour de l'Horloge. This clock tower also displays numerous examples of scientific achievements from the Renaissance period.

② Vic-le-Comte The town of Vic-le-Comte, the heart of the Comté, founded by Gauls and Romans, lies only around 5 km (3 miles) away from the A 75 Clermont-ferrand to Montpellier highway, just near the town of Enval, which has been settled since prehistoric times and is known for its cave dwellings. From the 13th century until the time of Richelieu (1585–1642), the French kings tried in vain to deprive the local counts, who resided in stately castles in the volcanic hills, of their independence.

The Old Town, with its pastel-shade houses, the Porte Robin city gate, Ste-Chapelle, a late-Gothic 16th-century chapel with unique choir windows, and the Romanesque Church of St-Jean (12th C.) lie between the Allier River and the mountains of the Livradois in the Parc des Volcans.

Once the capital of the former County of Auvergne, Vic-le-Comte is a prime destination for lovers of jazz festivals, antique and horse markets, motocross, canoeing, hang-gliding and paragliding. The bank notes of the Banque de France are printed on special paper made here.

② Billom The medieval ambiance of Billom, with its half-timbered houses, is popular for film sets. A university existed here as early as the 13th century, and the Maison du Chapître at the Place des Écoles was part of the complex. The crypt (11th C.) of the St-Cerneuf Church is one of the oldest in Auvergne. A sixth of all of France's famously fragrant garlic bulbs are harvested here.

Remains of the Gallo-Roman inter-city road from Lyon to Bordeaux can be seen in the town's east, at the transition from the Limagne to the Livradois. Today, it is worth making a détour to the Livradois-Forez Nature Park (see column on the left).

Top: Since its restoration in the 19th century, the interior of the St-Austremoine Church in Issoire has had an Oriental feel, despite actually being a Romanesque building.

Landscape with sunflower fields in the Parc Naturel Livradois-Forez

Parc Régional des Volcans d'Auvergne Europe's largest nature park covers several mountain ranges and the Artense granite plateau. It has numerous information centers.

St-Nectaire The thermal springs resort is one of the finest in the country. In terms of both architecture and décor, the St-Nectaire Church is considered one of the most important Romanesque places of worship in the Auvergne region.

Lavaudieu In this village, an 11th-century abbey boasting exquisite frescoes has stood the test of time. Pictured is the refectory.

Orcival The pagoda-like 12th-century Notre-Dame d'Orcival Basilica, partly embedded in the hillside, is striking even from afar. It marks the site where a statue of the Virgin Mary came to life.

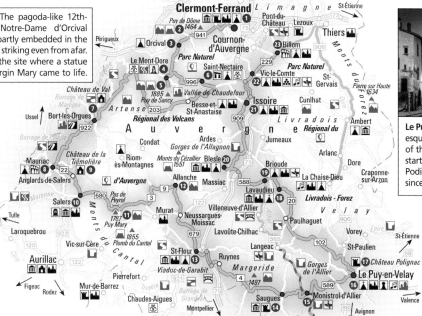

Le Puy-en-Velay The picturesque town on the margins of the Auvergne has been a starting point for the Via Podiensis pilgrimage route since the 10th century.

Gorges de l'Allier The River Allier is a paradise for white-water enthusiasts. The deep gorges in the upper reaches are a top challenge for those with some experience.

Clermont-Ferrand The history of the twin cities dates back to Celtic times; the first cathedral was built in Clermont in the 5th century. The Notre-Dame-du-Port Basilica (12th C.) is one of the most famous Romanesque churches in the region. Adjacent Montferrand experienced its heyday from the 13th to the 17th century. The towns merged as Clermont-Ferrand in 1731.

Château de la Trémolière The cute little castle belonging to the Montclar family is home to first-rate artistic treasures. The château boasts wood panels, paintings and ten elaborate 16th-century wall tapestries depicting animals, mythical creatures, castles and cities are particularly famous. It features historic architectural styles.

Saugues At one time, all pilgrims following the Way of St James trail through the Allier Gorge would reach the small town, but in the 18th century, the "Bête de Gévaudan", a wolf-like, man-eating creature, is said to have caused trouble here. Pictured is the St-Médard collegiate church.

173

Route 10
Côte d'Azur, Provence, Rhône-Alpes

The alpine landscape between the Côte d'Azur and Lake Geneva is accessed via two pass routes whose names say it all: the Route Napoléon was used by the French Emperor on his way back from the island of Elba in 1815, while the Route des Grandes Alpes is the ultimate roadway over some of the highest passes in the Alps.

Between the Côte d'Azur and the Mont Blanc Massif the Alps run predominantly in a north-south direction – a journey from the coast to Lake Geneva thus more or less runs directly along the main ridge. The Route Napoléon, situated somewhat west in the outlying hills, connects Cannes with Grenoble and, continuing on via Chambéry and Annecy, is the quickest way to Geneva. Napoleon, who had landed on the shores of the present-day Juan-les-Pins on 1 March 1815, needed seven days to cover the 330-km-long (205-mile) stretch to Grenoble.

The passes along the way are only moderately high: the Col de Valferrière in the Alpes Maritimes is the highest of these at 1,169 m (3,835 ft), while the Col de Lèques in the Alpes de Provence reaches a height of almost 1,148 m (3,767 ft). At

1,248 m (4,095 ft), the Col Bayard north of Gap in the Hautes Alpes between the vast Durance Valley and Grenoble, is not a giant either. North of Grenoble, the wide Isère Valley keeps the tall peaks at bay, as do the Lac du Bourget and the Lac d'Annecy farther north.

However, the easily navigable route does also unlock a variety of landscapes which could not be more diverse. The fragrant clouds wafting over the city of Grasse are only 40 km (25 mi) as the crow flies from the steep rock faces of the Grand Canyon du Verdon; from the Alpes de Provence, you'll suddenly find yourself in the fruit plantations of the Durance Valley. The monumental fortress in Sisteron vies with the mighty bulwark of the Notre-Dame-de-la-Salette Basilica in Corps. The hustle and bustle of the metropolis of Grenoble is only 20 km (12 miles) in a straight line from the absolute remoteness of the Grande Chartreuse. With their picturesque lakes, Aix-les-Bains and Annecy are the showpieces of the Haute-Savoie département, but are only the prelude to the grandeur of the old lady, Geneva.

On the other hand, the Rout des Grandes Alpes betwee Geneva and Nice is a completel different challenge. It consis tently follows the main ridge o the Alps, its passes like pearl on an exquisite necklace. N fewer than nine alpine passe and 691 km (429 miles) of as phalt roads must be covered But apart from the continuou alpine and pass routes, th contrasts also never cease t amaze: the lovely Lake Genev is only around 50 km (31 miles by air from the 4,000-m-hig (13,124 ft) western slopes o Mont Blanc.

The highest point of the alpin route, the Col de l'Iseran, i around 2,765 m (9,072 ft above Nice. The journey fron the northern side of the Galibie to its southern side involve passing through a climatic di vide: instead of the cool, north ern alpine climate, visitors ar

Above: The 12-km-long (7.5-mile) glacier descent through the Vallée Blanche from the Aiguille du Midi to Chamonix is the dream of many an ambitious skier.
Left: The Lac d'Annecy in the Haute-Savoie département is the jewel in the Savoy Alps' crown. Cold mountain streams supply the lake with crystal-clear water.

now met by the sun in the Midi, the South of France. And some 230 km (143 miles) farther south, the expansive coastal landscape around Nice follows the rocky scenery of the narrow Gorges de Daluis.

The short description above already indicates that scenic beauty is the main focus of this route. Alongside historic monuments and art-historic highlights, there are also vast, seemingly untouched stretches to discover. The "alpine hike" by car takes you to the glaciers of Mont Blanc, the Pelvoux (3,914 m/12,842 ft) and the Meije (3,983 m/13,068 ft). Briançon, perched at an altitude of 1,321 m (4,334 ft), is

Europe's highest city, while the Southern Alps are home to a series of other stunning passes, all exceeding 2,000 m (6,562

ft). The pass route does not end until you reach the 2,326-m-high (7,632-ft) Col de la Cayolle. Although the Var Valley

heads out as far as Nice, the Daluis Gorges make for one last highlight before you reach the lights of the Côte d'Azur.

This route is characterized by exciting contrasts – left, an orange tree in the perfume city of Grasse; right, mist over the Canyon du Verdon.

The St-Honorat Monastery on the Îles de Lérins, just off the coast of Cannes, dates back to the fourth century.

Grand hôtels

Whether it be Cannes, Antibes or Nice, all owe their early heyday to the luxury hotels built mostly by Britons on the shores of their respective bays. In Cannes, it was the Englishman Lord Brougham who attracted the European nobility to the Croisette in 1834. The elegant Hotel Carlton, with its white façade, was built for them, and is now a favorite with film stars.

Another example is the Eden Roc Hotel, located at the southern tip of the Cap d'Antibes peninsula. The palace-cum-hotel, situated in 8 ha (20 acres) of park, was opened in 1870 and achieved legendary status thanks to Scott Fitzgerald's novel, *Tender is the Night*. Surpassing all these is the Hotel Negresco, however, whose opening in Nice in 1913 saw the high society of the time gather around seven crowned heads of state. It was built by a young waiter from Bucharest, Henri Negrescu, who, with the help of a French indus-

The luxurious Hotel Carlton on the Croisette in Cannes

trialist, realized his dream of establishing the most luxurious hotel on the Côte d'Azur. The Negresco has 121 rooms, each appointed in a different style. The dome was created by Gustave Eiffel. The *grand hôtel* has been listed as a protected historical site since 1974 and continues to present itself as the finest Grand Hôtel of the Belle Époque.

The full splendor of the French Alps: the Route Napoléon heads from Cannes through France's lavender region, past Europe's largest gorge and through gently rolling terrain until it reaches the shores of Lake Geneva. From there, continue along the Route des Grandes Alpes, over the highest passes and back south toward the Côte d'Azur.

❶ Cannes See p. 177.

❷ Antibes The ancient Greek town of Antipolis, present-day Antibes, which also incorporates Golfe-Juan and Juan-les-Pins, lies around 11 km (7 mi) east along the coastal road. Antibes' quaint, labyrinthine Old Town is worth a visit. The cathedral, with its 17th-century baroque façade, sits on the town's eastern hillside. Its transept and chancel date back to the 12th century. Just next to

Above: Cannes' Old Town is best seen from the old port. The castle towers above the city with its La Suquet tower – today it houses the Musée de la Castre which shows local art and ethnography.

the cathedral is the impressive, solid construction of the former Grimaldi Palace, with a 17th-century defense tower. The most upscale addresses along the Côte d'Azur are located on the Cap d'Antibes peninsula south of the city. Exclusive estates with old pine trees and superb villas lie concealed be-

hind what are usually very high walls and security cameras. From Antibes, you can either follow the coastal road to Cannes and continue on to Grasse from there, or return to

Cannes' Old Town presents itself from its most attractive side in the old port area.

Travel information

Route profile
Length: c. 1600 km bei nur wenigen Abstechern
Time required: 2–3 weeks
Start: Cannes
End: Nice
Route: Cannes, Grasse, Sisteron, Grenoble, Chambéry, Annecy, Geneva, Chamonix/Mont-Blanc, Val d'Isère, Briançon, Nice

Safe driving:
The Route Napoléon is open all year round, but the Route des Grandes Alpes can only be used in the summer. Take extra care in unlit tunnels.

When to go:
From June until mid-October. Depending on the snow situation, the larger alpine passes may only open toward the end of July. For information check: www.alpineroads.com/passstatus.php

Where to stay:
There are attractive country inns along the entire route.

Information:
Cannes: www.cannes.fr
Grenoble:
www.ville-grenoble.fr
Chambéry: www.chambery-tourisme.com
Geneva: www.ville-ge.ch
Chamonix:
www.chamonix.com
Val d'Isère: www.valdinet.com
Briançon:
www.ot-Briancon.fr
Nice:
www.nicetourism.com

Cannes

As the meeting place of the rich and famous, Cannes is one of the most glamorous cities on the Côte d'Azur.

The Golfe de la Napoule was settled as early as Celtic and Roman times, but it was not until the arrival of the British in the 19th century that the bay became an attractive destination. They initially built splendid villas here, before adding comfortable hotels and the Boulevard de la Croisette, which runs around the entire bay.

The Old Town, know as Le Suquet, is perched above the old port on the 67-m-high (220-ft) Mont Chevalier, on whose summit stands an 11th-century watchtower. The nearby Musée de la Castre displays exhibits on

The Boulevard de la Croisette extends around the entire bay.

ancient history. The Gothic church of Notre-Dame-de-l'Espérance dates back to the year 1648. The lookout platform behind the building provides a spectacular view over the entire Bay of Cannes, the Îles de Lérins (Île Sainte-Marguerite and Île St-Honorat) just offshore from the city, and the nearby Massif de l'Esterel. At the edge of the Old Town you'll find the Marché Forville, housed in a giant covered market hall.

Cannes is the city of festivals, bringing together in one place show-business stars, film, TV and music producers, and not least the big players of high finance at the Boulevard de la Croisette. May is strictly reserved for the world-famous Cannes Film Festival, where the Palme d'Or, or Golden Palm, is awarded to the best film.

Grasse's medieval alleyways and the surrounding flower fields were the perfect backdrop for the film adaptation of the novel *Perfume* (2008).

Grasse – the city of fragrance

Grasse owes its importance as the world's perfume capital to a fashion dating back to the Italian Renaissance, when perfumed gloves suddenly became in vogue. At the time, most people bought their gloves in Grasse, and so it was only logical that glove-makers used Provençal herbs to perfume their gloves. The combination was such a resounding success that the entire region was very soon able to live off perfume production.

Today, the three perfume factories of Molinard, Fragonard and Galimard dominate the market. All three are open to the public.

Nowadays, the production of raw materials has become much more important than the retailing of the end products. Manufacturers of essential oils have long been procuring

Notre-Dame-du-Puy Cathedral (12th./13th C.)

their base products (aromatic plants) from all corners of the earth, and in turn supplying their extracts to leading perfume manufacturers around the world. While the vast majority of fragrances and aromatic substances are today being sent to yoghurt, ice-cream and soup manufacturers, the essences produced in Grasse are also indispensable in the world of cosmetics, scented soaps, aromatic dishwashing detergent and fine washing powder – as well as of course in perfumes.

Cannes. The D 6285, which ends in Cannes, and the D 6185/ D 6085 trace Napoleon's historic route to Grenoble.

3 Grasse The city is home to a very well-preserved Old Town with medieval alleyways and the quaint Place aux Aires lined with arcades. The Notre-Dame-du-Puy Cathedral dates back to the Romanesque period and also houses three paintings by Rubens from the time when he was still an unknown artist.

4 Castellane The village by the bridge over the Verdon is dominated by a mighty chalk cliff, , 164-m-high (538-ft). Perched atop its vertical rock faces is the Notre-Dame-du-Roc Chapel, which can be accessed on foot in one hour. The St-Victor Church (12th century) in the village itself is just as interesting. Castellane is the ideal starting point for continuing on to the rather spectacular Grand Canyon du Verdon situated in the far south-west.

The D 952 runs parallel to the river toward the town of Moustiers-Ste-Marie on the northern side of the gorge.

5 Grand Canyon du Verdon West of Castellane, the small Verdon River flows for 21 km (13 miles) between soaring rock faces which are not even 6 m (10 yds) apart in some areas of the canyon floor. This natural wonder can be experienced by boat, on foot or by car – the road heads along the top right on the edge. The Route des Crêtes along the northern side was completed in 1973, while the Route de la Corniche Sublime on the southern side was built as early as 1947. Both routes provide access to the best views on either side of the canyon.

The next stretch of the Route Napoléon from Castellane to Digne-les-Bains leads over the Col de Lèques pass and is particularly famous for its magnificent scenic beauty.

6 Digne-les-Bains The health resort town with its mineral springs lies in the Bléone Valley, and impresses visitors with its historic city center. The 15th-century St-Jérôme Cathedral is perched high above the town, while the Notre-Dame-du-Bourg Cathe-

dral is a superb Romanesque building which since 1437 has only been used as a cemetery chapel.

Continue on the N 85, initially heading south-west following the Bléone before turning north-westward into the Upper Durance Valley.

7 Sisteron The city on the Upper Durance, situated at an altitude of just under 500 m (1,641 ft), was developed as the road station of Segustero on the Via Sinistra under Emperor Augustus. The fortress complexes were built in the mid-14th century.

The citadel, perched atop a high mountain ridge, continues to dominate the landscape around Sisteron today. Opposite the fortress, the Rocher de la Baume, with its vertical limestone strata, displays a piece of living geology. The Notre-Dame-des-Pommiers Cathedral was built in Lombard style between 1160 and 1220. The Old Town, with its winding lanes sloping down toward the Durance, is particularly attractive. It is just under 50 km (31 miles) to Gap, the bustling town in

The Grand Canyon du Verdon stretches westward into a vast hilly landscape with extensive woodland and hedges.

Parc National des Écrins

The N 85 between Gap and Vizille (take the D 1091 east from there) offers several opportunities to drive through the national park situated to the east. Following the Route des Grandes Alpes, the park can be accessed via Briançon on the N 94 (as far as L'Argentière-la-Bessée) and the side road D 994E to Ailefroide on Mont Pelvoux.

Barre des Écrins (4,101 m/ 13,455 ft).

The 91,800-ha (226,838 acre) Parc National around Mont Pelvoux is the largest and newest of France's five national parks. It was established in 1973 and sprawls around the Massif des Écrins. There is a 178,600-ha (441,320-acre) designated reserve around the central area. At 4,102 m (13,459 ft), the highest point of the park is the summit of the Barre des Écrins (first climbed in 1864), yet it was long overlooked. As the summit is not visible from any valley, it did not pose an attractive destination to mountaineers, who preferred the 3,914-m-high (12,842-ft) Pelvoux. This mountain is visible from afar and from all angles as a striking peak, and was thus climbed for the first time by the French mountaineer, Durand, as early as 1828.

The round dance of sublime peaks in the Massif des Écrins is completed with the three individual summits of the Meije. The Meije Orientale is 3,890 m (12,763 ft) high, while the Meije Centrale comes in at 3,974 m (13,039 ft), and the Grand Pic de la Meije at 3,983 m (13,068 ft).

the hilly landscape of the Alpes du Dauphiné.

8 Gap The town rose to prominence as a result of its location at the intersection of the Route Napoléon and the inter-city road between Briançon and Valence. The mausoleum for François de Bonne, Duke of Lesdiguières, is worth seeing, before following the 1,248-m-high (4,095-ft) Col Bayard (12% incline) to Corps.

9 Corps A street in this small village leads to one of France's most famous pilgrimage sites; over 100,000 pilgrims each year visit the Notre-Dame de la Salette Basilica.

From this pilgrimage town, it is 60 km (37 miles) to Grenoble, which marks the end of the Route Napoléon. Before reaching the city, however, it is worth making a detour to the Parc National des Écrins (see column on the right).

10 Grenoble The old capital of the Dauphiné province is picturesquely situated at a bend in the Isère River, nestled among mountains reaching

Top left: Some houses in the small town of Sisteron, on the Durance River, nestle close up against the heavily eroded Rocher de la Baume.
Above: St-Laurent, one of the oldest districts of Grenoble, has a Mediterranean feel.

The gorge formed by the Verdon River – French "Gorges du Verdon" or "Grand Canyon du Verdon" – in Provence is one of Europe's most impressive landscapes. A spectacular road provides access to the gorge between Castellane and Moustiers-Sainte-Marie, offering fantastic views down into the abyss, parts of which are up to 700 m (2,297 ft) deep. However, the

routes through the Verdon Gorge by boat or on foot are even more impressive. It is advisable to have proper equipment and an experienced escort in order to better explore the narrow, 21-km-long (13-mile) canyon, along whose floor the turquoise river Verdon snakes its way. The steep rock faces are also popular with rock climbers and abseilers.

Charming city squares –
pictured left, the Elephant
Fountain – and arcades
await visitors in Chambéry.

heights of up to 3,000 m (9,843 ft). Place Grenette is the lively heart of the Old Town, while the adjacent Grande Rue existed as early as Roman times. Farther east, the Place St-André is also worth seeing. The church of the same name was built between 1220 and 1236 as the castle chapel of the Counts of Albon, and the Notre-Dame Cathedral is just a few steps farther east.
From Grenoble, the Route continues north over the Col de Porte (D 512) to St-Pierre-de-Chartreuse in the Massif de la Chartreuse.

⑪ Monastère de la Grande Chartreuse The mother house of the Carthusian Order was established in the "Déserte de Chartreuse" with the permission of the Bishop of Grenoble in the late 11th century. The buildings of the present complex date back to the 17th cen-

tury. The monastery itself is not open to the public. A small museum near the car park – 1.5 km (0.9 mi) from the monastery – provides information on the Carthusian Order and the lives of the Carthusian monks.

⑫ Col du Granier The northern border of the Chartreuse Mountains is marked by the 1,134-m-high (3,721-ft) Col du Granier. In 1248, a giant rockslide here buried an entire village of 5,000 people; the vast scale of the catastrophe is still visible today: the field of debris is called "Abymes de Myans". The northern slope of the Col du Granier leads directly down to Chambéry.

⑬ Chambéry The city located to the south of Lac du Bourget was the capital of Savoy from 1232 to the mid-1500s. At the center of the Old Town stands the Fontaine des Eléphants,

built in 1838, while the arcaded Rue de Boigne runs from the city's main landmark to the castle – the former residence of the Dukes of Savoy (the oldest sections date back to the 14th and 15th century) and today a museum. Chambéry Cathedral was erected in the 13th century, and work on its façade, today still incomplete, began in the 1400s. Don't miss the St-Pierre-de-Lémenc Church, the center

of the Christianization of Savoy in the early Middle Ages.

⑭ Aix-les-Bains The city on the eastern bank of the Lac du Bourget is home to thermal springs which were used as early as Roman times. The first real bathhouse was built in 1779 – and was developed into two large city bath complexes which still exist today. The Thermes Nationaux (19th C.)

The Wilson Globe standing
outside the European
headquarters of the United
Nations in Geneva

are open to the public. Apart from the modern health resort facilities, the remains of the Roman complex can also be seen. The castle of the Marquis d'Aix, built in the 16th century, today serves as the town hall. From Aix-les-Bains, the A 41 and the parallel D 1201 head to Annecy, one of the most attractive cities in the French Alps.

15 Annecy The city at the northern end of Lac d'Annecy is surrounded by snow-covered peaks. It was built around a fortified castle on the site of a prehistoric settlement in the 12th century, and the medieval Old Town is clustered picturesquely around several canals of the Thiou. The St-Pierre Cathedral dates back to the 16th century. Its interior is Gothic, while the superimposed façade is from the Renaissance. The St-Maurice Church, built by Dominicans in the 15th century, is even

more interesting. Inside, it has a wide Gothic nave and beautiful frescoes.
Continue along the D 1201, which heads north to the southern end of Lake Geneva (Lac Léman in French). North of Annecy, long stretches of the small Usses River have carved their way deep into the limestone. The original suspension bridge, the Pont de la Caille, still stands at the point where the D 1201 intersects with the valley. It can only be crossed on foot.

16 Le Salève From Cruseilles, a detour to Mont Salève is an absolute must. Although the tallest point of the mighty ridge is only 1,380 m (4,528 ft) high, this is still 1,000 m (3,281 ft) above Lake Geneva situated directly below. The view at the Grande Gorge suddenly opens out over the lake and the city of Geneva, while from the information board at the highest

point you'll have a great view of the mountains between the Dents du Midi and Mont Blanc. Looking north, the vista extends as far as the Swiss canton of Jura. The descent heads down to Annemasse by the lake and then directly to Geneva.

17 Geneva/Genève The capital of the canton of the same name, at the south-western end of Lake Geneva, is built on the site of an ancient settlement. A Celtic "oppidum" existed on the city's present-day hills centuries before Roman times; it was not until Caesar that the city was named Geneva. It fell under Calvinist control during the Reformation, and it became part of the Swiss Confederation in 1814. The St-Pierre Cathedral, which dates back to initial Christian buildings from the fourth and fifth centuries, forms the center of Geneva's Old Town. Construc-

tion of the present-day cathedral began in Romanesque style around 1150 and was completed largely in Gothic style in 1232. Its finest furnishings include the richly decorated late-Gothic choir stalls and the late-Romanesque capitals on the cluster columns in the nave. The 15th-century city hall situated south-west of the cathedral has interesting Renaissance façades and a tower dating back to 1455. The 15th-century town hall situated south-west of the cathedral has interesting Renaissance

**Above: Geneva lies in a picturesque spot at the western end of Lake Geneva, and is today the European headquarters of the United Nations.
Middle left: The 12th-century Palais de l'Isle on the bridge over the Thiou is the most famous landmark building in Annecy's Old Town.**

Perched at an altitude of 1,800 m (5,906 ft) in the Isère Valley after which it is named is the wintersports resort of Val d'Isère. Right, the old village center

Mont Blanc – Monte Bianco

Only philistines would want to count its glaciers, which clad it in ice like a king clad in his ermine-fur coat, stretching down 3,500 m (11,484 ft) from Mont Blanc's summit to the ice tongue. As is right and proper for a "King of the Mountains", Mont Blanc has also long kept itself clear of its subjects. Apart from the cable cars, this remains the case even today. Vehicles can only go 1,461 m (4,794 ft) up on the northern side, and Chamonix lies at an altitude of just 1,034 m (3,393 ft), rendering it another 3,773 m (12,379 ft) below the summit. The story is not much different on the southern side. In Courmayeur in the upper Aosta Valley, the first crops grow barely 100 m (161 yds) from the glacier. Here, the southern face of the Mont Blanc Massif soars up as a giant 3,500-m-high (11,484-ft), 25-km-wide (16-mile) wall.

Mont Blanc – Europe's highest mountain

A true rarity exists as a bonus at the south-western Italian foot of the grand mountain, in the Veny Valley: a natural glacial lake similar to those found in Greenland. The Lac du Miage is a product of the Miage Glacier, whose breakaway edge soars up approximately 20 m (66 ft) above the lake. The forward-pushing motion of the glacier means that large pieces constantly break off from the ice wall and drift on the lake's waters like icebergs in Arctic seas. The deciduous larches all along the shore attest to the fact that all this glacial action takes place well below the timber line.

façades and a tower dating back to 1455. The council chamber is decorated with valuable paintings (15th–17th C.). The city's most interesting museum is the Musée d'Art et d'Histoire, but the symbol of Geneva is its Jet d'Eaux, the world's highest fountain on the southern shores of the lake, which shoots water 145 m (476 ft) into the air. The Palais des Nations, nestled in vast park grounds, is a world on its own. The old League of Nations Palace, clad in pale marble, was completed in 1937 and, at 25,000 sq m (269,000 sq ft), is the second largest in Europe after the Palace of Versailles.

From Geneva, follow the highway (A 40/E 25) until you reach the outskirts of Chamonix.

⑱ Chamonix/Mont-Blanc The old mountain village situated at an altitude of 1,030 m (3,379 ft) at the foot of Mont Blanc is today a strange mix of luxury hotel and campsite, casino and snack bar. The focal point is not found in the valley, but rather up high. You get the best view from a cable-car ride up to the 2,524-m-high (8,281-ft) Le Brévent.

West of Chamonix, the D 1212 branches off to the south-west, leading to the host city of the 1992 Winter Olympic Games.

⑲ Albertville The city lies at the confluence of the Arly and the Isère, providing natural access to the Massif de la Vanoise in the south. Located in the valley, it was built with a regular, checkerboard layout in the 19th century at the orders of King Charles-Albert of Savoy. Conflans, perched on a mountain spur above the New Town, is the predecessor settlement and the Old Town of Albertville. It makes for a picturesque sight with its ogival city gates, mighty defense walls, a castle, baroque church and old houses.

The route now heads upstream through the Isère Valley as far as Val d'Isère: it initially follows a south-easterly direction to Moûtiers (which provides access to the ski regions in the Massif de la Vanoise), then north-easterly to the garrison town of Bourg-Saint-Maurice, where the road forks: the D 1090 continues on over the Col du Petit St-Bernard to Courmayeur, while the D 902 branches off south. Driving through the Tarentaise Valley up to Val d'Isère finally marks the start of the adventure that is the Route des Grandes Alpes.

⑳ Val d'Isère The climb up to Lac de Chevril has an incline of 9 to 13%! But it is a paradise for skiers after that, with ski lifts one after another around Val d'Isère and Tignes. In Lac de Tignes, you can take the cable car up to the Grande Motte (3,656 m/11,995 ft). The ascent to the Col de l'Iseran in the Parc National de la Vanoise begins once you have passed through Val d'Isère. At 2,764 m

The 2,650-m-high (8,695-ft) Col du Galibier, one of the highest of all alpine passes, provides stunning views across the mountains.

The most spectacular stage of the Tour de France: the Col du Galibier

Europe's most famous bike race has been held with varying routing every year since 1903. Spanning a total length of between 3,000 an 4,000 km (1,864 and 2,486 miles), the race demands sheer superhuman endurance over a variety of flat, hilly and mountainous stages.

One of the best-known ascents in the Alps is the 2,650-m-high (8,695-ft) Col du Galibier. Normally approached from the north, the ascent also involves an additional challenge in the form of the 1,570-m-high (5,151-ft) Col du Télégraphe in front. On the latter's southern side, riders must

The ninth stage of the Tour (2007) at the Col du Galibier

first descend around 200 m (656 ft), before re-climbing this same distance as they head toward the Galibier. The total difference in elevation which must be overcome on the northern slope is thus 2,070 m (6,792 ft), while the subsequent descent to Briançon on the southern side is 1,321 m (4,334 ft).

As if that wasn't enough, the weather adds further perils for the riders. If a low passes by from the north-west, the entire northern slope is enveloped in thick cloud, meaning rain at the bottom and snow at the top. If a low comes from the south, the northern slope will be warm with fierce headwinds, while the southern slope will have fog, rain or even snow flurries. This explains why the Col du Galibier stage sometimes decides who wins the Tour.

(9,069 ft), it is the highest alpine pass, whose northern side has a 12% uphill incline and an 11% downhill gradient.

21 Lanslevillard The village at the southern foot of the Col de l'Iseran is home to a unique gem in the form of the unimposing St-Sébastien chapel. Its interior is painted with thirty-five frescoes from the Life of Christ and sixteen scenes from the Legend of St Sebastian. Continue along the D 10006 through the Arc Valley as far as St-Michel-de-Maurienne.

22 Col du Galibier The climb (15% incline) up to the Col du Galibier begins in St-Michel. The 2,650-m-high (8,695-ft) pass is one of the most scenic routes in Haute-Savoie. With their steep northern faces and formidable glacial cataracts, the soaring Meije (3,983 m/13,068 ft) and Barre des Écrins (4,102 m/13,459 ft) are a breathtaking sight. Farther south, beneath the Col du Galibier, the pass route intersects with the D 1091 from Briançon to Vizille on the Route Napoléon. Head back the other way, over the 2,058-m-high (6,752-ft) Col du Lautaret, to Briançon.

23 Briançon The city lies at an altitude of 1,321 m (4,334 ft), thus claiming to be the highest city in the European Union. From Roman times onward, Briançon was always a military town. In 1692, Louis XIV commissioned the famous fortress builder, Vauban, to build a new defensive complex. He created the present-day citadel and surrounded the city with an immense circular wall, which was completed in 1722. The city's old main road, the Grande Rue, is lined with beautiful old houses and fountains.

24 Col d'Izoard One you are south of Briançon, you will start to feel the South; it is apparent just by passing over the Col d'Izoard (2,361 m/7,746 ft; incline of up to 12%). However, things really become interesting on the southern slope of the Col d'Izoard, when the Casse Déserte suddenly appears: reddish-brown blocks and pyramids – some rock and some a mixture of stones and rubble – soar up from the gravel slopes. From Guillestre it is approximately 20 km (12 miles) and an altitude difference of 1,110 m (3,641 ft) until the next pass, the Col de Vars.

25 Col de Vars Its northern slope (12% incline) provides an excellent view of the Massif de Pelvoux, while the rocky

Top left: The Glacier d'Argentière slides down from Mont Dolent, a peak in the Mont Blanc mountain range, and almost reaches Argentière. Above: Lac Blanc lies high above Chamonix at an altitude of 2,352 m (7,717 ft), flanked by the Mont Blanc Massif.

The epitome of all Mediterranean glamor: Nice on the Côte d'Azur with the port in the foreground

City of art: St-Paul-de-Vence

St-Paul-de-Vence was the artists' village on the Côte d'Azur. It was here that Modigliani, Bonnard, Soutine and Signac would meet in the 1920s. Today, the village's most important art address is the Fondation Maeght, which combines studios, an art gallery and an open-air museum in an extremely interesting manner.

Sculpture by Joan Miró at the Fondation Maeght

Aimé Maeght donated his entire collection of modern and contemporary art to the Maeght Foundation, which is today under the patronage of the French government. A large summer exhibition is held there every year, while other examples of the foundation's collection are displayed the rest of the time.

massifs of the southern Cottian Alps can be seen from the top of the pass (2,109 m/6,920 ft). The route through the valley from Col de Vars passes by pyramidal earth mounds before arriving in St-Paul-sur-Ubaye. The center of the Southern Alps – still at 1,132 m (3,714 ft) – is reached at Barcelonette.

26 Col de la Cayolle The climb up the 2,326-m-high (7,632-ft) Col de la Cayolle begins just beyond Barcelonette. The D 902 initially follows the Bachelard Valley upstream, heading south as far as the north-western corner of the Parc National Le Mercantour. The Gorges du Bachelard become so narrow that *garages*, or passing points, have had to be created. Once the vertical rock faces retreat somewhat, the route, which initially runs along the northern border of the national park, climbs up the slope (10%), providing spectacular valley vistas over the wild Gorges du Bachelard. After this pass region free from virtually all vegetation (with a downhill gradient of up to 11%), the pass route leaves the national park, winding its way towards the Var Valley and beyond to Guillaumes.

27 Gorges de Daluis Over the millennia, the upper reaches of the Var River beyond Guillaumes have created a particularly beautiful natural monument: the colors lighting up the several-hundred-foot-high gorge walls from below range from brown, to brick red and purple. High above the Var's narrow riverbed, the route snakes along the slopes as a corniche, providing stunning views down into the valley. South of the gorge, it joins the D 4202, later the D 6202, which reaches the coast to the west of Nice.

28 Vence Some 10 km (6 mi) from the coast, a smaller road branches off in a westerly direction, leading to Vence. The small town was established by the Romans as Vintium, and was home to a bishop as early as the fourth century. The former cathedral today still impresses visitors. Construction on the St-Véron Church began in the 10th century. Many parts of the medieval city wall have been preserved. The Tour du Peyra dates back to the 12th century, while the Porte de Peyra was built in 1441. Henri Matisse founded the Chapelle du Rosaire on the north-west edge of Vence in 1951.

Somewhat farther south lies the small town of St-Paul-de-Vence (see column on the left) one of the most famous examples of "villages perchés" Such is the French term used in this region to describe the high-up medieval villages surrounded by mighty ramparts and which were once fortified to protect against the invading Saracens.

We quickly reach our destination, Nice, via Cagnes-sur-Mer and the highway/coastal road.

29 Nice The capital of the Alpes-Maritimes département lies picturesquely at the southern foothills of the Maritime Alps. Its Promenade des Anglais is a large seaside boulevard lined with Belle-Époque buildings such as the Hotel Negresco, while its particularly beautiful Old Town is characterized by a maze of winding alleyways.

Nice was founded by the Greeks as Nikaia, before the Romans settled inland in Cemenelum, the present-day suburb of Cimiez. The thermal springs and arenas from the Roman settlement can still be visited here today. Nice later belonged to the ancient county of Provence, and was part of Italy from 1388 to 1860. Wealthy Britons chose it as the base for their retirement homes in the 19th century. The 92-m-high (302-ft) Castle Hill, the city's oldest settlement site, provides the best views over all of Nice and the old port. Sprawling out to the west is the Old Town with its labyrinth of lanes; its northern district is dominated by the Ste-Réparate Cathedral.

Above: All of Nice gathers at the Cours Saleya, whether for the picturesque flower market during the day, or in one of the many cafés, bars and restaurants by night.

Perched watchfully on a hill:
St-Paul-de-Vence in the Côte
d'Azur hinterland

Geneva Geneva The city by Lac Léman is the seat of many international organizations. Its landmarks are the world's highest fountain and the Palais des Nations.

Annecy The city by Lake d'Annecy in the Haute-Savoie has a pretty medieval center. One of the main attractions is the Palais d'Isle in the middle of the River Thiou.

Grand Canyon du Verdon The 21-km-long (13-mile), up to 700-m-deep (2,297-ft) and in some places very narrow gorge carved into Provence's limestone by the Verdon is one of Europe's most imposing natural wonders and a paradise for outdoor sports fans of all descriptions.

Sisteron The town boasts a spectacular location at the Durance River gap between two very steep mountain ranges. The castle and the cathedral offer particularly stunning views.

SWITZERLAND

Lausanne
Lake Geneva
Yvoire
Thonon-les-Bains
Geneva
Annemasse
Bourg-en-Bresse
Le Salève
Bonneville
Cluses
Martigny
la Roche-sur-Foron
Sallanches
Chamonix-Mont-Blanc
Annecy
St-Gervais-les-Bains
4807
Mont Blanc
Aosta
Rhône-Alpes
Ugine
Aix-les-Bains
Col du Petit St-Bernard (2188)
Lyon
Chambéry
Albertville
Conflans
Bourg-St-Maurice
Aiguebelle
Moûtiers
Val d'Isère
Col de Granier (1134)
Monastère de la Grande Chartreuse
Château du Touvet
902
St-Pierre-de-Chartreuse
Pralognan
3795
P.N.de la Vanoise
Col de l'Iseran (2764)
St-Egrève
Goncelin
St-Jean-de-Maurienne
Valence
Val-Thorens
Grenoble
Col du Télégraphe (1566)
1006
Lanslevillard
Vizille
43
Modane
Turin
Sisteron
le Bourg-d'Oisans
902
Col du Galibier (2650)
la Mure
N.D.de la Salette
Col du Lautaret (2058)
la Bérade
ITALY
P.N.des Écrins
Briançon
Barrage du Sautet
Corps
Ailefroide
l'Argentière-la Bessée
Col de l'Izoard (2361)
St-Bonnet
Château Queyras
Mont Dauphin
902
Gap
Guillestre
Montagne de Céuse
Embrun
Col de Vars (2109)
Serres
Tallard
St-Paul-sur-Ubaye
Avignon
Grand Bérard 3048
la Motte
Seyne
Barcelonnette
Cuneo
902
Col de la Cayolle (2326)
Provence-Alpes-Côte d'Azur
Colmars
P.N.du Mercantour
Château-Arnoux
Digne-les-Bains
Marseille
Guillaumes
Beuil
Barrème
Gorges de Daluis
Annot
Puget-Théniers
Turin
Clue de Chabrières
Moustiers-Ste-Marie
Castellane
Entrevaux
6202
Lac de Ste-Croix
Plan-du-Var
Gorges de la Vésubie
Bargeme
Le Logis-du-Pin
Vence
Genoa
Grand Canyon du Verdon
2204
Grasse
Monaco
Nice
Marseille
Cannes
Antibes
St-Tropez
Côte   d'Azur

Mont Blanc Europe's highest and intensely glaciated peak (4,807 m/ 15,772 ft) should only be climbed by seasoned mountaineers. It forms the divide between the Po and Rhône river systems. Cable cars provide access to the surrounding mountainscape.

Briançon Europe's highest city is surrounded by mighty circular fortifications. Also worth seeing are the Notre-Dame Church and the arched bridge over the Durance River.

St-Paul-de-Vence Picasso was just one of many world-famous artists to settle in the walled Provençal town for a while, and the village keeps its artistic vocation alive.

Nice Its mild climate and its location at the foot of the Maritime Alps by the Mediterranean predestined Nice as the most popular summer resort of wealthy Britons as early as the 19th century. The labyrinthine Old Town hints at the town's proximity to Italy.

Cannes Exclusive hotels and elegant boutiques symbolize this playground of the rich and beautiful, whose International Film Festival has made the town world famous. Particularly worth seeing are the long, sandy beaches next to the Boulevard de la Croisette, the Old Town, the indoor market at the town hall and the old port.

187

Route 11
The Mediterranean Coast

The coastline along the Côte d'Azur, the Golfe du Lion and the Costa Brava could hardly be more diverse or enticing. At the southern edge of the Alps, the Côte d'Azur showcases a landscape of breathtakingly unique beauty. Provence is a paradise for nature lovers and culture enthusiasts, while the Camargue is a near pristine delta landscape. The Côte Vermeille gets its name of "vermillion coast" from the reddish foothills of the Pyrenees which drop away steeply into the sea.

An incredibly varied stretch of coast between Menton on the Côte d'Azur and Collioure on the Côte Vermeille greets visitors with all the beauty the French Midi and the Roussillon, which touches onto Catalonia. Directly behind Monte Carlo's sea of houses and apartments are the captivating mountains of the Alpes-Maritimes, which only begin to flatten out near Nice, allowing the famous cities of Cannes and Antibes to sprawl a bit. The foothills of the Massif des Maures once again straddle the coast beyond St-Tropez where there is really only enough room for small, picturesque villages – your search for sandy beaches will be in vain. But not to worry, you'll find them again around Hyères and other offshore islands in the area. Wine lovers will get their money's worth between Toulon and Cassis –

the wines grown between Bandol and Le Castellet are some of the best in the Midi. Marseille then presents itself as the port city with two faces. Founded by the Greeks, and later a stronghold of the Romans, its cultural history dates back 2,500 years. At the same time, it was for a long time the gateway to the cultures on other Mediterranean shores – Europe, North Africa and the Middle East are all represented in Marseille's multicultural population.

West of Marseille, in the delta between the two mouths of the Rhône, sprawls a breathtakingly beautiful wetland of ponds, marshes, meadows and plains abundant with springs, grass, and salt fields – the Camargue. North of here is where you'll discover the heart of Provence. Cities such as Arles, Avignon and Nîmes are strongholds of European cultural history with unique examples of Roman architecture. The Languedoc-Roussillon region begins west of the Rhône delta and stretches to the

Spanish border with a mix of endlessly long beaches and mountainous hinterland. The Languedoc is home to the troubadours, and the Roussillon was part of Spain until the 1659 Treaty of the Pyrenees. The Catalán legacy in this region can still be seen at every turn.

The Languedoc was also home to the Cathars, who broke away from the Catholic Church in the 13th century. Between Narbonne and Carcassone in the hills of Corbières, where an invitation to taste the local wine should never be refused, are numerous ruins of the proud Cathar castles that once stood here. With its fortress complexes, Carcassonne takes you back in time to the Middle Ages. South of Narbonne, near Leucate, marks the start of and endlessly long, brilliantly white sandy beaches stretching to

St-Tropez: The international jet set discovered this sleepy fishing town in the 1950s and since then yachts and fishing boats have been anchored in perfect harmony side by side in the cosmopolitan port (above). Left: Lavender has been called "the blue gold of Provence". The plants have many uses – the flowers and their oil are used by the perfume industry, in ice-cream, sweets and drinks, as well as in natural medicine; the nectar attracts bees.

ne Franco-Spanish border and the eastern foothills of the Pyrenees.

The last of the French villages before reaching Spain are self-assured fishing villages virtually embedded into the mountains. The Côte Vermeille, the vermilion coast, has largely been spared the concrete jungle in its worst proliferation. Since this part of the coast attracts mainly art lovers and those who love ancient villages we can assume hat it will stay this way.

The coast here was named after the pink or vermillion hues – "vermeille" is the term used to describe the pinkish vermillion of young buds. On

the Côte Vermeille you can expect to find a landscape that is not scorched by drought as well as stunningly beautiful

ocher coastal strips. On this, the French Catalán side, some of the best Pyrenean wines are made, such as the Rouge de

Collioure. In this port village the "Fauves" (the wild ones) once experimented with the colors they saw in the bay.

Left: The wildly romantic Calanques cliffs near Cassis. The Old Town of Carcassonne is enclosed by a double wall of ramparts (right).

The sleepy port of the little town of Menton, located in the farthest eastern corner of the Côte d'Azur.

Detour

The Principality of Monaco

The area where the skyscrapers of "Manhattan on the Côte d'Azur" soar above Monaco's modest 190 ha (222 acres) was first settled by the Greeks, followed by the Romans, and then later ruled by the powerful maritime city-state of Genoa. In 1297, the coastal strip came under the rule of the mighty Grimaldi family, aristocrats from Genoa who later created the principality in 1612.

The Grimaldis built their residence on a rock south of the port and have been able to weather all the storm through the ages, retaining their mini-principality to this day.

Monaco owes its wealth to Prince Charles III, who built a casino on the still-bare headland north of the port in 1865. The revenues were so great that five years later the prince was able to abolish all taxes and thus lay the second foundation for the small state's successful history as a tax

The world-famous casino of Monte Carlo in Monaco.

haven. In his honor, the rock on which the casino was built was given the name of Monte Carlo in 1878, a name that now applies to the entire region north of the port.

The most important sights are the Palais de Monaco (16th–17th centuries); the casino, built by Charles Garnier in 1878; the Musée Océanographique, one of Europe's best aquariums; and the Jardin Exotique, a botanical garden with a unique cactus collection.

Along the north-western Mediterranean coast – our dream route from Menton to Collioure takes you into the hinterland of Provence, along impressive rocky coasts, white beaches, the Rhône delta and the foothills of the Pyrenees, and passes through famous seaside resorts on a journey that includes 2,000-year-old towns in a region rich in cultural history.

① Menton Rich Englishmen discovered the pleasant climate of the Côte d'Azur quite late – around 1870. Villas and magnificent hotels from this Belle Époque recall the glory days of their "winter residences" between the Alps and the sea. The most beautiful view over Menton and the bay here can be seen from the cemetery above the city. Its attractions include the baroque Church of St-Michel, the Register Office in the town hall with frescoes by Jean Cocteau, and the Musée Cocteau in a 17th-century fort.

A few miles beyond Menton is the Principality of Monaco, where a steep street heads into the mountainous interior towards Èze.

② Èze This tiny village sits on the top of a 427-m-high (1,401-ft) rock formation overlooking the Mediterranean Sea as if from a throne. It is one of Provence's most beautiful medieval fortified villages, the so-called "villages perches". A thick stone wall surrounds the houses, which are clustered around a castle donjon high in the mountains. An exotic garden surrounds the former fort, and the view from here reaches as far as Corsica on a clear day. Following the D 6098 toward Nice, the route continues along the sea to Villefranche-sur-Mer.

③ Cap Ferrat In the shadow of mighty pines and hidden behind high walls, the magnificent villas of millionaires cling to the coastline of Cap Ferrat which drops steeply into the sea. The Fondation Ephrussi de Rothschild, probably the most beautiful villa on the Cap Ferrat peninsula, is today open to the public. The stately building, in gorgeous gardens, displays the furnishings bequeathed by Baroness Rothschild.

④ Nice The "unofficial" capital of the Côte d'Azur is a city of contrasts – the grand boulevards try to rekindle the memories of the Belle Époque while parts of the Old Town still have the general appearance of an Italian village.

The Greeks founded Nikaia here, the "Victorious City", in the fifth century BC, but the Romans preferred the hills higher up to establish their vil

The view from the higher mountains to the hilltop village of Èze reveals its exposed position.

age of Cemenelum, present-day Cimiez. The most powerful con of Nice is the Promenade les Anglais, which is directly on he sea. Wealthy British made Nice their retirement home in he mid-19th century and the most impressive mansions from hat era are the Hotel Négresco and the Palais Masséna. The central square in the Old Town, with its maze of small alley-ways and Italian-style houses, is the Cour Saleya, which is home to an attractive flower and vegetable market. The castle hill provides a great view over the Old Town and the Mediterranean sea.

Above: Antibes was founded by the Greeks as Antipolis. The French fortification engineer Vauban constructed the port and the Fort Carrée. The cityscape is defined by medieval towers and the beautiful Château Grimaldi.

Travel information

Route profile
Length : approx. 1,200 km (746 miles)
Time required: 2–3 weeks
Start: Menton
End: Collioure
Route: Menton, Monaco, Nice, Toulon, Marseille, Aix-en-Provence, Arles, Avignon, Orange, Nîmes, Narbonne, Perpignan, Elne, Collioure

When to go:
Spring and fall are the best seasons for the Mediterranean coast. Summer is often very hot. An unpleasant peculiarity of the region around the Rhône delta is the Mistral, an ice-cold northerly wind, which starts up al of a sudden. In winter it can get cold and rain a lot, particularly on higher ground.

Information:
Monaco:
www.visitmonaco.com
Camargue:
www.camargue.fr
Nice:
www.nicetourisme.com
Cannes:
www.cannesinfo.com
www.festival-cannes.com
Côte d'Azur:
www.frenchriviera-tourism.com
Pont du Gard:
www.pontdugard.fr
Provence:
www.decouverte-paca.fr/fr
Avignon:
www.ot-avignon.fr
Montpellier:
www.montpellier.fr
Perpignan:
www.perpignantourisme.com
Collioure:
www.collioure.com

Detour

Antibes and Picasso

Antibes dates back to the ancient Greeks, who originally founded it as Antipolis. Over time the village was fortified, the port and Fort Carrée both being creations of French architect Vauban. Medieval towers and the beautiful Grimaldi Castle dominate the Antibes cityscape, and the old watchtower is now used as the bell tower for the Église de l'Immaculée Conception.

The Château Grimaldi (12th century) was the residence of the Grimaldis of Monaco between 1385 and 1609, and the city allowed Pablo Picasso to use some rooms as his studio in the autumn of 1946, after the war, to "free himself from the evils of civilization". He produced around 150 works in a very short time, which he then gave to what is now the Musée Picasso in return for the hospitality.

The famous Promenade des Anglais in Nice extends for around 8 km (5 miles).

The city's most interesting museums are the Musée d'Art Contemporain as well as the Musée Chagall and the Musée Matisse in Cimiez, which displays works by the artist, who moved to Nice in 1916. One of the most impressive Roman ruins in Nice is the 67-m-long (220-ft), 56-m-wide (184-ft) arena, which at one time used to accommodate about 5,000 Romans. The city's most exotic landmark is the Cathédrale Orthodoxe Russe St-Nicolas dating from 1912.

Enchanting Nice: the Cours Saleya, one of the city's most attractive squares (top); the legendary Négresco Hotel on the Promenade des Anglais (middle), opened in 1913; and the port at night, with fishing boats (bottom).

The picturesque Old Town of Cannes on the slopes of Mont Chevalier.

After passing the airport, the route now leaves the coastal road for a trip into Provence's hilly interior. For art lovers, it is worth taking the 10-km (6-mile) detour into St-Paul-de-Vence, a medieval town where the Fondation Maeght displays modern works of art. From the coast, the D 2085 heads to Grasse, the most important perfume-manufacturing center.

5 Grasse Perfume brought this town its early prosperity, traces of which can still be seen in the medieval alleys and streets of the Old Town. The International Perfume Museum will tell you everything you ever wanted to know about the manufacture of these valuable essences, and the large factories hold daily tours.
From Grasse, the D 6185 heads back to the sea toward Cannes, probably the swankiest place on the entire Côte d'Azur.

6 Cannes This city is of course known for its annual film festival, where the world's rich and famous – and those who want to be – gather on the Boulevard de la Croisette. Cap d'Antibes, with the holiday resorts of Juan-les-Pins and Antibes, is just 11 km (7 miles) from here.
The D 6098 heads from Cannes to Fréjus along the Corniche d'Esterel, which is one of the highlights of the journey with its red rocks, cliffs, many gorges and secluded bays.

7 Fréjus The Roman legacy of this settlement, founded by Julius Caesar in 46 BC, is still clearly visible in the cityscape. Parts of the Roman city wall, the aqueduct and, most importantly, the amphitheater have all been very well preserved.

Red cliffs fringe the coast of the Corniche de l'Esterel between St-Raphaël and Agay.

View from the walls of the
citadel across St-Tropez

The area around the Cathédrale St-Léone is also worth
seeing. The fortified church and
the monastery were founded in
the 12th century, and the considerably older baptistery dates
back as far as the 5th century.

8 **St-Tropez** Between Fréjus
and Hyères, thick pine, oak and
chestnut forests line the coast,
and the hills drop away steeply
into the sea, leaving no room
for urban developments of any
great size on the Corniche des
Maures. The coastal road is all
the more spectacular here,
since it winds its way hugging
the hills at half height and continually providing stunning
views of the sea. Small villages
that were once dedicated to
fishing are nestled tidily into

the small bays, many of them
retaining most of their original
village charm.
St-Tropez is no exception. In
this town – which first became
famous after the film *And God
Created Woman* (1956) with
Brigitte Bardot – it's all about
seeing and being seen. The image of the extravagant life in
the film captivated the youth of
the world and ultimately drew
mass tourism to the sleepy
coastal town.

9 **Hyères** This small town
east of Toulon is the oldest seaside resort on the coast. The medieval Vieille Ville, with its Place
Massillon, is delightful.
The old castle ruins provide an
amazing panoramic view of the
coast. Offshore from Hyères are

the Iles d'Hyères, a group of
islands that President Pompidou
had declared a nature reserve in
1971. A visit to Porquerolles
allows you to imagine how the
entire Côte d'Azur must have
looked before the age of mass
tourism.

10 **Toulon** The capital of the
Var département owes much
of its importance to the large
natural port basin here, which
continues to be an important
marine base even today. It was
the famous architect Vauban
who developed Toulon into a
war port in the 17th century
under King Louis XIV.

11 **Route de Crêtes** La Ciotat
is the starting point for a trip
over the Route des Crêtes to

Cassis. The so-called "Mounta
Ridge Road" leads over th
steep slopes of the Montagr
de la Canaille and provide
magnificent views of the Med
terranean sea and the count
behind the coast. The small po
town of Cassis has been able
retain much of its early charr
particularly in the old alle
directly behind the port whe
the shops and businesses gi
an insight into the original Mi
way of life. West of Cassis, bri
liant white limestone walls ris
straight out of the crystal blu
waters. You can take a boat ric
to the cliffs from Cassis.
If you take the departmenta
road D 559 direct toward Ma
seille and turn left, you'll se
narrow access roads leading t
three bays that are all wort
exploring – Port Miou, Port Pi
and En-Vau. To drive into th
heart of Provence, take th
highway A 50 or the D 559 t

**Top: The Vieux Port in Marseill
has been used as a place of
anchorage for more than
2,500 years. Above left: Two
forts, St Jean and St Nicolas,
once protected the Old Port
from hostile attack.**

Marseille

The second-largest city in France and the country's most important port town boasts a long history of 2,500 years.

Marseille was originally founded as Massalia by Greeks from Asia Minor who built the city on the hill where Notre Dame de la Garde now stands. It came under the yoke of the Romans, who initially were allies, when Caesar eventually conquered the Greek republic in 49 BC. The port city experienced its first big boom in the 12th century when legions of crusaders embarked from here on their journeys to Jerusalem. For the next few centuries, Marseille was the most important port in the Mediterranean.

Notre-Dame-de-la-Garde guards the city and its port.

The heart of Marseille continues to beat in the Old Port quarter. It marks the beginning of the city's main road, the Canebière, which connects the port with the rest of the city and was once the icon of a lively town that liked to celebrate. The entrance to the Old Port is flanked on the north side by the Fort St-Jean and on the south side by the Fort St-Nicolas. The best view over the port and the city is from the Plateau de la Croix in front of the Basilica of Notre Dame de la Garde, Marseille's most visible landmark.

Attractions include the St-Victor Basilica, a 5th-century fortified church with crenellations, in whose crypt are housed early-Christian sarcophagi and sculptural fragments; the Notre Dame de la Garde Basilica (19th century), a neo-Byzantine church with a gold-plated figure of Mary on the bell tower and the Chateau d'If (1516–1528) on the rock in front of the port, accessed from the Quai des Belges. The citadel was the state prison from 1580.

Sip a coffee or an apéro in one of the many inviting open-air cafés in Aix-en-Provence and soak up the southern joie de vivre.

The Romans in southern France

When the Romans elected to overrun and conquer southern France, the decision was strategic in nature – after the victory over Carthage in the 2nd century BC they needed a safe land route to Spain. The hammer fell in 102 BC when Marius crushed the Teutons at the foot of the St-Victoire Massif. As a result, Aquae Sextiae Saluvorium was founded – today's Aix-en-Provence. One after the other in quick succession, the Greek settlements throughout the entire region were remodeled as Roman towns to reflect the design of Rome. The streets were built according to a checkerboard grid pattern with each block approximately 100 m (328 ft) long. This layout can most clearly be seen

The amphitheater in nearby Orange represents the 2,000 years of Roman heritage.

in Orange and Arles. A Roman city's center point was its forum, a square lined with colonnaded walkways around which temples and other important public buildings were grouped. Extravagant stages and large amphitheaters satisfied the Romans' need for high culture as well as more lowbrow entertainment. The triumphal arches, public baths and aqueducts continue to provide testimony to this day to the architectural and engineering achievements of the Roman occupation army in France.

Aubagne and then the D 96 to Aix-en-Provence.

⑫ Marseille (see p. 209).

⑬ Aix-en-Provence It was the Romans originally founded the colony of Aquae Sextiae Saluvorium on the former Celtic-Ligurian town of Entremont in 122 BC – what is now Aix-en-Provence. This spa and university town eventually became the capital of Provence at the end of the 12th century and remained so for hundreds of years. It also developed into a city of artists and academics. The Old Town is tucked between the Cours Mirabeau, an avenue of plane trees with gorgeous 18th-century city palaces, and the Cathedral of St-Sauveur (12th to 17th C.) with a Merovingian baptistery.
Sights worth exploring include the city hall (17th-century), the Musée des Tapisseries and the Atelier de Paul Cézanne. A frequent subject for the city's most famous son was the Mont St-Victoire in the east of the town. The shortest route to Arles heads along the A 8 and A 7 to Salon-de-Provence and from there crosses the eastern part of the Rhône delta on the A 54.

⑭ Arles The gateway to the Camargue was an area settled by the Celts, the Greeks and the Romans. Emperor Constantine had a splendid residence here, where he summoned a council in AD 314. Today, Arles still has important Roman buildings – the amphitheater, an oval structure of 137 m (446 ft) by 107 m (351 ft) wide with a capacity of 20,000; and the theater, which could fit 12,000 people into its semicircle. The Romanesque Church of St-Trophime is a masterpiece of Provençal stone masonry, with a portal from 1190. The Romanesque-Gothic cloister adjacent to the church is considered the most beautiful in all of Provence.
From Arles, the D 17 heads

north-east to one of Provence's best-known villages, Les Baux.

⑮ Les Baux-de-Provence This rock village is perched on a 900-m-long (2,953-ft) by 200-m-wide (656-ft) rocky ridge that rises dramatically out of the Alpilles range. In the Middle Ages, troubadours performed their courtly love songs in the once proud fort of Les Baux. The fort's unique location on a rock combined with the stunning views over the expanses of the Camargue and the Rhône delta draw countless visitors to this car-free town every year. From Les Baux, the road crosses the Alpilles to St-Rémy, a 24-km-long (15-mile) mountain range between Rhône and Durance.

⑯ St-Rémy-de-Provence Nostradamus was born in this quintessential Provencal town in 1503, and van Gogh painted his picture of *A Wheatfield, with Cypresses* here in 1889.

In Aix-en-Provence you can discover magnificent town houses, such as the entrance to the Tribunal de Commerce, embellished with figurative columns.

The popes of Avignon built a castle here in the 14th century. Today, the wine from this region is one of the best in the Côtes du Rhône region.

If you have enough time, make a detour into the Luberon or to Villeneuve-les-Avignon before continuing on your journey to Orange (see Detour p. 211).

18 **Orange** Emperor Augustus founded this location as the Roman town of Arausio in 35 BC. The theater was built soon after, and today it is one of the most beautiful Roman works in Provence. The large stage wall is 103 m (338 ft) wide and 37 m (121 ft) high. On the north side

Large picture: view of Avignon, capital of the Vaucluse département, from the opposite Rhône bank. Only four of the arches of the Pont d'Avignon of the song still stand today. Above left: Les Arènes in Arles, the remains of the two-tiered Roman Amphitheater.

St-Rémy's predecessor was the Roman city of Glanum, about 1 km (0.6 miles) south of the present center. An 18-m (59-ft) mausoleum dates back to this time and the Arc Municipal to the time of Emperor Augustus.

17 **Avignon** This former papal city dominates the left bank of the Rhône and is still surrounded by a 4.5-km-long (3-mile) city wall. The Rocher des Doms and the enormous Palais des Papes (Papal Palace) are an impressive sight even from a distance. Seven French popes resided here between 1309 and 1377, the time of the Papal Schism. The last "antipope" did not flee his palace until 1403. The mighty fort-like Palais des Papes was built during this century-long schism, but next to nothing remains of the once ostentatious interior decor. The famous bridge, Pont St-Bénézet (perhaps better known as Pont d'Avignon), was built in 1177, but only four of its original 22 arches still stand today. From Aix, the journey heads north to two more of Europe's most beautiful Roman constructions. Near Sorgues, the D 17 turns off toward Châteauneuf-du-Pape.

The village of Roussillon in the Luberon was a center for the quarrying of ocher until the end of the 18th century. The quarries around the village yielded more than 15 different hues. You can now explore some of the former ocher quarries on educational trails. The shining ocher tones also provide the facades of the houses in Roussillon with a special charm.

As well as vineyards and wheatfields, it is sunflowers that dominate the country-side in the Luberon massif.

Detour

Luberon and Haute Provence

East of Avignon, halfway between the Alps and the Mediterranean, extends the sprawling limestone Luberon massif. The rocky region, home to lonely oak forests, small mountain villages and ancient stone houses, has managed to preserve its natural beauty. The mountains, which reach 1,125 m (3,691 ft) in places, still contain wide swathes of uninhabited land where over 1,000 different types of plants thrive. The Parc Naturel Régional du Luberon was established in 1977 to protect the vegetation.

However, the seclusion of many parts of the Luberon today belies the fact that this tertiary limestone range has been settled by humans for thousands of years. In the Middle Ages, this place was home to villages nestled in vales and hollows, with thick-walled houses and churches that also doubled as refuges. Inhabitants of the region lived on the sparse results of agricultural cultivation. When incomes were no longer sufficient, the villages in the northern sections were abandoned.

One of the symbols of the South are some 3,000 one- or two-storey stone huts located seemingly randomly in the fields either on their own or in picturesque groups. Known here as *bories*, they were made using lime slabs without mortar and were used by farmers as

stalls and sheds. For their construction, each row of stones was staggered a little toward the middle so that when a height of about 3–4 m (10–13 ft) was reached, the final opening on top could be closed with a single slab. The most beautiful bories are found around Gordes, at the edge of the Plateau de Vaucluse on the northern side of the Luberon massif.

Nestled into a hilly knoll, Gordes welcomes visitors with arcaded lanes and a 16th-century castle. To its south is the Village des Bories with about twenty restored bories.

Another of the Luberon's landmarks are its ocher quarries, which are grouped around the pretty village of Roussillon. One of the most impressive is the now-closed quarry at Sentier des Ochres.

You'll understand why the Luberon is so arid after a visit to Fontaine de Vaucluse. Here, in a grotto at the foot of a massive rock formation is the source of the Sorgue River, the largest spring in France and one of the largest karst springs in the world with up to 90,000 liters (409,090 gal) of water bubbling up from the mountains of the Luberon and the Vaucluse per second.

Hidden in a small gorge on the Plateau de Vaucluse is a very different sort of attraction – the Abbey de Sénanque.

Founded in 1148 by Cistercians, the abbey had its heyday in the early 13th century and was destroyed in 1544. It wasn't until 1854 that seventy-two monks took the risk of rebuilding it. Lavender fields surround the monastery with its church and cloister.

If you wish to appreciate the fascinating Luberon countryside from above, a hike up the 1,125-m (3,691-ft) Mourre Nègre, located east of Apt, is recommended. The 1,909-m (6,263-ft) Mont Ventoux is the highest point in Provence and also provides fabulous views. The summit can be reached on foot or by car. On your ascent, you will

notice an impressive change in the vegetation on the mountain – from the lavender fields and vineyards at the foot of the mountain, to oak, beech and pine forests, and finishing with the bare rock summit with groundcover plants.

A purple sea of lavender surrounds the venerable Abbaye de Sénanque (top), founded in 1148. Middle: A farm in Haute Provence, nestled at the foot of the Mont de Vaucluse. Purple lavender fields extends for miles, the quintessential image of Provence (above).

The **Pont du Gard**, a three-tiered aqueduct bridge, represents masterpiece of Roman engineering. It is all that remains of an approximately 50-km-long (31-mi) water conduit from Uzès to Nîmes. From the first century AD, some 20,000 cu m (707,000 cu ft) of water were transported every day in a covered canal on the uppermost tier. The 49 m-high (161-ft) and 275 m-long (902-ft)

bridge was built without mortar from vast stone blocks, some of which weighed up to six tons. An army of slaves transported them with the aid of a pulley system. After around 500 years, however, the conduit finally had to be abandoned because it nd calcified. The impressive stone bridge was assigned the coveted UNESCO World Cultural Heritage status in 1985.

The Saint-Jean-Baptiste Cathedrale on the Place Gambetta in Perpignan also has the tomb with the marble statue of King Sanchos of Mallorca, who commissioned the building of the cathedral in 1324.

The Camargue

Covering a marsh, meadow and grasslands area of roughly 140,000 ha (345,940 acres), the delta between the two main forks of the mouth of the Rhône is one of the largest wetlands in Europe. Agriculture – predominantly rice cultivation – is concentrated on the northern part of the Camargue, while salt is extracted in the flat lagoons of the south-eastern section.

The southern part, on the other hand, is a nature paradise not found anywhere else in Europe. The delta's lush grassy meadows are home to not only the well-known Camargue horses and Camargue bulls, but also to numerous water and marsh birds – around 10,000 pairs of flamingos breed in the marshes, the largest of which is the Etang de Vaccarès. Twice a year, more than 350 species of birds stop at the Parc Ornithologique du Pont de Grau in the south-west.

Camargue horses

The white Camargue horses are a semi-wild race that already features in the Solutré cave paintings. Their physical characteristics include a compact body, angular head and thick mane. The horses are born black or brown and only grow their famous white coat after the age of five. If the wild horses are broken in to saddles and bridles at a young age, they can be enduring mounts and very useful to herdsmen in the supervision and control of their herds of cattle. A number of providers offer the chance to go for a ride into the marshes, to the beaches or to see the bull herds, even to amateur riders accompanied by experienced *guardiens*.

of the city is the triumphal arch of its kind, with a height of 20 m (66 ft), which is actually a town-founding arch.

Driving south-west along the A 9 you reach the Pont du Gard, a superb Roman aqueduct.

⑲ Nîmes This city of temples, public baths and theaters was founded in AD 16, by Emperor Augustus. The Romans' most impressive building is the amphitheater, with an oval arena and tiered stone benches that seated 25,000 spectators. The Maison Carrée, dating from the second and third centuries AD, counts as one of Europe's best-preserved Roman temples, with columns and decorative friezes. Many public baths, temples and a theater (today a park) are concentrated around the Jardin de la Fontaine.

About 20 km (12 miles) north-east of Nîmes is the Roman

aqueduct Pont du Gard. From Nîmes, the route heads along the north-western Camargue to the town of Aigues-Mortes.

⑳ Aigues-Mortes This town impresses visitors with the mighty ramparts, which are still intact – you can walk along sections of them. Aigues-Mortes, or "Place of Dead Water", was constructed by Louis XI in the 13th century to consolidate his

power on the Mediterranean coast. The Tour de Constance has the best view over the city and the Camargue.

㉑ Saintes-Maries-de-la-Mer A 30-km-long (19-mile) road heads through the Camargue to the main village, Les Saintes-Maries-de-la-Mer, known for the Sinti and Roma pilgrimage held each May. The Romanesque church with its battlements

Visible from afar is the Saint-Nazaire Cathedrale, the landmark of Béziers on the Canal du Midi. The Romanesque and Gothic church was built between the 12th and the 14th centuries. In the foreground the 13th-century Pont Vieux spanning the River Orb.

Detour

Canal du Midi

Since time immemorial people have dreamed of connecting the Mediterranean and the Atlantic but this didn't become reality until Paul Riquet, an engineer from Béziers, took on the task between 1666 and 1681. With the 240-km-long (149-mile) Canal du Midi he connected the Mediterranean port town of Sète to the industrial city of Toulouse, where he joined it with the Garonne River, navigable from Toulouse onward, thus creating a route through to the Atlantic. The canal, with its countless dams, aqueducts, bridges and locks, was an engineering masterpiece for the 17th century and, for the trade it became the backbone of the transportation of goods in the Languedoc region.

Today, the canal is a romantic waterway for leisure skippers for whom the French way of life is more important than a quick journey. Houseboats can be rented in Sète, Béziers, Narbonne, Carcassonne, Castelnaudary and Toulouse, allowing you to make some interesting journeys. The journey is done at a leisurely pace and in some parts passes beneath long avenues of plane trees, through impressive landscapes, past vineyards and cultural attractions. Along the way, there is still time for

nd crenellated platform looks ke a medieval castle.

2 Montpellier The capital of he Hérault département is ome to France's oldest Botani Garden, among other things. he focal point of the city is the lace de la Comédie, with a 9th-century opera house. Its ttractions include the 17th-entury patrician houses.

3 Béziers The route now eads via Montpellier to this ovely city on the Canal du Midi. he town's landmark is the nassive 14th-century Cathé-rale St-Nazaire, perched like a ort on a mountain ridge.

4 Narbonne This town was nce the an important Roman ort. The Horreum, an under-round granary built in the first entury BC, is visible evidence f this time. The Cathédrale

St-Just, with its beautiful sculptures and vivid stained-glass windows, dates back to the 13th century. The Palais des Archevêques is a fort-like complex with massive towers (14th century). Some 60 km (37 mi) west of Narbonne is Carcassonne, the fortified medieval town par excellence.

25 Carcassonne This city on the banks of the Aude is visible from afar. Its double ring of crenellated ramparts dates back to King Louis IX, who began to enlarge the Roman city in the 13th century. The Porte Narbonnaise takes you to the Old Town, where the most important sights are the Château Comtal as well as the Basilique St-Nazaire, home to France's finest stained-glass windows. The castle was built in the 12th century and has five defense towers.

The journey heads toward Perpignan on the D 118 to Quillan, then continues on the D 117. Here it's worth making a detour to the Château de Peyrepertuse, the most impressive Cathar castle ruins in the Corbières hills.

26 Perpignan The capital of Roussillon had its heyday under the kings of Mallorca in the 13th and 14th centuries. The fortified Palais des Rois de Majorque, picturesquely built around an arcaded courtyard, is evidence of this time. The two-storey chapel, a Gothic masterpiece featuring Moorish

Top: The ancient fortified city of Carcassonne was declared a UNESCO World Cultural Heritage Site in 1997.
Large picture: The Maison Carrée in Nîmes is an important Roman relic. The temple, built in 19 BC, avoided destruction.

The Canal du Midi, a World Cultural Heritage Site.

fishing, swimming or simply relaxing. A boat permit is not required to charter a boat –all important instructions are given at the start.

Some of France's most select wines are cultivated in the mountainous countryside of the Languedoc region.

elements, is a real gem. The Cathédrale de St-Jean was begun in 1324 and completed in 1509 and the houses on the palm-lined River Têt promenade are painted in turquoise or pink. Catalán influence in

Perpignan is noticeable particularly in the summer months when the Place de la Loge becomes a stage for Sardana, a Catalán dance. You'll also find the most beautiful building in the city here, the Loge de Mer,

built in 1397. You'll now continue southward on the D 114 to reach Elne.

27 Elne Once the main in the Roussillon, Elne today only has some 7,000 inhabitants. Its

11th-century cathedral is visible from afar, towering above the Old Town. Its beautiful cloisters date from the 12th to 14th centuries and are remarkable for their column capital. Also worth seeing here is the

Pont du Gard The 49-m-high (161-ft) bridge was built by the Romans over 2,000 years ago and also served as a water channel. For 500 years it supplied the citizens of Nîmes with cool mountain water.

Arles This city, located at the gateway to the Camargue, was for a while Vincent van Gogh's place of residence and has many Roman buildings. The amphitheater seats 20,000 people.

Carcassonne This city is encircled by a double ring of ramparts dating back to the 13th century. These enclose the 12th-century Château Comtal Castle.

Nîmes The most impressive buildings in this city, which was founded in the year AD 16, are the Roman amphitheater with a former seating capacity of 25,000, and the Maison Carrée, one of Europe's best-preserved Roman temples. Other sites in the city include the Romanesque Cathédrale Notre Dame et St-Castor and the 18th-century Jardin de la Fontaine.

Eine The cloister of the small town's cathedral is a remarkable place, featuring an abundance of vivid late-Romanesque motifs.

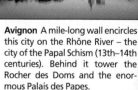

Avignon A mile-long wall encircles this city on the Rhône River – the city of the Papal Schism (13th–14th centuries). Behind it tower the Rocher des Doms and the enormous Palais des Papes.

Carmargue Black bulls, semi-wild white horses, huge mountains of salt as well as flocks of flamingos and other unique birds are typical of the vast Rhône delta.

FRANCE · Castres · Clermont-Ferrand · Nîme · Montpellier · 22 · La Grande-Motte · 20 · Aigues-Mortes · Saintes-de-la · Toulouse · Carcassonne · 25 · Lézignan-Corbières · 6113 · Coursan · Béziers · 23 · Pézenas · Frontignan · Sète · 612 · Agde · Cap d'Agde · Limoux · 118 · Abbaye de Fontfroide · Narbonne · 24 · Quillan · Couiza · Château de Peyrepertuse · Leucate-Plage · St-Paul-de-Fenouillet · 117 · Salses-le-Château · Bourg-Madame · 116 · Perpignan · 26 · 914 · Pic du Canigou · 2784 · Elne · 27 · Collioure · 28 · Banyuls · Cap Cerbère · Pyrénées · Ripoll · Figueres · 260 · Sant Pere de Rodes · Cap de Creus · Cadaqués · l'Escala · SPAIN · Vic · Girona · Pals · Palafrugell · Berga · Parc Natural de Montseny · Llagostera · Palamós · 253 · Lleida · Circuit de Catalunya · 16 · Blanes · Sant Feliu de Guíxols · Tossa de Mar · Lloret de Mar · Malgrat de Mar · Mataró · Monestir de Sant Cugat · BARCELONA · València · 32

The Château Royal fortress and the fortified church of Notre-Dame des Anges in Collioure were built to plans by Vauban.

uthern gallery with its rather zarre fabled creatures, animals and bluish white marble gures.

hen the bishops' see moved Perpignan in the 17th century, ne still remained a lively market town. The route continues south-east on the D 914 to Collioure. The coastal road snakes along the vermillion rocks of the Côte Vermeille, where ancient fishing villages are tucked into picturesque bays.

28 Collioure The picturesque fishing village is an attractive destination especially for artlovers. in the early 20th century, the Fauves lived here, among them Matisse and Derain. On the "Chemin du Fauvisme" trail you can discover the places that inspired them. The village panorama is characterized by the protruding spit of land with the church Notre-Dame-des Anges and the royal castle – both designed by Vauban.

Luberon The limestone massif, up to 1,125 m (3,691 ft) high, is known for its flora and fauna. Typical of the region are bories,huts and shelters for shepherds built from stone without mortar at the edge of the vineyards and lavender fields. Other sights include the ocher quarries of Roussillon and the Vaucluse spring.

Antibes Pablo Picasso used the 12th-century Château Grimaldi as his studio in 1946. Many of his works can be seen here.

Monaco The principality is a mix of high-rise and magnificent mansions including the cathedral and the Grimaldi palace. The views of Monte Carlo, a spit of land that juts out into the Mediterranean below an 800-m-high (2,625-ft) high rock, make you swoon.

Nice The Promenade des Anglais, the Hotel Négresco and the Palais Masséna are symbols of the unofficial capital of the Côte d'Azur. Also worth seeing are the maze-like old town, the flower and vegetable market, the Musée d'Art Contemporain and the Musée Chagall.

Marseille France's largest port city has many tourist attractions. High above the city is the Basilique of Notre Dame de la Garde. Narrow, stepped lanes and idyllic squares, but most of all the lively port and fish market lend the city its charm. The Château d'If is located on an island offshore from the city.

Cannes The trendiest place on the Côte d'Azur has a city wall around the Old Town. The Boulevard de la Croisette is world renowned.

St-Tropez This fishing village, located on a little peninsula, has been one of the most popular Côte d'Azur seaside resorts since the 1950s. The former citadel dates back to the 16th/17th centuries.

Route 12

A tour of Corsica

White limestone in Bonifacio, red granite in the Calanche and a verdant wilderness in the Castagniccia – it is no coincidence that the Greeks once gave Corsica the name *kalliste* – "the beautiful". The island offers a welcome dose of untouched scenery in a hectic, modern world, with spectacular coastlines, towering mountains and lush green forests.

Corsica, the third-largest island in the Mediterranean after Sicily and Sardinia, covers an area of 8,580 sq km (3,315 sq mi) and could aptly be described as a "mountain range in the sea". The natural contrasts here are mind-blowing, from temperate seas to chilly mountain peaks. But it is not just the magnificent mountains that impress visitors to Corsica. There are vast pine and chestnut groves, long sandy beaches in the east and hidden coves in the west that are ideal for a swim.

Corsica is just 85 km (55 mi) at its widest point across from east to west. From north to south the island extends for 185 km (110 mi) between its farthest points. The island of Elba, to the north-east, is visible on a clear day, and Sardinia is just 12 km (8 mi) off the southern tip of the island over the Strait of Bonifacio. It is only

80 km (50 mi) to the Italian mainland and 180 km (110 mi) to the French coast. In the north,

Corsica is bordered by the Ligurian Sea and in the east by the Tyrrhenian Sea.

The island has had a long ar eventful history. In the sevent millennium BC, Ligurian imm grants arrived in Corsica ar mixed with the original inhab tants of the island. The resu was a rich megalith cultu that produced numerous cham bered tombs and menhirs tha can still be seen today. Aft being occupied by the Greek and Romans, Corsica became territory of Pisa in 1077. The followed 500 years of Genoes rule to which the citadels Corte, Bastia and Calvi as we as the watchtowers along th coast attest. In 1769, the islan finally became part of France. Corsica is blessed with a stu ning natural interplay of ligh and color, and captivating de lightful scents emanating from the maquis shrubland, which dotted with wild rosemar thyme, lavender, fennel an gorse. To get to know all of th

Above: The surf has whittled soft curves into the high cliffs below the Ville Haute, or upper town, of Bonifacio.
Left: Not far to the south-east is the dramatically rugged coastline of Cape Pertusato, the southernmost point of Corsica on the narrow strait across from the Italian island of Sardinia.

various facets of Corsica we recommend a tour that covers the entire island. From the lively port city of Bastia your journey will first take you around the fascinatingly diverse Cape Corse before continuing along the west coast. From Porto you will head into the heartland of the island until you reach Corte, after which you will travel back to the coast to Ajaccio, where Napoleon was born and a number of cultural offerings as well as superb beaches await you. Bonifacio, once a hideaway for Mediterranean pirates, extends in a spectacular spot atop white limestone cliffs and invites vis-

Left: A portrait of Napoleon in his coronation regalia in the Museum Fesch in Ajaccio.
Right: Red rocks and the blue sea make out the spectacular scenery of Les Calanche in the Gulf of Porto.

itors to meander through the labyrinthine lanes in the Old Town. Via the Col de Bavella, one

of the most beautiful mountain sceneries on the island, and the dreamy Castagniccia region

you'll arrive back at the starting point of the route in the ferry port of Bastia.

Picturesque coastal towns
with boats in the port at the
northern tip of Corsica –

Napoleon – Corsica's most famous son

This legendary Corsican was born in Ajaccio in 1769 but he soon left his home island, in 1779. After a series of military successes Napoleon then managed to usurp power in France and in 1804 even declared himself

Statue of Napoleon in the Place St-Nicolas in Bastia

emperor. An ingenious commander, he soon looked to conquer Europe but ultimately failed during an attempt to invade Russia in 1812 and during the Battle of Leipzig in 1813. After his return from exile on Elba, he lost the Battle of Waterloo in 1815 and was banished to the island of St-Helena in the southern Atlantic where he died in 1821.

Hiking, swimming and a bit of culture – the leisure activities on Corsica are as diverse as the countryside. In addition to its many cultural landmarks, the imposing landscape of the island's heartland will excite any walking enthusiast, as a number of long-distance trails lead you through fascinating mountain scenery. Those who prefer the embrace of the sea will enjoy more than 1,000 km (600 mi) of coastline.

❶ Bastia Most visitors will begin their Corsica tour in Bastia, the second-largest city and main business center of the island. The city's main landmark is the majestic baroque Church of St-Jean-Baptiste (1636–1666) From the castle above the city built between 1480 and 1521 you'll enjoy expansive views o the port up to Cap Corse, the next stop on this tour.

Take the D 80 out of Bastia t the north. The 40-km (24-mi scenic route will take yo around the 12- to 15-km-wide (7- to 9-mi) peninsula.

Travel information

Route profile
Length: c. 700 km (435 miles)
Time required: 2–3 weeks
Start: Bastia
End: Bastia
Route: Bastia, Erbalunga, Centuri-Port, St-Florent, L'Île Rousse, Speloncato, Calvi, Corte, Ajaccio, Filitosa, Sartène, Bonifacio, Porto-Vecchio, Col de Bavella, Ponte Leccia, Bastia.

Safe driving:
When ascending from the flat coastal regions up into the high mountains especially, the roads are often narrow, featuring many bends and steep gradi-

ents. Make sure therefore that you allow plenty of time when driving on minor roads, especially on the way to Corte.

Where to stay:
Along the coast there are plenty of opportunities for camping in glorious surroundings. French campsites are classified as one to five stars. Wild camping is forbidden in the summer because of the great danger of starting forest fires. There is also a diverse selection of accommodation ranging from country homes to rent (list from Gîtes de

France) and hotels (book in good time for high season) to well-equipped and attractive holiday villages and resort towns along the coast.

Information:
Agence du Tourisme de la Corse
17, boulevard du Roi Jerôme
20181 Ajaccio Cédex 01
Tel 04 95 51 00 00
www.visit-corsica.com

Gîtes de France
56, Rue Saint-Lazare
75439 Paris Cédex 9
Tel 01 49 70 75 75
www.gites-de-france.com

Centuri-Port near Cap Corse
(far left) and St-Florent
(left) with the Church of
Santa Maria Assunta

Erbalunga and Cap Corse
Like a giant finger, Cap Corse points straight out into the Gulf of Genoa. The road takes you through a number of mountain hamlets and fishing villages, among them Erbalunga, a postcard town if ever there was one, with picturesque old houses built on rock foundations that reach right down to the waterfront. Overlooking it all is a Genoese watchtower dating from 1512.

Centuri-Port and Cap Corse Another quaint village: weathered gray, yellow and pink houses with slate roofs line the only natural port on the north-western end of Cap Corse, at Centuri-Port. The ancient Greeks and Romans were already well aware of the town's ideal location.
Beyond Nonza, along the western coast of Corsica, the steep mountains drive straight down into the sea. Following the D 80 and D 81 you will eventually reach St-Florent.

St-Florent This idyllic resort town with rows of bright

houses is also home to one of Corsica's largest yacht marinas. The quaint corners of the port invite you for a stroll while the Genoese citadel from 1568 is also worth a look despite being somewhat more modest than other Genoese structures on the island. The D 81, N 1197 and N 197 will take you to the next point on your tour.

L'Île Rousse This port town owes its name to the island Île de la Pietra just off the coast, which turns blood-red in the sunset: L'Île Rousse. The sandy beaches and the charm-

ing Old Town are a major draw for tourists, who arrive all year long. Winding mountain roads take you toward Monticello and on to Speloncato.

Speloncato and Balagne An important part of any Corsica tour is a foray across the hilly Balagne region. Speloncato, situated high up on a rocky promontory, is one of the most beautiful towns in the area with its baroque collegiate church and the palazzo providing impressive testimony of this village's former importance. Passing through Nessa,

Muro and Cateri you will once again follow the N 197.

Calvi Calvi was once an important Genoese staging point with a citadel stretching out into the sea, and it would have likely lost its significance after the French took over if it

Top left: The natural harbor of Bastia was already prized by the Genoese. Top right: The best views are from up high – pictured the Citadel in Calvi above the harbor and the mountain village of Speloncato (above) in the Balagne.

The Scandola Nature Reserve with its reddish rock formations in the Gulf of Girolata

hadn't been for its undeniably attractive location. The sizable bay and lively port district give the town a real Mediterranean ambience and are a big draw for tourists.

8 Porto Surrounded by bright red cliffs on one side and the deep blue sea on the other, the resort town of Porto sits atop rocky cliffs with a massive Genoese tower at the entrance to the harbor. The town at the mouth of the Porto River consists of two parts connected by an avenue lined with eucalyptus trees: Porto and Marine de Porto. Numerous hotels, an enchanting natural landscape and a beach in the town all make Porto a popular tourist destination with plentiful options nearby for entertaining excursions. The next two points are among those.

9 Les Calanche Between Porto and Piana lies Corsica's most impressive coastline, the Calanche, a range of red rocks 2 km (1.2 miles) long that was given UNESCO World Natural Heritage status. Touring the Calanche on foot is the only way to truly enjoy the interplay

of red stone, blue sea and green vegetation. The charming Piana, a village perched high up in the mountains with pastel-shade houses and an 18th-century church, is one starting point for an excursion into this stunning landscape.

10 Girolata/Scandola From Porto you can also take an excursion to the heritage-listed fishing village of Girolata, which is closed to motorized traffic and only accessible on foot or by boat. Once a popular hideaway for pirates, Girolata is now considered one of the most beautiful towns in the Mediterranean precisely because of its remoteness. West of the town is a mountainous peninsula, Scandola, boasting reddish rock formations. This area is also a UNESCO World Natural Heritage site, in addition to being under special protection as a Réserve Naturelle. Many birds nest here including ospreys.

11 Gorges de Spelunca From Porto, the D 84 begins to twist and turn, with many steep inclines, through the spectacular Spelunca Gorge and into the

hilly landscape of the interior. The Porto River has cut deeply through the land here creating some awe-inspiring formations with chestnut and pine forests that have long been a popular destination for hikers.

In Évisa you'll get an unforgettable view of the surrounding mountains and the sunny harbor of Porto. A summer resort, this town at an altitude of 800 m (2,640 ft) not only offers old chestnut groves and stunning views, but also a cooler climate during the often scorchingly hot summer months.

Continuing on the route by car you'll turn from the D 84 onto the N 193 at Francardo, in a southerly direction. From there you head toward Corte, the "Heart of Corsica".

12 Corte The fortress or citadel is Corte's landmark. Rising well above the rooftops it is now home to the important Musée de la Corse. The buildings here were reconstructed by Italian architect and UNESCO representative Andrea Bruno. Ville Haute, the upper town of Corte, has charming narrow alleyways and old houses that climb the eastern

flank of the mountain. Corte also home to Corsica's on university, which gives it a spe cial flair and a lively studen population.

In the Corsican battle for inde pendence, Corte has been th focus of much drama. Locate in the deep interior, the cit was controlled by Corsican na tionalists. Pasquale Pao (1725–1807) a patriot and th president of the Corsican Re public, even made Corte th capital of the island from 175 to 1769. The city is now a per fect starting point for excur sions into the surroundin mountains of the interior. Th magnificent Restonica Valle south-west of Corte deserve at least a one-day trip.

13 Gorges de la Restonic This valley with its wild strear is bound by steep rock walls. T the west it narrows and take the form of a gorge where th vegetation is dominated b chestnut trees, Corsican blac pines and the Corte pine, whic only exists on this small patc of the island. The classic hikin trail through the valley begin a short way beyond the bridg over the Timozza, a small rive

Nested on a rocky point high above the town: the Citadel of Corte

It traverses a number of different vegetation zones and takes some four to five hours to complete. Refreshment awaits you along the way with the cool Restonica River tempting you for a swim or a splash around in its many pools. In the year 2000, the valley suffered a devastating forest fire. In order to avoid any further such catastrophes the area was designated a nature reserve. Hikers should ask at the tourist information office in Corte about the rules of the park.

14 Ajaccio In 1811, Napoleon Bonaparte, the most famous Corsican in history, named his hometown the capital of the island, and this has not changed since then. The town of his birth, founded in 1492, is still defined in many ways by the memory of its most famous son.

Top left: The heavily eroded porphyry rocks are typical of the Calanche region near Piana. Top right: The town of Corte in the very heart of Corsica, shrouded in clouds. Left: The old Genoese bridge Pont de Zaglia leads across the Spelunca Gorge.

U Trinichellu

The train from Ajaccio to Bastia takes about three and a half hours during which it covers a distance of 158 km (100 mi) on the "Trinichellu". The

The Vecchio Viaduct by Gustave Eiffel

journey from coast to coast passes through Corte in the very heart of the island. The line was opened in 1888 and is still considered a pioneering effort. Between Vivario and Venaco the train crosses the Vecchio River over the Pont du Vecchio, a viaduct designed by Gustave Eiffel. Corsica's rail network covers a total of 230 km (144 mi) and has 38 tunnels and 76 bridges. Trains offer a good way to enjoy the beautiful mountain landscapes, the exquisite aromas of the maquis shrubland and the overall diversity of the island.

The Îles Sanguinaires are an extension of a promontory in the Gulf of Ajaccio.

Genoese towers – landmarks of vigilance

Most of the *tours* or towers, marked on Corsican maps are of Genoese origin, some are Pisan, some Florentine. Unlike the rectangular Pisan towers, Genoese towers were round structures that measured between 12 and 17 m (40 to 56 ft) in height and had imposing diameters of up to 10 m (33 ft). Roughly 150 of them line the coast of Corsica and give the island its unique look. About sixty towers have been restored while the rest have fallen into disrepair. Mostly they are classed as *monuments historiques*.

A majority of the watchtowers in Corsica were built in the 16th century on commission from the Bank of St George – Genoa mortgaged the island to the bank's financiers. The youngest of the towers are from the 17th century. As a whole, they represented a defense system against

The Genoese tower in Erbalunga on Cap Corse

attack from the sea. Tower watchmen used smoke, fire and conch signals to warn the population as soon as enemies approached. Within hours the signal could be passed from tower to tower all the way around the island.

The most impressive example of a Genoese tower stands near Campomoro by Propriano. The strategic advantages of this tower, which was restored in 1989, are immediately obvious. Once you have climbed the stone stairs and caught a glimpse of the superb views across the water and of the Gulf of Valinco you will no longer be regret having made the slightly arduous ascent.

The cathedral, built between 1582 and 1593 and featuring a modest façade but a rich interior, is well worth visiting, while the Old Town offers its visitors plentiful options for a meander among the Italian-influenced cafés, bars and pizzerias. The Rue Cardinal Fesch – which is also the main street of the old port district of Borgo – is a great place for a stroll to take it all in. For those interested in delving deeper into Napoleon's turbulent story, a visit to the gigantic Maison Bonaparte on Place Letizia is a must. His birthplace, it displays documents, portraits and other memorabilia of the Bonaparte family. The Musée Fesch in the Palais Fesch has an important collection of Italian paintings.

⑮ Îles Sanguinaires On the Route des Sanguinaires, the D 111 coastal road, you'll pass many picturesque beaches before coming to Pointe de la Parata, the other end of the Gulf of Ajaccio. From here you

can enjoy stunning views of the Îles Sanguinaires, four islands that are probably the most popular photo motif in the Ajaccio area. The largest of the four, Grande Sanguine, is 1,200 m long (750 mi) and 300 m wide (190 mi). In the evening sunset, the islands are bathed in a flaming blood-red light which is why they received their poetic name of "blood islands". The La Parata peninsula is a particularly wonderful place to enjoy panoramic views of this natural spectacle. From

the Genoese tower there you not only see the four offshore islands but also the southern Gulf of Sagone with its rocky coastline.

⑯ Filitosa Just as few miles north of Propriano you will find what is probably the most interesting and most important prehistoric excavation site in the entire Mediterranean. In the middle of gentle rolling hills is the ancient settlement of Filitosa with its 30 menhir statues and numerous round

Mighty limestone rocks, often mushroom-shaped, off the coast of Capu Pertusato

Stone witnesses of the past

Dolmen (chambered tombs), menhirs (standing stones) and stone alignments – Corsica has a rich history of megalithic sites. In fact, the most important prehistoric discovery in the entire Mediterranean is here: Filitosa near Propriano.

The megalithic culture, with its religious concepts, belief in the afterlife and the associated cult of the dead, is divided into three distinct periods. Evidence of the first epoch are the dolmen, or megalithic tombs, most of which are guarded by tall vertical stones known as menhirs that were rammed straight into the ground. Their significance is still unclear. In

Dolmen of Fontanaccia near the megaliths of Cauria (top); steles at Filitosa

houses that have survived from the mysterious Torrean civilization. The area here has been inhabited since 6000 BC and the museum at the site gives a good chronological overview of the findings.

tourist-brochure beaches await visitors along the Gulf de Valinco which you will pass on the way to Sartène.

⑰ Sartène Perched high above the Rizzanèse valley, Sartène is billed as the "most Corsican of all Corsican cities". It owes its reputation to the labyrinth of lanes with fortress-like granite houses and dark courtyards in Santa Anna, the Old Town district, as well as its somewhat shady history as an outlaw stronghold. Due to its strategically advantageous location, the entire area of the Sartenais was hotly contested for many years.

Its bloody history may also have been the inspiration for the "Catenacciu" Easter procession in which a repentant

believer in iron chains drags a 32-kg (70-lb) crucifix through the city, in imitation of Jesus Christ's march to Golgotha. He is followed by other penitents. The famous Easter spectacle draws lots of onlookers every year on Good Friday.

⑱ Bonifacio Located on top of 60-m-high (190-ft) limestone cliffs, Bonifacio has a fabulous view of the strait that divides Corsica from Sardinia, 12 km (miles) away. It is the southernmost city on the island and also the most stunning, surrounded on three sides by the sea and perched atop a narrow promontory that has been hollowed out from below by the surf over millions of years. In the port of Bonifacio you'll find the La Marine quarter, a yachting marina. In the Ville Haute is the Old Town with its many narrow alleyways and tower-like buildings constructed this way over centuries due to lack of space to spread horizontally and repeated sieges. Many of

the houses have their own wells and cisterns as well as storage rooms for provisions. Steep, narrow wooden stairs that could be retracted when under threat lead to the upper floor of the houses.

⑲ Capu Pertusato It is easy to get lost in the narrow lanes of Bonifacio, but if you're looking to escape the medieval fantasy and enjoy the wonderful contrast of the open sea you should take the hike out to Capu Pertusato. The Promenade des Falaises starts at the Chapel of St-Roch and follows the cliffs for 5 km (3 mi) to the southern tip of the Pertusato peninsula. The beach, lighthouse and spectacular views are ample reward for those who make their way out here,

Top: The fortress of Bonifacio, the southernmost town on Corsica, watches over the perfect natural harbor.
Left: Fishing boats bob in the harbor of Ajaccio

the second epoch, around 2000 BC, the cult sites took on more intelligible forms, often defined by so-called alignments, orderly rows of menhirs. The third epoch began around 1600 BC and is evidenced by a profusion of menhir-statues equipped with daggers and long swords. These statues may have been stone depictions of the Filitosan enemies.

The systematic exploration and study of Corsica's prehistory and early history did not begin until 1954 when the archeologist Roger Grosjean started what ultimately became years of excavations on the sites.

Spectacular beaches like this one at Olmeto line the Gulf of Valinco, one of the four big gulfs of western Corsica. The beach stretches about 3 km (2 mi) from the mouth of the small Taravo River along the northern coast of the bay. Visitors to the area will discover numerous Genoese towers such as the Tour de Micalona or the Tour de la Calanca. Just a few miles inland

are the important prehistoric archeological sites of Filitosa and the picturesque mountain village of Olmeto from where you can enjoy wonderful panoramic views of the gulf and Propriano. The latter is the main town and tourist destination of the region, featuring a yacht harbor and ferry connections to Marseille and to the island of Sardinia.

Remote mountain land-
scapes and magnificent
beaches on the south-east
coast of Corsica –

Col de Bavella

The 1,218-m-high (4,020-ft) Col de
Bavella is the most beautiful pass on
Corsica. Views of the bizarre Aiguilles
de Bavella rock formations at 1,600
m (5,280 ft) are spectacular. Behind
them Monte Incudine rises to 2,134 m
(7,042 ft). The pass has a number of
restaurants and with any luck you
will even spot a moufflon.

particularly if the return trip is
done in the late afternoon– it is
at this time of day that the setting sun baths the Old Town
atop the white cliffs in warm
Mediterranean hues.
Now follow the N 198 north to
Porto-Vecchio.

20 Porto-Vecchio Like many
Corsican towns, Porto-Vecchio,
the third largest on the island,
sits atop a hill on the craggy
gulf of the same name and features a charming fishing port
and yacht marina. Settlers from
the Torrean civilization landed
here in around 1600 BC and
built forts and villages. The cur-
rent city, however, dates back
to a Genoese settlement in
1539, after which repeated
battles destroyed the city and
required new fortifications.
The city's worst enemy, however,
for centuries was malaria. The
deadly disease killed off much
of the indigenous population
as well as the Genose settlers.
It was not brought under control until the 1950s. After that
the city enjoyed a period of
great prosperity. With nearby
fine sandy beaches, green pine

trees and crystal-clear blue
seas, Porto-Vecchio has become a very popular tourist
destination. Not far away is the
largest forest of cork oaks on
the island, still an important
source of income for local inhabitants.
From Porto-Vecchio it is worth
taking the route from the coast
into the interior. On the very
windy mountain road D 368 you
will head toward Zonza before
turning north and traversing the
Bavella range on the D 268.

21 Col de Bavella Along the
winding pass rises the rock
face of the Aiguilles. Depending on the weather and time of
day this area can deliver a
wonderful spectacle of light
and colors. The legendary Corsican long-distance trail also
passes through here (GR 20); it
offers superb mountain tours
and hiking trips. For more information go to the offices of the
Parc Naturel Régional de la
Corse in Ajaccio.
A curvy road leads down into
the Forêt de Bavella – a forest
and now a reserve for moufflon
sheep – and farther along into

the sunny and youthful beach
resort town of Solenzara with
its 20 km (13 mi) of sand
beaches. Here you can get back
on the N 198, heading north.

22 Castagniccia The coast
road passes through Aléria, the
ancient capital of Corsica that
is now famous for its archeological sites. Near Prunete the
D 71 branches off and leads
once again toward the interior
and the Castagniccia, an expansive chestnut forest – one
of the largest in Europe – that
is one of the major landscape
highlights of the island. Until
well into the 19th century, the
Castagniccia was one of the
most densely populated regions on Corsica, with numerous towns from which the inhabitants of the island wished
to enjoy the spoils of the forest's most valuable commodity
and the basic staple of island
life: chestnut meal.
The area was forgotten in the
20th century, however, but the
population later began focus-
ing on tourism. Indeed, this enchanting landscape, virtually
untouched by modern civilization, has a mild mountain climate and a plethora of offerings for visitors. In addition to
attractive villages there are the
thermal hot springs near Eaux
d'Orezza, the historic sites such
as Morosaglia (the birthplace
of Corsican freedom fighter
Pasquale Paoli), and the ruins
of the Franciscan monastery of
Orezza, which looks back on an
eventful history as the center
of the Corsican independence
movement.
From Ponte Leccia you follow
the N 193 back to the coast
and your starting point, the
lively port town of Bastia.

**Above and left: Storm-beaten
pines line the ridges and
plateaus on Col de Bavella,
a 1,218-m (4,020-ft) peak in
south-eastern Corsica.**

a mountain village in the densely forested Castagniccia (far left) and a splendid beach near Porto-Vecchio

Calvi The once mighty Genoese base is situated beautifully on the splendid blue Gulf of Calvi. The icon of Calvi is the Citadel perched high up on the rocky point – the views at sunset are stunning.

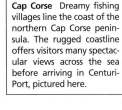

Cap Corse Dreamy fishing villages line the coast of the northern Cap Corse peninsula. The rugged coastline offers visitors many spectacular views across the sea before arriving in Centuri-Port, pictured here.

Erbalunga The historic fishermen's houses in the small port and the ruined Genoese tower set atop rocks surrounded by the sea make for a popular postcard subject. The village is also known for its Good Friday procession.

Golf von Porto Steep rock walls, green forests and the inviting blue sea distinguish this magnificent landscape. A Genoese watchtower built atop the cliffs is Porto's most famous landmark.

Bastia This lively harbor town is the most important commercial center of Corsica and the island's second-largest city.

Ajaccio The most famous native son of this port town in western Corsica is Napoleon Bonaparte, born here in 1769. In 1811, Ajaccio was named the capital of the island and it remains so today.

Porto-Vecchio Superb sandy beaches, green pine forests and electric blue waters make the island's third-largest city – known as "St-Tropez" of Corsica – a popular tourist destination.

Filitosa With its numerous dolmens, menhir-statues and Torrean complexes, Filitosa is among the most significant prehistoric excavation sites in the entire Mediterranean region.

Bonifacio Boasting a superb location on a rocky plateau 60 m (190 ft) above the sea, Corsica's southernmost city offers great views across the strait to the island of Sardinia.

The UNESCO World Heritage

No fewer than 35 sites in France have been declared a part of the UNESCO World Cultural and Natural Heritage. On the following pages we'll present in detail these cultural and natural monuments, which are of an extraordinary and universal importance and whose preservation is the responsibility of all of humankind.

Belfries of Belgium and France

The belfries were built as a symbol of the self-confidence of the civil authorities in the cities in the face of feudalism. They form a transnational world heritage property.

Year of inscription: 1999
Extension: 2005

Initially the World Heritage property comprised 32 belfries – as the bell towers are known here – in several cities in Belgium's Flanders and Wallonia. In 2005 the property was extended to include the belfries of the French provinces of Artois and Picardie, making it a transnational cultural heritage site. Originally the belfries, built between the 11th and the 17th centuries, held the town bell that would warn the citizens of imminent danger from enemies or fire. Over time the belfries then became prestigious municipal buildings in the prosperous cities, equipped with splendid clockworks and carillons. The towers are powerful symbols of the greater liberties that the citizens had wrought from the aristocracy and the clergy. Some were also the place of assembly of the aldermen, others served as prison or as municipal archives. Twenty-three belfries represent the architectural history of northern France, including those in the cities of Cambrais, Dunkerque, Lille, Calais and Amiens. It is worth mentioning here the Romanesque and Gothic belfries of Boulogne and Arras, for example. The tower in Comines was built as a Renaissance structure but its roof was later remodeled in the baroque style.

Between the 11th and the 17th centuries the citizens of Flanders and northern France built numerous belfries. Worth mentioning from an art historical perspective are the splendid belfries of Calais (top right; below right with Auguste Rodin's sculpture, *The Citizens of Calais*), Dunkerque (top left), Arras (left) and Bergues (below left).

The defense installations of Vauban, named after the master builder, are outstanding examples of Western European military architecture. They were copied all over the continent, in America and even the Middle East.

Year of inscription: 2008

The 17th century is known as the century of great wars and sieges of the fortified towns, and Sébastien le Prestre de Vauban (1633–1707) was an architect, town planner and a pioneering fortress designer under Louis XIV at the time. He was responsible for designing no fewer than thirty-three new fortresses and redesigning more than 160 battlements for the purposes of war, and he himself conducted more than fifty sieges as a commander. In 1677, he became the General Commissar of Fortifications and was promoted to Marshall of France in 1703. Although he used mainly traditional means and materials, the genius of Vauban as construction engineer becomes apparent in the complexes he built on difficult terrain. Some of the master builder's fortifications remained in use until World War I.

Fortifications in twelve French villages – on the seashore, in the mountains and on river banks – were chosen as World Heritage sites to represent the most successful examples of Vauban's engineering skills. Located on France's western, northern and eastern borders,

they are mostly still in an excellent condition. The different types of fortification and the geographical challenges mastered by Vauban can be seen in Arras, Longwy, Neuf-Brisach, Besançon, Briançon, Mont-Dauphin, Villefranche-de-Conflent, Mont-Louis, Blaye/Cussac-Fort-Mèdoc, Saint-Martin-de-Ré, Camaret-sur-Mer and Saint-Vaast La-Hougue.

Vauban's fortifications represent a daring combination of urban and natural architecture. Saint-Martin-de-Ré on the Atlantic coast (large picture) is a walled coastal town, whereas the fortifications of Besançon (top and left) are matched to the hilly terrain and the river on which the towns are located.

The Cathédrale Notre-Dame d'Amiens is one of the greatest church buildings of the French High Gothic. Its dimensions are vast – it covers a total area of 7,700 sq m (82,852 sq ft), making it the largest church in France.

Year of inscription: 1981

The first church that was built in Amiens went up in 1137 and was located on the site where today the mighty Cathedral of Our Lady rises majestically above the sea of houses. Two years after being destroyed by a massive fire in 1218, Bishop Évrard de Fouilloy decided to lay the foundations for a new cathedral that would be 145 m (476 ft) long. Most of the structure was completed quite quickly – by the end of the 13th century – based on plans by Robert de Luzarches.
The Cathedral consists of a triple-aisled nave that reaches an impressive height of 42.3 m (139 ft). The west façade features three portals and is crowned by two wide towers. It boasts a large rose window and elegant detailing.
The portals are embellished with three large scenes from

the Old and New Testaments that are considered some of the highlights of medieval sculptures in the whole of Europe. Among the numerous sculptures on the portals, the "Vierge Dorée" and the "Beau Dieu" are particularly worth seeing. A total of 126 flying buttresses stabilize the church which is famous for its impressive spatial relations as well as for its rich decorative figures.

Amiens Cathedral boasts an impressive western façade (below left) with two towers and richly ornamented portals (left: a detail from the main portal featuring scenes from the Last Judgment and Christ as "Beau Dieu" in the tympanum). More than 40 m (130 ft) tall, the central nave with its elegant Gothic arches (below right), seems to strive toward heaven

The city has been a bulwark of the Catholic Church for centuries. Three structures are World Heritage Sites: the Notre-Dame Cathedral, the archiepiscopal Palace of Tau and the former Abbey of Saint-Remi with its basilica.

Year of inscription: 1991

Reims is located in the heart of the Champagne region and looks back on a glorious history. Clovis was anointed King of

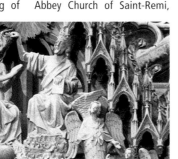

the Franks here by St Remigius in around 500. The archbishop's bones are kept in the Abbey Church of Saint-Remi, built in the 11th century. The narrow central nave from the ninth century is attached to an early-Gothic choir. The windows date from the 12th century.

The Gothic Notre-Dame Cathedral was once the coronation church of French kings and was built in 1211 on the site of an earlier church that had burned down. The structure is adorned with expressive stone sculptures and stained-glass windows that have been lovingly restored. Some were done by Marc Chagall and are vivid masterpieces of light and color. The Archbishops' Palace of Tau,

built around 1500, once served as a temporary residence for the French kings and as a festival hall. It features magnificent tapestries.

Notre-Dame Cathedral in Reims is a masterpiece of the high-Gothic. It has a west front richly adorned with sculptures (below; left: a detail). Above the three pointed-arch portals, 56 sculpted figures sit enthroned in the gallery of the kings. The bright stained-glass windows by Marc Chagall (below left) are works of art in light and color.

On a rocky islet in the English Channel, about 1 km (½ mi) off the Normandy coast, is the former Benedictine Abbey of Mont-Saint-Michel. The World Heritage Property also comprises the Bay.

Year of inscription: 1979

The history of the Abbey of Mont-Saint-Michel begins with a vision of the Archangel Michael that Bishop Aubert is said to have had in the eighth century. The bishop proceeded to build a small prayer hall for pilgrims. In 1022 construction was begun of a new building on the site of the old church of Notre-Dame-sous-Terre, incorporating the original walls as substructures. First the crypt and the chancel were built, the latter possibly the first ambulatory without radial chapels. After its collapse in 1421 it was rebuilt in the late-Gothic style.

In the time of Abbot Ralph de Beaumont, in the 11th century, work continued on the crossing piers and the transept. The nave was completed under Abbot Roger I at the beginning of the 12th century. The cross

vaults in the side aisles and the wall of the central nave are only preserved on the south side. The west façade and its two towers, completed in 1184, burned to the ground in 1776. The refectory with its tall windows is exceptionally beautiful. A good example of the Norman Gothic style is the cloister with its double arcades. A village soon grew up below the abbey; some of the 14th-century houses still stand today.
Because of the quicksand and the strong currents Mont-Saint-Michel was difficult to reach even at low tide, and so

it was never conquered. The Abbey lost in importance an became a state prison betwee 1811 and 1863. The building were restored and are toda accessible via a bridge.

The island fortress of Mont-Saint-Michel with the famous abbey at its tip is the emblem of Normandy (left and below). The Monastic Fraternities of Jerusalem handle the administration and support of the pilgrims. They also conduct services in the Gothic abbey church (above).

In 1944, Allied bombs destroyed the port city of Le Havre, which was occupied by Germany. After the end of World War II, the city was completely rebuilt as a unified architectural ensemble under the direction of Auguste Perret.

Year of inscription: 2005

Auguste Perret, one of the pioneers of reinforced concrete construction, originally wanted to rebuild Le Havre, on the south of the River Seine, on a concrete platform 3 m (11 ft) above the rubble. It was an impracticable plan, however. The present town, rebuilt between 1946 and 1964, is rather less unified than was originally planned. During the redevelopment of the parceled up terrain the few remaining buildings – the 16th-century cathedral and the 19th-century law courts – were incorporated into the new urban planning concept.

The old street network was retained in part. The most important street is the Avenue Foch, which runs from the city hall to the Porte Océane from where you have views of the sea. It is lined by trees and some seven-storey houses. A grid of squares each with 100-m-long (328-ft) sides was laid over the terrain that was to be developed with singular consistency, and building was undertaken with precast blocks measuring a standard length of 6.25 m (20.5 ft). Despite this uniform grid the ensemble does not appear monotonous. The individual

concrete slabs were not plastered so that joints and the skeleton construction method remain clearly visible. The social idea was innovative too: the density of buildings was reduced and apartments were assigned to cooperatives.

A positive object lesson in the prefabrication of buildings was given by the rebuilt port city built mostly from precast concrete. Auguste Perret was responsible also for the church of Saint-Joseph (below: inside the tower) and the City Hall (left). The Halles Centrales (top) were designed by André la Donné, Charles Fabre and Jean Le Soudier.

Palace and Park of Versailles

The Palace of Versailles outside Paris is the prototype of an absolutist ruler's residence and as such became the ideal model for many European palaces. The lavish baroque complex built for Louis XIV, the "Sun King", is surrounded by an extensive park.

Year of inscription: 1979

Starting in 1661, King Louis XIV of France converted his father Louis XIII's former hunting lodge into a palace that was later to become the permanent seat of his government. Architects Le Vau and Hardouin-

Mansart created a truly extravagant complex comprising roughly 700 rooms surrounded by a massive palace park – a unified work of art consisting of plants, fountains and sculptures as well as the garden palaces of

the Petit and the Grand Trianon. Versailles was the political center of France for the next 100 years. At its height, 5,000 people lived at the palace, including a considerable number of French nobles. As many as 14,000 soldiers also lived in the various outbuildings and the village of Versailles itself.

Of the many magnificent rooms in Versailles, the Hall of Mirrors is historically the most significant. It is where the German Emperor Wilhelm was crowned in 1871, and where the Versailles Treaty was signed in 1919. Overwhelming visitors

with its sheer size alone, the Hall of Mirrors owes its name t the seventeen mirrors tha reflect the light from the wir dows opposite them.

Wrought-iron railings separate the Place d'Armes from the Palace of Versailles (top). The Hall of Mirrors (left) is one of a series of rooms spanning the entire garden façade that counts as a masterpiece of baroque decoration. Louis XIV conducted his morning and evening audiences, the "lever" and the "coucher", in his bed chambers (below).

Paris, one of the world's truly cosmopolitan cities, boasts an incredible abundance of historic buildings and cultural highlights. The stretch of the Seine between Pont de Sully and Pont d'Iéna, which has been declared a World Heritage Site in and of itself, is particularly steeped in history.

Year of inscription: 1991

The heritage section of the Seine starts at the Île Saint-Louis, where the statue of Sainte Geneviève, Paris's patron saint, overlooks the river. The Île de la Cité, farther to the west, is the heart of spiritual Paris with the Gothic Cathedral of Notre-Dame and La Sainte-Chapelle, a filigree masterpiece of the High Gothic. Farther along is the Conciergerie, once part of the medieval royal palace and the state prison. Opposite that is the Louvre, the Renaissance palace of the French kings, which houses one of the world's most outstanding collections of art. Down river are the Musée d'Orsay, the Grand and the Petit Palais and the National Assembly. The site ends with the Eiffel Tower, a steel structure that was revolutionary in its day.

From the Pont de Sully, views open out to the two Seine islands, Île Saint-Louis and Île de la Cité, with the Cathedral of Notre-Dame de Paris (top). Below: inside the glass pyramid of the Louvre. Left: the Avenue des Champs-Elysées and the Arc de Triomphe. Far left: the emblem of Paris – the Eiffel Tower, built for the World Exhibition.

Palace and Park of Fontainebleau

The Palace of Fontainebleau about 60 km (37 mi) south of Paris is the ancestral home of the kings of France. Over centuries it was rebuilt and remodeled by numerous architects and artists. The palace park is also worth exploring.

Year of inscription: 1981

In the 12th century, King Louis VII commissioned a small hunting lodge in the forest of Fontainebleau. After being abandoned, however, it was completely rebuilt in 1528 on the orders of François I. Only one of the building's original towers was spared demolition in the process. Italian artists like Rosso Fiorentino and Francesco Primaticcio were commissioned to furnish the interior. Their work ultimately came to represent a version of Mannerism known as the "School of Fontainebleau". The palace was later enlarged, remodeled and embellished many more times, in particular by Henry IV and Emperor Napoleon. Today the palace houses a number of outstanding works from the Italian and French Baroque, Rococo and Neoclassicism. Among the most impressive structures in the Palace of Fontainebleau, which over time has been expanded to include five different inner courtyards, are the horseshoe-shaped staircase and the majestic ballroom.

The vast gardens surrounding the palace were created in the 17th century by André Le Nôtre, the eminent landscape and garden designer of Louis XIV who also established the park at Versailles. The Grand Parterre is the largest formal garden in Europe.

The Palace of Fontainebleau overwhelms visitors with its generously proportioned rooms such as the 80-m-long (262-ft) Gallery of Diane (left) and the neoclassical Throne Room (top). The renowned landscape architect André Le Nôtre designed the Grand Parterre of the Park of Fontainebleau in 1645 (below).

One of Europe's most fascinating cultural landscapes extends along the mostly unregulated Loire River. It features an incredible array of châteaux and abbeys.

Year of inscription: 2000

The stretch of the Loire from Sully-sur-Loire in the east to Chalonnes, a few miles downriver from Angers, is 200 km (124 mi) long. Here France's longest river meanders its way eastward toward the Atlantic, through the historic regions of the Orléanais, Blésois, Touraine and Anjou, an area that boasts an unique abundance of cultural monuments.

The rise of settlements on the Loire began with Saint Martin, Bishop of Tours from 371 to 397 and patron saint of the Franks, whose tomb in Tours became an important pilgrim-age site. In 848, Charles the Bald was crowned king in Orléans and the river valley became the preferred residence for the Capetian dynasty in the 10th and 11th centuries.

There are major Romanesque sites here: the abbey churches of Saint-Benoît-sur-Loire with its narthex and crypt from the 11th century; Germigny-des-Prés with a 12th-century mosaic; frescoes in Liget and Tavant; and the Church of Notre-Dame in Cunault. One of Europe's largest monastic complexes is the Fontevraud Abbey with the burial church of the Planta-

genets. When Henry Planta-genet was crowned as king of England in 1154, a vast empire was created with centers in Angers and Chinon. Here Joan of Arc took on Charles VII in 1429 before he was crowned, during the Hundred-Years' Wa. Then she set off to liberate Orléans from English troops.

Under Francis I, a number of castles were rebuilt or remodeled: the water Château of Azay-le-Rideau (1527), the Loire's archetypal Renaissance castle; Château de Chenonceau built on a bridge; the Château de Chambord and the châteaux

of Blois and Amboise. The châteaux of Villandry and Saumur are also worth a visit and feature vineyards lining the Loire with its islands, sand-banks and water meadows

Chambord, the largest of the Loire châteaux with more than 400 rooms, has a remarkable roof landscape of numerous turrets and chimneys (below). The Château of Chenonceau meanwhile boasts a unique and enchanting location – sited on a bridge, its buildings are washed on all sides by the small River Cher (top).

Provins, Town of Medieval Fairs

The authentically medieval town architecture of Provins, a small town between Paris and Troyes, epitomizes the political, social and economic structure of a flourishing community in the 12th and 13th centuries.

Year of inscription: 2001

Provins, once forming a part of the territory of the counts of Champagne, stood at the intersection of the trading routes between the North Sea and the Mediterranean, between Flanders and Italy. No fewer than nine major as well as eleven minor trade routes ran through the town. As a result, in the 12th and 13th centuries Provins became a major international trade fair town where goods of all kinds were exchanged on a large scale. Among the best-known events were the annual cloth and leather fairs. When a count brought a damask rose back from the crusades, Provins also became a center for the cultivation of roses.

At the base of the impressive Tour César, a 12th-century octagonal watchtower that was

later also used as a prison, extends a superb example of a beautifully preserved medieval town. The old town encompasses the ancient town ramparts and gates, underground galleries, the Romanesque collegiate church of Saint Quiriace and the church of Saint Ayoul as well as the 13th century Grange aux Dîmes a tithe barn that once served a a covered market square.

The Tour César is unique thanks to its octagonal layout (top). Legend ascribes it to Caesar, but it was not built until the 12th century. Construction of the collegiate church of Saint Quiriace was begun in around 1160. Its choir anticipates elements of the Gothic style (left and below).

Notre-Dame de Chartres is the undisputed mother of all high-Gothic structures. Unlike many other cathedrals, it has retained almost all of its original furnishings. Its elegance and simplicity embody the triumph of Gothic art.

Year of inscription: 1979

The cathedral towers over Chartres, capital of the Eure-et-Loire département, located about 100 km (62 mi) south-west of Paris. The triple-aisled basilica with transept and five-aisled choir, surrounded by radial chapels, is one of the very first purely Gothic edifices and quickly became a model for the cathedrals of Reims as well as Amiens. Construction here began early in the 12th century and the church was consecrated in 1260. As if by some miracle, the early-Gothic west façade from 1140 managed to survive the fire of 1194. Below the choir is St Fulbert's crypt from 1024. At a length of 108 m (354 ft), it is the largest Romanesque crypt in France. A number of new architectural techniques were employed during the construction of the cathedral, including the flying buttresses, which made it possible to interrupt the long walls with large windows. The colorful stained-glass windows from the 12th and 13th centuries provide the interior with a unique light and the rich sculptures and reliefs of the portals were groundbreaking.

The towers of Notre-Dame de Chartres (below left) date from the 12th and 15th centuries. Vertical lines are emphasized inside the Cathedral (below: a view of the nave). It is an art historical gem thanks to its rich sculptural décor (left: the ambulatory) and its stained-glass windows (top).

Stanislas Leszczynski, the deposed King of Poland, nominally became the Duke of Lorraine in 1737, and it is to him that Nancy owes its squares. Three of them are World Heritage Sites: Place Stanislas, Place de la Carrière and Place d'Alliance.

Year of inscription: 1983

Place Stanislas was meant to be an architectural bridge between the Old Town and the New Town to the south. As Place Royale it was to become the new heart of Nancy. Designed and built in 1752 to 1755 under the supervision of the architect Emmanuel Héré de Corny, the square's most prominent building is the Hôtel de Ville (city hall) on the south side. Its interior was lavishly decorated, and the staircase is particularly impressive: it seems even larger than it is thanks to a trompe-l'oeil painting on the back wall. The pavil-

ions on the west and east side of the square were designed in a similar style.

The square is crowned by a triumphal arch, on the other

side of which is the elongated Place de la Carrière. This square was built in the 16th century and completed under Stanislas. The Palais de Justice and the

Bourse des Marchands opposite were also designed by Héré. Work on the Place d'Alliance began in 1753. It is particularly impressive thanks to the uniform façades of its houses, a look that continues in the adjacent streets.

Wrought-iron latticework by Jean Lamour and the Neptune Fountain by Barthélemy Guibal (left) adorn the north side of the generously proportioned Place Stanislas (below). The Place de la Carrière, once an exercise ground, ends with the Palais du Gouverneur (top).

The remarkably well-preserved buildings of the Cistercian Abbey of Fontenay, built by Bernard of Clairvaux in 1119, are a very vivid illustration of medieval monastic life.

Year of inscription: 1981

he Cistercian order goes back o a reformist movement within he Benedictine community, triving for a stricter adherence o the rules of Benedict of Nur-ia. The Cistercians founded a irst abbey in 1098 in den narshy grounds of Cîteaux, but hen followed this with many nore, all of them erected in ru-al isolation. The order rejected ll excesses, and the community f monks lived solely from the arvest they themselves could eap and in decidedly modest lwellings. The Abbey of Fonte-ay, located some 50 km (31 ni) north-west of Dijon, was

dedicated by Pope Eugene III in 1147. It was partly overhauled and replaced by new buildings in the 18th century, yet the ideal plan of a Cistercian abbey is still easy to make out today. The abbey's plain and harmo-nious complex is surrounded by a high wall. The church and abbey form a strictly closed, largely unadorned unit. The abbey church, for its part, was originally intended only for the devotions of the monastic com-munity, which is also why stairs connect it directly with the dor-mitory. Several ancillary build-ings are loosely grouped around the twin structures, be-tween green spaces and trees.

A forge and a mill dating from the 12th century have also been lovingly preserved here. They document the very signifi-cant economic impact made by the Cistercians, whose monas-teries also featured the first factory-like complexes in the Middle Ages.

The abbey church of Fontenay subscribes to the very strict ideals of the Cistercians. The choir (below) has the tombs of noblemen form Burgundy. An impressive Romanesque cloister surrounds the green courtyard (top and left).

The medieval Old Town of Strasbourg is located on the Grande Île (big island), in the River Ill. An area of conflict between France and Germany, the historic center contains a high concentration of beautifully preserved buildings.

Year of inscription: 1988

The main landmark of Strasbourg is its Minster, one of the most important religious buildings of the Middle Ages. Begun in 1015, the Minster was originally Romanesque, but since construction extended over several centuries, it also features Gothic style elements. Particularly interesting is the western façade, praised for its proportions as well as its portals, which are bedecked with elaborate stone sculptures. Having taken on the financing of the vast structure in 1286, the citizens of Strasbourg built the cathedral as much as a place of worship as a monument to their own efforts. Other highlights in the church are the superb stained-glass windows and the astronomical clock.

The Minster square is lined by rows of up to five-storey-tall half-timbered houses like the Maison Kammerzell and the Palais Rohan, built in about 1740 in the style of Louis XV. Also worth seeing are the picturesque tanners' district La Petite France from the 16th and 17th centuries, the Ponts Couverts – bridges that were once covered – and the weir built by Vauban.

Its mixture of rural and urban building traditions is typical of Strasbourg. Whereas urban elegance predominates in the arcades and townhouses of the Rue Mercière, leading up to the Minster (bottom), visitors will also still come across many quaint timber-frame houses with steep gables, for example in the Petite France district (top and below).

The Basilica of St Mary Magdalene is perched on a hilltop above the Old Town of Vézelay, which is surrounded by mighty ramparts. The largest abbey church in France, it is a masterpiece of the French Romanesque style.

Year of inscription: 1979

The 9th-century church of the abbey allegedly holds the relics of St Mary Magdalene, and so the church was soon unable to accommodate the stream of pilgrims. In 1096 a new building was begun and Vézelay developed as one of the most important sites for the veneration of saints in the Middle Ages and a major spiritual center during the crusades – it was here that Bernard de Clairvaux began the second Crusade. The abbey church became the gathering point for pilgrims on their way to Santiago de Compostela. However, in 1279, when the re-

putedly genuine bones of Mary Magdalene were found in Provence, it brought about a sudden decline in the abbey's fortunes. The church's barrel vaulting, which reaches 18 m

(59 ft) in height and 62 m (203 ft) in length, is unique in Romanesque architecture and the plain furnishings of the bright interior were enlivened by the use of colored blocks. The stat-

ues above the main portal were restored in the 19th century; the most sophisticated sculptures from the Middle Ages, they illustrate both biblical scenes and heroic legends and myths.

The ninth-century Vézelay Abbey Church is perched high on top of City Hill (top). Some parts of the church were built much later than the Romanesque central nave (left) and already feature early Gothic style elements. The capitals and the tympanum of the narthex are particularly lavish in their designs (below).

Bourges Cathedral

In the former capital of the dukes of Berry it is the five-aisled cathedral that stands out among the architectural gems. With its five large portals, the concept of the church as a gateway to heaven found its strongest expression here.

Year of inscription: 1992

St Stephen's Cathedral was built in two stages. The choir and apse were built between 1195 and 1215, whereas the nave and the main façade went up between 1225 and 1260. Two asymmetric towers rise proudly above the church. The north tower collapsed in 1506 and was rebuilt by 1542. Parts of the Gothic structure such as the southern side portal date from the Romanesque period. The sculptures adorning the west front, which contains five portals that correspond with the aisles, are of particular significance. Biblical subjects such as the Last Judgment as well as legends from the life of St Stephen (Saint-Étienne) are depicted here.

The interior is illuminated by "sacred" light falling through

the intricate stained-glass windows that date from the 13th century. The crypt underneath the choir dates from the 12th century. In fact, this is an independent and well-proportioned church in its own right, built a a lower level, with remarkabl sculptures and large clerestor which rises above the groun because of the differences i height levels.

The west façade of the high-Gothic cathedral at Bourges (left) is in the heart of a densely built-up town.
A veritable forest of pillars supports the five-aisled nave an its ambulatory (below with the astronomical clock from 1424). The church also has the tomb of Jean Duc de Berry in its crypt (top).

The Royal Saltworks of Arc-et-Senans, around 30 km (19 mi) south-west of Besançon, were built in 1779 featuring a revolutionary architectural style and are today an important monument of France's early industrial architecture.

Year of inscription: 1982

The saltworks built between 1775 and 1779 by Claude-Nicolas Ledoux in an exaggerated neoclassical style represent a microcosm of late Absolutist society in both aesthetic as well as political and social terms. The heart of the saltworks where the workers also had to live (four to a room), is the director's house, and like the entrance to the complex it featured a portico. Arranged round it in a semi-circle are four buildings with three wings each, serving as living quarters and as work places. Ledoux placed the large workshops where the brine was processed at the sides of the residential blocks. Originally an entire city was planned where the workers would live, but this was never happened.

The director's house with portico (left and below) and embossed columns quickly reveals the social hierarchy at the saltworks even in its architectural features. The entire complex with the workshops at the sides and the workers' living quarters arranged in a semi-circle (top) was tailor-made for his person.

Abbey Church of Saint-Savin sur Gartempe

With its 11th- and 12th-century frescoes, the so-called "Sistine Chapel of the Romanesque" holds the greatest cycle of paintings from that period in France. Its walls once served as visual aids to instruct the faithful.

Year of inscription: 1983

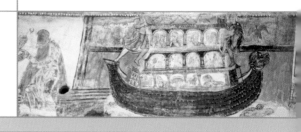

As if by a miracle, this abbey church was spared from destruction and looting over the centuries, but it began to decay after the French Revolution. In 1836, writer Prosper Mérimée, who became the Inspector of Historic Monuments in France in 1831, discovered it some 35 km (22 mi) east of Poitiers and immediately placed it on the list of protected buildings. Fortunately, the expressive cycle of paintings dating from the 11th and early 12th centuries could largely be rescued thanks to new technology employed in the restoration work undertaken in the 1970s.

On a surface area of more than 400 sq m (4,304 sq ft), the images preserved in the vaults of the central nave represent a self-contained cycle of scenes from the Old Testament ranging from Genesis to the Exodus and the Passion of Christ. The murals in the rood loft and narthex depict the Life of Christ and the Apocalypse of John. The images of of St Savin and St Cyprian in the crypt are less elaborate in their execution. Aside from these invaluable wall paintings, the abbey church also boasts precious Romanesque altars.

The frescoes of the Abbey Church of Saint-Savin (below) aimed to use popular imagery to introduce the contents of the Bible to the faithful, who were mostly illiterate (below left: Cain and Abel, above: Noah's Ark). Below right: the painted barrel vault of the church.

Concentrated along an approximately 40-km-long (25-mi) stretch of the Vézère Valley in the Périgord Region is a series of prehistoric sites and caves with rock paintings that give us valuable insights into human life during the Paleolithic and the Neolithic Ages.

Year of inscription: 1979

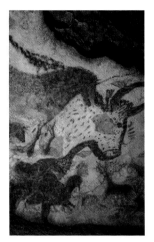

his World Heritage Region omprises an impressive 147 rehistoric sites and twenty-ve caves with rock paintings hat were discovered over the ourse of the 19th and 20th enturies. The most important tes in this treasure trove of arly humanity are all in a row n a hill slope above the ézère River: Le Moustier, La Madeleine, Lascaux and Cro-Magnon. At Cro-Magnon, five keletons dating from the late aleolithic Age were found in he year 1868. They are the ori-in of the name given to the ype of homo sapiens.

Lascaux is the most famous of the caves. In 1940, about 100 paintings were discovered, dating back roughly 15,000 years and displaying remarkably realistic hunting scenes; finds in other caves meanwhile confirm that the hunters and gatherers, who settled in southern France during the Ice Age, were responsible for the first works of art in Europe as far back as 30,000 years ago.

The images document the religious imagination of Stone Age humans. Animals played a central role in the fight for survival for these early humans and they

therefore also figured prominently in the religious cults. For reasons of conservation, visitors can only see a reproduction of the cave at Lascaux and its priceless prehistoric works.

The cave of Lascaux is located on the River Vézère (top) near Montignac. In the Galerie Lascaux II faithful reproductions are all that can today be admired of its prehistoric works of art (left and below: realistic images of horses and aurochs) because the steady stream of visitors made their conservation problematic

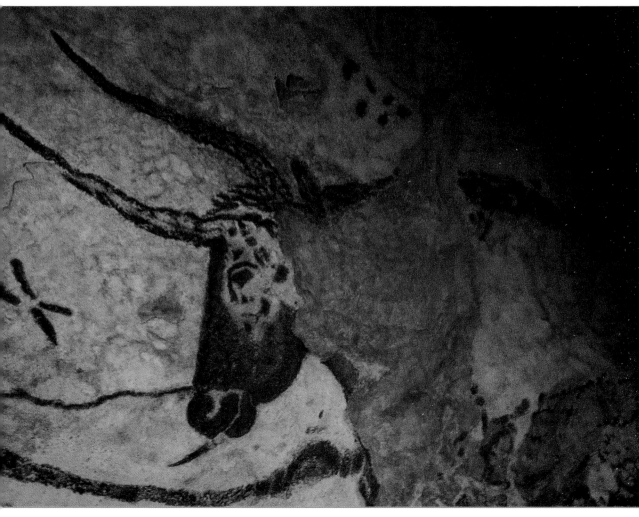

The history of this former Roman colony founded at the confluence of the Saône and Rhône rivers is reflected in the numerous buildings dating from different periods.

Year of inscription: 1998

Lyon – the second-largest metropolitan area in France after Paris– developed as one of Europe's foremost fair towns in the 16th century thanks to its large number of silk mills, which are today remembered by a museum, and its book printing works. In 1506, France's first stock exchange was established here as well, and today Lyon still counts as one of the most important banking centers in France.

Narrow, winding alleyways and fabulous medieval buildings characterize the oldest part of the city, Fourvière, adapted from

the Roman "forum vetus" (old forum). St John's Cathedral built from the 12th to the 15th centuries stands here with its early-Gothic stained-glass windows and a clever astronomical clock from the 14th century. Not far form the cathedral are the impressive façades of some superb Renaissance houses. On a hill above the River Saône, where the Romans founded the city in a strategic location, is the pilgrims' basilica of Notre-Dame de Fourvière, built in the 19th century. On the 5-km (3-mi) peninsula between the two rivers are the 17th-century town hall, the Palais des Arts (a former Benedictine abbey), the Stock Exchange as well as several late-medieval churches. The heart of the peninsula and the center of Lyon is the Place Belle cour. A short way south of her is the Church of Saint-Martin d'Ainay, which was built in the 12th century in Romanesque style and dates back to a ninth century basilica.

The façade of the town hall was designed by Jules Hardouin Mansart (below). The restaurant of the nearby opera house boasts fine views of Lyon (left). The St-Jean Cathedral (top) in Fourvière, Lyon's Old Town, is the bishop's see.

Saint-Émilion, about 30 km (19 mi) east of Bordeaux, and another seven communities in its environs, was the first historic wine-growing area to be given the coveted status of World Heritage Site.

Year of inscription: 1999

was the Romans who originally introduced viticulture to the fertile Aquitaine Region. In the Middle Ages grapes were extensively cultivated, and today the village of Saint-Émilion, spread across the tops of two hills east of Bordeaux, is renowned for its outstanding wines far beyond the borders of France.

Today, this protected territory includes – aside from Saint-Émilion itself – the communes of Saint-Christophe des Bardes, Saint-Étienne-de-Lisse, Saint-Hippolyte, Saint-Laurent-des-Combes, Saint-Pey-d'Armens, Vignonet and Saint-Sulpice-de-Faleyrens.

Saint-Émilion rose around the grotto in which the Breton monk and hermit Émilion lived in seclusion in the 8th century, succeeded by other monks from the Benedictine order. Later a subterranean church, the triple-aisled Église Monolithe was hewn into the rock next to the hermitage. A direct passageway links the church with the catacombs, where St Émilion is said to be buried. Other historic buildings worth seeing in Saint-Émilion are the Cloître de la Collégiale with its magnificent cloisters and the Chapelle de la Trinité. The latter was built in the 13th century to honor St Émilion, the patron saint of vintners. Thanks to its location on the pilgrimage route to Santiago de Compostela, many monasteries, churches and hospices were built in the region starting in the 11th century.

During the period of English rule St.-Émilion was awarded the special status of a free town with its own jurisdiction in 1199. This is celebrated each year in spring by the Jurade – a festival and the procession of ermine-robed aldermen to the Eglise Monolithe. Each year in September the gentlemen of the confrèrie (the wine fraternity) get together in the Tour du Roi, the remains of a 13th-century palace, in order to ceremoniously open the vendange, the wine harvest.

Saint-Émilion, its bell tower (below) rising high above the rock church (top: sculptural decoration in the interior), is the leading wine village of the Bordeaux region and has its own appellation contrôlée, or controlled area of origin.

Historic Center of Bordeaux

The Old Town of Bordeaux hugs the left bank of the River Garonne. It is impressive not only because of its many outstanding buildings but even more thanks to the grand layout of the town, dating back to the Enlightenment.

Year of inscription: 2007

Bordeaux, located some 50 km (31 mi) from the Atlantic coast on the Garonne River, has served as a port city since Roman times. One of its most important commercial products is the wine for which the town and its environs are still world-famous today.

Until way into the 18th century, Bordeaux had preserved its medieval character, but the Enlightenment paved the way for an intellectual movement that transformed the city into a neoclassical gem. First, Jacques Gabriel designed the Place de la Bourse in about 1730. Louis-

Urbain Aubert, the marquis of Tournay and administrator of the local community from 1743 to 1757, then played a key role in the restructuring of Bordeaux, replacing the medieval gates with neoclassical structures. He also designed the Place Gambetta, the Place d'Aquitaine, the Place de Bourgogne and the Place Tourny, and he had new streets laid out

and gardens and parks esta[b]lished. It was also during t[his] time that the town houses [and] the quays along the Garon[ne] began to be built. Betwe[en] 1810 and 1822 the first sto[ne] bridge was constructed acr[oss] the Garonne. The old p[ort] on the left bank, however, [re]mained unchanged.

Among the buildings and squares of Bordeaux the Pla[ce] de la Bourse (top), the Place Gambetta (left) and the neo[-]classical theater built betwe[en] 1773 and 1780 by Victor Lou[is] stand out (below).

Albi has remained virtually unchanged since the early Modern Age. Its importance in clerical history is reflected by the city's architecture with its Gothic buildings and the systematic use of brick as a construction material.

Year of inscription: 2010

The small town of Albi is located in the south of France, some 80 km (50 mi) north-east of Toulouse. Mainly two buildings stand out from the mostly low houses in the Old Town of the town on the River Tarn: the Sainte-Cécile Cathedral and the episcopal palace, Palais de la Berbie. Construction of the Gothic church began in 1282, and it was finally completed in 1492. With its more than 70-m-tall (230-ft) steeple the cathedral is one of the largest brick churches on Earth. The entire historic district of the bishops' see of Albi was also built from brick. The mighty Palais de la Berbie originally served as a fortress, intended to demonstrate the power the bishops of Albi had from the 13th century. Its walls today contain a fascinating museum of the painter Henri Toulouse-Lautrec (1864 –1901). The baroque garden established in the 17th century is a beautiful work of art. The World Heritage Site also comprises the historic bridge spanning the River Tarn, the church of Saint-Salvi as well as the district surrounding it.

The mighty cathedral of Ste-Cécile, the heart of the episcopal quarter, towers high above the River Tarn and its venerable bridge (top). Left: the western façades with a mural of the Last Judgment. Below: view of the main altar (right) and the choir (left).

Orange looks back on some 2000 years of history. Many remains of buildings can still be seen here from the time of its Roman settlement, including one of the best-preserved amphitheaters in Europe.

Year of inscription: 1981

The Romans founded Arausio on the site of a Celtic settlement they had conquered in the Rhône Valley. The "Triumphal Arch", completed in about AD 25, is the best and most completely preserved Roman arch in what was known then as Gaul. In fact, it isn't a triumphal arch at all but an arched gateway that commemorates the founding of the town by the Romans. The structure, which measures 20 m (66 ft) wide, 18 m (59 ft) high and 8.5 m (28 ft) deep, marks the entrance to the city on the Via Agrippa. It has three openings with the central one larger than the other two. The gate's parapet wall had a second level added. A relief wraps around it glorifying the "Pax Romana" under Emperor Augustus.

The Théâtre Romain was one of the largest in the Roman Empire. It even impressed King Louis XIV with its vast front measuring 103 m (338 ft) long and 37 m (121 ft) tall. Due to its spectacular location on a city hill, several corridors had to be dug into the rock. Up to 10,000 spectators could be accommodated here and admire the stage and its magnificently decorated stage set. After centuries of decay and the plundering of materials for new buildings as well as being used as a prison, it has been restored from the 19th century and is once more a popular festival venue.

The Roman theater in Orange, built just after the beginning of the Christian Era, boasts an impressive stage set, adorned by a statue of Augustus (below). The relief-adorned Triumphal Arch guards the northern entrance (left and top a detail).

This bridge aqueduct across the River Gard is a masterpiece of Roman engineering. It was part of an approximately 50-km-long (31-mi) water supply channel extending from the source of the River Eure to Nîmes.

Year of inscription: 1985

During the reigns of Emperors Claudius and Nero, between roughly AD 40 and 60, an impressive bridge aqueduct was built over the rocky valley of the River Gard. It was a daring feat at the time in terms of its construction methods. The purpose of this engineering marvel was to supply the fast-growing ancient town of Nemausus (present-day Nîmes) with water. The row of arcades on three levels were slightly offset from each other, the uppermost level measuring 275 m (902 ft) in length. The lowest level has six arches, varying in width from 15 to 24 m (49 to 79 ft) while the middle level has a total of eleven arches. Water was transported on the top level, supported by thirty-five smaller arches, each 5 m (16 ft) in width. The structure was built using limestone blocks without mortar; the blocks were held together merely by the pressure they exerted on each other. Some 40,000 cu m (1,412,587 cu ft) water were transported along the aqueduct to Nîmes every day during peak periods. The aqueduct began to decay in the fourth century. In the Middle Ages, the pillars on the middle level were tapered so it could be used as a road bridge. The structure was not restored until the 18th century.

A museum and visitor center near the Pont du Gard explain the story of the bridge's construction.

The Pont du Gard, 49 m (161 ft) high above the River Gard near Nîmes, is one of the best-preserved Roman bridge aqueducts. The installation has a slight incline from one side of the valley to the other of about 1 cm (½ in), which allowed the water to flow.

The Romans selected Arles, on the northern edge of the Camargue, for its strategic location on the Rhône canal. Aside from remarkable remains from Roman times, there are also important French Romanesque structures to be seen.

Year of inscription: 1981

The subterranean passages of the Cryptoporticus below the Forum are among the oldest Roman structures in Arles. These vast corridors, more than 100 m (328 ft) long and about 70 m (230 ft) wide, likely served as grain storage silos. Two amphitheaters built in the first and second centuries are also Roman. One of them, Les Arènes, is 135 m (443 ft) wide and 100 m (328 ft) long, making it the largest ancient open-air stage still standing. Its vast arena is now used for bullfights. The Thermae on the right bank of the Rhône are from late Roman times and were part of a 200-m (656-ft) palace complex. Thanks to its well-preserved sarcophagi, the necropolis of Alyscamps gives us insight into some of the funerary methods from early- and pre-Christian times. Saint-Trophime Cathedral, with a nave from the 11th/12th centuries, is one of France's most remarkable Romanesque buildings. Its most valuable components are an exquisite portal and magnificent cloisters.

Arles also entered art history as the place where Vincent van Gogh painted some of his most famous pictures.

In Arles you'll wander in the footsteps of the Romans wherever you go, for example the Roman Amphitheater (large picture) or the remains of the former Forum with the Cryptoporticus (top). One of the city's Romanesque gems is the Cathedral Saint-Trophime (left, behind the city hall).

This World Heritage Site on the Rhône, where the popes resided for sixty-seven years in the 14th century, includes the Old Town with its Papal Palace, the surrounding Episcopal Ensemble and the often sung about Pont d'Avignon.

Year of inscription: 1995

etween 309 and 1377, during e "Babylonian Captivity", the pacy found refuge from the political upheavals in Rome in e southern French town of vignon. And thus Avignon, hich Pope Clement VI had

bought from Joan of Naples in 1348, was the center of Christendom during the pontificate of seven popes. Later, two antipopes also resided here.
The Palais des Papes consists of the Old and New Palaces. On

the north side is connected to the 12th-century Romanesque Cathedral of Notre-Dame des Doms. Also part of the Episcopal district, on the west side of the Place du Palais, is the Petit Palais, built in 1317, which was given to the bishop in recompense for the demolition of his former palace.
Since the 14th century, the town had been encircled by almost 5 km (3 mi) of ramparts, reinforced by defense installations and watchtowers including the Tour des Chiens and the Tour du Châtelet. The latter controlled access to the Saint

Bénézet Bridge, built between 1171 and 1185 and also known as the Pont d'Avignon, which today is only a rump jutting halfway into the river.

"Sur le Pont d'Avignon" is the song that made the bridge at the foot of the Papal Palace (below) famous around the world. In the year 1660, half the bridge was washed away by floods. The Papal Palace also contains liturgical rooms such as the Sacristie Nord (left) as well as the Saint John's Chapel with its magnificent paintings (top).

Routes of Santiago de Compostela in France

The Way of St James actually consists of a dense network of trails that cover the continent, converging into four main routes in south-western France: Via Turonensis, Via Lemovicensis, Via Podiensis and Via Tolosana.

Year of inscription: 1998

The alleged grave of St James in north-western Spain was one of the most important pilgrimage destinations in the Christian world. Four main routes traverse France: the Via Turonensis starts in Paris and continues via Tours, Poitiers and Bordeaux to Ostabat, where it merges with the Via Lemovicensis from Vézelay and the Via Podiensis from Le Puy. These routes cross the Pyrenees together. The Via Tolosana starts in Arles and continues via Toulouse and the Somport Pass to Jaca and Puente la Reina. There, all routes com-bine as Camino Francés, which ends in Santiago de Compostela.

Medieval pilgrimages were certainly comparable to modern tourism. To draw pilgrims into the villages along the route, hostelries, hospitals and especially impressive sacred buildings were erected along the way. Becoming popular pilgrimage destinations in their own right thanks to the valuable relics collected, they now feature some of the most remarkable works of medieval architecture. The Way of St James thus gained great impor-tance in the evolution of Romanesque art and inspired individual centers in return. Thus, for example, architecture and sculpture flourished in Burgundy under the influence the Cluniac order in the 11 and 12th centuries, and it w.

The routes join up together just behind the Spanish border at Puente la Reina and become the Camino Francés, the pilgrimage route through northern Spain to the longed-after end of the journey – the Cathedral of Santiago de Compostela.

Year of inscription: 1998

the pilgrimage route in return which created the preconditions for the spiritual and political influence of the order and the material wealth of Cluny. The churches in Tours, Poitiers, Bordeaux, Vézelay, Bourges, Le Puy, Conques, Cahors and Arles, for example, are an expression of people's devoutness in the Middle Ages and of the power of the church. The four routes of the Way of St James in southern France were assigned the status of World Cultural Heritage Sites as important witnesses of the Christian traditions of the region.

In Saint-Côme-d'Olt on the Via Podensis is an attractive 16th-century parish church (top left). The towers of the Sainte-Foy Abbey Church in Conques (left). A popular pilgrims' destination on the Via Tolosana is Saint-Guillhem-le-Désert (opposite, bottom left). Sarrance (opposite bottom right: the cloister) is on the Spanish border. The scallop shell, the symbol of the Apostel James (right: in Saint-Jacques of Châtellerault), shows pilgrims the route (below). St-Eutrope (top: the crypt) is on the Via Turonensis in Saintes.

Canal du Midi

The Canal du Midi links Toulouse (and thus, via the River Garonne, the Atlantic Ocean) with the Mediterranean. It is one of the greatest achievements of engineering from the period of absolutist rulers.

Year of inscription: 1996

Together with its various auxiliary channels like the Canal de la Robine, this artificial waterway was largely completed with amazing swiftness – fourteen years, from 1667 to 1681 – and extends over an impressive length of about 350 km (217 mi). It also features over 300 structures including locks, aqueducts, tunnels and bridges. On the roughly 50-km-long (31-mi) long stretch between Toulouse and its highest point near Naurouze, the canal has to overcome a difference in height of 63 m (207 ft) with the help of 26 locks. Dozens of additional locks are then needed to master the descent of 190 m (623 ft) down to its estuary at the Mediterranean near Agde. And yet the riskiest undertaking by engineer Pierre-Paul Riquet was the construction of the 150-m-long (492-ft) Malpas Tunnel near Béziers, where for the first time explosives were used to clear a path.

The Canal became the most important transport route in southern France, leading to a great boom in the Languedoc Region, where shipping traffic did not decline until the rise of the railroads. In the 1970s, the

Canal was rediscovered as a tourist attraction, and since then it has been used mostly by houseboats whose operators can enjoy the French countryside and the culture of the adjacent towns and villages at a leisurely pace.

In Béziers the Canal du Midi crosses the little Rover Orb via a bridge (top). Today it is possible to cruise down the Canal du Midi in all manner of craft, enjoying the landscape and the villages gliding past the tree-lined riverbanks at leisure (left and below).

The fortified Old Town of Carcassonne, with its double ring of ramparts and numerous gates and towers, is one of the most impressive examples of medieval European fortification architecture.

Year of inscription: 1997

eople from Iberia had already ettled in Roman times on the ill above the River Aude, along he old trading routes between the Mediterranean and the Atlantic. In 418, Gallo-Roman Carcasso was conquered by the Visigoths, who built the inner ramparts in 485. In 725, the Moors took over, and in 759 they were followed by the Franks. In 1229, Carcassonne finally came under the control of the French Crown.

The impressive Romanesque Basilica of Saint-Nazaire was built during the town's expansion in the Middle Ages, roughly between 1096 to 1150, before being remodeled later in the Gothic style in the 13th century. The superb stained-glass win-dows date from the 14th to 16th centuries. Around 1125, the Château Comtal was inte-grated into the inner ramparts. At the end of the 13th century, construction began on the outer ramparts and watchtowers. In the process, the inner ramparts also acquired an impressive gate, the Porte Narbonnaise. The Porte d'Aude dates from the 13th century.

Starting in 1660, the fortifica-tions were no longer needed and began to fall into disrepair. In 1844, a decision was made to reconstruct the medieval city, but the historic quarter had long since become a slum. Master builder and art historian Eugène Viollet-le-Duc (1814 to 1879), a pioneer of modern restoration, supervised the work on the ancient ramparts and the Cathedral, which took until 1960 to complete.

The towers and ramparts of Carcassonne with their meter-thick (three-feet) walls formed a virtually impenetrable fortress in the Middle Ages. The nighttime illuminations allow visitors today to dream of romantic stories of castles, knights and fair maidens.

Pyrénées – Mont Perdu

The landscape around 3,352-m (11,000-ft) Mont Perdu, straddling the French-Spanish border in the Pyrenees, was granted Natural as well as Cultural Heritage status because of the impressive geological formations and its unique culture.

Year of inscription: 1997; extension: 1999

The protected site around Mt Perdu covers a surface area of 300 sq km (11.5 sq mi) world heritage and includes parts of the Spanish Parque Nacional de Ordesa y Monte Perdido and the French Parc National de Pyrénées. In 1999, the site was extended to include the French commune of Gèdre. The specific geomorphology of the region in the area of tension between Atlantic and Mediterranean climates created particularly impressive rock formations here. Añisclo and Ordesa canyons – two of Europe's deepest – are the main attractions on the Spanish side of the border whereas the three valleys of Troumouse, Estaubé and Gavarnie belong to the French administrative department of Hautes-Pyrénées. The U-shaped valleys were formed by glaciers and are among the most beautiful in Europe.

The most striking feature of this imposing landscape is its unspoilt state. Focused on pastoral farming, life here has remained virtually unchanged for centuries, and the trappings of modern technology have failed to leave any real mark on the villages, farms and fields that are still connected by old mountain roads. The landscape bears unique testimony to a high mountain lifestyle that has long since ceased to exist in other parts of Europe.

The mountain region around the Mont Perdu massif (left and below) features impressively rugged limestone peaks, such as here those of the Pic de Pinède and of the Pointe de Forcarral (top).

This World Natural Heritage Site along the middle of the west coast of Corsica includes the coastal region around the Gulf of Porto as well as local underwater habitats and the islands of Elbo and Gargallo.

Year of inscription: 1983

In 2006, the official name of this site was changed to "Gulf of Porto: Calanche of Piana, Gulf of Girolata, Scandola Reserve". The inclusion of the names of the two bays and peninsulas reflected the full extent of the land covered by this protected area. It was listed not only for the beauty of its landscape, but also for its flora and fauna, and the traditional methods of agricultural and pasture management used by the inhabitants.

The nature reserve is part of a larger Corsican regional park. It provides an ideal nesting and breeding ground for many seabirds including seagulls, cormorants and the now rare sea eagle. The rocky peninsula of La Girolata is largely covered in unspoiled wild forests,

and there are large areas of the characteristically Mediterranean maquis to be found here. Dense eucalyptus forests line the many sandy yellow beaches, and the waters around the bays and coves along the deeply fissured rocky cliffs are alive with flora and fauna the likes of which are hard to find anywhere else. Rare algae are just one example of the underwater life that has survived here.

Both rough and smooth rock formations can be found on the Scandola peninsula which can only be reached on foot (below). The steep coast features impressive reddish-brown rock formations (top). Left: bizarre worlds of stone in the Calanche de Piana.

253

The fertile volcanic landscape of the Île de la Réunion ("island of encounters"), located around 800 km (500 miles) east of Madagascar in the Indian Ocean, is home to a rich and varied, often endemic fauna and flora.

Year of inscription: 2010

La Réunion, which together with the neighboring islands of Mauritius and Rodrigues forms the Mascarenhas Archipelago, was created out of fire and water around two million years ago when the Piton des Neiges volcano rose from the Indian Ocean. Today this volcano is the tallest peak in a chain of volcanoes that traverses the island. Also part of the volcanic landscape that was assigned World Heritage status are the Cilaos, Salazie and Mafate "cirques" – three valley basins located in the middle of the island, so named for their circular shape.

The newly protected area largely overlaps with the Parc National de la Réunion surrounding the Piton des Neiges, which was founded in March 2007.

Volcanoes up to 3,000 m (9,843 ft) high (left the 2,205-m 7,235-ft Piton Maïdo) and low cirques (top the Grand Etang lake) feature extreme differences in altitude and in micro climates, making the island of La Réunion a refuge for a unique animal and plant world. Below: a waterfall in the Cirque du Salazie, located in the middle of the island.

The lagoons of New Caledonia and their associated unique reef systems are a refuge to a great many endangered marine animals. The World Heritage Site encompasses six ecosystems with a total surface area of almost 16,000 sq km (6,200 sq mi).

Year of inscription: 2008

New Caledonia covers an area of some 18,600 sq km (7,240 sq mi) and includes both the eponymous main island as well as several smaller coral and two volcanic islands. The group came under French rule in 1853 and is now a French Overseas Territory.

The main island and the islands to its south are surrounded by – along with the Australian Great Barrier Reef – one of the largest coral reef systems in the world. The untouched mangrove forests are home to a wide variety of animal life and lush vegetation. Meanwhile, numerous species of rare fish, including parrot fish, leopard whipray and requiem sharks, as well as the slipper lobster, a type of crustacean only found in New Caledonia, live in the largely intact ecosystems of the lagoons. The shallow coastal waters are the home of the Indo-Pacific tarpon or oxeye, a bony fish whose ancestors populated the tropical seas already during the Cretaceous period. Extensive fields of sea grass provide perfect sustenance for the world's third-largest population of dugongs, which are also also known as sea cows.

The New Caledonian barrier reef (large picture with a ship wreck) is home to a greatly diverse flora and fauna, and provides an ideal habitat for numerous species of corals and fish, such as for example the speckled blue grouper (left) and the violet shining table coral (top).

Despite many later extensions, the Château de Saumur, located high above the city's Old Town and the Loire, has largely maintained its original 14th-century appearance.

Travel atlas France

The maps on the following pages represent France at a scale of 1:340,000. The geographical details are complemented by a large number of additional tips and ideas for tourists including, for example, a detailed reproduction of the road network as well as icons that indicate the location and type of all the important sights, attractions and leisure destinations. The UNESCO World Heritage Sites are clearly identified, and there's an index of place names to make it easy for visitors to locate a particular spot.

Legend

Legend 1 : 340.000

Motorway (under construction)		**A6** Motorway number		**Güter** Freight haulage-Station	
Dual carriageway (under construction)		**E 15** Number of main European road		✈ Important airport	
Trunk road/Federal road (under construction)		**N79** Federal road number		✈ Airport	
Important main road (under construction)		㉔ Motorway junction number		✈ Airfield	
Main road (under construction)		○ Motorway junction		Ferry-harbour	
Secondary road		Filling station		Harbour	
10,5 Distances on motorways		⊗ ⊗ Restaurant, Restaurant with motel		Restricted area	
10 Distances on other roads		⋈ Pass		National and nature park	
Trunk road in tunnel		XII-II Closed in winter		**COLMAR** Place of interest	
16% Gradient		Not recommended for caravans		● Border crossing point	
Other railway		Closed for caravans		International boundary	
T.G.V. railway		**TGV** T.G.V.-Station		Administrative boundary	
Ferry		Car-loading terminal			

Significant points of interest

Road route	Aquarium	Castle/fortress/fort	Olympics
Rail route	Crocodile farm	Castle ruin	Arena/stadium
Highspeed train	Island	Palace	Race track
Shipping route	Beach	Technical/industral monument	Golf
UNESCO-World Natural Heritage	Underwater reserve	Dam wall	Horse racing
Mountain landscape	Spring	Disused mine	Skiing area
Rock landscape	UNESCO-World Cultural Heritage	Working mine	Harbour
Ravine/canyon	Pre- and early history	Impressive lighthouse	Fishing
Cave	Roman antiquity	Wind mill	Sailing
Glacier	Place of Celtic history	Amazing bridge	Diving
Waterfall/rapids	Place of Buddhist cultural interest	Theatre of war/battlefield	Wind surfing
Lake country	The Ancient Orient	Graves	Canoeing/rafting
Sand dunes	Place of Islamic cultural interest	Monument	Waterskiing
Depression	General church	Memorial	Beach resort
National park (landscape)	Church ruin	Tower of interest	Leisure bath
National park (flora)	Christian monastery	Remarkable building	Mineral bath/thermals
Protected area for birds	Roman church	State Historical Park	Amusement/theme park
Biosphere reserve	Gothic church	Space telescope	Gaming casino
Nature park	Baroque church	Market	Viewpoint
Coastal landscape	Renaissance church	Feasts and festivals	Rambling/rambling area
Botanic gardens	Byzantine/orthodox church	Museum	Climbing area
Fossil site	Cultural landscape	Theatre	Mountain refuge/alpine pasture
Zoo/safaripark	Historical picture of the city	Water mill	Remarkable hotel
Wildlife reserve	Impressive skyline	World exhibition	

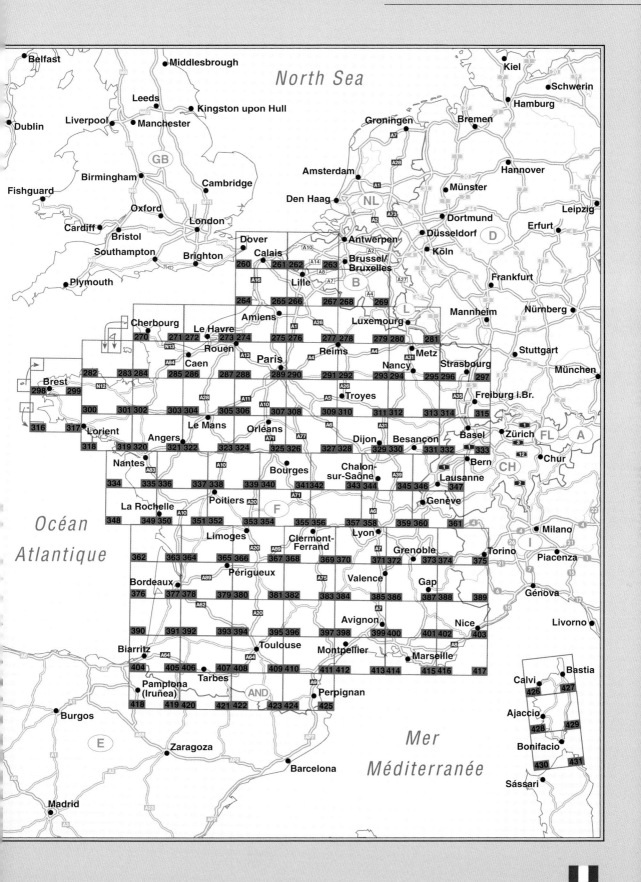

South Channel

MARGATE

Foreness Point
Margate Cave
Cantium

HERNE BAY

Reculver
St. Mary's Church
Birchington
Reculver
Salmestone Grange

BROADSTAIRS

Dickens House Museum
Maritime Museum

Whitstable 5 km
A2990

A299

Chatham 41 km
Maidstone 49 km
London 98 km

Brambles Wildlife Park

Hillborough
Beltinge
Broomfield
Hunters Forstal
Herne
Marshside
Maypole
Chislet
Sarre
West Stourmouth
Monkton

A253

Kent International Airport

RAMSGATE

Pegwell Bay

Ashford 23 km
A28

A2

Chatham 38 km
Maidstone 45 km
London 94 km

Hythe 24 km

Broad Oak
Herne Common
Westbere
Chilham Castle
Whitstable
Fordwich
A291
Preston
Grove
Wickhambreaux
Hoaden
Ware

Richborough Castle

Sandwich Bay

CANTERBURY
Canterbury Cathedral

Ramsgate-St-Augustine

SANDWICH

Woodnesborough

The Small Downs

St-Augustie's Abbey
Lower Hardres

Higham Park
Chillenden
B2046

Ickham
Shatterling
Ash
Marshborough
Eastry
Worth
Sholden

DEAL

Deal Castle
Kingsdown

The Downs

A257
Wingham
Goodnestone
Ingleshan
Betteshanger
Northbourne

Ashford 21 km
Maidstone 42 km
London 94 km
M20

London
TGV **EST**
Ashford 24 km
A261

A259

New Romney 14 km
Rye 35 km
Hastings 53 km

Upper Hardres Court
Bossingham
Kingston
Snowdown
Aylesham
Elvington
Great Mongeham
Time Ball Tower
A258
Kingsdown

A250
Derringstone
Breach
Wingmore
Shepherdswell of Sibertswold
Eythorne
East Studdal
Ripple
Sutton
Ringwould

Walmer Castle

Kingsdown

Stelling Minnis
Waldershare House
Martin
A260
Wootton
Ewell
East Langdon
Martin Mill

St. John Commandery

St. Margaret's at Cliffe

Elham
Swingfield Minnis
Swingfield Street
Kearsney Abbey
 Atkham
Whitfield
West Cliffe

St Margaret's Bay

Liminge
Kent Battle of Britain Museum
Densole
Buckland
St. Radigund's Abbey

South Forelands Lighthouse

Dover Castle

Paddlesworth
Hawkinge
West Hougham

Etchinghill
Capel-le-Ferne
M20

DOVER

11A
Saltwood
Saltwood Castle
Sandgate

East Wear Bay

FOLKESTONE

HYTHE

Strait of Dover

Pas de Calais

Côte d'Opale

Tunnel sous la Manche
Eurotunnel

CAL

Blériot-Pl

Sangatte
Fort Ni
Tunnel sous la M
Coquelle
Coquelle
Signal
Fréthun
Gare TGV

D 940
Peuplingues
Bonningues-
les-Calais
Sombre
Hervelinghen
St-Inglev
Wissant
Wadech

Cap Blanc-Nez
Escalles
Mont d'Hubert 114

Cap Gris-Nez

Cap Gris-Nez
Tardingheo
Framzelle
Audembert
Mont de Couple 163
St-Inglevert
Leubringhen
Château de Blacourt
Mon
de Be
Fergue

Cran aux Œufs
Musée du Mur de l'Atlantique
Audinghen
les Deux Caps
Onglevert
Marquise/
Wissant
Leulinghen-
Bernes
Elinghen

Audresselles
Raventhun
Bazinghen
A16
Marquise

Ambleteuse
Fort Mahon
Slack
Offrethun
Beuvrequen
Rinxent
Re

Dunes de la Slack
Pointe aux Oies
Wacquinghen
Offrethun
l'Epître
Wierre-
Effroy

Hydrequ
D 127

le Wast

2 4 6 8 10 km

Boulogne-sur-Mer

Boulogne-sur-Mer 6 km

D 940

A16 Boulogne-sur-Mer 7 km
Étaples 38 km

TGV Boulogne-sur-Mer

le Wast
Desvres

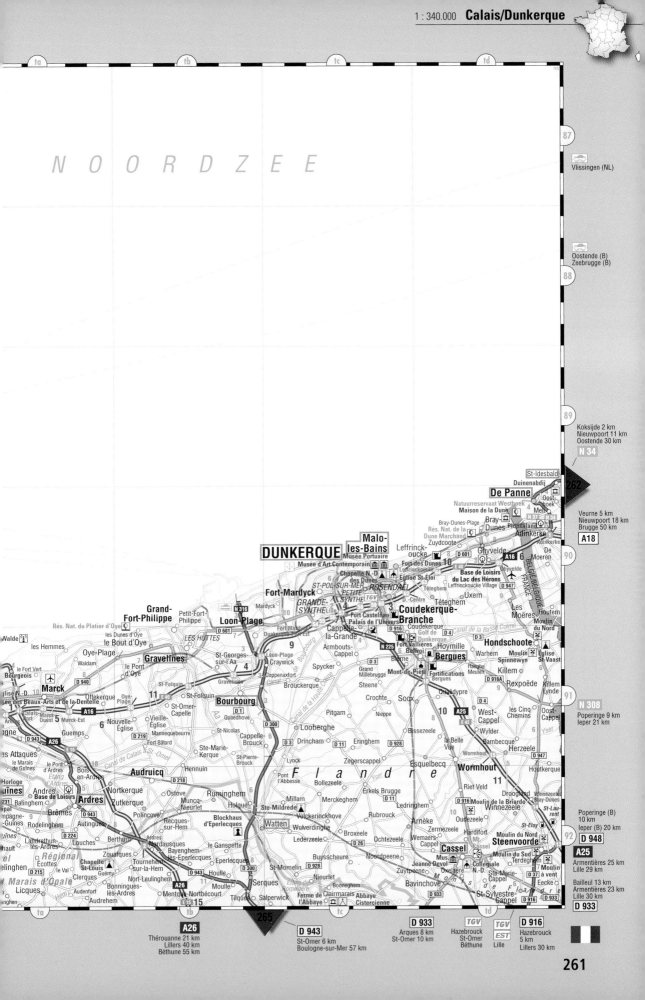

N O O R D Z E E

Felixstowe (GB)  Kingston-upon-Hull (GB)

ub   uc   ud

Dover (GB)

87

Dover (GB)

88

KNOKKE
♪ Scharpoord
Duinbergen
ZEEBRUGGE Heist
Schapenbrug
Westkapelle
Columbus Lissewege Oostkerke Lapsche
BLANKENBERGE
Wenduine Vierwegen Dudzele Damme
De Haan Zuienkerke Koolkerke Moerkerke
Vosseslag Strooienhaan St-PIETERS Schewe
Vlissegem Meetkerke Kroosdij **BRUGGE**
Bredene-aan-Zee Houtave Groeninge Museum Sint-Salvatorskathedraal
OOSTENDE Bredene Stalhille Gruuthusemuseum
Sint-Petrus en Pauluskerk Sas-Slijkens Noordede Memlingmuseum Sijsele
MARIAKERKE Zandvoorde St-Andries Onze-Lieve-Vrouwekerk
Raversijde-Bad Oudenburg St-MICHIELS ASSEBROEK
Raversijde Zandvoorde Jabbeke Steenbrugge Doorn
Middelkerke Effelgem Varsenare Tillegem Kasteel Moerbrugge
Driewegen Snaaskerke **Jabbeke** Loppem **Oostkamp** Beernem
Westende Leffinge Westkerke Snellegem Bloemendale
Ratevalle Slijpe Gistel Bekegem Heidelberg Kasteel Waardamme
NIEUWPOORT St-Godelieveabdij **Zedelgem** Zuidwege Drie Koningen Beernem Hertsberge
St-Joris Zevekote Zande Moerdijk Eernegem Ruddervoorde Wildenburg
Koksijde Middelkerke-Kapelle Moere Aartrijke Molenhoek Doomk
Oostduinkerke Schore Leke Wijnendale Kasteel Lakebos
Nieuwpoort **Ichtegem** De Engel Veldegem **Wingene** St-Jan
Ramskapelle Mokker Koekelare Ermietshoek Baliebrugge
Booitshoeke Keiem Soldatenkerkhof Vladslo **TORHOUT** Hille Zwevezele
VEURNE Avekapelle Pervijze Kasteel Ter Heide KROMMEN-HAAK Koolskamp
Steenkerke Stuivekens-kerke Moskou Edewalle **Lichtervelde** Egem
Bakkerijmus. Zoutenaaie Beerst Bovekerke Kortemark Egem Bergmolen Pittem
Eggewaarts-kapelle Vladslo St-Henricus Koolskamp
Bulskamp Oostkerke IJzertoren Kruisstraat Handzame Gits Gidsberg **Ardooie**
Kasteel van Beauvoorde Lampernisse Esen Werken Korte Wandeling **Liechtervelde**
Vinkem Fortem St-Jacobs-Kapelle **Diksmuide** Predikboom Zarren Geite Kasteel Vijfwege
Wulveringem Oudekapelle Woumen Klerken Terrest Hooglede Ardooie Meulebe
Nieuwe Nieuwe-kapelle **Staden** Gidsberg St-Antonius Kazantwijk
Izenberge Alveringem Sleihage Stadenberg Roeselare-Beveren
Leisele Sint-Rijkers N 364 Houthulst Oostnieuw-kerke Tinnenpot
Gijverinkhove Hoogstade Natuurreservaat De Blankaart Jonkershove Vijtwegen **ROESELARE**
Lo-Reninge Noord-schote Merken Madonna Westrozebeke Kasteel van Rumbeke Haan Kachtem
Pollinkhove Reninge Hoekske Roes-Haven **Ingelmunster**
Weegscheede Linden Fintele Mangelare **Poelkapelle** Rumbeke Roeselare-Rumbeke
Beveren Stavele Bikschote Soldatenkerkhof Langemark Kruiske Vossemolen
Oostvleteren Poelkapelle **IZEGEM**
Roesbrugge-Haringe Westvleteren Langemark- Passendale Kruishoek
D 916A Haringe Eikhoek Boezinge Tyne Cot Cemetery Beitem Ooigem
91 Krombeke Woesten Sint-Juliaan **Moorslede** Lendelede Hulste Dess
Proven Abdij der Trappisten Elverdinge Calvaire-Dolmen Rollegem-Kapelle St-Eloois-Winkel Bavikhove
Kasteel De Lovie Vogelhoek Ieper-Centrum Zonnebeke Beitem Kuurne
Kasteel Koudhof Watou Kasteel De Drie Torens Sint-Jan **Zonnebeke** Moorsele **Gullegem** St-Maarten
Sint-Jan-ter-Biezen Vlamertinge Ieper Noord Beselare Dadizele Industr. Vortr. **KORTRIJK**
POPERINGE Saint-George Memorial Church Zillebeke Sint-Martenskath. Geluveld Wevelgem Nationaal Vlasmuseum
Bergues 24 km Nationaal Hopmuseum Brandhoek Weethoek Moorsele Kortrijk Zuid
Dunkerque (F) 35 km Mus. Mergheynck Ouderdom Zwarte Leen Zandvoorde Kruiseke Lauwe Rekkem
A25 Abele Lijssenthoek Cemetery **IEPER** Hollebeke Vormezele **Wevelgem** Bellegem
92 Reningelst Dikkebus Vierstraat Timbrele **MENEN** HALLUIN Rollegem
D 948 Boeschepe Westouter Klijte Scherpenberg Ossuaire Wijtschate Houthem **WERVIK** **Mouscron**
Godewaersvelde Mont des Cats 158 Berthen Kemmelberg 159 Mesen Oosttaverne **COMINES-** Wervied-Sud Bousbecque Roncq
Caëstre St-Jans-Cappel Mont Noir 138 Dranouter Loker Wulvergem **Warneton** Comines Tourcoing

2   4   6   8   10 km

262

ua

ub   **N 58**   uc   ud

Armentières (F) 9 km   Lille 13 km   D 617   Tourcoing 2 km   N 58   A17
Lille (F) 25 km   A22   Roubaix 8 km   Tournai   Tournai
Roubaix 9 km   Lille 14   29 km   26 km
Lille 13 km
Tournai
Lille (F)

A25
Bailleul 8 km
Armentières 19 km
Lille 31 km

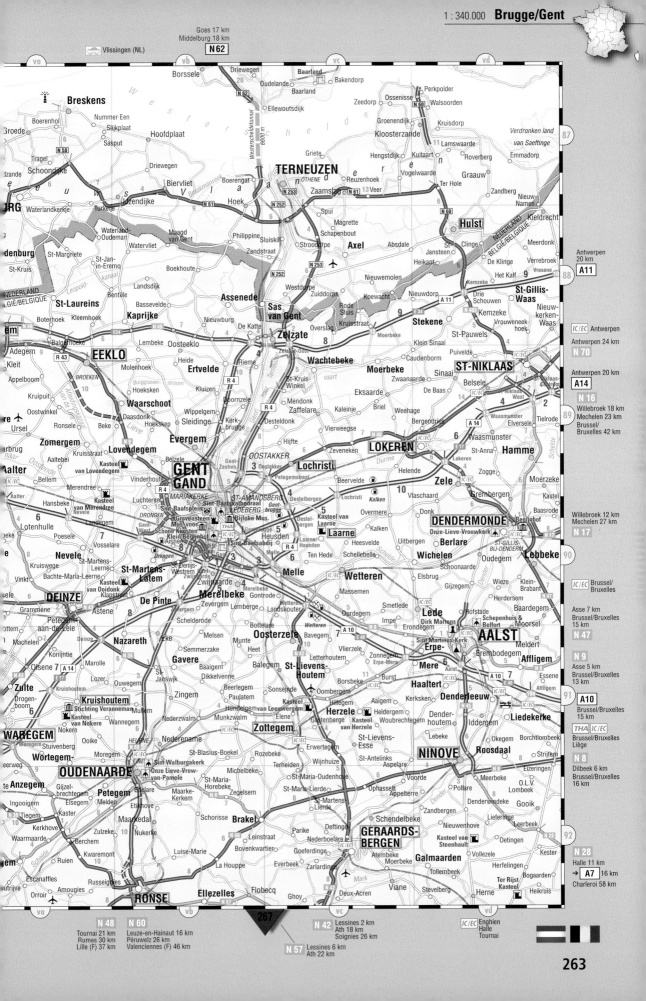

Goes 17 km
Middelburg 18 km
N 62

Vlissingen (NL)

va   vb   vc   vd

Borssele   Driewegen   Baarland   Bakendorp   Perkpolder
Oudelande   Baarland   Ossenisse   Walsoorden
N 62   Ellewoutsdijk   Zeedorp   Groenendijk   Kruisdorp   87

Breskens   Nummer Een   Slijkplaat   Verdronken land
Boerenhol   Hoofdplaat   Sasput   Griete   Hengstdijk   Kuitaart   Roverberg   van Saeftinge
Groede   Tragel   Lamswaarde   Emmadorp
Schoondijke   Biervliet   Boerengat   TERNEUZEN   Reuzenhoek   Graauw
JRG   Waterlandkerkje   Turkeije   IJzendijke   Hoek   Zaamslag   Veer   Ter Hole   Zandberg
Waterland-   Maagd   N 61   Spui   Nieuw-
Oudeman   van Gent   Magrette   Namen
St-Margriete   Philippine   Sluiskil   Schapenbout   HULST   Kieldrecht
denburg   St-Jan-   Watervliet   Zandstraat   Axel   Absdale   Jansteen   Meerdonk
St-Kruis   in-Eremo   Boekhoute   Westdorpe   Zuiddorpe   Heikant   De Klinge   Verrebroek   A11   88
St-Laureins   Bentille   Landsdijk   Nieuwemolen   Rode   Nieuwdorp   Het Kalf   Vrasene   St-Gillis-
em   Boterhoek   Kleemhoek   Bassevelde   Assenede   Sluis   Kruisstraat   Drie   Kemzeke   Waas   Nieuw-
Kaprijke   Nieuwburg   Sas   Schouwen   kerken-
EEKLO   De Katte   van Gent   Overslag   Koewacht   Waas
Kleit   Balgerhoeke   Lembeke   Oosteeklo   Zelzate   Moerbeke   St-Pauwels   IC/EC Antwerpen
Adegem   Heide   Rieme   Wachtebeke   Klein Sinaai   Antwerpen 24 km
Appelboom   Molenhoek   St-Kruis-   Caudenborm   ST-NIKLAAS   N 70
Kruipuit   Waarschoot   Ertvelde   Winkel   Moerbeke   Sinaai   Belsele   Antwerpen 20 km
Oostwinkel   Daasdonk   Wippelgem   Doornzele   Eksaarde   Zwaanaarde   A14
Ursel   Ronsele   Beke   Hoekske   Sleidinge   Desteldonk   Kaleinje   Briel   Weehage   Bergendries   Willebroek 18 km
Zomergem   Lovendegem   Evergem   Vierweegse   Niklaas   89
Aaltebie   Belzele   OOSTAKKER   Lochristi   West   Mechelen 23 km
Aalter   Merendree   Kruisstraat   Vinderhoute   Gent-Zeh.   Oostakker   Beervelde   Helende   Lokeren   Brussel/
Bellem   GENT   Petegemstraat   LOKEREN   St-Anna   Hamme   Bruxelles 42 km
Hansbeke   Landegem   GAND   Destelbergen   Zogge   Moerzeke
Lotenhulle   Nevele   MARIAKERKE   Overmere   Waasmunster   Kastel
Poesele   DRONGEN   Kasteel van   Donk   Baasrode
Nevele   Luchteren   Heusden   Laarne   DENDERMONDE   Willebroek 12 km
Vosselare   Vinkt   St-Martens-   Melle   Laarne   Heesvelde   Schellebelle   Berlare   Mechelen 27 km
Leerne   Ten Hede   Wichelen   Oudegem   N 17
Kruiswege   Bachte-Maria-Leerne   St-Denijs-   Melle   Uitbergen   Schoonaarde   Lebbeke   90
Vinkt   Westrem   Zwijnaarde   Wetteren   Massemen   Gijzegem   Wieze   Klein-
DEINZE   Merelbeke   Gontrode   Schepenhuis &   Brabant   IC/EC Brussel/
Grammene   De Pinte   Zevergem   Landskouter   Belfort   Asse 7 km   Bruxelles
Astene   Scheldeode   Bottelare   Bavegem   Lede   N 47   Brussel/Bruxelles
Machelen   Nazareth   Eke   Melsen   Oosterzele   Vlierzele   Dirk Martens   AALST   15 km
Olsene   Deinze   Semmerzake   Heet   Zonnegem   Erpe-   N 9
Zulte   Marolle   Gavere   Baaigem   Balegem   St-Lievens-   Erpe-Mere   Mere   Affligem   Asse 5 km
Drogen-   Lozer   Ouwegem   Dikkelvenne   Houtem   Borsbeke   Burst   Haaltert   Meldert   Brussel/Bruxelles
boom   Zingem   Beerlegem   Paulatem   Oombergen   Aaigem   Denderleeuw   13 km
Kruishoutem   Mullem   Leeuwergem   Hillegem   Herzele   Heldergem   A10   91
WAREGEM   Stichting Veranneman   Nederzwalm   Munkzwalm   Woubrechtegem   Idegem   Liedekerke   Brussel/Bruxelles
Kasteel   Wannegem   Herzele   15 km
van Nokere   Zottegem   Lebeke   Roosdaal   THA IC/EC
Wortegem-   Nokere   Ooike   Nederename   St-Lievens-   Okegem   Borchtlombeek   Brussel/Bruxelles
Moregem   St-Blasius-Boekel   Esse   NINOVE   Liège
OUDENAARDE   Rozebeke   Erwetegem   Meerbeke   N 8
Anzegem   Gijzel-   Elsegem   Sint-Walburgakerk   Wijnhuize   St-Antelinks   O.L.V.   Dilbeek 6 km
brechtegem   Michelbeke   Terheiden   Aspelare   Lombeek   Brussel/Bruxelles
Petegem   Melden   St-Maria-   St-Maria-Lierde   Voorde   Pollare   Gooik   16 km
Etikhove   Horebeke   Zegelsem   St-Martens-   Meerbeke
Maarkedal   Maarke-   Lierde   Zandbergen   Appelterre
Tiegem   Nukerke   Kerkem   Denderwindeke
Kerkhove   Zulzeke   Brakel   Deftinge   Schendelbeke   92
Waarmaarde   Berchem   Leinstraat   Nederboelare   Nieuwenhove   GERAARDS-   Kasteel van
Kwaremont   Goeferdinge   BERGEN   Steenhault   N 28
Ruien   Luise-Marie   Bovenkwartier   Atembeke   Galmaarden   Halle 11 km
La Houppe   Moerbeke   Oetingen   A7 16 km
Escanaffles   Everbeek   Zarlardinge   Tollembeek   Vollezele   Kester   Charleroi 58 km
Orroir   Amougies   Russeignies   Ghoy   Mark   Viane   Stevelberg   Herne   Heikruis
RONSE   Ellezelles   Flobecq   Deux-Acren

va   vb   267   vc   N 42   vd   IC/EC

N 48   N 60   N 57   Lessines 2 km   Enghien
Tournai 21 km   Leuze-en-Hainaut 16 km   Lessines 6 km   Ath 18 km   Halle
Rumes 30 km   Péruwelz 26 km   Ath 22 km   Soignies 26 km   Tournai
Lille (F) 37 km   Valenciennes (F) 46 km

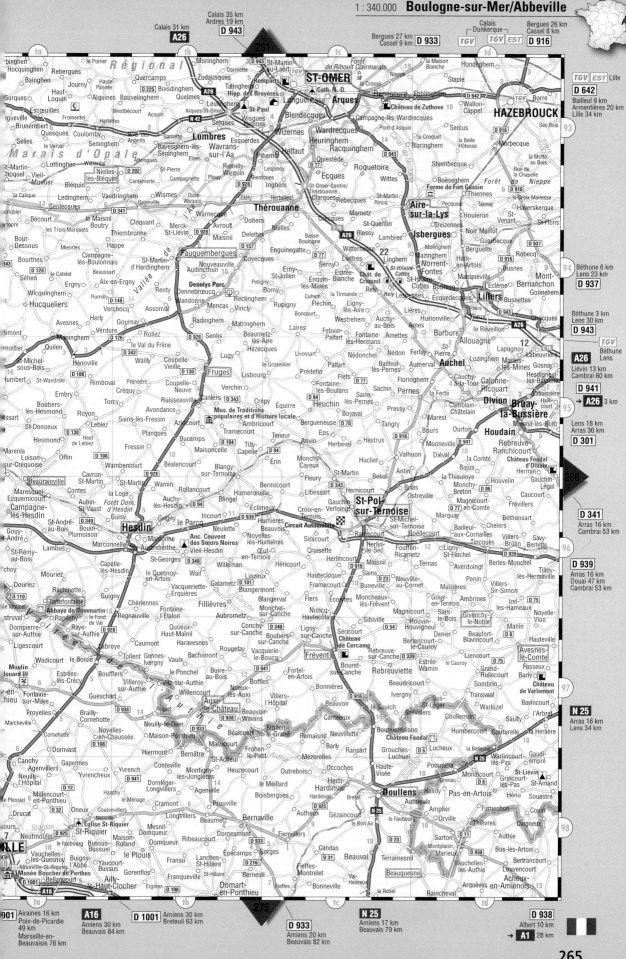

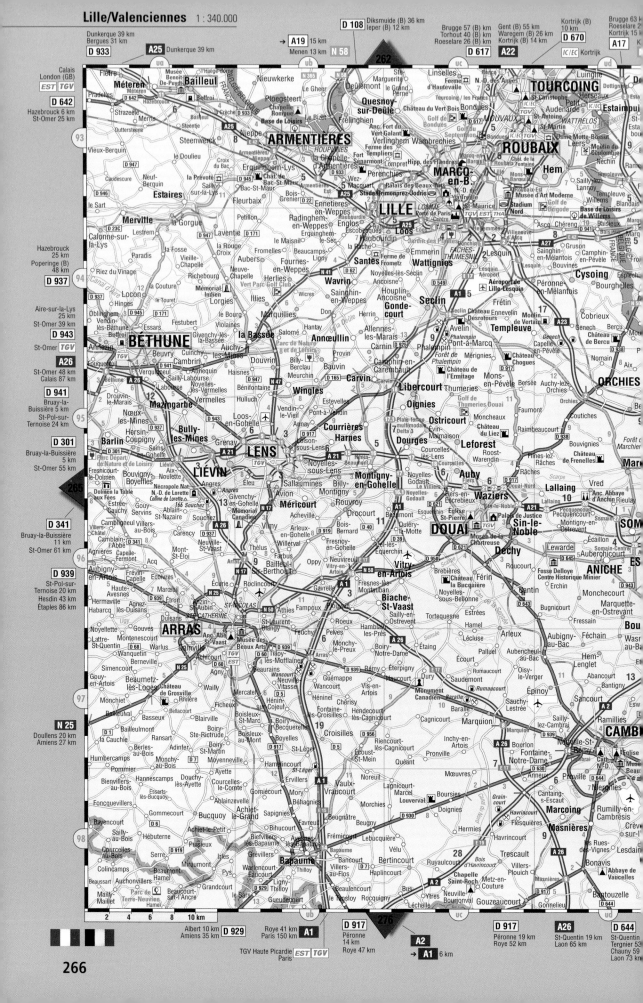

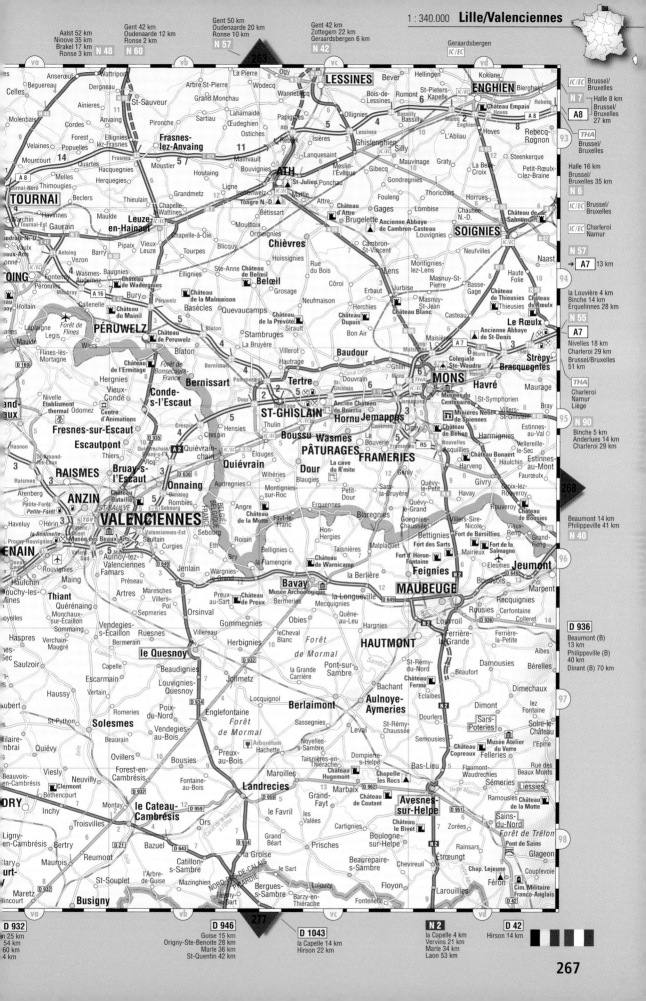

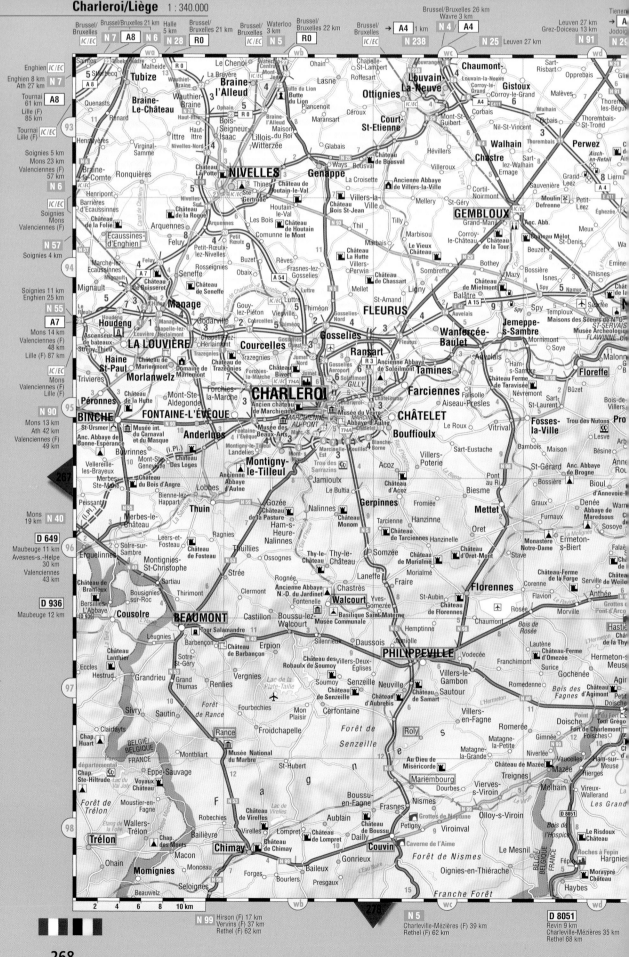

Weymouth (GB)

Rosslare (IRL)
Cork (IRL)

Portsmou
Poo

oa

ob

oc

od

99

100

Rosslare (IRL)

101

Champ de tir

du Castel Vendon

★

Phare du
Cap de la
Hague

Cap de
la Hague

Goury

St-Germain-
des-Vaux

Pointe Jardeheu

Rocher du
Castel-Vendon

Auderville

Omonville-
la-Petite

Omonville-
la-Rogue

Pointe de
Nacqueville

Cap Lévy

Cosqueville

Réthoville

Néville-
sur-Mer

P
de Gatte

Alderney (GB)

102

Digulleville

Éculleville

Landemer

Urville-
Nacqueville

Fort de
Chavagnac

Fort de
l'Ouest

Fort de
l'Est

Pointe du Bruay

Fermanville

le Brick

St-Pierre-Église

Carneville

Varouville

Gouberville

Tocqueville

D 116

D 901

Jobourg

Usine
de retraitement

Gréville-
Hague

Beaumont-
Hague

Manoir de
Dur-Écu

Querqueville

Fort de
Querqueville

**CHERBOURG-
OCTEVILLE**

Maupertus-
sur-Mer

Clitourps

Ste-Geneviève

D 90

Nez de
Jobourg

Dannery

Herqueville

D 901

Branville-
Hague

Domaine de
Nacqueville

Tonneville

le Hameau
de la Mer

Abb. N.-D. du Vœu

Fort des
Flamands

Bretteville

Cherbourg
Maupertus

Tourlaville

le Brick

Ar
An

D 901

le Petit Beaumont

Ruines Mégalithiques
les Pouquelées

Vauville

Équeurdreville-
Hainneville

Château
de Tourlaville

Digosville

Gonneville

D 355

Valcanville

le Vicel

Canteloup

Arse
de Vauville

Réserve Naturelle
de la Mare
de Vauville

Ste-Croix-
Hague

Nouainville

Octeville

le Fort Neuf

Fort
du Roule

la Glacerie

le Mesnil-
au-Val

les Hauts-Vents

le Theil

les Aunays

D 120

Brillevast

Manoir de la Crasviller

Hameau
Valognes

la Pernelle

Champ de tir
de Biville

Calvaire des
Dunes

Biville

Acqueville
(l'Église)

le Saussey

D 64

Sideville

Hipp. de
la Glacerie

Martinvast

Golf de Cherbourg

Man. de Barville

le Poteau

Hameau au
Gallis

le Doucet

Parc Animalier
St-Martin

Hameau
Néel

Hameau
Bonhomme

D 25

D 26

le Tronquet

Quettehou

Fort

le Pont des Sablons

Pénitot

Vasteville

Teurtheville-
Hague

Domaine
de Beaurepaire

Hardinvast

Hameau au
Comte Saussemesnil

Hameau
Mouchel

Hameau
Dubost

Montaigu-
la-Brisette

Piédrechou

Teurthéville-
Bocage

St-Vaas

Clairefontaine

Héauville

D 64

la Croix
Cosme

Virandeville

Helleville

Baudretot

Tollevast

D 56

Délasse

les Planques

la Coucourie

Videcosville

Morsalines

Fort

Diélette

Siouville-
Hague

D 650

D 900

D 24

D 902

D 14

Aumeville-Le

103

Centrale Nucléaire
de Flamanville

le Bois

la Petite
Siouville

St-Christophe-
du-Foc

Couville

St-Martin-
le-Gréard

Rauville-
la-Bigot

Brix

Château de
Chiffrevast

St-Joseph

Tamerville

St-Martin-
d'Audouville

Chap. St-Mic

Flamanville

★

Tréauville

Sotteville

Manoir de la
Grande Maison

Breuville

le Lieu
Jourdan

Hameau
Fouquet

N 13

E 46

St-Germain-
de-Tournebut

Lestre

D 42

Quine

Cap de Flamanville

Dolmen la Pierre au Rey

Houel

Bréval

D 4

les Pieux

Benoîtville

la Belle Étoile

Bricquebosq

Grosville

la Caudière

Sottevast

Chât. du
Pont Rilly

la-Briqu

Valognes

Vaudreville

D 421

Anse
de Sciotot

le Rozel

St-Germain-
le-Gaillard

D 23

la Vauvicard

Quettetot

St-Martin-
le-Hébert

Abb. N.-D.
de Grâce

la Luzerne
du Bas

la Cour

Rocheville

Ruines Romaines
d'Alauna

Ancienne Abbaye

Anc. Abb.

St-Floxel

Fontenay-
sur-Mer

Ozeville

Chât. de
Courcy

Danguevi

le Pou

D 650

Pierreville

la Croix
Morain

D 900

Négreville

Yvetot-
Bocage

D 902

St-Cyr

D 24

N 13

Montebourg

Joganville

St-Marcou

Pointe du Rozel

Surtainville

D 66

le Vrétot

la Vente
aux Sauniers

Bricquebec

D 66

Village
Ste-Anne

l'Étang-
Bertrand

Morville

Hameau
du Mesnil

Colomby

Flottemanville
(le Ruage)

Sortosville

Éroudeville

D 42

Écousseville

Azeville

Sénoville
(l'Épivent)

Soye

les Perques

Magneville

Magnenville
(le Val)

Urville

Hémevez

Fresville

Neuville-
au-Plain

104

Baubigny (l'Église)

Sortosville-
en-Beaumont
(Hameau-Costard)

le Valdécie

les Fourquettes
(le Férage)

Golleville

Biniville

Hameau Gravot

la Gare

Cibrantot

Foucarv

les Moitiers-
d'Allonne

la Vallée

St-Pierre-
d'Arthéglise

Man. de
Gonneville

D 900

St-Jacques-
de-Néhou

Néhou

Hautteville-
Bocage

Orglandes

Gourbesville

Reigneville-
Bocage

D 24

Amfreville

Ste-Mère-
Église

Turquevi

la-Haye-
d'Ectot

St-Maurice-
en-Cotentin

D 50

Fierville-
les-Mines

le Pont-
aux-Moines

Forêt de la
Blauderie

Saudr

Crosville-
sur-Douve

D 2

la Bonneville

D 15

Gueuttevill

Écqu

Rocher du Rit

ob

284

oc

od

2 4 6 8 10 km

D 650

→ D 903 10 km
la Haye-du-Puits 20 km
Carentan 47 km

D 2
la Haye-du-Puits 11 km
Lessay 20 km
Coutances 42 km

N 13
Carentan 13
Bayeux 64 k

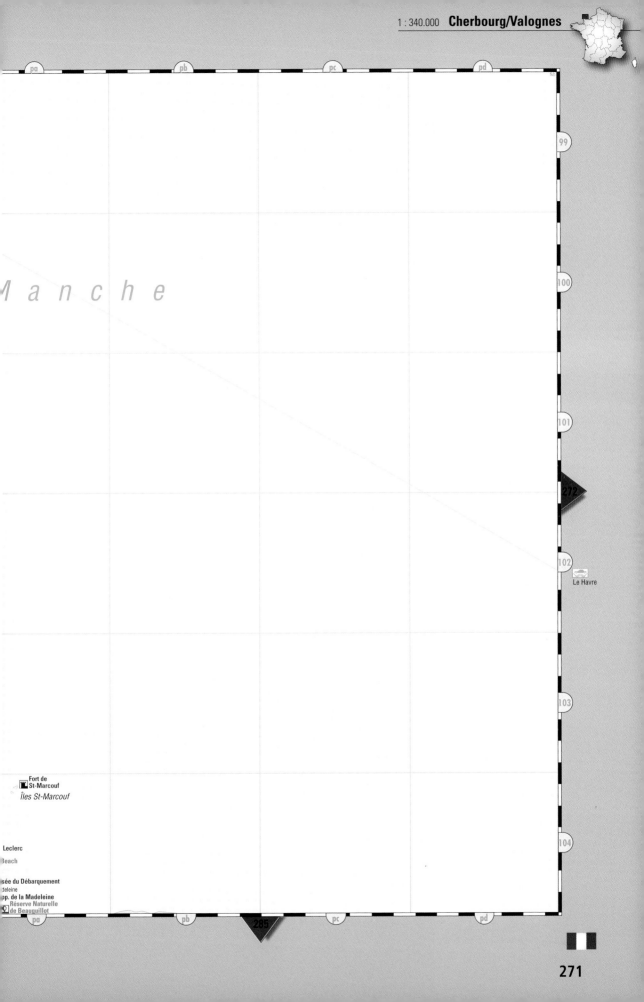

99

100

M a n c h e

101

272

102
🚗
Le Havre

103

Fort de
St-Marcouf
Îles St-Marcouf

104

Leclerc
Beach

sée du Débarquement
deleine
pp. de la Madeleine
Réserve Naturelle
de Beauguillot

285

La Manche

Portsmouth(GB)

99

100

101

271

Rosslare (IRL)
Cork (IRL)

102

103

104

Côte d

Vat

Falaise d'Amont Bénou
Étretat Ch
Falaise d'Aval Ay
D 39
D 39

Cap d'Antifer le Tillé
Phare d'Antifer
la Poterie- Pierre
Cap-d'Antifer
Ste-Ma
au-Bosc
Port Pétrolier du Havre-Antifer Bruneval Villai
Plage de Bruneval Gonneville-
St-Jouin-Bruneval la-Mallet
D 139

Anglesquevi
D 940 l'Esnev

Heuqueville
12 St-Martin-
du-Bec
Cauville Mannevillette He
N.-D
Château du Bec du-B

Écqueville Rolleville
St-Barthélémy Fontenay Épouvi
Octeville- D 925
sur-Mer Cim. des
St-Andrieux D 31 Brisegaret

Montivilliers
Edreville Fontaine St-Martin-au-Mano
le Havre- la-Mallet Royelles Man de
Octeville Devilliers Ga
le Mont Forêt de
Gaillard Montgeon
Cap de la Hève Fort de Harfleur
Tourneville Graville l'Or
Phare de la Hève Bléville TGV
Ste-Adresse Stade Jules Prieuré de Gr
Deschaseaux Complexe
LE HAVRE 13 Pétrochimique
Canal du

Baie de

la Seine

Côte de Grâce Phare de la Falaise
des Fonds
Vasouy N.-D.
Cricquebœuf de Grâce
Villerville D 62 D 579

2 4 6 8 10 km

Ouistreham D 513
Dives-sur-Mer 25 km
Caen 45 km → A13
Caen

272

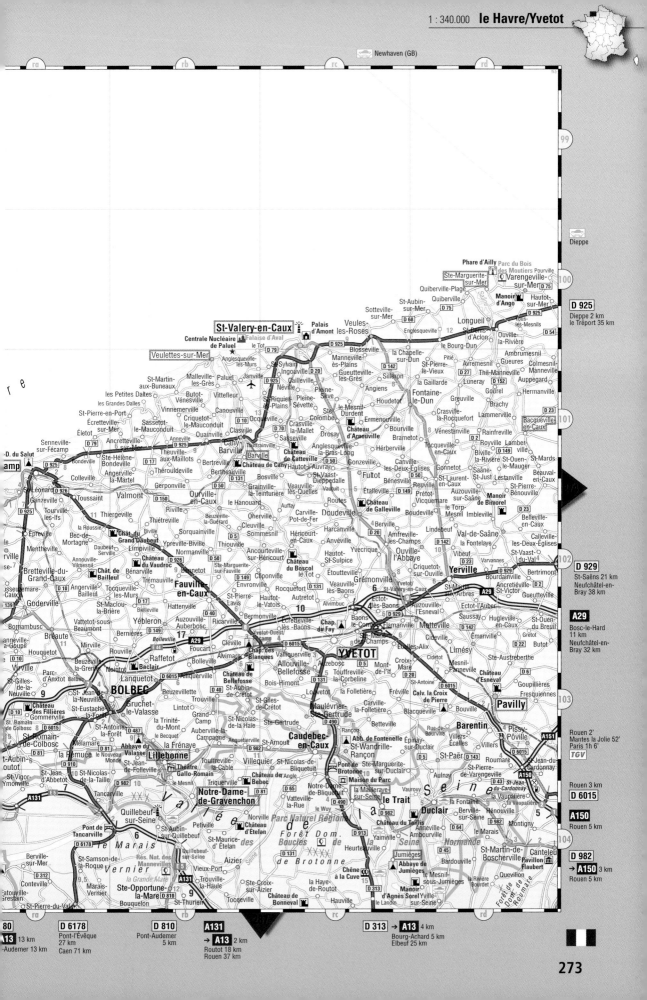

Newhaven (GB)

ra rb rc rd

99

Dieppe

Phare d'Ailly · Parc du Bois
des Moutiers Pourville
Ste-Marguerite- Varengeville-
sur-Mer sur-Mer D 75
Quiberville-Plage Quiberville Manoir
St-Aubin- d'Ango
sur-Mer Hautot-
Sotteville- D 68 sur-Mer
St-Valery-en-Caux sur-Mer D 925
Palais Veules- Englesqueville Tous-
Centrale Nucléaire d'Amont les-Roses Longueil les-Mesnils

D 925
Dieppe 2 km
le Tréport 35 km

100

de Paluel le Tot Blosseville la Chapelle- Ste-Denis-
Veulettes-sur-Mer Angiesville- D 79 sur-Dun d'Aclon Ouville-
lès-Murs St-Sylvain Manneville- St-Pierre- la-Rivière
St-Martin- Ingouville D 20 ès-Plains le-Vieux Pitié Avremesnil Ambrumesnil
aux-Buneaux Malleville- Paluet Janville Gueutteville- la Gaillarde D 142 Gueures Colmesnil-
les-Grès Néville Caiileville- lès-Grès Angiens Luneray Thil-Manneville Manneville
les Petites Dalles Butot- Vittefleur Pleine- D 27 Auppegard
Vénesale Sève Houdetot Fontaine- Greuville Brachy
les Grandes Dalles Vinnemerville Canouville le Mesnil- le-Dun Crasville- Hermanville
St-Pierre-en-Port Criquetot- Riquier- Durdent Bourville Venestanville la-Rocquefort Lammerville D 23
Sassetot- le-Mauconduit Plains le Colombe Ermenouville 8 Rainfreville Bacqueville-
Ancretteville- le-Mauconduit Ocqueville Drosay Brametot Royville en-Caux
Sennevile- sur-Mer Clasville Crasville- Château Tocqueville- Biville- la-Rivière St-Ouen- Lamber-
sur-Fécamp D 79 Anneville la-Mallet Sassevillle d'Arnouville en-Caux la-Baillie le-Mauger St-Mards
Életot Théuville Touffrainville Hautot-l'Auvray Hérberville Canville- la-Rivière Beauval-
D du Salut Barville Château D 925 Gonzeville les-Deux-Églises eri-Caux
amp D 925 Ste-Hélène- Barville de Catteville Hautot- D 50 Reuville St-Laurent- Gonnetot Saâne- St-Pierre-
Bondeville Angerville- Bertrevelle- St-Vaast- sur-Saâne St-Just Lestanville Bénouville
D 926 la-Martel Château de Cany Dieppedalle Bénesville en-Caux Auzouville- D 23
Colleville Gerponville Bertheauville Grainville- Vauquit Prétot- sur-Saâne Manoir Belleville-
St-Léonard Toussaint la-Teinturière Veauville- Vicquemare le Torp- de Bimorel en-Caux
Ganzeville D 150 Ourville- le Hanouard lès-Quelles Étalleville Mesnil Imbleville D 23
Tourville- Riville en-Caux D 149 Routes Calleville-
les-Ifs Thiergeville Oherville Carville- Doudeville Boudeville D 20 Val-de-Saâne les-Deux-Églises
Épreville Thiétreville Beuzeville- Pot-de-Fer Berville Amfreville- la Fontelaye St-Vaast-
Bec-de- la-Guérard Sorquainville Harcanville les-Champs D 142 Vibeuf du-Val
Mortagne la Roussel Ypreville-Biville Thiouville Héricourt- Anvéville Yvecrique Ouville- Varvannes D 102
Menthéville D 5 Normanville en-Caux l'Abbaye
Annouville- Ancourteville- Hautot- Criquetot- **D 929**
Bretteville-du- Vilmesnil Château sur-Héricourt St-Sulpice Grémonville sur-Ouville Yerville D 929 St-Saëns 21 km
Grand-Caux Chât. de du Vaudroc D 50 Ste-Marguerite- Cliponville St-Mesnil Ancretiéville- D 2 Neufchâtel-en-
Bailleul sur-Fauville Environville St-Victor Bray 38 km
Caux- Angerville- D 926 Bonnetot Rocquefort D 131 Veauville- Ectot- Gueutteville
se Bailleul Trémauville Fauville- St-Pierre- Autretot lès-Baons 4ès-Baons l'Esneval **A29**
Godervile St-Maclou- en-Caux Lavis Hautot- 10 Bosc-le-Hard
Bornambusc la-Brière Bielleville St-Pierre- le-Vatois Alvimbuc Ectot- Saussay 11 km
Breauté Yébleron Hattenville Baons- l'Auber Ste-Ouen- Neufchâtel-en-
anneville- Mirville Auzouville- Ricarville D 40 Bermonville le-Comte Flamanville Gretot du-Breuil Bray 32 km
à-Goupil Houquetot Bernières Auberbosc Ste-Marie- Émanville D 22 Butot
Virville Rouville Bolleville 17 Cléville Chap. des Champs Metteville
D 10 Raffetot A29 Foucart Chap. Cideville Limésy
St-Gilles- Parc- Neintot Bolleville Alvimare Vallquerville du Fay Écalles-Alix Ste-Austreberthe
de-la- d'Anxtot Baclair D 6015 YVETOT Mont- Château D 6
Neuville 9 Lanquetot Château de Allouville- St-Antoine d'Esneval Goupillières
BOLBEC Beuzevillette Bellefosse Bellefosse Touffreville- Croix- D 6015 Fresquiennes
D 10 Gruchet- Trouville Bois-Himont la-Corbeline Mare Mesnil-
St-Romain- le-Valasse St-Aubin- Freville Panneville
Château de-Crétot Louvetot la Folletière Calv. la Croix **PAVILLY**
des Fillieres Grand- St-Gilles- Maulévrier- Blacqueville de Pierre
Gommerville St-Eustache- Lintot Camp de-Crétot Ste-Gertrude Bouville
la-Forêt la Trinité- Betteville D 103
St-Romain- Mélamare du-Mont Anquetierville Rue-de- **BARENTIN** Pissy-
de-Colbosc St-Antoine- le Becquet Sticy-Nicolas-de-la-Haie Abb. de Fontenelle Bourville Villers- Pôville
St-Jean- la-Forêt Aubervillle- St-Wandrille- Épinay- Villers A151
outot D 81 Abbaye du la-Campagne Rançon sur-Duclair St-Paër D 143 Rouen 2'
St-Vigor- Valasse la Frénaye Villequier D 6015 Roumare Mantes la Jolie 52'
d'Ymonville D 910 Lillebonne Touffreville- St-Nicolas-de- St-Pierre- Paris 1h 6'
A131 St-Nicolas- Théâtre la-Cable Bliquetuit Pont de Ste-Marguerite- de-Varengeville **TGV**
de-la-Taille Gallo-Romain Le Mesnil Triquerville Brotonne sur-Duclair Aulnay St-Jean-
Tancarville Vallée Château de Notre-Dame- Maison du Parc D 43 du-Cardonnay
Quilleboeuf- la Bebec de-Bliquetuit la Mailleraye- Vaupiry Rouen 3 km
Pont de sur-Seine Notre-Dame- D 81 sur-Seine Seine la Vaupalière D 6015
Tancarville D 6178 St-Aubin- de-Gravenchon Vatteville- le Trait D 982 la Vaupalière **A150**
le Marais sur-Quilleboeuf Petiville la-Rue le Wuy Berville- Rouen 5 km
Berville- D 6178 St-Maurice- Norvile Château Parc Naturel Régional Château du Taillis sur-Seine Hénouville 104
sur-Mer St-Samson- d'Ételan d'Ételan Yainville Anneville- D 64 Montigny **D 982**
de-la-Roque Forêt Dom. Ambourville le Marais → A150 3 km
Conteville Quillebeuf- des Boucles de la Jumièges D 45 St-Martin-de- Rouen 5 km
atouville- Vernier Aizier Vieux-Port Seine D 131 Abbaye de Boscherville
Gestain la Grande Mare de Brotonne Heurteauville Jumièges Mesnil- Bardouvile Canteleu
Marais- A131 Ste-Croix- la Haye- Chêne sous-Jumièges la Rivière Quevillon Gustave
Vernier Trouville- de-Aizier de-Routot à la Cuve Bourdet Flaubert
Berville- la-Haule D 313 Manoir Forêt de Dom.
sur-Mer Ste-Opportune- St-Thurien d'Agnès Sorel Yville- de Roumare
D 312 la-Mare Tocqueville Bonneval le Landin sur-Seine
St-Pierre-du-Val Bouquelon

ra rb rc rd

273

80 | D 6178 | D 810 | **A131** | | **D 313** → **A13** 4 km
13 13 km | Pont-l'Évêque 27 km | Pont-Audemer 5 km | → **A13** 2 km | | Bourg-Achard 5 km
-Audemer 13 km | Caen 71 km | | Routot 18 km | | Elbeuf 25 km
| | | Rouen 37 km

La Manche

Newhaven (GB)

DIEPPE

LE TRÉPORT
Calvaire des Terrasses

EU

le Crotoy 34 km
St-Valery-sur-Somme 20 km
Ault 4 km

D 940

Abbeville 14 km

D 925

Centrale Nucléaire de Penly

Blangy-sur-Bresle
Manoir de Fontaine

Manoir de Briançon
Criel-sur-Mer
Mt. Jolibois
106

D 925
St-Valery-en-Caux 33 km
Fécamp 64 km

D 929
Yerville 10 km
Yvetot 25 km
le Havre 66 km

Tôtes

A29
Yvetot 27 km
le Havre 69 km

A151

A150 5 km

A151

le Havre **TGV**

Malaunay

D 6015
Pavilly 12 km
Yvetot 33 km

A150
Pavilly 17 km
Yvetot 38 km
le Havre 89 km

Notre-Dame-de-Bondeville

Bois-Guillaume

D 982
Duclair 14 km
Lillebonne 47 km
le Havre 83 km

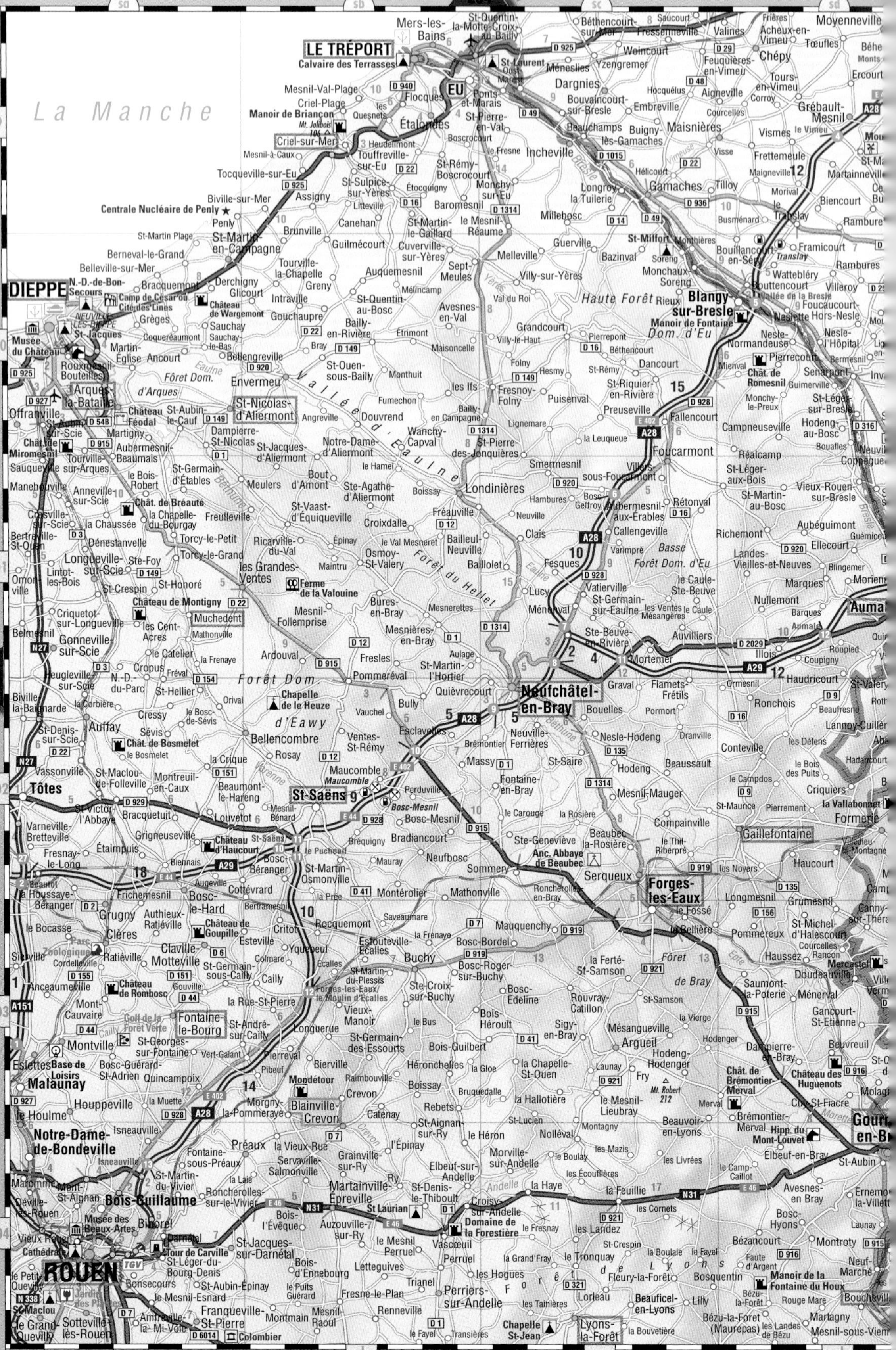

ROUEN

Neufchâtel-en-Bray

St-Saëns

Forges-les-Eaux

Gournay-en-Bray

Aumale

Forêt d'Eawy

Forêt du Hellet

Vallée de l'Eaulne

2 4 6 8 10 km

N 338 | **D 18E** | **D 7**

A13 10 km
Mantes-la-Jolie 76 km

TGV
Mantes-la-Jolie
Paris

D 6014
les Andelys 32 km
Gisors 47 km
Pontoise 84 km
Paris 115 km

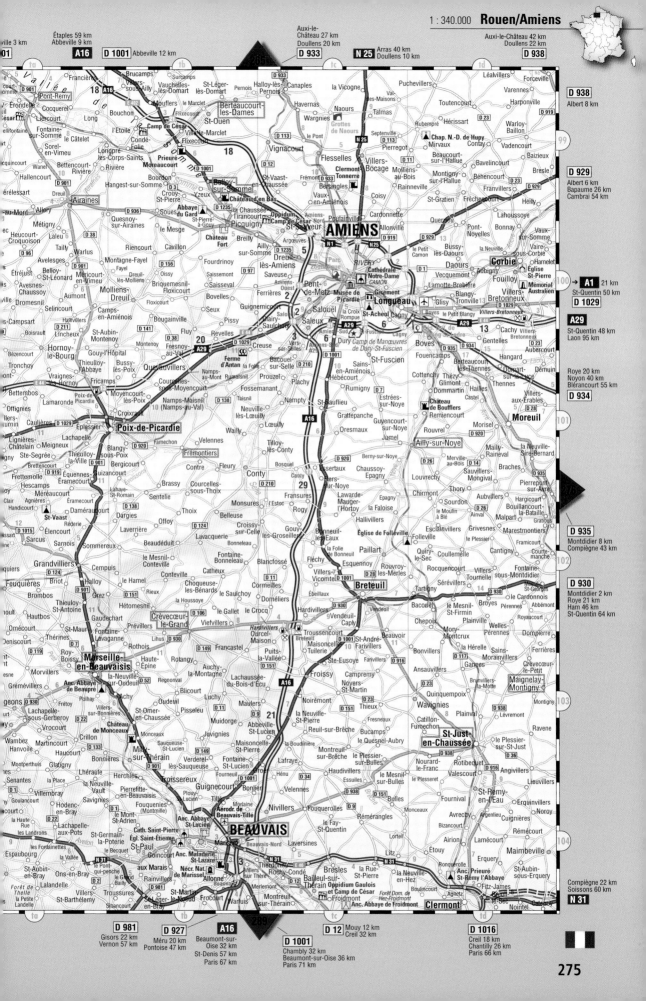

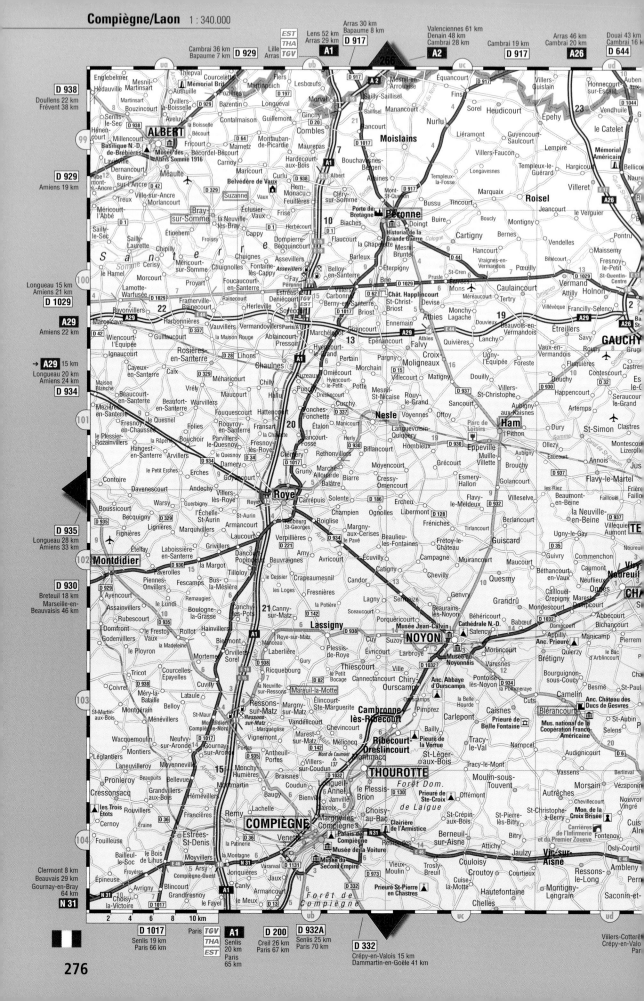

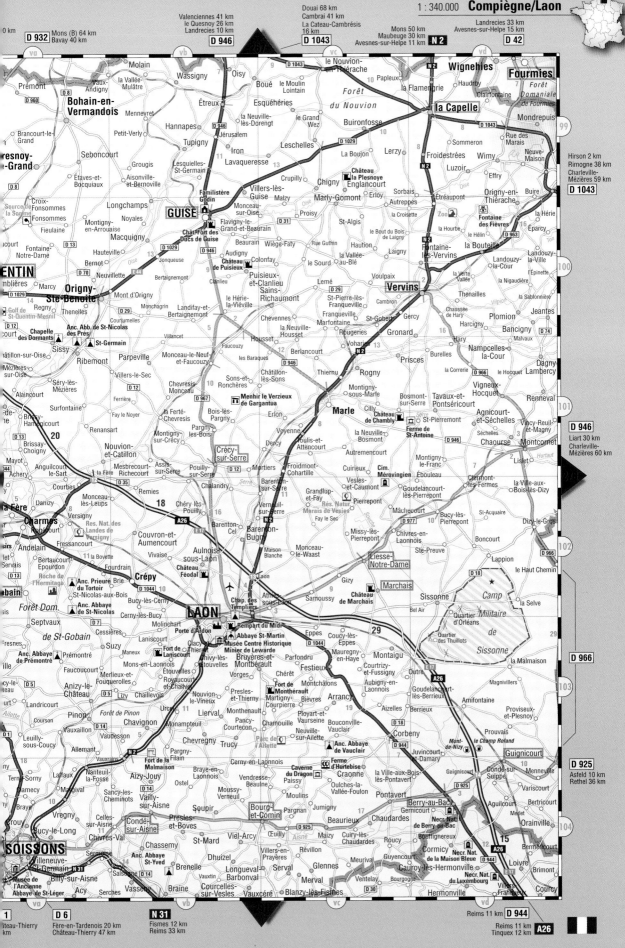

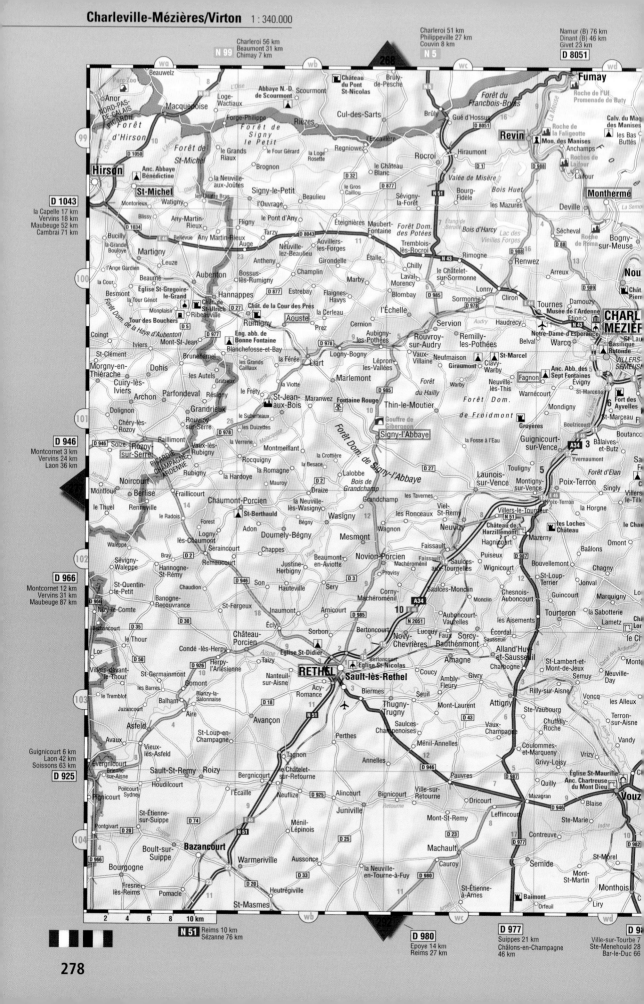

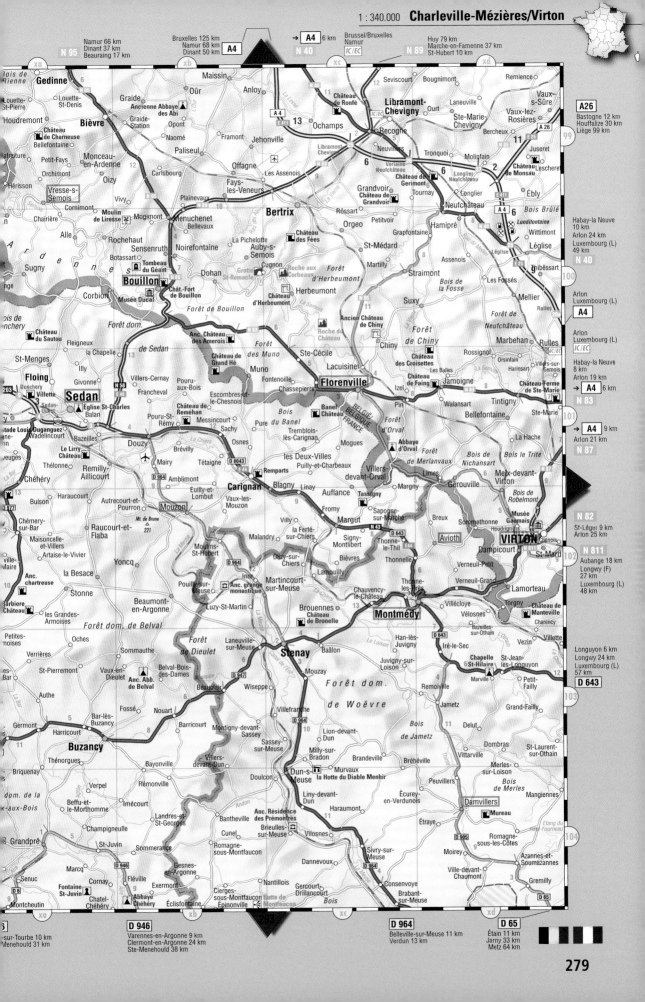

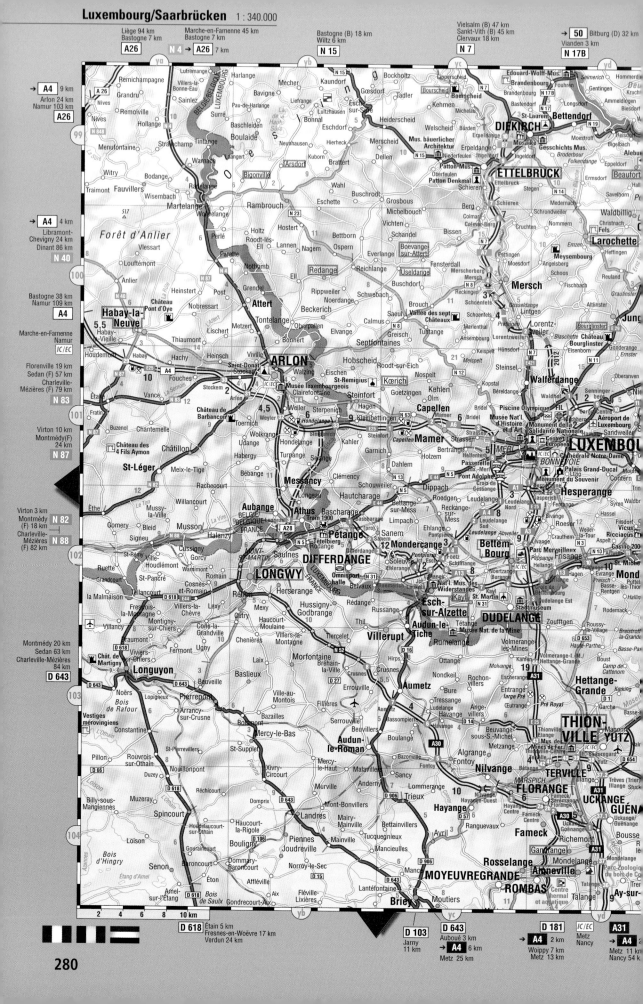

La Manche

Plymouth (GB)

Weymouth

Cork (IRL)

ma
mb
mc
nc

105
101

106
102

Guernsey

nc
md

107

108

Côte de Goëlo

Chenal de Bréhat

The Swinge
Bra
St. Anne

Telegraph Bay

109

Perros-Guirec 5 km
Lannion 8 km
Trébeurden 24 km
D 6

D 786
Lannion 4 km
Trébeurden 14 km
Morlaix 35 km
D 767
110

Pointe de Carn
Île Tomé
Île Baëlanec
Port-Blanc
Buguélès
Trévou-Tréguignec
Trélévern
Louannec
Mabiliès
St-Nicolas
Camlez
Kermaria-Sulard
Coatréven
Trézény
Lochrist
Rospez
Langoat
Lanmérin
Quemperven
Lanvézéac
Mantallot
Caouënnec-Lanvézéac
Confort
Berhet
Kerrod
Prat
Cavan
Tonquédec
Kerel
Coatascorn

Pointe de Plougrescant
Maison de Plougrescant
Porz Bugalé
Île d'Er
le Roudour
Plougrescant
Kerautret
Kergall
Keralio
D 74
D 8
St-Gonery
Penvénan
Plouguiel
Tréguier
Minihy-Tréguier
Trédarzec
D 6
D 786
la Roche-Derrien
Troguéry
Hengoat
Pouldouran
Boloi
Château de la Roche Jagu
Bois de Penhoat-Lancerf
Ploëzal
la Roche Jagu
D 787
D 787
Plourivo
Kermaria
Runan
Trévoazan
D 33
Plouëc-du-Trieux
le Cabaret

Île Loaven
St-Antoine
Brestan
Pleubian
Kerbors
le-Paradis
Lanmodez
St-Adrien
Kermenguy
Lézardrieux
Kergrist
Pleudaniel
Moulin à Marée
Lancerf
Kerfot
Yvias
Pontrieux
Quemper-Guézennec
le Faouët
St-Jacques
Tréméven
Lézoën
D 15
Temple de Lanleff
Lanleff
Manoir de Boisgelin
St-Laurent

Lanros
Île Modez
l'Armor
Chaire
Centre d'Études et de Valorisation des Algues
Kermouster
D 33
D 20
Pleumeur-Gautier
Lannévez
Perros Hamon
Placen al-Louédec
Plouézec
le Vieux Bourg
Kermaria
le Danot
Pléhédel

Phare du Paon
Île de Bréhat
Phare du Rosédo
St-Michel
Île-de-Bréhat
Loguivy
Pointe de l'Arcouest
Porz Even
Île St-Rion
Paimpol
Kérity
Abbaye de Beauport
Port Lazo
D 789
D 7
Pointe de Guilben
Pointe de Plouézec
St-Riom
Minard
Pointe de Minard
Plouézec
la Madeleine
le Questel
Lanloup
Pointe de la Tour
Manoir de la Noé Verte
Port-Moguer
Kerouziel
Kermaria
Run Bellec
le Palus
D 786
Plouha
St-Quay-Binic

2 4 6 8 10 km

mb
mc
md

D 767 Bégard 6 km
Guingamp 20 km
St-Brieuc km 52 km

D 787 Guingamp 13 km
→ **N 12** 13 km

D 7 Guingamp 23 km
St-Brieuc 35 km

D 786 St-Quay-Portrieux 8 km
St-Brieuc 31 km

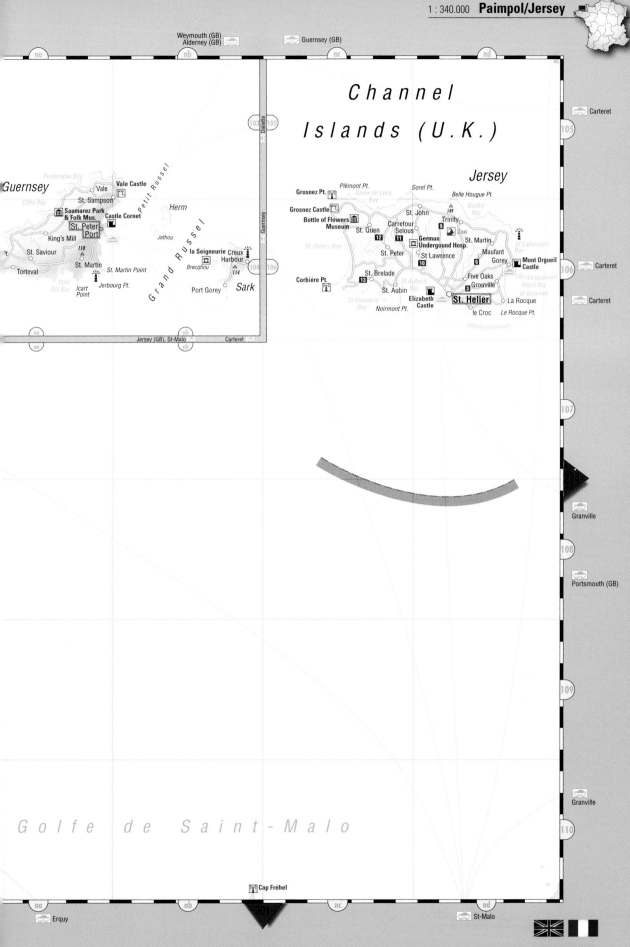

Weymouth (GB)
Alderney (GB)

Guernsey (GB)

Carteret

Channel

Islands (U.K.)

Guernsey

Pembrocke Bay

Vale Castle

St. Sampson

Saumarez Park
& Folk Mus.

Castle Cornet

St. Peter
Port

King's Mill

St. Saviour

110

St. Martin

St. Martin Point

Torteval

Petit
Bôt Bay

Icart
Point

Jerbourg Pt.

Côbo Bay

Vale

Herm

Jethou

Grand Russel

Petit Russel

Guernsey

la Seigneurie

Brecqhou

Creux
Harbour

114

Port Gorey

Sark

Jersey

Grosnez Pt.

Plémont Pt.

Grève de Lecq
Bay

Sorel Pt.

Belle Hougue Pt.

Grosnez Castle

Bottle of Flowers
Museum

St. Quen

St. John

△ *149*

Trinity

Carrefour
Selous

St. Ouen's Bay

St. Peter

German
Undergound Hosp.

St Lawrence

St. Brelade

St Brelade's
Bay

Corbiére Pt.

St. Aubin

Noirmont Pt.

Bouley
Bay

Zoo

St. Martin

St Catherine's
Bay

Maufant

Gorey

Mont Orgueil
Castle

Five Oaks

Grouville

Elizabeth
Castle

St. Helier

le Croc

La Rocque

Le Rocque Pt.

Royal Bay
of Grouville

Carteret

Carteret

Carteret

Jersey (GB), St-Malo

Carteret

Granville

Portsmouth (GB)

Granville

G o l f e   d e   S a i n t - M a l o

Cap Fréhel

Erquy

St-Malo

Cherbourg-Octeville 41 km
St-Germain-le-Gaillard 13 km
D 650

Valognes 14 km
D 2

Cherbourg-Octeville 41 km
Valognes 21 km
N 13

270

Passage de la Déroute

105

106 Gorey (Jersey, GB)

St. Hélier (Jersey, GB)

107

108 St. Hélier (Jersey, GB)

109

St-Malo

110

Cap de Carteret
Phare de Carteret
Carteret
Barneville-Carteret
St-Jean-de-la-Rivière
Barneville-Plage
Barneville-sur-Mer
St-Georges-de-la-Rivière
Golf de la Côte des Isles
St-Siméon
Gennetot
Baptistère
Hipp. des Pins
Portbail
Chât. d'Omonville
Varreville
Lindbergh-Plage
Denneville
Denneville-la-Plage
St-Rémy-des-Landes
Surville
la Poudrière
Glatigny
Bretteville-sur-Ay
la Plage
St-Germain-sur-Ay
St-Germain-sur-Ay-Plage
le Gué de l'Orme
Anc. Abb.
Créances
Printania-Plage
Armanville-Plage
Pirou
Bourgogne
Pirou-Plage
Chât. de Pirou
la Grande Maresquière
Geffosses
Anneville-sur-Mer
la Mielle
le Sénéquet Phare
Gouville-sur-Mer
Boisroger
Gonneville
St-Malo-de-la-Lande
Blainville-sur-Mer
le Vieux Coutainville
Coutainville
Hipp. du Martinet
Agon
Coutainville
Regnéville-sur-Mer
Pointe d'Agon
Montmartin-sur-Mer
Hauteville-sur-Mer
Hauteville-sur-Mer-Plage
Annoville
Lingreville
Bricqueville-sur-Mer
Golf de Bréhal
St-Martin-de-Bréhal
Hipp. des Mielles
Aérodrome de Granville
Golf de Granville
Bréville-sur-Mer
Donville-les-Bains
Yquelon
Granville
Pointe du Roc
la Maison Brûlée
St-Pair-sur-Mer
le Petit Kairon
Jullouville
Hipp. la Cale
Bouillon
Carolles
Cabane Vauban
Angey
la Pierre de Herpin
Pointe du Grouin
Île des Landes
Pointe du Meinga
Port-Mer
Basse Cancale
le Verger
St-Pierre-Langers
St-Aubin-des-Préaux
Champeaux
St-Jean-le-Thomas
Ronthon
Falaises de Champeaux
Dragey-Ronthon
Château de Brion
Bacilly
Marcey-les-Grèves
St-Jean-de-la-Haize
St-Brice
Ponts

St-Sauveur-le-Vicomte
Rauville-la-Place
Anc. Abb.
Étienville
Picauville
Chef-du-Pont
Mais. de Barbey d'Aureville
Besneville
Taillepied
Vindefontaine
Carentan
le Mesnil
Neuville-en-Beaumont
Catteville-et-l'Adrienne
Varenguebec
Château de Francquetot
St-Côme-du-Mont
St-Lô-d'Ourville
St-Sauveur-de-Pierrepont
Anc. Corps de Garde
les Novailles
Houtteville
la Rue Mare
Neufmesnil
Prétot-Ste-Suzanne
Appeville
le Rivage
Baudreville
Bolleville
Anc. Abb. de Blanchelande
St-Jores
Baupte
Auvers
St-Symphorien-le-Valois
la Haye-du-Puits
D 903
Lithaire
la Roquette
Montgardon
Hameau Blémont
Mobecq
Nerduit
le Pautet
Carbassue
Méautis
Gonfreville
D 903
Angoville-sur-Ay
Vesly
Laulne
la Boetterie
Longueville
Sainteny
D 900
Pissot
St-Patrice-de-Claids
Nay
Corbauville
Gorges
Bléhou
Rés. Nat. de la Tourbière de Mathon
St-Germain-sur-Sèves
Raids
la Martinerie
Auxais
Lessay
la Doderie
la Banserie
Milbières
D 900
St-Sébastien-de-Raids
le Haut Mesnil
la Feuillie
Périers
St-Martin-d'Aubigny
Marchésieux
la Gislarderie
Maison des Marais
Vaudrimesnil
D 68
Feugères
le Mesnil-Vigot
l'Eventard
Corbuchon
St-Michel-de-la-Pierre
St-Aubin-du-Perron
le Haut de Bingard
la Ronde-Haye
les Mares
le Mesnilbus
Vichard
Montsurvent
Muneville-le-Bingard
Ancteville
Hauteville-la-Guichard
la Laiserie
le Val
la Carrie
St-Sauveur-Lendelin
Montcuit
le Pont au Lorey
la Rue
la Fouberdière
Servigny
la Vendelée
Cambernon
Camprond
Grato (le Pavement)
D 244
Guesnay
Cametou
Tourville-sur-Sienne
Bricqueville-la-Blouette
Coutances
Hôtel-Dieu
Savigny
Heugueville-sur-Sienne
le Pont de la Roque
St-Pierre-de-Coutances
Courcy
la Hongrie
Orval
Belval
le Castel
Montpinchon
Cerisy
Ouville
le Castelet
Roncey
Saussey
le Boulay
l'Auriole
Montchaton
Hyenville
Contrières
Quettreville-sur-Sienne
St-Denis-le-Vêtu
Guéhébert
Hérenguerville
la Jouannerie
St-Ma de-Ce
Trelly
le Mesnil-Aubert
St-Denis-le-Gast
D 971
le Bourg Sey
la Baleine
l'Abbaye
Muneville-sur-Mer
Lengronne
Cérences
la Croix le Gros
Gavray
la Planche Guillemette
Bricqueville-sur-Mer
Ver
Bréhal
Chanteloup
le Castillon
la Violette
Chât. de Chanteloup
Coudeville-sur-Mer
le Loreur
le Mesnil-Amand
la Blout
Hudimesnil
le Mesnil-Rogues
le Mesnil-Villeman
la Meurdraquière
le Mesnil-Garnier
Fleury
Longueville
Anctoville-sur-Boscq
St-Sauveur-la-Pommeraye
Equilly
Zoo
Villedieu-les-Poêles
Malicorne
Folligny
St-Jean-des-Champs
Beauchamps
Champrepus
la Lande-d'Airou
Pieuré de l'Oiselière
St-Aubin-des-Préaux
St-Pierre-Langers
Hocquigny
St-Ursin
la Haye-Pesnel
la Mouche
Bourguenolles
la Loge Guibert
la Duretière
Anc. Abb. de la Lucerne
la Lucerne-d'Outremer
Champcervon
la Rochelle-Normande
les Chambres
Ste-Pience
le Luot
St-Michel-des-Loups
D 973
Sartilly
Montviron
Lolif
Sublignyi
Chavoy
St-Jean-le-Thomas
le Tilleul
Champcey
Baie Somb
Tiépied
la Gohannière

A84

Îles Chausey
Grand Romont
Grande Île
les Huguenans
le Pignon

2 4 6 8 10 km

D 911
Avranches 12 km
→ **A84** 13 km

A84
Avranches 2 km
Rennes 79 km

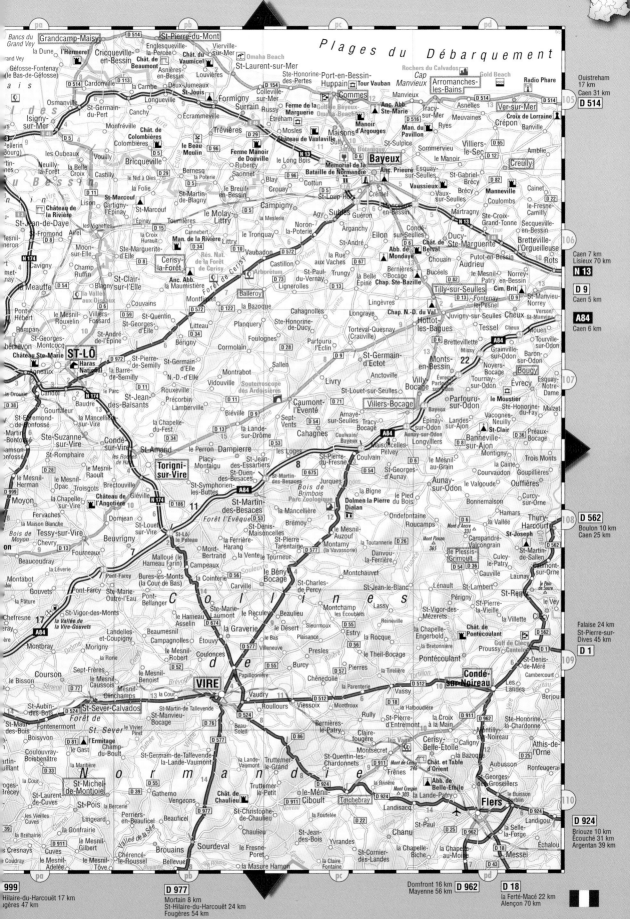

Plages du Débarquement

Bancs du Grand Vey
Grandcamp-Maisy
St-Pierre-du-Mont
D 514
l'Hermerel
Cricqueville-en-Bessin
Chât. du Vaumicel
Omaha Beach
St-Laurent-sur-Mer
Englesqueville-la-Percée
Vierville-sur-Mer
Rochers du Calvados
Gold Beach
Ouistreham 17 km
Caen 31 km
D 514

la Dune
Géfosse-Fontenay (le Bas-de-Géfosse)
Chât. de Beaumont
Asnières-en-Bessin
Louvières
Ste-Honorine-des-Pertes
Port-en-Bessin-Huppain
Tour Vauban
Cap Manvieux
Arromanches-les-Bains
Radio Phare
Ver-sur-Mer

Osmanville
Cardonville
D 113
La Cambe
Deux-Jumeaux
St-Jouis
Colleville-sur-Mer
Commes
Manvieux
Asnelles
Meuvaines
Croix de Lorraine
Caen 7 km
Lisieux 70 km
N 13

Isigny-sur-Mer
St-Germain-du-Pert
Canchy
Longueville
Formigny
Russy
Golfe Bayeux
Omaha Beach
Tracy-sur-Mer
Crépon
Banville
Amblie

les Oubeaux
Monfréville
Écrammeville
Surrain
Ferme de la Marguerie
Étréham
Anc. Abb. Ste-Marie
Manvieux
Sommervieu
le Manoir
Villiers-le-Sec
Creully

Neuilly-la-Forêt
Vouilly
Bricqueville
le Beau Moulin
Mosles
Château de Vaulaville
Sully
Manoir d'Argouges
Man. du Pavillon
St-Sulpice
Ryes
D 65
Cainet
le-Fresne-Camilly

la Belle Croix
Bernesq
le Nid à Oies
Ruberry
le Long Bois
Mémorial de la Bataille de Normandie
Bayeux
Anc. Prieuré
Esquay-sur-Seulles
Martragny
Secqueville-en-Bessin
Bretteville-l'Orgueilleuse
Rots
Caen 5 km
D 9

Château de la Rivière
D 11
Lison
St-Marcouf
Cartigny-l'Épinay
le Breuil-en-Bessin
la Poterie
Blay
Crouay
Vaussieux
Brécy
Manneville
Coulombs
A84
Caen 6 km

Château de la Rivière
St-Jean-de-Daye
Fromond
Airel
Ste-Marguerite-d'Elle
Moon-sur-Elle
le Molay-Littry
la Croix
Noron-la-Poterie
Arganchy
St-André
Ellon
Condé-sur-Seulles
Ducy-Ste-Marguerite
Putot-en-Bessin
Audrieu
Norrey-Patry-en-Bessin
St-Manvieu-Norrey
Verson

Cavigny
Champ Ruffin
St-Clair-sur-l'Elle
Tournières
Castillon
la Rue aux Vaches
Trungy
la Belle Épine
Chap. Ste-Bazille
Tilly-sur-Seulles
Bucéels
le Mesnil-Patry-en-Bessin
Cim. Brit.

St-Georges-Montcocq
Cerisy-la-Forêt
Anc. Abb. la Maumistière
Balleroy
Arboretum
Ligerolles
Lingèvres
Chap. N.D. du Val
Hottot-les-Bagues
Fontenay-le-Pesnel
Cheux

ST-LÔ
Haras National
Montfiquet
la Bazoque
Cahagnolles
Ste-Honorine-de-Ducy
Torteval-Quesnay (Crauville)
St-Germain-d'Ectot
Monts-en-Bessin
Bretteville
Missy
Grainville-sur-Odon
Noyers-Bocage
Baron-sur-Odon

Château Ste-Marie
Agneaux
St-Pierre-de-Semilly
St-Germain-d'Elle
N.D.-d'Elle
Vidouville
Souterroscope des Ardoisières
Sallen
Cormolain
Livry
Anctoville
Villy-Bocage
Évrecy-Parfouru-sur-Odon
Bougy
Tourville-Odon
Évrecy

le Parc
St-Jean-des-Baisants
Rouxeville
Précorbin
Lamberville
Biéville
Caumont-l'Éventé
Amayé-sur-Seulles
Tracy-Bocage
Villers-Bocage
Épinay-sur-Odon
Landes-sur-Ajon
St-Clair
Préaux-Bocage
le Moustier
Ste-Honorine-du-Fay
Malzac

la Mancellière-sur-Vire
la Chapelle-du-Fest
la Lande-sur-Drôme
Sept-Vents
Cahagnes
Couvain/Bayeux
Aunay-sur-Odon
Longvillers
Banneville-la-Campagne
Montigny
Vacognes-Neuilly

Ste-Suzanne-sur-Vire
St-Romphaire
St-Amand
le Perron
Dampierre
Placy-Montaigu
St-Jean-des-Essartiers
St-Georges-d'Aunay
Aunay-sur-Odon
le Mesnil-au-Grain
la Caine
Courvaudon
le Valgoude
Trois Monts
Goupillières
Ouffières

le Mesnil-Herman
Moyon
Torigni-sur-Vire
St-Ouen-des-Besaces
St-Symphorien-les-Buttes
Jurques
Bois de Brimbois Parc Zoologique
la Bigne
le Pied du Bois
Ondefontaine
Roucamps
Hamars
la Vallée
Curcy-sur-Orne

la Chapelle-du-Fest
le Mesnil-Opac
Troisgots
Brectouville
Château de Gièville d'Angoterie
St-Martin-des-Besaces
la Mancellière
Brémoy
le Mesnil-Auzouf
Montamy (la Vavassorie)
Danvou-la-Ferrière
Mont Pinçon 365
le Plessis-Grimoult
Campandré-Valcongrain
Culey-le-Patry
St-Martin-de-Sallen
Caumont-sur-Orne
Thury-Harcourt
D 562
Boulon 10 km
Caen 25 km

le Mesnil-Raoult
Fervaches
la Maison Blanche
Domjean
St-Louet-sur-Vire
Fourneaux
la Ferrière-Harang
St-Pierre-Tarentaine
Montchauvet
la Toutannerie
la Vallée
Campandré-Valcongrain
Cauville
St-Joseph
Launay
le Mesnil-Herman

Chevry
Beuvrigny
St-Lô le Poteau
Mont-Bertrand
Malloué (le Hameau Farin)
le Bény-Bocage
St-Charles-de-Percy
St-Jean-le-Blanc
Lénault
St-Lambert
St-Rémy
le Vey
Clécy

Beaucoudray
la Léverie
Pont-Farcy
Ste-Marie-Outre-l'Eau
Bures-les-Monts (la Cour de Bas)
la Cointerie
Carville
Périgny
St-Pierre-la-Vieille
la Villette

Montabot
la Pâture
Pont-Bellanger
la Graverie
Beaulieu
Montcharny les Écoublets
Lassy
St-Vigor-des-Mézerets
Falaise 24 km
St-Pierre-sur-Dives 45 km
D 1

Gouvets
St-Vigor-des-Monts
la Vallée de Vire-Gouvets
le Hameau Asselin
Landelles-et-Coupigny
Beaumesnil
le Reculey
Sieurmoux
Reineville
la Chapelle-Engerbold
Chât. de Pontécoulant
Golf de Clécy
Proussy
Cantelou

Chefresne
Montbray
Morigny
Campagnolles
Étouvy
le Désert
le Bas
Plaisance
Estry
la Rocque
la Bretonnière
Pontécoulant
D 562
D 109

Courson
le Bisson
Sept-Frères
le Mesnil-Robert
Coulonces
Villeneuve
Presles
Burcy
le Theil-Bocage
Pierres
la Tirelière
Condé-sur-Noireau
St-Denis-de-Méré
Cambercourt
Berjou

la Pâture
le Mesnil-Benoist
Brévogne
Papillonne
D 55
Chênedollé
la Parenterie
Vassy
D 512
Proussy
Les Landes

VIRE
Vaudry
Roullours
Viessoix
Montfroux
Rully
la Halboudière
D 911
Ste-Honorine-la-Chardonne
Athis-de-l'Orne

St-Aubin-des-Bois
St-Sever-Calvados
Forêt de St-Sever
St-Manvieu-Bocage
le Vivier Piret
Beau-Soleil
Bernières-le-Patry
St-Pierre-d'Entremont
la Croix à la Main
Montilly-sur-Noireau
Caligny

St-Maur-des-Bois
Fontenermont
Boisyvon
l'Ermitage
le Gast
Champ-du-Boult
St-Germain-de-Talfevende-la-Lande-Vaumont
Truttemer-le-Grand
St-Quentin-les-Chardonnets
Montsecret
Mont de Cerisy 246
Chât. et Table d'Orient
Cerisy-Belle-Étoile
la Bazoque
Aubusson
Ronfeugeral

Coulouvray-Boisbenâtre
la Maritière
Truttemer-le-Petit
la Rivière
Mont Crespin 303
Abb. de Belle-Étoile
St-Georges-des-Groseillers
Flers

St-Michel-de-Montjoie
St-Laurent-de-Cuves
St-Pois
Gathemo
Vengeons
Chât. de Chaulieu
le Ménil-Ciboult
Tinchebray
Landisacq
la Lande-Patry
le Buisson-Corblin
Landigou

les Vieilles Cuves
la Gonfrairie
Perriers-en-Beauficel
Beauficel
le Mesnil-Gilbert
Brouains
Sourdeval
Bellevue
St-Christophe-de-Chaulieu
Chaulieu
la Fouterie
D 22
St-Paul
Chanu
D 962
la Selle-la-Forge
Messei

le Mesnil-Adelée
le Mesnil-Tôve
la Masure Hamon
St-Jean-des-Bois
Yvrandes
la Chapelle-Biche
la Chapelle-au-Moine
D 18

999
St-Hilaire-du-Harcouët 17 km
Fougères 47 km

D 977
Mortain 8 km
St-Hilaire-du-Harcouët 24 km
Fougères 54 km

Domfront 16 km
Mayenne 56 km
D 962

D 18
la Ferté-Macé 22 km
Alençon 70 km

D 924
Briouze 10 km
Écouché 31 km
Argentan 39 km

285

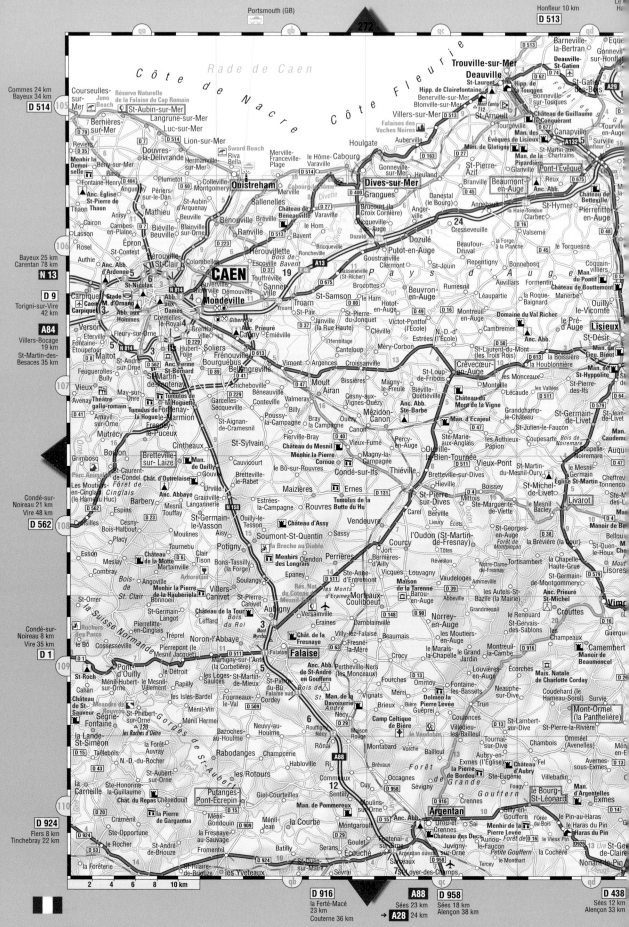

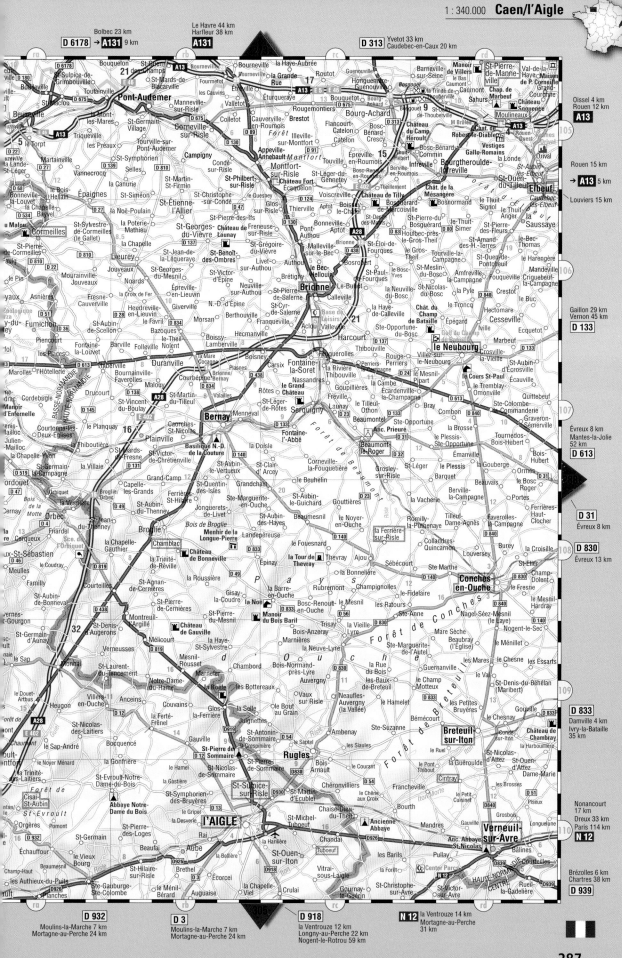

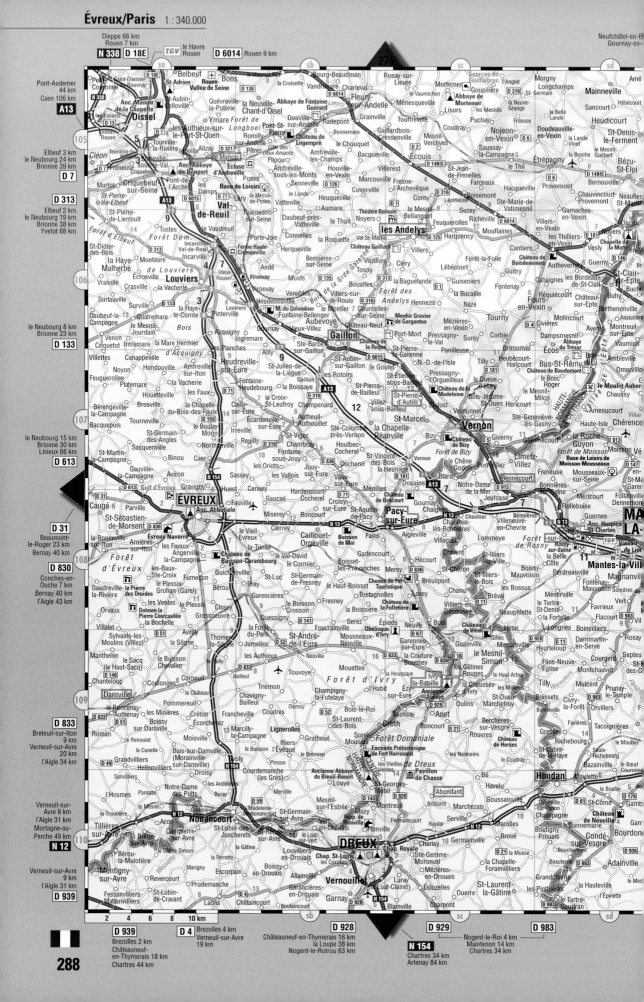

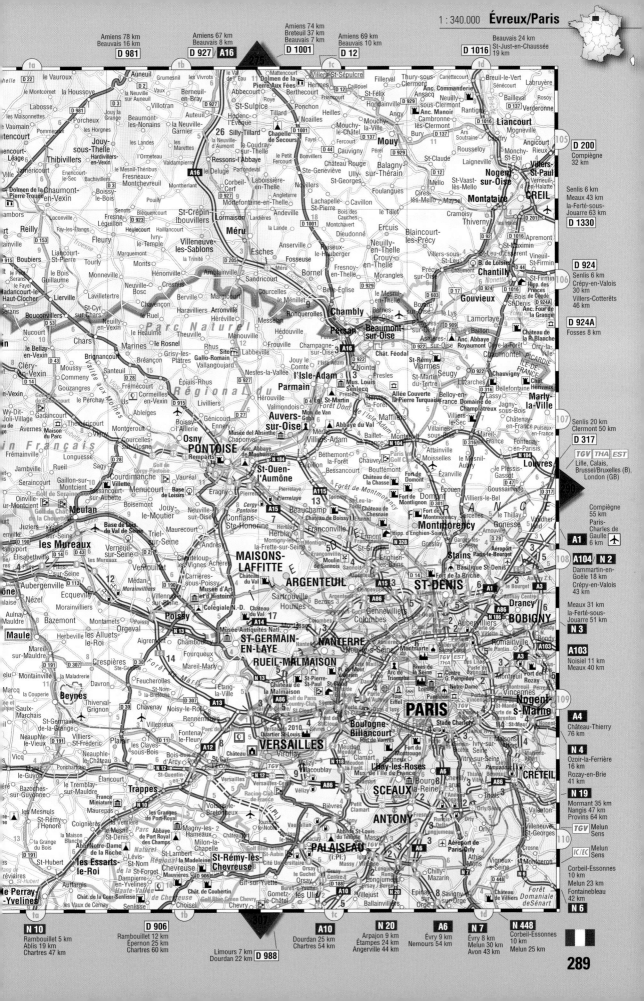

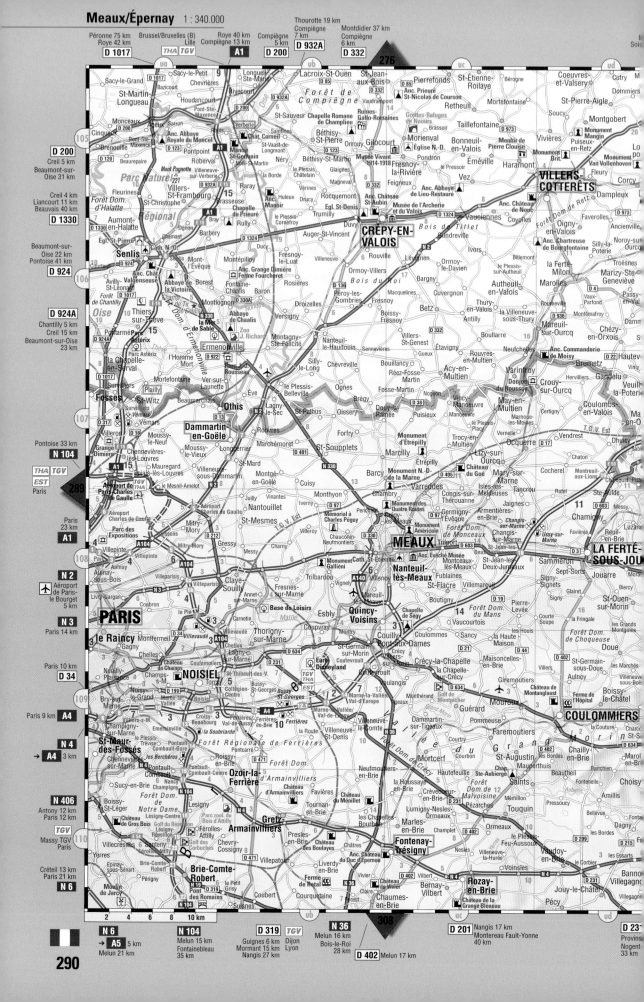

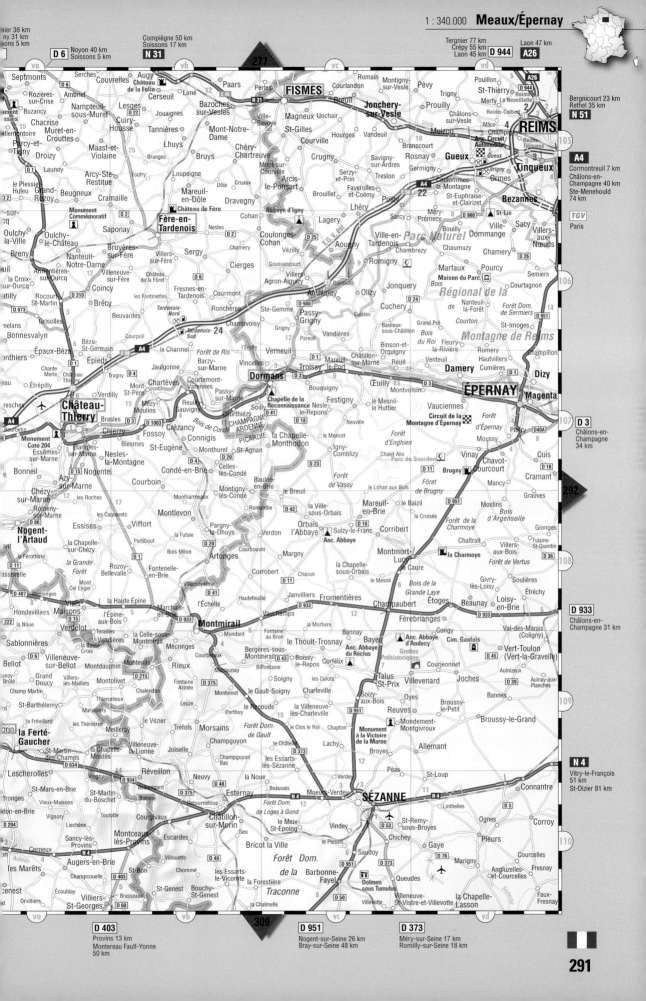

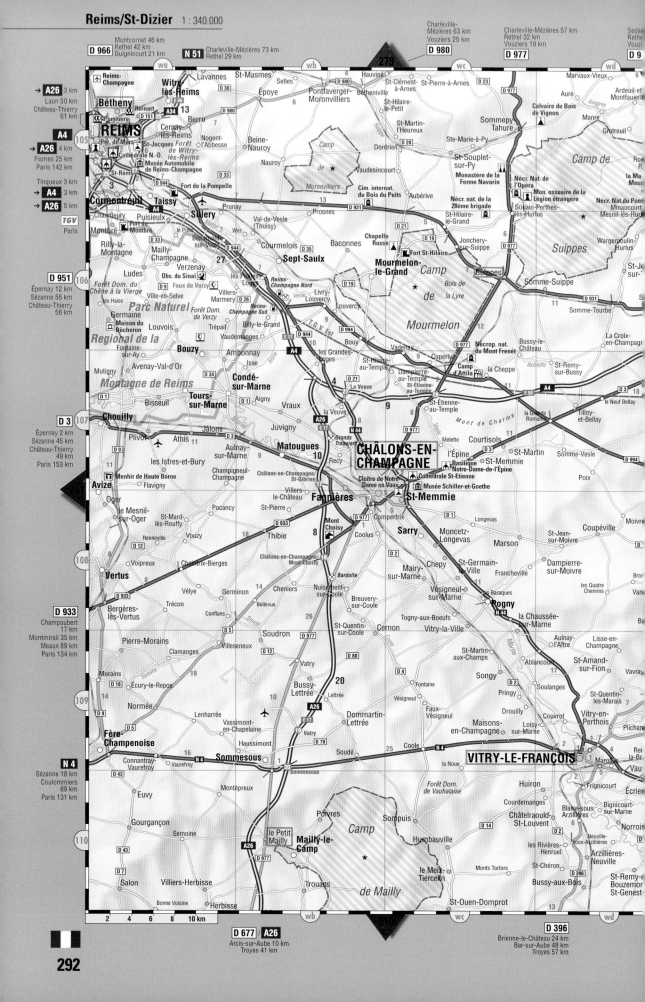

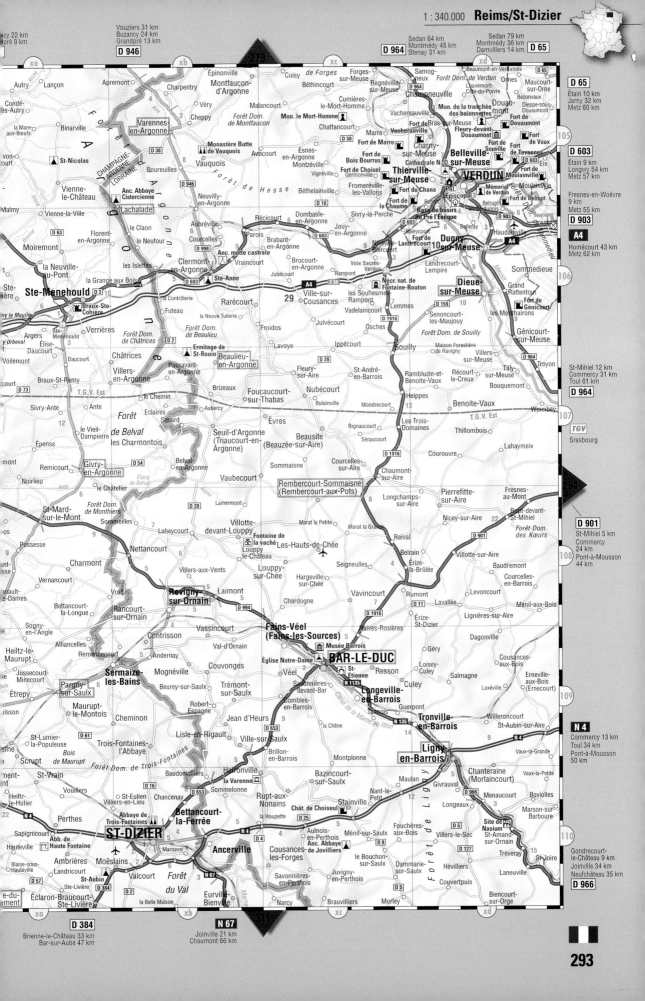

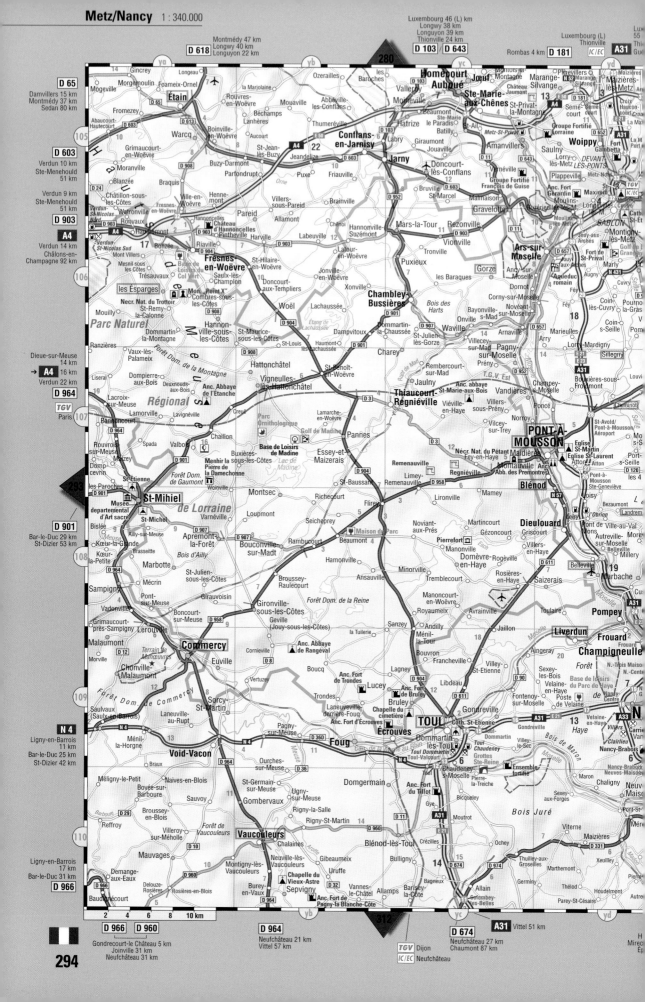

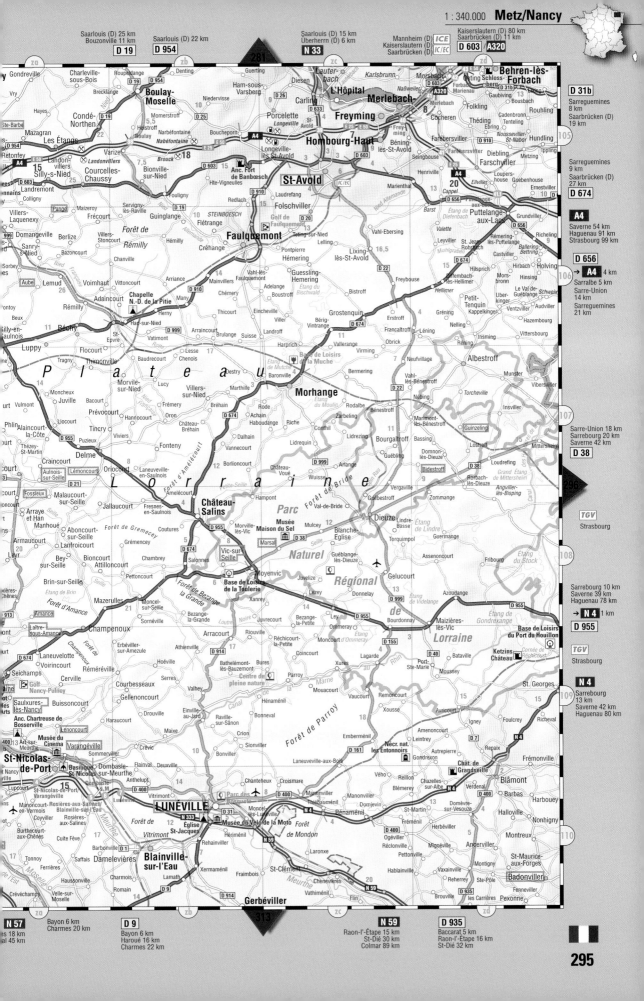

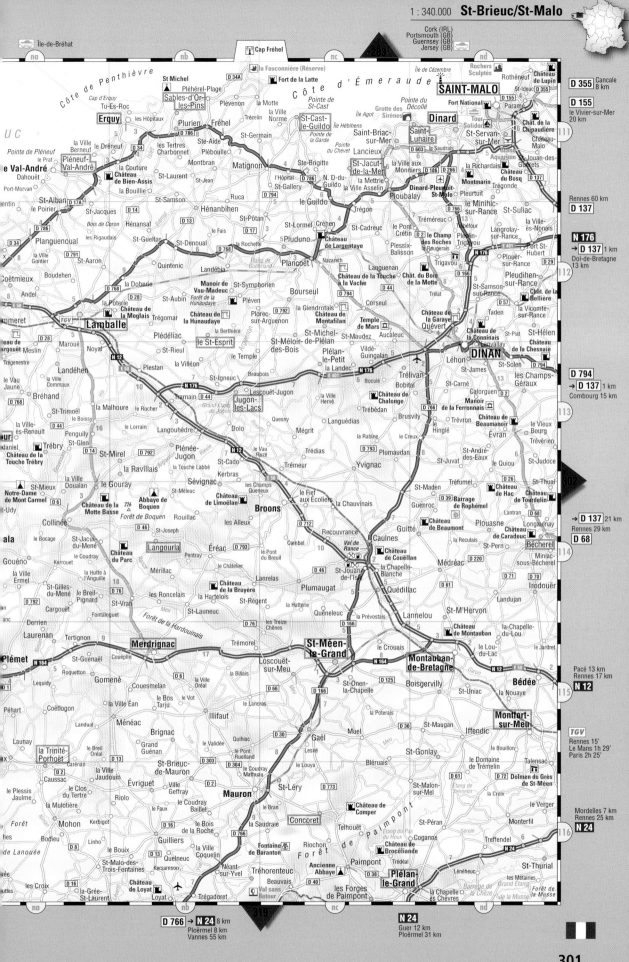

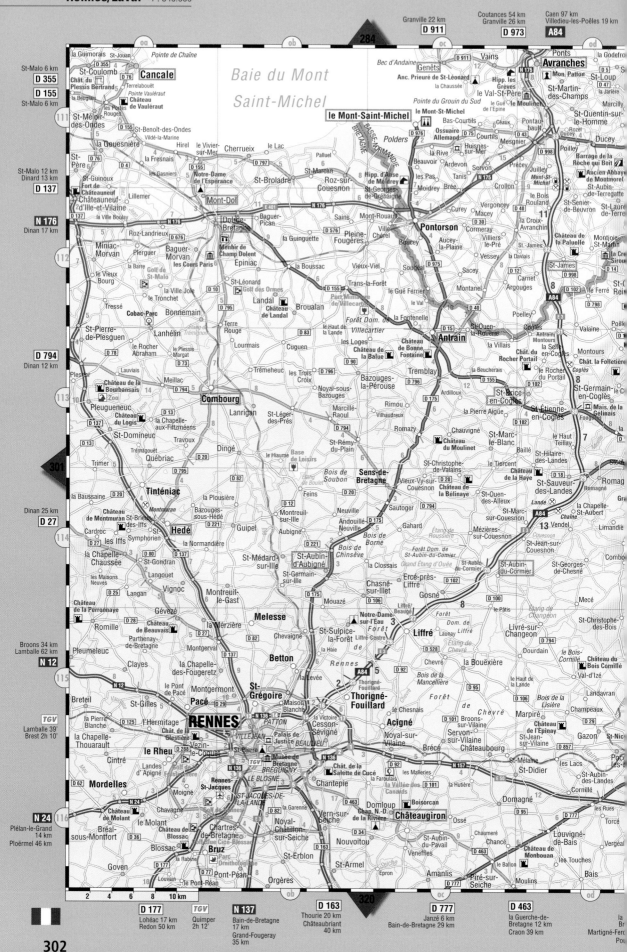

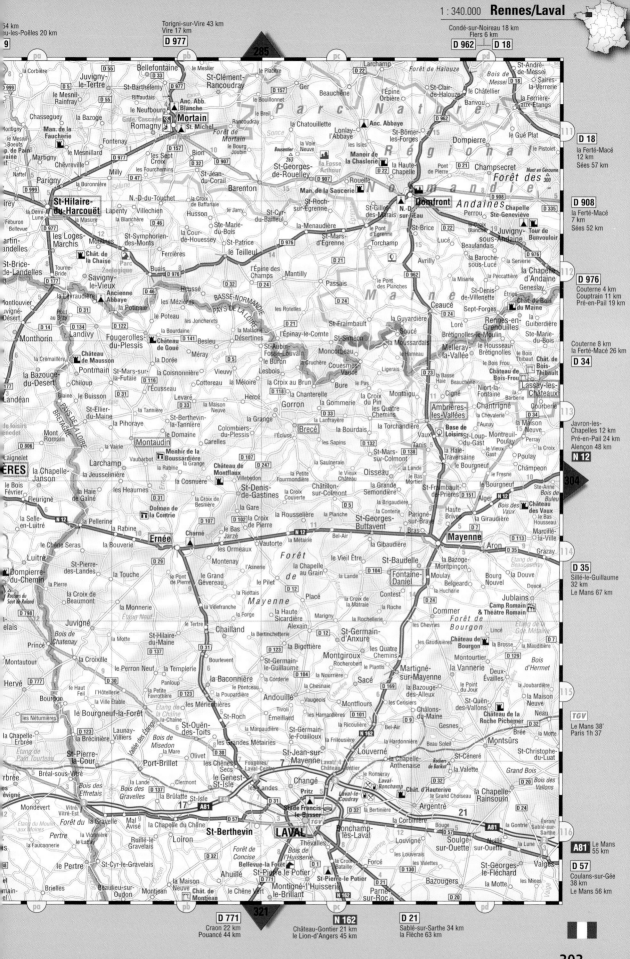

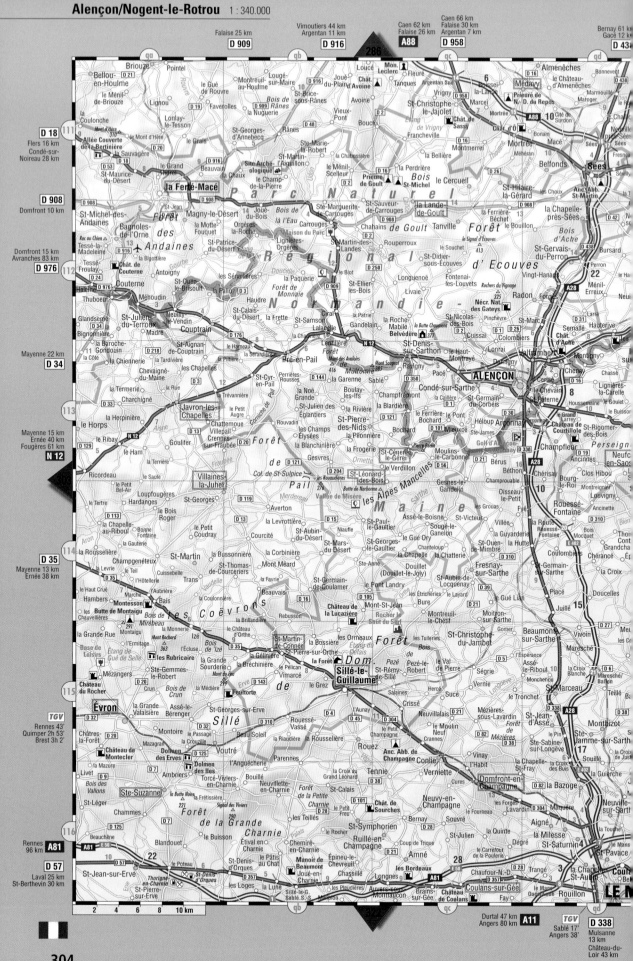

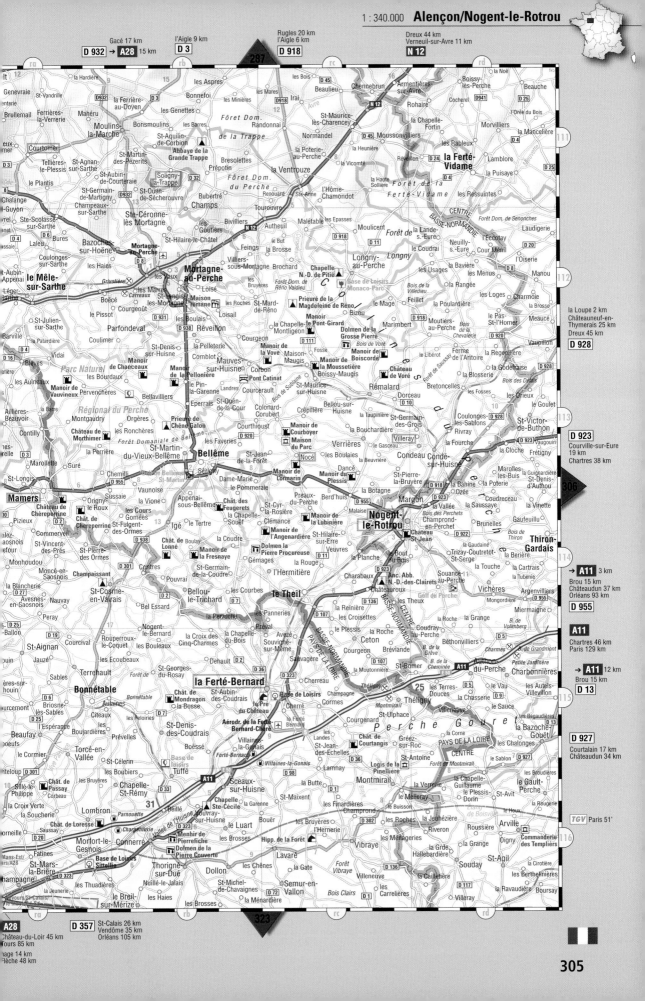

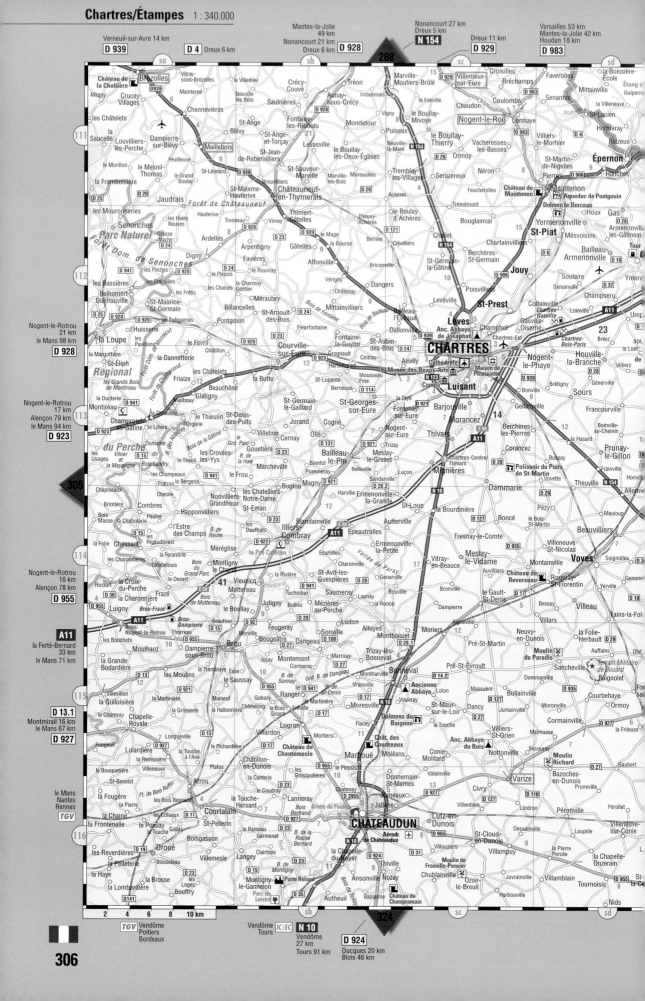

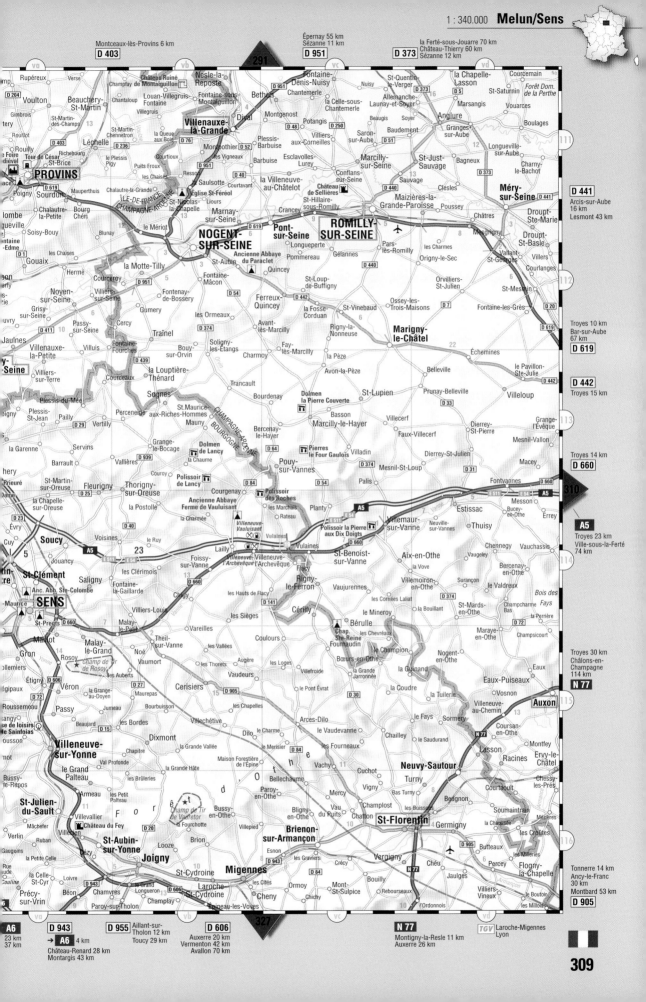

Montceaux-lès-Provins 6 km
D 403

Épernay 55 km
Sézanne 11 km
D 951

la Ferté-sous-Jouarre 70 km
Château-Thierry 60 km
Sézanne 12 km
D 373

291
vb
vc
vd

Rupéreux
Verse
Champfay de Montaiguillon
Château Ruiné
Nesle-la-Reposte
Fontaine-Denis-Nuisy
Nuisy
St-Quentin-le-Verger
la Chapelle-Lasson
Courcemain
Forêt Dom. de la Perthe

D 204
Voulton
Beauchery-St-Martin
Chantaloup
Louan-Villegruis-Fontaine
Fontaine-sous-Montaiguillon
Béthon
Chantemerle
la Celle-sous-Chantemerle
Allemanche-Launay-et-Soyer
St-Saturnin
Marsangis
Vouarces

Gimbrois
St-Martin-des-Champs
Villegruis
Montgenost
Potangis
Beaugis
Soyer
Baudement
Anglure
Granges-sur-Aube
Boulages

Rouillot
Léchelle
St-Martin-Chennetron
la Queue aux Bois
Divat
Plessis-Barbuise
Villiers-aux-Corneilles
Saron-sur-Aube
Marcilly-sur-Seine
St-Just-Sauvage
Longueville-sur-Aube

111

Roully
Richebourg
le Plessis Pigy
D 236
Montpothier D 52
Barbuise
Esclavolles-Lurey
Conflans-sur-Seine
Sauvage
Charny-le-Bachot

Tour de César
St-Brice
les Chaises
D 951
Courtoivry
la Villeneuve-au-Châtelot
Château de Sellières
Maizières-la-Grande-Paroisse
Poussey
Châtres
Méry-sur-Seine
D 441
D 441

PROVINS
D 619
Sourdun
Chalautre-la-Grande
St-Nicolas-la-Chapelle
Liours
Église St-Féréol
Cloncey
St-Hillaire-sous-Romilly
Mesgrigny
Droupt-Ste-Marie

Arcis-sur-Aube 16 km
Lesmont 43 km

Poigny
Chalautre-la-Petite
Bourg Chéri
le Mériot
Marnay-sur-Seine
Pont-sur-Seine
ROMILLY-SUR-SEINE
Pars-lès-Romilly
Vallant-St-Georges
Droupt-St-Basle

Soisy-Bouy
Blunay
D 619
Longueperte
Pommereau
Gélannes
les Charmes
Origny-le-Sec
Villers
Courlanges

NOGENT-SUR-SEINE
St-Aubin
Longueperte
112

Fontaine-Edme
les Chaises
Hermé
la Motte-Tilly
Ancienne Abbaye du Paraclet
Quincey
St-Loup-de-Buffigny
Orvilliers-St-Julien
St-Mesmin
D 20

Gouaix
Courceroy
Fontaine-Mâcon
Ferreux-Quincey
St-Vinebaud
Ossey-les-Trois-Maisons
Fontaine-les-Grès

Noyen-sur-Seine
Villiers-sur-Seine
Fontenay-de-Bossery
D 54
la Fosse-Corduan
D 7

Grisy-sur-Seine
Gumery
D 442
Rigny-la-Nonneuse
D 619

Troyes 10 km
Bar-sur-Aube 67 km
D 619

Jaulnes
Passy-sur-Seine
Cercy
les Ormeaux
Avant-lès-Marcilly
Fay-lès-Marcilly
MARIGNY-le-Châtel

Villenauxe-la-Petite
Villuis
Traînel
D 374
Soligny-les-Étangs
Rigny-la-Nonneuse
la Pèze
22

Fontaine-Fourches
Bouy-sur-Orvin
Charmoy
Avon-la-Pèze
Échemines
D 619

Villiers-sur-Terre
Courceaux
la Louptière-Thénard
Trancault
Belleville
le Pavillon-Ste-Julie

Plessis-du-Mée
Sognes
Bourdenay
Dolmen la Pierre Couverte
St-Lupien
Prunay-Belleville
Villeloup
D 442

Troyes 15 km

Plessis-St-Jean
Pailly
Perceneige
St-Maurice-aux-Riches-Hommes
Basson
Marcilly-le-Hayer
Villecerf
D 33

D 29
Vertilly
Mauny
Bercenay-le-Hayer
Faux-Villecerf
Dierrey-St-Pierre
Mesnil-Vallon
113

la Garenne
Servins
Grange-le-Bocage
Dolmen de Lancy
Pierres le Four Gaulois
Villadin
Dierrey-St-Julien
Grange-l'Évêque
Macey

Barrault
Vallières
D 939
la Chaume
Pouy-sur-Vannes
Mesnil-St-Loup
D 31
Fontvannes
D 660

Troyes 14 km
D 660

Prieuré
St-Martin-sur-Oreuse
Couroy
Dolmen de Lancy
D 84
Polissoir des Roches
Palis
D 54
E 511
A5
310
A5

la Chapelle-sur-Oreuse
Fleurigny
Thorigny-sur-Oreuse
D 25
Ancienne Abbaye Ferme de Vaulisant
Planty
E 511
Messon
Bucey-en-Othe
Errey

Évry
D 23
D 40
la Postolle
la Charmée
Villeneuve-Vaulisant
les Marchais
Rateau
Vulaines
Polissoir la Pierre aux Dix Doigts
Villemaur-sur-Vanne
Neuville-sur-Vannes
Thuisy

Cuy
Voisines
23
le Ruy
Lailly
Villeneuve-l'Archevêque
Vulaines
D 660
St-Benoist-sur-Vanne
Chennegy
Vauchassis
114

Soucy
Jouancy
A5
E 511 E 54
Foissy-sur-Vanne
Villeneuve-l'Archevêque
Flacy
Aix-en-Othe
la Vove
Bercenay-en-Othe
le Valdreux

St-Clément
Saligny
Fontaine-la-Gaillarde
D 660
Rigny-le-Ferron
Vaujurennes
Villemoiron-en-Othe
Surançon

Ste-Colombe
Villiers-Louis
D 141
Cérilly
les Cornées Laliat
la Bouillant
St-Mards-en-Othe
D 72
la Perrière

SENS
Malay-le-Petit
les Sièges
le Mineroy
Bois des Fays
Champcharme Bas

St-Prégts
D 660
Vareilles
Coulours
Bérulle
le Chevréaux
Maraye-en-Othe
Champsicourt

Maillot
Theil-sur-Vanne
les Vallées
Chap. Ste-Reine Fournaudin
le Champion
Nogent-en-Othe
Eaux

Gron
Malay-le-Grand
Noé
Augère
les Thorets
les Loges
Villefroide
la Grande Jarronnée
la Guinand
Eaux-Puiseaux

Rosoy
Champ de Tir de Rosoy
Vaumort
les Auberts
Vaudeurs
le Pont Évrat
la Coudre
la Tuilerie

Étigny
D 606
Véron
la Grange-au-Doyen
D 27
Maurepas
Bourbuisson
Cerisiers
15
D 905
les Chapelles
D 30
Vosnon

Roussemeau
D 72
Passy
Jumeau
Arces-Dilo
le Fays
Sormery
Villeneuve-au-Chemin
Auxon
N 77

Beaujard
D 15
les Bordes
Villechétive
Dixmont
Dilo
le Charme
le Vaudevanne
les Fourneaux
Chailley
le Saudurand
Coursan-en-Othe
115

de loisirs de Sainfoias
Chapitre
Val Profonde
la Grande Vallée
le Merisier
D 84
Vachy
Cuchot
Turny
Beugnon
Montfey
Racines

Bussy-le-Repos
Villeneuve-sur-Yonne
le Grand Palteau
la Grande Hâte
Maison Forestière de l'Épine
Bellechaume
Vigny
Bas Turny
Courtaoult
Chessy-les-Prés
Ervy-le-Châtel

St-Julien-du-Sault
Armeau
les Petit Palteau
Château du Fey
Villepied
Paroy-en-Othe
Mercy
Champlost
les Buissons
Soumaintrain
Lasson

Mâchefer
Villevallier
D 20
Bussy-en-Othe
la Fourchotte
Bligny-en-Othe
Chatton
St-Florentin
Germigny
la Chaussée
Mézières
les Croûtes

Verlin
Cézy
Looze
Brion
Brienon-sur-Armançon
Esnon
Vergigny
N 77
les Milleries
116

Joigny
St-Cydroine
les Graviers
Crécy
Chéu
Percey
Flogny-la-Chapelle

Précy-sur-Vrin
Béon
D 943
le Grand Longueron
D 606
Laroche-St-Cydroine
Ormoy
Chichy
Rebourseaux
Jaulges
Villiers-Vineux
le Boutoir
Armançon

la Celle-St-Cyr
Chamvres
Champlay
Épineau-les-Voves
Cheny
Mont-St-Sulpice
Bouilly
l'Ordonnois
les Millas

Migennes
les Cités
Paroy-sur-Tholon
D 84
327
vc
vd

Tonnerre 14 km
Ancy-le-Franc 30 km
Montbard 53 km
D 905

A6
23 km
37 km

D 943
A6 4 km
Château-Renard 28 km
Montargis 43 km

D 955
Aillant-sur-Tholon 12 km
Toucy 29 km

D 606
Auxerre 20 km
Vermenton 42 km
Avallon 70 km

N 77
Montigny-la-Resle 11 km
Auxerre 26 km

TGV
Laroche-Migennes
Lyon

309

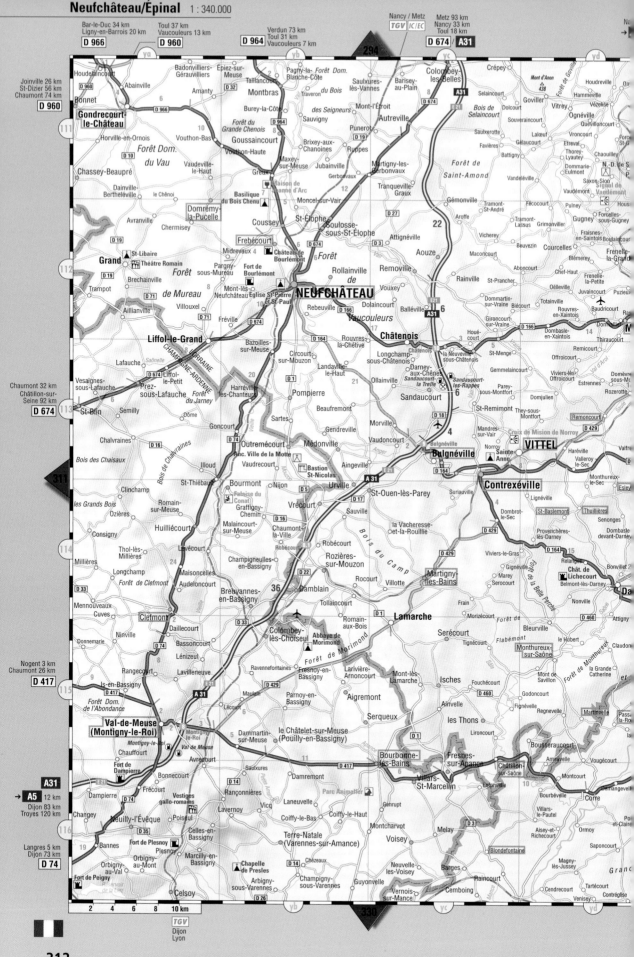

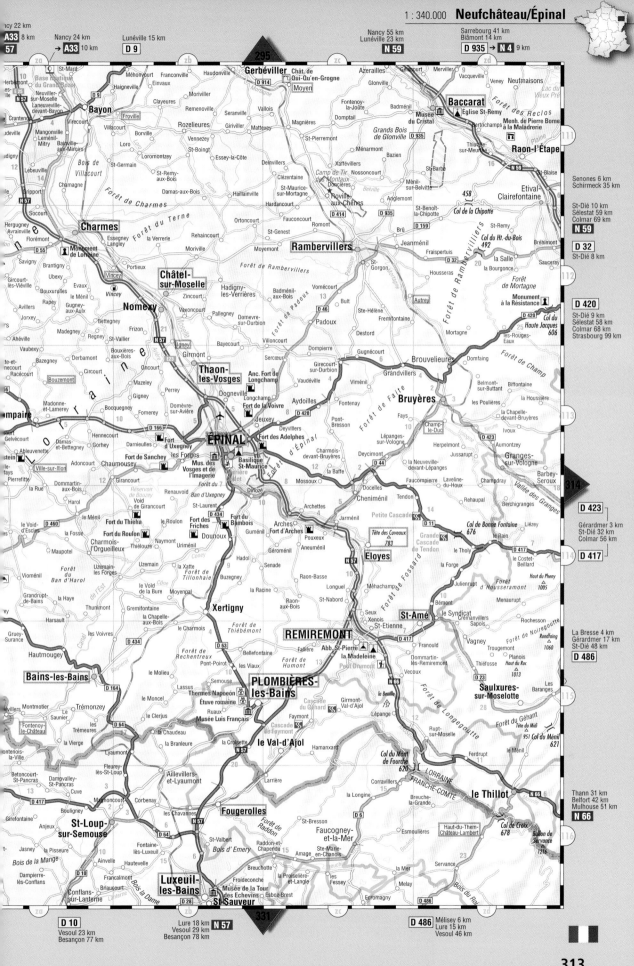

295

Gerbéviller   Chât. de Qui-Qu'en-Grogne

Baccarat

Raon-l'Étape

Senones 6 km
Schirmeck 35 km

St-Dié 10 km
Sélestat 59 km
Colmar 69 km

N 59

Étival-Clairefontaine

Col de la Chipotte

Charmes

Rambervillers

Col du Ht.-du-Bois 492

D 32
St-Dié 8 km

Châtel-sur-Moselle

Nomexy

D 420
St-Dié 9 km
Sélestat 58 km
Colmar 68 km
Strasbourg 99 km

Col de la Haute Jacques 606

Brouvelieures

Thaon-les-Vosges

Bruyères

D 113

Granges-sur-Vologne

ÉPINAL

Basilique St-Maurice

314

D 423
Gérardmer 3 km
St-Dié 32 km
Colmar 56 km

D 417

Éloyes

St-Amé

REMIREMONT
Abb. St-Pierre
la Madeleine

D 486
La Bresse 4 km
Gérardmer 17 km
St-Dié 48 km

Saulxures-sur-Moselotte

D 115

Bains-les-Bains

PLOMBIÈRES-les-Bains
Thermes Napoléon
Étuve romaine
Musée Luis Français

le Val-d'Ajol

Col du Ménil 621

le Thillot

N 66
Thann 31 km
Belfort 42 km
Mulhouse 51 km

LORRAINE
FRANCHE-COMTÉ

Col du Mont de Fourche 620

St-Loup-sur-Semouse

Fougerolles

Col de Croix 678

Ballon de Servance 1216

Luxeuil-les-Bains
Musée de la Tour des Échevins
St-Sauveur

331

D 10
Vesoul 23 km
Besançon 77 km

Lure 18 km   N 57
Vesoul 29 km
Besançon 78 km

D 486   Mélisey 6 km
Lure 15 km
Vesoul 46 km

313

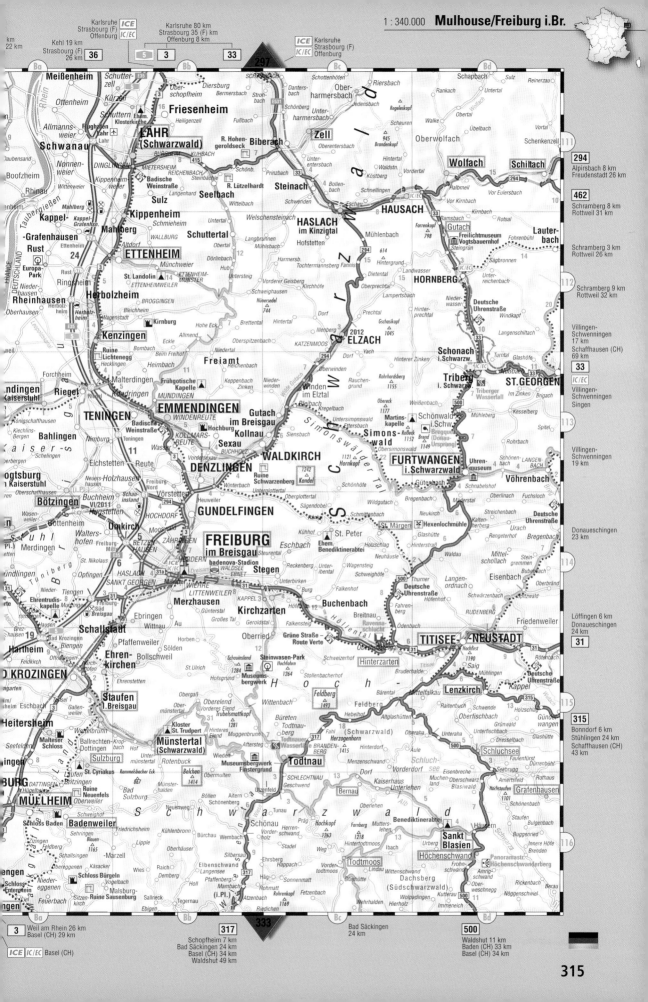

Camaret-sur-Mer
0,5 km
D 8

298

Brest 46 km
Landerneau 25 km
D 791   N 165

Camaret-sur-Mer
D 791
10

Phare de la Parquette

Alignements
de Lagatjar
Lannilien
Pointe de Pen-Hir
Pointe de la Tavelle
Anse de Dinan
Gaoulac'h
Kerguéréon
Luguniat
Marros
Rosnoër
D 60
Bellevue
Keréon
Tal ar
Groaz
Argol
Trégarvan
Château de Dinan
Rochers
Pointe de Dinan
Lost Mar'h
Morgat
D 887
Petites
Grottes
Telgruc-
sur-Mer
Forêt Com. d' Argol
Kerivin
Toul ar
Gloët
Pointe de Lost Marc'h
la Palue
Île de l'Aber
Anse de Morgat
Ménez Hom
Dinéault
St-Hernot
Grandes
Grottes
Maison des
Minéraux
Penquer
Lézargol
Manoir
Guerveur
330
Ste-Marie
du Ménez Hom
D 255
Pointe de Rostudel
Pointe du
Bellec
Porslous
St-Nic
Rostudel
Pointe du Dolmen
Pentrez-Plage
St-Côme
Toul Hoat
Cap de la Chèvre
Pointe de Talagrip
Plomodiern

**Parc Naturel Régional
d'Armorique**

Baie de Douarnenez
Plage de Ste-Anne
Ste-Anne
la Palud
Ty Job
Ploéven
Ca
D 63
Kerhant
Lanzent
D 107
D 7

Île-de-Sein

Pointe de Leydé
Pointe de la Jument
Pointe du Millier
Pointe de Tréfeuntec
Plonévez-Porzay
Manoir
du Moëllien
la Bonne
Nouvelle
Kergo

Pointe de Beuzec
Quillouarn
St-Jean
Douarnenez
D 7
Locronan
Pointe de Penharn
Réserve
du Cap Sizun
Pors-Péron
Poullan-
sur-Mer
Tréboul
Kerlaz
Plogonnec
St-Th
Pointe de Brézellec
Lesven
Beuzec-
Cap-Sizun
Ploaré
le Juch
Plogonnec
Lezmel
Pointe du Van
Kermeur
Notre-Dame
de Kérinec
Kerfinidan
St-Pierre
Plaisance
le Cro
St-They
Moulin-
Castel
9
a
Kerflous
Île-de-Sein
Baie
des Trépassés
Cléden-
Cap-Sizun
Goulien
Quatre-Vents
Pont-Croix
Confort
5
10
u
Stang
ar Guell
Guengat
Pointe du Raz
Plogoff
Lescoff
Primelin
Toulemonde
D 765
Goyen
Mahalon
C
Pouldergat
Trézent
le Fort
D 765
Plonéis
Kerf
Lescoff
Pennéac'h
Esquibien
St-Tugen
la Trinité
Guiler-
sur-Goyen
D 143
Goyen
Gourlizon
3
QUIM
Cath
Se
St-Evette
Trébeuzec
Audierne
Plouhinec
D 784
Hent-Meur
8
Landudec
D 784
2
Pointe de Lervily
le Pouldu
Pointe de Mezpeurleuch
Plage de Guendrez
Pointe de Souc'h
Poulhan
4
Plozévet
Kerlaéron
D 784
Kerstridic
D 765
Château
du Hilguy
Pluguffan
D 40
Pointe de
Pluguffan
Penhars

Baie
Laban
Plogastel-
St-Germain
St-Germain
Quimper-
Cornouaille

d'Audierne
Pouldreuzic
Kervéyen
D 2
St-Joseph
Penhors
Peumérit
Tréogat
Stang
ar Bacol
Chap.
St-Sébastien
Plomelin
12
Site des Vire-C
Plovan
Chapelle
de Languidou
Chapelle
de Languivoa
Château du
Pérennou
Ménez
Tréméoc
D 785
Chapelle
de Languidou
Plonéour-
Lanvern
Kerdréanton
Combrit
Tréguennec
Manoir
de Trévilit
D 57
Keréon
D 785
Kerbascol
St-Jean-
Trolimon
6
Pont-l'Abbé
D 44
Ste-Marine
Notre-Dame-de-Tronoën
Notre-Dame
de Tréminou
D 2
Île-Tudy
le Sillon
Plage de Tronoën
Beuzec
de Co
Pointe de
la Torche
Plomeur
Château
de Kernuz
5
Manoir
de Kérazan
Loctudy
St-Guénolé
la Madeleine
Notre-Dame
de la Joie
1
Phare
d'Eckmühl
St-Pierre
Plobannalec-
Lescouil
Manoir
de Kerhoas
Pointe de K
Pointe de Ke
Penmarc'h
Treffiagat
D 53
Lodonnec
Pointe de
Penmarc'h
Guilvinec
Léchiagat
Lesconil
Pointe St-Qual

Camaret-sur-Mer

118

115

115

Pointe du Van
St-They
Baie
des Trépassés
Ar Men
Chausée de Sein
Île-
de-Sein
Île de Sein
Pointe du Raz
Lescoff
Audierne
119

O

116

116

ATLA

2   4   6   8   10 km

300

Loudéac 39 km
Pontivy 15 km
D 768

Mûr-de-Bretagne 31 km
Pontivy 14 km
D 767

Pontivy
D 764

D 769
Gourin 35 km

D 62
Quimperlé 18 km
→ N 165 18 km

N 165
Quimperlé 25 km
Quimper 70 km

TGV
Lorient 2'
Quimperlé 11'
Quimper 36'

D 781
Port-Louis 0,5 km

Lorient

Plouay
Inzinzac-Lochrist
Hennebont
Caudan
Lanester
Languidic
Pluvigner
Baud
Locminé
St-Avé
VANNES
Séné
Sarzeau
Auray
Carnac
Quiberon
Belle-Île
le Palais
Erdeven
Plouharnel
Étel
Arzon
Locmariaquer
St-Gildas-de-Rhuys
St-Pierre-Quiberon

Presqu'île de Quiberon

Côte des Mégalithes

Baie de Quiberon

Passage de la Teignouse

Phare de la Teignouse

Île d'Houat
Île aux Chevaux
Île d'Hœdic
Hœdic

OCÉAN ATLANTIQUE

Grand Phare de Belle-Île
Aiguilles de Port Coton
Citadelle Vauban
Fort Sarah-Bernardt
Pointe des Poulains
Sauzon

2 4 6 8 10 km

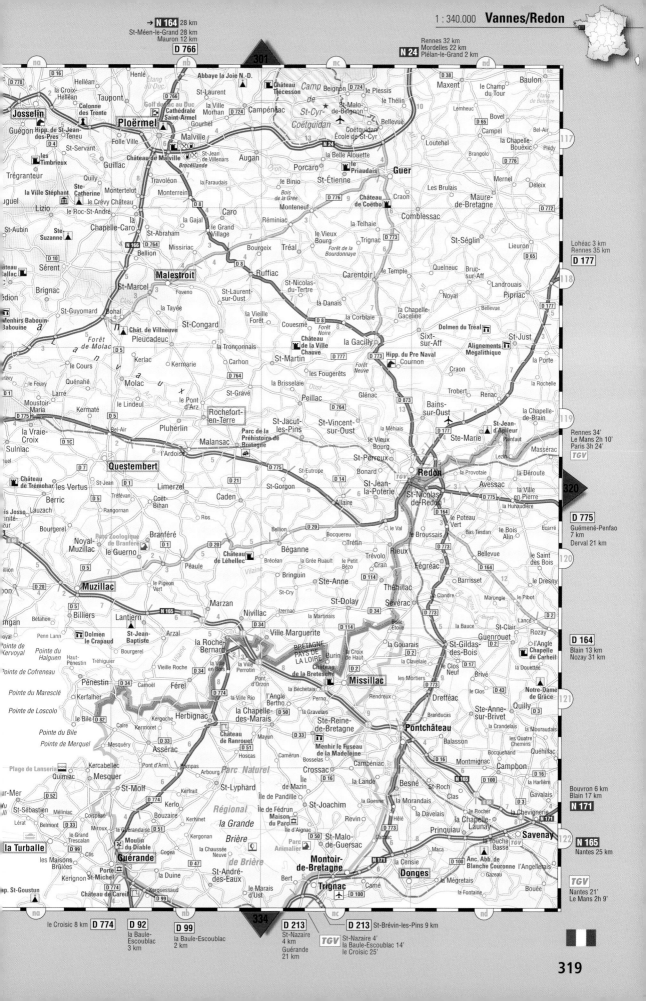

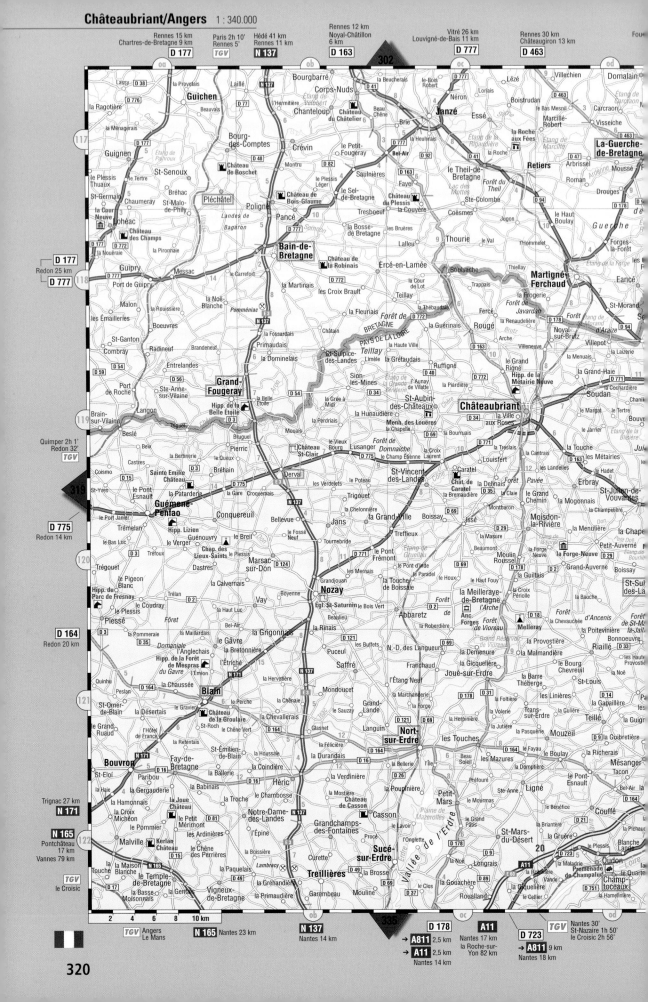

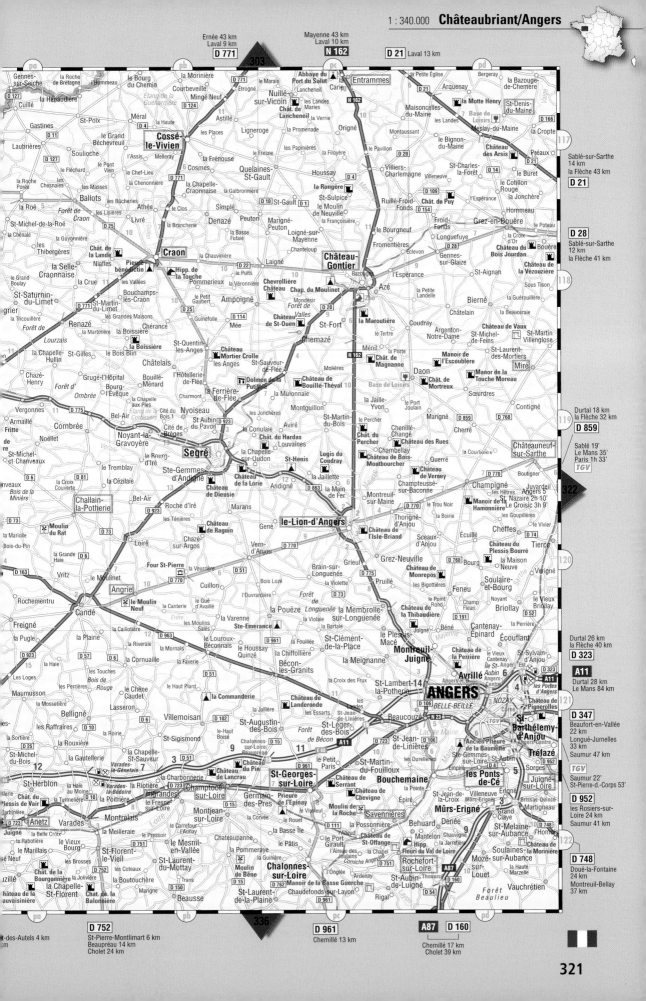

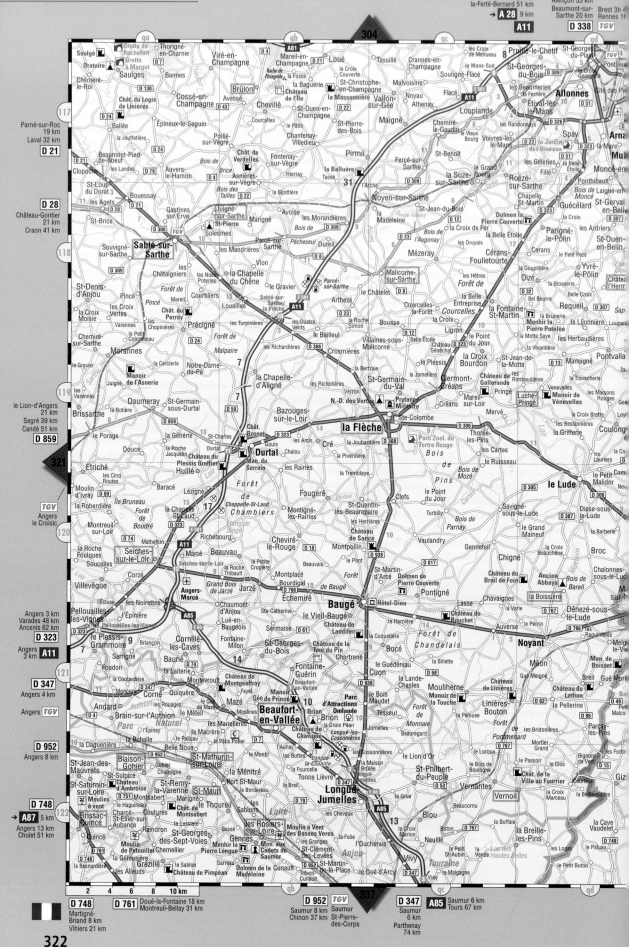

305

A28 Alençon 55 km   D 357 → A 28 7 km

D 357
Fréteval 15 km
Orléans 79 km

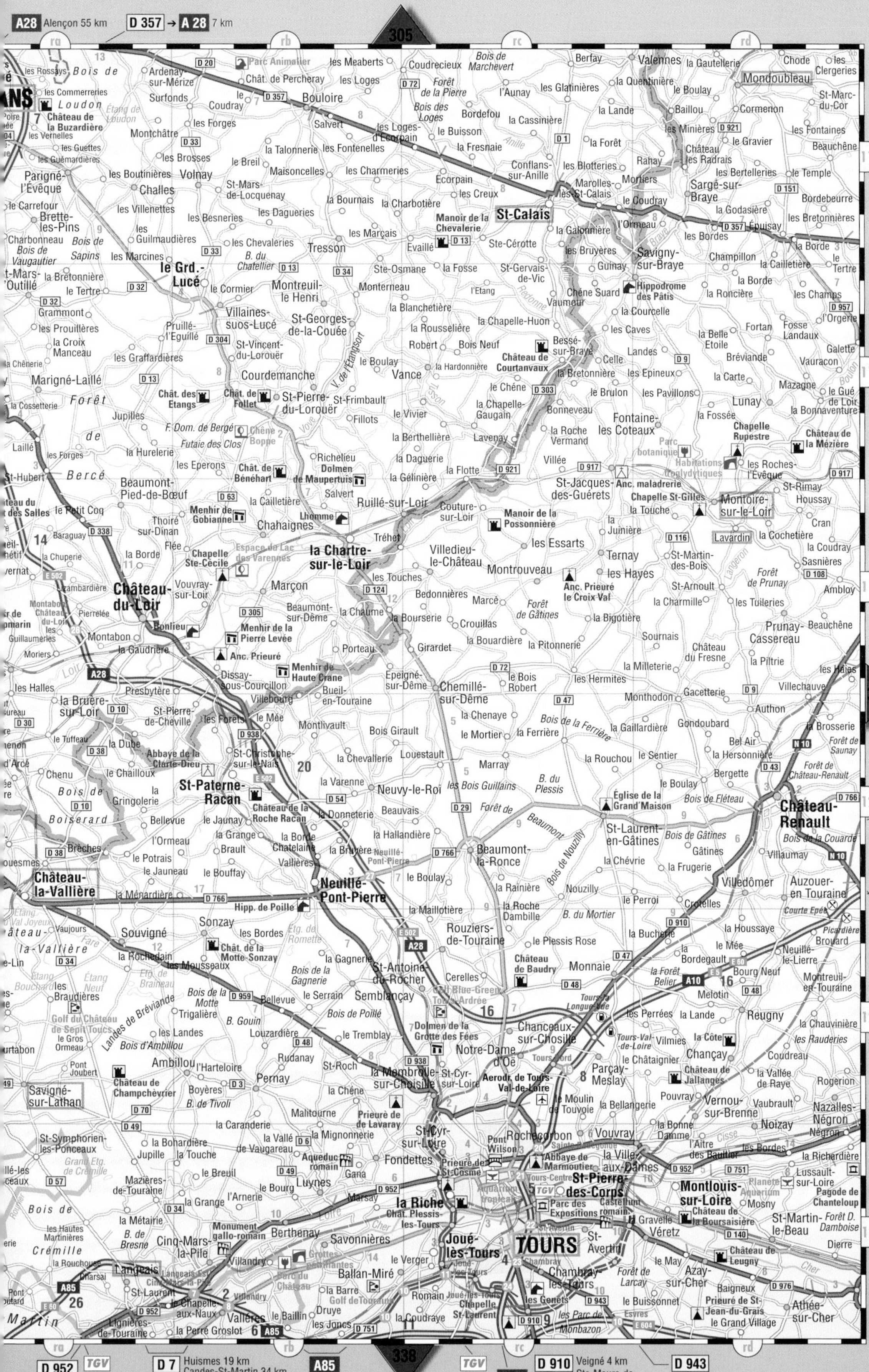

Vendôme 9 km
Blois 44 km
D 957

N 10
Vendôme 17 km
Châteaudun 62 km

IC/EC Chartres
Châteaudun

324

Herbault 14 km
Blois 31 km
D 766

TGV Vendôme-
Villiers 19'
Paris 1h 11'
Blois 30 km
Orléans 86 km
A10

D 31
Amboise 20 km
Loches 59 km

D 952
Amboise 3 km
Blois 41 km

Amboise 11 km
Blois 41 km
D 140

D 976
Bléré 2km
Montrichard 23 km
Loches 29 km

D 952
la Chapelle-sur-
Loire 13 km
Saumur 40 km

TGV Angers 51'
Saumur 30'

D 7
Huismes 19 km
Candes-St-Martin 34 km
Saumur 48 km

A85

338

TGV Poitiers 44'
la Rochelle
2h 19'
Bordeaux 2h 44'

A10
Ste-Maure-de-
Touraine 25 km
Châtellerault 57 km

D 910
Veigné 4 km
Ste-Maure-de-
Touraine 26 km
Châtellerault 62 km

D 943
Cormery 6 km
Loches 28 km

TOURS

le Mans

Château-du-Loir

St-Calais

Montoire-sur-le-Loir

Château-Renault

Neuillé-Pont-Pierre

Château-la-Vallière

St-Paterne-Racan

Joué-lès-Tours

St-Pierre-des-Corps

Montlouis-sur-Loire

Athée-sur-Cher

la Chartre-sur-le-Loir

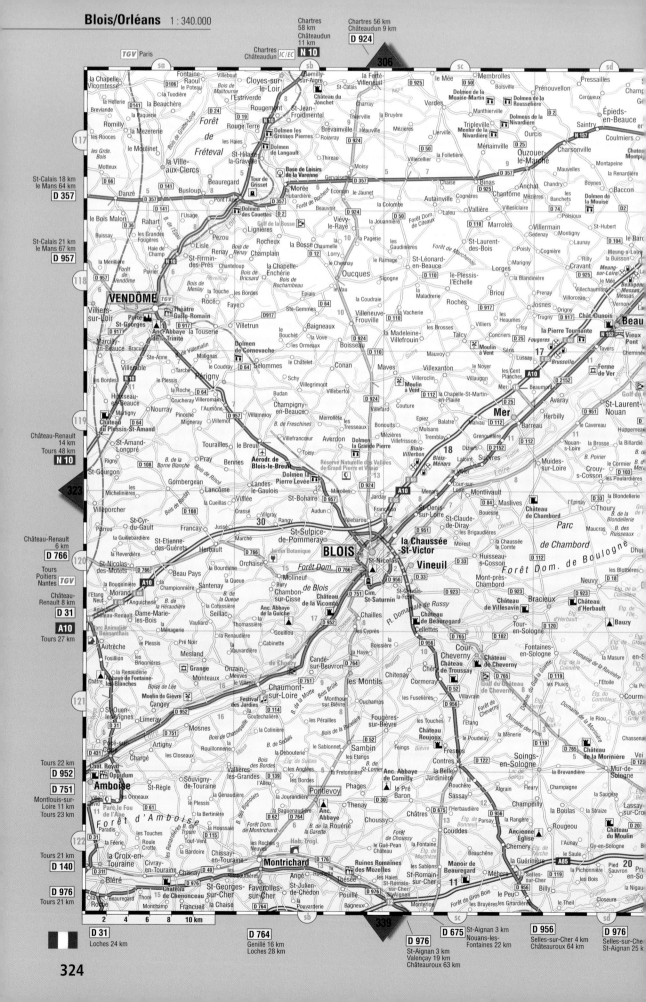

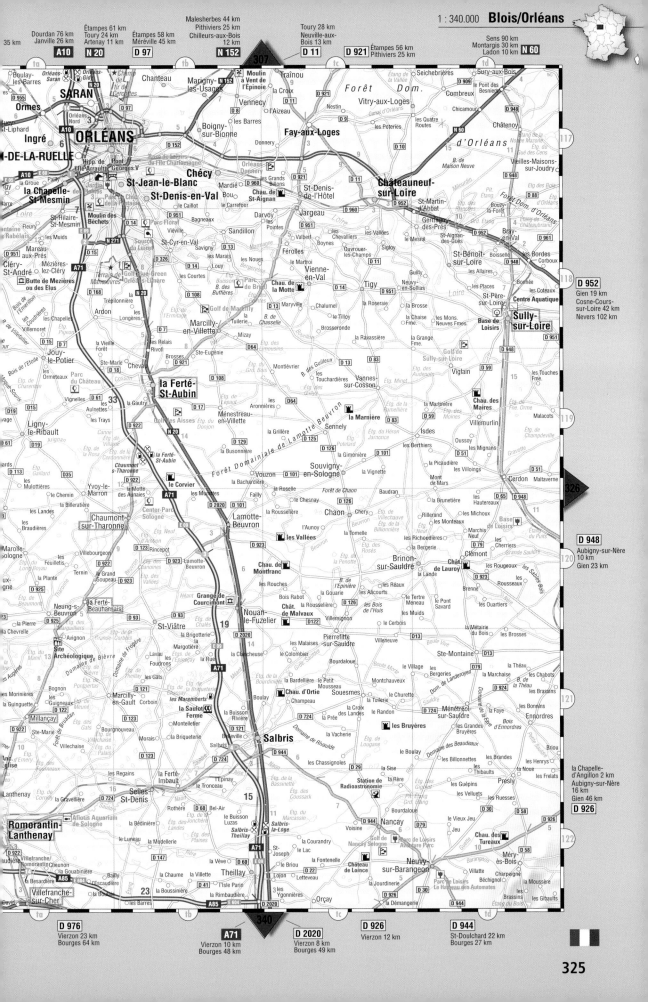

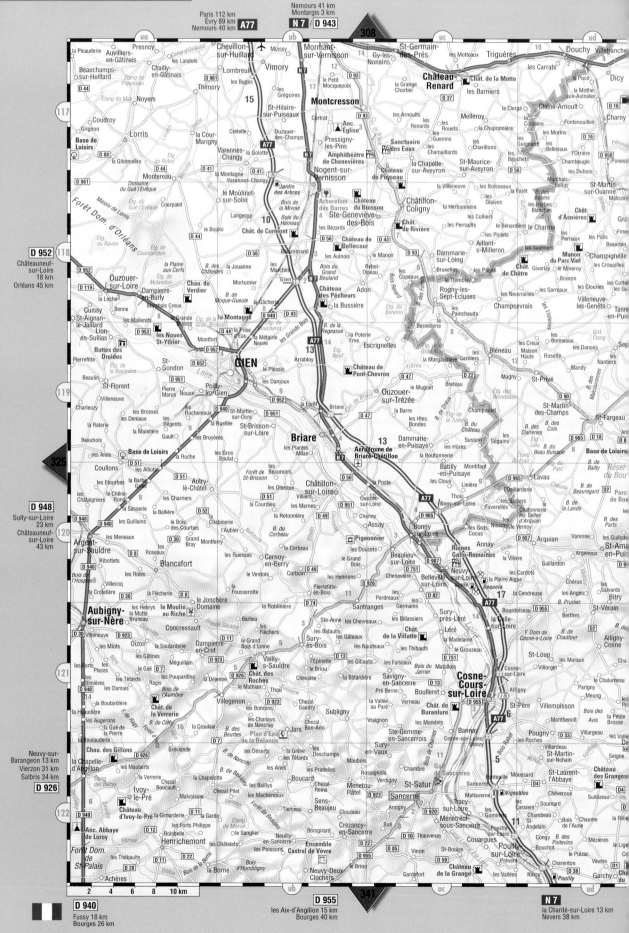

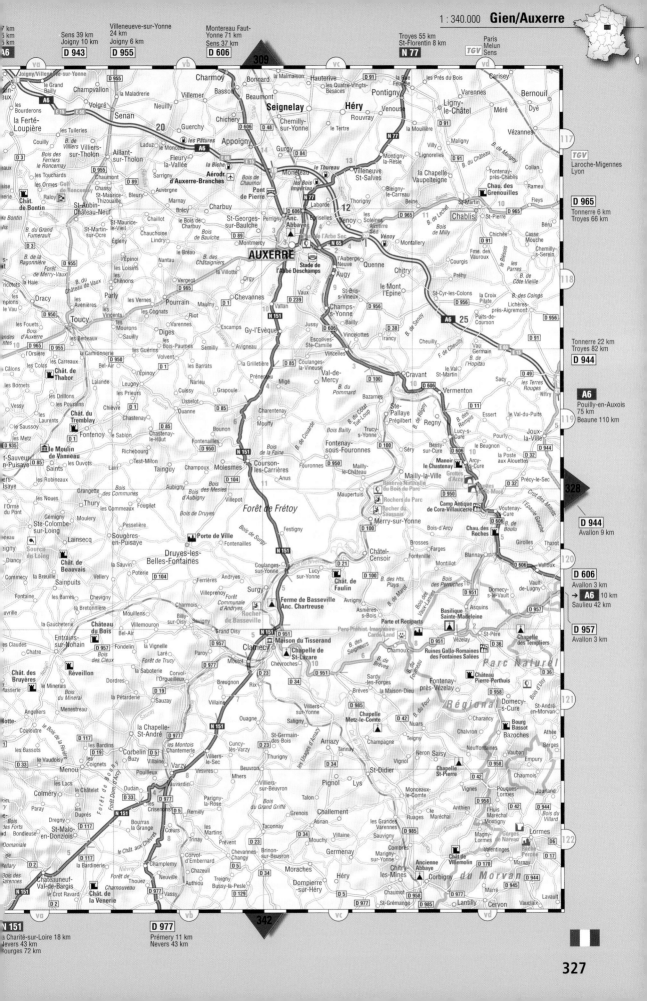

Sens 67 km
St-Florentin 17 km
D 905

D 944 Troyes 52 km
Chaource 19 km

Troyes 60 km
Mussy-sur-Seine 11 km
D 971

TGV
Sens
Melun
Paris

D 965
Chablis 9 km
Auxerre 35 km

→ A6 3 km
Joux-la-Ville 9 km
Avallon 27 km
D 944

A6
Auxerre 36 km
Nemours 121 km
Paris 188 km

D 944
Joux-la-Ville
7 km

D 606
Cravant 37 km
Auxerre 57 km

D 957
Vézelay 10 km
Clamecy 34 km

Tonnerre
Tanlay
Argentenay
Lézinnes
Ancy-le-Franc
Chassignelles
Ravières
Nuits
Montbard
Semur-en-Auxois
Avallon
Noyers
Montréal
Époisses
Saulieu
Parc Naturel Régional du Morvan
Maulnes
Laignes
Molosmes
Dannemoine
Forêt Dom. du Grand Jailly
Anc. Abbaye Cistercienne de Fontenay
Quarré-les-Tombes
St-Léger-Vauban
2 4 6 8 10 km

D 15
Autun 34 km
Le Creusot 64 km

TGV
Le Creusot
Lyon

D 906
Arnay-le-Duc 10 km
Chagny 50 km
Chalon-sur-Saône 68 km

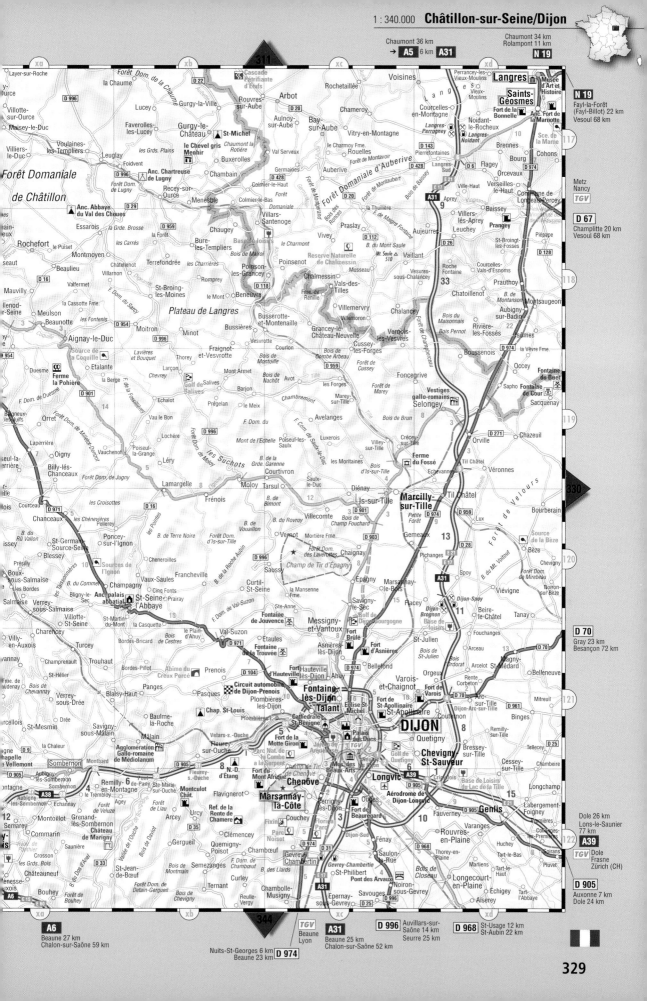

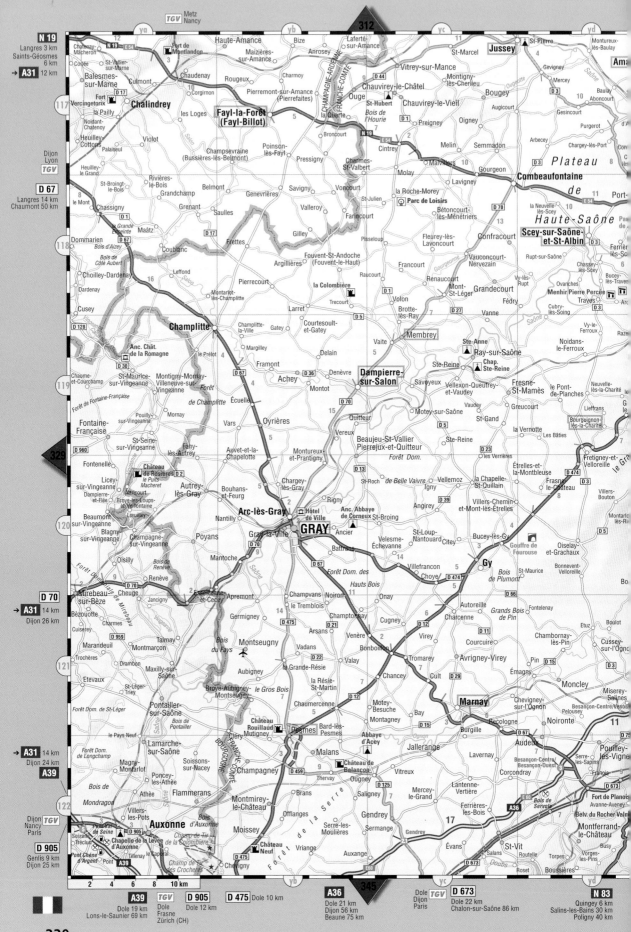

Plombières-les-Bains 30 km
Bains-les-Bains 25 km
St-Loup-sur-Semouse 8 km
D 10

Vittel 83 km
Épinal 51 km
Plombières-les-Bains 22 km
Luxeuil-les-Bains 3 km
N 57

313

Remiremont 42 km
le Thillot 17 km
D 486

D 12
Belfort 17 km
le Thillot 34 km
Bussang 35 km
Masevaux 36 km
117

Belfort 5 km
→ **A36** 7 km
Delle 29 km
Mulhouse 48 km
N 19

Belfort 10 km
Delle 24 km
D 483
118

Montbéliard 6 km
119

Montbéliard 7 km
→ **A36** 3 km
D 663

JC/EC Montbéliard
Belfort
A36 Belfort
24 km
Mulhouse
64 km
332

120

121

D 437
Maîche 8 km
la Chaux-de-Fonds
(CH) 32 km
122

VESOUL

BESANÇON

346

D 67 Ornans 7 km
Pontarlier 39 km

N 57 / **D 50**
Pontarlier 24 km
Lausanne (CH) 88 km

D 461 / **D 437**
Morteau 8 km
Pontarlier 41 km

ICE Offenburg
IC/EC Freiburg i.Br.

3 Freiburg i.Br. 40 km
Müllheim 10 km

317

315

Freiburg 45 km
Titisee-Neustadt 40 km
Todtnau 15 km

St. Blasien 19 km
Todtmoos 7 km

500 Titisee-Neustadt 38 km
St. Blasien 14 km

Kandern
Zell i.Wiesental
SCHOPFHEIM
WEHR
Görwihl
WALDSHUT
STEINEN
Maulburg
Rickenbach
Albbruck
LÖRRACH
Laufenburg (Baden)
Böttstein
WEIL am Rhein
Möhlin
BAD SÄCKINGEN
RIEHEN
RHEINFELDEN
RHEIN-FELDEN
Brugg
BIRS-FELDEN
GRENZACH-WYHLEN
Windisch
BINNINGEN
MUTTENZ
PRATTELN
Füllinsdorf
Frick
Frenkendorf
Gelterkinden
Arlesheim
LIESTAL
Lausen
Dornach
Sissach
Mörikenenz-Niederlenz
Aesch
Bubendorf
Lenzburg
AARAU
Buchs
Suhr
Gränichen
Seon
Trimbach
Schönenwerd
Ober-entfelden
OLTEN
Balsthal
Aarburg
Oftringen
Kölliken
Oensingen
Rothrist
Zofingen
Reinach
Strengelbach
Menziken
Niederbipp
Brittnau
Reiden
Langenthal
Aarwangen
Roggwil
Sursee
Herzogenbuchsee
Deren-dingen
Biberist
Ruswil
Gerlafingen
Bätter-kinden
Huttwil
Wolhusen
Utzenstorf
Kirchberg
BURGDORF
Sumiswald

Stühlingen 23 km
Schaffhausen (CH) 36 km

34

7 Baden 18 km
17 Zürich 42 km

5 Klingnau 6 km

118 Baden Zürich
ICE IC/EC

3 Baden 8 km
Zürich 32 km

3 → 1 4 km

Baden 11 km
Zürich 35 km
Winterthur 60 km

TGV Zürich

119

1 Wohlen 7 km
Zürich 33 km
Cham 38 km

120

26 Hochdorf 15 km
Luzern 31 km

23 Hochdorf 15 km
Luzern 31 km

121

2 Emmen 12 km
Luzern 16 km

IC/EC Luzern

2 Emmen 11 km
Luzern 15 km

122

10 → 2 10 km
Emmen 12 km
Luzern 14 km
Cham 33 km

12
ICE/EC
TGV
Bern 13 km
Thun 37 km
Interlaken 63 km

1 Bern
Interlaken
Bern
Neuchâtel

23 Langnau i.
Emmental 19 km

23 Langnau i. Emmental 15 km
Burgdorf 23 km

Schüpfheim 9 km
Langnau i. Emmental 32 km
Bern 67 km

10

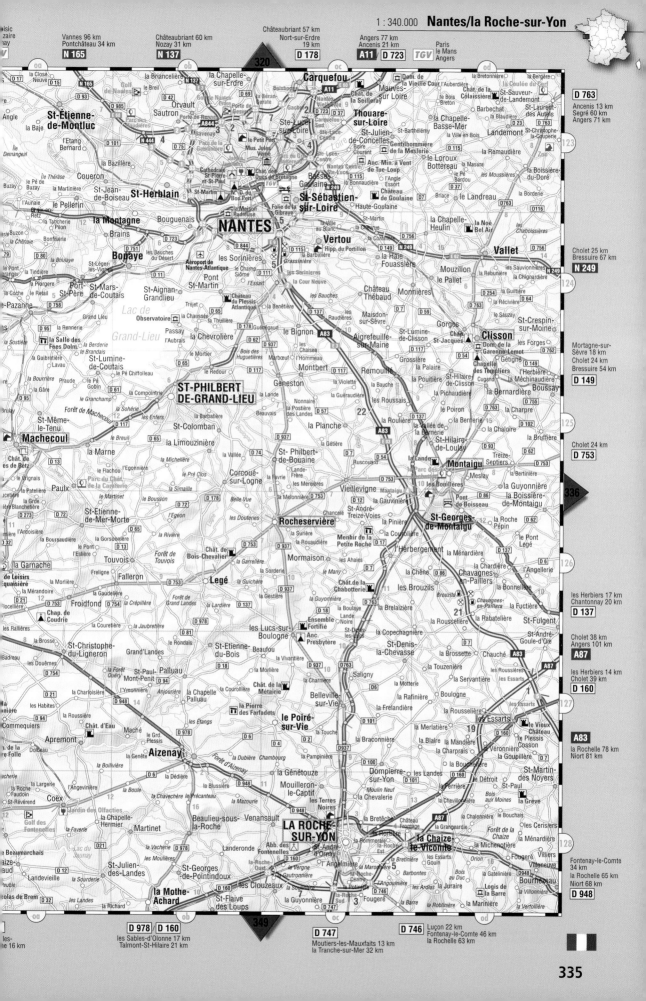

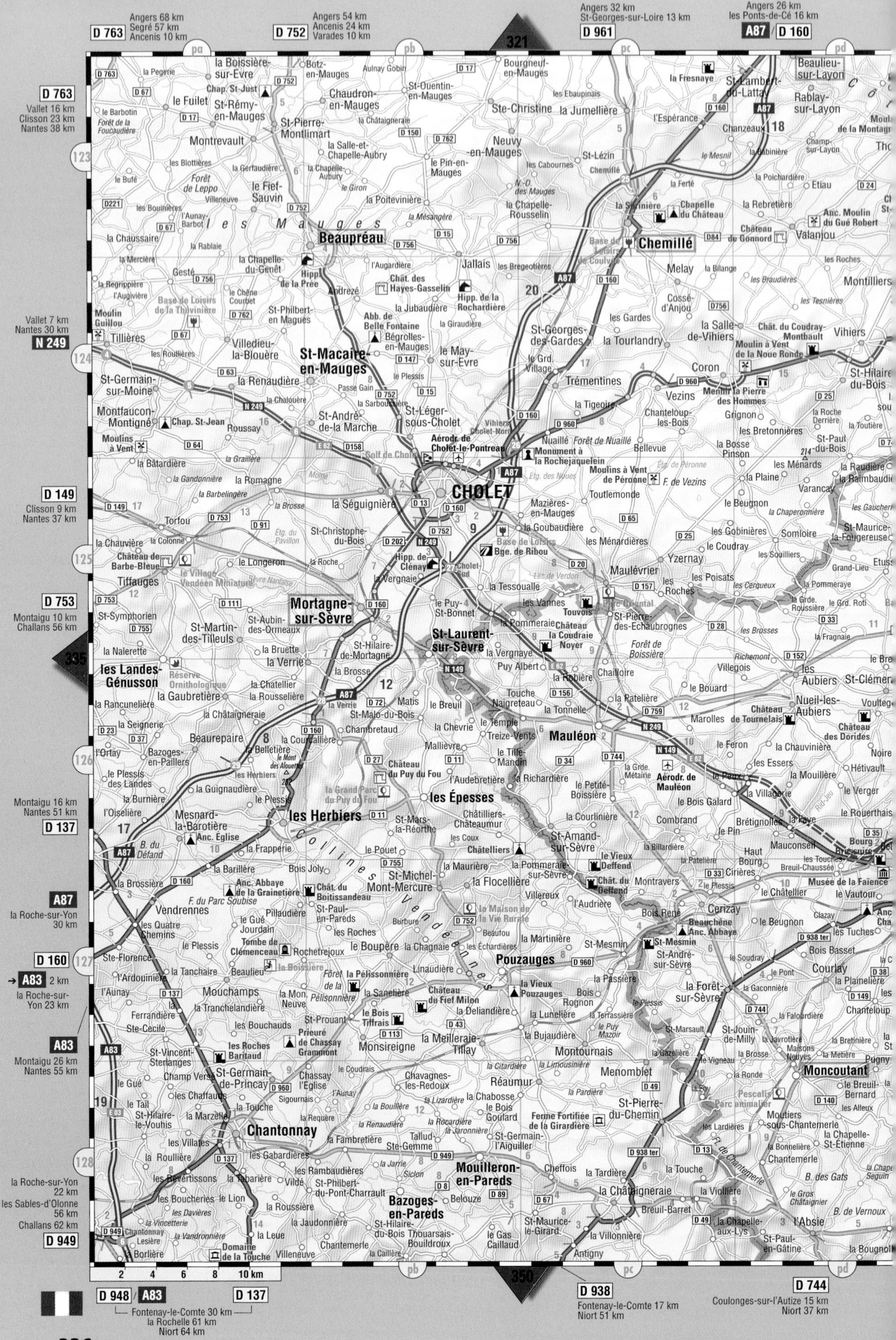

D 763 Angers 68 km Segré 57 km Ancenis 10 km
D 752 Angers 54 km Ancenis 24 km Varades 10 km
321
D 961 Angers 32 km St-Georges-sur-Loire 13 km
A87 / D 160 Angers 26 km les Ponts-de-Cé 16 km
D 763 Vallet 16 km Clisson 23 km Nantes 38 km
Vallet 7 km Nantes 30 km N 249
D 149 Clisson 9 km Nantes 37 km
D 753 Montaigu 10 km Challans 56 km
335
Montaigu 16 km Nantes 51 km D 137
A87 la Roche-sur-Yon 30 km
D 160
A83 2 km la Roche-sur-Yon 23 km
A83 Montaigu 26 km Nantes 55 km
la Roche-sur-Yon 22 km les Sables-d'Olonne 56 km Challans 62 km D 949
D 948 / A83 D 137 Fontenay-le-Comte 30 km la Rochelle 61 km Niort 64 km
2 4 6 8 10 km
350
D 938 Fontenay-le-Comte 17 km Niort 51 km
D 744 Coulonges-sur-l'Autize 15 km Niort 37 km
Beaupréau
Chemillé
CHOLET
St-Macaire-en-Mauges
Mortagne-sur-Sèvre
St-Laurent-sur-Sèvre
les Landes-Génusson
Mauléon
les Herbiers
les Épesses
Pouzauges
Chantonnay
Mouilleron-en-Pareds
Bazoges-en-Pareds
Moncoutant
Montrevault
Jallais
Vihiers
Tiffauges
Montfaucon-Montigné
Maulévrier
Cerizay
la Châtaigneraie
Collines Vendéennes
les Mauges

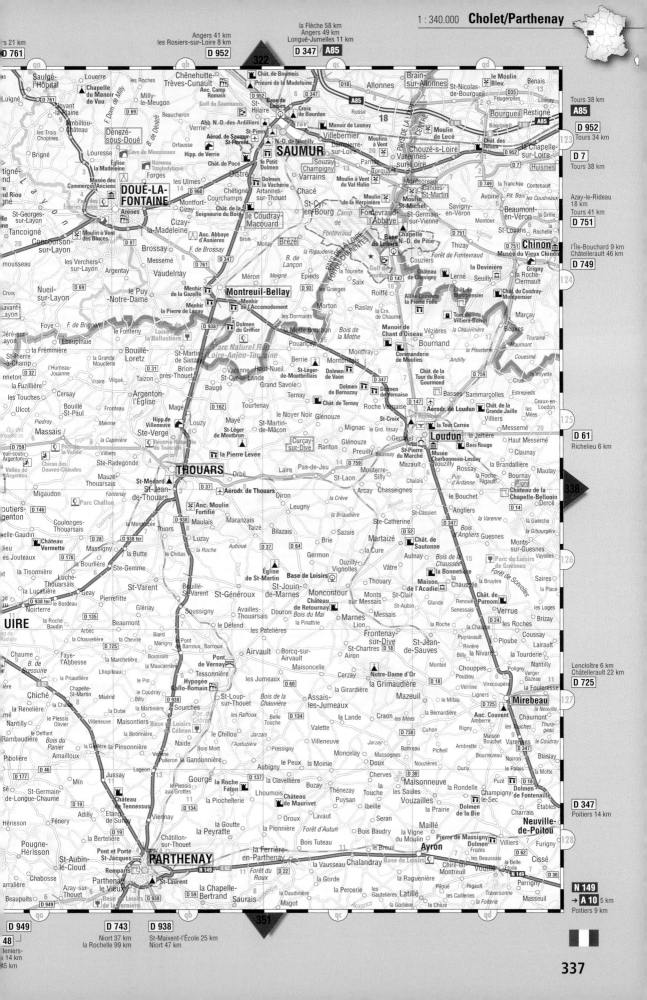

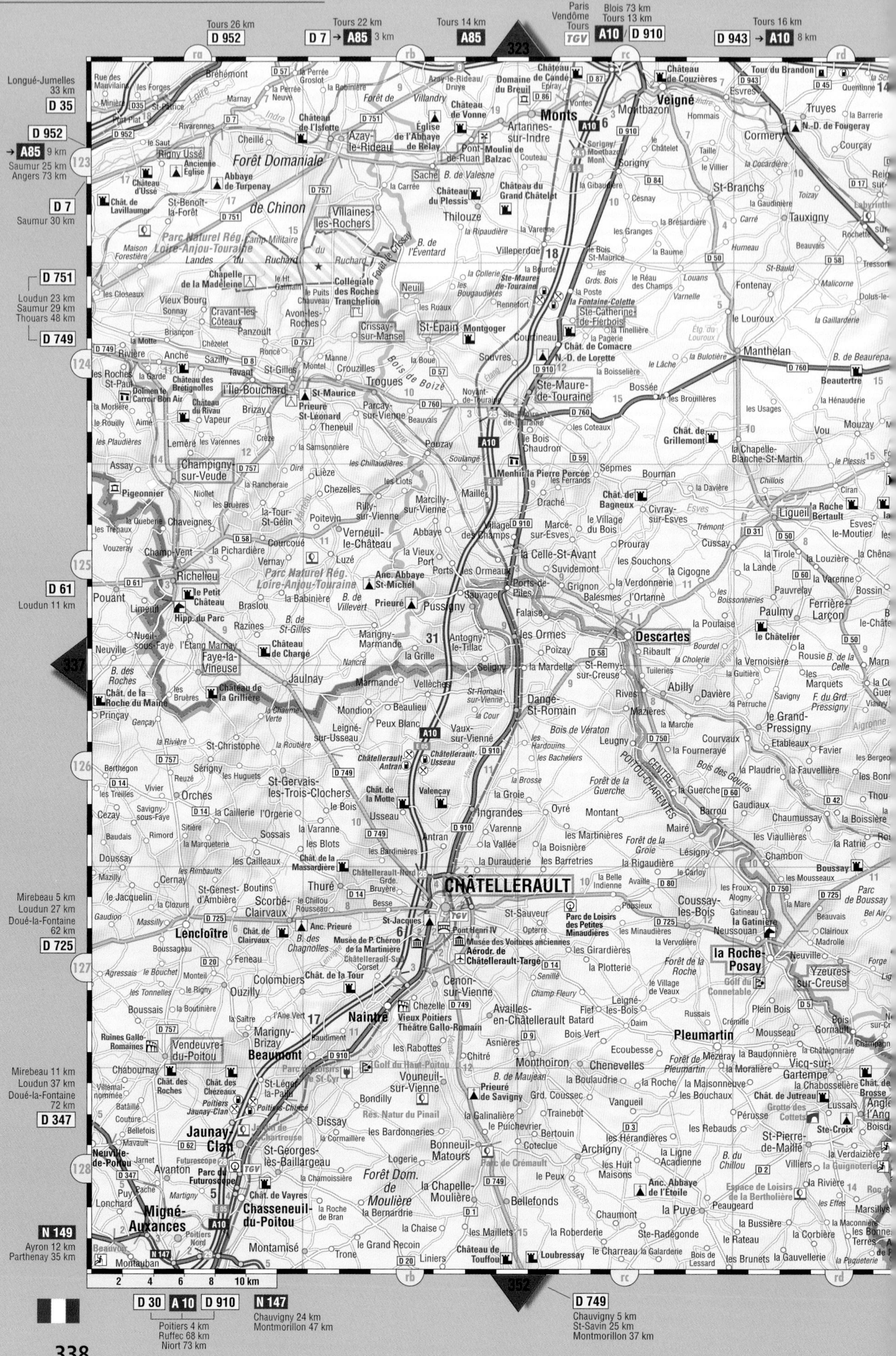

Tours 26 km — D 952
Tours 22 km — D 7 → A85 3 km
Tours 14 km — A85
Paris Vendôme Tours — TGV
Blois 73 km Tours 13 km — A10 D 910
Tours 16 km — D 943 → A10 8 km

Longué-Jumelles 33 km — D 35
D 952 → A85 9 km
Saumur 25 km
Angers 73 km

D 7
Saumur 30 km

D 751
Loudun 23 km
Saumur 29 km
Thouars 48 km

D 749

D 61
Loudun 11 km

Mirebeau 5 km
Loudun 27 km
Doué-la-Fontaine 62 km
D 725

Mirebeau 11 km
Loudun 37 km
Doué-la-Fontaine 72 km
D 347

Neuville-de-Poitou
N 149
Ayron 12 km
Parthenay 35 km

D 30 A10 D 910 N 147
Poitiers 4 km
Ruffec 68 km
Niort 73 km

Chauvigny 24 km
Montmorillon 47 km

D 749
Chauvigny 5 km
St-Savin 25 km
Montmorillon 37 km

Major towns: Montbazon, Veigné, Monts, Azay-le-Rideau, Sainte-Maure-de-Touraine, Sainte-Catherine-de-Fierbois, Descartes, Ligueil, Richelieu, l'Île-Bouchard, Champigny-sur-Veude, Châtellerault, Naintré, Beaumont, Jaunay-Clan, Migné-Auxances, Chasseneuil-du-Poitou, La Roche-Posay, Pleumartin, Le Grand-Pressigny, Lencloître, Dangé-St-Romain

Scale: 2 4 6 8 10 km

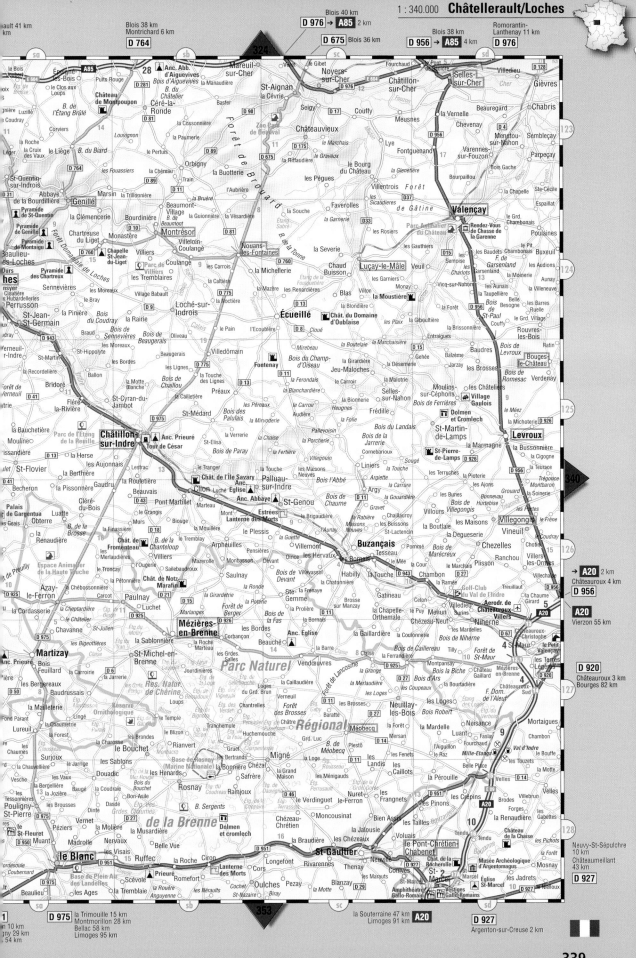

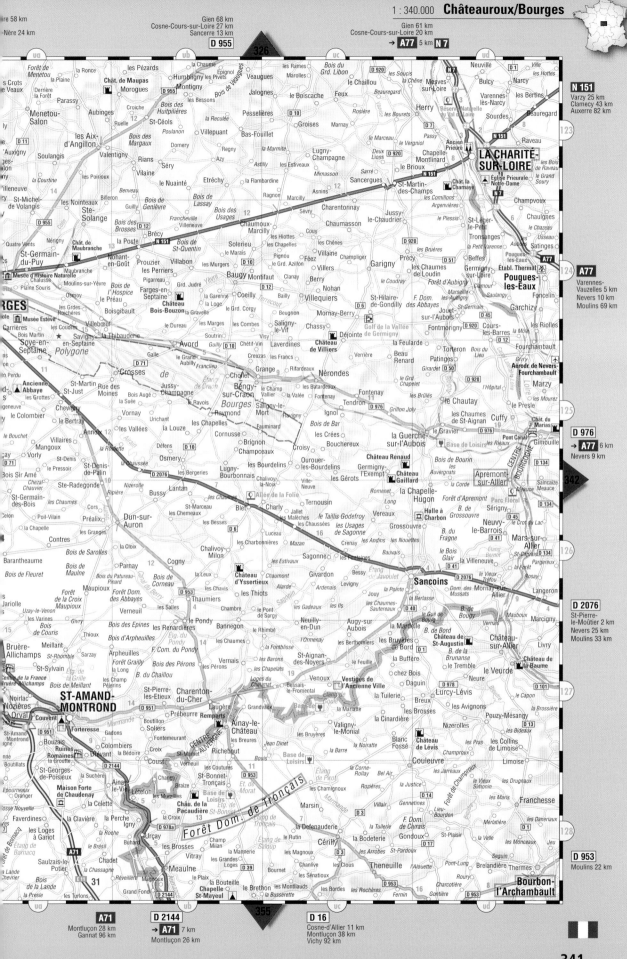

ire 58 km

Nère 24 km

Gien 68 km
Cosne-Cours-sur-Loire 27 km
Sancerre 13 km
D 955

Gien 61 km
Cosne-Cours-sur-Loire 20 km
→ **A77** 5 km **N 7**

326

N 151
Varzy 25 km
Clamecy 43 km
Auxerre 82 km

Forêt de Menetou
les Crots Veaux
la Plaine
Derrière la Forêt
Parassy
Aubinges
Menetou-Salon
les Aix-d'Angillon
d'Auxigny
les-ges-ion
St-Michel-de-Volangis
la Courtine
St-Germain-du-Puy
RGES
Musée Estève
Carrières
Bois Martin
Soye-en-Septaine
Polygone
Crosses
Annoix
Vorly
St-Denis-de-Palin
Ste-Radegonde
Bussy
Dun-sur-Auron
Parnay
Cogny
Baranthaume
Bois de Fleuret
Maupiou
Bruère-Allichamps
St-Sylvain
Noirlac
Orval
ST-AMAND-MONTROND
Colombiers
St-Georges-de-Poisieux
Ainay-le-Vi
Urçay
Meaulne

A71
Montluçon 28 km
Gannat 96 km

D 2144
→ **A71** 7 km
Montluçon 26 km

D 16
Cosne-d'Allier 11 km
Montluçon 38 km
Vichy 92 km

LA CHARITÉ-SUR-LOIRE
Église Prieurale Notre-Dame
Pougues-les-Eaux

A77
Varennes-Vauzelles 5 km
Nevers 10 km
Moulins 69 km

D 976
→ **A77** 6 km
Nevers 9 km

342

D 2076
St-Pierre-le-Moûtier 2 km
Nevers 25 km
Moulins 33 km

D 953
Moulins 22 km

Sancoins
Apremont-sur-Allier
la Guerche-sur-l'Aubois
Château-sur-Allier
Bourbon-l'Archambault

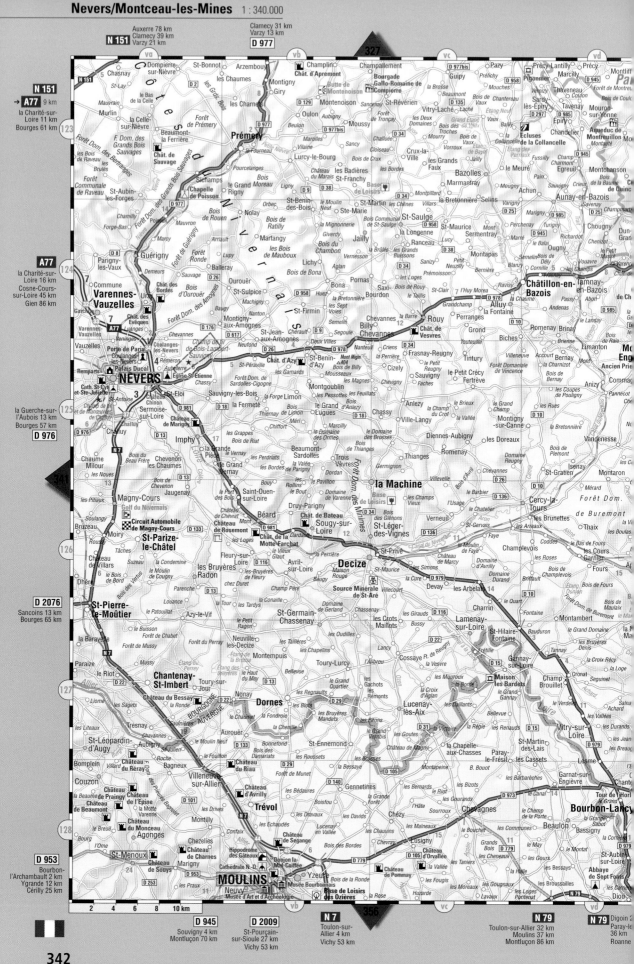

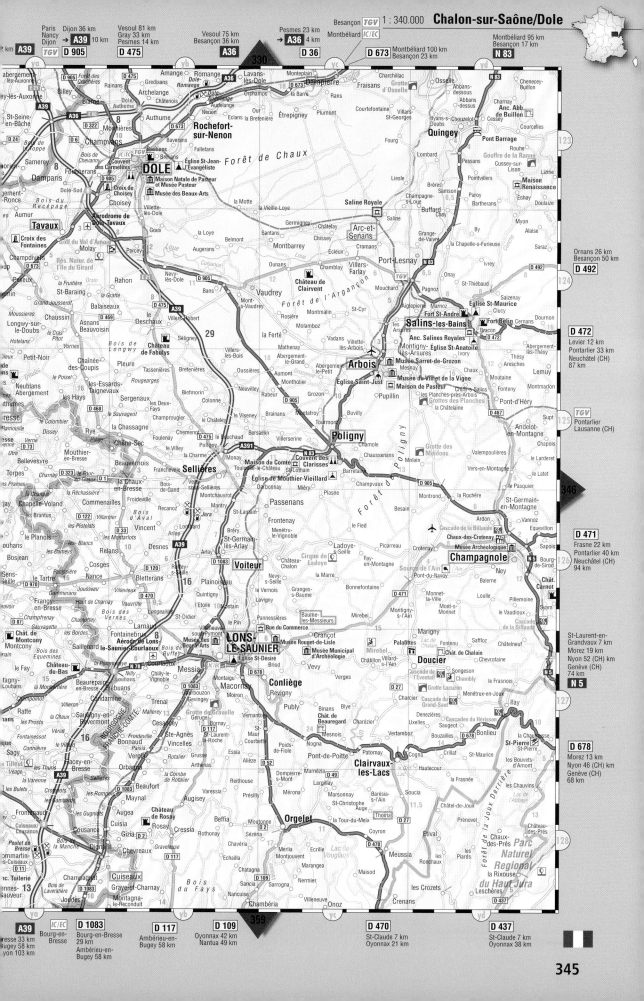

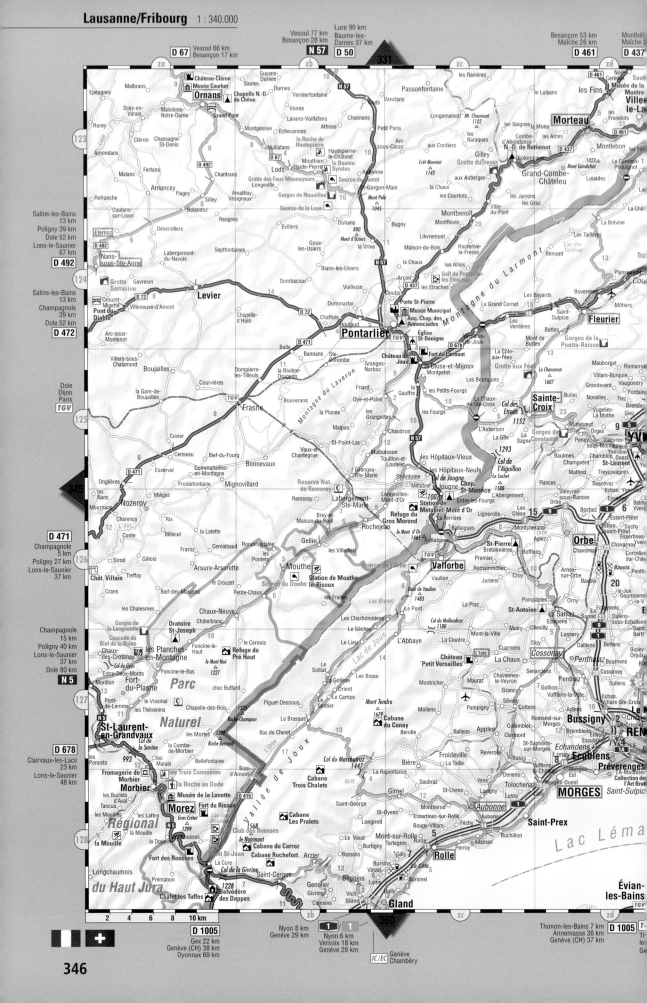

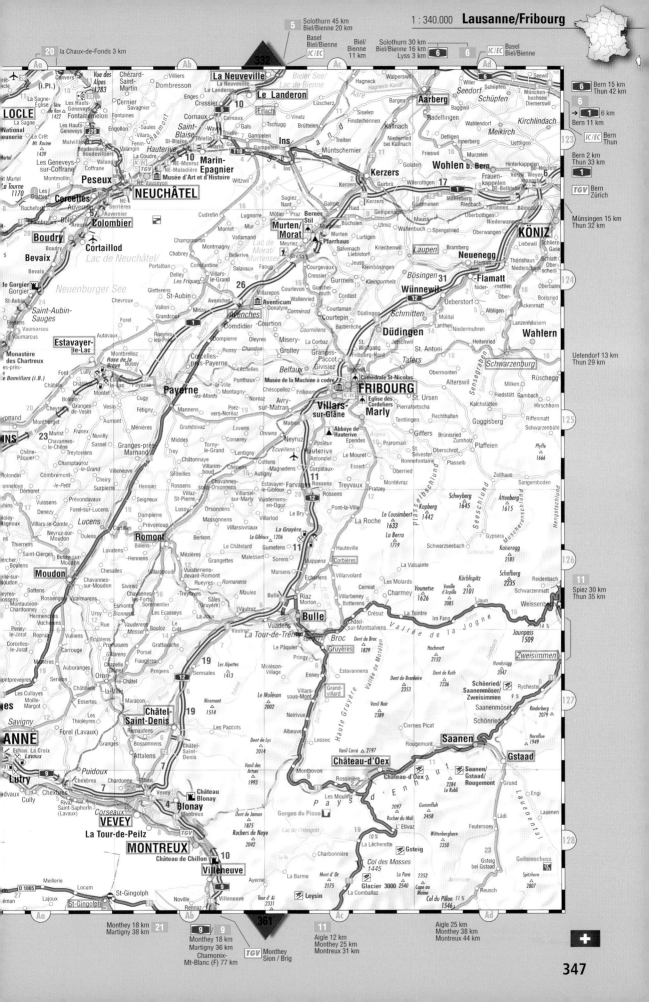

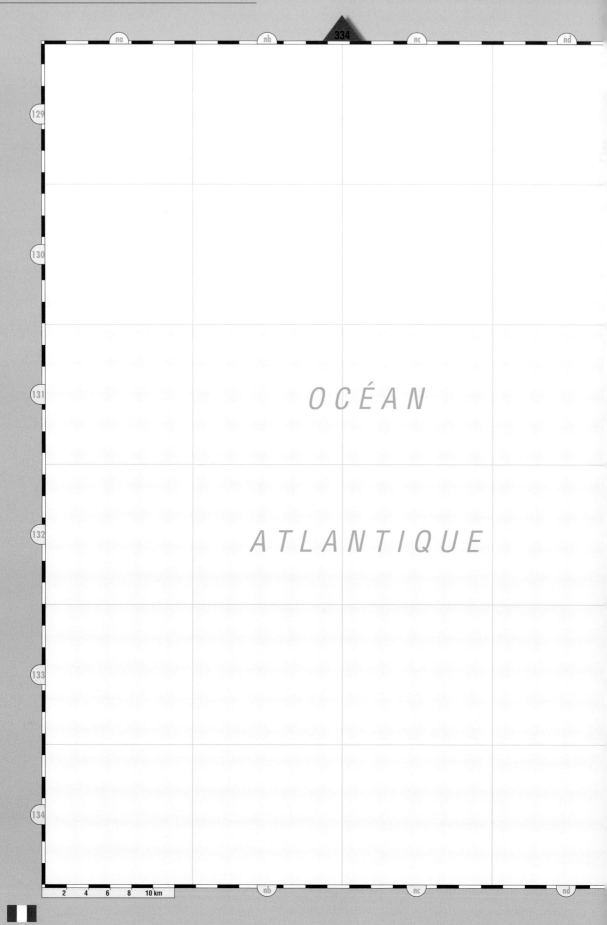

OCÉAN

ATLANTIQUE

2 4 6 8 10 km

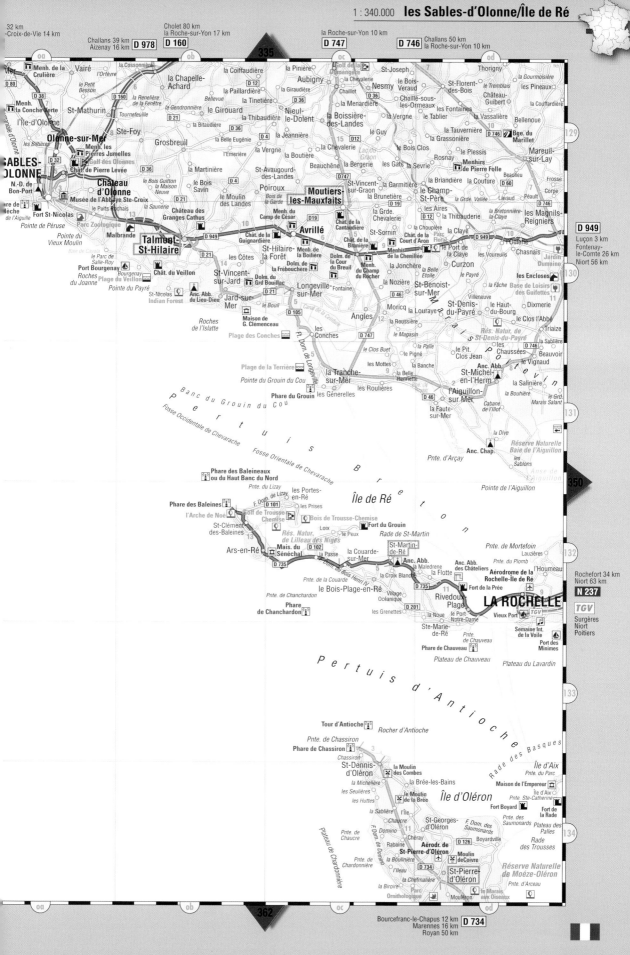

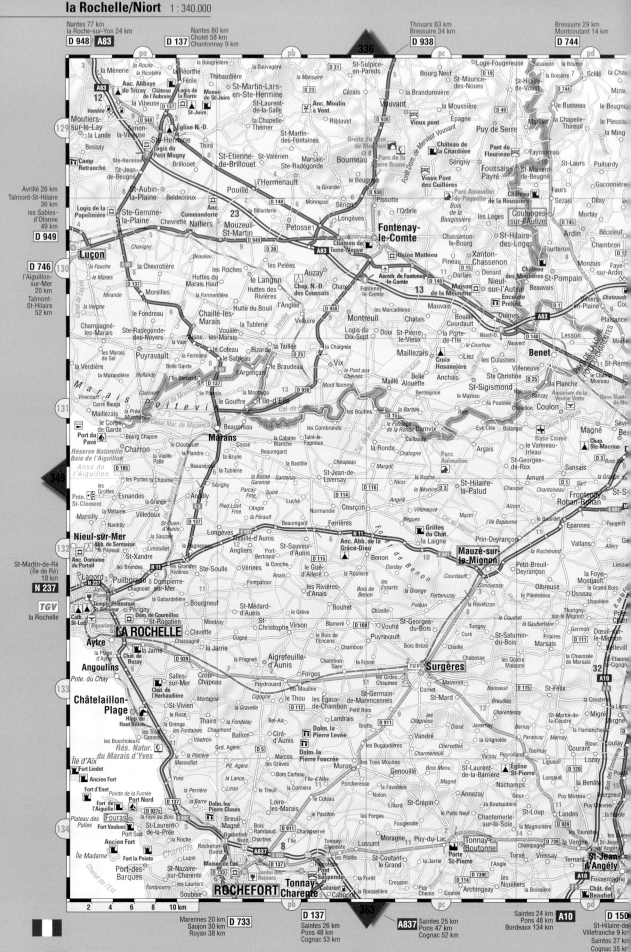

Nantes 77 km
la Roche-sur-Yon 24 km
D 948 | A83

Nantes 80 km
Cholet 58 km
Chantonnay 9 km
D 137

Thouars 63 km
Bressuire 34 km
D 938

Bressuire 29 km
Montcoutant 14 km
D 744

336

pa | pb | pc | pd

Avrillé 26 km
Talmont-St-Hilaire 36 km
les Sables-d'Olonne 49 km
D 949

D 746 | 130
l'Aiguillon-sur-Mer 20 km
Talmont-St-Hilaire 52 km

St-Martin-de-Ré (Île de Ré) 18 km
N 237

TGV
la Rochelle

LA ROCHELLE

Marans

Fontenay-le-Comte

Benet

Mauzé-sur-le-Mignon

Surgères

Châtelaillon-Plage

Fouras

ROCHEFORT
Tonnay-Charente

349
131
132
133
134

2 4 6 8 10 km

pb
363

350

Marennes 20 km
Saujon 30 km
Royan 38 km
D 733

Saintes 26 km
Pons 48 km
Cognac 53 km
D 137

A837 Saintes 25 km
Pons 47 km
Bordeaux 134 km

Saintes 24 km
Pons 48 km
A10

D 150
St-Hilaire-de-Villefranche 9 km
Saintes 27 km
Cognac 35 km

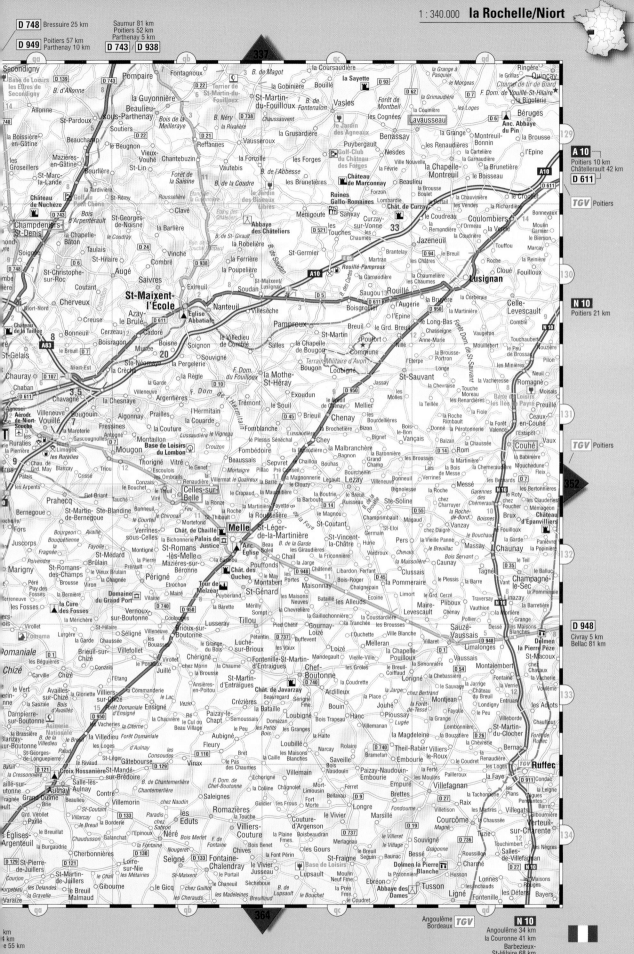

D 748 · Bressuire 25 km

D 949 · Poitiers 57 km
Parthenay 10 km

Saumur 81 km
Poitiers 52 km
Parthenay 5 km

D 743 / D 938

A 10
Poitiers 10 km
Châtellerault 42 km
D 611

TGV Poitiers

N 10
Poitiers 21 km

TGV Poitiers

D 948
Civray 5 km
Bellac 81 km

Angoulême TGV
Bordeaux

N 10
Angoulême 34 km
la Couronne 41 km
Barbezieux-
St-Hilaire 68 km

351

Parthenay 39 km
Mirebeau 24 km
D 347 / **N 149**
Châtellerault 28 km
A 10 **D 910** **N 147**
Futuroscope
Tours
Paris
TGV

D 749 Châtellerault 24 km

338

ra   rb   rc   rd

Buxerolles
POITIERS
B. de Mortier
Bignoux
Lavoux
Bonnes
Base de Loisirs
de la Plage
Nalliers
Roussac
le Pré
Boisherpir

★ Champ de tir
★ de Biard
Vouneuil-
sous-Biard
Aéroport de
Poitiers-Biard
Jardin des Plantes
Baptistère
St-Jean
B. de Lirec
Breuil-
Mingot
Anxaumont
B. du Bois-
Doussé
les Mesdières
le Breuil
Jardres
D 20
les Courlis
D 749
Forêt Domaniale
de Mareuil
la Forge
la Chaise
Babousseau
Lauthiers
Paizay-le-Sec
D 951
la Maranchère
D 9
les Sables
Chalache
la Chaise
Chauvigny

St-Maixent-
l'École 39 km
Niort 59 km
A 10

St-Benoît
Mignaloux-
Beauvoir
Sèvres-
Anxaumont
Barleng
Pigeron
St-Julien-
l'Ars
Puygirault
Chât. d'Harcourt
Chévrie
Peuron
Asnières
les Églises
Abbaye Poitevine
St-Savin
St-Germ
Ville

D 611
Lusignan 13 km
St-Maixent-l'École
42 km
Niort 65 km

Ligugé
Smarves
Nouaillé-
Maupertuis
Anc. Logis Abbatial
Anc. Abbaye
St-Martin
Parc
Animalier
Jardin Médiéval
Col de Mignaloux
Bois de
Poitiers
le Bouchet
Tercé
la Thibaudière
St-Martin
le Mazeau
la Coulonnière
les Chaumes
Leignes-
sur-Fontaine
Jouhet
Moulin de Roche
Peufa
Puist

TGV
Niort
la Rochelle

129
130

Dolmen de Pouzac
Roches-Prémarie-
Andillé
Nieuil-
l'Espoir
Chapelle-
Morthemer
l'Épine
Fleuré
la Roche
Morthemer
Bourpeuil
les Brousses
Parthenay
D 8
Ribes
la Forge
Servon
Chapelle-
Viviers
Pindray
la Roche-
au-Baussan
Prunier
D 11
D 54
Soulage
Concise

N 147
N 10
Ruffec 47 km
Angoulême 65 km

la Villedieu-
du-Clain
Gizay
Dolmen d'Arlait
Vivonne
Château-
Larcher
St-Maurice-
la-Clouère
Gençay
Chât. de
la Roche
Verrières
St-Laurent-
de-Jourdes
Montmorillon
D 727
D 729
Lussac-
les-Châteaux

351
TGV
Ruffec
Angoulême
Bordeaux
131
132

Champagné-
St-Hilaire
Abbaye
de Moreau
Sommières-
du-Clain
Château-
Garnier
Chât. de
Vareilles
Usson-
du-Poitou
Chât. de
Monchandy
Chabanne
D 741
l'Isle-
Jourdain
St-Martin-
l'Ars
Circuit
Automobile
Millac
D 729

D 948
Ruffec 17 km
Melle 33 km
Niort 63 km
133

St-Pierre-
d'Exideuil
Civray
Grottes
du Chaffaud
Charroux
Hippodrome
de Breuil
Anc.
Abbaye
Pressac
Menhir de la
Pierre Fade
Availles-
Limouzine
Abzac
Château
de la Fayolle
Oradour-
Fanais
St-Martial-
sur-Isop

Genouillé
Chatain
Vieux Pont
Château
de Cibioux
Chât. d'Ordières
Parc Animalier
de la Colline Enchantée
Hiesse
Dolmen de
Ste-Madeleine
St-Germain
de-Confolens
Brillac
Bussière-
Boffy

134
St-Georges
Nanteuil-
en-Vallée
Champagne-
Mouton
Allone
D 740
St-Barthélemy
Pont Vieux
Confolens
Ansac-
sur-Vienne
D 29
St-Christophe
D 28

Couture
St-Sulpice-
de-Ruffec
Turgon
St-Laurent-
de-Céris
Manot
St-Maurice-
des-Lions
Chabanais
Chabrac
Brigueuil
D 16
D 948

2 4 6 8 10 km

D 951
la Rochefoucauld 24 km
Angoulême 51 km

365

rb   rc   rd

D 948
St-Junien 6 km
Limoges 37 km
St-
Roche

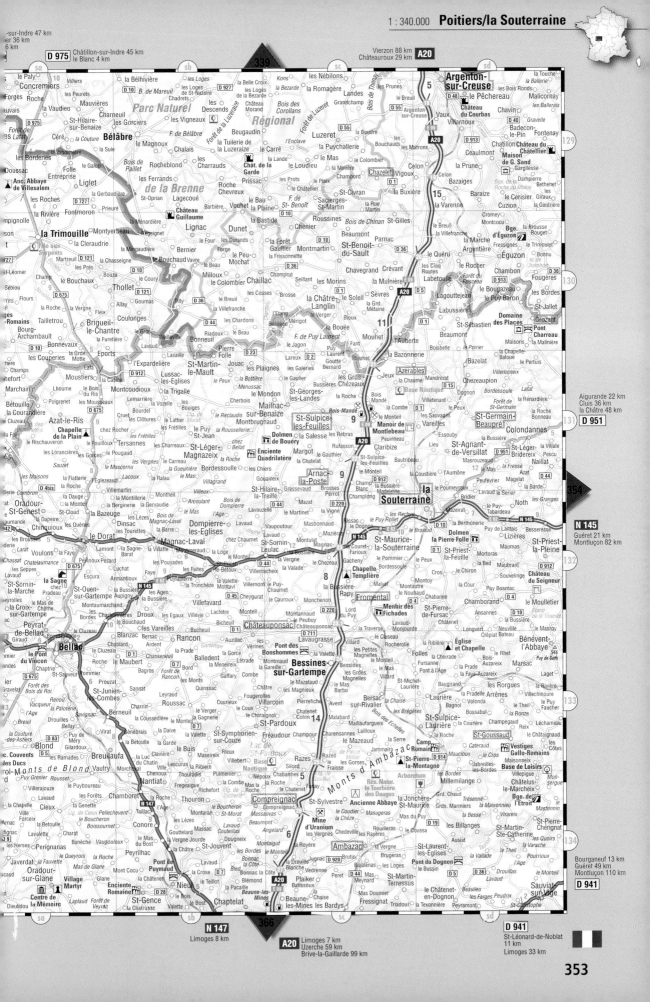

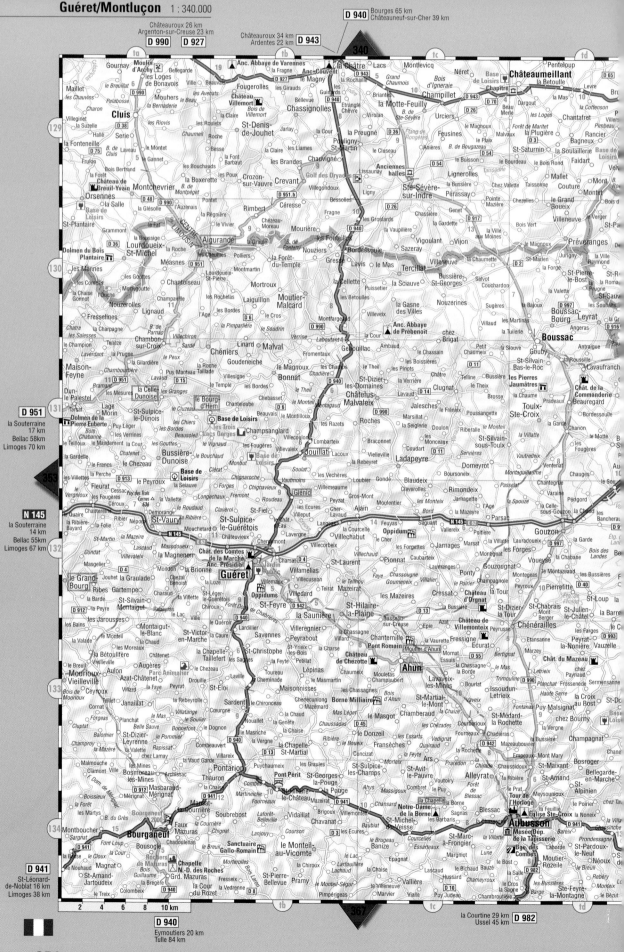

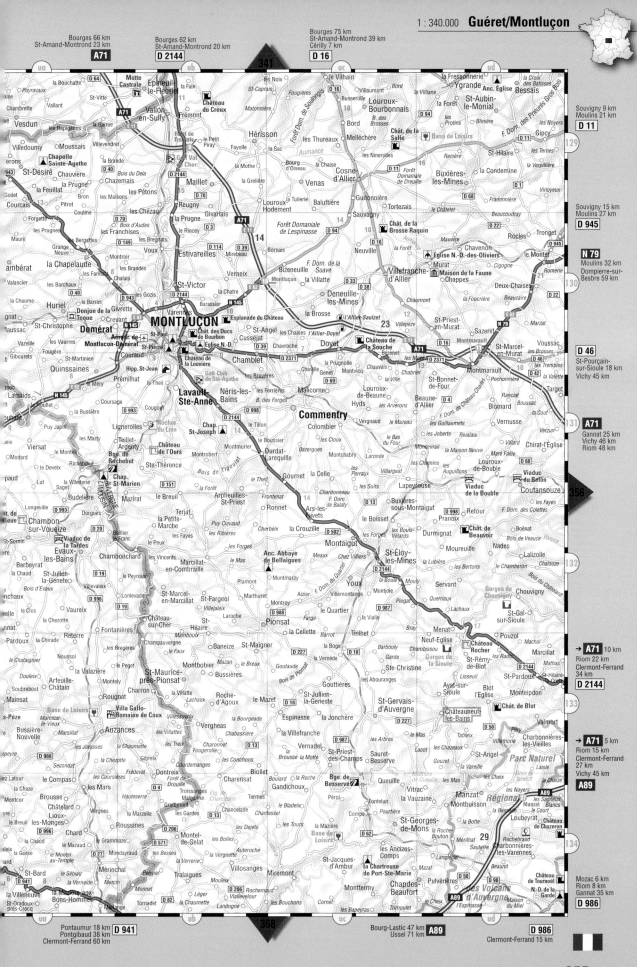

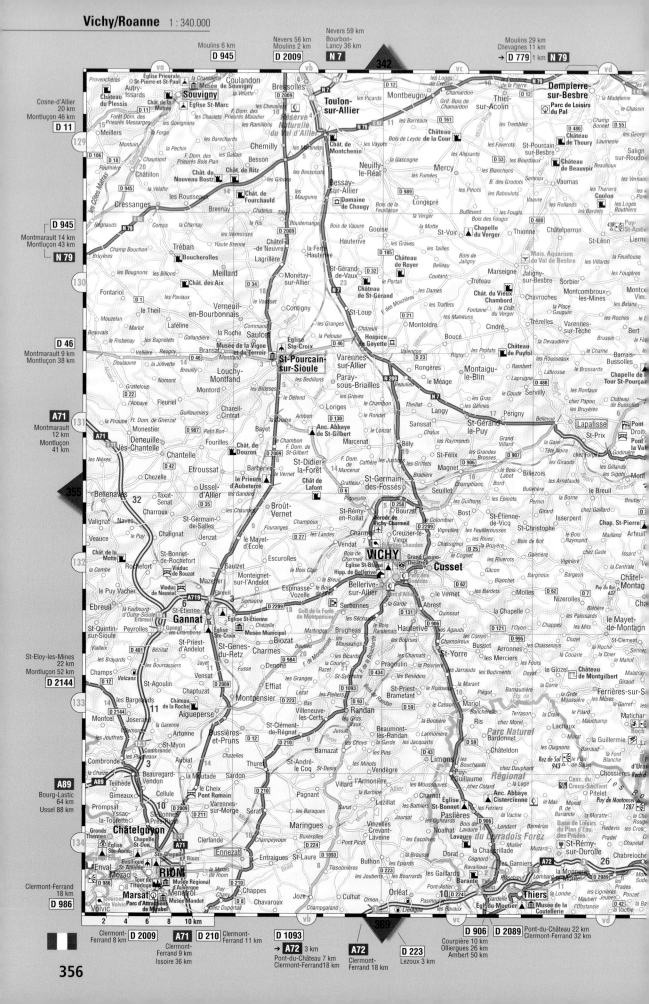

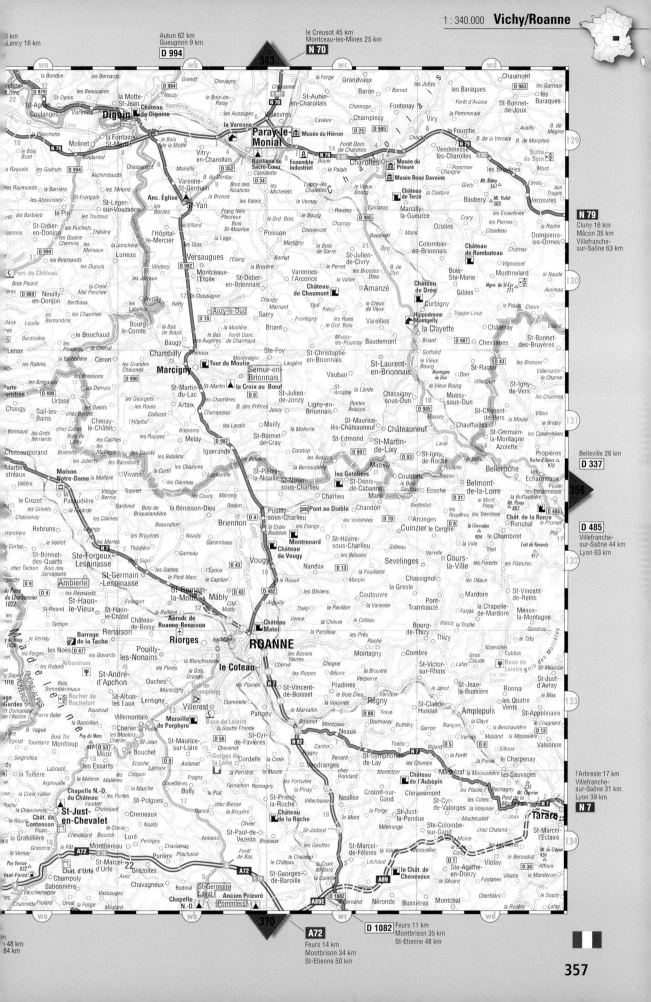

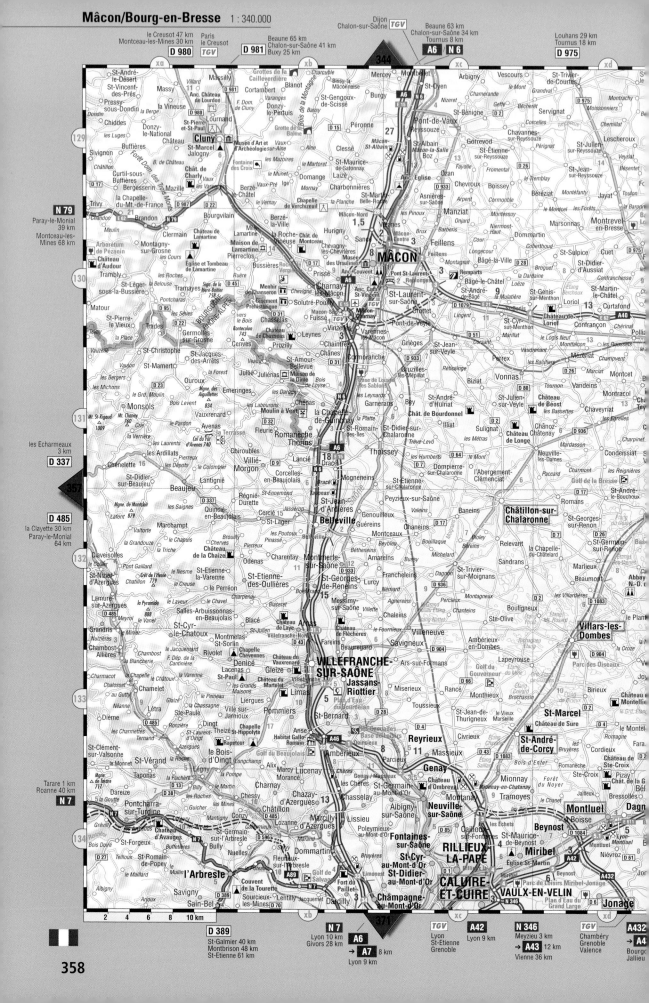

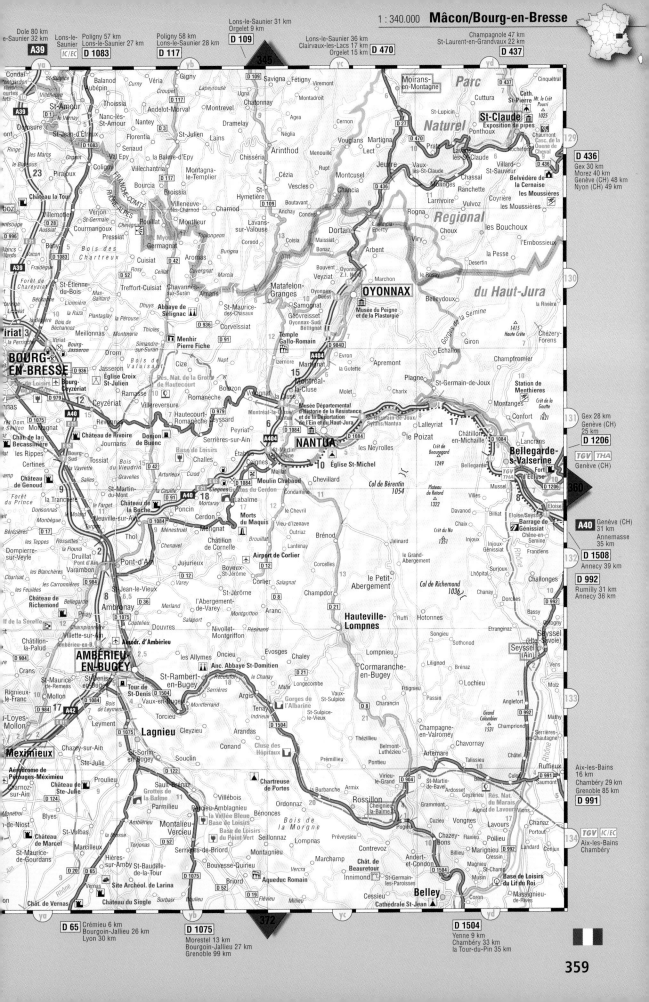

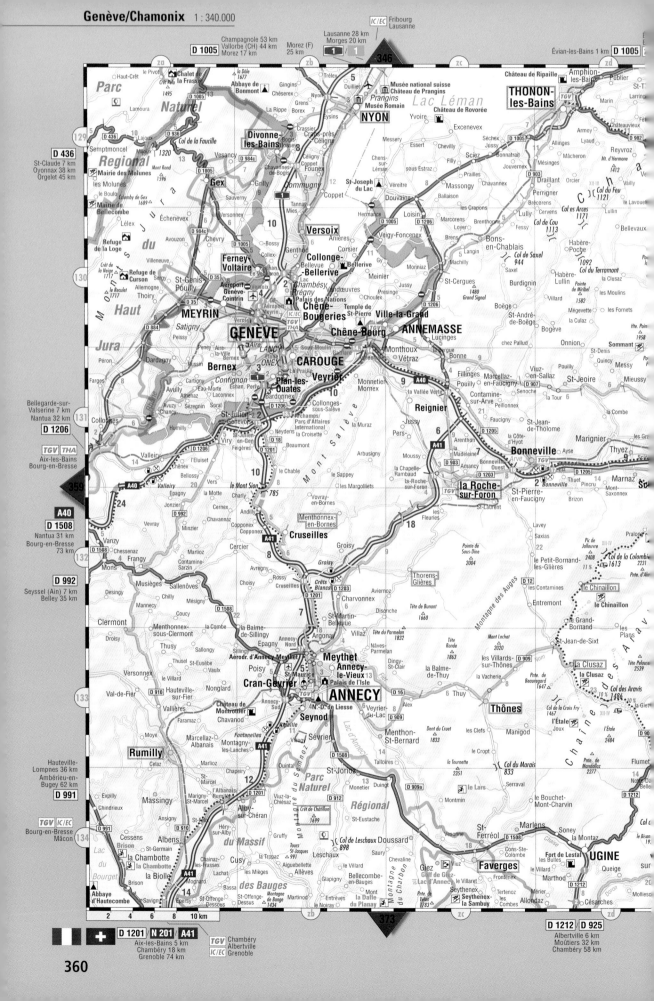

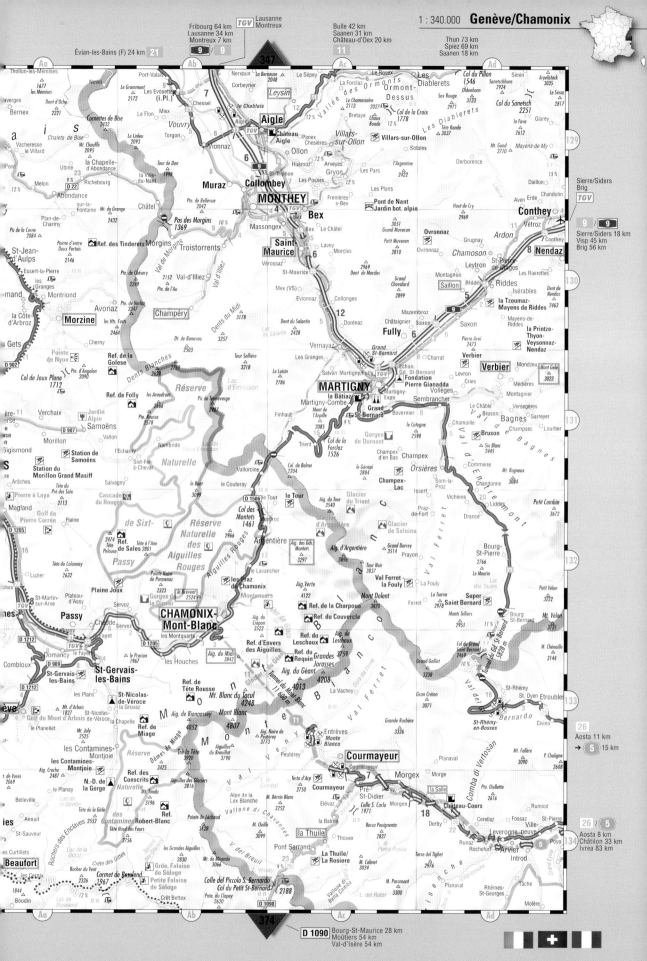

St-Denis-d'Oléron 25 km [D 26]
St-Pierre-d'Oléron 12 km

Aquarium — la Matonnière
Dolus-d'Oléron — les Bardière
la Remigeasse   le Château-d Po
                 [D 26]
                 [D 126] la Citadel
Vert-Bois   le Deu
Plage le Grand Village   la Chevalerie
le Grand Village-Plage   **Bou**
                                 le
St-Trojan-les-Bains
la Grande Plage

Lannelongue

Pointe   Plage
de Maumusson   Ron
                          [D 25]
Côte Sauvage Plage
                          Forêt Dom
                          2
                          de la Co
                          la-Tremb

Phare de la Coubre   Presq

                          [i] Bor
Bonne-Anse
Pointe de
la Coubre
                          Plage de

Grande Passe de l'O

Embouchure de l

Plateau de Cordouan
                          Phare de Co

O C É A N

A T L A N T I Q U E

Passe du Sud ou d

Plage de Soula

Côte d'Argent

Plage de Montalive
les-Bain

| 2 | 4 | 6 | 8 | 10 km |

362

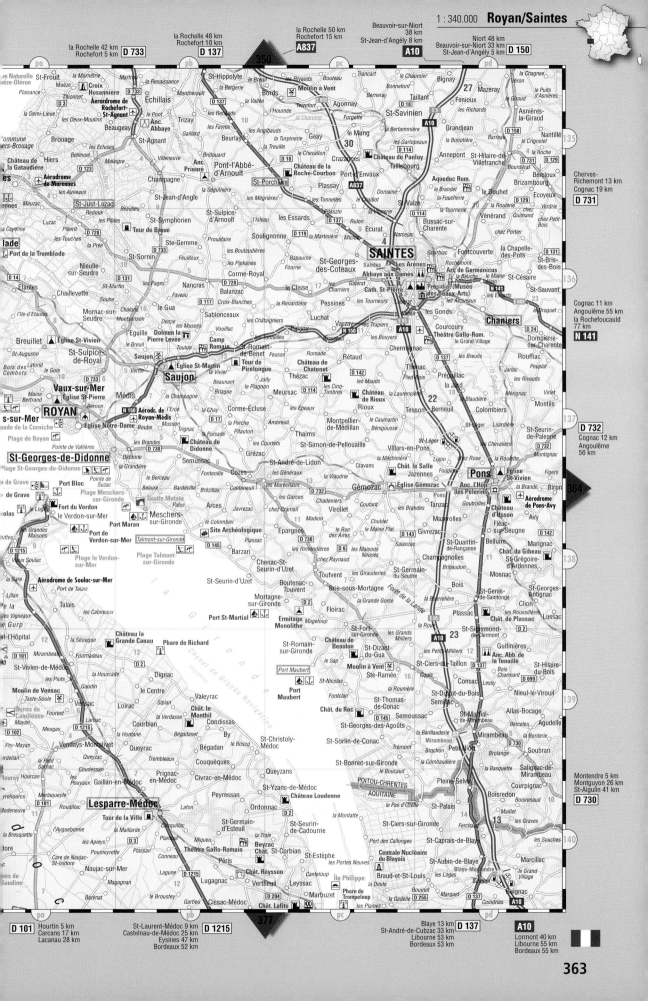

Bellac 48 km
Confolens 14 km
D 951

D 948 Confolens 12 km

352

N 141 Limoges 27 km
St-Léonard-de-Noblat 44 km

135

136

137

366

138

Thiviers 1 km
Châlus 30 km
Aixe-sur-Vienne 51 km
N 21

139

Excideuil 14 km
Saint-Yrieix-la-Perche 42 km
D 705

140

D 708

D 709 Mussidan 22 km
Bergerac 51 km

379

D 939 Périgueux 5 km
Bergerac 54 km

N 21 Périgueux 10 km
Bergerac 59 km

Gijon-Ménestérol 26km
Ste-Foy 47 km

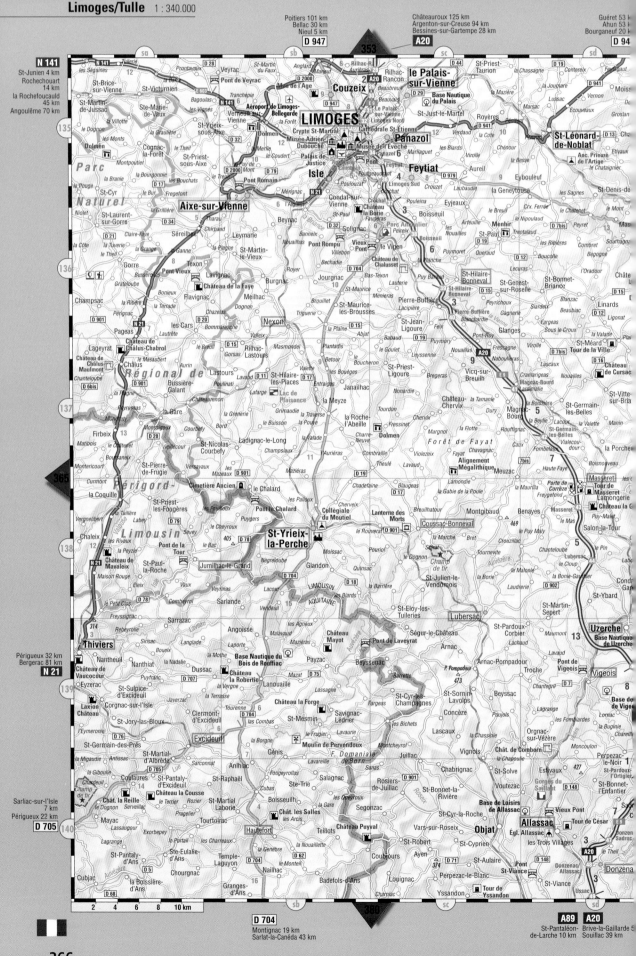

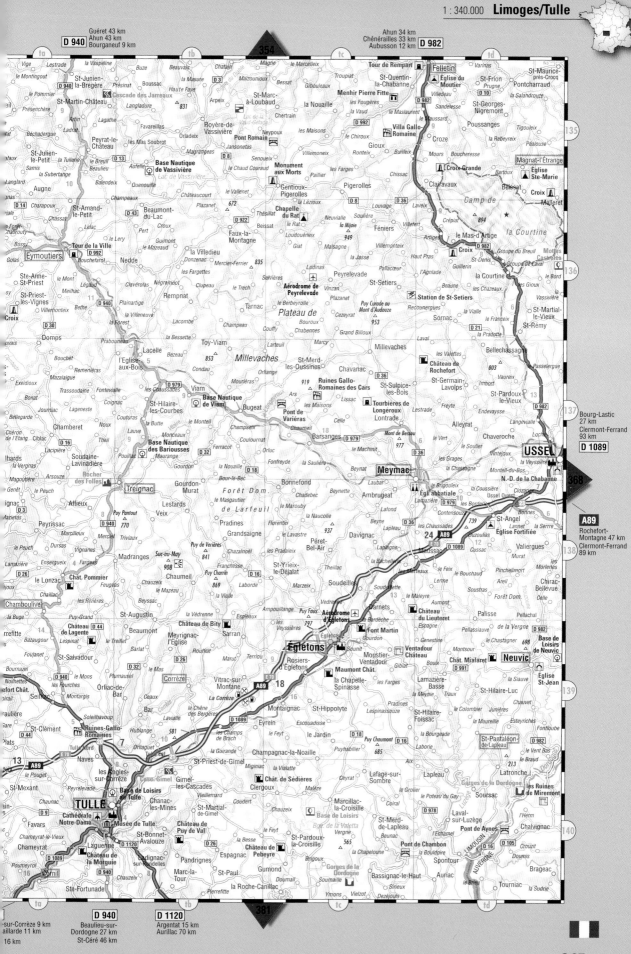

354

Guéret 43 km
Ahun 43 km
D 940
Bourganeuf 9 km

Ahun 34 km
Chénérailles 33 km
Aubusson 12 km D 982

381

D 940
Beaulieu-sur-
Dordogne 27 km
St-Céré 46 km

D 1120
Argentat 15 km
Aurillac 70 km

367

355

→ A71 24 km
Combronde 23 km
A89

Crocq · Basville · la Celle · Chaupeyrat · St-Avit · 744 la Rodde · Pontaumur · Provenchère · Maleret · Pranal · St-Ours · D 943 · Puy de Louchadière 1198

Longeaigue · Dimpoux · Parsange · Marcolanges · Condat-en-Combrailles · Montglandier · la Goutelle · Lamothe · Fougères · Château de Dauphin · Puy Chopine · Beauregard

la Villette · D 833 · Motte Feodèle · les Molles · Combrailles · 19 · Bromont-Lamothe · Pontgibaud · Puy de Côme 1181 · Pontgibaud

St-Agnant-près-Crocq · Lépinas · Fernoël · Giat · D 204 · les Aymards · St-Hilaire-les-Monges · Feuillassou · les Betz · Bonnabaud · Château · D 986 · St-Pierre-le-Chastel · Forêt de Mazaye

Flayat · Doumareix · Villevergne · Angoilas · D 987 · Puy-St-Gulmier · Sauvagnat · Pérol · 23 · Gelles · la Narse · Vareilles · Couhei · Montmeyre · Allagnat · Puy de Dôme 1464

D 996 · Gourseix · 805 · Barmontel · les Barrichons · l'Éclache · le Montel · Villevieille · Banson · Monges · D 204 · Olby · Bravant · Temple de Mercure

St-Oradoux-de-Chirouze · le Bessaud · St-Merd-la-Breuille · Dolmen · Ronzet · Chadeaux · Tortebesse · Massages · St-Pierre-Roche · D 2089 · Nébouzat

le Mourcy · le Besth · les Barlauds · Teissonnières · Lastic · Rozet · Buzaudon · Heume-l'Église · Montcheneix · St-Bonnet-près-Orcival · Château de Cordès

Bongue · le Brasseix · Laroche-près-Feyt · 793 · Montel Brut · Combrar · Muratel · Bourgeade · Rochefort-Montagne · Orcival · Aurières

Forêt de Châteauvert · Bigoulette · Feyt · les Combes · Cornes · Vialatte · Bajouve · Puy-Laveze · Perpezat · Légalie · Soussat · Vernines · Base de Loisirs Lac d'Aidat

Couffy-sur-Sarsonne · Lamazière-Haute · Chardoux · Veynières · Artiges · Bosjean · St-Julien-Sanc · Vilevieille · la Chabanne · Fontsalie · D 983

Croix · Charbouède · Chassergues · Merlines · Monestier-Merlines · Tauzin · 23 · Bourg-Lastic · Bauberty · St-Sulpice · Roche Tuilière · Puy de Combe Perret 1380 · Pessade

Courteix · la Roussanie · Motte Feodèle · la Garde · Vedrine · Puits-St-Louis · D 31 · Chorlol · Rigaud · 1512 · 1481 · Puy Corde · Station de Beaume-le-Froid

St-Pardoux-Aix-le-Neuf · la Jarrige · Faux · le Bialon · 6 · D 82 · Musée la Cluze · Laqueuille · Puy Loup · Station de Guéry · Puy d'Alou 1098

la Doulange · 880 · la Marsalouse · Gioux · Messeix · Brogros · Chomadoux · St-Sauves-d'Auvergne · Murat-le-Quaire · le Prégnoux · Puy de Barbier 1702 · Beaume-le-Froid

A89 · Ussel Est · les Sauvettes · Ruère · Avèze · Méjanesse · Portique Renaissance · la Bourboule · Mont-Dore · Murol

St-Dezery · St-Etienne-aux-Clos · Froides Maisons · Savennes · Mercœur · Menhir dit Pierre de Quatre Curés · 988 · Fougeolles · Station de Charlannes · Rigolet Haut · Col de la Croix-St-Robert · Chambon-sur-Lac

USSEL · Marsinchal · Gorges d'Avèze · Pradelles · Ardot · Granges · Escladines · D 29 · Station de la Tour Sancy la Stèle · Puy de Chambourguet · Roche de Vendeix · la Grande Cascade

367 · Rastoix · Gorges du Chavanon · Singles · Serre · Ribbes · la Roche · Noilhat · 1373 · Station de Mont Dore · 1737 · Puy de Sancy · Chambon des Neiges · Courbanges

16 · la Subrange · 747 · St-Exupéry-les-Roches · Montassou · Confolent-Port-Dieu · Larodde · 873 · Aulnat · Eglise St-Pardoux · la Tour-d'Auvergne · Station de Chastreix-Sancy · Mont Redon 1582 · Chambon Cre

A89 · Egletons 25 km · Naves 54 km · Tulle 54 km · Mestes · Fumarettes · St-Bonnet-près-Bort · Montaux · Chastreix · Chapelle Notre-Dame · Puy de Paillaret 1721 · Super-Besse · D 978

138 · Veyrières · Monestier-Port-Dieu · Labessette · Trémouille-St-Loup · 1021 · Tialle · la Pluneyre · Peut · la Morangie · Station de Picherande · Puy de Montchal 1407

la Vialatte · D 979 · St-Victour · les Bosdeveix · Crouzet · 724 · Bourboulou · Nugerolle · Chassagnoux · Cisternes · Chaumiane · Compains

Chaumerliac · St-Etienne-la-Geneste · Vaux · Andregeat · Beaulieu · Journiac · Saussat · Cros · Ponet · Plateau · Arfouilllouze · Lamur · Puy de la Vaisse 1358

Sainte-Marie-Lapanouze · Margerides · Base de Loisirs de Bge. Dordogne · Château de Val · Labanut · Régional · des · Escouaillous · Puy de Montchal

D 20 · Liginiac · Chap. St-Blaise · Lanobre · 808 · Gravière · la Renonfeyre · Dressondeix · Eglise-neuve-d'Entraigues · la Chaux d'Espinhal · 1230 · Brion

Roche-le-Peyroux · Chât. de Pierrefitte · Bort-les-Orgues · Champs-sur-Tarentaine Marc · Marchal · 1052 · Lamareugie · Chanterelle · la Tabastie · Espinchal · la Godivelle

Peyroux · Chât. de Mareges · Mareges · 859 · St-Pierre · Fournols · Base de Loisirs de Lastioulles · la Crégut · le Coudert · Courteilles · Labro · Lascombe · Domaine Nordique du Cézallier-Sancy

Sérandon · Belv. de Gratte Bruyère · Champagnac · Ludiès · Cheyssac · Saut de la Saute · le Bouchet · le Chambon · Trémouille · Chastelanay · Montboudif · Espinasouze · Margnat · Montgreleix · 1476 · Burron de Chaussigué-Hut

la Moransane · Prodelles · Ydes · Vebret · Château Couzans · 926 · Gorges de la Rhue · Coindze · Condat · Marvaud · Laveissière · le Lac · le Saillant

139 · Veyrières · Serviolle · Ydes Bourg · Saïgnes · Antignac · St-Etienne-de-Chomeil · Jointy · St-Amandin · Feniers · Marcenat · Monts Cézall

Clemensac · Serandon · Bassignac · Sauvat · la Monselie · Château de Murat-la-Rabbe · Embesse · Hab. Préhist. de Chateauneuf · Chassagny · Marcenat · le Greil · Volcas

Arches · Tiolade · Parensol · D 922 · Tour de la Ville · le Monteil · Jalanlac · Menet · Montsistrier · Château St-Angeau · Riom-ès-Montagnes · Lugarde · D 16 · St-Bonnet-de-Condat · Landeyrat

140 · Vendes · Chabrespine · Marladet · Alsac · la Ribbe · Crayssac · Rignac · Valette · la Ribeyre · Marchastel · Soulages · Clavières · Chât. de Combes · Courbières

Ortigier · Sourniac · Jaleyrac · Marlat · Auzers · Lieuchy · 1168 · Apchon · Chât. de Peyrelade · Pierrebesse · la Vergne · 1118 · 1238 · Vernols · Cascade de Veyrines

Aymons · Angles · Montbrun · Méallet · Lachassagnes · Trizac · Collandres · la Morel · St-Hippolyte · Ségur-les-Villas · la Gazelle · Puy de

Basilique Romane · Conrut · le Vigean · Boissières · Chanterelle · St-Vincent-de-Salers · Cheylade · la Bussinie · 1232 · le Monteil · Aynas · Roche du Pic 1261 · Mouret

Mauriac · D 922 · Chap. N.-D. de Claviers · Chât. la Trémolière · Anglards-de-Salers · Gorges de St-Vincent · N.-D. de la Font-Sainte · Cascade de la Roche · 1398 · 1284 · Fortuniès · Suc Grand 1165

Mazerolles · D 22 · Egl. Romane · 968 · Nuzerolles · Fageolles · 1156 · le Vaulmir · Broussouze · Fouilloux · Cascade du Sartre · Plateau du Limon · 1330 · Sauvages

382

2 4 6 8 10 km

D 922 St-Cernin 25 km
Aurillac 43 km

Murat 10 km D 3
St-Flour 36 km

368

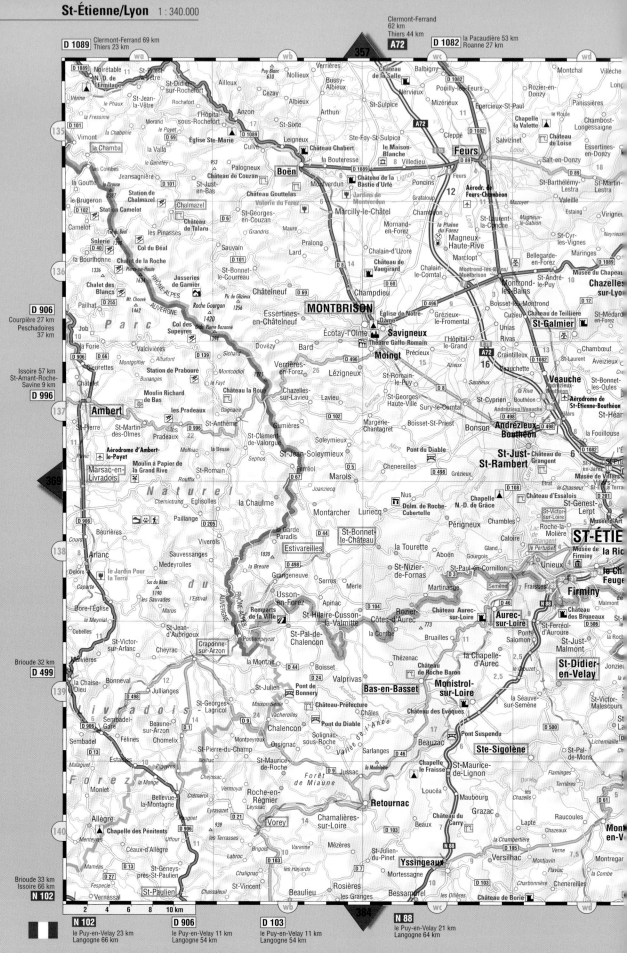

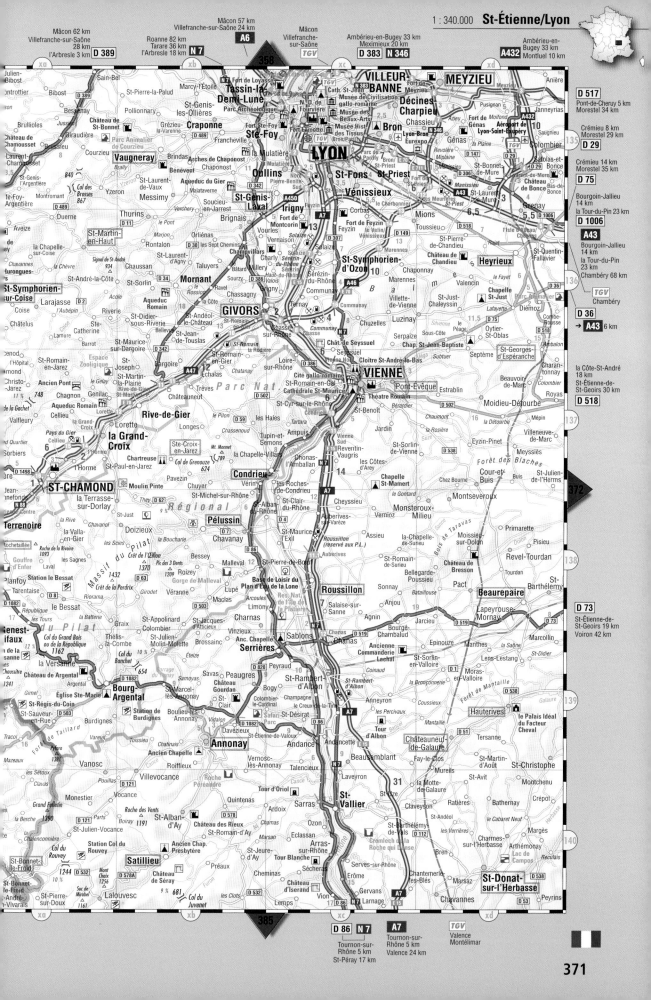

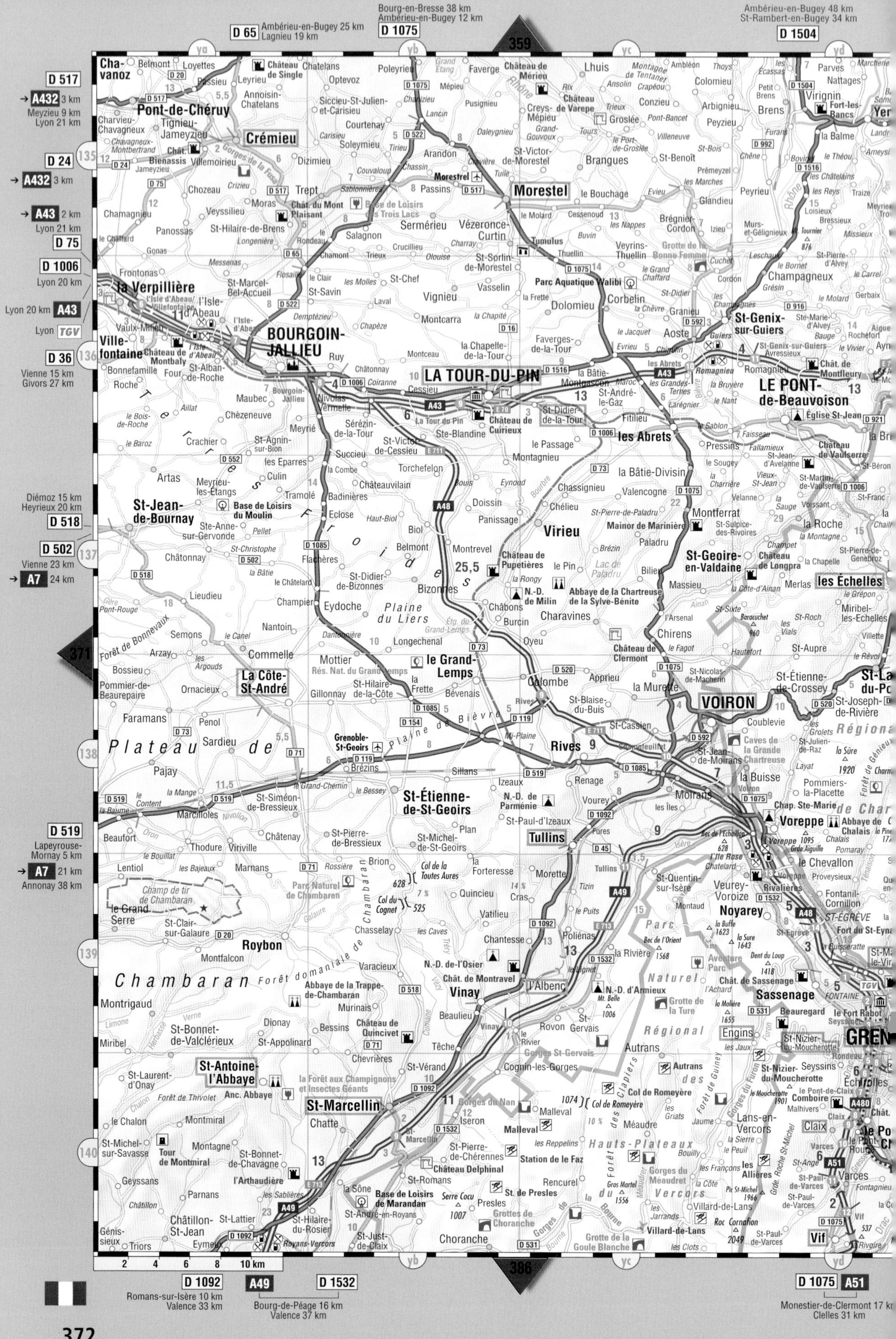

Chavanoz
Pont-de-Chéruy
Crémieu
Morestel
LA TOUR-DU-PIN
LE PONT-de-Beauvoison
Bourgoin-JALLIEU
la Verpillière
l'Isle-d'Abeau
Villefontaine
St-Jean-de-Bournay
La Côte-St-André
le Grand-Lemps
VOIRON
Rives
Voreppe
Tullins
St-Étienne-de-St-Geoirs
Roybon
St-Marcellin
Vinay
Sassenage
GREN...
Vif

D 65 · Ambérieu-en-Bugey 25 km · Lagnieu 19 km
D 1075 · Bourg-en-Bresse 38 km · Ambérieu-en-Bugey 12 km
D 1504 · Ambérieu-en-Bugey 48 km · St-Rambert-en-Bugey 34 km

D 517
→ A432 3 km · Meyzieu 9 km · Lyon 21 km
D 24
→ A432 3 km
→ A43 2 km · Lyon 21 km
D 75
D 1006 · Lyon 20 km
A43 · Lyon 20 km
TGV · Lyon
D 36 · Vienne 15 km · Givors 27 km
D 518 · Diémoz 15 km · Heyrieux 20 km
D 502 · Vienne 23 km
→ A7 24 km
D 519 · Lapeyrouse-Mornay 5 km
→ A7 21 km · Annonay 38 km

359
371
386

D 1092 · Romans-sur-Isère 10 km · Valence 33 km
A49
D 1532 · Bourg-de-Péage 16 km · Valence 37 km
D 1075 · A51 · Monestier-de-Clermont 17 km · Clelles 31 km

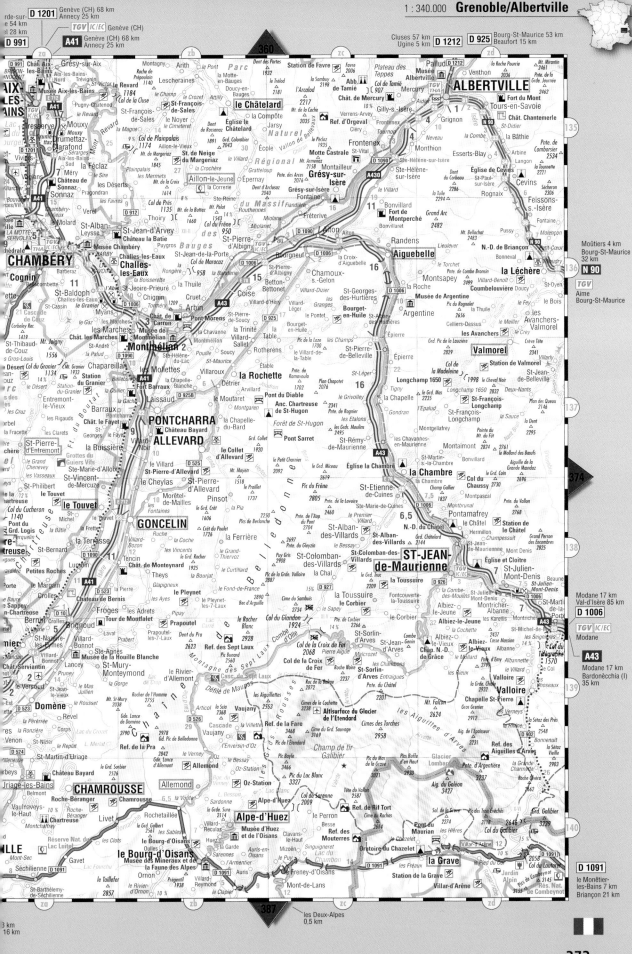

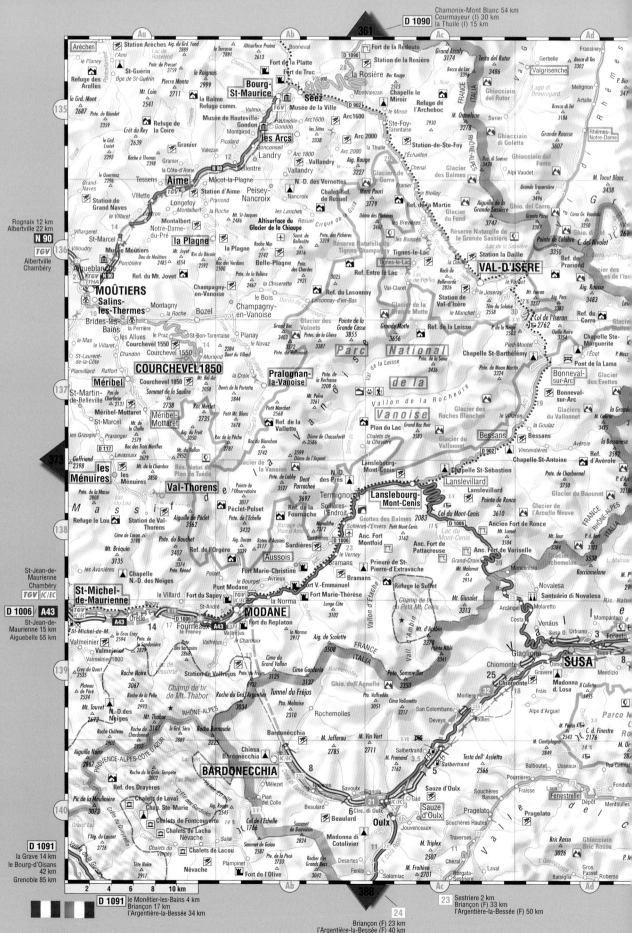

OCÉAN

ATLANTIQUE

362

od

oo

ob

oc

od

141

142

143

144

145

146

A r g e n t

A r g e n t

d '

c ô t e

C

Hou
Hourt

Phare d'H

Carcans-Pla
Carcans-Plage

Lacanau-Océan
Plage de Lacanau-Océan

Forêt D
de

le Porge Océan

Fo
d

Dunes de Lescour
Forêt Dor
de Lege et

le Grand Crohot

Centre d'I

Lège-Cap

Réserve Naturelle des Prés
d'Arès Lège-Cap-

Dunes Boisées

la Pigna

Piclaoue

les Jacquets

le Truc Vert

les Arbousiers

25 le Canon

Pîraillan

î

île aux

l'Herbe

la Vigne

D 106 **ARCACH**
Egl. Notre-Dam

Bélisaire

le Moulleau

Phare du Cap-Ferret
Lavergne

Plage le Cap-Ferret la Pointe

Plage de

Cap Ferret Pyla sur Mer

Pyla-sur-Mer

Réserve Naturelle du Banc d'Arguin

Banc d'Arguin

Pilat Plage

Pointe d'Arcachon

Forêt Usagè

D 218

LA
DE

Dune
Iro

Hourn Laur

le Petit N

2 4 6 8 10 km

ob

390

oc

od

376

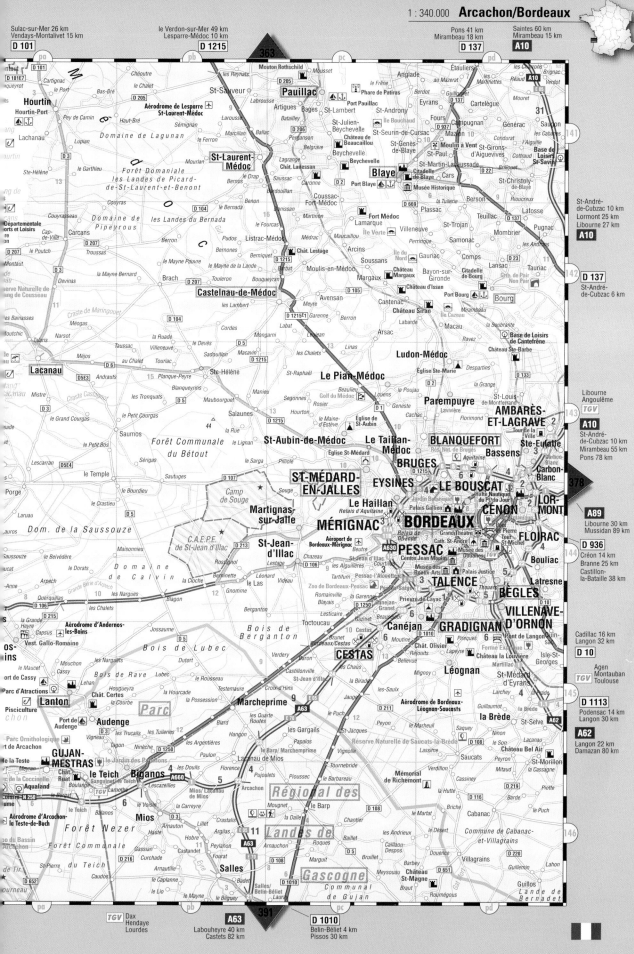

Sulac-sur-Mer 26 km
Vendays-Montalivet 15 km
D 101

le Verdon-sur-Mer 49 km
Lesparre-Médoc 10 km
D 1215

363

Pons 41 km
Mirambeau 18 km
D 137

Saintes 60 km
Mirambeau 15 km
A10

St-André-
de-Cubzac 10 km
Lormont 25 km
Libourne 27 km
A10

D 137
St-André-
de-Cubzac 6 km

Libourne
Angoulême
TGV
A10
St-André-
de-Cubzac 10 km
Mirambeau 55 km
Pons 78 km

378

A89
Libourne 30 km
Mussidan 89 km

D 936
Créon 14 km
Branne 25 km
Castillon-
la-Bataille 38 km

Cadillac 16 km
Langon 32 km
D 10

Agen
Montauban
Toulouse
TGV

D 1113
Podensac 14 km
Langon 30 km
A62

A62
Langon 22 km
Damazan 80 km

Hourtin
Lacanau
Lanton
GUJAN-
MESTRAS
Biganos
Mios
Salles

St-Laurent-
Médoc
Castelnau-de-Médoc
Pauillac
Blaye
Bourg

Le Pian-Médoc
St-Aubin-de-Médoc
Le Taillan-
Médoc
BLANQUEFORT
Bassens

ST-MÉDARD-
EN-JALLES
Le Haillan
BRUGES
EYSINES
LE BOUSCAT
LOR-
MONT
CENON

Martignas-
sur-Jalle
MÉRIGNAC
BORDEAUX
FLOIRAC
Bouliac

St-Jean-
d'Illac
PESSAC
TALENCE
Latresne

CESTAS
Canéjan
GRADIGNAN
BÈGLES
VILLENAVE-
D'ORNON

Marcheprime
Léognan
la Brède

TGV Dax
Hendaye
Lourdes

A63
391

D 1010
Belin-Béliet 4 km
Pissos 30 km

Labouheyre 40 km
Castets 82 km

377

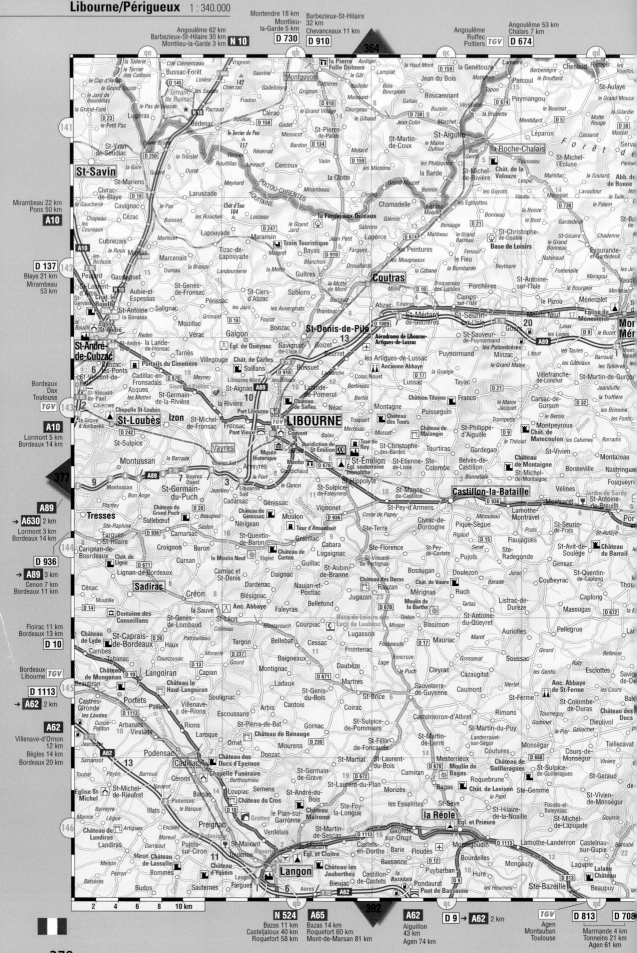

Aixe-sur-Vienne 82 km
St-Yrieix-la-Perche 52 km
Thiviers 32 km

N 21

365

PÉRIGUEUX

Chancelade

St-Astier

Neuvic

Mussidan

BERGERAC

Lalinde

A89

Brive-la-
Gaillarde 58 km

A89

Thenon 12 km
Terrasson-
Lavilledieu 31 km

D 6089

les Eyzies-de-
Tayac-Sireuil
19 km
Sarlat-la-Canéda
40 km

D 47

le Buisson-
de-Cadouin 12 km
Sarlat-la-Canéda
33 km
Fumel 67 km

D 710

380

le Buisson-
de-Cadouin 1 km
Sarlat-la-Canéda
37 km
Fumel 56 km
Gourdon 58 km

D 29

Villefranche-
du-Périgord
20 km
Fumel 41 km
Cahors 62 km

D 660

Eymet

**Miramont-
de-Guyenne**

Monflanquin

393

SARLAT-LA-CANÉDA

D 710	D 673	
Fumel 4 km		
Villeneuve-sur-Lot 33 km		
Montauban 80 km		
D 911		
Fumel 8 km		
Villeneuve-sur-Lot 37 km		
D 811		
Puy-l'Évêque 8 km		
Fumel 26 km		
D 811		
Cahors 9 km		
Caussade 49 km		
D 820		
Cahors 7 km		
Caussade 47 km		
A20		
Caussade 43 km		
Montauban 66 km		

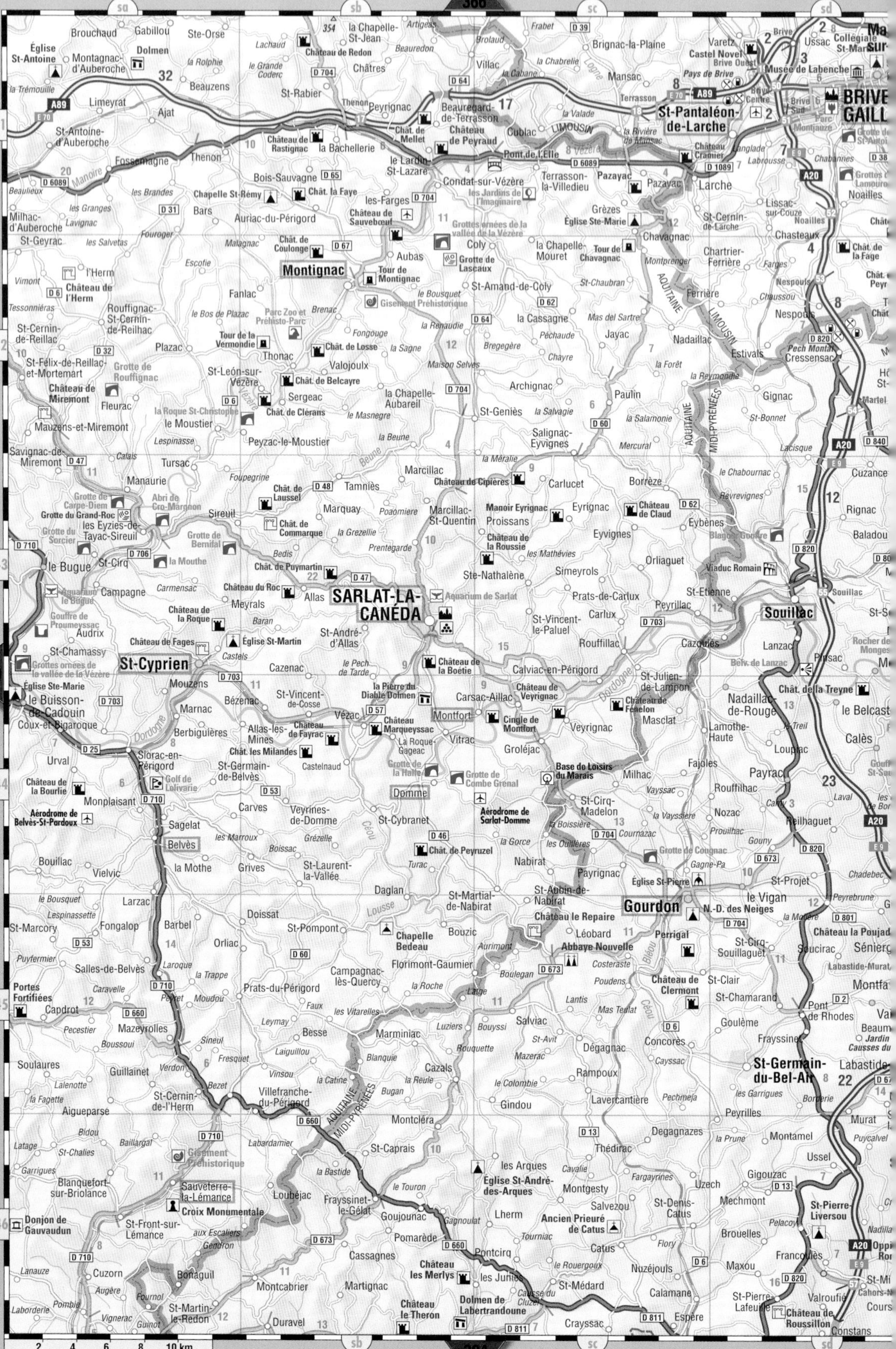

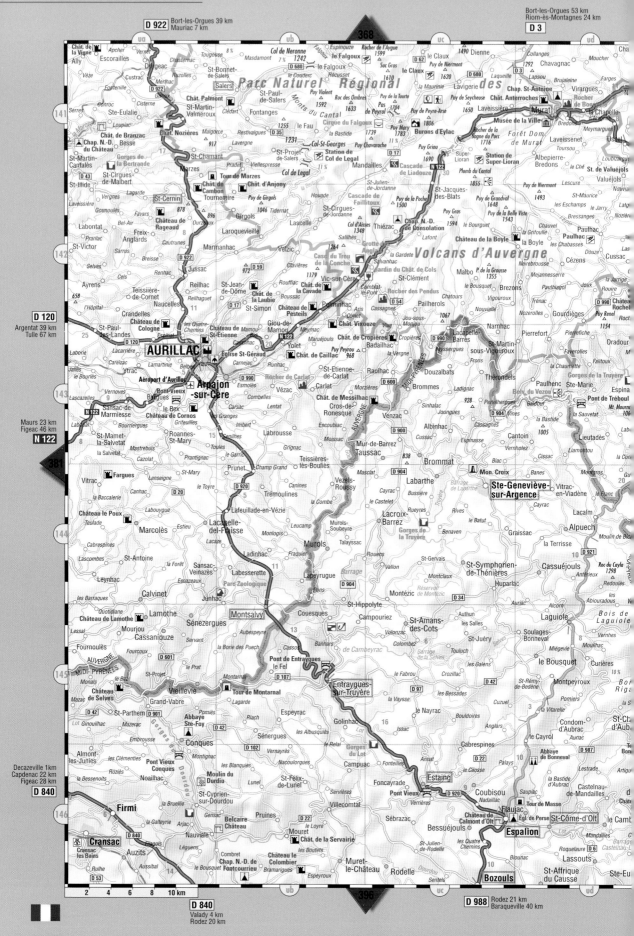

Bort-les-Orgues 39 km
Mauriac 7 km
D 922

Bort-les-Orgues 53 km
Riom-ès-Montagnes 24 km
D 3

Parc Naturel Régional des **Volcans d'Auvergne**

AURILLAC

Arpajon-sur-Cère

Aéroport d'Aurillac

D 120
Argentat 39 km
Tulle 67 km

Maurs 23 km
Figeac 46 km
N 122

381

Ste-Geneviève-sur-Argence

Laguiole

Entraygues-sur-Truyère

Montsalvy

Estaing

Espalion

Decazeville 1km
Capdenac 22 km
Figeac 28 km
D 840

Cransac

Firmi

Bozouls

2 4 6 8 10 km

D 840
Valady 4 km
Rodez 20 km

D 988
Rodez 21 km
Baraqueville 40 km

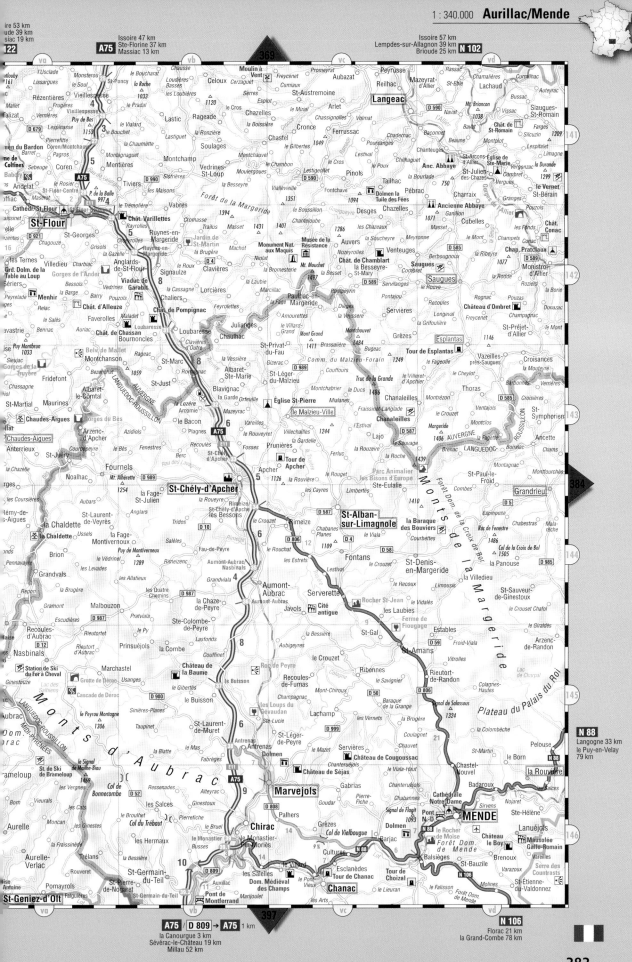

A75 D 809 → **A75** 1 km
la Canourgue 3 km
Sévérac-le-Château 19 km
Millau 52 km

N 102 Brioude 32 km
Ambert 57 km
Arlanc 42 km
D 906
Bas-en-Basset 40 km
Retournac 23 km
D 103
370
St-Étienne 50 km
Yssingeaux 5 km
N 88

LE PUY-EN-VELAY

Brives-Charensac

Tence

Langogne

Largentière

Fix-St-Geneys
Château de la Rochelambert
Vazelles-Limandre
Loudes
Aérodr. du Puy-Loudes
St-Jean-de-Nay
Chaspuzac
le Thiolent
St-Rémy
Montpignon
Vergezac
Bains
la Visseyre
St-Privat-d'Allier
Chapelle St-Roch
St-Christophe-sur-Dolaison
Dolmen de Séneujols
Séneujols
St-Didier-d'Allier
St-Jean-Lachalm
Station de Cayres
Bizac
le Brignon
Cayres
Mt. Chant
Ouides
l'Herm
Alleyras
le Bouchet-St-Nicolas
le Cros
les Souls
St-Christophe-d'Allier
St-Haon
Landos
Praclaux
Chambon-le-Château
Condres
Laval-Atger
la Gardette
Ste-Colombe-de-Montauroux
Fabrèges
Briges
Fontanes
Auroux
le Sap
le Villaret
Chastanier
St-Jean-la-Fouillouse
Meyrilles
l'Hermet
Langogne
Aérodrome de Langogne-Lespéron
Lespéron
Chaudeyrac
Pierre Branlante
Argentière
Châteauneuf-de-Randon
l'Habitarelle
Mont-A Du Guesclin
Ancien Abbaye de Mercoire
la Bastide-Puylaurent
Gourgons
Laubert
Montbel
le Moure de la Gordille
St-Frézal-d'Albuges
Laubert
Chasseradès
Puylaurent
Allenc
Chadenet
Bagnols-les-Bains
St-Jean-du-Bleymard
St-Julien-du-Tournel
Clocher de Tourmente
le Bleymard
Cubières
Cubiérettes
le Bleymard-Mont-Lozère
Mont Lozère
Montagne du Goulet
Castanet
Villefort
la Garde-Guérin
Col du Mas de l'Air
Gravières

Lavoûte-sur-Loire
Malrevers
Chanceaux
Chaspinhac
Blanzac
Vialette
Polignac
Pont de la Chartreuse
Blavozy
St-Germain-Laprade
le Pertuis
St-Étienne-Lardeyrol
St-Pierre-Eynac
St-Julien-Chapteuil
Latour
Volhac
Coubon
Bouzols
Lantriac
Laussonne
Chadron
Agizoux
Onzillon
le Monastier-sur-Gazeille
Freycenet-la-Tour
Moudeyres
St-Front
Cascade de la Beaume
St-Martin-de-Fugères
Goudet
Alleyrac
Vachères
Château de Beaufort
Arlempdes
Salettes
les Arcs
le Chabanis
le Béage
Station le Béage
la Sauvetat
St-Arcons-de-Barges
Vielprat
Lafarre
Issarlès
Barges-Haut
Pigeyres
Chanteloube
le Lac-d'Issarlès
Ste-Eulalie
Lachapelle-Graillouse
St-Paul-de-Tartas
Coucouron
les Chirals
Pradelles
Peyre Beille
Auberge de Peire-Beille
Lavillatte
Issanlas
les Epveriers
Lanarce
Abbaye
Mazan-l'Abbaye
Station de St-Cirgues-en-Montagne
St-Cirgues-en-Montagne
le Plagnal
St-Alban-en-Montagne
Cellier-du-Luc
le Cros
Col de la Chavade
Astet
Mayres
Thueyts
Laveyrune
Huédour
St-Étienne-de-Lugdarès
Col de la Croix de Bauzon
Borne
Col de Meyrand
St-Laurent-les-Bains
Loubaresse
Valgorge
le Tanargue
Laboule
des Monts d'Ardèche

Station de Queyrières
Monibrand
les Moulins
Chazeaux
Mendigolles
Queyrières
Recharinges
Salettes
le Chambo-sur-Lignon
Station de Mazet-St-Voy
Mazet-St-Voy
Champclause
St-Julien-Chapteuil
Boussoulet
St. de Boussoulet
Montusclat
Chaudeyrolles
Fay-s.-Lignon
les Vastres
Montbrac
Station de St-Front
Chaudeyrolles
les Estables
Station les Estables
Anc. Chartreuse de Bonnefoy
Base de Loisirs St-Martial
le Sagnas
Cros-de-Géorand
Sagnes-et-Goudoulet
Usclades-et-Rieutord
Château de Pourcheyrolles
Montpezat-sous-Bauzon
Château du Bruget
Jaujac
la Souche
Mont Aigu
les Chambons
St-Cirgues-de-Prades
Château du Montlaur
Château de Chadenac
Meyras
Laval-d'Aurelle
Pradon
Chalbos
Dompnac
Pourcharesse
Beaumont
St-Mélany
Largentière
Sablières
Largerou
Tastavin
St-André-Lachamp
St-Jean-de-Pourcharesse
Thines
Faugères
Payzac
Planchamp
Ste-Marguerite-Lafigère
Malarce-sur-la-Thines
les Salelles
St-Genest-de-Beauzon
Lablachère
Ribes
Joyeuse
Notre-Dame de Bon Secours

2 4 6 8 10 km

398

D 104
St-Ambroix 20 km
Alès 39 km

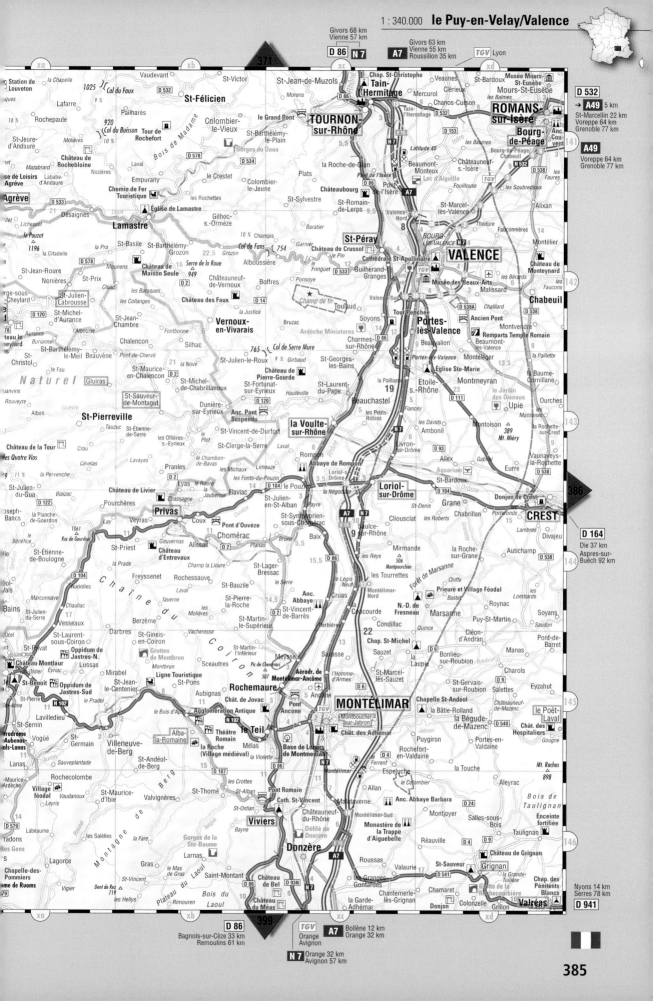

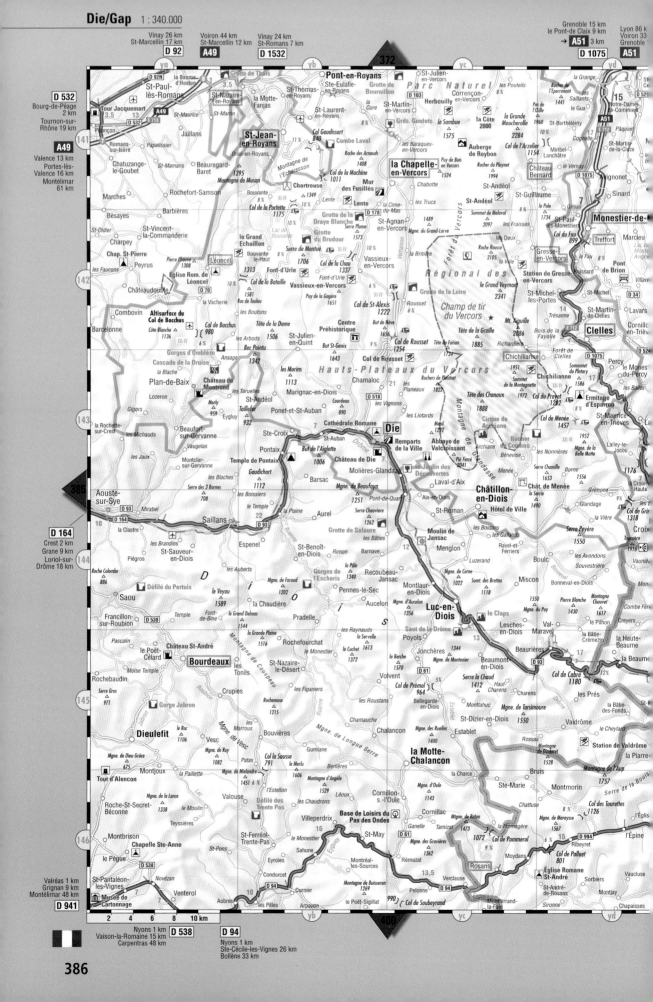

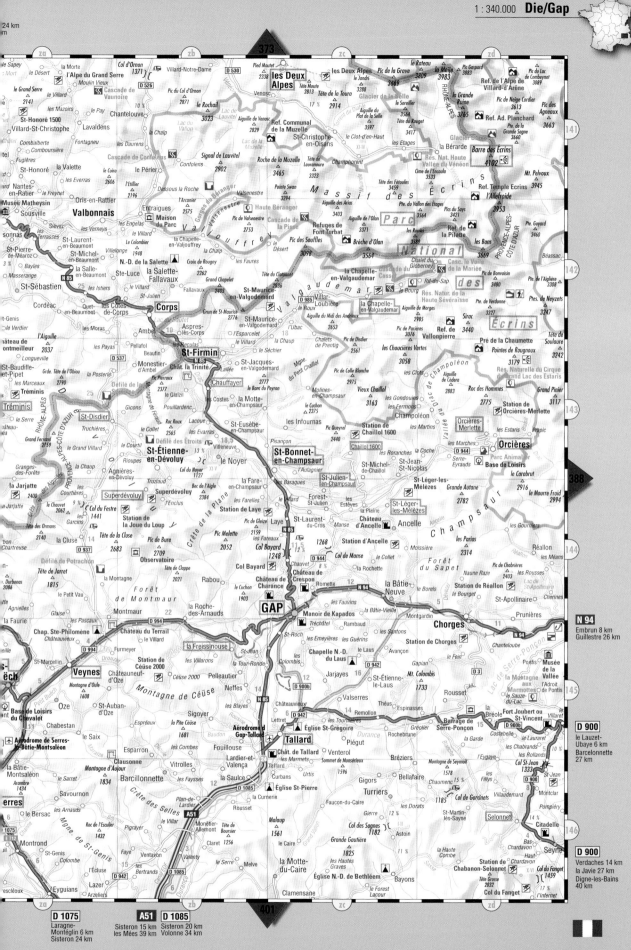

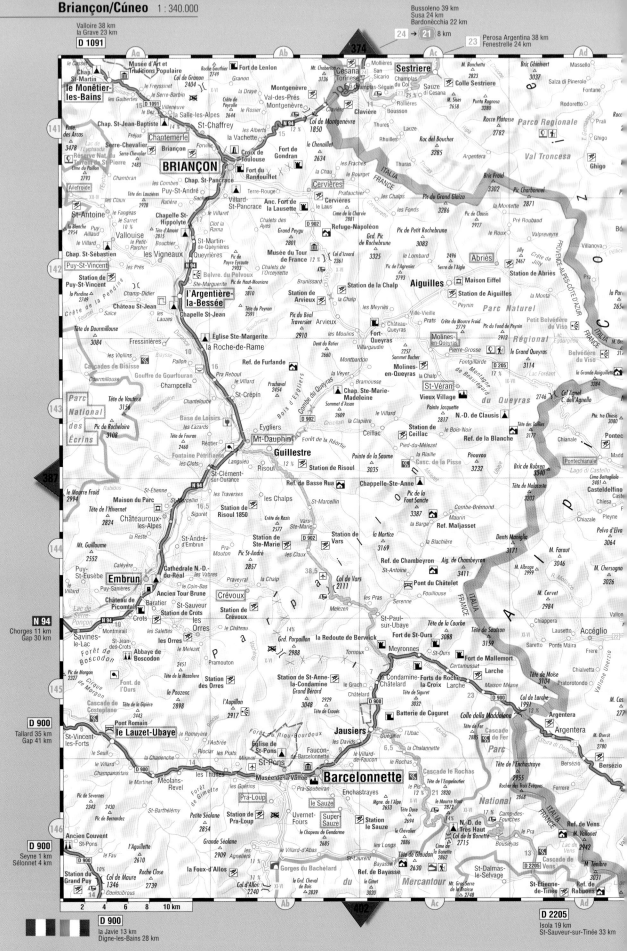

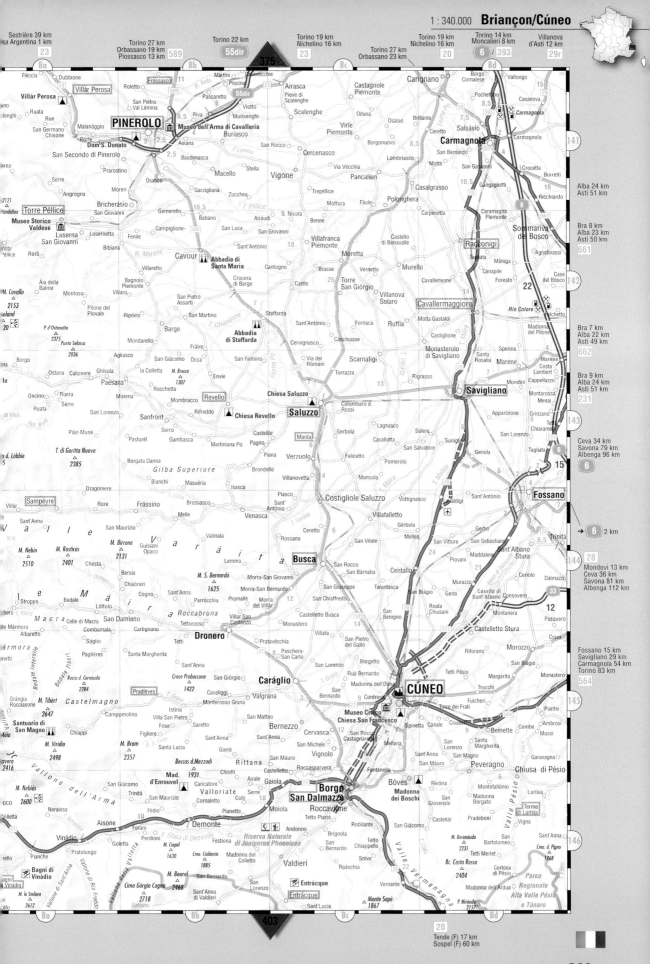

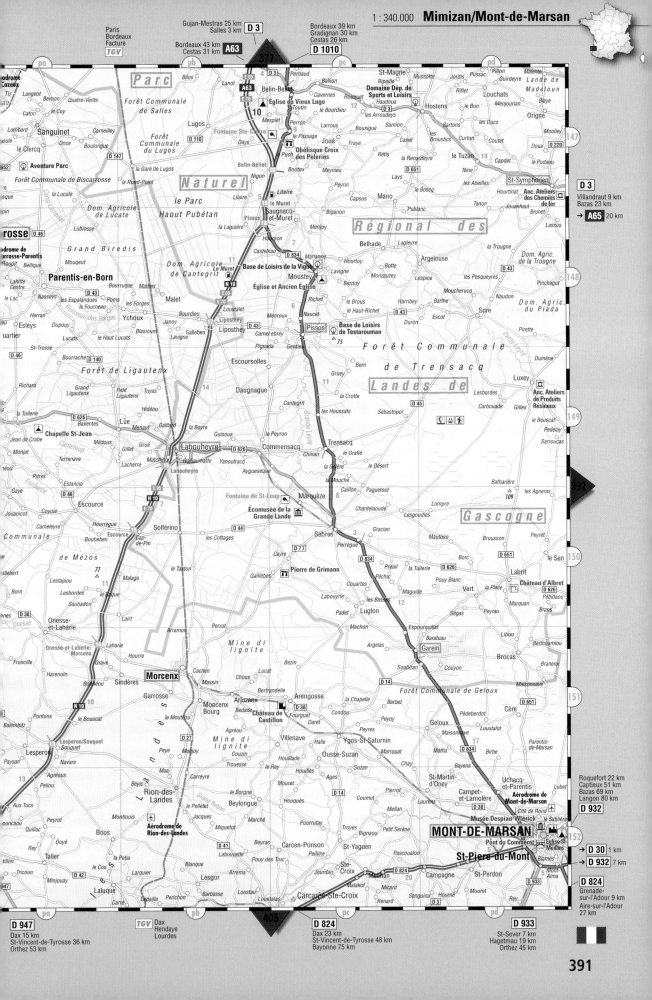

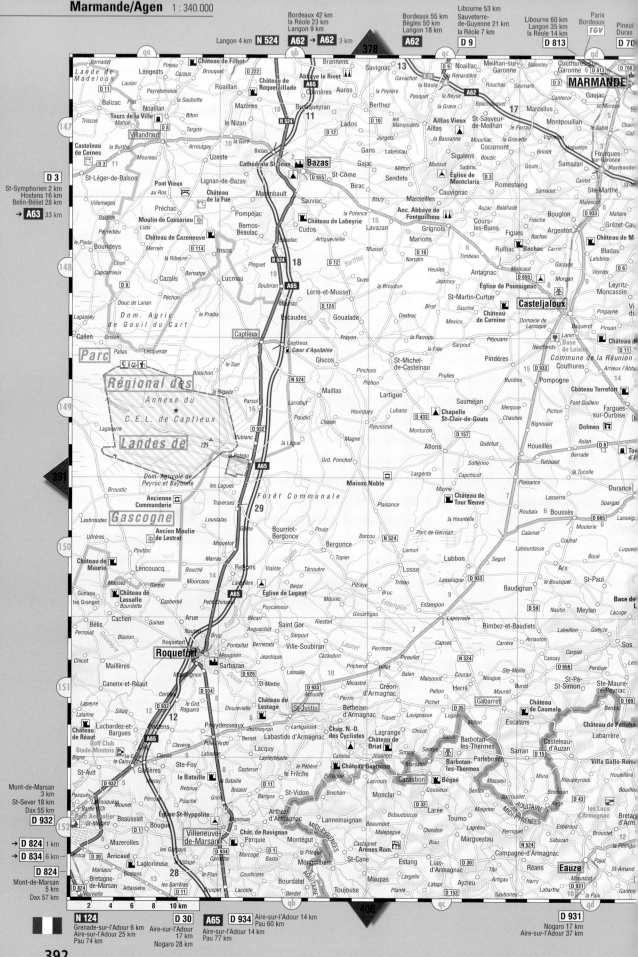

Bergerac 57 km
Miramont-de-Guyenne 11 km
D 933

Bergerac 44 km
Castillonnès 17 km
N 21

379

D 911
Fumel 7 km
Cahors 51 km
Gourdon 63 km

147

148

D 656
Tournon-
d'Agenais 15 km
Cahors 62 km

Ste-Abondance
St-Pierre-de-Londres
D 933
Puymiclan
le Vieux Château
Agmé
St-Barthélémy-d'Agenais
D 124
Tourtres
Cabannes
Lavassale
Soulaudres
Castelnaud-de-Gratecambe
Calviac
D 124
Fillol
Savignac-sur-Leyze
Monségur

Birac-sur-Trec
Labretonie
Montastruc
St-Pastour
Combe-Borie
Beaugas
Trabade
Labarthe
D 676
Reyssous
Montmarès
St-Aubin

Grouillé
Baquey
Pigousset
Chât. Gontaud-de-Nogaret
Verteuil-d'Agenais
Coulx
Balade
Madorine
Rastel
Maurasse
Pradié
Paille loles
Fadèze
Gaffard
D 133
Bernardet
Lédat
La Castagnal
Pechagut
Bord
Ladignac
Trentels

Fauguerolles
Gontaud-de-Nogaret
Hautesvignes
Brugnac
Verdegas
Monclar
Cassenueil
N 21
Seubirous
VILLENEUVE-SUR-LOT

D 641
Tolzac
Varès
D 120
Ste-Marthe
Roudeyrou
St-Rémy
St-Étienne-de-Fougères
D 217
Rabanel
Château de Favols
Bias
Vieux Pont
Tour de Romaine d'Eysses
St-Aignan
Anc. Moulin de Moudoulens
Moudoulens
D 911

D 813
Fauillet
Castelmoron-sur-Lot
Fongrave
Halle de Laparade
Tour de Paris
Musée de la Vallée du Lot
N. D. de Peyragude
Vieux Pont de Penne
Château de Noillac

Tonneins
St-Gayrand
St-Étienne
Laparade
Base de Plein Air
Ste-Livrade-sur-Lot
Pujols
Tour de Pujols
Aérodrome de Villeneuve-sur-Lot
Penne-d'Agenais

de l'Étang de la Mazière
Calonges
Grateloup-St-Gayrand
Granges-sur-Lot
le Temple-sur-Lot
Laurier
D 118
Château de la Sylvestrie
Moulin de Penne

Clairac
Bugassat
la Loup
Biardel
Marchiol
Rogo
Malaure
Cazeneuve
St-Colombe-de-Vielleneuve
Bonneval
Pech
Gautier
Bequé
St-Léger
Escarbisses

le Queyran
Monheurt
Hunet
Lafitte-sur-Lot
Dolmayrac
Lamaurelle
Filbol
St-Antoine-de-Ficalba
Grottes de Lestournelles
Château de Donjon
Auradou
Massoulès
148

Mouret
Chât. Maurin
Nicole
D 666
Bourran
St-Sardos
Montpezat
D 13
St-Médard
les Mathieux
Renaud
Castella
Grottes de Préhist.
D 103
Hautefage-la-Tour
Tour de Hautefage
Musée de Frespech

Aiguillon
St-Martin
Dremes
Ste-Radegonde-sur-Lot
Tour de Pigeonnier
Lacépède
Cours
Floirac
Castella
Parc de Préhist. de Fonters
Monbalen
Fontbaysse
Frespech
D 656

Damazan
Galapian
St-Vincent
la Parie
Arpens
Lesterne
Sembas
Tour de Laugnac
Laugnac
la Croix-Blanche
Tour de la Croix-Blanche
Tournier
les Bordiels
Tour de Hautefage
D 656
Cauzac
Beauville

Tour Gallo-Romaine
Buzet-sur-Baïse
St-Avit
St-Salvy
Frégimont
Prayssas
le Quey
Tillote
Boscia
Quissac
Bascau
Marsac
232
Bazès
Arnaud
Tibé
la Garrigue
Goutges
Rougayrès
D 215
Dondas

A62
Mongaillard
Xaintrailles
Clermont-Dessous
Port-Ste-Marie
Anc. Prieuré
Ventamil
Lusignan-Petit
le Ga
Gardonnet
Château de Madaillan
la Garrigue
St-Julien-de-Terre Fosse
Trésorré
D 13
Argues
Anc. Église
D 656
Carpillou
D 110
Château de Combebonnet

149

Moulin de Auvignon
Sérignac-sur-Garonne
St-Hilaire-de-Lusignan
D 813
St-Cirq
Pont-du-Casse
Castella
Sauvagnas
St-Robert
St-Martin-de-Beauville
Baillarguet

Mongaillard
Bruch
Montesquieu
D 119
Colayrac-St-Cirq
Brax
le Passage
TGV
Monbran
164
Méras
Toutza
Musée des Beaux-Arts
Castel Noubel
St-Caprais-de-Lerm
Lásbrugués
Rigal
Tayrac

Vianne
D 930
Laverny
Agen-Porte d'Aquitaine
A62
Enf. des Jacobins
AGEN
Cath. St-Caprais
St-Pierre-de-Clairac
Puymirol
Perville

Pont Vieux
Lavardac
Dourde
le Balesté
Roquefort
Ance. Evêche
Boé
Bon-Encontre
St-Jean-de-Thurac
St-Urcisse
St-Romain-le-Noble
Crayssas
394

Barbaste
Moulin de Henri IV
Espiens
Ste-Colombe-en-Bruilhois
Estillac
Agen
Aérodrome d'Agen-la-Garenne
D 305
Sauveterre-St-Denis
D 813
Val. d'Agen
Moissac
Lauzerte 28 km
Montcuq 40 km
Cahors 69 km

le Béas
Ricane
Nérac
Pont Vieux de Nérac
Montagnac-sur-Auvignon
Moncaut
Aubiac
Moirax
Marsan
Cabos
Rabés
Bouhoben
St-Nicolas-de-la-Balerme
St-Sixte
Château Clermont-Soubiran
Golfech
D 953
TGV
Montauban
Toulouse

Ste-Catherine de Rey
Tauzié
Calignac
Fontarède
Saumont
Barthes
Gaugelin
Slailles
D 931
Château de Lassalle
Layrac
Tourillon
Carrefour
Caudecoste
Donzac
D 813
VALENCE
D 813
Moissac 16 km
Castelsarrasin 24 km
Montauban 48 km

Lisse
Andiran
D 656
Galin
Autièges
Larroudé
Nomdieu
Pachère
St-Lary
Laplume
Brimont
Joannenque
Fals
Cuq
Pédauba
Bonnehé
25
Dunes
Roquet
A62
D 12

Mézin
D 5
Fréchou
Pichotte
Château de la Pomarède
D 930
Fieux
Bénésit
D 15
Pécaillou
Moulin de Astaffort
la Carreté
le Boiron
Andiran
Mariné
A62
A62
Castelsarrasin 19 km
Montauban 43 km
Toulouse 80 km

Lamarque
Pouy
Lasserre
D 112
Francescas
St-Vincent-de-Lamontjoie
le Château d'Escalup
Lamontjoie
Pradet
Barbéroux
Astaffort
le Bilain
Pergain-Taillac
le Tanddouret
Gimbrède
Boubées
Berné
Sistels
Église de St-Cirice
St-Antoine

D 149
Artigues
Moncrabeau
Estrépouy
Ligardes
Pouy-Roquelaure
222
Pont Vieux
Barbonvielle
Nauté
Rouillac
Larché
Marquehaut
Mansonville
D 3

la Grangerie Château
D 5
Lannes
D 117
Lialores
Mousseau
St-Mézard
Berrac
Sempesserre
D 19
Miradoux
Gruat
Peyrecave
Lachapelle

Château Ste-Raphine
Château de Mothes
Gazapouy
Château de St-Aignan
D 41
la Tapie
St-Martin-de-Goyne
Petit
Tour Ste-Mère
Ste-Mère
20
N 21
Castet-Arrouy
St-Avit-Frandat
Bouhebent
Lucas
D 40
Poupas

Heux
Aquitaine
MIDI-PYRÉNÉES
Condom
Cath. St-Pierre
Château de Cugnac-Armagnac
la Romieu
Larressingle
D 931
Milhac
Larroque-Engalin
Lagarde
Moulin de la Mothe
Château de Lacassagne
Larroque
Marsac
Maltroutet

Beaumont
D 15
Larressingle
Musée de l'Armagnac
Caussens
Blaziert
D 7
Tressens
Marsolan
Lectoure
Église Ste-Marie
Beaulieu
D 7
Gramont
D 7
Marsac
D 7
St-Créac
St-Martin
Gaudonville

D 15
apelle de Lanne
Château des Evêques de Condom
10
Béraut
le Camus
Bordes
Roquepine
Tour de Bourreau
Terraube
Lac des Trois Vallées
Bourcio
l'Isle-Bouzon
Naudin
St-Clar
152

Taulet
le Baradé
Mouchan
Cassaigne
Château de Tauzia
Maignaut-Tauzia
D 42
Mas-d'Auvignon
Bouillas
le Ramier
Arenque
Ancien Moulin à Vent
Lac de St-Clar
Castéron
Tourneicoupe
D 18

Gondrin
D 35
Polignac
Roques
Anc. Abbaye
Château du Busca-Maniban
Mansencôme
Valence-sur-Baïse
St-Puy
Lamothe-Goas
Pauilhac
Pont de Aurenque
Magnas
Castelnau-d'Arbieu
Avezan
D 13
Estramiac
D 654

Mahé
D 113
Cadignan
Laca
Couchet
Courrensan
Lagardère
D 930
10
Boutan
Dauzère
les Trouils
Château du Bosc
Bréchan
Noguès
Périssé
Historique Edifice de Fleurance
Urdens
St-Léonard
Brugnens
Bivès
Lusat

Beaucaire
D 939
Ayguetinte
la Bourdille
Larroque-St-Sernin
Château de Argentens
Ste-Radegonde
Gavarret
N 21
Fleurance
Cadeilhan
le Brana
D 654
Nasous
Daube à Boué

D 930
Auch 29 km
l'Isle-Jourdain 40 km

407

N 21
Auch 23 km
Mirande 48 km
Tarbes 91 km

393

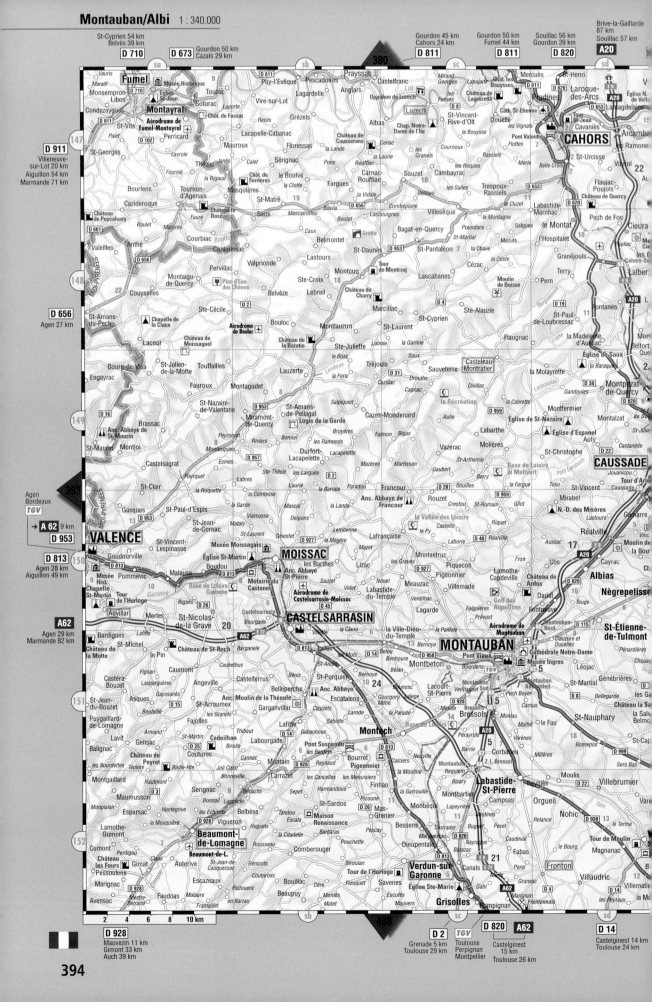

Figeac 48 km
Decazeville 19 km
D 840

D 920 Aurillac 76 km
Espalion 10 km

382

Lugan Escandolières St-Christophe-Vallon **Marcillac-Vallon** Dolmen D 904 Barriac Trou de Bouzols **Bozouls** Coudournac

Bournazel Glassac **Valady** Ste-Austremoine Lagarde Bezonnes Curlande La Viguerie Gabriac Cruéjouls Malescom

Villefranche-de-Rouergue 27 km
Caussade 72 km
Cahors 82 km **D 1** 147

Château de Cantuel **Salles-la-Source** Cascade *Causse du Comtal* Concourès Aboul Tour Gabriac D 28 Maymac Château des Bourines

les Hemps Clairvaux-d'Aveyron Seveyrac Souyri Sébazac-Concourès Montrozier Pont Vieux Anglars Banc

le Cayrou Goutrens **D 840** **D 988** Gages-le-Haut Parc Zoologique Cayssac Bertholène Palmas

la Remise Chapelle N.-D. Buenne Cantemerle D 901 Vabre Ortholès Trebosc *Forêt des Palanges* 21 Laissac

Rignac 11 Balsac **Rodez-Marcillac** 18 Onet-le-Château Aveyron Canabols Agen-d'Aveyron Reilhac Séverac-l'Église

Prévinquières Belcastel Mayran Abbas le Pas Anc. Abbaye Capelle Château de Fontenge 3 **RODEZ** D 29 la Bouldoire Douzoumayroux

Talespues Druelle 13 Musée Fenaille Pont Vieux Ste-Radegonde Église St-Martin le Mazet

Lasserre-Lissosse D 997 **Olemps** Cathédrale Notre-Dame Barry Larnaldesq le Vibal Arques Vaysse-...

Rivières Colombiès Gaugeac Moyrazès Agnac **le Monastère** Frayssinhes la Trémolière la Fabrègue St-Agnan

Querbes Combrouze le Verdier Ruols Luc Iniès la Vayssière Château de Viel-Vayssac St-Étienne-de-Viauresque

Villefranche-de-Rouergue 24 km
Cahors 84 km **D 911** 148

D 911 les Angles les Combettes D 57 Château le Luzet N 88 la Capelle St-Martin Flavin Vayssac Réservoir de Pont-de-Salars D 29

la Baraque de Cussan Salayrac **Baraqueville** le Lac la Primaude les Bastries Cambolas **Pont-de-Salars** Buscastels St-Julien-de-Fayret

Lardeyrolles St-Julien Lacombe la Vernhe Église du Poujol la Verhe Crespiaguet Trappes 22 Prades-Salars Mas 2...

Castanet Gramond Pinsou Cayrac le Cayrou Réservoir du Bage Lestang Viarouge

Salettes Parc Animalier Jouels **Calmont** Tremouilles Espinassettes D 56 Canet-de-Salars

Lacombe Noyès Magrin Comps-la-Grand-Ville Conquettes Paulhe Boulouis D 95

Pradinas Château de la Garcie Lugan a Mothe Ste-Juliette-sur-Viaur Carcenac la Bastide Pareloup *Lac de Pareloup* Charouzech Salleles la Fabrègue

Villelongue **Sauveterre-de-Rouergue** Quins 14 Camboulazet le Piboul Ventajou Céor Arviou Église N.-D. d'Aurès Bonnevale **Salles-Curan** Chât. Larguiès Curan

Castelmary Cabanès **Naucelle** Rancillac Sabin Tayac la Barthe Vabre les Faux Connes Nayrac

Favols Crespin Bouvert D 10 le Lac Blanc Frons Maury Salmiech Caplongue la Rouquette Calméjane les Canabières D 44 Bouloc

Château le Bosc Centrès Magrinet le Caucard Auriac-Lagast la Capelle-Farcel D 25 St-Jean le Froid Tour de Peyrebrune

Château de Thuriès Tauriac-de-Naucelle Lande Calmèze Taurines **Aérodrome de Cassagnes-Bégonhès** **Cassagnes-Bégonhès** D 902 Pyramide du Lagast Alrance Figeaguet Coupiaguet

las Planques Mesmajou Teillet Malphettes Castelpers Meljac la Cailholie Fournols Durenque le Jouanesq *Lac de Villefranche-de-Panat* Ladepeyre St-Symphorien

Pampelonne **Tanus** Viaduc du Viaur St-Just-sur-Viaur Grascazes Rullac-St-Cirq Garrissous Savinhac Mon...

Carmaux 8 km
Albi 24 km **N 88** 150 Lunaguet Bibel Tréban St-Cirq la Selve Montautut la Cammazie-Basse Villefranche-de-Panat Château de Linas la Beloterie Cor...

Moularès Lédas-et-Penthiès Blaye les Vialettes la Gardelle Lebous Linars Ayssènes Viala-du-Tarn

St-Jean-de-Marcel Lacapelle-Pinet D 53 le Bousquet St-Jean-Delnous Serieux Taysses D 44 Lestrade-et-Thouels le Truel St-Victor-et-Melvieu

Crespin le Renayresc l'Herm Padiès Fausserguès Château Belair l'Hôpital-Bellegarde Thouels Arnac la Romiguière D 31 St-...

St-Julien St-Géraud Cougourez D 903 le Dourn Moudelorgues **Réquista** Connac Sabuc Broquies les Thomps la Sabaterie

Dolmen Gaulène St-Michel-Labadié Laval Lincou Lavabre **Brousse-le-Château** Broquies le Moulin du Len Bous...

Valdériès Anc. Prieuré Saussenac St-Julien-Gaulène D 74 Serméja 524 Cadix D 33 Brasc Château Brousse le-Château l'Hôpital Béjan la Carayral Château des Évêques de Valore Bournac Touloup

D 903 Energues la Calmette Cadix Lautanous Montclar **St-Izaire** D 25 le Cambon Sauveplane Savignac **St-A...**

St-Grégoire Crespinet Sérénac Assac Fraissines la Bastide-Solages Faveyrolles D 902 Bedos **Vabres-l'Abbaye**

Ambialet Gaycre Trébas Coupiac Farret Calmels-et-le-Viala Vabres-l'A...

les Avalats la Condomine St-André le Truel Plaisance Martrin Ennous Mas de Gros Salmanac D 999 Rayssac *de...*

Marsal Fabas Courris la Barthe 595 la Cayla St-Christophe St-Juéry Segonzac 11 le Moulin-Neuf Montlaur

D 999 Albi 6 km Château de Montels Foncouverte Cambon du Temple Lacalm Château Lugan Balaguier-sur-Rance la Serre Rebourguil le Moulin-Neuf Montlaur

→ **A 68** 15 km Gaillac 34 km Toulouse 85 km Bellegarde **Villefranche-d'Albigeois** le Fraysse **Alban** la Martinié Monteils 15 la Trivalle St-Pierre D 12

Fréjairolles Teulet 25 Ginestières D 999 le Puget **St-Sernin-sur-Rance** Bétirac Buffières Verrières Briols

Mouzieys-Teulet Château de Lalgayrie Notre-Dame d'Ourtiguet Massals Pousthomy la Lauze St-Maurice Combret St-Julien Galamans

Terre-Clapier Sirvens la Cabane-de-Canabou N.-D. d'Ourtiguet Paulinet Jouvens Monastère de N.-D. d'Orient la Verdolle Lascazes **Aérodrome de St-Affrique-Belmont** Cama...

Fauch St-Étienne-de-Terabusset Pommardelle Montfranc **Belmont-sur-Rance**

152 la Teulière le Lauzié Vernières St-Jean-de-Jeannes D 82 Pourencas Château du Pujol Vic Gorges de Rance Prohencoux Moun...

Ronel D 86 le Travet Teillet Rayssac la Bessière Pouzats **St-Crépin** la Loubière l'Albespy Prohencoux Peux...

Chât. de la Bancelié Mont-Roc St-Antonin-de-Lacalm le Masnau-Massuguiès St-Salvi-de-Carcavès Laval-Roquecézière St-Sever-du-Moustier le Cros

Roumégoux la Cassanie la Bancalié St-Paul la Tibarié Dadou le Masnau D 32 Gorges de Rance

410

2 4 6 8 10 km

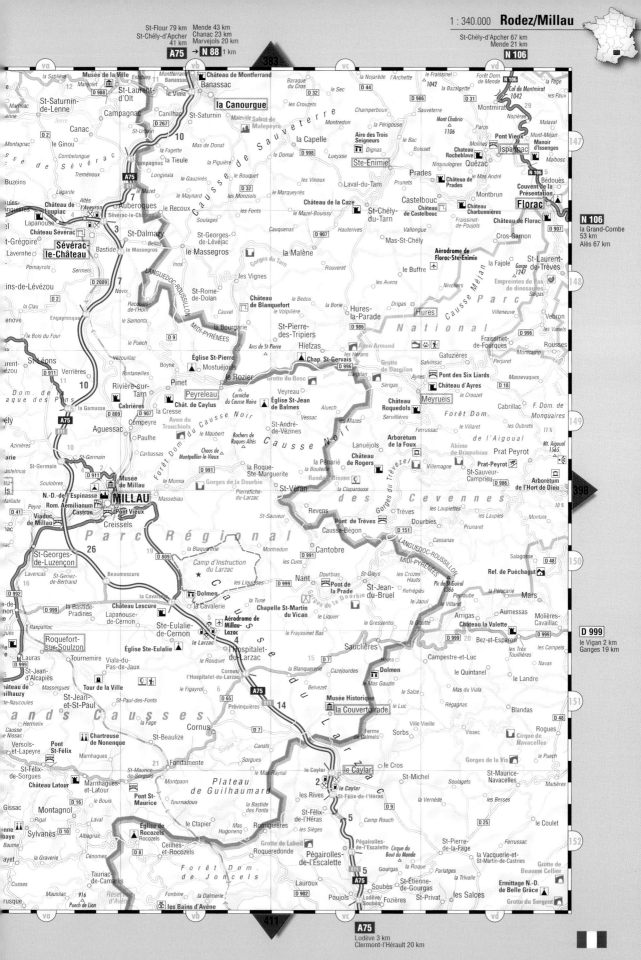

St-Flour 79 km   Mende 43 km
St-Chély-d'Apcher   Chanac 23 km
41 km   Marvejols 20 km
A75 → N 88 1 km

St-Chély-d'Apcher 67 km
Mende 21 km
N 106

la Sablière   Musée de la Ville   Château de Montferrand
St-Laurent   Banassac   Baraque   le Fraissinet   Forêt Dom.   la Fage
d'Olt   la Canourgue   du Cros   l'Archette   1042   de Mende   les Faux
le Viala   le Sec   D 44   la Bazalgette   N 106   Col de Montmirat   1042
D 988   St-Saturnin   Maleville   les Crouzets   D 986   D 31   Montmirat   29
St-Saturnin-   Campagnac   Canilhac   Sabot de   Sauveterre   Molines   Nozières   Malaval
de-Lenne   Canac   St-Urbain   Malepeyre   Montredon   la Périgouse   Mont Chabrio   Paros   Pont Vieux   Mont-Méjan
D 2   le Ginou   10   la Fagette   Mas de Donat   la Capelle   Aire des Trois   1106   Château   Ispagnac   Manoir
Combelongue   la Tieule   la Piguière   le Domal   D 998   Seigneurs   Rocheblave   Quézac   d'Issenges
de Sévérac   Tremenoux   Longviala   le Gauzinès   Dignas   Ste-Enimie   Nissoulorgues   Malbosc
Buzeins   le Mazet   le Maynard   D 32   les Vinoux   Prades   Château de   le Mas André   N 106
Lagarde   Château de   Altès   le Recoux   D 32   les Monziols   le Marqueyrès   Castelbouc   Prades   Montbrun   Bédouès
Château de   Loupiac   l'Aveyron   Auberoques   Château de la Caze   St-Chély-   Château   Château   Couvent de la
Lapanouse   Lapanouse   A75   Sévérac-le-Château   le Mazel-Bouissy   du-Tarn   de Castelbouc   Charbonnières   Présentation
Château Sévérac   St-Dalmazy   St-Georges-   les Fonts   Hauterives   Fraissinet-   Florac
St-Grégoire   Sévérac-   3   de-Lévéjac   Cauquenas   D 907   de-Poujols   Château de Florac
Lavernhe   le-Château   Bastide   les Massegros   Mas-St-Chély   Vallongue   D 907   N 106
Pomayrols   Bella   le Massegros   la Malène   Aérodrome de   Cros-Garnon   la Grand-Combe
la Clau   Sermels   7   Inos   les Vignes   Florac-Ste-Enimie   la Fajole   St-Laurent-   53 km
enove   D 2   St-Rome-   Gorges du Tarn   Rouveret   la Fajole   de-Trèves   Alès 67 km
le Bois du Four   Recoules-   de-Dolan   le Buffre   Gargo   St-Laurent-
Engayresque   Novis   de-l'Hom   Château   les Avens   Empreintes de Pas   1247   de-Trèves
le Puech   de Blanquefort   le Bedos   la Borie   de dinosaures   148
St-Léons   le Samonta   le Volpilière   St-Pierre-   Drigas   Salgas
D 911   Verrières   Vézouillac   la Bourgarie   des-Tripiers   Hures-   Nivollers   Villeneuve   Vebron
Fontaneilles   Boyne   Arcs de St-Pierre   D 986   la-Parade   Parc   les Vanels
Dom. de   10   Rivière-sur-   Église St-Pierre   Hielzas   Hures   les Herans   Gatuzières   Rousses
aque des Pins   11   Tarn   Mostuéjouls   Chap. St-Gervais   D 986   National   Perjuret   D 996
ély   Pinet   le Rozier   D 996   Aven Armand   Montcamp   Fraissinet-   11 %
Peyreleau   Grotte du Bosc   Grotte   de-Fourques
A75   Cabrières   Chât. de Caylus   Corniche   Veyreau   de Dargilan   Pont des Six Liards   Massevaques
E11   D 809   D 907   la Cresse   du Causse Noir   Église St-Jean   Aluech   Sérigas   Ayres   Château d'Ayres   D 18   F. Dom. de
Aguessac   Compeyre   Aven du   de Balmes   Vessac   les Mazes   Château   Meyrueis   le Crouzet   Cabrillac   Monquaires
10   Paulhe   Trouchiols   St-André-   Roquedols   Servillières   Forêt Dom.   les Oubrets   11 %
arie   St-Germain   Carbassas   de-Vézines   Rochers de   Lanuéjols   Ferrussac   le Villaret   de l'Aigoual   Mt. Aigoual
Soulobres   D 991   Roques-Altés   Chaos de   Arborétum   Abîme   Prat Peyrot   1565
N.-D.-de-l'Espinasse   Musée   Montpellier-le-Vieux   la Roque-   de la Foux   de Bramabiau   149
D 41   Rom. Aemilianum   de Millau   le Monna   Ste-Marguerite   la Pénarié   Château   Villemagne   Prat-Peyrot   Arborétum   398
Viaduc   MILLAU   Castron   Gorges de la Dourbie   la Bouteille   de Rogers   Prat-Sauveur-   de l'Hort de Dieu
de Millau   Peyre   Pont Vieux   Massebiau   Randals Bisons   Camprieu   D 986
Creissels   Pierrefiche-   St-Véran   la Claparouse   des   Cévennes   10 %
Parc   Régional   du-Larzac   St-Sauveur   Revens   Trèves   les Laupiettes   Montals
St-Georges-   26   19   la Blaquèrene   Pont de Trèves   Dourbies   les Laupies   D 48   150
de-Luzençon   D 809   Montredon   Causse-Bégon   D 151   Prunaret   Cassanas
Lavencas   Camp d'Instruction   Cantobre   Salagosse   Ref. de Puéchagut
St-Geniez-   Beaumescure   du Larzac   D 991   Languedoc-Roussillon   D 48
de-Bertrand   les Cuns   Dourbias   St-Gleys   Pic de St-Guiral   Mars
D 992   la Cavalerie   les Liquisses   Nant   Douric   les Crozes   1366   Peyraube   la Pélucarie
la Bastide-   Château Lescure   D 999   Hauts   Refrégiès   le Villaret   Midi-Pyrénées   D 999
Pradines   Lapanouse-   Dolmen   la Tune   Pont de   St-Jean-   le Jaoul   Arrigas   Aumessas   Molières-
D 999   de-Cernon   la Cavalerie   la Prade   du-Bruel   la Goutte   Château la Valette   Cavaillac
Ste-Eulalie-   Aérodrome de   Chapelle St-Martin   le Liquier   les Gressentis   Bez-et-Esparon   D 999
Roquefort-   de-Cernon   Millau-   du Vican   le Frayssinet Bas   D 999   20   les Très   les Campels
sur-Soulzon   le Larzac   Lazac   Saulières   Touillères   Navas
D 999   Église Ste-Eulalie   l'Hospitalet-   Homs   Campestre-et-Luc   le Landre
Lauras   Tournemire   du-Larzac   15   D 7   Cazejourdes   le Quintanel   Blandas
St-Jean-   Viala-du-   le Rouquet   Cornus   Dolmen   le Salze   Mas du Viala
d'Alcapiès   Pas-de-Jaux   le Figayrol   6   la Blanquerie   Réganas
hâteau de   Massergues   Tour de la Ville   D 65   l'Hospitalet-du-Larzac   Musée Historique   le Luc   151
ilhauzy   St-Jean-   A75   Prévinquières   la Couvertoirade   Ville Vieille   Vissec   Rogues
nds   Causses   et-St-Paul   la Fage   14   D 7   Sorbs   D 48   Cirque de
Hermelix   Chartreuse   St-Beauzile   Ferme   Navacelles
usse   de Nonenque   Cornus   de Calmels   le Puech
e Nissac   Pont   Canals   le Caylar   Gorges de la Vis
Versols-   St-Félix   Marnhagues   Sorgue   le Cros   St-Maurice-
et-Lapeyre   21   Fondamente   le Mas Raynal   le Caylar   St-Michel   Navacelles
St-Félix-   Marnhagues-   Sorgues   2   St-Félix-l'Héras   Soulagets   Madières
de-Sorgues   Château Latour   et-Latour   Montpaon   les Rives   St-Félix-   le Besses   Grotte de
Gissac   D 16   le Bouis   Tournadous   la Bastide   de-l'Héras   D 9   la Vernède   Beaume Cellier
Montagnol   Pont St-   des Fonts   5   Camp Rouch   St-Pierre-
baye   Rigal   Maurice   le Clapier   Mas   Romiguières   de-la-Fage   la Vacquerie-et-
Sylvanès   D 10   Laval   Plateau   Hugoneng   les Sièges   D 25   le Coulet   St-Martin-de-Castries
Baume   Albagnac   de Guilhaumard   Grotte de Labeil   E11   Pégairolles-   152
ayet   D 8   Église de   Ceilhes-   Roqueredonde   de-l'Escalette   Cirque du   la Roque   Grotte de
Gars   Rocozels   et-Rocozels   A75   Bout du Monde   Parlatges   Beaume Cellier
Maussac   916   Forêt Dom.   Pégairolles-   Gourgas   la Trivalle   Ermitage N.-D.
rusque   Puech de Lion   la Dalmerie   de-l'Escalette   Laurolx   Soubès   St-Étienne-   les Salces   de Belle Grâce
Réserve   Fonbine   de Joncels   D 902   5   de-Gourgas   St-Privat   Grotte du Sergent
d'Avène   les Bains d'Avène   Poujols   Lodève/   Fozières
les Bains d'Avène   Soubès

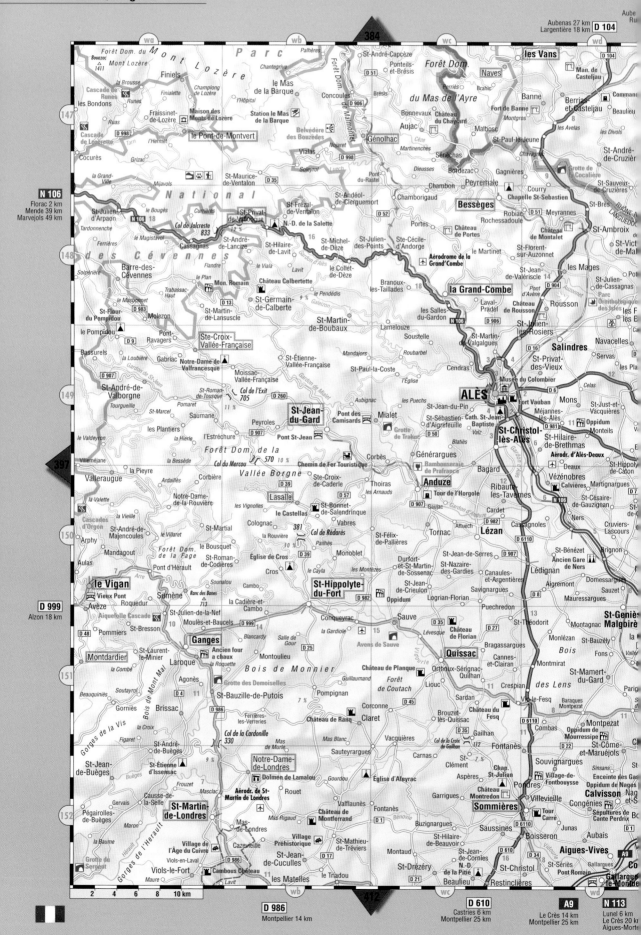

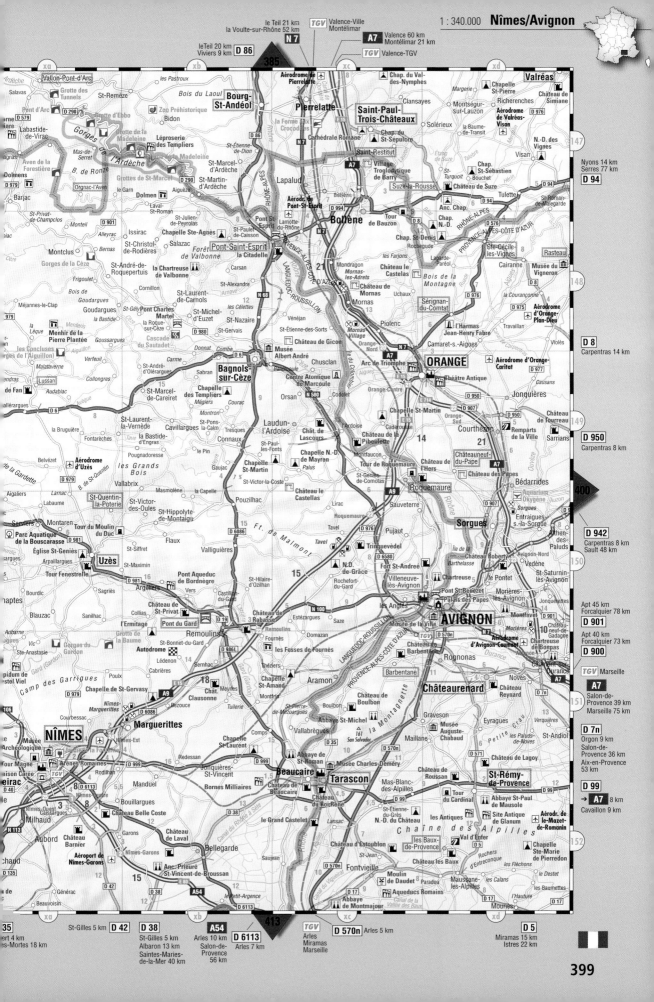

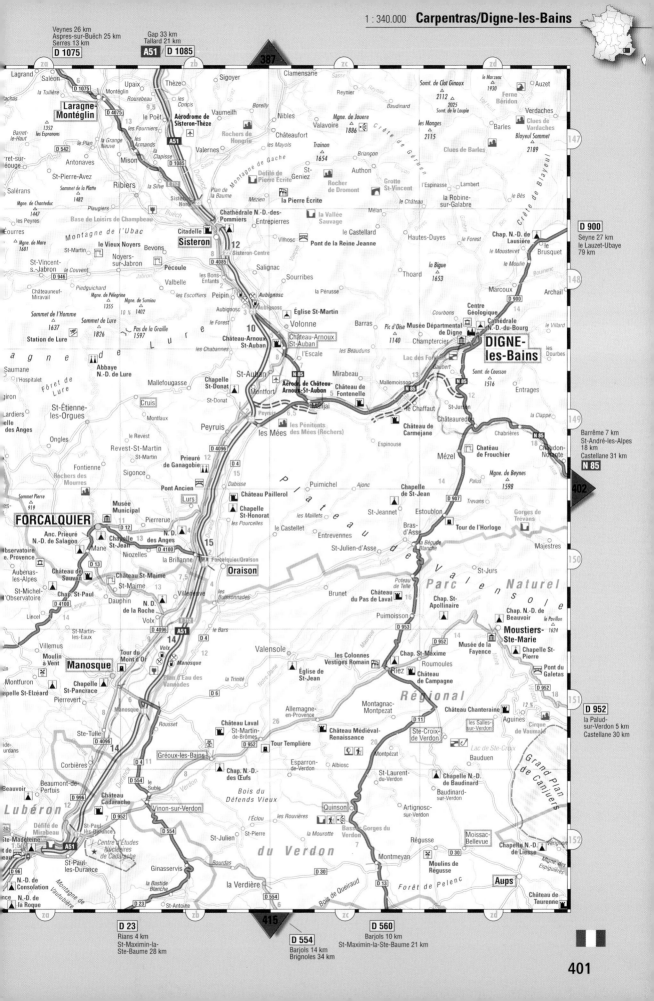

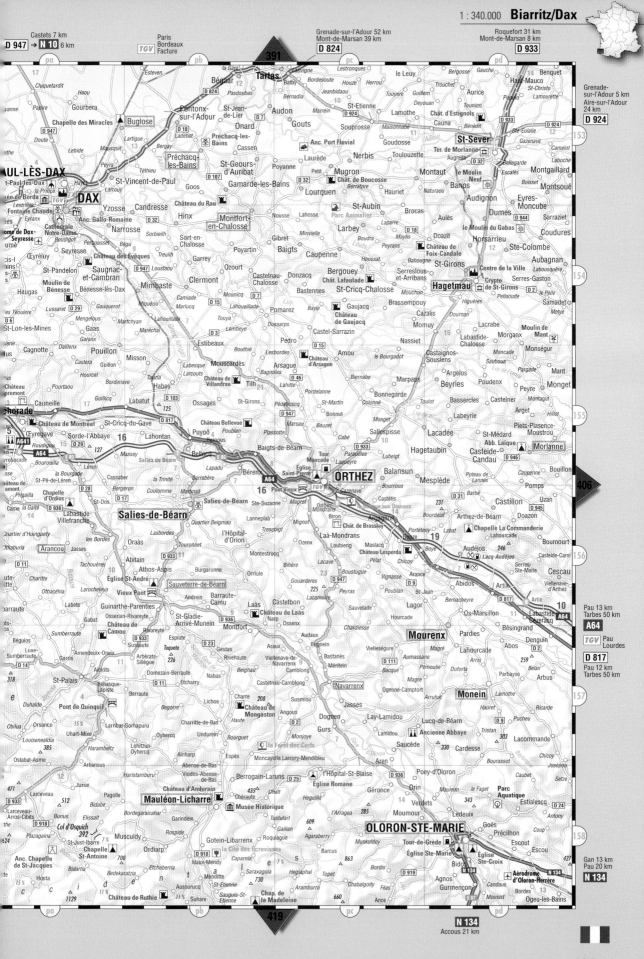

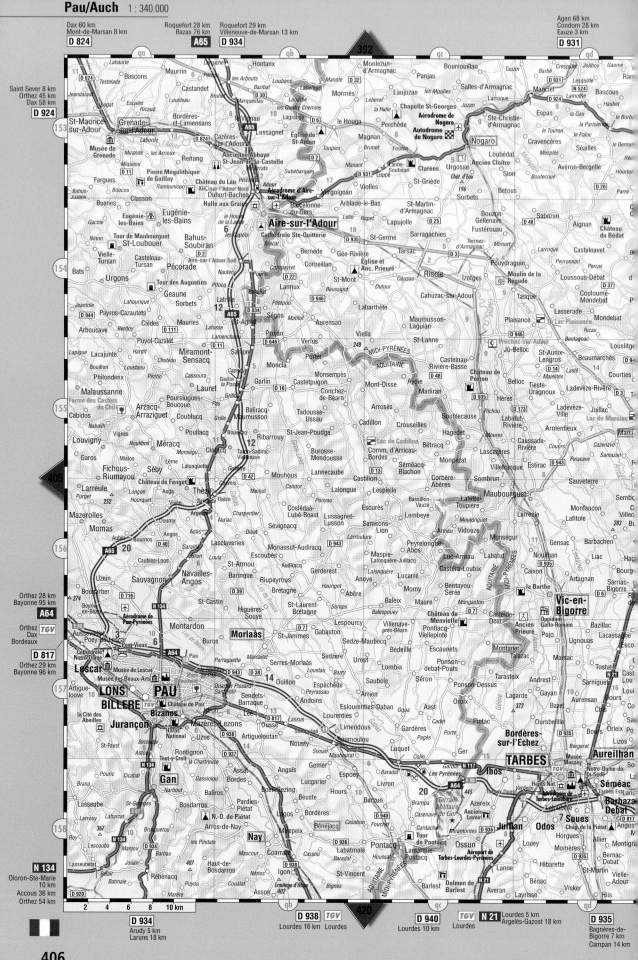

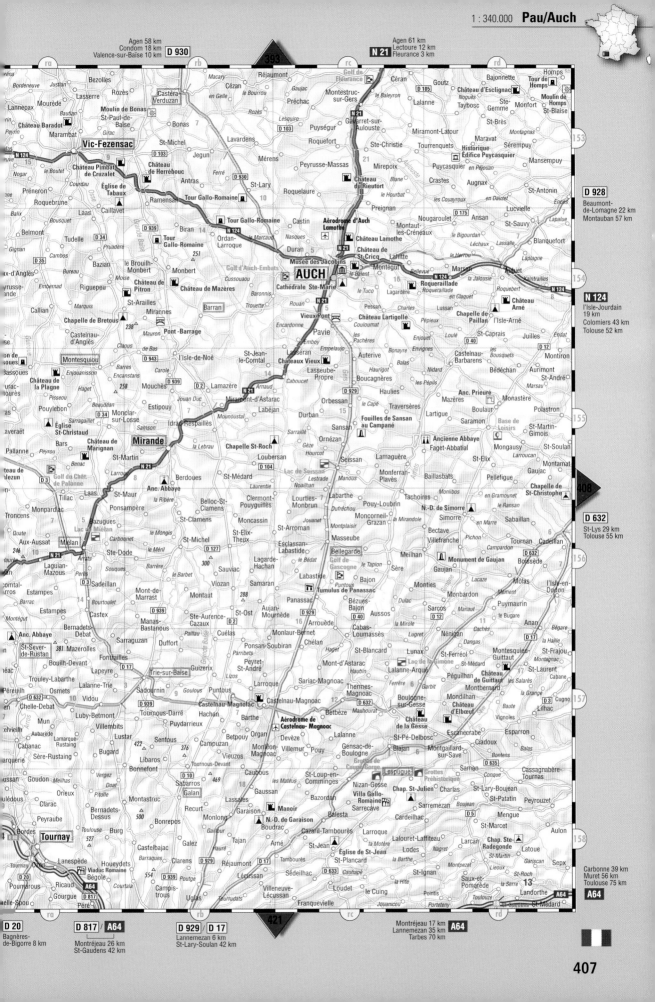

Golfe du

Lion

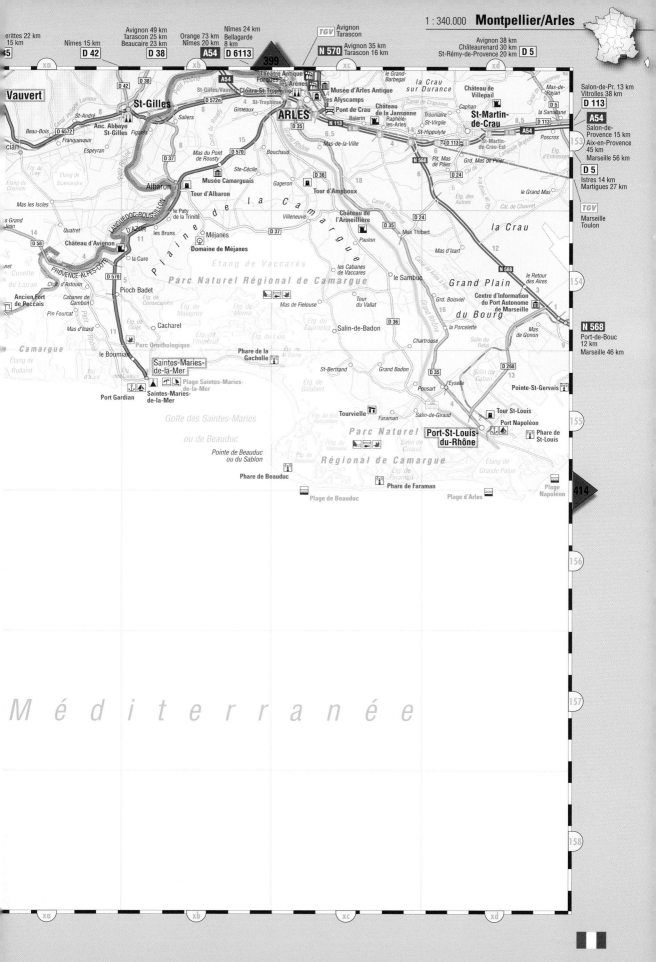

Vauvert

St-Gilles

ARLES

St-Martin-de-Crau

Parc Naturel Régional de Camargue

Étang de Vaccarès

Saintes-Maries-de-la-Mer

Port-St-Louis-du-Rhône

M é d i t e r r a n é e

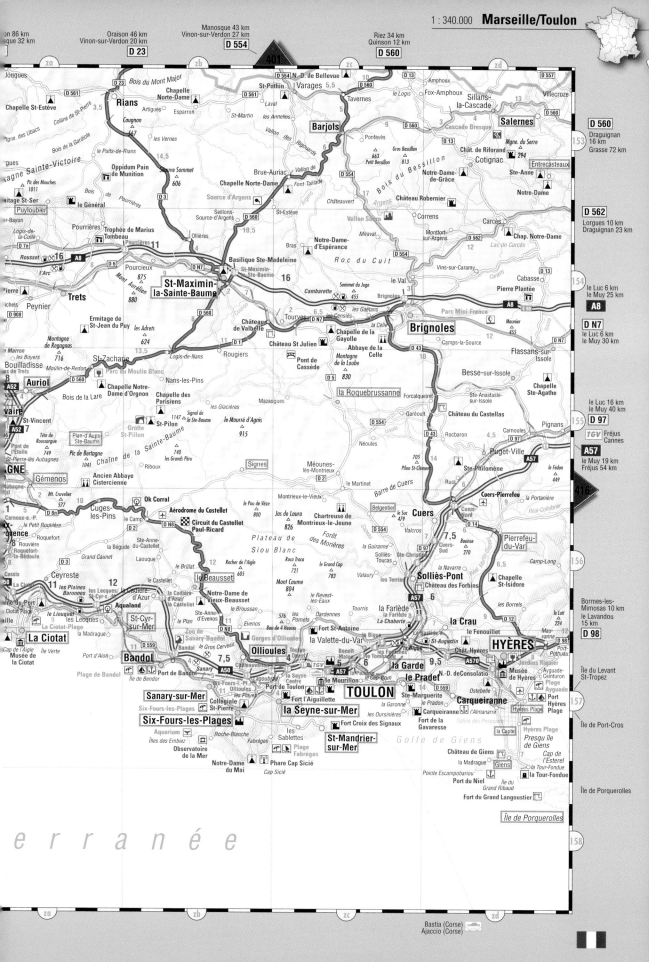

arlo 48 km
m
ur-Mer   Cagnes-sur-Mer
          13 km
D 6007   TGV Nice
               Antibes

Nice 21 km

Antibes

403

Ba   **Bb**   **Bc**   **Bd**

Bocca

CANNES
Cannes Festival du Film Plage de Cannes Batt. du Graillon
Cap de la Croisette

Golfe de la
Napoule

Île Ste-Marguerite
Fort Île Ste-Marguerite
Île St-Honorat
Abbaye Île
St-Honorat

Théoule-s.-Mer

Îles de Lérins

Pointe de l'Esquillon
de Miramar

Côte d'Azur

age du Trayas

l'Estérel

Anthéor

M é d i t e r r a n é e

153

154

155

156

157

158

Ba   **Bb**   **Bc**   **Bd**

Bayonne (F) 53 km
Ustaritz (F) 40 km
Cambo-les-Bains (F) 33 km

Hendaye (F) 35 km
Bera-Vera de Bidasoa 23 km

N-121-A

N-121-B

Cambo-les-Bains 31 km
St-Martin-d'Arrossa 9 km

D 948

Salies-de-Béarn 56 km
Cambo-les-Bains 37 km

D 933

404

oo   ob   oc   od

Andoain 29 km
Donostia/
San Sebastián
38 km

NA-170   159

A-15 8 km
Lekunberri
(Larraun)
15 km
Tolosa 40 km
Donostia/
San Sebastián
63 km

NA-411

160

Lekunberri
(Larraun)
18 km
Donostia/
San Sebastián
66 km

N-240

AP-15

Altsasu-Alsasua
29 km
Vitoria-Gasteiz
68 km

161

Estella/Lizarra
24 km
Logroño 70 km

NA-700

162

Estella/Lizarra
21 km
Logroño 67 km

A-12

163

NA-132

Estella/Lizarra
23 km
Logroño 69 km

164

**PAMPLONA/
IRUÑEA**

Berriozar
Ansoain
Barañain
Zizur Mayor

Tafalla

Olite

France
España

Orreaga / Roncesvalles

N-135

Sangüesa/Zangoza

Sos del Rey
Católico

A-127

2 4 6 8 10 km

ob   oc   od

NA-115   A-15   N-121 Tudela 45 km

NA-115
San Adrián 37 km
Calahorra 41 km

A-15
Tudela 44 km

A-127
Sadaba 26 km
Ejea de los Caballeros 53 km

418

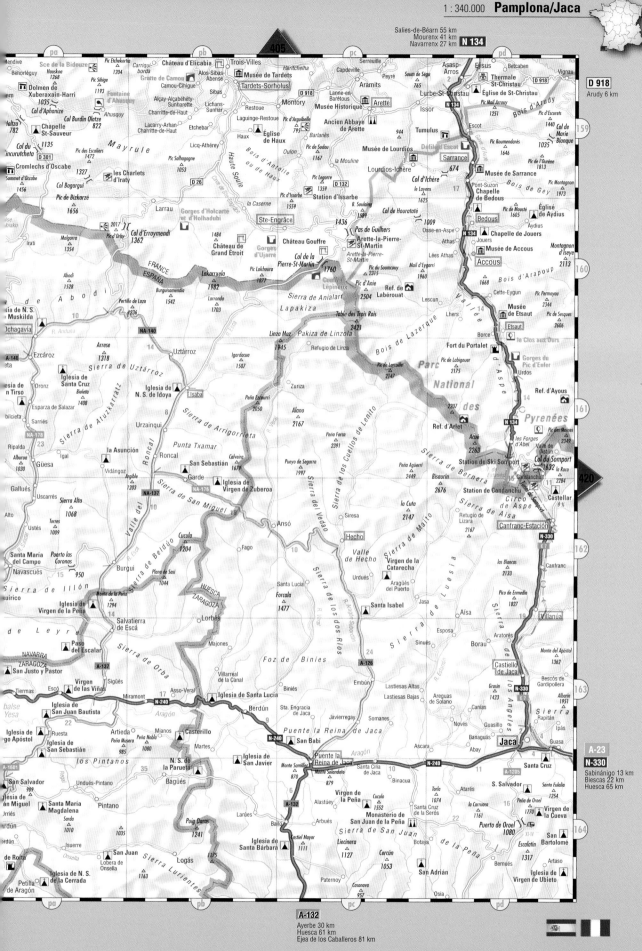

D 918
Arudy 6 km

405

pa   pb   pc   pd

Sce de la Bidouze
Béhorléguy
Hauskoa
1268
Pic Etchekortia
1204
Carriqui-
borda
Château d'Elicabia
Trois-Villes
Musée de Tardets
Tardets-Sorholus
Héritchelhia
Capdeville
Serreuille
Asasp-
Arros
2
Elsus
Betcaben
Vignau

Pic Sihige
1193
Grotte de Camou
Alos-Sibas-
Abense
Aramits
Peyré
Soum de Séga
765
Lurbe-St-Christau
Thermale
St-Christau
Église de St-Christau

Dolmen de
Xuberaxain-Harri
1035
Fontaine
d'Ahusquy
Camou-Chigue
Sibas
Lanne-en-
Barétous
Issor
Pic Mail Arrouy
1251
Bois d'Escures

Col d'Aphanize
Alçay-Alçabéhéty-
Sunharette
Montory
Musée Historique
Arette
Escot
1440
Col de
Marie
Blanque

Chapelle
St-Sauveur
1135
Charritte-de-Haut
Lacarry-Arhan-
Charritte-de-Haut
Restoue
Laguinge-Restoue
Pic d'Arguibelle
795
Ancien Abbaye
de Arette
944
Tumulus
Pic Roumendarés
1646
1035

Col du
Incurutcheta
Etchebar
Haux
Licq-Athérey
Église
de Haux
Oulan
Pic de Sudou
1167
la Mouline
Musée de Lourdios
Lourdios-Ichère
Défilé l'Escot
Sarrance
674
Pic de l'Ourène
1813

Cromlechs d'Oscabe
Sommet d'Occabe
1456
Pic des Escaliers
1472
les Charlets
d'Iraty
1327
D 301
D 26
Pic Salhagagne
1053
Barlanès
Col d'Ichère
le Layens
1625
17
Musée de Sarrance
Pic Montagnon
1973
Bois de Gey

Pic de Bizkarzé
1656
Larrau
Gorges d'Holcarté
et d'Holhadubi
Pic d'Issarbe
1359
D 132
Station d'Issarbe
1559
B. Soulaing
1589
Col de Houratate
1009
Pont-Suzon
Chapelle
de Bedous
Bedous
Pic de Mousté
1605
Église
de Aydius

2017
Pic d'Orhy
Col d'Erroymendi
1362
Ste-Engrâce
1436
Pas de Guilhers
Osse-en-Aspe
Athas
N 134
Aydius
Montagnon
d'Iseye
2113

Malgarra
1354
Col Bagargui
1484
Château de
Grand Étroit
Château Gouffre
Arette-la-Pierre-
St-Martin
Pic du Soumcouy
2315
Lées Athas
Jouers
Chapelle de Jouers
Musée de Accous

Irati
Abodi
1528
Portillo de Laza
2236
Col de la
Pierre-St-Martin
1760
Lakarxela
1677
Arette-la-Pierre-
St-Martin
Pic d'Anie
2504
Mail d'Eygarri
1960
Accous
Cette-Eygun
1668
Pic Permayou
2344

de Abodi
Burgusamendia
1542
Lorrondo
1703
1982
Sierra de Anialart
Lapakiza
Réf. de
Labérouat
Lhers
Vallée
14
Musée de Etsaut
Pic de Sesques
2606

Iglesia de N.S.
de Muskilda
10
NA-140
Table des Trois Rois
2421
Bois de Lazerque
Borce
Etsaut
Le Clos aux Ours

Ochagavía
Uztárroz
Linza Maz.
Pakiza de Linzola
Refugio de Linza
Fort du Portalet
Gorges du
Pic d'Enfer

Ezcároz
Arrese
1318
14
Igardacua
1507
1945
Pic de Labigouer
2175
Urdos

A-140
Sierra de Uztárroz
Zuriza
Pic de Lortailde
2147
Parc
Réf. d'Ayous

Iglesia de
N Tirso
Iglesia de
Santa Cruz
Bioleta
1408
Isaba
Iglesia de
N.S. de Idoya
Alano
2167
National
2207
N 134

Esparza de Salazar
Sarriés
8
Urzainqui
Sierra de Arrigorrieta
Peña Ezkaurri
2050
Zuriza
Pic Agüerri
2449
des
Réf. d'Arlet
Pyrenées
les Forges
d'Abel
Pic des Moines
2349

Ripalda
Igal
NA-178
23
la Asunción
Punta Txamar
Peña Forca
2391
Acüé
2263
Station de Ski Somport
1632
Col du Somport
2284

Alburué
1030
Güesa
Vidángoz
Argibe
1203
Roncal
San Sebastián
Calveira
1679
Pueyo de Segarra
1997
Bisaurín
2676
la Roca
Station de Candanchú
Castellar

Gallués
Uscarrés
Sierra Alta
1068
NA-137
Garde
NA-176
Iglesia de
Virgen de Zuberoa
Sierra del Vedao
la Cuta
2147
Refugio de
Lizara
2167
Circo
de Aspe
Canfranc-Estación

Ustés
Torres
1009
Sierra de San Miguel
10
Ansó
Siresa
Sierra de Aísa
N-330
Canfranc

Santa María
del Campo
Navascués
Puerto los
Coronas
950
15
Cucula
1204
Fago
Hecho
Valle
de Hecho
Virgen de la
Catarecha
las Blancas
2133
Villanúa

Sierra de Illón
quírico
Burgui
Monte de la Peña
1294
Plana de Sasi
1044
Santa Lucía
Urdués
Aragüés
del Puerto
Pico de Enmedio
1827
19

Iglesia de
Virgen de la Peña
14
Salvatierra
de Escá
Lorbés
Forcala
1477
Santa Isabel
Jasa
Aísa
Esposa
Sinués
Borau
Castiello
de Jaca
Bescós de
Gardipollera
1362

de Leyre
Paso
del Escalar
Sierra de Orba
Majones
Foz de Biniés
N-126
24
Aratorés
Grosín
1423
N-330
Sierra

NAVARRA
San Justo y Pastor
A-137
Villarreal
de la Canal
Biniés
Lastiesas Altas
Lastiesas Bajas
Areguas
de Solano
Canías
Albarín
1951
163

ZARAGOZA
Virgen
de las Viñas
Sigüés
Asso-Veral
Miramont
17
N-240
Berdún
Embún
Sta. Engracia
de Jaca
Javierregay
Somanes
Novés
Guasillo
Rapitán
Sierra

Iglesia de
San Juan Bautista
Aragón
Puente la Reina de Jaca
9
Ascara
Banaguás
Ipás

Iglesia de
go Apóstol
22
Artieda
Mianos
Peña Musera
985
Casterillo
Martes
N-240
San Babi
Puente la
Reina de Jaca
Santa Cilia
de Jaca
Abay
Jaca
Guasa
A-23
N-330

Iglesia de
San Sebastián
Ruesta
Peña Noblo
1080
Aragón
N-230
Binacua
Santa Cruz
Sabiñánigo 13 km
Biescas 22 km
Huesca 65 km

A-1601
San Salvador
989
Undués-Pintano
Bagüés
N.S. de
la Parueta
Monte Samillán
870
Monte Solandato
879
Virgen de
la Peña
Alastuey
Cuculo
1552
Torla
1074
S. Salvador
Santa Eulalia
1254
A-1205

Iglesia de
n Miguel
Santa María
Magdalena
Pintano
Sarda
1010
Larrés
A-132
Arbués
Santa Cruz
de la Serós
la Carruaca
1161
Peña de Oroel
1770
Virgen de
la Cueva

ardún
Iglesia de
N.S. de la Cerrada
Puig Daras
1241
Baílo
Castiel Mayor
Iglesia de
Santa Bárbara
1111
Monasterio de
San Juan de la Peña
Sierra de San Juan
Liecinera
1127
Cercán
1053
Puerto de Oroel
1080
22
San
Bartolomé
Artaso
164

de Roíta
Petilla
de Aragón
San Juan
Lobera de
Onsella
Logás
1175
Sierra Lurientes
1163
Paternoy
Casanava
957
San Adrián
Bernués
Iglesia de
Virgen de Ubieto
Osia

pa   pb   pc   pd

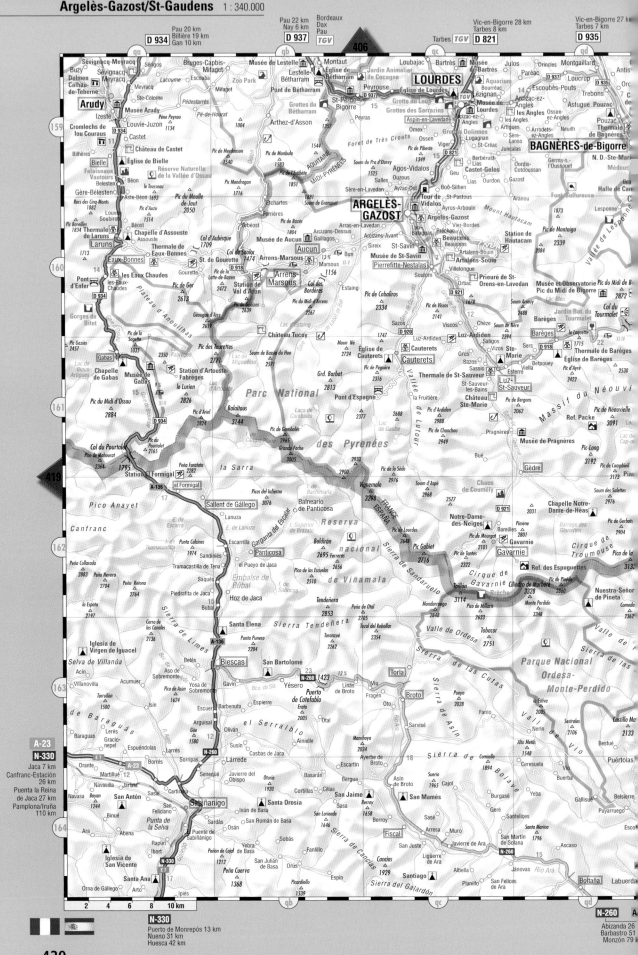

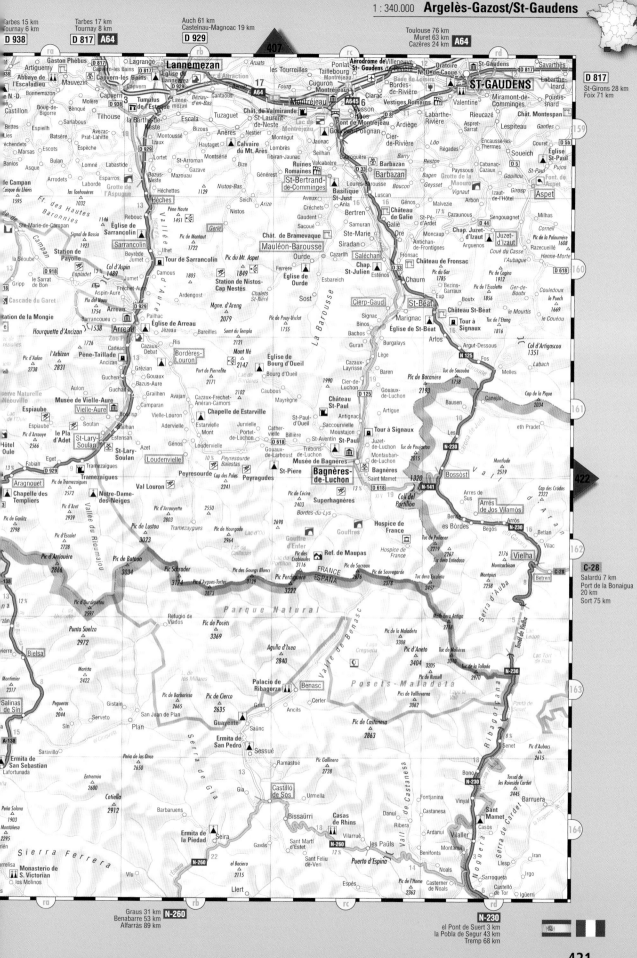

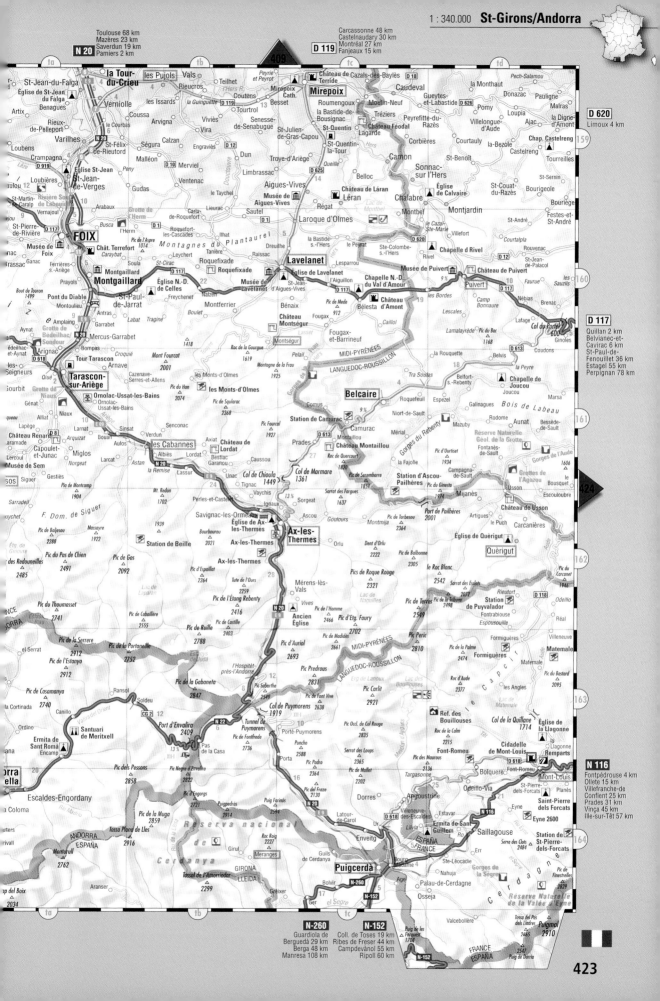

N 20
Toulouse 68 km
Mazères 23 km
Saverdun 19 km
Pamiers 2 km

409

D 119
Carcassonne 48 km
Castelnaudary 30 km
Montréal 27 km
Fanjeaux 15 km

D 620
Limoux 4 km

D 117
Quillan 2 km
Belvianec-et-
Cavirac 6 km
St-Paul-de-
Fenouillet 36 km
Estagel 55 km
Perpignan 78 km

N 116
Fontpédrouse 4 km
Olette 15 km
Villefranche-de-
Confient 25 km
Prades 31 km
Vinça 45 km
Ille-sur-Têt 57 km

N-260
Guardiola de
Berguedà 29 km
Berga 48 km
Manresa 108 km

N-152
Coll. de Toses 19 km
Ribes de Freser 44 km
Campdevànol 55 km
Ripoll 60 km

Carcassonne 20 km
Preixan 11 km
D 118

410

D 623
Fanjeaux 22 km
Villasavary 22 km
Castelnaudary 37 km

D 118
D 623
Pieusse
D 620
Gaja-et-Villedieu
Greffeil
Pont de Greffeil
Gardie
Villebazy
Forêt Dom. de Castillou
Labastide-en-Val
Taurize
Prieuré
Église N.-D. de l'Aire
Coustouge
Fontjoncouse

LIMOUX
St-Polycarpe
Villar-St-Anselme
Clermont-sur-Lauquet
Château de Clermont
Plateau de Lacamp 697
St-Martin-des-Puits
Caunettes-en-Val
St-Pierre-des-Champs
Talairan
Église N.-D. de Fontjonc

159
Magrie
Cournanel
Vendémies
Arce
Aquaduc Romain
Belcastel-et-Buc
D 129
Caunette-sur-Lauquet
Forêt Dom. de Lacamp
D 40
Lairière
Mayronnes
D 212
Église de St-Martin
D 613
Tréviac-Bas
Albas
Durban-Corbières

Château des Ducs de Joyeuse
Alet-les-Bains
Roquetaillade
Ancien Abbey
Conilhac-de-la-Montagne
Cathédrale Notre-Dame
Pont du Diable
Montazels
Luc-sur-Aude
Missègre
la Pouzanque
Montjoi
Bouisse
Château de Durfort
Vigneveille
Château de Termes
Termes
Félines-Termenès
Villerouge-Termenès
Château de Villerouge-Termenès
Pont de Cascastel
Cascastel-des-Corbières
Château de Durban
Villeseque-des-Corbi

Château de Quillan
Château des Ducs de Joyeuse
Couiza
D 613
Cassaignes
Château de Arques
Arques
Musée de Arques
Peyrolles
Salza
Mouthoumet
Laroque-de-Fa
Divejean
Église de Quintillan
Palairac
Quintillan
Embres-et-Castelmaur

D 117
Puivert 14 km
Belcaire 26 km
Lavelanet 33 km
Foix 67 km

Fa
Espéraza
Rennes-le-Château
Serres
Pont de Serres
175
Savignan
les Moulines
Auriac
Dolmen Dernacueillette
Dernacueillette
Château de Auriac
Massac
Maisons
Nouvelle
Château d'Aguilar

Tour de Fa
D 118
Granès
Rennes-les-Bains
Sougraigne
Fourtou
D 212
Montgaillard
D 613
Pech de Fraysse 942
Tuchan
Église de Tuchan
D 611
Terrass

160
St-Ferriol
le Bézu
Col de Bugarach 680
le Linas
D 14
Cubières-s.-Cinoble
Soulatgé
Rouffiac-des-Corbières 614
Château de Peyrepertuse
Padern
Château de Padern
Paziols
Vingrau
la Se

QUILLAN
Château de Quillan
St-Just-et-le-Bézu
1029
Château de Bugarach 1231
Camps-sur-l'Agly
969
Duilhac sous-Peyrepertuse
Cucugnan
508
288
455
Espira

Belvianes-et-Cavirac
Cap de Fer 1044
St-Julia-de-Bec
Parahou Grand
Pic de Bugarach
Roc Paradet 900
Gorges de Galamus
Grau de Maury
Château de Quéribus
Mas de las Frèdes
Coume de l'Arago
Château de Tautavel
Musée de Tau
Tautavel
Tour de Tau

D 117
Col Campérié 517
Caudiès-de-Fenouillèdes
13
la Boulzane
Ermitage de St-Antoine
St-Paul-de-Fenouillet
Église de St-Paul-de-Fenouillet
Maury
D 611
9
Ermitage St-Vincent
Cases-de-Pène
Église N.-D. Dame d

161
Caïla
Lapradelle
Château St-Pierre
Fenouillet
D 117
Castel Fizel
les Cabanes
10
Musée de la Ville
Lesquerde
436
Latour-de-France
Estagel
D 117
Calce
17

Défilé de Pierre Lys
Quirbajou
Artigues
Château de Puilaurens
Axat
Pic d'Estable 1512
Salvezines
les Bordes
Col de Mars 551
Vira
le Vivier
Felluns
St-Martin
St-Arnac
Rasiguères
Planèzes
Ansignan
Lansac
Montner
Église Notre-Dame Ste-Catherine

le Clat
D 118
Gorges de St-Gorges
le Cauni
Forêt de Boucheville
Pont-Aqueduc Romain
Prats-de-Sournia
Trilla
Caramany
Cassagnes
Col de la Dona 200

423
Roquefort-de-Sault
Ste-Colombe-sur-Guette
Montfort-s.-Boulzane
Sal. Naou 1314
Rabouillet
Pézilla-de-Conflent
Barrage de l'Agly

162
Counozouls
Pic Dourmidou 1845
Chapelle St-Michel
Sournia
D 619
Château de Campoussy
Trévillach
Bélesta
Musée de Bélesta
Corneilla-la-Rivière
Pézilla-la-Rivière
Vil
la
N 11

1750
Col de Jau 1513
Rer. du Roussillon 1314
Chapelle de Campoussy
Campoussy
Col des Auzines
Montalba-le-Château
Orgues
Néfiach
d'Avall
Millas
16

Forêt de Lapazeuil
Forêt de Salvanère
Mosset
Raque Jalère 1104
Tarerach
Château de Montalba-le-Château
Marcevol
Ille-sur-Têt
Chaleppe de Ille-sur-Têt
Corbère-les-Cabanes
Corbère
12
Musée de Thuit
Thui

Arguelle
St-Berthomeu
Ref. de Caillaou
Molitg-les-Bains
Campome
Arboussols
Ancienne Prieuré
Eus
Retenue de Vinça
Rodès
Musée de Ille-sur-Têt
St-Michel-de-Llottes
D 615
Parc Botanique
Église de Thur
Llupia
Terrats

Madres 2471
2236
Urbanya
N.-D. de Riquér
Catllar
N 116
Marquixanes
Vinça
Rigarda
Dolmen St-Michel
Camélas
Castelnou
Castelnou
Ste-Colombe-de-la-Commanderie

Puig d'Escoutou 2293
Mont Coronat 2165
Nohèdes
Conat
PRADES
Ria-Sirach
Chapelle de Prades
Espira-de-Conflent
Joch
Finestret
Estoher
Prieuré de Serrabone
Casefabre
Boule-d'Amont
Église de Montauriol
Fourques

163
Sansa
Railleu
Château de Evol
Ayguatébia-Talau
Évol
Chapelle de Evol
Jujols
Serdinya
Musée de Villefranche
Fort Libéria
Villefranche-de-Conflent
Musée de Prades
Tour de Cours
Villerach
Clara
Taurinya
Baillestavy
la Bastide
Chapelle de la Trinité
Belpuig
Col Xatard 754
Calmeilles
Col de Llauro
Llauro 380
Église St-L

Caudiès-de-Conflent
Talau
Oreilla
Chapelle de Evol
Château de Fillols
Vernet-les-Bains
Fillols
Corneilla-de-Conflent
Abbaye de St-Martin-du-Canigou
Valmanya
St-Marsal
Église de Calmeilles
Oms
Col de Fourtou 655
Vivès
Tordères
St-Ferréol Ermitage

2000
Canaveilles
Souanyes
Escaro
Nyer
Sahorre
Castell 1018
Pic de l'Alzina
Pic Joffre 2413
Los Masos
Col Paloumère 1036
Taillet
Veinat

N 116
Thuès-Entre-Valls
Thuès-les-Bains
Parc Animalier
Mont Canigou 2748
Puig Barbet 2785
2495
Forêt Domaniale de Corsavy
Céret
Musée de Palada
Palada

Sauto
Fontpédrouse
Puig de Tres Estelles 2096
Tour de Goa
Puig des Tres Vents 2763
Montbolo
Reynès
Musée d' Moderne

N 116
Mont-Louis 5 km
Saillagouse 20 km
Bourg-Madame 30 km
Puigcerdà (E) 31 km

Pont Gisclard
Gorges de la Carança
Col de Mantet 1765
Py
Réserve Naturelle de Py
Pla Guillem 2302
1933
Musée de Corsavy
Corsavy
Gorges de la Fou
Amélie-les-Bains Palalda
D 115
Amélie-les-Bains Palalda
Musée d'
1093

164
2556
Pic de Gallinas 2634
Pic Redoun 2678
Pic del Racó Gras
Mantet
Cime de Pomarole 2457
Réserve Naturelle de Mantet
Esquerdes de Rotja
Réserve Naturelle de Prats-de-Mollo-la Preste
Puig Ca de Llors
Pic de la Coumelle 1699
la Souque 1621
Musée de Montferrer
Montferrer
Tour de Cos
Roc de France
Stèle des Évadés
1278
Pic de Fontfreda

Pic de la Dona
Bastiments 2704
2779
Pic d'Eina 2786
Pic de Noucreus 2799
Torreneules 2711
Réserve Naturelle de Py
Costabona 2882
les Bains de la Preste 2465
la Preste
Prats-de-Mollo la Preste
le Tech
Musée de Serralongue
Serralongue
Forge del Mitg
1446
Castell de Cabrera
Maçanet de Cabrenys

Nuria
Fresèr
Reserva Nacional Setcases
Serra del Catllar
les Barreges 2675
Tech 1765
Remparts de Fort
Musée de Prats
Tour de Mir
les Bains de la Preste
13
Musée de St-Laurent
St-Laurent-de-Cerdans
Mont Capell 1194
la Sort
Tapis

2 4 6 8 10 km

XII-I 1621 Montfalgars
D 115
Mollo 13 km
Camprodon 19 km
Sant Pau de Ségúries 25 km

Col d'Arós 1513
Lamanère
Tours de Cabrens
Villeroge
Golf de France
FRANCE
ESPAÑA
Rocabruna
Comanegra 1558

Marseille
Nice

Mer

Méditerranée

Punta di l'Acc
Anse de

Tour de Pe
Anse de l'I

Phare de la Pietra
Île de la Pietra

Plage de
l'Île Rousse

l'Île Rousse
l'Île Rousse Lozari

N 197

Punta di Vallitoni
Marine de Davia

Gimebaru

4,5

Plage de Algajola
Algajola

Corbara

Monticello
Couvent de Corbara

Chapelle St-Fran

16

Marine de Sant' Ambrogio
Punta Spano
Île de Spano
Baie Agajo

Citadelle
de Algajola

9,5

Pigna

Santa-Reparata-
di-Balagna

San Se

San
Roccu

**Phare de Punta
di a Revellata**

Punta Caldanu

Lumio

Couvent de
Marcasso

Sant'Antonino

Belgodere

Costa

Punta di a Revellata

Punta Bianca

Citadelle
de Calvi

Golfe de
Calvi

St-Pierre

Lavatoggio

Aregno

Cateri

Avapessa

Monte Longo

Ancien Couvent
de Tuani

455

Nessa

Ville-di-Paras

Fort Mozzela

Grote des Veaux Marins

N 197

Capu di Corduvella
336

Église San Raineru

Muro

Pioggiola

Église de Notre-
Dame de la Serra

Calvi

Port de Calvi

4

Lunghignano

St-Albanu

Feliceto

Monte Tollu
1332

Punta Guale
Baie de Nichiareto

Capu di a Conca
725

Aérodr. de
Calvi-Ste-Catherine

D 151

Montegrosso

Zilia

San Parteo
1680

Mausoléo

Forêt de
Melaja

Punta di Cantaleli

Capo Cavallo

Capu Pianu
848

9

Moncale

Ancien Couvent
d'Alzi Pratu

Cima all' Altare

Torre Truccia

D 81

Calenzana

Tarazone

Église
Santa Restituta

GR 20 Capu di Pratu

Forest

Punta di Vigatoggio
256

Bocca di Marsolinu
443

San Quilico

Suare

828

Punta Rodiche
1781

Riu di Tartagine

Sant'A

Capu di a Mursetta

Plage de Crovani

Église St-Jean

Argentella

891

Ref. de l'Ortu di u Piubbu
Capu Jovu
1629

2012

Forêt Domaniale de
Tartagine-Melaja

Monte Padru
2393

Cima di a Statoja
2305

Asc

Punta Farrajola

Punta di Cluttone

Golfe de Galéria

Forêt de
Calenzana

18

Capo Ghineparo

Capo di Vegno
1389

Punta Scaffa

Capu Ladroncellu
693

Ref. de
Carrozzu
2145

Cascade de Rotello

33

Plage de Galéria

Punta di Stollu

Tour Maraghiu

Olmo

Filosorma

Église de
Santa Lucia

Cirque
de Bonifatu

Punta Gialla
2085

a Muvrella
2148

Fore
Vecc

Port de Galéria

Pt. Muvareccia

D 351

Galéria

D 81

le Fango

Capu a u Ceppu
1951

Haut Asco

Capu Biancu
2562

Punta Bianca

Punta Validori
407

Calca

Château
l'Ambiu

Tuarelli

Château
de Tuarelli

Manso

Punta a Scala
1409

Punta Missoju
2201

2018

Capu a u Perdatu
2583

Capu Terri Cou
2109

Punta Palazzu

Punta Nera

Baie de Focolara

Parc Naturel

Fangu

Forêt de
Tetti

Barghiana

Riu de Bocca Bianca

Bocca a e Poste
1437

Punta Minuta
2556

Monte Cinto
2706

Cascade d'Ercu

Rau

Phare di Gargalu

Isola di Gargalu

Baie
d'Elbo

HAUTE-CORSE
CORSE-DU-SUD

Capu Licchia
639

Forêt Domaniale
du Fangu

Santa Maria
Couvent

Monte Estremo

Riu di Cavichia

Paglia Orba
2525

Tighiettu
Ref.

Monte Albanu
2018

Lac d'
Cinto

Lozzi

Réserve Naturelle
de Scandola

Girolata

Punta Salisei
927

Capu à Giallichiccia

Grotte des Anges

Poggio

S.P
Cala

Baie de Solana

Cala di Gattaja

Golfe
de Girolata

Tour de Girolata

Col de la Croix
269

Osani

Curzu

D 81

Ref. Ciuttulu di i Mori

Punta Licciola
2235

Régional de la

Musée Albertacce
Albertacce

Cascade de Radule

Pont
Casama

Punta Muchillina

Punta Scandola

Capu Seninu

2 4 6 8 10 km

Porto

Porto 12 km

D 81

428

Livorno (I)

Piombino (I)
Portoferráio
(Isola d'Elba, I)

Mer

Ligurienne

Savona (I)
Génova (I)

Marseille
Nice
Génova (I)

Phare de
Île de la Giraglia
Île de la Giraglia
Tour de Tollare
Pointe d'Agnello
Tour d'Agnello
Baie de Capandola
Plage de Capandola
Capo Grosso
Tollare
Barcaggio
Cap Corse
Monte Maggiore
359
Capo Bianco
Capo Bianco
Poggio
Cannelle
Botticella
Granaggiolo
Église de
Sant'Antonino
Église de Santa Maria
Îles Finocchiarola
Chapelle Santa Restituta
Baie de Tamarone
Tour Centuri-Port
Centuri-Port
Château de Camera
Morsiglia
Camera
Bettolacce
Rogliano
Tomino
Port de Macinaggio
Macinaggio
Plage de Macinaggio
Mucchieta
N.D. des Gréces
608
Punta di Gulfidoni
Capu Corvoli
Église de San Paolo
Pastina
Marine de Méria
Tour Marine de Méria
Golfu Alisco
Col de Santa Lucia
381
Pino
St-François Anc. Couvent
Poggio
Piazza
Campu
Port Santa Severa
Fiero
Mt. Grofiglieta
837
Minerbio
Castello
Santa Severa
Plage Santa Severa
Couv. d'Oveglia
Barrettali
Carbonacce
Tour de Giottani
Marine de Giottani
Conchiglio
Ortale
Marine de Porticciolo
Tour de l'Ossa
Martinco
Pinzuta
Lapedina
Pietracorbara
Marine de Pietracorbara
Tour de Castella
Punta di Canelle
Canari
Abro
Cima di e Follicie
1324
San Michele
4,5
Marine de Canelle
Ogliastro
Balba
Crosciano
Punta Bianca
Sisco
Moline
Santa Catalina Ancien Couvent
Marine de Sisco
Marine d'Albo
Olcani
Marie de Sisco
Église de San Michele
Monte Stello
1307
Silgaggia
Santa Maria di e Nevi
Plage de Nonza
Nonza
Erbalunga
Tour de Erbalunga
Couvent de Nonza
Celle
Chapelle
St-Jean
Pozzo
Poretto
Plage de Erbalunga
Monte Foscu
Lavasina
Miomo
Tour Negru
1102
Figarella
San Martino-
di-Lota
San Hyacinthe
Plage de Bastia
Punta Negra
Punta
di Mignola
Plage de Saleccia
Punta di Curza
Marine
de Farinole
Bracolaccia
Pietranera
Grigione
Malfalcu
Plage de Loto
Phare de Mortella
Punta Vecchia
Punta Mortella
Farinole
Ville-di-Pietrabugno
Cardo
Musée de Bastia
Patrimonio
Bastia
Port de Bastia
Cima d'Ortella
416
Golfe de St-Florent
Serra di Pigno
960
Monserrato
Phares la Citadelle
Cima d'Itona
479
Monte Genova
421
Port St-Florent
Citadelle de
St-Florent
Anc. Cathedral
du Nebbio
Suerta
Lupino
La Citadelle de Bastia
Plage de Lupino
Bocca di Vezzu
311
Casta
Château Stélo
Baccialu
Rosajola
San Pancrace
Dolmen
St-Florent
Col de Teghime
536
Montesoro
Plage de la Marana
la Marana
Monte Filetto
842
Champ de tir
de Casta-Sud
Furiani
Poggio-
d'Oletta
Reserve Naturelle
de l'Étang de Biguglia
Plage de Pineto
Cima Alta
362
Monte Vicinasco
1018
Moulin d'Isola
Église San-Pietro
Sto-Pietro-di-Tenda
Couvent
St-François
Cima di u Zuccarellu
955
Oletta
Biguglia
Casatorra
Pineto
Île San Damianu
Chapelle
San Michele
Cima di Mitielli
652
Monte Asto
1535
San-Gavino-
di-Tenda
Rapale
Pianello
Sant'Antone
368
Église San Michele
Vallecalle
Fusaja
Col de S. Stefano
Ortale
Etang de
Biguglia
M. Musso
Plage de M. Musso
Chapelle
San Michele
Cima di Pristofe
573
Chapelle
San Jabicu
Château
Assigliani
Sorio
Murato
Pieve
Rutali
Rivincino
la Marane
Aéroport de Bastia-Poretta
Chapelle
an Roccu
Pietralba
Grottu d'Erbajolu
Forêt Dom.
de Stella
Borgo
Église de la Canonica
Castellu
an Colombanu
obanu
Chapelle
Sant'Agostinu
Église San Michele
Vignale
Lucciana
Croceta
Cité Antique
Plage de la Marane
Castiglione
ntu
Monte Reghia di Pozzo
1469
Bigorno
Campitello
Volpajola
Scolca
Casamozza
San Giustu
Camp du Cap Sud
Plage Camp du Cap Sud
Cima di Pristofe
573
Monte Tassu
1372
Lento
Marcello
Barchetta
Campile
Cappuccini
Couvent
Prunelli-di-
Casacconi
Olmo
Marina di Sorbo
rre di
nosa
Castifao
Monte Tevisi
1146
Costa Roda
Cavanaggia
Torre d'Asinaja
Bisinchi
Divina
Prunelli-di-
Casacconi
Vescovato
Venzolasca
Querciolo
Anghione
Plage de Anghione
ncescu
Couv.
Moltifao
Pont Génois
San Thomaso
di Pastoreccia
Crocicchia
Penta
Loreto-di-
Casinca
Sorbo-
Ocagnano
Penta-
di-Casinca
Valandella
Tour San Pellegrinu
Château
Sepula
Grotte de
Petralbellu
Forêt Communale
de Moltifao
Santa Maria
di Riscamone
Valle-di-
Rostino
Pastoreccia
Ortiporio
Silvareccio
Porri
San Pellegrinu
Plage San Pellegrinu
Piedigriggio
Taverna
Morosaglia
Giocatoggio
Casalta
Taglio-
Isolaccio
Terre Rosse
Castellu di
Serravalle
Ruines de
Tribuna
San Pantaléo
Stoppia
Nove
Scata
Pruno
Isolaccio
Figaretto
Plage de Figareto
San Nicolao
Prato-di-
Giovellina
Castineta
la Porta
San Petru d'Accia
Poggio-
Casevecchie
Talasani
Château Francardo
Croix de
Setonia
Aiti
Église San Cristofano
Croce
Alzi
Ste-Lucie de Moriani
Forêt Dom. de
Castiglione
Saliceto
Campana
Mte. San Petrone
1767
Francolacce
Velone-Orneto
Piazzole
Poggio-
Mezzana
Venzolasca
Sant'Angelu
San Michele
Lano
San Lorenzo
Piedicroce
Couvent d'Orezza
San-Giovanni-
di-Moriani
Moriani-Plage
Sant'Angelu
Omessa
Grotte de
Carbuccia
Château Vigne
Piedipartino
Carticasi
San Giorgio
Parata
Cascade de
Lecchiuline
San-Nicolao
N 198
Plage de Prunete
Galghellu
Zuccarellu
Chapelle
Santa Servanda
Forêt de San
Petru d'Accia
Carpineto
Felce
Forci
Sta-Maria
Poggio
Port de Campoloro
Chapelle
Sta-Marione
Sta-Lucia
di-Mercuriu
Mt. Pianu Maggiore
1558
Monte Murvaje
1697
Col d'Arcarotta
819
Perelli
la Madonna Chap.
Valle-d'Alesani
Cervione
Valle-di-
Campoloro
Chapelle Santa Cristina
Padulone
Prunete
Sermano
Bustanico
1408
Anc. Couvent d'Alesani
Pietricaggiu
429
Sant' Andréa-
di-Cotone
Ortale
Musée Cervione
San Giuliano
Plage de Prunete

N 193 Corte 500 m
Aléria 48 km
Ajaccio 83 km

N 198 Aléria 24 km
Porto-Vecchio 92 km
Bonifacio 120 km

Bastia 71 km
l'Île Rousse 68 km
Ponte Leccia 23 km
N 193

Bastia 48 km
→ **N 193** 27 km
Vescovato 25 km
N 198

427

Fa   Fb   Fc   Fd

Musée de Corte
Corte
Église et Bapt.de San-Giovanni
Aérodrome de Corte
Chapelle St-François
San Martino
Erbajolo
N 200
Punta di Gianfena
N 193
1408
St-Christophe
Santo-Pietro-di-Venaco
Château de Pozzo di Borgo
Col de Bellegranaje
526
St-Alexis
Venaco
2458
723
Serraggio
Pont Génois
Castellare
Punta Bagliacone
Noceta
784
Pont du Vecchio
di Petra Facciata
Église Sta-Maria
1733
Muracciole
Fortin de Pasciolu
Vizzavone
Col de la Serra
807
Viviano
Forêt Domaniale de Rospa-Sorba
Punta Muru
1565
Col de Sorba
1478
Monte d'Oro
2389
D 69
Saparelle
Chapelle Sant'Andréa
Vizzavona
Col de Vizzavona
1163
Forêt Domaniale de Vizzavona
Chapelle de Ghisoni
Ghisoni
Punta di u Oriente
2112
Capannelle
Barrage de Sampolo
Punta di Serra
881
Punta Kyrie-Eleison
1535
Lugo-di-Nazza
Monte Renoso
2352
Poggio-di-Nazza
Forêt Communale de Ghisoni
Punta di Campiglione
1579
St-Antoine
Ajola
Forêt Dom.de Pietra Piana
Ghisonaccia Gare
Aérodrome de Ghisonaccia-Alzitone
Plateau d'Ese
Ref. San Pietro di Verde
Col de Verde
Punta di Prutu
1289
1954
Valcaccia
Chap. San Giovanni
Padula
Ref. de Prati
Acciani
Prunelli-di-Fiumorbo
Ghisonaccia
Punta Scaldasole
2101
Punta di a Capella
1950
Forêt Dom.de Saint-Antoine
Isolaccio-di-Fiumorbo
Egl. de la Curse
Serra-di-Fiumorbo
Abbazia
Morta
Migliacciaru
Mt. Giovanni
1759
Pietrapola
Pietrapola
San Michele
Casamozza
Punta di a Vena
1872
Palneca
San Gavino-di-Fiumorbo
San Quilicus
Ania
Pinellu
Château de Coasina
Ciamannacce
Église Sta-Lucia
Ref. d'Usciolu
Punta Bianca
1954
Punta di a Faiu
1568
Pedi Querciu
Sampolo
Cozzano
Chisa
le Travo Riviera
Ventiseri
Vix
Aérodrome de Solenzara
Zicavo
San Roccu
Monte Occhiatu
Parata
Cité de l'Air
San Petru
Chapelle San Giacomu
Punta d'Alluccia
1590
Solaro
Travo
Lustinchellu
Pielza
Marine de Solaro
D 69
Forêt Dom.du Coscione
Monte Malo
1850
Punta Mozza
711
Punta di u Castellu
1122
Église de Solenzara
1623
Punta di Frauletu
2018
Punta di Tintennaja
D 268
Togna
Solenzara
HAUTE-CORSE
2134
Punta di Buccaragiu
N 198
Castellu d'Ornucciu
Ref. d'Asinao
608
Sari-Solenzara
D 268
15
Col de la Vaccia
1193
Punta d'Ariola
1456
Coscione
14
Punta di Ferriate
1089
Cannella
Cantoli
Col de Bavella
1218
Ref. de Paliri
Punta di Monte Sordu
1117
Chapelle de St-Sébastien
Quenza
Punta Veloco
1483
Favone
Favone
Église Ste-Marie
Zonza
Punta di Quercitella
1461
D 420
Massif de San Martinu
Punta d'Ortu
695
Musée de Conca
Tarcu
Sorbollano
Castellu de Cucuruzzu
Conca
N 198
Pacciunituli
GR 20
Figa
San-Gavino-di-Carbini
Massif de Barocagio-Marghese
Carabona
Musée de Levie
Tour di Fautea
D 268
Guardiariccu
991
Tagliu Rossu
Punta di Fautea
Levie
Monte Rossu
1058
Forêt Domaniale de l'Ospedale
Ste-Lucie de Porto-Vecchio
Carbini
D 368
Cascade de Piscia di Gallo
Nevatoli
Plage de Pinarellu
Punta di a Vacca Morta
Agnarone
Lecci
Porto-Vecchiaccio
Pinarellu
Pt. de Finaggia
1058
Tour Île de Pinarellu
D 59
1315
l'Ospedale
Castellu d'Araghju
San Cipriano
Mégal. Monument
N 198
Punta Capicciola
Punta d'Arasu
Île San Cipriano
Ste-Trinité
Cala Rossa
Phare San Cipriano
Marina di Fiori
Plage Cala Rosa

431

Fa   Fb   Fc   Fd

Mazzola
San Nicolao
Santa Servanda
Novale
Barrage de l'Alesani
Chapelle Sant'Antone
Favalello
Sant'Andréa-di-Bozio
Pietra-di-Verde
Chiatra
Plage de Sumaltu
Monte Alhu
1151
Moita
Torre a i Caselli
Tour de Sumaltu
Punta di Mangolo
1036
Matra
Canale-di-Verde
Phare d'Alistro
Zuani
Campi
1093
Ancien Couvent
Zalana
Punta di a Campana
Linguizzetta
Tour d'Alistro
Ampriani
Tox
Rau di Alistro
Chapelle Sta-Maria
Altiani
Pietraserena
Chapelle Sta-Brigida
Spazzola
Rau di Chiusura
Plage d'Alistro
Piedicorte-di-Gaggio
Sta-Maria
Giuncaggio
Pancheraccia
Pianiccia
Marine de Bravone
Site Préhistorique
Rau de Vadule
Tour de Bravone
Église de San Martinu
Plage de Bravone
Fagu
Château Vaccili
Casabertola de Licceto
N 198
11,5
Fontaine de Padula
Vezzani
Église St-Laurent
Antisanti
Frasciccia
Étang de Terrenzana
Pietroso
Casevecchie
Chapelle Sta-Maria
Teppa
N 200
12,5
Étang de Diane
Tour de Diane
4,5
Église San Michele
Campo-Quarciu
Rvoir de Teppe-Rosse
la Gare
Caterragio
Aghione
Casone
Teppe Rosse
Fort de Matra
Aléria
Plage d'Aléria
Maison Pierraggi
Casabianda
Musée d'Aléria
Étang del Sale
Samuletu
Pénitencier de Casabianda
D 343
12
Rvoir d'Alzitone
4,5
Campolidori
Vadina
Étang d'Urbino
10,5
Piana Fme
Tour de Vignale
Calzarellu
Plage de Quercioni
Mignataja
Étang de Palu
5

Livorno (I)

Mer

Tyrrhénienne

Génova (I)

Ajaccio
(Corse, F)

Marseille (F)
Nice (F)

Propriano (Corse, F)

428

Ajaccio 95 km
Propriano 15 km
Sartène 2,5 km **N 196**

Ea

Eb

Ec

Ed

Cala d'Agulia

Église de
San Giovanni

Monte Grosso
625

Pt. di Mucchiu Biancu

Punta d'Eccica

211

Menhir de
Vaccil - Vacchiu

Giuncheto

Cala d'Arana

Tour de
Senetosa

6

Cala di Conca

D 48

Alignement de
Pagliaju Menhirs

15

N 196

Phare de Senetosa

Punta di Patania
321

13,5

Capu di Senetosa

Fort de Tizzano

Mégalithes
de Cauria

Giar

124

Plage de Tizzano

Tizzano

Golfe de Tizzano

Serragia

Mo
d'A

Capu di Zivia

Zivia

Punta di u Grecu
266

Punta di Valanincu
429

Plage de Zivia

Golfe de Murtoli

Punta di Murtoli

Roccapina

7

Golfe de Roccapina

Plage de Roccapina

Cala di
Roccapina

F
Ca

Capu di Roccapina

Tour d'Olmeto

Ce

Punta di Caniscione

125

Anse
d'Arbitru

Îles Bruzzi

Anse de

126

M a r

M e d i t e r r á n e o

127

Punta d
Portobello

Nuraghe Tuttusoni

Sarra Tamburu
217

128

Cala Sarraina

Vaccaggi

Punta Cruzitta
267

Iu Colbu

Costa Paradiso

Porto Léccio

23

Monte
Pitrighino
377

Punta li Canneddi

M. Tinnari

G

Baia Trinità

Ísola Rossa

Ísola Rossa

Paduledda
la Scalitta

Trinità d'Agultu
e Vignola

Sant'António
de li Colti

San Pie
di Ru

San Pietro
Martire

129

90

Badesi Mare

Badesi

Monte Littigheddu

20

la Tozza

Monte
693

Muntiggioni Punta Bianca
618

Camping Int'l.
Valledoria

Azzagulta

Codaruina

S. Maria
Maddalena

248

Monte Naragu

Monte Stazzoni
829

Mar

Castel-
sardo

Cala
Ostina

la Ciaccia

Iu Razzoni

l'Avru

Valledoria

2

13

Fiume

Ec

Ed

Eb

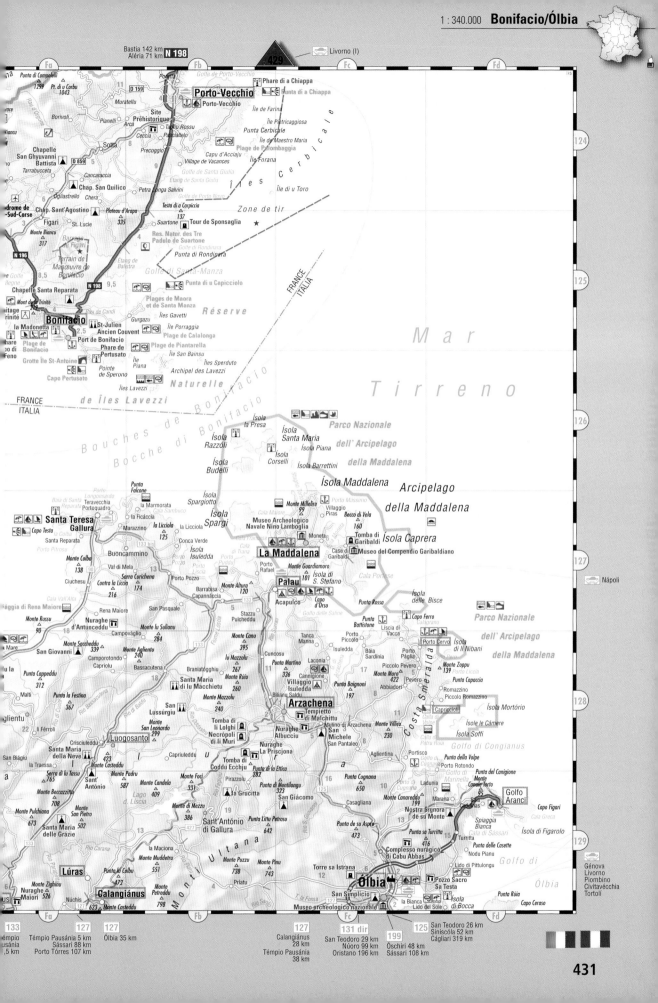

435

441

Picture Credit

abbreviations:

A = Alamy
BB = Bilderberg
C = Corbis
G = Getty Images
H = Bildagentur Huber
L = Laif
M = Mauritius Images
Schapo = Schapowalow

Cover front: L/REA
Cover back: L/Huber; L/Meyer; Huber/Gräfenhain

p. 10/11: H/Simeone, p. 12/13 t.: Bridgemanart, p. 12 b.: L/Hemis/Colin Matthieu, p. 13 m.: L/Hemis/Bruno Barbier, p. 13 b.: L/Hemis/Bertrand Rieger, p. 14 t.: A/Picture Contact, p. 14/15: L/Hemis/Bruno Barbier, p. 15 r.: L/Hemis/Bruno Barbier, p. 16/17: A/Art Kowalsky, p. 18 l.: imagep.de/Stephane Frances, p. 19 t.: A/Robert Harding, p. 19 m.: A/Danita Delimont, p. 20 t.: L/Hemis/Bertrand Rieger, p. 20 m.: L/Boening, p. 21 t.: H/von Dachsberg, p. 21 m.: H/Spilla Riccardo, p. 21 r.: Bridgemanart, p. 22 l.: G/John Miller, p. 23 t.: L/Fulvio Zanettini, p. 23 m.: L/REA, p. 23 b.: L/Hemis, p. 24 t.: A/Jon Arnold, p. 24 m.: L/Hemis, p. 25 t.: A/Guichaoua, p. 25 m. l.: L/Hemis, p. 25 m. r.: L/Hemis, p. 25 b.: Schapo/Doormann, p. 26 t.: L/Hemis, p. 26 m.: Biosphoto/Jean Luc Ziegler, p. 26 l. t.: L/Hemis, p. 26 l. b.: L/Hemis, p. 27 t.: L/Michael Amme, p. 26/27: L/Hemis, p. 28 t.: L/Hemis, p. 29 t.: L/Hemis, Karte 28/29 from l. to r., from t. to b.: L/Hemis, L/Fulvio Zanettini, L/Hemis, Visum/Alfred Buellesbach, 4 x L/Hemis, p. 30/31 t.: Panstock, p. 30/31 m.: DFA/Mayer, p. 30 b.: Jon Arnold, p. 31 b.: H/Spilla Riccardo, p. 32 t.: L/Gilles Rigoulet/Hemis, p. 32 l.: Lescourret, p. 32/33: Panstock, p. 33 t.: M/Photononstop, p. 34/35: L/Jean Erick Pasquier, p. 36 t.: H/Simeone, p. 36 l.: C/Richard Klune, p. 36/37: Panstock, p. 37 t.: L/Jonkmanns, p. 37 b.: Diaf, p. 38/39: Jon Arnold, p. 40 t.: C/Richard Bickel, p. 40 l.: L/Linke, p. 40/41: C/Yann Arthus-Bertrand, p. 41 t.: C/Philippe Giraud, p. 41 b.: C/Aldo Pavan, p. 41 r. t.: A/images of Europe, p. 41 r. m.: A/Harald Theissener, p. 41 r. b.: A/Adam Woolfitt, p. 42 r. t. C/Atlantide, p. 42 r. b.: C/Robert Estall, p. 43 t.: Jon Arnold, Karte 42/43 from l. to r., from t. to b.: Diaf, Diaf, Panstock, Christopher Haigh, Jon Arnold, Herb Hartmann, C/Richard Klune, Premium, C/Hubert Stadler, Jon Arnold, Premium, p. 44/45: G/Martin Child, p. 44 b.: L/Hemis, p. 45 m.: L/Eric Martin, p. 45 b.: Visum/Andia, p. 46 l. t.: L/Hemis, p. 46 l. b.: L/Hemis, p. 46 t.: L/Hemis, p. 46 m. l.: f1-online/Prisma, p. 46 m. r.: L/Hemis, p. 47: Schapo/Sime, p. 48 t.: L/Hollandse Hoogte, p. 48 l.: C/Adam Woolfit, p. 49 t.: C/Charles Platiau, p. 49 m.: L/VU, p. 49 r.: L/Andreas Herzau, p. 50 l.: G/RDA, p. 50 t. l.: Wilhelm Mierendorf, p. 50 t. r.: Wilhelm Mierendorf, p. 50/51: A1-Pix/Your Photo Today, p. 51 t.: A/Peter Bowater, p. 51 r.: Bridgemanart, p. 52 t.: M/A/Lourens Smak, p. 52 m.: Schapo, p. 52 b.: M/A/Lourens Smak, p. 53 t.: A/Jeremy Hoare, p. 53 r.: A/Danita Delemont, p. 54 t.: Schapowalow/SIME, p. 54 m.: A/Jeremy Hoare, p. 55 t.: A/Isifa Image Service, p. 55 r.: M/Photononstop, p. 56 t.: A/Cephas, p. 56/57; L/Olivier Roux, p. 57 t.: A/Bon Appetit, p. 57 r.: A/Bon Appetit, p. 58 t.: M/A, p. 58 m.: A/Cephas, p. 58 b.: A/Cephas, p. 59 t. l.: Biosphoto/Bidault Frederique, p. 59 t. r.: Schapo/Pratt-Bries, Karte p. 59 from l. to r., from t. to b.: H/von Dachsberg, Andia/Jolyot, L/Hemis, L/Hemis, A/Cephas A1-Pix/Your Photo Today, p. 60/61: A/Digital Vision, p. 60 b.: A/Art Kowalski, p. 61 m.: Bridgemanart, p. 61 b.: A/F1-online, p. 62 t.: L/Hemis, p. 62 m.: look/Karl Johaentges, p. 63 t.: A/Peter Horree, p. 63 m.: L/Hemis, p. 63 b.: H/Graefenhain, p. 64/65: A/Rainer Jahns, p. 66 t.: M/A/David Colena, p. 66 m.: A/Collection, p. 66 b.: Jalag/Frank Owen, p. 67 t.: L/Top, p. 67 m.: A/jon Arnold, p. 67 r.: A/Paul Ahowcross, p. 68/69: L/Hemis, p. 70 t.: F1-online/Austrophoto, p. 70 m.: L/Hemis, p. 70 l.: A/F1-online, p. 70 b.: L/Heeb, p. 71 r.: L/Hemis, p. 72/73: A/Guichaoua, p. 74 t.: A/Guichaoua, p. 74 m.: H/Graefenhain, p. 74 b.: L/Le Figaro Magazine, p. 75 t.: Bridgemanart, p. 75 m.: L/Le Figaro Magazine, p. 75 r.: L/Hemis, p. 76/77: L/Eric Martin, p. 78 t.: A/Cubo Imnages, p. 78 l.: L/Hemis, p. 78/79: M/A, p. 79 t.: A/Jon Arnold, p. 79 r. t.: L/Hemis, p. 79 r. b.: L/Hemis, p. 79 b.: A/Robert Harding, p. 80 t.: L/Sylvain Somet/Hemis, p. 80/81: look/Brigitte Maerz, p. 81 t.: L/Hemis, p. 81 r.: Bridgemanart, p. 81 b.: H/Stadler, p. 82 l.: M/Photolibrary, p. 83 t.: L/Hemis, Karte p. 83 from l. to r., from t. to b.: L/Hemis, A/Peter Horree, L/Le Figaro Magazine, L/Hemis, L/Hemis, Andia/Blondel, A/Guichaoua, p. 84/85: G/Travelpix, p. 84 b.: L/Max Galli, p. 85 m.. C/Macduff Everton, p. 85 b.: G/t. Anger, p. 86 t.: Freyer, p. 86 m.: DFA, p. 86 b.: L/Linke, p. 87: L/Martin Kirchner, p. 88/89: L/Max Galli, p. 91 t.: Blickwinkel/Mc Photo, p. 91 m.: L/Martin Kirchner, p. 92 t.: J. Bieker, p. 92/93: L/Max Galli, p. 93 t.: L, p. 93 b.: L/Melanie Dreysse, p. 94 t.: Caro/Kaiser, p. 94/95: L/Martin Kirchner, p. 95 t. l.: G/Flickr, p. 95 t. r.: G/John Miller, p. 96 t.: L/Hemis, p. 96 m.: Picture Press/Kaefer, p. 97 t.: L/Max Galli, Karte p. 97 from l. to r., from t. to b.: L/Melanie Dreysse, DFA, L/Martin Kirchner, L/Max Galli, Bieker, Bieker, L/Kirchner, p. 98/99 t.: Monheim, p. 98/99 m.: Premium/Pau, p. 98 .: C/Archivo Iconographico, p. 99 b.: C/Frank Owen, p. 100 t.: L/Heiko Meyer, p. 100/101: L/Tom Craig, p. 100 b.: H/Ripani Massimo, p. 101 t.: laif/Heiko Meeyer, p. 101 b.: C/Craig Aurnes, p. 103: M/Superstock, p. 104/105: G/David Barness, p. 107: G/grant, p. 108/109: G/Jules Hardouin Mansart, p. 110 t.: H/Stadler, p. 110/111: Panstock, p. 110 l.: C/Krist, p. 111 t.: H/Stadler, p. 112 t.: Jon Arnold, p. 112/113: L/Hemis, p. 113 t.: L/Linke, p. 113 b.: A/Mark Jones, p. 114/115: L/Hemis, p. 116 t.: C/Loviny, p. 116 l.: A/Monheim, p. 116/117: H/Spilla Riccardo, p. 117 t.: M/A, p. 117 r.: L/Sebastian Hartz, p. 118 t.: imagep.de/IPN/Clay Mc Lachlain, p. 118/119: H/von Dachsberg, p. 119 t.: L/Hemis, p. 120/121: A/Mark Zypbler, p. 122 t.: G/Medio Images, p. 122 m.: C/Adam Woolfit, p. 122 b.: C/Robert Holmes, p. 123 t.: G/Slvia Otte, Karte p. 123 from l. to r., from t. to b.: H, C/Adam Woolfit, C/Christopher Loviny, G, C/Hubert Stadler, C/Buselle, p. 124/125: A/David Norton, p. 124 b.: A/Cmarl, p. 125 m.: L/Hemis, p. 125 b.: A/David Plummer, p. 126 t.: Visum/Andia, p. 126 m.: Helga Lade, p. 127 t.: M/A, p. 127 m.: A1-Pix/Sat, p. 127 b. l.: A1-Pix/Your Photo Today, p. 127 b. r.: A1-Pix/Your Photo Today, p. 128 t.: M/A/Cro Magnon, p. 128: A/Andre Jenny, p. 129 t.: Schapo/Harding, p. 129 m.: look/Brigitte Maerz, p. 130/131: A/AM Corporation, p. 132 t.: A/Guichaoua, p. 132/133: A/David Noton, p. 133 t.: A/Guichaoua, p. 133 b.: A/Guichaoua, p. 134 t.: F1-online, p. 134 l.: Bridgemanart, p. 134/135: Andia/Blondel, p. 135 t.: A/Andia, p. 135 r. t.: A/Tor Eigeland, p. 135 r. b.: A/David Giral, p. 136 l.: A/Art Kowalsky, p. 137: L/Hemis, p. 138 t.: L/Hemis, p. 138/139: M/A, p. 139 t.: L/dDieter Klein, p. 139 r. t.: A/Chad Ehlers, p. 139 r. b.: G/Foodpix, p. 140/141: H/G. Simeone, p. 142 t.: M/A, p. 142 m.: H/von Dachsberg, p. 142 m. b.: L/Hemis, p. 142 l. t.: L/Heuer, p. 142 l. b.: L/Heuer, p. 143 t.: look/Brigitte Maerz, Karte p. 143 from l. to r., from t. to b.: die Bildstelle/Rex Features, A/Mike Blenkinsop, A/Andre Jenny, L/Hemis, F1-online, A/Art Kowalsky, p. 144/145: A/David Noton, p. 144 b.: A/Sami Sarkis Frances, p. 145 m.: G/Altrendo Travel, p. 145 b.: A/Jupiter, p. 146 t.: A/Monheim, p. 146 m.: A/Jupiter, p. 146 b.: L/Hemis, p. 147 t.: L/Hemis, p. 147 m.: L/Hemis, p. 148 t.: G/Samuel Magal, p. 148 l.: L/Hemis, p. 148/149: L/Raach, p. 149 t.: G/Samuel Magal, p. 149 b.: A/David A. Barnes, p. 150 t.: A/Andia, p. 150 l.: actionpress/die Bildstelle, p. 150/151: A/Jupiter, p. 151 t.: A/Jupiter, p. 152 l.: H F. Damm, p. 152/153: A/Dfwalls, p. 154 t.: G/Bruno Morandi, p. 154 l.: A/Bernard O Karl, p. 154/155: L/Hemis, p. 155 t.: M/A, p. 155 m.: G/Creative Commons, p. 155 r.: L/Hemis, p. 156/157: L/Hemis, p. 158 t.: L/Rapho, Karte p. 158/159: from l. to r., from t. to b.: A/Jupiter, F1-online/Dieter Ziegler, L/Hoa-Qui, A/David A. Barnes, A/David Noton, L/Raach, Stephane Frances, Bildagentur-Online/Harald Theissen, A/Jupiter, p. 160/161 t.: L/Heiko Meyer, p. 160 b.: A/Jupiter, p. 161 m.: L/Hemis, p. 161 b.: A/Emammanuel Lattes, p. 162 t.: A/Jupiter, p. 162 m.: L/Hemis, p. 163: L/Hemis, p. 164 t.: L/Hemis, p. 164 b.: L/Hemis, p. 165 t.: L/Hemis, p. 165 b.: A/Jupiter, p. 166 t.: L/Hemis, p. 166 m.: L/Lenain Herve, p. 166 b.: L/Le Figaro Magazine, p. 167 t.: A/Robert Harding, p. 167 m. l.: A/F1-online, p. 167 m. r.: A/Jaubert Bernard, p. 168 t.: G/Jupiterimages, p. 168 m.: H/Schulte-Kellinghaus, p. 168 b.: A/John C. Doornkamp, p. 169 t.: Andia/Aucouturier, p. 169 m.: H/Schulte-Kellinghaus, p. 169 b.: Schapo/Aspect, p. 170: C/Jose Fuste Raga, p. 171 t.: L/Hemis, p. 171 m.: L/Hemis, p. 172 t.: G/Bernard Jaubert, p. 172 m.: imagep.de/Marie Docher, p. 172 l. t.: L/Hemis, p. 172 l. b.: L/Hemis, p. 173 t.: L/Hemis, Karte p. 173 from l. to r., from t. to b.: L/Hemis, A/Jaubert Bernard, L/Hemis, L/Heiko Meyer, A/F1-online, Biosphoto/Querlioz Ht, p. 174/175: Caro/Riemiller, p. 175 b.: Arco/Barrett m., p., p. 175 m.: Andie/Piel, p. 175 b.: Look/Millenium, p. 176 t.: Andia/Zintzmeyer, p. 176 m.: Schapo/SIME, p. 176 l.: Visum/Cooperphotos, p. 176 r.: L/Iris Kuerschner, p. 178 t.: L/Hemis, p. 178 m.: Schapo/SIME, p. 178 b.: look/Juergen Richter, p. 179 t.: Schapo/SIME, p. 179 l.: C/Grand Tour, p. 179 r.: L/Iris Kuerschner, p. 180/181: Schapo/Spilla Riccardo, p. 182 t. l.: A/imagebroker, p. 182 t. r.: A/imagebroker, p. 182/183: Jon Arnold, p. 182 b.: Schapo/SIME, p. 183 t.: Ba-Online/G. Fischer, p. 184 t. l.: G/David Barbier, p. 184 t. r.: L/REA, p. 184 m.: G/Yohann Eustache, p. 184 l. b.: BB/Aren Sommer, p. 185 t.: M/A, p. 185 m.: G/Rudi Sebastian, p. 185 r. b.: G/AFP, p. 186 t.: G/Jean-PierrePieuchot, p. 186 m.: L/Dreben, p. Kristensen, p. 186 b.: L/Hartmut Krinitz, p. 187 t.: C/Sandra Raccanetto, Karte p. 187 from l. to r., from t. to b.: L/Joerg Modrow, L/Hoa-Qui, Schapo/SIME, L/Iris Kuerschner, Schapo/SIME, L/Sabine Bungert, Schapo/SIME, p. 188/189: Panstock, p. 188 b.: Jon Arnold, p. 189 m.: Panstock, p. 189 b.: Jon Arnold, p. 190 t.: Premium/Sixty Six, p. 190 l.: H/Radel, p. 190/191: A/David Entrican, p. 191 t.: H, p. 192 t.: Panstock, p. 192 l. t.: G/Gallo, p. 192 l. m.: G/Robert Harding, p. 192 l. b.: G/Scott R. Barbour, p. 192/193: H, p. 193 t.: M, p. 194 t.: Panstock, p. 194 m.: A/Art Kowalsky, p. 194 b.: Panstock, p. 195 r.: Diaf, p. 196 t.: M/age, p. 196 l.: L/Krinitz, p. 196/197: Panstock, p. 197 b.: H/Giovanni, p. 198: Premium, p. 199 t.: Panstock, p. 199 m.: Premium, p. 199 r. Reihe t.: Panstock, p. 199 r. Reihe b.: Panstock, p. 200/201: Look/Richter, p. 202 t.: L/Hemis, p. 202 l.: R. Maier, p. 202 m.: H/Cogoli Franco, p. 202/203: A/Images Etc, p. 203 t.: M/A, p. 203 r. b.: Premium, p. 204 t.: Premium, Karte p. 204/205 from l. to r., from t. to b.: TPC, H/Giovanni, Panstock, Jon Arnold, Jon Arnold, Premium, Harris, A/Mathias Wassermann, R. Maier, Diaf, Jon Arnold, Jon Arnold, p. 205 t.: H/Fantuz Olimpio, p. 206/207 t.: Schapo/SIME, p. 206 b.: Andia/Belzid-Media Sud, p. 206/207 m.: Schapo/SIME, p. 207 b.: Schapo/SIME, p. 208 t.: look/Juergen Richter, p. 208 m.: Visum/Norbert Henn, p. 208 b.: L/Gerd P. Mueller, p. 209 t.: Schapo/SIME, p. 209 m.: L/Karl-Heinz Raach, p. 209 b.: L/Karl-Heinz Raach, p. 210 t.: Schapo/SIME, p. 210 m.: H/G. Simeone, p. 211 t.: L/Hemis, p. 211 m.: Jalag, p. 211 b. l.: Mediacolores/Peters, p. 211 b. r.: Andia/Segmin, p. 212 t.: Schapo/SIME, p. 212 l.: look/Juergen Richter, p. 212 b.: L/Karl-Heinz Raach, p. 212/213: G/David Madison, p. 213 t.: Schapo/SIME, p. 213 r. t.: Look/Widmann, p. 213 r. b.: Look/Widmann, p. 214/215: H/Spilla Riccardo, p. 216 t.: Look/Widmann, p. 216 m.: L/Karl-Heinz Raach, p. 216 b.: Aura, p. 217 t.: G/John Miller, Karte p. 217 from l. to r., from t. to b.: Monheim, look/Juergen Richter, L/Karl-Heinz Raach, L Visum/Norbert Henn, L/Raach, L/Mueller, Jose Fuste Raga, Schapo/SIME, p. 218/219: M/Age, p. 220 t. l.: L/Hemis, p. 220 t. r.: L/hemis, p. 220 m.: A/Images-of-france, p. 220 b. l.: L/Hemis, p. 220 b. r.: M/Steve Vidler, p. 221 t.: A1 Pix/Sat, p. 221 M: L/Hemis, p. 221 b.: L/hemis, p. 222 t.: M/Photononstop, p. 222 m.: Bildagntur-online/Guichaoua, p. 222 b. l.: L/Hemis, p. 222 b. r.: Eberhard Grames, p. 223 t.: Schapo/SIME, p. 223 m.: M/Rene Mattes, p. 223 b. l.: L/Hemis, p. 232 b. r.: C/Sandro Vannini, p. 224 t.: M/Iconotec, p. 224 M: BB/Felipe Alcoceba, p. 224 b.: L/Hemis, p. 225 t.: L/Hemis, p. 225 m.: L/Hemis, p. 225 b.: L/Hemis, p. 226 t.: L/Hemis, p. 226 m.: L/Hemis, p. 226 b.: L/Hemis, p. 227 t.: L/Heiko Meyer, p. 227 m. l.: Premium, p. 227 m. r.: A/Visa, p. 227 b.: M/A, p. 228 t.: L/Hemis, p. 228 m.: C/Ludovic Maisant, p. 228 b.: A/Jon Arnold, p. 229 t.: Focus/Harf Zimmermann, p. 229 b.: G Waite, p. 230 t.: C/Richard Hamilton, p. 230 m.: M/Photononstop, p. 230 b.: akg/Monheim, p. 231 t.: BB Andrej Reiser, p. 231 m.: C/Sandro Vannini, p. 231 b. l.: L/Hemis, p. 231 b. r.: BB/Andrej Reiser, p. 232 t.: M/A, p. 232 m.: L/Hemis, p. 232 b.: M/A, p. 233 t.: M/Bridge, p. 233 m.: Premium/Roda, p. 233 b.: M/age, p. 234 m.: L/Christian Heeb, p. 234 t.: L/Hemis, p. 234 b.: BB/Hans-Joachim Ellerbrock, p. 235 m.: L/Hemis, p. 235 t.: Andia/Boelle, p. 235 b.: L/Hemis, p. 236 t.: L/Hemis, p. 236 m.: L/Frank Heuer, p. 236 b.: L/Hemis, p. 237 m.: L/REA, p. 237 t.: L/REA, p. 237 b.: L/Hemis, p. 238 m.: Monheim/Paul m. R. Mayart, p. 238 t.: C/Vannini Archive, p. 238 b. l.: C/Vannini Archive, p. 238 b. r.: C/Vannini Archive, p. 239 m.: L/Hemis, p. 239 t.: BB/Thomas Ernsting, p. 239 b.: L/Hemis, p. 240 m.: L/hemis, p. 240 t.: L/Hemis, p. 240 b.: L Heuer, p. 241 t.: L/Hemis, p. 241 b.: Premium/Roda, p. 242 m.: A/Images/Europe, p. 242 t.: M/A, p. 242 b.: A/Art Kowalsky, p. 243 m.: Schapo/Cora, p. 243 t.: M/A/David Angel, p. 243 b. l.: M/A/John Kellerman, p. 243 b. r.: M/A/John Kellerman, p. 244 m.: BB/Berthold Steinhilber, p. 244 t.: M/A/Philipus, p. 244 b.: M/A, p. 245 m.: L/Hartmut Krinitz, p. 245 t.: M/A, p. 245 b.: BB/Berthold Steinhilber, p. 246 m.: L/Hemis, p. 246 t.: BB/Rainer Drexel, p. 246 b.: Uwe Schmid, p. 248 m.: L/Hemis, p. 248 t.: H, p. 248 b. l.: BB/Christophe Boisvieux, p. 248 b. r.: BB/Christophe Boisvieux, p. 249 m.: BB/Christophe Boisvieux, p. 249 t.: L/Hemis, p. 249 b.: BB/Berthold Steinhilber, p. 250 m.: Look/Bernhard Limberger, p. 250 t.: Jon Arnold, p. 250 b.: L/Kreuels, p. 251 m.: BB/Thomas Ernsting, p. 251 t.: BB/Thomas Ernsting, p. 251 b.: M/age, p. 252 m.: M/A, p. 252 t.: Biosphoto/Pierre-Paul Feyte, p. 252 b.: A/Charles Bowman, p. 253 m.: M/imagebroker/Otto Stadler, p. 253 t.: H/Giovanni, p. 253 b.: Schapo/SIME, p. 254 m.: A/Ariadne Van Zandbergen, p. 254 t.: G/Daniel Cheong, p. 254 b.: L/Hemis, p. 255 m.: A/Sami Sarkis, p. 255 t.: A/Sami Sarkis, p. 255 b.: A/Authors Image

All facts have been researched with the greatest possible care, to the best of our knowledge and belief. However, the editors and publishers can accept no responsibilty for any inaccuracies or incompleteness of the details provided. The publishers are pleased to receive any information or suggestions for improvement.

MONACO BOOKS is an imprint of Verlag Wolfgang Kunth
© Verlag Wolfgang Kunth GmbH & Co.KG, Munich, 2011
Concept and design: Verlag Wolfgang Kunth GmbH & Co.KG
English translation: Sylvia Goulding, Emily Plank,
Katherine Taylor, Kevin White

For distribution please contact:
Monaco Books
c/o Verlag Wolfgang Kunth, Königinstr.11
80539 München, Germany
Tel: +49 / 89/45 80 20 23
Fax: +49 / 89/ 45 80 20 21
info@kunth-verlag.de
www.monacobooks.com / www.kunth-verlag.de

ISBN 978-3-89944-635-7

Printed in Slovakia

All facts have been researched with the greatest possible care to the best of our knowledge and belief. However, the editors and publishers can accept no responsibility for any inaccuracies or incompleteness of the details provided.
The publishers are pleased to receive any information or suggestions for improvement.

UNESCO